The
Pub

CW01455548
2004

Contents

How to use the Guide

The Guide is divided into two parts. At the front is the main section, which lists pubs throughout Britain selected for the quality of their food, drink and atmosphere; the selections are based on reports from the general public backed up by independent inspections. Towards the back you will find the 'Round-up' section, which features more than 350 additional pubs which are also well worth a visit. These have been selected less on the basis of the food they offer (some do not offer food at all; in other cases, we have had insufficient feedback to be able to assess cooking), but rather for other qualities that set them apart – perhaps for their superlative beers, hospitality, character, setting, history or other attribute.

Layout
Both parts of the Guide are further divided into the following sections: London (main section only), England, Scotland and Wales. Pubs are listed alphabetically by locality (by name of pub in the London Section); they are put in their true *geographical* location, rather than at their postal address. If a pub is difficult to find, directions are given (after the address and telephone number). It is always worth checking by telephone if you are unsure about the exact location of an out-of-the-way pub.

How to find a pub in a particular area
Go to the maps at the back of the book and choose the general area that you want. Cities, towns and villages where pubs in the Guide are located are marked with a tankard symbol; turn to that locality in the appropriate section of the book, where you will find details of the pub (or pubs) there.

Symbols and awards
🍴🍴 denotes a pub where the quality of the bar food is comparable to that of a 'serious' restaurant – i.e. ingredients are consistently first-class and imagination and style are hallmarks of the kitchen. See page 9 for a list of these pubs.

🍴 signifies that the pub offers above-average bar food that shows ambition and good ideas, or simple pub fare prepared particularly well. See pages 9–11 for list.

🍺 denotes a pub serving exceptional draught beers. See pages 12–13 for list.

🍷 indicates a pub serving better-than-average wines, imaginatively chosen and decently priced, with a good selection (usually six or more) by the glass. See pages 14–15 for list.

▲ indicates a pub which offers accommodation.

NEW ENTRY appears after a pub's name if it did not feature in the last edition as a main entry. See pages 16–18 for list.

BREW PUB

'*Flashes*' These highlight a particular point of interest in selected main entries. For this edition we feature four: 'fish', 'waterside', 'vegetarian' and 'brew pub'.

Sample dishes

These are listed at the end of each main entry and are examples of typical dishes from the menu. Prices are based on figures provided by the pub licensee; in most cases, prices have been rounded up to the nearest 25 pence. Note that items listed may not always be available (particularly if they are 'specials').

Food and drink

Details of bar food mentioned in the entries are based on all the feedback we have received since the last edition of the Guide was published, including official inspections, notes from readers, and information provided by the licensees. Many pubs vary their menus from day to day, so specific items may no longer be in the kitchen's repertoire. If dishes are available in a separate restaurant and not in the bar, we mention that in the entry. Similarly, the range of draught beers may differ from time to time, especially if a pub has guest brews. Any real ciders are also listed. Information about wine is geared to what is generally available in the bar; in some pubs with a separate restaurant, you may need to request to see the full wine list (most pubs will oblige). The number of wines available by the glass is usually given in the text.

'Details'

The information given in the section at the end of each entry has been supplied by the pub and may be subject to change. If you are making a special journey, it is always worthwhile phoning beforehand to check opening and bar food times, and any other details that are important to you, such as restrictions on children or dogs, wheelchair access, the availability of no-smoking areas, etc.

- ✪ Licensee: the current licensee is given, followed by the name of the pub's owner (such as a brewery) in brackets; 'freehouse' is given if that is the case.
- ✪ 'Open' times: these are the pub's full licensing hours. (Sunday hours are given separately if different.) Opening times may vary, especially in pubs that rely heavily on seasonal trade; days and times when a pub is closed are also listed.
- ✪ Bar food (and restaurant) times: these denote when food is served in the bar (and restaurant, if there is one).
- ✪ Children: often children are allowed in a family room or eating area of a pub, but not in the main bar area. Any restrictions on children are listed.
- ✪ Car park: if a pub has its own car park, this is noted.
- ✪ Wheelchair access: this means that the proprietor has confirmed that the entrance to the bar/dining-room is at least 80cm wide and passages at least 120cm across – the Royal Association for Disability and Rehabilitation (RADAR) recommendations. If 'also WC' is given, it

means that the proprietor has told us that the toilet facilities are suitable for disabled people.

- ❂ Garden/patio: this is noted for pubs with outside seating areas. If a pub has a children's play area or another interesting feature – e.g. a boules pitch – this is mentioned in the text.
- ❂ Smoking: restrictions on smoking or special areas designated for non-smokers are noted.
- ❂ Music: if background or live music is ever played, or if a pub has a jukebox, this is stated.
- ❂ Dogs: any restrictions on dogs *inside* the pub are listed. Most pubs will allow dogs in their gardens. Guide dogs are normally exempt from restrictions, although it is best to check beforehand if you have special requirements.
- ❂ Cards: major credit and debit cards are listed if a pub accepts these as a means of payment. If a pub does not accept cards, we note this.
- ❂ Accommodation: if a pub offers overnight accommodation, the number of bedrooms and a range of B&B prices – from the lowest you can expect to pay for a single room (or single occupancy of a twin/double) to the most you are likely to pay for a twin/double – are listed. Pub bedrooms have not been officially inspected for this guide.

Report forms

At the very back of the book are report forms which you may use to recount your pub-going experiences. The address is FREEPOST, so no stamp is necessary (full details on the report forms; or email us at *whichpubguide@which.net*). Because *The Which? Pub Guide*, like its sister publication *The Good Food Guide*, relies to a great extent on unsolicited feedback from readers, your comments are invaluable to us and will form a major part of our research when we prepare future editions.

The top-rated pubs

❀ ❀ indicates a pub where the quality of the bar food is comparable to that of a 'serious' restaurant – i.e. ingredients are consistently first class, and imagination, skill and an individual style are hallmarks of the kitchen.

ENGLAND

Cambridgeshire
Old Bridge Hotel, Huntingdon
Pheasant Inn, Keyston
Three Horseshoes, Madingley

Cumbria
Punch Bowl Inn, Crosthwaite

Devon
Dartmoor Inn, Lydford

Dorset
Museum Inn, Farnham

East Sussex
Jolly Sportsman, East Chiltington

Gloucestershire
Falcon Inn, Poulton
Old Passage Inn, Arlingham

Greater Manchester
White Hart, Lydgate

Hampshire
Greyhound, Stockbridge

Herefordshire
Lough Pool Inn, Sellack
Stagg Inn, Titley

North Yorkshire
Angel Inn, Hetton
Blue Lion, East Witton
Durham Ox, Crayke
Star Inn, Harome
Yorke Arms, Ramsgill

Northamptonshire
Falcon Inn, Fotheringhay

Oxfordshire
Boar's Head, Ardington
Sir Charles Napier, Chinnor

Shropshire
Sun Inn, Marton
Waterdine, Llanfair Waterdine

Wiltshire
Vine Tree, Norton

WALES

Monmouthshire
The Foxhunter, Nant-y-derry

LONDON

Admiral Codrington, SW3
Anglesea Arms, W6
Cow Dining Room, W2
Drapers Arms, N1
Eagle, EC1
Ealing Park Tavern, W5
Fox Dining Room, EC2
Golborne House, W10
Grand Union, W9
Havelock Tavern, W14
The House, N1
Lansdowne, NW1
St Johns, N19
Salisbury Tavern, SW6
Salusbury Pub and Dining Room, NW6
Sutton Arms Pub and Dining Room, EC1
Waterway, W9
White Horse, SW6

✿ indicates a pub offering distinctly above-average bar food that shows ambition and good ideas, or simple pub dishes prepared particularly well.

ENGLAND

Berkshire
Dundas Arms, Kintbury
George & Dragon, Swallowfield
Red House, Marsh Benham
Royal Oak, Yattendon

Buckinghamshire
Chequers Inn, Wooburn Common
Crooked Billet, Newton Longville

Cambridgeshire
Anchor Inn, Sutton Gault

Co Durham
The County, Aycliffe
Rose and Crown, Romaldkirk

Cumbria
Bay Horse Hotel, Ulverston
Drunken Duck Inn, Ambleside
Queens Head Hotel, Troutbeck
Snooty Fox Tavern,
    Kirkby Lonsdale

Derbyshire
Red Lion, Hognaston
Red Lion Inn, Hollington

Devon
Arundell Arms, Lifton
Drewe Arms, Broadhembury
Jack in the Green, Rockbeare
Nobody Inn, Doddiscombsleigh
Peter Tavy Inn, Peter Tavy

Dorset
Fox Inn, Corscombe

East Riding of Yorkshire
Wellington Inn, Lund

East Sussex
Best Beech Inn, Wadhurst
Griffin Inn, Fletching
Tiger Inn, East Dean

Essex
Bell Inn, Horndon on the Hill
White Hart, Great Yeldham

Gloucestershire
Bell at Sapperton, Sapperton
Churchill Arms, Paxford
Fox Inn, Lower Oddington
Kings Arms, Stow-on-the-Wold
New Inn, Coln St Aldwyns
Trouble House, Tetbury
Village Pub, Barnsley
White Horse, Frampton Mansell
Yew Tree, Clifford's Mesne

Hampshire
East End Arms, East End
Hampshire Arms, Crondall
Peat Spade, Longstock
Red House Inn, Whitchurch
Three Tuns, Romsey
Wykeham Arms, Winchester

Herefordshire
Roebuck Inn, Brimfield
Three Crowns Inn, Ullingswick

Isle of Wight
Seaview Hotel, Seaview

Kent
Dove, Dargate
Harrow Inn, Ightham
Sportsman, Whitstable
White Horse, Bridge

Lancashire
Bay Horse Inn, Forton
Feilden's Arms, Mellor Brook
Mulberry Tree, Wrightington
Spread Eagle, Sawley

Leicestershire
Red Lion, Stathern

Lincolnshire
Wig & Mitre, Lincoln

Norfolk
Hoste Arms, Burnham Market
Three Horseshoes,
    Warham All Saints
Wildebeest Arms, Stoke Holy Cross

North Lincolnshire
George, Winterton

North Yorkshire
Appletree, Marton
Black Bull Inn, Moulton
Crab & Lobster, Asenby
Fox and Hounds, Sinnington
   North Yorkshire
Galphay Arms, Galphay
General Tarleton, Ferrensby
Golden Lion, Osmotherley
Sandpiper Inn, Leyburn
Sportsman's Arms,
   Wath-in-Nidderdale

Northumberland
Cook and Barker Inn,
   Newton-on-the-Moor
General Havelock Inn,
   Haydon Bridge
Manor House Inn,
   Carterway Heads
Queens Head Inn,
   Great Whittington

Nottinghamshire
Martins Arms, Colston Bassett

Oxfordshire
Lamb at Buckland, Buckland
Three Horseshoes, Witney
Trout at Tadpole Bridge,
   Tadpole Bridge
White Hart, Wytham

Rutland
Finch's Arms, Upper Hambleton
Olive Branch, Clipsham

Shropshire
Hundred House Hotel, Norton
Malthouse, Ironbridge

Somerset
Three Horseshoes, Batcombe

Suffolk
Cornwallis, Brome
Swan Inn, Monks Eleigh

Warwickshire
Howard Arms, Ilmington
Kings Head, Aston Cantlow

West Sussex
King's Arms, Fernhurst
Lickfold Inn, Lickfold

West Yorkshire
Fleece, Addingham
Millbank, Millbank
Ring O' Bells, Thornton
Shibden Mill Inn, Halifax
Three Acres Inn, Roydhouse
Travellers Rest, Sowerby

Wiltshire
Angel Inn, Hindon
Angel Inn, Upton Scudamore
Bell, Ramsbury
Cross Keys, Corsley
George & Dragon, Rowde
Pear Tree Inn, Whitley
Seven Stars, Bottlesford

Worcestershire
Bell and Cross, Holy Cross
Walter de Cantelupe Inn, Kempsey

SCOTLAND

Argyll & Bute
Crinan Hotel, Crinan

Glasgow
Ubiquitous Chip, Glasgow

WALES

Conwy
Queen's Head, Glanwydden

Gwynedd
Penhelig Arms Hotel, Aberdovey

Isle of Anglesey
Olde Bulls Head Inn, Beaumaris

Monmouthshire
Bell at Skenfrith, Skenfrith
Clytha Arms, Clytha

Powys
Bear Hotel, Crickhowell
Felin Fach Griffin, Felinfach
Nantyffin Cider Mill Inn,
   Crickhowell
Wynnstay Hotel, Machynlleth

Pubs serving exceptional draught beers 🍺

Most pubs in the Guide serve acceptable real ales. This list includes establishments which are making a special effort to provide excellent choice in terms of styles and strengths, and demonstrate knowledgeable cellar work. Pubs that support independent local and regional country breweries have been given preference.

LONDON
Crown, E3
Duke of Cambridge, N1
White Horse, SW6

ENGLAND
Bath & N.E. Somerset
Salamander, Bath

Berkshire
Bell Inn, Aldworth
Dundas Arms, Kintbury

Buckinghamshire
Crooked Billet, Newton Longville
Lions of Bledlow, Bledlow
Red Lion, Chenies
Stag & Huntsman Inn, Hambleden

Cambridgeshire
Cock, Hemingford Grey

Cheshire
Albion, Chester
Bhurtpore Inn, Aston
Grosvenor Arms, Aldford
Old Harkers Arms, Chester

Cornwall
Maltsters Arms, Chapel Amble
Napoleon, Boscastle
Plume of Feathers, Mitchell
Royal Oak, Lostwithiel
Trengilly Wartha Inn, Constantine

Cumbria
Britannia Inn, Elterwater
Drunken Duck Inn, Ambleside
Masons Arms, Cartmel Fell
Queens Head, Tirril
Queens Head Hotel, Troutbeck

Devon
Anchor Inn, Cockwood
Drewe Arms, Broadhembury
Duke of York, Iddesleigh
Maltsters' Arms, Tuckenhay
Masons Arms, Branscombe
Nobody Inn, Doddiscombsleigh
Peter Tavy Inn, Peter Tavy
Tower Inn, Slapton
Union Inn, Dolton

Dorset
Langton Arms, Tarrant Monkton

East Sussex
Griffin Inn, Fletching
Jolly Sportsman, East Chiltington
Queens Head, Icklesham

Essex
Bell Inn, Horndon on the Hill

Gloucestershire
Bell at Sapperton, Sapperton
Kings Arms Inn, Didmarton
Kings Head, Bledington

Greater Manchester
Church Inn, Uppermill

Hampshire
Flower Pots Inn, Cheriton
Hawkley Inn, Hawkley
John of Gaunt, Horsebridge
Peat Spade, Longstock
Sun, Bentworth
Wykeham Arms, Winchester

Herefordshire
Riverside Inn, Aymestrey
Stagg Inn, Titley

Kent
Gate Inn, Marshside
Hare, Langton Green
Rose & Crown, Perry Wood
Royal Harbour Brewhouse, Ramsgate
Shipwright's Arms, Oare
Three Chimneys, Biddenden

Lancashire
Eagle & Child, Bispham Green

Leicestershire
Bell Inn, East Langton

Merseyside
Baltic Fleet, Liverpool

Norfolk
Darby's, Swanton Morley
Fishermans Return, Winterton-on-Sea
Lifeboat Inn, Thornham
Recruiting Sergeant, Horstead
Three Horseshoes, Warham All Saints

North Yorkshire
Buck Inn, Thornton Watlass
Malt Shovel, Brearton
Stone Trough Inn, Kirkham Priory
White Swan Hotel, Middleham

Northumberland
Dipton Mill, Hexham
Feathers Inn, Hedley on the Hill
General Havelock Inn, Haydon Bridge

Nottinghamshire
Martins Arms, Colston Bassett
Victoria Hotel, Nottingham

Oxfordshire
Falkland Arms, Great Tew
Royal Oak, Ramsden
Tite Inn, Chadlington

Rutland
Exeter Arms, Barrowden

Shropshire
Burlton Inn, Burlton
Crown, Munslow
Hundred House Hotel, Norton
Three Tuns, Bishop's Castle
Waterdine, Llanfair Waterdine

Somerset
Horse & Groom, East Woodlands
Royal Oak Inn of Luxborough, Luxborough

Suffolk
Angel, Lavenham
Crown, Westleton

De La Pole Arms, Wingfield
Moon & Mushroom Inn, Swilland

Surrey
Plough Inn, Coldharbour

Warwickshire
Fox & Hounds Inn, Great Wolford
Howard Arms, Ilmington

West Sussex
Halfway Bridge Inn, Halfway Bridge
The Fox Goes Free, Charlton
King's Arms, Fernhurst
Lickfold Inn, Lickfold
Three Horseshoes, Elsted

West Yorkshire
Bar T-at, Ilkey
Chequers Inn, Ledsham
Old Bridge Inn, Ripponden

Wiltshire
Dove Inn, Corton
George & Dragon, Rowde
Pear Tree Inn, Whitley

Worcestershire
Talbot, Knightwick
Walter de Cantelupe Inn, Kempsey

SCOTLAND
Borders
Traquair Arms, Innerleithen

Edinburgh
Baillie, Edinburgh
Café Royal, Edinburgh

WALES
Gwynedd
Harp Inn, Llandwrog

Isle of Anglesey
Ship Inn, Red Wharf Bay

Monmouthshire
Clytha Arms, Clytha

Pembrokeshire
Nag's Head Inn, Abercych

Vale of Glamorgan
Plough and Harrow, Monknash

Wrexham
Pant-yr-Ochain, Gresford

Pubs serving better-than-average wine 🍇

This award goes to pubs where wines have been chosen with imagination and in keeping with the dishes on offer; where there is good global choice (from easy-drinking house wines to classics) at fair prices; where the lists themselves give useful information to aid choice; and where there is at least a good handful available by the glass. Judging has been stricter for this edition of the Guide, as wines in country pubs continue to improve; as a result, some wine-award winners in the previous edition are not in the list below.

LONDON
Atlas, SW6
Salusbury Pub and Dining Room, NW6
Sutton Arms Pub and Dining Room, EC1

ENGLAND
Bedfordshire
Knife & Cleaver, Houghton Conquest

Berkshire
Bird in Hand, Knowl Hill
Dundas Arms, Kintbury

Buckinghamshire
Bull and Butcher, Turville
Chequers Inn, Wooburn Common
Crooked Billet, Newton Longville

Cambridgeshire
Anchor Inn, Sutton Gault
Old Bridge Hotel, Huntingdon
Pheasant Inn, Keyston
Three Horseshoes, Madingley

Cheshire
Bhurtpore Inn, Aston

Co Durham
Morritt Arms, Greta Bridge
Rose and Crown, Romaldkirk

Cornwall
Pandora Inn, Mylor Bridge
Rising Sun, St Mawes
Trengilly Wartha Inn, Constantine

Cumbria
Bay Horse Hotel, Ulverston
Drunken Duck Inn, Ambleside

Devon
Anchor Inn, Cockwood
Arundell Arms, Lifton
Dartmoor Inn, Lydford
Kings Arms Inn, Stockland
New Inn, Coleford
Nobody Inn, Doddiscombsleigh
Rock Inn, Haytor Vale

Dorset
Fox Inn, Corscombe
Museum Inn, Farnham

East Riding of Yorkshire
Wellington Inn, Lund

East Sussex
Griffin Inn, Fletching
Jolly Sportsman, East Chiltington
Star Inn, Old Heathfield

Essex
Bell Inn, Horndon on the Hill
White Hart, Great Yeldham

Gloucestershire
Bell at Sapperton, Sapperton
Village Pub, Barnsley
White Horse, Frampton Mansell

Greater Manchester
White Hart, Lydgate

Hampshire
Wykeham Arms, Winchester

Herefordshire
Lough Pool Inn, Sellack
Roebuck Inn, Brimfield
Stagg Inn, Titley
Three Crowns Inn, Ullingswick

Kent
Three Chimneys, Biddenden

Lancashire
Inn at Whitewell, Whitewell
Leicestershire
Red Lion, Stathern

Merseyside
Red Cat, Crank

Norfolk
Hoste Arms, Burnham Market
Lifeboat Inn, Thornham
Walpole Arms, Itteringham
White Horse, Brancaster Staithe
White Horse Hotel, Blakeney

North Yorkshire
Abbey Inn, Byland Abbey
Angel Inn, Hetton
Black Bull Inn, Moulton
Blue Lion, East Witton
Nag's Head, Pickhill
Red Lion, Burnsall
Sportsman's Arms,
    Wath-in-Nidderdale
Star Inn, Harome
Stone Trough Inn, Kirkham Priory
White Swan, Pickering
Yorke Arms, Ramsgill

Northamptonshire
Falcon Inn, Fotheringhay

Northumberland
Cook and Barker Inn,
    Newton-on-the-Moor

Oxfordshire
Boar's Head, Ardington
Lamb at Buckland, Buckland
Sir Charles Napier, Chinnor
Trout at Tadpole Bridge, Tadpole
    Bridge

Rutland
Olive Branch, Clipsham

Somerset
Blue Ball Inn, Triscombe

Suffolk
Angel, Lavenham
Cornwallis, Brome
Crown Hotel, Southwold
Star Inn, Lidgate

West Yorkshire
Millbank, Millbank
Old Bridge Inn, Ripponden
Ring O' Bells, Thornton

Wiltshire
Angel Inn, Upton Scudamore
George & Dragon, Rowde
Pear Tree Inn, Whitley
Seven Stars, Bottlesford
Three Crowns, Brinkworth

SCOTLAND
Argyll & Bute
Creggans Inn, Strachur

Borders
Burt's Hotel, Melrose

Glasgow
Ubiquitous Chip, Glasgow

Perthshire & Kinross
Killiecrankie Hotel, Killiecrankie

WALES
Gwynedd
Penhelig Arms Hotel, Aberdovey

Monmouthshire
Bell at Skenfrith, Skenfrith
Clytha Arms, Clytha

Powys
Bear Hotel, Crickhowell
Nantyffin Cider Mill Inn,
    Crickhowell

Wrexham
West Arms, Llanarmon Dyffryn
    Ceiriog

New entries

The following pubs did not appear as main entries in the previous edition of the Guide, although some may have been in the Round-up (previously 'Out and About') section, or may have appeared as main entries in previous editions.

LONDON
Admiral Codrington, SW3
Albert, NW1
Anglesea Arms, W6
Atlas, SW6
Barnsbury, N1
Bollo, W4
Chapel, NW1
Cow Dining Room, W2
Crown, E3
Drapers Arms, N1
Duke of Cambridge, N1
Eagle, EC1
Ealing Park Tavern, W5
Engineer, NW1
Fentiman Arms, SW8
Fire Station, SE1
Fox Dining Room, EC2
Golborne House, W10
Grand Union, W9
Havelock Tavern, W14
The House, N1
Ifield, SW10
Lansdowne, NW1
Lock Tavern, NW1
Lord Palmerston, NW5
Lots Road Pub & Dining Room, SW10
Peasant, EC1
Perseverance, WC1
St Johns, N19
Salisbury Tavern, SW6
Salusbury Pub and Dining Room, NW6
Sutton Arms Pub and Dining Room, EC1
Swag & Tails, SW7
Waterway, W9
White Horse, SW6
William IV, NW10

ENGLAND
Bath & N.E. Somerset
Hop Pole, Bath
Ring O' Bells, Bath
Rose & Crown, Hinton Charterhouse
Salamander, Bath

Berkshire
George & Dragon, Swallowfield
Sun in the Wood, Ashmore Green
Winterbourne Arms, Winterbourne

Bristol
Clifton Sausage, Bristol
Spring Gardens, Bristol

Buckinghamshire
Chester Arms, Chicheley

Cambridgeshire
Cock, Hemingford Grey
Exhibition, Godmanchester
King William IV, Heydon

Cheshire
Albion, Chester
Calveley Arms, Handley
Netherton Hall, Frodsham
Old Harkers Arms, Chester

Co Durham
The County, Aycliffe
Fox & Hounds, Cotherstone
Seven Stars Inn, Shincliffe

Cornwall
Heron Inn, Malpas
Napoleon, Boscastle
Plume of Feathers, Mitchell

Cumbria
Farmers Arms, Ulverston
King's Head, Thirlspot

Derbyshire
Chequers Inn, Calver
Plough Inn, Hathersage
Red Lion Inn, Hollington

Devon
Agricultural Inn, Brampford Speke
Blue Ball, Sandy Gate
Church House Inn, Marldon
Culm Valley Inn, Culmstock
Hunters Lodge Inn, Cornworthy
Merry Harriers, Clayhidon

Ship Inn, Noss Mayo
Thorverton Arms, Thorverton

Dorset
Museum Inn, Farnham

East Riding of Yorkshire
St Vincent Arms,
    Sutton upon Derwent

East Sussex
Best Beech Inn, Wadhurst
George Inn, Alfriston
Giants Rest, Wilmington
Queens Head, Icklesham

Essex
Carved Angel, Earls Colne
Whalebone Inn, Fingringhoe

Gloucestershire
Bell at Sapperton, Sapperton
Egypt Mill Hotel, Nailsworth
Falcon Inn, Poulton
Horse & Groom, Upper Oddington
Kings Arms, Stow-on-the-Wold
Old Passage Inn, Arlingham
Trouble House, Tetbury
White Hart, Winchcombe
White Horse, Frampton Mansell

Greater Manchester
Barça, Manchester
Church Inn, Uppermill
Kro 2 Bar, Manchester
Oddfellows Arms, Mellor
Ox, Manchester

Hampshire
Bush Inn, Ovington
Chestnut Horse, Easton
Greyhound, Stockbridge
Hampshire Arms, Crondall
Three Tuns, Romsey
White Star Tavern, Southampton
Wykeham Arms, Winchester

Herefordshire
Eagle Inn, Ross-on-Wye
Verzons Country Inn, Trumpet
Alford Arms, Frithsden

Hertfordshire
Alford Arms, Frithsden

Isle of Wight
New Inn, Shalfleet

Kent
Chequers Inn, Crouch
Fountain Inn, Cowden
Red Lion, Stodmarsh
Rose & Crown, Perry Wood
Royal Harbour Brewhouse,
    Ramsgate
Sankey's, Tunbridge Wells
Wheatsheaf, Bough Beech
White Horse, Bridge

Lancashire
Feilden's Arms, Mellor Brook
Lunesdale Arms, Tunstall
Red Lion, Mawdesley
Spread Eagle, Sawley

Lincolnshire
Hare & Hounds, Fulbeck
Wig & Mitre, Lincoln

Merseyside
Baltic Fleet, Liverpool
Philharmonic, Liverpool
Red Cat, Crank

Norfolk
King's Head, Coltishall
Ratcatchers Inn, Eastgate
Recruiting Sergeant, Horstead

North Lincolnshire
George, Winterton

North Yorkshire
Appletree, Marton
Black Bull, Boroughbridge
Charles Bathurst Inn, Langthwaite
Durham Ox, Crayke
Galphay Arms, Galphay
Golden Lion, Osmotherley
Rose and Crown Hotel, Bainbridge
Royal Oak, Dacre Banks
Stone Trough Inn, Kirkham Priory
White Swan Hotel, Middleham
Wyvill Arms, Constable Burton

Northamptonshire
Red Lion Hotel, East Haddon
Windmill, Badby

Northumberland
Cottage Inn, Dunstan
Crown and Anchor Hotel,
    Holy Island
Ship Inn, Low Newton-by-the-Sea

Nottinghamshire
Caunton Beck, Caunton
Robin Hood Inn, Elkesley
Victoria Hotel, Nottingham

Oxfordshire
Lord Nelson, Brightwell Baldwin
Masons Arms, Swerford
Three Horseshoes, Witney
White Hart, Wytham

Rutland
Exeter Arms, Barrowden
Jackson Stops Inn, Stretton
Sun Inn, Cottesmore
White Horse, Empingham

Shropshire
Lime Kiln, Porth-y-waen
Malthouse, Ironbridge
Sun Inn, Marton

Somerset
Ring O' Roses, Holcombe

South Yorkshire
Waggon and Horses, Oxspring

Staffordshire
Holly Bush Inn, Salt

Suffolk
Buxhall Crown, Buxhall
Crown Hotel, Southwold
Kings Head, Laxfield
Swan Inn, Monks Eleigh
Three Horseshoes, Charsfield

Surrey
Red Lion, Betchworth
White Swan, Richmond

Tyne & Wear
Magnesia Banks, North Shields

Warwickshire
Crabmill, Preston Bagot
Rose and Crown, Warwick

West Midlands
Malt Shovel, Barston
Orange Tree, Chadwick End

West Sussex
Fountain Inn, Ashurst
Royal Oak, East Lavant

West Yorkshire
Bar T-at, Ilkey
Chequers Inn, Ledsham
Fleece, Addingham
Gray Ox, Hartshead
Shibden Mill Inn, Halifax
Travellers Rest, Sowerby

Wiltshire
Bridge, Upper Woodford
Cross Keys, Corsley
Linnet, Great Hinton
Vine Tree, Norton

Worcestershire
Bell and Cross, Holy Cross

SCOTLAND
Argyll & Bute
Loch Melfort Hotel, Arduaine

Edinburgh
Baillie, Edinburgh
Café Royal, Edinburgh
Ship on The Shore, Edinburgh

Glasgow
Babbity Bowster, Glasgow
Brel, Glasgow
Corinthian, Glasgow
Rab Ha's, Glasgow
Ubiquitous Chip, Glasgow

Moray
Swish, Elgin

Perthshire & Kinross
Killiecrankie Hotel, Killiecrankie

South Ayrshire
Apple Inn, Troon

WALES
Monmouthshire
Bell at Skenfrith, Skenfrith
The Foxhunter, Nant-y-derry

Pembrokeshire
Castle, Little Haven

Powys
Felin Fach Griffin, Felinfach
White Swan, Llanfrynach

Introduction

So, it is farewell to *The Which? Guide to Country Pubs* and hello to *The Which? Pub Guide*. The principles by which we have selected the pubs featured in this new edition have not changed: we still look for pubs serving good, fresh food competently cooked, offering an impressive range of drinks, and possessing a charm and character that make them stand out from the crowd. Our standards are still high, but now we can lead you to some really good pubs in towns and cities as well as in country villages. Nevertheless, the best of the best country pubs still feature very strongly in the pages of this Guide, so if urban pubs do not appeal to you, you have still plenty to choose from.

Sup in the city

When setting out to expand the book to include urban pubs, we were full of optimism: surely, every city in the UK is full of great pubs for food, drink and atmosphere. We were, alas, disappointed. There are tens of thousands of town and city pubs that just can't cut the mustard when it comes to providing fresh food. While those serving good beer were relatively easy to find, it was often the case that the atmosphere it was served in involved a mostly young clientele enjoying a thumping sound track. How different from the image of a thatched country inn by a shimmering brook . . . .

But is that really a surprise? City life is very different from country life and what we require of our city pubs is different too. Customers in urban areas are easier to come by, for a start, so (with higher turnover) the focus is naturally more towards drinking; rural pubs, meanwhile, are much more dependent on the income from food to survive, attracting a good portion of their customers from further afield. Many of the very best city pubs don't make food a priority, or indeed offer any food at all, so they do not qualify for the main section of this Guide – but you will find lots of great ones in the Round-up section at the back of the book. There is no need for a successful town or city pub to turn to food if it can thrive without it, and it would be much better if some of them just didn't bother – we don't need all these identikit menus from catering packs offering frozen lasagne and Thai curry. Why not stick to what they do best – perhaps providing a particularly inviting ambience, fascinating décor, unique setting, or (again) great beer – and not bother trying to compete in the culinary stakes by offering sub-standard food?

London seems to be a unique case – although it may well be an indicator of what the future will bring elsewhere in the country. Good food pubs seem to be everywhere in the capital and are proving highly successful. We've 36 main entries listed in the London section and that number will undoubtedly grow with each new edition. The very best offer food of a high standard (fresh ingredients, skilfully cooked by a professional chef) served in an informal, relaxed and cheerful environment. Some places, however, are more pubby than others.

The term 'gastro-pub' has entered the vernacular over the last few years and will undoubtedly find its way into the *Oxford English Dictionary* soon, if it hasn't already. The term is overused and often misused. Imagine the scenario: a pub is taken over by a businessman who removes the original interior, strips the woodwork back to nakedness, hangs a few pieces of modern artwork on the walls, and offers a modern menu of confit of duck with plum chutney and such like. Is it still a pub? So far, perhaps, but what if he puts tablecloths on the tables, offers waiter service, and doesn't allow customers who only want a drink? Then, surely, it is a restaurant, not a pub, and many places that are labelled gastro-pubs are really restaurants in attitude and operation. Real gastro-pubs not only offer excellent food but also welcome drinkers and still offer a relaxed and informal environment. Converting a pub to a restaurant can be a logical step that makes sound business sense, particularly in an area overloaded with good drinking pubs; there may be a gap in the market for a slightly more formal dining experience, and so we wish such places well. In our view, however, they are no longer pubs and should not promote themselves as such.

A sense of place
The reality of 'pub as centre of the community' has been fading for a few generations, but pubs can still fly the flag for their area or region by using local ingredients in the food they serve, and by selling local beers – or even wines. Pubs in some of the most beautiful parts of the country are listed in the Guide, and nothing can beat, say, eating fine local cheese and drinking beer from the nearest independent brewery, while taking in the vista of the landscape from whence these came.

The use of local produce makes sense at so many levels: the food doesn't travel so far (clocking up so-called 'food miles'), and the local community will benefit (e.g. the man who grows the salad leaves will spend his profits locally). The loyalty to regionalism seen throughout European countries such as France, Spain and Italy gives these areas their character, and we in the UK head off to these places to admire their individuality and proud identities – based at least in part on the prevalence of local foods and drinks. We have such riches in this country, but they tend to get a bit lost among the pre-packaged, pre-frozen food that dominates. Often local influence here is more akin to a theme-park-like touting of ye olde England in terms of a commercial pork pie or Cornish pasty, or Scottish heritage in terms of a frozen haggis.

This year, though, has seen a significant increase in the number of food awards (157 versus 107 in the previous edition), and we are happy to reward some truly excellent cooking. The very best menus use ingredients that are grown or made in the region – see for example the entries for the Crinan Hotel in Crinan, Argyll & Bute; the Nantyffin Cider Mill Inn in Crickhowell, Powys; the Stagg Inn in Titley, Herefordshire; and the Waterdine in Llanfair Waterdine, Shropshire (though a good number of others could be listed). Many pubs in the pages of the Guide offer food in both bar and restaurant, and we indicate in the entries if there is a difference in style and price. Some truly excellent kitchens serve simpler food in the bar, although – because of the sourcing of ingredients and the skills in the kitchen – the standard remains very high throughout.

Beer, too, should be as rooted in its locale as food. The very best pubs for real ale have been awarded a beer symbol and are listed at the front of the book. The range of ales in some pubs is disappointing, with many places (even some in this Guide) offering a predictable assortment from major producers. We don't expect every pub to make real ale a specialty and aim to stock a dozen, although it is great that some do. There is, though, no excuse for offering a dull array of brand leaders and ignoring the exciting local or regional brewers. The large breweries target the young with their powerful mass-marketing techniques, while often playing the 'traditional' card. You might be drinking in an area with several small breweries in close proximity, but chances are the bar you'll find yourself propping up against (if you've taken pot luck) is selling only the big brands, with no local beers on offer at all. Many of the otherwise very good pubs included in the Guide could go much further when it comes to supporting small breweries. So, publicans, please take a look at your pumps and see if you can hold your heads up high. If not, get on the phone to your local brewer.

Time gentlemen, please
The expression 'Time gentlemen, please' is likely to stay with us for a few generations to come, despite planned changes to the licensing laws. We all know the story about the munitions workers during the First World War, and I dare say it was probably sensible to stop workers handling ordnance after a few ales and a late night. But didn't that war end in 1918? Unique in the world, our licensing

laws are a curiosity. Bad enough for visitors to these shores, but especially galling for those of us that live here and have to put up with them all the time. Change is afoot, and three cheers for that.

The new Licensing Bill was given the go-ahead by Parliament in summer 2003, and promises more flexible opening hours, clarification over the laws related to alcohol and children, less red tape, and a greater say by local residents when pubs ask for licensing applications. In Scotland, when the last major change to licensing laws took place in 1976, pubs in main cities may apply for extended hours well past usual closing time, and – depending on the local authority – it is usually possible to have a drink in most places between 11am and midnight.

Take a glance at the opening times at the bottom of the entries in the England and Wales sections, too, and you will notice that quite a few establishments now have taken up the option to open through the middle of the day. Many choose to open all day on Fridays and weekends (sometimes just in the summer, though), and tend to close in the afternoons midweek. This trend has not brought about the end of the world as we know it; in fact, it makes sound economic sense for some places to open all day – particularly in towns and cities where the turnover of customers is greater – but by no means for all.

The allocation of licences is likely to be a big issue as the proposed new changes to licensing hours are implemented. Local communities may not want their village pubs to open until the small hours, attracting a large crowd from miles around, and all pouring into the streets at 3 in the morning rather than 11 at night. The long-awaited change in the laws will allow the licensing boards to judge each case on its own merits. Such flexibility will inject a new lease (pun intended) of life into the pub business, enabling those best suited to take advantage of the new choices to do so, while not forcing change on those who wish to carry on as before.

Commercial break

Pubs are seriously big business. You cannot open the pages of a newspaper without reading about the sale of a thousand or so pubs from one company to another, or about the profits crisis of yet another. Therefore, it may seem a little puzzling that the majority of pubs listed in this Guide are not owned by these big companies. Instead, most belong to private individuals. The independently run freehouse is often a one-off business, a labour of love even, with a landlord or landlady who is hands-on, *in situ*, behind the bar, delivering the kind of hospitality that cannot be surpassed. These proprietors can pick and choose where they put themselves in the market – sandwiches and real ale, perhaps, or fresh fish and fine wine. They work extremely long hours to bring us what we love and we reward them by going and spending our money – and returning whenever we can again and again.

The owner of a single pub and that of a large pub-owning company both have a bottom line: each has to make the business succeed in its own right. No one is going to subsidise poor business practice. But the reality of owning a large chain of pubs takes that enterprise into different territory, and there is usually a tendency to submerge the individual 'units' in conformity, make them all the same – same beers, same look (you can bulk buy that nice Irish green paint), and a series of managers who pass through. Such practice makes sound business sense (economies of scale etc.), but it doesn't make for a very interesting product. (Yes, 'product' is the right word.) There are some excellent managers and tenants out there, and we're pleased to have some managed houses in the Guide; however, in those cases the success is more often down to the hard work of an individual who is trying to make a difference.

We do list a good number of tied houses attached to the good independent breweries – such as Harveys in Sussex and Greene King in Suffolk – which successfully enable their tenants to offer a good quality of food and service and, in most cases (and not unsurprisingly), their respective companies' range of beers.

Reports, please
Please tell us about your experiences in pubs, about what you love, what drives you mad, and tell us where we should send our researchers. There are over 1,000 pubs listed within the pages of this Guide and they are the best we have found. We visited many others that did not make the grade, where the food was poor, the beer deadly dull, and the atmosphere sadly lacking. The British pub is unique, but so many are being allowed to stagnate, their grubby patterned carpets and indifferent service testaments to a bygone age. The very best pubs featured here offer what is truly great about the British pub: an informal, relaxed approach to hospitality, where you can eat a little or a lot, depending on your mood, or just come in for a drink.

Cheers

Andrew Timm

Editor

London

All the entries in the London section are, of course, new, as the Guide in its previous format did not include city pubs. In order to avoid typographical tediousness, however, we have omitted the 'New Entry' symbol from the entries in this section.

Admiral Codrington ✿   map 12
17 Mossop Street, SW3 2LY   TEL: (020) 7581 0005

An unassuming neighbourhood dining pub, tucked away in a Chelsea back-water, the Cod (as it's affectionately termed) is under the same ownership as the Salisbury Tavern (see entry). The pubby bar upfront – with banquettes and sofas around panelled walls with polished floorboards – delivers a sepa-rate lunchtime menu running from eggs Benedict to a steak sandwich with chips and béarnaise, or cottage pie. On handpump are Wells Bombardier Premium Bitter and Flowers Original. Out back, a long, thin, bright and cheerful dining room – with a sliding glass roof to let in those summer rays, piscatorial prints, banquettes and some booth seating – cranks things up a culinary gear. True to its name, fish is a speciality, with namesake cod baked with tomato and mushrooms in a soft herb crust, while potato and spring onion rösti and a soft-poached egg could accompany pan-fried red snapper. Meat eaters are not forgotten, with fairly straightforward combinations: maybe roast British lamb chops with baby button mushrooms and confit shallots. Puddings of perhaps lemon tart, or banana tarte Tatin with butter-scotch and banana ice cream, round things off nicely. Virtually every bottle of wine on the short list is available by the glass from £3, £12 a bottle. SAMPLE DISHES: tuna carpaccio with wasabi and crème fraîche dressing £7.25; pan-fried fillet of sea bass with a crispy scallop parcel and courgette chutney £13.25; lavender crème brûlée with plum jam £5.25.

Licensee Alex Langlands Pearse (Longshot Estates)
Open 11.30 to 11, Sun 12 to 10.30; bar food 12 to 2.30, restaurant 12 to 2.30, 7 to 11 (10 Sun); closed 25 and 26 Dec
Details Children welcome   Garden and patio   Background music   No dogs   Amex, Delta, MasterCard, Switch, Visa

Albert   map 12
11 Princess Road, NW1 8JR   TEL: (020) 7722 1886

The Albert, in an area heavily populated with gastro-pubs, earns plaudits for being more recognisably pub-like than some of its rivals. Indeed, it is consid-ered 'a good all-rounder', appealing as much to drinkers as eaters. The décor in the main bar features bare floorboards, prints of Prince Albert on the walls, and fittings including some 1950s dining room furniture and traditional cast-iron-framed tables. Towards the rear is a no-smoking conservatory extension and beyond that a leafy patio. The kitchen is open to view, so you can watch as they prepare heartily appealing dishes like ribeye steak with wild mushroom sauce, pancetta-wrapped roast cod on mushroom and pine-nut ratatouille, or Irish stew with warm soda bread. The printed menu changes monthly and is supplemented by blackboard specials: perhaps salmon fillet baked with black pepper and rum on wilted spinach. Fuller's London Pride, Greene King IPA and Bass are the real ales on offer. There are also some interesting Continental beers, such as Hoegaarden and Pilsner Urquell. Half a dozen wines are available by the glass from the good-value list of 15 bottles, with prices starting at £9.95. SAMPLE DISHES: tempura prawns with sweet chilli dip £6.50; chicken thighs roasted with sea salt served with sautéed new potatoes and wilted spinach £8; baked strawberry crumble cheesecake with crème Chantilly £4.25.

Licensees A.E.L. and M.L. Campbell (Simply Pubs)
Open 11 to 11, Sun 12 to 10.30; bar food Mon to Fri 12 to 2.30 (3 Fri), 6.30 to 10, Sat 12 to 10, Sun 12 to 9.30
Details Children welcome Wheelchair access (not WC) Patio No smoking in conservatory
Background music Dogs welcome Delta, MasterCard, Switch, Visa

Anglesea Arms 🏵

map 12

35 Wingate Road, W6 0UR TEL: (020) 8749 1291

The Anglesea Arms has been around in its current guise long enough to be considered a stalwart of London's pub dining scene. It remains one of the foremost exponents of the genre: still recognisably a pub (bar and dining areas are distinct but not really separate), with an informal and unpretentious atmosphere, but offering a menu that shows a serious attitude to food. The cooking style shows a broad range of influences, subject to predominantly modern and British sensibilities: this means starters of Cornish mackerel rillettes with beetroot, horseradish and chives, or a warm salad of duck confit with grapes, green beans and sherry vinegar. Among main courses, expect the likes of seared gilt-head bream on savoury polenta with peperonata, black olives and basil oil, or pot-roast saddle of lamb with white beans, curly kale and rosemary gravy, and to finish there might be cherry clafoutis with crème fraîche ice cream. One of the quirks of this place is its ordering system – the kitchen cooks to order, but only when it is ready to do so. This means you might get your food very quickly, or you might be in for a wait. If it's the latter, then at least there are the real ales and wines with which to amuse yourself in the interim: Fuller's London Pride, Old Speckled Hen and Shepherd Neame Spitfire Premium Ale among the former, the latter featuring a broad selection of Old and New World bottles priced from £10.50 and including at least a dozen by the glass from £2.50. SAMPLE DISHES: pigeon, quail and foie gras terrine with brioche and onion marmalade £6; roast cod fillet with new potatoes, clams, fennel, slow-cooked tomato and dill butter £10; buttermilk pudding with passion fruit £4.50.

27

Licensees Fiona Evans and Jamie Wood (freehouse)
Open 11 to 11, Sun 12 to 10.30; bar food 12.30 to 2.45, 7.30 to 10.45, Sun 1 to 3.30, 7.30 to 10.15; closed 1 week Christmas
Details Children welcome before 9pm Wheelchair access (not WC) Patio Occasional background music Dogs welcome exc in eating areas Delta, MasterCard, Switch, Visa

Atlas 🍇 map 12

16 Seagrave Road, SW6 1RX TEL: (020) 7385 9129

This revamped old pub is nowadays more orientated towards dining than drinking, but it happily caters to all-comers. The deep, oblong-shaped room has a long bar with comfortable seating (banquettes and chairs) and old-fashioned wrought-iron pub tables, and to the rear is a dining area. There is also a garden with patio heaters. Soft background music and friendly young staff give the place a happy atmosphere. The short menu goes in for hearty pubby cooking, with around a dozen choices and no distinction between courses. But despite this seemingly casual approach, there is a good degree of flair behind it. A starter of roast tomato risotto, for example, comes with slow-roasted tomatoes, Gorgonzola, rocket, pine nuts and Parmesan, making it 'creamy, colourful and very tasty'. Among main courses, pan-roast whole poussin is cooked 'in dazzling style', giving it crispy skin and moist meat, and is served on a ragoût of flageolet beans, while braised duck leg flavoured with rosemary and garlic likewise has crispy skin and 'meltingly tender' meat and comes with sweet potato and parsley mash with thyme and chilli and salsa verde. Fuller's London Pride and Wells Bombardier Premium Bitter are among the real ales. Wines are good value (outstanding value when you consider that this is Fulham), and the short list is chosen with care and flair, sporting modern classics like Quinta do Crasto, Cape Mentelle and Domaine de l'Hortus – and not a boring bottle in sight. A dozen come by the glass from £2.60. SAMPLE DISHES: linguine with green beans, melted sweet onions, parsley and pesto £7; roast leg of lamb with rosemary and garlic, mashed potato, roast garlic and horseradish, and tomato chilli jam £11.50; pannacotta with red berries and vanilla and hazelnut crunch £4.

Licensees George and Richard Manners (freehouse)
Open 12 to 11 (10.30 Sun); bar food 12.30 to 3, 7 to 10.30 (10 Sun); closed Christmas, Easter
Details Children welcome before 7pm Garden Background music Dogs welcome on a lead Delta, Diners, MasterCard, Switch, Visa

Barnsbury map 12

209–211 Liverpool Road, N1 1LX TEL: (020) 7607 5519
WEBSITE: www.thebarnsbury.co.uk

Two front doors open straight from the pavement into the more or less square room that makes up the Barnsbury. Floorboards, oak half-panelling, with walls above painted a shade of eggshell blue-grey, a central bar also of oak, with 'chandeliers' above it made from inverted stemmed wine glasses, pine tables, church chairs and pews – all create an impression of bareness. Two coal-effect gas fires add cheer, and decoration and colour are provided by changing exhibitions of paintings, a gilt-framed mirror and bunches of flowers, and atmosphere by the satisfied clientele. The short, lively menu sticks largely within the Mediterranean sphere of influence: for instance, starters of Parma ham with caramelised beetroot and red onions (described as 'sweet and earthy at the same time'), aubergine and piquillo pepper ravioli with cherry tomato sauce, and main courses of roast chicken breast with pesto and sun-dried tomatoes, or venison sausages braised in red wine with pancetta and juniper. Good old Bakewell tart and plum crumble take their places with tarte Tatin and Vin Santo with apricot and almond biscotti at dessert stage. The weekday set lunch, at £6.50 for two courses, is good value, and those wanting just a snack might find croque monsieur or Welsh rarebit to soak up a pint of Greene King Abbot Ale, Fuller's London Pride or a guest beer on draught. Around half the wines on the list of twenty-plus bottles are organic, and eight are served by the glass. SAMPLE DISHES: chorizo and butter-bean salad with cherry tomatoes and parsley £5.25; chargrilled spatchcock poussin with lemon and rosemary sauce £8.50; warm chocolate cake with caramelised oranges £4.

Licensee Jeremy Gough (freehouse)
Open *12 to 11 (10.30 Sun); bar food Mon to Sat 12 to 2.45, 6.30 to 9.45, Sun 12.30 to 5.45*
Details *Children welcome   Wheelchair access (also WC)   Patio   Background music   No dogs Delta, MasterCard, Switch, Visa*

Bollo   map 12

13–15 Bollo Lane, W4 5LR   TEL: (020) 8994 6037
WEBSITE: www.thebollo.co.uk

A huge green awning over the front of this large, part-brick, part-green-painted building – with tables and chairs outside – announces this 'neighbourhood gastro-pub' in residential Chiswick. Although a lively pub serving imaginative food, it's also 'a top place' just for drinks and a chat. The large open-space interior offers two options: a relaxed bar area with a mix of brown-leather sofas and wooden furniture, and a slightly more formal dining space. Here you can also choose between a sofa (this time in green) and regular chairs and sit beside an open fire. Dark-wood and red-painted walls, a glass dome in the ceiling, and pleasant and friendly service catch the mood. The daily-changing well-priced menus are chalked up on blackboards (also printed), with food ordered at the bar. The sensibly compact, modish and appealing repertoire could lead with steamed mussels ('big and fresh') with leeks, bacon, cream and white wine, while, from six main courses, choose perhaps roast duck breast with turnip and potato dauphinois and 'fantastic' Savoy cabbage, or pan-fried fillet of sea bass in a crunchy crust of fennel and olives with provençale Jerusalem artichokes. Pure chocolate torte ('very rich and good for sharing') with crème fraîche makes a satisfying way to finish. On handpump are Greene King IPA and Abbot Ale, and there's a selection of around 10 wines by the glass. SAMPLE DISHES: king prawn risotto £8; grilled ribeye steak with chips and salad £10.50; pears poached with saffron served with mascarpone and cantuccini £4.

Licensees Rob Claasen and Nick Mash (Greene King)
Open 12 to 11 (10.30 Sun); bar food and restaurant 12.30 to 3.30, 7 to 10
Details Children welcome   Wheelchair access (not WC)   Patio   Background music   Dogs welcome
in bar on a lead   Amex, Delta, Diners, MasterCard, Switch, Visa

Chapel   map 12

48 Chapel Street, NW1 5DP   TEL: (020) 7402 9220

There are no sermons to be heard at this chapel, a Victorian building on a
corner set back off the Edgware Road; rather, its congregation flock here to
enjoy the wares of a modern-day gastro-pub. Spacious and open-plan, with
stripped floorboards and cream walls, it's a 'classy' yet 'no-nonsense' space.
The large, traditional bar is painted dark green, while well-spaced wooden
tables are accompanied by bentwood chairs. Beside the bar there's an open-
plan kitchen and large charcoal grill. The menu, on blackboards, steps out on
typically modern lines, perhaps featuring pan-fried sea bass ('full of flavour')
with salad, cherry tomatoes and teriyaki sauce to start. That big chargrill
comes into play for T-bone steak, accompanied by French beans, dauphinois
potatoes and wild mushrooms, while another main course could be chicken
breast stuffed with goats' cheese and bacon and teamed with spiced ratatouille.
Finish with raspberry bavarois, or date and toffee pudding. Blackboards also
display the globe-trotting wine options (with eight or nine by the glass), while
beers on handpump deliver Adnams Bitter and Greene King IPA. SAMPLE
DISHES: duck's liver with Cognac and green pepper terrine £5; pan-fried skate
with French beans £13; banoffi pie £4.

Licensees Alison McGrath, Sebastian Leach and Mr P. Hondrogiannis (Punch Taverns)
Open 12 to 11 (10.30 Sun); bar food 12 to 2.30 (12.30 to 3.30 Sun), 7 to 10
Details Children welcome   Wheelchair access   Garden   Background music   Dogs welcome
Amex, Delta, Diners, MasterCard, Switch, Visa

Cow Dining Room 😕   map 12

89 Westbourne Park Road, W2 5QH   TEL: (020) 7221 0021

The Cow, at the Chepstow Road end of Westbourne Park Road, describes
itself as 'saloon bar and dining rooms', the latter upstairs and accessed either
through the bar or separately. The bar itself, reached up some steps from a
small raised patio, has lots of dark wood, chairs and tables in various styles, and
some leather-covered banquettes, all looking as though nothing has changed
since the 1950s, and menus painted on mirrors add to the feeling of working
man's pub meets French bistro. The room is loosely separated into two halves,
with a sign at the entrance to the back half informing that this area is for eating
(and people can be asked to return to the drinking area 'pretty sharpish' once
they've finished eating). The surroundings may be of the 'grunge/shabby chic
genre', but food is taken seriously here and materials are of good quality.
Oysters and a seafood platter (for two) kick off the short printed menu, with
other items written on a blackboard. Robustly flavoured dishes are what to
expect: Catalan fish stew, a 'great' salad of black pudding with French beans,
lardons and a perfectly poached egg, sausage and mash with onion gravy, and

cassoulet with duck confit. Fuller's ESB and London Pride are on draught, along with Guinness (to pair with those oysters) and various lagers, and around a dozen wines are served by the glass, from £3, from a short, well-chosen list. SAMPLE DISHES: six Irish rock oysters £7.50; warm porcini mushroom tart £6.75; braised oxtail with mash £10.

Licensees Humphrey Barber and Bardi Berisha (freehouse)
Open 12 to 11, Sun 12 to 10.30; bar food 12 to 4, 6 to 10.30; closed 25 and 26 Dec, 1 Jan
Details Children welcome   Patio   Occasional background music   No dogs   Delta, MasterCard, Switch, Visa

Crown 🍺   map 12

223 Grove Road, E3 5SN   TEL: (020) 8981 9998
WEBSITE: www.singhboulton.co.uk

This Victorian pub, a substantial end-of-terrace building opposite Victoria Park, is under the same ownership as the Duke of Cambridge in Islington (see entry), which means it also has a policy of using only organic materials, right down to the ketchup, and is endorsed by the Soil Association. Its large open-plan main room has a simple unadorned look, with a few plants, mismatched wooden chairs and large tables. Food is listed on a blackboard by the bar, and like the décor it takes a straightforward approach, with dishes ranging from simple snacks to full-blown main courses and some items available in small or large portions. Bruschetta with mushrooms, a poached egg and herb butter might appear alongside salt-cod with Puy lentils, French beans, egg and olive salad in aïoli, or penne pasta with roasted pumpkin, kale and pesto cream. Wines are also listed on boards – about twenty of each colour, with five of each by the glass – and beers include Eco Warrior and Shoreditch Organic Stout. There is also a good choice of fruit juices and cordials. SAMPLE DISHES: chicken liver pâté with pickled onion jam and toast £6.50; chargrilled lamb leg steak with dauphinois and Savoy cabbage £14.75; lemon tart with vanilla ice cream £5.

Licensees Jon Paul and David Roome (freehouse)
Open Mon 5 to 11 (bank hol Mons 10.30 to 11), Tue to Fri 12 to 11, Sat and Sun 10.30 to 11; bar food and restaurant Mon 6.30 to 10.30, Tue to Fri 12.30 to 3, 6.30 to 10.30, Sat and Sun 10.30 to 4, 6.30 to 10.30; closed 25 Dec, restaurant closed Mon to Thur winter
Details Children welcome   Wheelchair access (also WC)   Patio   No-smoking area in bar, no smoking in restaurant   No music   Dogs welcome   Amex, Delta, MasterCard, Switch, Visa

Drapers Arms ✿   map 12

44 Barnsbury Street, N1 1ER   TEL: (020) 7619 0348

In the heart of Islington, but away from the hustle and bustle of Upper Street, the Drapers Arms is a top-class modern pub in a Georgian house with an attractive seating area to the rear, traditional bar on the ground floor and a dining room upstairs. Downstairs, food is limited to a 'bar bites' menu. This is a short list of simple but out-of-the-ordinary snacks priced around £3 to £3.50 – things like spicy chorizo sausage, chilli squid, chargrilled bread with hummus, and chunky chips with chilli crème fraîche. Upstairs, the menu goes in for sophisticated eclectic cooking, but still keeping things simple, with starters of roast figs with Parma ham, or mussels with beer and bacon, and main courses like lamb shank with harissa and couscous, herb-crusted cod with Puy lentils, or pan-fried calf's liver with celeriac and garlic mash and onion gravy. Desserts might include lemon cheesecake with tamarillo compote, alongside more traditional sticky toffee pudding with custard. Beers are Old Speckled Hen, Courage Best and a guest ale in winter, and there is a list of around 60 superior-quality but good-value wines, of which 18 are served by the glass. SAMPLE DISHES: seared squid and octopus with butter beans and chorizo £7.50; pheasant with creamed mushroom and barley, and roast salsify £14; amaretto espresso pot and biscotti £4.50.

Licensees Mark Emberton and Paul McElhinney (freehouse)
Open 11 to 11, Sun 12 to 10.30; bar food all week 12 to 3 (Sun 12 to 4), Mon to Sat 7 to 10.30; closed 1 week Christmas/New Year
Details Children welcome in eating areas Wheelchair access (not WC) Garden Background music Dogs welcome in ground floor and garden only Delta, MasterCard, Switch, Visa

Duke of Cambridge 🍺
30 St Peter's Street, N1 8JT   TEL: (020) 7359 3066

map 12

This mid-nineteenth-century Islington pub claims to be 'London's first organic gastro pub', having, along with it sister pub, the Crown E3 (see entry), gained Soil Association endorsement. Green credentials are evident not just in food but across the board: décor is basic and minimalist, with original features restored using reclaimed building materials, while furniture is all second-hand. The overall effect is very pleasant, and friendly staff enhance the generally upbeat mood. Shortish menus offer modern-sounding dishes with a broad scope of influences (mostly French and Italian) that are less economical than the décor. Start perhaps with bruschetta of chicken livers and dandelion leaves with sherry and crème fraîche, then something like pan-fried red mullet with linguine, lemon and chilli sauce; or home-smoked lamb fillet with potato, aubergine and feta gratin. Beers, including the own-label Singhboulton, are from London organic brewers Pitfield, plus Organic Best Bitter from St Peter's brewery and Freedom organic lager. There is also Luscombe cider, some interesting bottled beers and a list of around 40 organic wines. SAMPLE DISHES: roast tomato soup with tapenade £4.50; chargrilled chicken thighs with sun-dried tomatoes, sweet potato and parsley salad £12; frozen chocolate and orange bombes with brandy syrup £4.50.

Licensee Geetie Singh (freehouse)
Open 12 to 11, Sun 12 to 10.30; bar food 12.30 to 3 (3.30 Sat and Sun), 6.30 to 10.30 (10 Sun); closed 25 and 26 Dec
Details Children welcome Courtyard No smoking in dining room No-smoking area in bar No music Dogs welcome Amex, Delta, MasterCard, Switch, Visa

🍺 *indicates a pub serving exceptional draught beers.*

Eagle ✿   map 12
159 Farringdon Road, EC1R 3AL   TEL: (020) 7837 1353

The Eagle is the original gastro-pub, still going strong after more than ten
years, and still the same large, casual and bustling single room on Farringdon
Road near the *Guardian*'s office. There is no division between drinking and
eating areas, and no bookings are taken, which often means getting here early
or fighting the crowds for a table. Food is listed on blackboards over the bar.
There isn't a huge range of dishes on offer, but the untypical ingredients and
inventive flavour combinations make a good impression. The style is hearty
and modern, with Spanish and Italian influences in evidence: start with
pumpkin, chilli, tomato and fava soup, perhaps, then move on to wild boar
casserole with polenta, or a stew of octopus, mussels, beans and cabbage. If
you're not in the mood for a full meal, you could stick to a marinated rump
steak sandwich. There is only one unchanging dessert option: pasteis de mata,
a Portuguese version of custard tart. Wells Bombardier Premium Bitter and
IPA are the real ales on offer, and all dozen or so reasonably priced wines
(from £10.50 to £15) are served by the glass (£2.50 to £3.75). SAMPLE DISHES:
spaghetti with asparagus, truffle oil and Parmesan £8; whole roast widgeon
with almond, blood orange and dried fruit couscous £11.50; Sardinian ewes'
cheese with crispy flat bread and a pear £6.50.

Licensee Mike Belben (freehouse)
Open *12 to 11, Sun 12 to 5; bar food 12.30 to 2.30 (3.30 Sat and Sun), 6.30 to 10.30; closed
Christmas and New Year, Easter Sun, bank hols*
Details *Children welcome   Wheelchair access (not WC)   Background music   Dogs welcome
Delta, MasterCard, Switch, Visa*

Ealing Park Tavern ✿   map 12
222 South Ealing Road, W5 4RL   TEL: (020) 8758 1879

The sign 'Dining Room' displayed outside announces its intentions and the
arrival of the Ealing Park Tavern to the gastro-pub fold, while its large
windows present passers-by with views of the high-ceilinged bar and dark-
panelled interior. There's still a 'pub style' here and the offer of tapas like charcuterie and cheese as bar snacks. The dining room has an open-to-view
kitchen in the larger of two areas, both set out with chunky wooden tables and
assorted wooden chairs. The compact, modern British menu comes chalked
up on a blackboard and moves with the times. Portions are 'well sized', ingredients are fresh and dishes are 'well presented', as witnessed by a main course
of watercress-crusted cod with gnocchi and saffron sauce, and maize-fed
chicken with mushroom velouté, rösti and red cabbage. Starters might feature
black pudding and chicken terrine that 'went down a treat', while treacle tart
with vanilla ice cream, and apple charlotte with crème anglaise both get the
thumbs up. The wine list offers 14 by the glass, while ales on handpump
include Fuller's London Pride, Adnams Broadside, Timothy Taylor Landlord
and Courage Directors. SAMPLE DISHES: salt-cod hash with poached egg and
shaved truffle £5.25; pork belly with mustard mash and pea and mint gravy £9;
bitter chocolate tart with maple syrup ice cream £4.50.

Licensee Nicholas Sharpe (Unique Pub Company)
Open 11 to 11, Sun 12 to 10.30; bar food 6 to 10.30 (9 Sun), restaurant Mon to Sat 12 to 3,
6 to 10.30, Sun 12 to 4, 6 to 9
Details Children welcome Wheelchair access Garden Background music Dogs welcome in bar
Amex, Delta, MasterCard, Switch, Visa

Engineer
map 12

65 Gloucester Avenue, NW1 8HJ TEL: (020) 7722 0950
WEBSITE: www.the-engineer.com

This brick and white-painted corner building, housing (another) one of
London's original gastro-pubs, is reputed to have been built by Isambard
Kingdom Brunel: hence its name. Whether the great man would approve of
today's modern, rustic interiors is another thing. They include an L-shaped
bar, an array of dining areas and a walled garden for summer days. In the bar
there are closely spaced chairs and settees, stripped-wood floors and a homely,
laid-back, buzzy atmosphere, while the informal dining areas exhibit modern
art. The trendy, crowd-pleasing modern European menu, with
Mediterranean and far-flung influences, shows its hand in eclectic dishes such
as roast red pepper stuffed with spicy couscous and pine nuts and served with
grilled halloumi cheese, and main-course roast free-range chicken breast with
a spicy stew of Spanish butter beans, chorizo and vine tomatoes accompanied
by wilted spinach. The modern globe-trotting wine list runs in tune with the
cooking and offers a handful by the glass, while Fuller's London Pride and a
guest ale such as Old Speckled Hen or Young's Bitter are on handpump.
SAMPLE DISHES: tempura of prawns with Chinese slaw and chilli jam aïoli
£7.25; grilled organic ribeye steak with watercress, baker fries and a herb,
garlic and horseradish butter £15; prune and Armagnac crème brûlée £5.

Licensees Abigail Osbourne and Tamsin Olivier (freehouse)
Open Mon to Fri 9 to 11.30, Sat and Sun 9 to 12; bar food and restaurant Mon to Fri 12 to 3,
7 to 11, Sat and Sun 9 to 12, 7 to 11 (10.30 Sun)
Details Children welcome Wheelchair access Garden Background music Dogs welcome
Delta, MasterCard, Switch, Visa

Fentiman Arms
map 12

64 Fentiman Road, SW8 1LA TEL: (020) 7793 9796

A new kid on the Vauxhall block, the Fentiman is setting a new trend in its
large beer garden, not with its bamboos, but with its vegetables – quite the
contemporary city kitchen garden. There are tables at the front under large
parasols on the pavement patio too. Inside, there's an informal feel, with large
windows, plank flooring and mix-and-match tables and chairs. On one side of
the U-shaped bar there's a chill-out area with large cushions and chairs in oak
and mahogany and a 'library-style' ambience, while on the bar's other side it's
more convivial to drinking. The menus move with the times and could feature
a baked shallot and goats' cheese tart to start. Main courses follow the trend,
with beef and Guinness sausages, smoked haddock and thyme fishcakes,
ribeye steak, and tagliatelle with wilted spinach. Greene King IPA and
Wadworth 6X are on handpump, while eight of the fairly priced wines are sold

by the glass from £2.80. SAMPLE DISHES: smoked salmon pâté £5; chicken breast filled with sun-dried tomatoes served with a white wine and lime sauce £11; Baileys cheesecake £4.

Licensees Talufik Yahia and Douglas Green (freehouse)
Open 11 to 11, Sun 12 to 10.30; bar food Mon to Sat 12 to 2.45, 7 to 9.45, Sun 12 to 4, 7 to 9
Details Children welcome   Garden   Background music   Dogs welcome   Delta, MasterCard, Switch, Visa

Fire Station   map 12
150 Waterloo Road, SE1 5SB   TEL: (020) 7620 2226
WEBSITE: www.wizardinns.co.uk

Even if the name didn't give the game away, the former identity of this popular, noisy bar/restaurant in the shadow of Waterloo Station would be easily recognisable – not least in the huge red doors that open on to the street, often with crowds spilling out. The front part is for drinkers only, though bar snacks are available here, along with a decent selection of real ales, including Young's Bitter, Fuller's London Pride and Adnams Bitter, plus a few interesting Belgian beers. Beyond is the cavernous dining room, with its open kitchen running along the back wall adding to the sense of drama. Menus offer inventive global cooking, starters taking in everything from onion tartlet with rocket salad and spicy chutney, to oriental shredded duck spring roll with sweet chilli sauce. Main courses might feature classic dishes like bouillabaisse, alongside eye-catching contemporary creations such as tandoori-seared yellow-fin tuna loin with banana raita, sag aloo, aubergine chutney and poppadoms. Desserts are conservative by contrast: tiramisù, for example. Most bottles on the list of around 40 wines are under £20, and 10 are available by the glass from £2.75. SAMPLE DISHES: salad of spinach, bacon, toasted pine nuts and croûtons with citrus vinaigrette £6.50; pan-fried John Dory with noodles, greens and sun-dried tomato dressing £12; plum bread-and-butter pudding with chilled custard £4.50.

Licensee Philippe Ha Yeung (Wizard Inns)
Open 11 to 11, Sun 12 to 10.30; bar food 11 to 10.30, Sun 12 to 9.30, restaurant Mon to Fri 12 to 3, 5.30 to 10.45, Sat 12 to 10.45, Sun 12 to 9.30
Details Children welcome   Wheelchair access (not WC)   Garden   Background music   No dogs
Amex, Delta, Diners, MasterCard, Switch, Visa

Fox Dining Room ✿   map 12
28 Paul Street, EC2A 4LB   TEL: (020) 7729 5708

The Fox is a new venture from the owner of the Eagle on Farringdon Road (see entry), one of the original genre-defining gastro-pubs. Like its sibling, the décor demonstrates a no-frills, rough-and-ready approach, with bare floorboards, plain wooden tables and mismatched seating. The food shows considerable panache while still keeping things simple. Listed on a blackboard over the bar might be hot salt-beef with mustard on rye bread, smoked haddock kedgeree, and even sausage rolls, while the upstairs dining room has a fixed-price menu of more ambitious dishes (also served in the bar): perhaps Cullen skink, followed by roast partridge with bubble and squeak, or rack of lamb with fennel and anchovies. To finish, there might be pear and almond tart, or rhubarb and blood orange salad. Wells Bombardier Premium Bitter is the only real ale offered, while wines run to a list of around 15 good-value bottles (the majority between £10.50 and £15), most of which are also available by the glass. SAMPLE DISHES: poached egg, red wine and bacon; belly pork with celeriac, potato and rosemary; Dorset apple cake: 2 courses £14, 3 courses £18.75.

Licensee Michael Belben (freehouse)
Open *Mon to Fri 12 to 11; bar food and restaurant Mon to Fri 12.30 to 3, 6.30 to 10; closed 10 days Christmas, bank hols*
Details *Children welcome Patio Background music Dogs welcome in bar Delta, MasterCard, Switch, Visa*

Golborne House ✿   map 12
36 Golborne Road, W10 5PR   TEL: (020) 8960 6260
WEBSITE: www.golbornehouse.co.uk

Golborne House, on the corner of Golborne and Elkstone Roads, has gone from traditional local boozer to thriving modern dining pub, but keeps an air of unpretentious informality and stays in touch with its pubby roots. It also has a 'trendy urban buzz' – partly due to the stylish décor of dark chocolate brown and terracotta walls, a light, polished wooden floor and casual dark wood chairs and tables. The food makes a similar impression: menus change twice daily, coming up with starters like cauliflower and cumin soup with poppadoms and yoghurt, or a simple puff pastry tart with goats' cheese, red peppers and rocket salad ('well-timed, well-balanced, the flavour shone through'). Main courses are things like ham hock on creamed cabbage with pancetta, mash and whole-grain mustard; whole sea bass with roast fennel and potatoes, zucchini and chilli; or penne pasta with tomato, chilli and radicchio sauce. Desserts might include crème caramel with kumquat compote, or poached warm winter fruits with honey and ginger ice cream. Eleven wines are offered by the glass from a good, varied list of forty-odd bottles with plenty under £20. Fuller's London Pride is the one real ale served. SAMPLE DISHES: bresaola with toasted pine nuts, rocket and Parmesan salad £6.75; pan-fried red snapper with chilli, coconut egg noodles, choy sum and shiitake mushrooms £12.75; mango and passion-fruit pavlova £4.

Licensees Tom Etridge and Beth Coventry (Enterprise Inns)
Open *Mon to Thur 12 to 11, Fri and Sat 12 to 12, Sun 12 to 10.30; bar food 12.30 to 3.45, 6.30 to 10.45 (10.15 Mon to Thur), Sun 12.30 to 4.30, 6.30 to 9.45*
Details *Children welcome Patio Background music Dogs welcome Delta, Diners, MasterCard, Switch, Visa*

After the main section of the Guide is the 'Round-up' section listing additional pubs where food may not be the main focus but which are well worth a visit for, perhaps, their inviting ambience, fine beers, a stunning setting, special history or other attribute. Reports on these entries are most welcome.

Grand Union ☺

WATERSIDE   map 12

45 Woodfield Road, W9 2BA   TEL: (020) 7286 1886

Overlooking the Grand Union Canal, this remodelled Victorian pub is not as attractively located as its name might first suggest, with Westbourne Park's bus depot opposite on the other bank and the concrete Westway more or less directly overhead. The décor is typically modern gastro-pub (bare floorboards, mix-and-match wooden furniture, a large red-leather sofa), while a wrought-iron spiral staircase leads to a basement dining room and a small terrace for fair-weather drinks. At heart, the Grand Union is 'definitely more pub than restaurant', as illustrated by food that is 'down to earth and hearty, rather than refined and classy'. Pies are a house speciality, from familiar beef and mush-rooms in red wine gravy to modern variants: perhaps pork, chorizo and baby clams, 'with a well-risen, flaky pastry lid'. Less traditional offerings could feature 'excellent' Scottish mussels in tomato and basil sauce to start, and gnocchi with beef, red wine, sage sauce, Emmental and mixed leaves at mains. Familiar desserts run the tiramisù comfort route. Adnams Broadside and Regatta are on handpump, and the short wine list offers five by the glass. SAMPLE DISHES: creamy pumpkin soup with crusty bread £3.50; fish pie topped with Cheddar mash £7.50; orange and poppy seed treacle sponge pudding with vanilla sauce £4.

Licensee Matthew Leitl (freehouse)
Open 12 to 11 (10.30 Sun); bar food Mon to Sat 12 to 3, 7 to 10, Sun 12 to 10
Details Children welcome   Wheelchair access   Garden   Background music   Dogs welcome
Delta, MasterCard, Switch, Visa

Havelock Tavern ☺

map 12

57 Masbro Road, W14 0LS   TEL: (020) 7603 5374
WEBSITE: www.thehavelocktavern.co.uk

If local estate agents don't mention proximity to the Havelock Tavern to prospective incomers to Brook Green, they are missing a unique selling point. This is the neighbourhood pub as it should be in the twenty-first century: casual and relaxed, and aiming high with food and drink. And it looks and feels like a pub. The blue-tiled frontage stands out among the surrounding terraced houses, while inside it oozes informality with unerring ease. The large open-plan space has plenty of standing room by the bar, wooden floorboards are well trodden, and mixed styles of wooden tables and chairs fill up quickly. Real ales include Brakspear Bitter, Marston's Pedigree and Fuller's London Pride, and the wine list, on blackboards as well as a printed sheet, offers a sensible range of food-friendly stuff, half of which comes in under £15 a bottle, with around a dozen by the glass. At lunchtime the food is aimed at one-course satisfaction, with perhaps poached salt-beef with bubble and squeak, or a bowl of mussels and clams with chorizo. In the evening you might start with fennel and parsley soup, go on to whole roast skate with new potatoes, fennel, baby spinach and aïoli (perfectly fresh and correctly cooked at inspection), and finish with lemon and vanilla cheesecake with poached plums, or a plate of Blue Wensleydale with toast and chutney. There's no pressure to eat more than one course, though, and watch out for dishes disappearing from the blackboard as the evening progresses. SAMPLE DISHES: tempura prawns with cucumber, spring onion and coriander salad £7; roast chump of lamb with couscous, grilled vegetables and minted yoghurt £12; strawberry pavlova with blackberry sorbet £4.

Licensees Peter Richnell and Jonny Haughton (freehouse)
Open 11 to 11, Sun 12 to 10.30; bar food 12.30 to 2.30 (3 Sun), 7 to 10 (9.30 Sun); closed 22 to 26 Dec, Easter Sat and Sun, second Mon in Aug
Details Children welcome   Wheelchair access (not WC)   Garden   No music   Dogs welcome   No cards

The House ✿   map 12
63–69 Canonbury Road, N1 2DG   TEL: (020) 7704 7410
WEBSITE: www.inthehouse.biz

This red-brick pub dating from the 1920s looks slightly austere outside, but inside it feels comfortable and relaxing. A drinking area around the entrance is furnished with deep armchairs and sofas, while the dining area has smartly laid tables with gleaming cutlery and glasses. Décor throughout is restful, although a fair amount of noise is generated by the lively clientele and a DJ. The concise menu blends modern and traditional ideas, as in starters of jambon persillé with warm potato salad, gherkins and Dijon mustard, or risotto of calamari with mascarpone and chives. Main courses typically feature marinated pork fillet with sage and garlic sautéed potatoes and spinach; roast duck breast with creamed cabbage, turnip gratin and Thai-spiced jus; and sausage of crab and scallop with wilted lettuce, tomato and shellfish bisque. At weekends, the regular lunch menu is replaced with a brunch menu of things like eggs Benedict, Caesar salad, and ribeye steak with black pudding and fried egg. The wine list is grouped into somewhat whimsical headings and covers a good range of styles and countries. Prices start at £11.50, and there are eight wines by the glass. Adnams is the one real ale on offer. SAMPLE DISHES: Stilton, red onion and rocket salad with peppered beef fillet and blue cheese dressing £5.50; vinaigrette of chicken with new potatoes and leeks, chillied hazelnuts and roasting juices £13.50; pear tarte Tatin (for two) £11.

Licensee Barnaby Meredith (freehouse)
Open 11 to 11, Sun 12 to 10.30; bar food Tue to Sun 12 to 3.30, 5.30 to 10.30 (9.30 Sun); closed 24 to 29 Dec
Details Children welcome   Wheelchair access (also WC)   Garden   No smoking in dining room   Live or background music   Dogs welcome   MasterCard, Switch, Visa

Ifield   map 12
59 Ifield Road, SW10 9AY   TEL: (020) 7351 4900

Formerly an old-fashioned 'community-style' pub, now more towards the gastro-pub end of the market, the Ifield caters for anyone looking for a good pint and some hearty yet sophisticated cooking. The long L-shaped room has a drinking area at one end and an eating area at the other, though there is no formal distinction and a convivial atmosphere prevails throughout. Menus are sensibly short and unfussy, but the cooking shows some panache, as in an inspector's starter of flash-grilled squid with chorizo and red peppers 'all oozing with flavour and freshness, and bouncing with colour and goodness'. Monkfish steaks with tiger prawns, pancetta, beans and tarragon oil is another lively and voguish creation among main courses, while more traditional ribeye steak with roasted shallots, chunky chips and green peppercorn sauce has also impressed. Desserts are along the lines of crème brûlée, and pecan and chocolate tart. Beers include Fuller's London Pride and Adnams, and the short, well-balanced wine list keeps prices respectably under £20, with four of each colour by the glass. SAMPLE DISHES: crispy duck salad £6.95; corn-fed chicken with noodles in soy sauce £11.95; tarte Tatin £3.50.

Licensees Sam Freeman and Clark White (Punch Taverns)
Open *Mon to Thur 5 to 12, Fri and Sat 11 to 12, Sun 11 to 11; bar food Mon to Thur 5 to 11, Fri to Sun 12 to 11*
Details *Children welcome   Background music   No dogs   Amex, Delta, MasterCard, Switch, Visa*

Lansdowne 😋   map 12

90 Gloucester Avenue, NW1 8HX   TEL: (020) 7483 0409

One of London's early gastro-pubs, and 'still a fine model for the genre', the Lansdowne offers a wide choice of drinks, hearty food and a 'laid-back', 'no-airs' atmosphere. The large ground-floor room has wooden furniture and floors and a well-worn look (a testimony to its popularity), while large windows give plenty of light. Upstairs is a more relaxing restaurant, with table service, which accepts reservations. Downstairs, order at the bar: 'best advice is to order everything first time around', maintained one reporter, though 'getting the bill involves the same queuing'. The modish blackboard menu changes regularly and could feature a risotto with red onions, goats' cheese and garlic leaves to start, perhaps followed by guinea fowl stewed with pancetta, sausage, chard and thyme, or, more familiarly, grilled ribeye steak with aïoli, watercress and chips. Desserts follow the route of chocolate and pecan brownie, and apricot tart. Woodforde's Wherry Best Bitter and Fuller's London Pride on handpump, plus around nine wines by the glass, help seal success for an 'efficiently run and friendly operation'. SAMPLE DISHES: home-made soup £4.25; seared salmon with baby leeks and Jersey Royal potatoes £12; grilled brioche with strawberries and ice cream £4.50.

Licensee Amanda Pritchett (freehouse)
Open *Mon 6 to 11, Tue to Sat 12 to 11, Sun 12 to 10.30; bar food Mon 7 to 10, Tue to Fri 12 to 3, 7 to 10, Sat 12 to 3.30, 7 to 10, Sun 12 to 4, 7 to 9.30, restaurant Sun 1 to 3.30, Tue to Sat 7 to 10.30*
Details *Children welcome in bar lunchtimes, restaurant evenings   Wheelchair access bar only (not WC)   No music   Dogs welcome in bar   Delta, MasterCard, Switch, Visa*

Lock Tavern   map 12

35 Chalk Farm Road, NW1 8AJ   TEL: (020) 7482 7163

This place must be handy for patrons of Camden Lock Market opposite. Having said that, though, anyone over 45 will wonder what hit them – even thirty-somethings could feel slightly superannuated – but the young, fashionable and vaguely alternative will lap it up (along with the Fuller's London Pride). Five evenings a week live DJs (Sunday afternoons too) play splendidly eclectic music, but the volume does permit conversation. There is a roof garden at the top, a garden at the bottom, and the two bars in between have a laid-back, fashionable but unpretentious feel and friendly, informal service to match. The menu is simple and good value: a couple of soups, a couple of puds, and in between hearty main dishes for vegetarians and meat eaters, though not fish-fanciers. These might well include a vegetable tagine in an earthen pot (harmonious spicing and tender, well-cooked vegetables contrasting with the crunch of peanuts), Cumberland sausage and mash, or a steak and cheese pie with mash and salad. Saturday breakfast has eggs with everything (plus Benedict, Florentine and Royale), while Sunday lunch offers chicken, beef and nut roasts. Around a dozen wines are listed, with six available by the glass. If you're young enough (in mind or body) to enjoy it here, enjoy it you will. SAMPLE DISHES: sweetcorn and red pepper chowder £3; steak and Guinness stew £6; mint and strawberry chocolate pot £3.

Licensee Rebekkah Potter (586 Ltd)
Open 12 to 11, Sun 12 to 10.30; bar food Mon to Fri 12 to 3, 5 to 9, Sat and Sun 12 to 5, 6 to 9; closed 24, 25 and 26 Dec
Details Children welcome in eating areas Garden and patio Background music, live music Wed to Sun evenings No dogs MasterCard, Switch, Visa

Lord Palmerston

map 12

33 Dartmouth Park Hill, NW5 1HU TEL: (020) 7485 1578

A substantial Victorian corner building, the Lord Palmerston 'remains a pub with an ambitious menu rather than a gastro-pub'. A large island bar dominates the interior, with plenty of high stools for drinkers. Bare-wood floors, tables and chairs – some with prayer-book ledges – and plain, unadorned walls create an unpretentious space with a neighbourhood atmosphere, while generous windows allow light to stream in. To the rear, one room has a glass roof and beyond it there's a small, if rather shady, garden for fair-weather drinks. Food, chalked on a large blackboard, is ordered at the bar and follows a modish Mediterranean slant. The menu is well balanced, with the fruits of the sea represented by moules marinière, or perhaps roast cod with ratatouille, tapénade and red pepper dressing. Toulouse sausage with mash and a red wine and onion jus might tempt carnivores, while vegetarian dishes could feature baked aubergine topped with roasted Mediterranean vegetables and goats' cheese with mixed leaves and basil dressing. Beers on handpump deliver Courage Best and Directors plus Marston's Pedigree, while more than 20 wines, chalked on boards, are available by the glass. SAMPLE DISHES: rigatoni with red pepper and crème fraîche sauce and Parmesan £5; pork fillet with roast sweet potato and ginger with honey sauce £10.50; chocolate tart £3.50.

Licensee Simon Palmer (freehouse)
Open 12 to 11 (10.30 Sun); bar food Mon to Sat 12.30 to 3, 7 to 10, Sun 1 to 4, 7 to 9
Details Children welcome Garden No music Dogs welcome Delta, MasterCard, Switch, Visa

Lots Road Pub & Dining Room
114 Lots Road, SW10 0RJ   TEL: (020) 7352 6645

map 12

On a corner site opposite the entrance to Chelsea Harbour, this erstwhile boozer has been reborn as a thoroughly modern gastro-pub. Inside, the décor is in contemporary-minimalist style, with dark wood floors, a zinc-topped bar counter, and red textile wall hangings adding splashes of colour to the cream-painted walls. There is a small, separate dining area, but one menu is served throughout. Value is good for this part of the world, and the cooking is sophisticated and cosmopolitan while remaining loyal to the pub ethos. Thus, the daily-changing menu may well offer home-made burger with chips alongside spaghetti nero with clams, crab, coriander, chilli and tomato. Both dishes were enjoyed at an inspection meal, demonstrating good ingredients and sound cooking skills, and portions were appropriately hearty. Other options might include pan-fried sea bass with a Parmesan potato cake and pak choi, and roast saddle of lamb with fondant potato and honeyed parsnips. Wadworth 6X, Brakspear Bitter and Fuller's London Pride will keep real ale fans happy, and wine drinkers should be equally pleased with a choice of 14 wines by the glass from £2.75 for the basic Italian white and red to £6 for Laroche's Chablis. Eleven more wines complete a short list that is well suited to the menu and the tone of the place. SAMPLE DISHES: smoked chicken and pear salad with raspberry vinaigrette £6; chicken breast with Mediterranean vegetables and veal jus £10; pear and almond tart with crème fraîche £4.

Licensee Letitia Creevy (Spirit Group)
Open 11 to 11, Sun 12 to 10.30; bar food and restaurant Mon to Fri 12 to 3, 5.30 to 10, Sat 12 to 11, Sun 12 to 10.30; closed 25 Dec
Details Children welcome   Wheelchair access (also WC)   Background music   Dogs welcome
Amex, Delta, MasterCard, Switch, Visa

Peasant
240 St John Street, EC1V 4PH   TEL: (020) 7336 7726
WEBSITE: www.thepeasant.co.uk

map 12

This handsome and imposing nineteenth-century building on a corner site looks very much the traditional London pub and makes the most of its original features, including an impressive mosaic floor and 'amazing' ceiling mouldings. Food is more contemporary. There's a bar menu of 'meze' nibbles – marinated olives, dolmades, asparagus with piquillo peppers, jamón and caper berries, prawns in white wine with chilli, and Spanish meatballs – either individually priced or as a selection platter. It's ideal pub food, perfect to soak up the beer. For those after a full meal the restaurant-like upstairs dining room offers a more substantial menu, typically featuring deep-fried plaice with chips, pea purée and tartare sauce; roast butternut squash stuffed with oyster mushroom risotto; and braised lamb shank with harissa, chickpeas and spiced aubergine. Charles Wells Bombardier is the only draught real ale, but there are a few interesting bottled beers, including Leiffman's Kriek and Leffe. The wine list runs to nearly 40 bottles, ranging from simple house wines at £11.50 to some fairly upmarket offerings for big spenders. Half a dozen of each colour are served by the glass. SAMPLE DISHES: meze selection platter £5.50/£11; baked halibut steak with artichoke hearts, black olives and sun-dried tomatoes £15.50; stewed pears with winter berries and cream £4.

Licensees Gregory and Patrick Wright (freehouse)
Open 12 to 12, Sun 12 to 5; bar food and restaurant Mon to Sat 12 to 3.30, 6 to 11, Sun 12 to 3.30
Details Children welcome Patio Background music Dogs welcome Amex, Delta, MasterCard, Switch, Visa

Perseverance
map 12

63 Lamb's Conduit Street, WC1N 3NB   TEL: (020) 7405 8278

The Perseverance is a retro-pub classic: think young men discussing the sinking of the *Titanic* or perhaps whether the war would be over by Christmas and you have the right time frame. We're talking real flock wallpaper here, faux crystal chandeliers, dark wooden floors, tables and chairs, and banquettes along dark red walls. Upstairs, the small dining room offers quite a contrast. Painted pink, with a couple of mirrors and modern artwork by way of decoration, it's a bright room, with large windows overlooking the street, and with white tablecloths lending a slightly serious tone. The restaurant menu doesn't follow the retro theme but instead moves with the times to deliver appealing and ambitious dishes: starters of rillettes of salmon with smoked salmon, cucumber and apple jelly, for example, might be followed by main courses of fillet of sea bass with asparagus and fennel, tomato tarte Tatin and rocket pesto, or roast chicken with tarragon mash and peppered goats' cheese sauce. Finish with something like strawberry and thyme soup with peach sorbet and champagne sabayon. A bar-only menu offers tapas-style dishes in the evenings. Courage Directors is the regular on handpump, plus a guest ale, and ten wines are sold by the glass. SAMPLE DISHES: red onion tart with goats' cheese and roast pepper £5; roast rump of lamb with minted salsa verde, spinach and roast cherry tomatoes £12.50; peach and apple crumble with vanilla ice cream £4.25.

Licensee Billy Drew (freehouse)
Open 12.30 to 11 (10.30 Sun); bar food and restaurant Mon to Sat 12.30 to 3, 7 to 10, Sun 12 to 4; tapas menu Mon to Fri 6 to 9.30.
Details Children welcome Wheelchair access Jukebox Dogs welcome exc on Sun Amex, Delta, MasterCard, Switch, Visa

St Johns ✿
map 12

91 Junction Road, N19 5QU   TEL: (020) 7272 1587

There's nothing about the exterior of this large Victorian pub, with its glazed-tile frontage and big windows on the humdrum main drag between Tufnell Park and Archway, that 'would tell you there is exceptional food inside'. The large, buzzy bar has high ceilings and wooden floors and is filled with pine and oak tables, wooden chairs (some school-room style), leather sofas and a coal fire. A few designer touches run to large sprays of flowers and modern artworks, but overall there's an unpretentious, welcoming, almost old-fashioned appeal that attracts the trendy, urbane thirty-somethings. At the back is the dining room (though you can eat anywhere), a vast space with magnificent glass chandeliers, another coal fire and simply laid tables – and it's a 'whole lot quieter than the bar'. The modish menu of 'sophisticated but hearty and appealing' dishes comes chalked on blackboards and could open with chargrilled squid, chorizo, red pepper and rocket salad, with perhaps roast monkfish with saffron, pea, red onion and mussel risotto to follow, or chicken breast stuffed with mushrooms in red pepper jus, and steamed apricot pudding with custard to finish. Beers, which change frequently, might include Fuller's London Pride and Adnams on handpump, while the compact wine list offers a few by the glass. SAMPLE DISHES: pork, duck, black pudding and leek terrine £5.50; seared tuna with sautéed potatoes, spinach and peppercorn sauce £12; raspberry crème brûlée £4.50.

Licensee Nick Sharpe (Unique Pub Company)
Open 11.30 to 11, Sun 12.30 to 11; bar food Mon 5 to 11, Tue to Sat 11 to 11, Sun 12 to 10.30; restaurant Mon 6.30 to 11, Tue to Sat 12 to 3.30, 6.30 to 11, Sun 12 to 4, 6.30 to 10.30
Details Children welcome   Wheelchair access   Patio   Background music   Dogs welcome   Amex, Delta, MasterCard, Switch, Visa

Salisbury Tavern ༝   map 12
21 Sherbrooke Road, SW6 7HX   TEL: (020) 7381 4005

Hidden away in Fulham, the Salisbury's stylish remodelled interior draws an affluent crowd to its dining-pub doors (it's under the same ownership as the Admiral Codrington; see entry). The large open space has light pouring through big windows, bright and cheerful paintwork and board floors. Seating is in booths, on sofas, armchairs or wooden chairs, and there's a real neighbourhood atmosphere, with TV screens installed above the bar. Fuller's London Pride and Wells Bombardier Premium Bitter are the regulars on handpump, along with a guest like Old Speckled Hen. Straightforward, traditional pub fare is offered at lunchtime only, from cottage pie and fish and chips to eggs Benedict or fishcakes. Meanwhile, in the evening, the separate, upmarket dining room at the rear cranks up the culinary gears with more ambitious idea such as warm salad of confit duck and braised lamb shank. All the wines on the 27-bottle list are available by the glass. SAMPLE DISHES: Italian cured meat with fresh Parmesan and olives £7.25; crispy salmon and smoked haddock fishcakes with curly kale £9.75; trio of home-made crème brûlée £4.95.

Licensee Kim Cottingham (Longshot Estates)
Open 11.30 to 11; bar food 12 to 2.30 (3.30 Sat and Sun), restaurant 7 to 10.30
Details Children welcome at lunchtimes   Wheelchair access (also WC)   Occasional live or background music   Dogs welcome in bar lunchtimes   Amex, Delta, MasterCard, Switch, Visa

---

༝ ༝ *indicates a pub serving food on a par with 'seriously good' restaurants, where the cooking achieves consistent high quality.*

Salusbury Pub and Dining Room 🍸 🍇 map 12
50–52 Salusbury Road, NW6 6NN   TEL: (020) 7328 3286

This double-fronted building on a busy street north of Queens Park tube station is clear about its roles. At the left, the sign reads 'Pub', and it gets packed with a lively young crowd who can generate decibels aplenty; lubrication comes in the form of periodically changing beers – maybe Adnams Bitter and Bass. On the right, behind the sign saying 'Dining Room', are bare wooden floors, a few oriental-looking prints on the plain walls and a hotchpotch of tables, chairs and benches of various shapes and sizes. The cooking is rustic Italian, so expect pasta (in the shape of maybe spaghetti with clams, chilli and garlic, or porcini ravioli), risotto – pumpkin, for example – and plenty of gusto in main dishes like osso buco with mash, or oven-fried hake with green beans and tomatoes. Start the meal with, say, cured goose breast with mushroom tartare and truffle oil, and round it off with 'diplomatico' (a version of chocolate and rum mousse) or tiramisù of panettone with white chocolate. Friendly, informally dressed staff cope well with the crowds. Eighty or so wines are crammed into two handwritten pages, with a dozen house wines offered by the glass from £2.60 to £4.15. The list ranges the world looking for great flavours, picking up a bigger-than-average Italian selection along the way, but not a lot of bottles will give you change out of £15. Wines are grouped together by style but the commentary is otherwise limited to quirky one-word summaries: 'funky, value, crowdpleaser, monster, spiceshop'. SAMPLE DISHES: borlotti bean and home-made sausage soup £4; pappardelle with duck ragoût £7; pannacotta with chocolate and coffee £4.

Licensees Nicholas Mash and Robert Classen (freehouse)
Open Tue to Sat 12 to 11, Sun 12 to 10.30, Mon 5 to 11; bar food Tue to Sun 12.30 to 3.30, all week 7 to 10.15, Sun 7 to 10; closed 25 and 26 Dec
Details Children welcome at lunchtimes Wheelchair access (not WC) Patio Background music Dogs welcome in pub only MasterCard, Switch, Visa

Sutton Arms Pub and Dining Room 🍸 🍇 map 12
6 Carthusian Street, EC1M 6EB   TEL: (020) 7253 0723

Rosie Sykes may be familiar to readers of the *Guardian*, since she is the paper's self-styled Kitchen Doctor. In 2002 she teamed up with Jon Flitney and opened this promising venture in a side-street pub within walking distance of the Barbican. The traditional downstairs bar, with wooden furniture, gets packed with drinkers, who can graze on a few tapas-style nibbles such as patatas bravas, leek tart with salad, and Manchego cheese with rocket and olive bread. Most of the culinary action takes place in the rustically decorated upstairs dining room, which also has a bar for beer and wine. The short menu often changes twice daily ('great for the regulars'), and vegetarians are well served with the likes of squash with sage, cream, Parmesan and toast ('an oven-to-table dish of melting comfort food'), and goats' cheese gnocchi with roast beetroot and shallots. Otherwise, the kitchen is keen on big earthy flavours: oxtail soup, roast belly pork with red cabbage, and braised rabbit with mash. To finish, there's an 'awesome' rendition of chocolate and praline marquise with crème fraîche, or Neal's Yard cheeses with oatcakes and sesame biscuits. Real ales are from Fuller's and Ridleys, and the pub boasts a smart contemporary wine list of over 30 bins with 18 available by the glass. Make that 27 if you add the fizz, sweeties and selection of three dry sherries for aperitifs. Prices start at a modest (especially for London) £10 per bottle. SAMPLE DISHES: lentil and Serrano ham soup £4.50; roast cod with white-bean stew and romesco £13.50; ricotta and saffron tart £5.

Licensee Jon Flitney (freehouse)
Open *Mon to Fri 12 to 11; bar food Mon to Fri 12.30 to 10.30, restaurant 12.30 to 2, 6 to 10*
Details *No children   Background music   No dogs   Amex, Delta, MasterCard, Switch, Visa*

Swag & Tails   map 12
10–11 Fairholt Street, SW7 1EG   TEL: (020) 7584 6926
WEBSITE: www.swagandtails.com

Tucked away in the quiet residential streets of exclusive Knightsbridge, the well-kept flower-adorned exterior of the Swag & Tails makes a charming first impression. The interior doesn't disappoint either. The informal but civilised bar is decked out with floorboards, wooden furniture and a fire, with cream walls packed with prints above the half-panelling. Behind it, the dining areas have a more contemporary edge, with mirrors, posters, prints and contemporary artwork on the walls, while the conservatory-style room beyond has a tiled floor. The menu brings together some contemporary, if not trendy, culinary notions, from a starter of pan-seared foie gras with rhubarb jam, spiced red wine reduction and sherry vinegar caramel, to main courses of chargrilled loin of tuna with peppery coriander noodles, pak choi, roasted shiitake mushrooms and a dressing of spring onions, sesame and soy, or 'excellent-quality' chicken breast stuffed with a vibrantly flavoured tarragon mousse served on a mixture of wilted green vegetables and bacon dauphinois, and desserts of perhaps vanilla rice pudding with honey-glazed peaches and cherry sorbet. Those after something more traditional could opt for ribeye steak braised in red wine with tomatoes, shallots and mushrooms, and lighter dishes of a sirloin steak sandwich or a burger are also possibilities. The wine list, arranged by grape variety, is a well-chosen selection, with nine, plus some dessert wines and a champagne, offered by the glass, including a white Menetou-Salon. Marston's Pedigree and Wells Bombardier Premium Bitter are on draught.

Licensee Annemaria Boomer Davies (freehouse)
Open *Mon to Fri 11 to 11; bar food 12 to 3, 6 to 10; closed bank hols*
Details *Children welcome in restaurant   Wheelchair access (also WC)   No music   Dogs welcome in evenings only   Amex, Delta, MasterCard, Switch, Visa*

Waterway ☼   map 12
54 Formosa Street, W9   TEL: (020) 7266 3557   WATERSIDE
WEBSITE: www.thewaterway.co.uk

Hard by the Grand Union Canal, with an outside wooden terrace making the most of the setting, the Waterway is an unprepossessing building of fairly recent construction. It makes a more favourable impression inside, with a

1960s lounge-bar feel to the décor – dark wooden floor, pale walls, low, dark leather sofas, and a brick fireplace. Here you can enjoy bar snacks like Toulouse sausage sandwich, chunky chips with aïoli, or cream of Jerusalem artichoke soup. A row of closely spaced pillars separates the bar from the main dining area, where a 'grown-up' menu offers starters of mackerel ceviche with rocket, shallots and fried breadcrumbs, or steamed mussels with ham hock, Pernod and tarragon, followed by main courses like roast halibut with olive oil mash and pipérade, or free-range chicken breast with baby vegetables and gratin dauphinois. Draught beers include Fuller's London Pride, Flowers Original and Hoegaarden, and there is a varied and respectable list of wines arranged by style and priced from £10.50. Ten wines are available by the glass. SAMPLE DISHES: crisp leek and rosemary dumplings with carrot velouté and white truffle oil £6.50; pot-roast lamb shank with flageolet beans, new potatoes and mint £13.50; upside-down pear and ginger cake with butterscotch sauce £5.50.

Licensee Mitch Upton (freehouse)
Open 12 to 11, Sun 12 to 10.30; bar food 12 to 11, Sun 12 to 10.30; restaurant 12 to 3, 7 to 10 (9.45 Sun); closed 25 and 26 Dec, 1 Jan
Details Car park   Wheelchair access (not WC)   Patio   Background music   Dogs welcome exc in restaurant   Amex, MasterCard, Switch, Visa

White Horse 😊 🍺   map 12

1 Parsons Green, SW6 4UL   TEL: (020) 7736 2115
WEBSITE: www.whitehorsesw6.com

The White Horse is a pub of considerable proportions, set on a corner by Parsons Green. Inside, the décor comprises crimson walls, oak panels, a flagstone floor, church pews and large pine tables, which all add up to give the place a traditional feel, though large plants, mirrors and Venetian blinds give a touch of modernity, and as well as the main bar there is a restaurant upstairs. Not only does the printed menu come with suggested wines, but unusually beers are recommended to match dishes: a Belgian blond to go with salmon fishcakes with tarragon mayonnaise and a poached egg, for example. They really know their beers here, and the range on offer is seriously impressive. As well as top-quality British real ales like Harveys Sussex Best Bitter, Adnams Broadside and Oakham JHB on draught, there are sixty classic bottled beers from around the world. And there is an impressive list of over seventy wines, some with three-figure price tags. Thirteen wines come by the glass. Food, though not cheap, also comes up to a high standard. Old favourites like lightly battered cod with chunky chips and mushy peas, or 'true butcher's sausages' on a mound of cabbage and mash are on the menu, but more unusual are teasmoked lamb rump with aubergine pickle and lemon couscous, or basil-infused chargrilled tuna with new potatoes, peppers and olives. Substantial starters (perfect for a light supper) might feature large field mushrooms topped with grilled goats' cheese with rocket salad, and to finish there might be rum and raisin bread-and-butter pudding. SAMPLE DISHES: chilli-salt squid with tomato and coriander salsa £6.75; pan-roast pork chop with caramelised apples and crackling £11.25; vanilla cheesecake £4.

Licensee Mark Dorber (Mitchell & Butlers)
Open *11 to 11, Sun 12 to 10.30; bar food and restaurant Mon to Fri 12 to 3, 6 to 10, Sat and Sun 12 to 10; closed 25 Dec*
Details *Children welcome in eating areas   Wheelchair access (also WC)   Garden and patio No smoking in restaurant   Occasional live music   Dogs welcome   Amex, Delta, MasterCard, Switch, Visa*

William IV   map 12
786 Harrow Road, NW10 5JX   TEL: (020) 8969 5944
WEBSITE: www.william-iv.co.uk

Its position opposite Kensal Green Cemetery may not induce the happiest of moods, but this tastefully refurbished Victorian pub draws the crowds. Bar and restaurant are separate entities, with a garden each for al fresco dining and drinks. 'There's something of the public school common room about the bar,' thought a reporter, as it occupies a large, high-ceilinged room painted in rather gloomy shades of pale green and cream, dotted with wooden tables, chairs and well-worn sofas. Though it may be cavernous, 'it feels comfortable and laid back'. The menu runs on modern lines and might feature steamed mussels with 'authentic-tasting' Thai red curry, slow-roast belly pork with artichokes and French beans, or beer-battered skate cheeks with chips and tartare sauce. There's a good-value one-course lunch option for £7.50 too, including a glass of wine: perhaps smoked haddock and dill fishcake with spinach and a poached egg. For beer drinkers there's Fuller's London Pride and Boddingtons, plus a guest, perhaps Timothy Taylor Landlord, while the short wine list offers seven or eight house wines by the glass. SAMPLE DISHES: poached asparagus with hollandaise and a poached egg £5.95; sirloin steak with mash and snail butter £13.75; strawberry jelly with blood orange coulis £4.50.

Licensee Jane Bower (freehouse)
Open *Mon to Wed 12 to 11, Thur to Sat 12 to 12, Sun 12 to 10.30; bar food and restaurant Mon to Fri 12 to 3, 6 to 10.30 (11 Thur and Fri), Sat 12.30 to 4.30, 7 to 11, Sun 12 to 4.30, 6 to 9.30*
Details *Children welcome   Wheelchair access   Garden   Occasional live or background music No dogs   Amex, Delta, Diners, MasterCard, Switch, Visa*

England

Fleece ✿   NEW ENTRY

Main Street, Addingham LS29 0LY   TEL: (01943) 830491
on A6160, off A65 W of Ilkley

This solid-looking stone pub on the main road through the village attracts a
mixed bunch of locals, diners and walkers, drawn as much by the atmosphere
as by the food. Black-painted beams, stone walls, flagstone floors, and a lovely
wood-burning stove and a log fire provide a comfortable environment, while
there are plenty of things to look at, from a stag's head to copper kettles and
pans hanging from the ceiling. There are lots of things to choose from on the
long, enterprising menu too. You could start with broccoli and Stilton soup
and proceed to a huge pie for main course – meat and potato, say, or chunky
fish – or the aptly described jumbo Whitby haddock with chunky chips and
mushy peas. Omelettes and sandwiches – perhaps rump of beef with dripping
and home-pickled onions – are possibilities, and a good range of farmhouse
cheeses is a good alternative to desserts of bread-and-butter pudding, or
crème brûlée. Black Sheep Best Bitter, Tetley Bitter and Timothy Taylor
Landlord are on draught, and a dozen wines are sold by the glass, with the
full, well-chosen selection approaching 40 bottles. SAMPLE DISHES: chicken
liver pâté with tomato chutney £4; seared sea bass with wild mushrooms and
garlic £12; plum and apple crumble £3.25.

Licensee Chris Monkman (Punch Group)
Open 12 to 11; bar food and restaurant Mon to Sat 12 to 2.15, 6 to 9.30, Sun 12 to 8
Details Children welcome   Car park   Wheelchair access (not WC)   Garden   No smoking in
restaurant   Occasional live music   Dogs welcome exc in restaurant   Delta, MasterCard, Switch, Visa

Valiant Trooper

Trooper Road, Aldbury HP23 5RW   TEL: (01442) 851203
off A41, 2½m E of Tring

It's a joyous surprise to find that Hertfordshire sub-suburbia runs out just
before you get to Aldbury, and suddenly you're in real country. And the
Valiant Trooper (né 1752) is a real country pub too, catering for walkers and
cyclists as well as obviously appreciative locals. Outside, it's small, pink-
washed and climber-grown; inside it seems larger than expected, although the
beams are low and plentiful, and there are open fires and wooden tables and

chairs with the look of long and faithful service. The bar serves Fuller's London Pride, Adnams Bitter and Morrells Oxford Blue, supplemented by two guest ales. You can have sandwiches, ciabatta and jacket potatoes, all with various fillings, in the bar, or you can eat in the restaurant (once a stable) at the back. Here blackboard menus offer starters like green-lipped mussels and mains like steak and ale pie. One couple used the blackboard devoted to game and fish to brighten a grey November day, choosing sautéed pheasant with field mushrooms, bacon and white onion ragoût, and roast partridge with roast fennel and tarragon sauce – both were generous portions and accompanied by lashings of vegetables. A list of 16 wines includes eight by the (large) glass, and bottle prices start at £9. SAMPLE DISHES: grilled goats' cheese £4; baked lemon cod fillet £9; sticky toffee pudding £3.50.

Licensee Tim O'Gorman (freehouse)
Open 11.30 to 11, Sun 12 to 10.30; bar food and restaurant all week 12 to 2 (2.30 Sun), Tue to Sat 6.30 to 9.15; closed 25 Dec
Details Children welcome in eating areas   Car park   Wheelchair access (also WC)   Garden and patio   No-smoking area in bar, no smoking in dining room   No music   Dogs welcome on lead Diners, MasterCard, Switch, Visa

ALDERMINSTER   Warwickshire   map 5

▲ Bell

Shipston Road, Alderminster CV37 8NY   TEL: (01789) 450414
WEBSITE: www.thebellald.co.uk
on A3400, 4m S of Stratford-upon-Avon

The Bell is a large yellow building, once a coaching inn, on the main road through the village. The spacious interior is traditionally decorated to create a soothing atmosphere, with plump low sofas in the lounge area, a number of plants, floors of boards, flagstones or carpet, and well-spaced tables and chairs of bare wood; a conservatory extension affords views of the Stour Valley as well as of the inn's own courtyard garden. Baguettes are served at lunchtime, while the menu, which changes every two months, deals in such favourites as wild mushroom risotto, or chicken drumsticks in barbecue sauce, followed by steak and kidney pudding, braised lamb shank, or fishcakes with chive hollandaise. From further afield come bobotie, lamb tagine with lemon couscous, and Thai green scampi curry with fragrant rice, while the choice of desserts runs from sticky toffee pudding to praline semi-freddo with summer fruits. Greene King IPA and guest ales, such as Hook Norton Old Hooky or Old Speckled Hen, are on handpump, and there are 15 wines to be had by the glass from a list of over 30 bottles. Special events are sometimes held, like a 'Flavours of France' or live 'Jazz' menu. SAMPLE DISHES: crab tart £6.25; duck breast on roasted vegetables with Cumberland dressing £12; treacle tart £4.25.

Licensee Keith Brewer (freehouse)
Open 12 to 2.30, 7 to 11 (10.30 Sun); bar food and restaurant 12 to 2, 7 to 9.30; closed evenings 24 to 27 Dec and 1 Jan
Details Children welcome   Car park   Wheelchair access (also WC)   Garden   No smoking exc in entrance bar   Occasional live music   Dogs by arrangement   Amex, Delta, Diners, MasterCard, Switch, Visa   Accommodation: 6 rooms, B&B £25 to £85

Grosvenor Arms 🍺

Chester Road, Aldford CH3 6HJ   TEL: (01244) 620228
WEBSITE: www.grosvenorarms-aldford.co.uk
just off B5130, 5m S of Chester

'A beacon for fine ales and superb cuisine' was one visitor's verdict on this 'immensely popular' pub overlooking the River Dee, formerly the alehouse for workers on the Grosvenor Estate. Several distinct areas surround the bar and servery at the heart of the building, each with a slightly different mood – the bright conservatory 'bursting with foliage', for example, and the 'snug' bar, which has a coal fire. A 'pleasing array of handpumps' dispenses Caledonian Deuchars IPA and beers from the local Robinson's and Weetwood breweries, among others – usually around six ales are on offer at a time. About 20 wines are available by the glass from a short but enthusiastic wine list. House wines are £9.95 and half the list is £15 or under. An enormous blackboard lists the food (admirably served all day) and the choice is extensive, ranging from hearty sandwiches through starters (salads, such as Roquefort, pear and walnut, or 'thick and warming' soups like sweetcorn and watercress) and main courses – simple affairs like ploughman's as well as more elaborate dishes such as pan-fried duck breast with black pudding, spring onions and white-bean casserole – finishing up with 'calorie-packed delights' along the lines of banoffi pie. Note that this pub is part of a small chain; see also Dysart Arms, Bunbury; the Hare, Langton Green; Old Harkers Arms, Chester; and the Pant-yr-Ochain, Gresford. SAMPLE DISHES: duck rillettes with orange marmalade and walnut toast £5.75; grilled plaice on stir-fried asparagus and cabbage with tomato and tarragon butter £11.25; cherry crumble £4.25.

Licensees R.G. Kidd and D.J. Brunning (Brunning & Price Ltd)
Open 11.30 to 11, Sun 12 to 10.30; bar food 12 to 10 (9 Sun)
Details *Children welcome; no under-14s after 6pm   Car park   Wheelchair access (also WC)
Garden   No-smoking area   No music   Dogs welcome in 1 bar   Amex, Delta, MasterCard, Switch,
Visa*

Bell Inn 🍺

Aldworth RG8 9SE   TEL: (01635) 578272
on B4009, 3m W of Streatley

The Bell has been in the hands of the Macaulay family for over 200 years; it has been a pub for 400, and the building is even older. Comfort then and now is different, so hard wooden chairs, narrow benches and odd tables are what you get. It stands opposite the old village well, and the garden and back field are edged by farms and woodland. Beer is the main focus here, and the pub stocks a decent selection of well-kept ales, among them West Berkshire Maggs, Magnificent Mild, Old Tyler Bitter, and Arkells 3B and Kingsdown Ale. Wine hardly counts, although Berry Bros and Rudd's Good Ordinary Claret, one of four house wines sold by the glass, is decent enough. Food in the bar (there is no restaurant) is limited to home-made soup, Aga-warmed rolls with generous and good-quality hot fillings ranging from Devon crab to ox tongue, ploughman's, and a dish of the day, which might be pasta, plus hot treacle pudding. Neither canned music nor gaming machines disturb the peace of the Bell's customers. SAMPLE DISHES: hot and crusty turkey roll £1.95; spinach and ricotta cannelloni with salad £4; sticky toffee pudding with pecan sauce £3.

Licensee H.E. Macaulay (freehouse)

Open Tue to Sun and bank hol Mon 11 to 3, 6 to 11; bar food 11 to 2.45, 6 to 10.35; closed 25 Dec

Details Children welcome in family room   Car park   Wheelchair access (not WC)   Garden   Occasional live music   Dogs welcome   No cards

ALFRISTON   East Sussex   map 3

▲ George Inn   NEW ENTRY

High Street, Alfriston BN26 5SY   TEL: (01323) 870319

In the pretty village of Alfriston much of a terrace on one side of the main street consists of the George's distinctive frontage: local flint with red-brick trimmings below, the upper floor zebra-striped half-timbering. The 'smashing and spacious' interior has two huge bar areas and a large dining room. The former offer Greene King IPA and Abbot Ale, Morland Original and Old Speckled Hen in spare surroundings dominated by old, dark wood – in floor, ceiling and the stripped studwork partitions – mellowed by the flickering of a roaring log fire. The dining room's apricot-coloured walls give a softer, more domestic feel. Portions are concise and timing accurate: witness one diner's three plump scallops in a beurre noir with chopped hazelnuts, lime zest and coriander leaves. Alternative starters might be chicken and duck terrine, or deep-fried Brie with Cumberland sauce. Lunchtime mains – like beer-battered salmon and chips, say, or beef braised in red wine with mushrooms and mash – come cheaper than the evening's trout Szechuan-style with chilli noodles, or pancakes filled with wild mushroom soufflé; a well-timed, tasty roast rack of lamb came with nicely textured sweet potato mash and subtle lemon and mint sauce. Desserts span treacle sponge pudding and glazed pears with almond zabaglione. From a list of 24, starting from £10, six wines are served by the glass. SAMPLE DISHES: seafood chowder £6; veal escalope stuffed with Parma ham and shrimps in sage and Marsala sauce £15; Key lime pie £4.

Licensees Roland and Cate Couch (Greene King)

Open 12 to 11, Sun 12 to 10.30; bar food 12 to 2.30, 7 to 9 (10 Fri and Sat); closed 25, 26 and 27 Dec

Details Children welcome in eating areas   Garden   No smoking in dining room   Occasional background music   Dogs welcome   Delta, MasterCard, Switch, Visa   Accommodation: 7 rooms, B&B £40 to £100

Which? Online subscribers will find The Which? Pub Guide *online, along with other Which? guides and magazines, at* www.which.net. *Phone (08459) 830254 for information on how to become a subscriber.*

ALNMOUTH   Northumberland   **map 10**

▲ Saddle Hotel

24–25 Northumberland Street, Alnmouth NE66 2RA   TEL: (01665) 830476
from A1, take Alnwick turn-off, then Alnmouth exit at mini-roundabout

The Saddle is in a terrace on the main street of this picturesque village on the
mouth of the Aln but is just minutes from the beach. Inside, fires, a striped
green carpet and busily patterned wallpaper create a homely and comfortable
atmosphere, and a separate restaurant deals in set-price menus, although
people just wanting one course can order from these in the bar. The bar menu
itself is long enough to satisfy most tastes, with starters of Craster kipper,
potato wedges with garlic dip, or egg and prawn cocktail. Sandwiches, salads –
crab when available, for instance – and vegetarian dishes are also listed, and
steak and kidney or shepherd's pie, chicken curry, or breaded plaice are what
to expect among main courses. Blackboard specials broaden the range to crab
and prawn cocktail, followed by chicken with noodles in a creamy leek sauce,
and then strawberry pavlova. Old Speckled Hen and Theakston Cool Cask
are among the real ales on draught, and three house wines are available by the
glass. SAMPLE DISHES: smoked mackerel with horseradish £3.50; chicken
pancake £10; knickerbocker glory £3.75.

Licensees Mr and Mrs M. McMonagle (freehouse)
Open 11 to 11, Sun 12 to 10.30; bar food 12 to 2, 6 to 9 (8.30 Sun), restaurant 6 to 8.30
Details Children welcome in eating areas   Wheelchair access (not WC)   No smoking in restaurant
Occasional background music   Dogs welcome   Delta, MasterCard, Switch, Visa   Accommodation:
8 rooms, B&B £33.50 to £67

ALRESFORD   Hampshire   **map 2**

Globe on the Lake

The Soke, Alresford SO24 9DB   TEL: (01962) 732294
WEBSITE: www.theglobeonthelake.co.uk   **WATERSIDE**
on lower end of Broad Street on B3046 Basingstoke road

The Globe sits beside Old Alresford lake, where ducks and swans provide a
summer diversion for outdoor drinkers and diners. Inside, log fires, low
beams and traditional dark wooden tables, plus a sofa next to an inglenook,
embody winter cosiness. Above the fireplace, the daily-changing blackboard
menu has dishes ranging from, say, variously filled baps to roast red pepper
stuffed with goats' cheese and lentils, or Balinese baby squid with Thai spicing and coconut rice – followed perhaps by orange and thyme pannacotta.
John Bullish alternatives may include pork and apple pie, or traditional
Sunday roasts, plus bread-and-butter pudding with custard. A generous
sixteen wines by the glass kick off a decent list, with both Old and New World
offerings coming in well under the £20 mark. Real ale drinkers are looked
after, too, with Fuller's London Pride, Wadworth 6X, Brakspear Bitter, and
Ringwood Best all on tap. SAMPLE DISHES: Cape Malay chicken curry and
poppadom £8.95; seared and crusted tuna with coriander and basil £10.50;
sticky toffee pudding with toffee sauce and ice cream £4.50.

Licensees Marc and Emma Duveen Conway (freehouse)
Open 11 to 3, 6 to 11 (Sat summer 11 to 11), Sun 12 to 3, 7 to 10.30 (Sun summer 12 to
10.30); bar food and restaurant 12 to 2, 6.30 to 9, Sun 12.30 to 2, 7 to 9; closed 25 and 26 Dec
Details Children welcome in restaurant   Wheelchair access (not WC)   Garden and patio
No smoking in restaurant   No music   No dogs   Amex, MasterCard, Switch, Visa

AMBLESIDE   Cumbria   map 8

▲ Drunken Duck Inn 😵 🍺 🌼

Barngates, Ambleside LA22 0NG   TEL: (015394) 36347
WEBSITE: www.drunkenduckinn.co.uk
off B5286, between Ambleside and Hawkshead, 3m S of Ambleside

Barngates is a few miles south of Ambleside, reached – if you are coming
from the south – by a twisting, undulating country lane (with some hair-rais-
ing gradients along the way). In fact, Barngates amounts to not much more
than this attractively well-maintained stone-built pub, which stands at a
crossroads with nothing but fields and trees for miles around. No surprise,
then, that many of the clientele are walkers. The various bar areas are done
out elegantly with polished dark floorboards and plain coloured walls covered
with a mix of prints, watercolours, advertising posters and so on. Among the
star attractions here are the excellent real ales from the Barngates brewery,
which is on the premises – one reporter was particularly impressed with the
latest addition to the range, a smooth, hoppy pale ale called Catnap. The wine
list does by-the-glass in high style, with a selection of 20 wines priced from
£2.80 for a simple vin de pays Sauvignon Blanc right up to £8.80 for a chance
to sample one of the top bottles. The full selection runs to over 50 bottles,
with something to suit all pockets. It's not just the drinks that impress: there's
the menu of classy modern British cooking too. Local produce is put to good
use, whether in a starter of smoked salmon with cream cheese, a light main
course of vegetable samosas with cardamom and lemon rice, or a more
substantial dish of ginger-marinated pork fillet on sautéed leeks and bacon
with roast potatoes, black pudding and garlic jus. The kitchen is self-
possessed enough to allow the quality of ingredients to shine through: an
inspector enthused about the unpretentious simplicity of grilled herring with
crisp skin and moist flesh, served on fresh-tasting leaves with an intense
tomato salsa. SAMPLE DISHES: grilled black pudding on cumin-roast squash
with chervil butter sauce £4.75; sea bass on rosemary and Parmesan risotto
with basil pesto £10; warm pecan pie with toffee banana ice cream £5.

Licensee Stephanie Barton (freehouse)
Open 11.30 to 11, Sun 12 to 10.30; bar food and restaurant 12 to 2.30, 6 to 9; closed to
residents, but bar open, 24 and 25 Dec
Details Children welcome   Car park   Wheelchair access (also WC)   Patio   No smoking in eating
areas   Background music in restaurant   Dogs welcome in bar only   Amex, Delta, MasterCard,
Switch, Visa   Accommodation: 16 rooms, B&B £56.25 to £165

🍺 indicates a pub serving exceptional draught beers.

APPLEY   Somerset   map 2

Globe Inn
Appley TA21 0HJ   TEL: (01823) 672327
from M5 junction 26 take A38 W for 3m; turn right to Greenham and after 1m turn right at
T-junction, signposted Stawley; pub further ½m on left

Down narrow, winding lanes you will find this rambling 500-year-old pub
hidden away in a secluded hamlet surrounded by unspoilt rolling countryside. Despite the isolated location, it is a popular place, both with travellers
stopping for refreshment (it is not far off the A38) and with locals out for a
meal. Four rustic but comfortable rooms radiate off a narrow, flagstoned
central passageway, and one menu operates throughout. Starters range from
home-made soups, via 'prawn Othello' (cold pancake filled with prawns,
celery and pineapple in a marie-rose sauce), to mushrooms cooked in garlic
cream and horseradish. Seafood – smoked haddock and bacon chowder, for
example, or grilled salmon in cream and wine sauce – and steaks help fill out
the main-course choices, along with venison pie and Thai chicken curry.
Beers on handpump include Palmer IPA, Cotleigh Tawny plus a guest. Four
wines are sold by the glass from a list that runs to 20-plus bottles. SAMPLE
DISHES: fish soup £6; half roasted duckling with Madeira sauce £12; hot
Toblerone crêpe £4.50.

Licensees A.W. and E.J. Burt (freehouse)
Open *Tue to Sat and bank hol Mon 11 to 3, 6.30 to 11, Sun 12 to 3, 7 to 10.30; bar food and
restaurant Tue to Sun 12 to 2, 7 to 10*
Details *Children welcome   Car park   Wheelchair access (also WC)   Garden   No smoking in
dining room   No music   No dogs   MasterCard, Switch, Visa*

ARDELEY   Hertfordshire   map 3

Jolly Waggoner
Ardeley SG2 7AH   TEL: (01438) 861350
off B1037 at Cromer, 5m E of Stevenage

At the heart of a pretty country village, the Jolly Waggoner is a warm and
welcoming cottagey-type pub with an attractive courtyard at the front. Horse
brasses, wooden beams and lots of knick-knacks set the tone well, although a
collection of empty champagne bottles hints at the high-life as well. Bar
snacks include salads of various descriptions (cheese, warm bacon and mushroom, say, or ham and Camembert), as well as home-made soups and sandwiches, while more substantial dishes encompass calf's liver sautéed with
butter and sage, steak and kidney pie, and perhaps vegetable and pasta bake.
Look at the board for puddings, which might include Bakewell tart with
vanilla custard, raspberry and toffee brûlée or chocolate sponge with a rich
chocolate sauce. Next door, a slightly smarter, but still tiny, restaurant, Rose
Cottage, seems almost like the dining room of a private house, and serves
more elaborate menu, from goats' cheese topped with mushrooms and tomatoes wrapped in puff pastry, to chicken and salmon roulade accompanied by
warm Italian vegetables. Greene King IPA and Abbot Ale are on tap, and the

wine list offers a compact selection, with just house red and white by the glass. SAMPLE DISHES: smoked salmon and goats' cheese croûtons £6.25; omelette Arnold Bennett £7.50; sticky date cake with toffee sauce and vanilla ice cream £4.25.

Licensee D.J. Perkins (Greene King)

Open Tue to Fri (and bank hol Mon) 12 to 2.30, 6.30 to 11, Sat 12 to 3, 6.30 to 11, Sun 12 to 3, 6.30 to 10.30; bar food Tue to Sun (and bank hol Mon) 12 to 2, Tue to Sat (and bank hol Mon) 6.30 to 9/9.30; closed Tue after bank hol Mon

Details No children under 7   Car park   Wheelchair access (not WC)   Garden and patio No-smoking area   Background music   No dogs   MasterCard, Switch, Visa

ARDINGTON   Oxfordshire   map 2

▲ Boar's Head 😺😺 🍇
Church Street, Ardington OX12 8QA   TEL: (01235) 833254
off A417, 2m E of Wantage

This handsome half-timbered pub is so neat and well maintained that you might think it was of modern construction, but it has in fact been an inn at least since the eighteenth century. The open-plan bar areas are simply decorated, and an informal mood is set by the crowd of drinkers congregating around the bar. It may look more like your local boozer than anything else – there is even a dartboard in one corner – but since Bruce and Kay Buchan took over the reins early in 2001 it has leaped up a few divisions in the pub food league, now providing both an excellent restaurant and top-notch bar meals. The restaurant menu goes in for an ambitious and inventive style: witness roast cod with sweetbreads, chorizo, rösti and port sauce. By contrast, the philosophy when it comes to bar food is to keep everything simple. The succinct blackboard menu mostly consists of one-dish meals, plus a few baguettes at lunchtime. A generous bowl of 'super-quality, super-fresh' mussels in wine and cream, and crispy duck in a mixed herby salad with warm fig segments and a five-spice dressing both made a favourable impression at inspection. Among other options might be grilled scallops with 'hazelnut crumb', a Portland crab and brandy omelette, or oak-smoked pork sausages with mash. Bread is a highlight: several interesting varieties are baked daily on the premises. Beer spotters will appreciate the rarely sighted Dr Hexter's Wedding Ale from the West Berkshire Brewery as well as the more common Brakspear Bitter. The wine list opens with an earnest selection of Burgundies and Bordeaux. If your heart sinks at the sight of three-figure price tags, fear not: there are rich pickings under £20 from all over the world, including these classic French regions, and even a few bottles under £15. Eight come by the glass from £2.45. SAMPLE DISHES: creamy pea and ham soup with bacon sandwiches £4.50; boeuf bourguignonne £8.75; pears poached in red wine with Cassis sorbet £5.50.

Licensees Bruce and Kay Buchan (freehouse)

Open 12 to 3, 6 to 11 (10.30 Sun); bar food and restaurant 12 to 2.15, 7 to 9.30 (10 Fri and Sat)

Details Children welcome   Car park   Wheelchair access (not WC)   Patio   No smoking in restaurant   Occasional background music   Dogs welcome in bar only   Amex, Delta, MasterCard, Switch, Visa   Accommodation: 3 rooms, B&B £75 to £120

ARKESDEN   Essex   map 3

Axe and Compasses

Arkesden CB11 4EX   TEL: (01799) 550272
WEBSITE: www.axeandcompasses.co.uk
off B1038, 1m N of Clavering

A tiny stream runs through this picture-postcard village, spanned by a succession of little footbridges that lead to a wicker gate, behind which stands this pretty, partly thatched pub. Set right in the centre, the Axe dates from 1650, the thatch covering one of its roofs indicating the original part of the brick building. The interior is traditional, with a profusion of oak beams, horse brasses and assorted farm accoutrements. The frequently changing bar menus might include focaccia with Stilton and red onions, pheasant and mushrooms sautéed in Madeira sauce served with straw potatoes, or pan-fried strips of chicken with red Thai sauce, rice and naan. The lengthy restaurant menu (not served in the bar) might take you from well-flavoured chicken liver pâté, garlic prawns, or mushrooms baked in white wine and cream and glazed with Stilton, to main courses of pink-roast rack of lamb with caramelised shallots, whole grilled lemon sole, or spinach and potato cakes on a tomato and basil sauce. Portions are generous, but those wanting a pudding could go for lemon meringue pie, hazelnut roulade or something fruity like fresh strawberries and cream. Drink Greene King IPA, Abbot or Old Speckled Hen or one of the guest beers. Around a dozen wines are sold by the glass, with the full list approaching forty bottles. SAMPLE DISHES: roasted strips of duck with plum hoisin sauce on noodles £6.50; baked fillet of monkfish wrapped in Parma ham carved on a tomato and basil sauce £14; crème caramel £3.50.

Licensees Themis and Diane Christou (Greene King)
Open 11 to 2.30, 6 to 11, Sun 12 to 3, 7 to 10.30; bar food and restaurant 12 to 2, 6.45 to 9.30; *restaurant closed Sun evening winter; closed 25 Dec*
Details Children welcome in restaurant   Car park   Garden and patio   No smoking in restaurant   No music   No dogs   Delta, MasterCard, Switch, Visa

ARLINGHAM   Gloucestershire   map 2

▲ Old Passage Inn ✿ ✿   NEW ENTRY

Passage Road, Arlingham GL2 7JR   TEL: (01452) 740547
WEBSITE: www.fishattheoldpassageinn.co.uk
of A38 and B4071, 13m SW of Gloucester

The name of this ancient inn derives from its position on the bank of the River Severn, beyond Arlingham village, at what was once the lowest fordable point. It is surrounded by fields, and views from the dining room are over the river to the Forest of Dean. Inside, the 'understated chic', with eau-de-nil the dominant colour, may seem more restaurant-like than pubby, but the atmosphere is completely relaxed, and those coming just for a drink are made just as welcome. First-class seafood cookery, however, is the real draw. Some dishes have a familiar ring – shell-on prawns with marie-rose sauce, and battered haddock with chips and tartare sauce, say – but more sophisticated options abound: fried sea bass with sauerkraut, canelet of carrots and juniper berry sauce, or maybe a warm sausage of salmon, scallop and lobster on creamed leeks with a red wine jus. Whatever you choose is made with first-rate ingredients and cooked with great skill and care, and that includes desserts such as summer pudding with fruit coulis, or layered dark and white chocolate truffle cake. Real ale is limited to draught Bass, but there are six wines by the glass on a list of around 40 bottles priced from £10.40. SAMPLE DISHES: steamed scallops in their shells with chilli, ginger, shallot and vermouth dressing £7; roast fillet of hake on garlic mash with olive oil, lemon and parsley infusion £14; glazed baked lemon tart £5.

Licensees Patrick Le Mesurier and Josephine Moore (freehouse)
Open Tue to Sun 12 to 3, Tue to Sat 6.30 to 11; bar food Tue to Sun 12.15 to 2, Tue to Sat 6.45 to 9; closed 24 and 31 Dec
Details Children welcome   Car park   Wheelchair access (also WC)   Garden and patio
No-smoking area in bar, no smoking in dining room   Occasional background music   Dogs welcome
Amex, Delta, MasterCard, Switch, Visa   Accommodation: 3 rooms, B&B £50 to £95

ARMATHWAITE   Cumbria   map 10

▲ Duke's Head Hotel

Armathwaite CA4 9PB   TEL: (016974) 72226
off A6, between Carlisle and Penrith

This unpretentious pub, its exterior of pink-washed stucco, is on the main road through the village, which is in the beautiful Eden Valley, a paradise for bird-watchers and walkers. Inside are two bar areas, one a slightly austere room with table skittles, the other a comfortable, homely lounge with a log fire; beyond the lounge is the restaurant. One menu is served throughout, offering a generous range of mostly straightforwardly prepared but interesting pub fare, such as potted shrimps, pork fillet in a creamy cider, brandy and apple sauce, stuffed roast duckling with apple sauce, and poached fillet of plaice with a cheese and prawn sauce. The blackboard specials might feature a starter of salmon goujons in a light parsley and chervil batter with lime crème fraîche, followed by griddled lamb's liver with bacon and sautéed potatoes, or venison and pheasant casseroled in red wine and juniper berries, then trifle, or bread-and-butter pudding. Old Speckled Hen and Cumberland Ale from Jennings are on draught, and four wines are served by the glass. SAMPLE DISHES: pork, venison and apricot terrine with Cumberland sauce £4.25; pan-fried loin of tuna with lime, coriander, chilli and garlic butter £9; profiteroles with a butterscotch and whisky sauce £3.25.

Licensee Henry Lynch (Pubmaster)
Open 11.30 to 3, 5.30 to 11; bar food and restaurant 12 to 1.45, 6.15 to 9; open all day Sat and Sun Easter to 1 Oct
Details Children welcome   Car park   Wheelchair access (also WC)   Garden   No smoking in restaurant   Background music   Dogs welcome in 1 bar   Delta, MasterCard, Switch, Visa
Accommodation: 6 rooms, B&B £32.50 to £55.50

🦃 indicates a pub serving better-than-average wine, including good choice by bottle and glass.

ASENBY   North Yorkshire   map 9

Crab & Lobster ☺
Dishforth Road, Asenby YO7 3QL   TEL: (01845) 577286
WEBSITE: www.crabandlobster.co.uk
off A168, between A19 and A1

With thatch-work crabs and lobsters scuttling across the thatched roof, and lobster pots hanging from external walls, you certainly know you've arrived at the right place. However, nothing quite prepares the uninitiated for the riot of bric-à-brac and memorabilia that fills almost every inch of the interior, from bar to pavilion (conservatory); 'it definitely deserves its reputation for eccentricity', remarked one reporter. Even their adjacent hotel (Crab Manor) continues the theme, with rooms designed to echo exotic locations around the world (from 'Tropical Beach House' to 'Bird Island Lodge'). True to its name, seafood is the main attraction on an equally exuberant and thoroughly modern global menu. One reporter enjoyed a starter of fish risotto made with smoked red mullet, followed by crab-coated halibut served with 'very fresh' vegetables, or there could be lobster thermidor, bouillabaisse or cod, crab or salmon fishcakes. There are plenty of meat dishes, too: oriental-spiced beef pancakes, for example, or roast venison with creamed celeriac and thyme jus, and for dessert 'quite irresistible' chocolate torte with liquorice ice cream is 'wonderful and huge'. Although the Guide was not able to see a wine list, the pub tells us that eight wines are available by the glass. The choice of handpumped ales on offer includes Courage Directors and XB, and John Smith's Bitter. SAMPLE DISHES: roast squash and pumpkin risotto with asparagus £5.50; croustade of cured haddock with curried leeks and mussels £14; baked blueberry cheesecake £5.25.

Licensee Mark Spencely (freehouse)
Open 11.30 to 11; bar food and restaurant 12 to 2.15, 6.30 to 9.15 (light lunch menu available 3.30 to 5.30)
Details Children welcome   Car park   Wheelchair access   Garden   Smoking permitted in bar only
Occasional live or background music   Dogs welcome   Wheelchair access to restaurant   Amex, Delta,
Diners, MasterCard, Switch, Visa

ASHLEWORTH   Gloucestershire   map 5

Queens Arms
Ashleworth GL19 4HT   TEL: (01452) 700395
village signposted off A417 Gloucester to Ledbury road at Hartpury

The sign at the front of this red-brick pub, with its neat lawn and flower borders, hangs between two splendid 200-year-old clipped yew trees. The sensitively modernised interior preserves the beams and iron fireplace, and the spacious lounge is homely yet bright, with Tiffany-style lamps in an otherwise conventionally decorated room. Clues to Tony and Gill Burreddu's background are a prominently displayed South African flag and the menu's bobotie and potjiekos (venison, vegetable and potato casserole). They describe the Queens Arms as 'a country village dining pub', but despite the emphasis on food three well-kept beers are on offer at any one time from a list that includes

Timothy Taylor Landlord, Adnams Bitter, Donnington BB, Shepherd Neame Spitfire, Rev James from Brains and Archers Village Bitter. The wine list, modest in length and prices, is strong on South African bottles; ten wines are sold by the glass. The blackboard menus might include moules marinière, or sweetbreads in sherry sauce. Follow them with a main course of perhaps pan-fried duck breast with a plum and port sauce, sea bass fillets in a prawn and white wine sauce with asparagus and mushroom risotto, or faggots with mash and peas in onion gravy. Vegetables are fresh and properly cooked, and among desserts might be meringues with strawberry mousse, or sticky fudge and walnut pudding. SAMPLE DISHES: seafood St-Jacques £5.50; roast partridge wrapped in bacon served on a bed of caramelised onions with a sage and port sauce £11.50; chocolate truffle tart £4.50.

Licensees Tony and Gill Burreddu (freehouse)
Open *12 to 3, 7 to 11; bar food and restaurant 12 to 1.45, 7 to 8.45 (9.45 Fri and Sat); closed 25 Dec*
Details *Children welcome   Car park   Wheelchair access (not WC)   Garden and patio No smoking in restaurant   Background music   Guide dogs only   Delta, MasterCard, Switch, Visa*

ASHMORE GREEN   Berkshire   map 2

Sun in the Wood   [NEW ENTRY]

Stoney Lane, Ashmore Green RG18 9HF   TEL: (01635) 42377
from roundabout junction of A339 and A4 in Newbury, take B4009 Shaw road, turn right at roundabout in Shaw on to Kiln road, then after ½m turn left into Stoney Lane; pub 1m on left

In a quiet semi-rural location, just a couple of miles from busy Newbury town centre, is this cream-painted inn with a woodland garden and children's play area to the rear. It lives up to its name with a bright interior colour scheme of sunny yellow and terracotta. There's a warming fire, walls are lined with food-related prints, and pots, pans and utensils hang from the ceiling. 'Something for everyone' sums up the menu: perhaps mushrooms in creamy garlic and white wine sauce, or smoked haddock with spinach and a poached egg to start, followed by anything from lamb shank braised with redcurrants and port to fillet of Scottish salmon on leek and smoked salmon risotto with creamy prawn sauce. Blackboard specials extend the choice even further, and there are hot and cold filled baguettes at lunchtime. The wine list opens with six 'special selections' at £9.75 a bottle, £2.60/£3.60 a glass, and efficiently covers the world in around 30 mostly good-value bottles. Wadworth 6X might be joined by Badger Tanglefoot and Henry's Original IPA among the real ale options. SAMPLE DISHES: crisp-fried Camembert with raspberry dressing £5; chargrilled marinated venison steak on garlic mash with red wine and thyme sauce £13; apple and blackberry crumble in a sweet pastry case with vanilla ice cream £4.25.

Licensee Philip Davison (Wadworth)
Open *Tue to Sat 12 to 2.30, 6 to 11, Sun 12 to 2.30, 7 to 10.30; bar food and restaurant Tue to Sun 12 to 2 (3 Sun), Tue to Sat 6 to 9.30*
Details *Children welcome   Car park   Wheelchair access (also WC)   Garden   No-smoking area in bar, no smoking in restaurant   No music   No dogs   Amex, Delta, MasterCard, Switch, Visa*

ASHURST   West Sussex   map 3

Fountain Inn   NEW ENTRY

Ashurst BN44 3AP   TEL: (01403) 710219
on B2135, 4m N of Steyning

A duck pond and attractive herb-filled gardens complete with a pergola-covered walkway add character and charm to this popular sixteenth-century village pub. No music disturbs the peace in the maze of dimly lit rooms, which have old brick and dark timbers in abundance. Printed lunchtime and evening menus are supplemented by blackboard specials, which often strike a colourful, modern note, as in caramelised onion, goats' cheese and cranberry tart, although old favourites such as Cumberland sausages with mash, or steak, ale and mushroom pie are not neglected. There are no starters, and the char-grill gets plenty of use, handling anything from fillet of salmon (served with hollandaise and chive sauce) to chicken breast (which shows up in a well-made salad with bacon and herbs). A limited menu operates on Sunday and Monday evenings, and there are a few homely puddings such as cherry pie and lemon tart. The beers on handpump are all from southern breweries, including Horsham Best Bitter from King, Sussex Best Bitter from Harveys, and Master Brew from Shepherd Neame, as well as guests such as Adnams. Wines are stacked on shelves behind the bar, and a weekly changing selection of five by the glass is chalked up on a blackboard: prices are fair, starting at £10.95 a bottle. SAMPLE DISHES: lasagne verde £7; chargrilled Scotch fillet steak with tomatoes, mushrooms and chips £14.50; Bakewell tart with custard £4.

Licensees Mark and Chris White (freehouse)
Open 11.30 to 2.30, 6 to 11 (10.30 Sun); bar food 11.30 to 2, 6 to 9.30; closed evenings 25 and 26 Dec, 1 Jan
Details No children under 12   Car park   Wheelchair access (not WC)   Garden   No music   Dogs welcome   No cards

ASKRIGG   North Yorkshire   map 8

Kings Arms

Main Street, Askrigg DL8 3HQ   TEL: (01969) 650817
WEBSITE: www.kingsarmsaskrigg.com
off A684 Hawes to Leyburn road, 1½m NE of Bainbridge

The Wensleydale trans-Pennine route was the M62 of coaching days, and this three-storey Georgian inn in Askrigg's attractive market square shows service stations were nicer then. White frames of small-paned sash windows contrast with soft grey stone, and there's a mounting block outside the door. Inside, characterful, Georgian-feeling rooms are beamed and panelled or decorated in cheerful yellowy-creamy tones. The two bars (one the Herriot Bar – this pub was 'the Drovers' in the TV series) serve Theakston Old Peculier, John Smith's Bitter and Black Sheep Best Bitter, and a lunchtime menu of baguettes, sandwiches and other dishes. The Silks restaurant operates only on Friday and Saturday nights, but the same menu appears on the bar blackboards every night. You might start with spicy Thai crab cake and chilli dip, or blue Wensleydale soufflé and dressed salad, before tackling monkfish and chorizo kebabs with rice and tomato and basil sauce, say, or a Barnsley chop on provençale vegetables, or maybe battered haddock, chips and mushy peas. Puds range from chocolate orange mousse with orange liqueur coulis to spotted dick and custard. From a short, mostly New World list six wines are served by the glass. SAMPLE DISHES: pea and mint soup £3.50; chicken korma with rice and poppadoms £7.25; tarte Tatin with sauce anglaise £4.50.

Licensee Stuart Gatty (freehouse)
Open Mon to Fri 11 to 3, 6 to 11, Sat 11 to 11, Sun 12 to 10.30; bar food 12 to 2, 6.30 to 9; restaurant Fri and Sat 6.30 to 9
Details Children welcome Patio No-smoking area in bar, no smoking in dining room Background music Dogs welcome MasterCard, Switch, Visa

ASTON   Cheshire   map 7

Bhurtpore Inn 🍺 🍇
Wrenbury Road, Aston CW5 8DQ   TEL: (01270) 780917
off A530, 5m S of Nantwich

In a pleasant hamlet, opposite a stunning half-timbered farmhouse dated 1667, the Bhurtpore takes its name from an Indian city, the scene of a successful nineteenth-century siege by a local landowner. Miniatures, a plan of the city and etchings relating to the siege are found within, with other Indian-themed pieces including rugs, carvings, wood, china and porcelain elephants; otherwise, the walls are hung with photographs and prints of local buildings, and countless water jugs are suspended from beams. The Indian connection is also found in a blackboard list of around six curries and baltis, all served with traditional accompaniments. Apart from these, expect to find dishes as varied as Thai crab cakes on a coconut, lime and coriander sauce, or a herb pancake filled with smoked haddock in a leek and cheese sauce among starters, with main courses running from lemon sole fillets rolled around Parma ham served in a cream and herb sauce to 'beautifully tender' venison casseroled in Belgian ale and pumpkin sauce or 'a mouth-watering mound' of pork medallions in mustard and apple sauce. Sandwiches and jacket potatoes are possibilities too, and vegetarians have around five main courses to choose from. Desserts run to brioche bread-and-butter pudding, and summer pudding. Real ales here are a choice from Hanby Drawwell Bitter or ten frequently changing guest brews; the pub gets through around a thousand a year. In addition, there are about 140 bottled beers, mostly Belgian, a long list of whiskies, mainly malts, and a farmhouse cider. Wine is not forgotten, with a short, imaginative list of fruity everyday drinking and a quirky selection of fine wines priced from £15 to £35. Eight wines are served by the glass and there are blackboard specials too. SAMPLE DISHES: chicken tikka kebabs with pitta bread, mini-poppadoms and mango chutney £4.25; salmon fillet in filo on basil sauce £8.25; baked blueberry cheesecake £3.25.

Licensees Simon and Nicky George (freehouse)
Open 12 to 2.30, 6.30 to 11, Sun 12 to 10.30; bar food and restaurant 12 to 2, 6.45 to 9.30, Sun 12 to 9
Details Children welcome in eating areas exc after 8pm Car park Wheelchair access (also WC) Garden and patio No-smoking area in bar, no smoking in restaurant Occasional live music Dogs welcome in games room Delta, Diners, MasterCard, Switch, Visa

ASTON CANTLOW   Warwickshire   map 5

Kings Head ✿

FISH

Aston Cantlow B95 6HY   TEL: (01789) 488242

village signposted off A3400 NW of Stratford or off A46 Stratford to Alcester road

A couple of wooden seats at the front and a patio and larger lawned area at the back are good places from which to enjoy the appearance of this ancient, creeper-covered, black and white half-timbered building. The most striking feature inside is the quantity of original beams, conveying an impression of great antiquity, together with particularly low ceilings, varnished floorboards, and bare wooden furniture. To the back is a light and airy restaurant done out in blond and slate-grey, but the same brasserie-style menu, supplemented by daily specials, is served throughout and people tend to gravitate towards the main bar area. The Kings Head duck supper – confit of leg and slices of breast on a bed of sticky and sweet braised red cabbage – is something of a signature dish, and fish are the main thrust of the specials: perhaps 'quite a brilliant little dish' of tuna ceviche with a salad of tomato, cucumber and coriander, followed by pan-fried red snapper with grilled courgettes and feta and olive salad, or whole baked sea bass with rocket and chilli jam. Otherwise, traditional-sounding dishes are given a modern twist: pan-fried calf's liver with a ginger, caper and herb compote and olive oil mash, or salmon and dill fishcakes with celeriac rémoulade and chips. Puddings include old favourites like warm chocolate brownie with vanilla ice cream, and Sunday lunch brings out the best of British, including roast leg of Warwickshire lamb. Greene King Abbot Ale, M&B Brew XI and Black Sheep Best Bitter are on tap, while wine drinkers are offered a list of around twenty bottles, with eight sold by the glass. SAMPLE DISHES: deep-fried chilli-crusted squid with sweet chilli sauce £5.75; roast rump of lamb with dauphinois potatoes and mint hollandaise £12.75; glazed lemon tart with mascarpone £4.75.

Licensees Miss S. Coll and Mr H. Fentum (Furlong Leisure)

Open Mon to Fri 11 to 3, 5.30 to 11, Sat and Sun 12 to 10.30; bar food and restaurant Mon to Sat 12 to 2.30, 7 to 10, Sun 12.30 to 3, 7 to 9; closed evenings 25 Dec and 1 Jan

Details Children welcome   Car park   Wheelchair access (also WC)   Garden and patio No smoking in 1 room   Background music   Dogs welcome in bar area   Amex, Delta, MasterCard, Switch, Visa

AWRE   Gloucestershire   map 2

Red Hart Inn

Awre GL14 1EW   TEL: (01594) 510220

off A48 Newnham to Chepstow road, 3m S of Newnham

Just alongside the Forest of Dean, a peninsula noses out from the west bank into a great meander of the River Severn. Here, peacefully on the way to nowhere, is the village of Awre, in the middle of which, close to the church, is a three-storey fifteenth-century building, white-plastered with black woodwork. Outside there's a neat garden; inside it has black beams draped in hops, a stone well and pump in the middle of the bar and the hay bale of Damocles hanging from the pitched roof. Red carpets, yellow walls and strong, sunny colours enhance the happy, unpretentious, spick-and-span feel. Fuller's London Pride is the odd man out in a Gloucestershire line-up of Freeminer Resolution (from Cinderford, five miles away), Goff's Jouster and Wickwar BOB, plus Stowford Press cider. Food at the bar runs from simple (whitebait) to aspirational (chicken liver pâté flavoured with apricots and Southern Comfort, plus red onion marmalade), and mains span beer-battered cod, sea bass en papillote, chicken jalfrezi and venison steak with red wine and blue-berry sauce (plus five vegetarian choices). Baileys cream profiteroles and butterscotch sauce, or Malteser cheesecake and honeycomb ice cream are there for the sweet-toothed, and from an attractive and sensibly priced list six wines come by the glass. Many of these dishes appear in the restaurant, supplemented by the likes of roast rack of lamb, or lemon sole fillets. SAMPLE DISHES: smoked salmon fettucine £5; suprêmes of pheasant with celeriac purée and parsnip ribbons £10; apple and cinnamon crumble £3.

Licensee Jerry Bedwell (freehouse)

Open Tue to Sat (Mon to Sat summer) 12 to 3, 6 to 11; Sun 12 to 3, 7 to 10.30; bar food and restaurant Tue to Sat (Mon to Sat summer) 12 to 2, 6.30 to 9, Sun 12 to 2, 7 to 9; closed 25 Dec and 1 Jan

Details Children welcome in bar eating area before 8.30   Car park   Garden   No-smoking area in bar, no smoking in dining room   Occasional background music   No dogs   Amex, Delta, MasterCard, Switch, Visa

AYCLIFFE   Co Durham   map 10

The County 😊   [NEW ENTRY]

13 The Green, Aycliffe DL5 6LX   TEL: (01325) 312273
WEBSITE: www.the-county.co.uk
from A1(M) junction 59, take A167 for Newton Aycliffe; turn half right at first roundabout, take second right then first right

On a corner by a village green, this cream-painted early nineteenth-century building seems pleasantly unexceptional. But green-louvred shutters on first-floor windows and the mauve-lettered name (in Durham?) hint at a less tradi-tional interior. This is a pub/brasserie that's serious about British beer: witness Charles Wells Bombardier, John Smith's Magnet and guests like Palmers Bridport Bitter or Wild Cat from Cairngorm. Nor is wine overlooked, with a two-dozen-strong selection of mostly New World bottles and eight by the glass. All this in a fresh and fairly minimalist, wood-floored and open-plan interior divided by a peninsula bar. Further, it transpires that Andrew Brown has trained under Raymond Blanc and Gary Rhodes, and two blackboards – for main menu and specials – encompass pub grub and poshish nosh. One reporter chose salmon and leek fishcake and got a deep fishcake 'the diameter of a beer mat: crisp, well-cooked batter, plenty of salmon and young leeks, and a very cutting, lemony sauce'. That filled him up, but he could have gone on to liver, bacon, mash and onion gravy (plus sherry sauce), or Chinese crispy beef with stir-fried peppers, mushrooms and noodles. There's yet posher nosh in the separate restaurant (dressed crab with lobster gratin; game pie). Desserts include crème brûlée, and tarte Tatin. SAMPLE DISHES: smoked salmon and scrambled egg muffin £5; curry of the day £8.50; 'enriched' tiramisù £5.

Licensee Andrew Brown (freehouse)

Open *Mon to Sat 12 to 2, 5.30 (6.45 Sat) to 11, Sun 12 to 3; bar food and restaurant Mon to Sat 12 to 2, 6 (6.45 Sat) to 9.15, Sun 12 to 3*
Details *Children welcome in dining room   Car park   Patio   No smoking in dining room Occasional background music   Guide dogs only   Amex, MasterCard, Switch, Visa*

AYMESTREY   Herefordshire   map 5

▲ Riverside Inn 🍺
Aymestrey HR6 9ST   TEL: (01568) 708440
on A4110, 6m NW of Leominster

This half-timbered inn, long and narrow, fronts the A4110 near a bridge over the River Lugg, but as it's been built on steeply rising ground the interior is on different levels, with the restaurant down a steep flight of stairs. Inside, the bar and an ancillary dining area with spindle-backed chairs and brightly patterned carpet are on the ground-floor level, and beams, bare wooden tables, decorative dried hops and log fires contribute to the simple country atmosphere. The bar has its own short menu of such dishes as hot smoked chicken and mushroom salad with apple mayonnaise, steak and ale pie, and pan-fried lamb's liver with bacon and red wine jus, although the Barn Restaurant's menu is served in here too. You might start with fillet of smoked Lugg trout with creamed horseradish, or vegetable terrine with a tomato and basil oil coulis, before proceeding to a main course of medallions of venison sautéed with a rosemary and juniper jus and garnished with a glazed apple and rowan jelly, or pan-fried duck breast with bramble sauce. The selection of English and Welsh cheeses from the Mousetrap in Leominster is not to be missed, and there might be tangy lemon tart accompanied by locally produced elderflower ice cream. The Wye Valley Brewery's Butty Bach and Dorothy Goodbody's Golden Ale are on draught along with Black Sheep Best Bitter and Weston's Stowford Press cider. All seven house wines are served by the glass (175ml or 250ml), while the full list runs to over thirty bottles. SAMPLE DISHES: smoked duck salad with home-made quince cheese £6.25; ox kidneys sautéed in their own suet with a creamy mustard sauce £11; Grand Marnier mousse with caramel and oranges £4.25.

Licensee Richard Gresko (freehouse)
Open *winter 11 to 3, 6 to 11, Sun 12 to 3, 6.30 to 10.30, summer 11 to 11 (10.30 Sun); bar food and restaurant 12 to 2, 7 to 9; open 12 to 2 25 Dec, closed to non-residents evening 25 Dec*
Details *Children welcome in bar eating area   Car park   Garden and patio   No-smoking area in bar, no smoking in restaurant   Live or background music   Dogs welcome   Delta, MasterCard, Switch, Visa   Accommodation: 7 rooms, B&B £45 to £85*

BADBY   Northamptonshire   map 5

▲ Windmill   [NEW ENTRY]
Main Street, Badby NN11 3AN   TEL: (01327) 702363
WEBSITE: www.windmillinn.info
off A361, 2m S of Daventry

In the pretty village of Badby, not far from Althorp Park and Canons Ashby House, this thatched stone-built country inn dating from the seventeenth century has been sensitively modernised and transformed so it is now more small hotel than pub. The public bar still has a pubby character, with a friendly atmosphere and locals propping up the bar. Its look is modern and under-stated, with scrubbed wooden furniture, red patterned rugs on the flagstone floor and plain coloured walls adorned with sporting memorabilia. The menu offers some familiar pub staples, like crispy whitebait, chilli con carne with rice, steaks and lasagne, alongside some slightly more unusual choices: for example, deep-fried jalapeño peppers stuffed with cream cheese, venison burgers with creamy pepper sauce, roasted Thai-marinated salmon suprême, or chicken breast with white wine, cream and Stilton sauce. Portions are generous, but for those who don't want a full meal there are snacky options, such as melted Gorgonzola and pears on toasted French bread, and various sandwiches. Flowers Original, Fuller's London Pride and Wadworth 6X are among the better-than-average selection of real ales, and four wines are served by the glass from the list of three dozen well-chosen bottles. House wines are £9.50. SAMPLE DISHES: smoked duck breast salad with honey and mustard dressing £5.50; loin of lamb wrapped in bacon with redcurrant and port sauce £13; rum and banana bread-and-butter pudding £3.50.

Licensees John Freestone and Carol Sutton (freehouse)
Open 11.30 to 3, 5.30 to 11, Sun 12 to 4, 6.30 to 10.30; bar food and restaurant 12 to 2, 7 to 9.30 (9 Sun)
Details Children welcome   Car park   Wheelchair access (also WC)   Garden   No smoking in eating areas   Background music   Dogs welcome   Amex, Delta, Diners, MasterCard, Switch, Visa   Accommodation: 10 rooms, B&B £57.50 to £75

BAINBRIDGE   **North Yorkshire**   map 8

▲ Rose and Crown Hotel   NEW ENTRY

Bainbridge DL8 3EE   TEL: (01969) 650225
WEBSITE: www.theprideofwensleydale.com
on A684, 4m E of Hawes

Standing on a large village green, along with imposing villas, old cottages and even a working watermill, the Rose and Crown is a long, low, white-painted building dating partly from 1445 – most is more recent than that, but still has plenty of character, both inside and out. The main bar features sepia photographs, old pews and settles, small-paned sash windows and a huge old fireplace of worn stone with a massive wooden lintel, while the bright Dust & Diesel bar is the social centre of the village where you may encounter darts matches in full swing. The style is more upmarket than the pub grub norm: expect moules marinière, crab cakes with a mild curry sauce and caramelised asparagus with crème fraîche among starters, with mains of beef Wellington wrapped in smoked ham and encased in pastry, served with new potatoes, or ragoût of smoked haddock, dill and tagliatelle, and to finish perhaps bread-and-butter pudding or a selection of local cheeses. Real ales are a local bunch, including Black Sheep Best Bitter and Theakston Old Peculier. Seven wines are served by the glass from the list of over 30 bottles. SAMPLE DISHES: smoked mackerel salad £5; breast of duck with orange sauce £15; chocolate mousse £5.

Licensee David Collinson (freehouse)
Open *11 to 11, Sun 12 to 10.30; bar food and restaurant 12 to 2.15, 6 to 9.15*
Details *Children welcome   Car park   Wheelchair access (also WC)   Patio   Occasional background music; jukebox   Dogs welcome exc in restaurant   Delta, MasterCard, Switch, Visa Accommodation: 12 rooms, B&B £40 to £74*

BALLINGER COMMON   Buckinghamshire   map 3

Pheasant

Ballinger Common HP16 9LF   TEL: (01494) 837236
WEBSITE: www.wimpennys.com
E of A413, 2m N of Great Missenden

By the cricket pitch and the playground in the village you will find a white-fronted brick building with a slate roof and a conservatory extension on the front: the Pheasant. There's a patio with picnic benches and parasols for summer eating and drinking, or, for wet days and cooler times, a homely, beamy, busily decorated interior. Supplementing the printed menu are black-boards that change once or twice a week: these might include starters of winter vegetable soup, or Thai fishcakes and sweet chilli sauce, and main dishes of lamb shank with rösti, roast salmon and chive cream, or steak, kidney and mushroom pie. If you've room, there might be chocolate and raspberry roulade, or treacle sponge pudding and custard to finish. Adnams Best Bitter is on draught, as is Stowford Press cider, and a world wine list of 20 or so bottles from £13 to £30 includes three by the glass. SAMPLE DISHES: woodland mushrooms with port and Stilton £4.75; crab, chive and ginger fishcakes with lime mayonnaise £9.25; treacle and walnut tart £4.50.

Licensee Nigel Wimpenny-Smith (freehouse)
Open *Tue to Sun 12 to 3, Tue to Sat 6.30 to 11; bar food Tue to Sun 12 to 2 (2.30 Sun), Tue to Sat 7 to 9*
Details *Children over 7 welcome   Car park   Wheelchair access (also WC)   Patio   No smoking in conservatory   Occasional background music   No dogs   Amex, Delta, Diners, MasterCard, Switch, Visa*

BANTHAM   Devon   map 1

▲ Sloop Inn

Bantham TQ7 3AJ   TEL: (01548) 560489
off A379, 4m W of Kingsbridge

FISH

A sixteenth-century, white-painted building, the Sloop is reached along a single-track lane with passing places. The drive is worth the effort just for the pub's cracking location just 500 yards from the Avon Estuary, sandy beaches and the Coast Path. Not surprisingly, the décor has a nautical theme, with rooms at the back decked out like a galleon, with sloping polished-wood walls and ships' windows and bar counters made of old boat timbers; at the front is a dark-beamed bar with stone walls, a flagstone floor and a log-burning stove. Fish is the strength of the menus, with unusual treatments taking in wok-fried crevettes with lime and ginger oil on herb couscous, and cod steak topped with a crust of smoked cheese and chives served with citrus sauce. Simpler ideas work well too: potted shrimps followed by chargrilled darne of salmon with orange butter, for instance. Vegetarians have plenty of choice, and meat eaters could go for something like breast of Barbary duckling with a creamy sauce of green peppercorns, apples and brandy. Basket meals, ploughman's and sandwiches are also possibilities, and for pudding there's Salcombe dairy ice cream, or perhaps hot chocolate fudge cake. Drinking options are just as wide and varied: beers are draught Bass and Palmer IPA and Copper Ale. Luscombe organic cider is also available, as well as 20-plus malt whiskies and West Country drinks like Somerset cider brandy. The West Country keeps its end up on the wine list too, with a page devoted to Devon's Sharpham Estate. Otherwise an extensive selection stays mostly well under £15 and a dozen are sold by the glass. SAMPLE DISHES: garlic prawns £5; steamed fillet of smoked haddock with a cream and spinach sauce £8; raspberry pavlova £3.75.

Licensee Neil Girling (freehouse)
Open 11 to 2.30, 6 to 11, Sun 12 to 2.30, 6.30 to 10.30; bar food and restaurant 12 to 2, 6.45 to 10
Details Children welcome   Car park   Garden and patio   No cigars/pipes   No music   Dogs welcome   Delta, Switch   Accommodation: 5 rooms, B&B £35 to £70

BARNSLEY   **Gloucestershire**   map 2

▲ Village Pub 🏮 🍇

Barnsley GL7 5EF   TEL: (01285) 740421
WEBSITE: www.thevillagepub.co.uk
on B4425, 4m NE of Cirencester

This Cotswold-stone inn-with-rooms is smack in the centre of the quiet village, diagonally opposite Rosemary Verey's Barnsley House gardens, horticultural enthusiasts will be delighted to hear. The pub itself has no garden, but it does have a well-designed brick courtyard crammed with tables and chairs for outdoor eating, while the interior is an inviting mix of the trendy and the rustically traditional, with botanical prints and faux bookcases contributing to the genteel feel. No distinction is made between the various eating areas in a warren of little rooms, and the same short menu is offered throughout. The cooking is ambitious and makes good use of some excellent raw materials, as in a starter of baked goats' cheese with olives, rocket and pesto, followed perhaps by grilled rib of beef with Roquefort-glazed mushrooms and roasted sweet potatoes, or grilled peppered halibut steak with tomato and coriander salsa. Finish with apricot and almond tart, or chocolate brownie with peanut butter ice cream. Lunchtimes might see snackier items like grilled ciabatta with chicken, tomato and goats' cheese. To drink are draught Stowford Press Scrumpy Supreme, and for devotees of the grain Hook Norton Best and Wadworth 6X are on tap. The enterprising wine list is arranged by style and includes a generous 17 wines by the glass from £2.80. There's a strong showing from Italy, and France includes the excellent Domaine de Clovallon in the Languedoc (£26). SAMPLE DISHES: steamed mussels with cider, onion and sage £5.50; grilled pork chop with caraway, black pudding and bubble and squeak £11; pain d'épice crème brûlée £4.50.

Licensees Tim Haigh and Rupert Pendered (freehouse)
Open 11 to 3.30, 6 to 11; bar food 12 to 2.30 (3 Sat and Sun), 7 to 9.30 (10 Fri and Sat); closed 25 Dec
Details Children welcome   Car park   Wheelchair access (not WC)   Patio   No music   Dogs welcome   Delta, MasterCard, Switch, Visa   Accommodation: 6 rooms, B&B £65 to £125

BARNSTON   Merseyside   map 7

Fox & Hounds

Barnston CH61 1BW   TEL: (0151) 648 1323
WEBSITE: www.the-fox-hounds.co.uk
on A551, 2m NE of Heswall

'Worth passing a few pubs for. . . . This solid village local draws them from near and far with quality of food and range of real ales.' Look for an imposing whitewashed building beside a farm at the top of a wooded ravine, whose trees give shelter in winter and grateful shade in a good summer. Built in 1911, it expanded into some barns in the 1980s – and the old farmyard behind now sports parasol-decked bench tables. The older part has a cosy old-style smoke room and snug, the newer section a largely open-plan lounge with solid wood tables and walls decked with old photos, paintings and an intriguing titfer collection (bowler, policeman's helmet, etc. – thereby must hang a tale or two). The regular ales are Theakston (Best, Cool Cask and Old Peculier) and Webster's Green Label, plus guests (maybe Everards Tiger, Marston's Pedigree, or Spooky Doo from Shropshire's experimental Hanby Ales) – or there are over fifty whiskies, as well as ten wines by the glass. Food is served only at lunchtime, with the bar menu offering sandwiches, quiches and plat-ters of mixed meats, fish or seafood, but excitement comes from the black-board dishes, which change with the seasons and availability of ingredients. There might be a Thai green curry or a large helping of leek and lamb pie ('lots of nicely hot, tender meat and decent gravy'). Waistband pressure may preclude the sticky toffee pudding. SAMPLE DISHES: home-made soup £2.45; braised steak £6; chocolate fudge cake £3.

Licensee Ralph Leech (freehouse)
Open 11 to 11, Sun 12 to 10.30; bar food 12 to 2
Details Children welcome in family room   Car park   Wheelchair access (not WC)   Garden
No music   Dogs welcome exc at food times   Amex, Delta, Diners, MasterCard, Switch, Visa

BARROWDEN   Rutland   map 6

▲ Exeter Arms ▐█ NEW ENTRY

Main Street, Barrowden LE15 8EQ   TEL: (01572) 747247   BREW PUB
WEBSITE: www.exeterarms.com
off A47, 9m W of A1

Beach Boys, Best Boys and Bevin Boys are just some of the beers produced by the Blencowe Brewing Company, which is housed in a stone barn adjacent to this old stone pub overlooking the village green and duck pond. You can sample the results at the long, wood-panelled bar: smokers head for the Tap Room, decorated with framed beer mats, while others settle into another low-beamed area, where food is the main order of the day. Menus are on a black-board, and the repertoire changes daily: doorstep sandwiches and things on toast give way to Billy Bunter-sized helpings of, say, cock-a-leekie soup, ham and eggs and more bistro-style offerings such as beef stroganoff, fillet of trout with dill and lemon butter, or vegetable moussaka. To finish, lemon and cran-berry cheesecake pleased one pre-Christmas visitor; otherwise there might be wacky-sounding offerings like chocky fridge cake. Live jazz is played every other Sunday evening, and other musical events are held; there's an outdoor pétanque court for fine days. At least eight house wines come by the glass or bottle. SAMPLE DISHES: grilled pear with Brie £4.75; game casserole £8.50; chocolate cookie pie £3.75.

Licensees Peter and Elizabeth Blencowe (freehouse)
Open *Tue to Sat 12 to 2, 6 to 11, Sun 12 to 3, 7 to 10.30; bar food Wed to Sun 12 to 2, Tue to Sat 6.30 to 9*
Details *Children welcome   Car park   Wheelchair access (also WC)   Garden and patio*
No-smoking area in bar, no smoking in eating area   Live or background music   Dogs welcome exc at bar and in eating area   Delta, Diners, MasterCard, Switch, Visa   Accommodation: 3 rooms, B&B £30 to £55

BARSTON   West Midlands   map 5

Malt Shovel   NEW ENTRY

Barston Lane, Barston B92 0JP   TEL: (01675) 443223
off A452, 1m W beyond Barston village

Situated about a mile outside the village, the Malt Shovel, a white-painted building with lots of trailing greenery, is a 'country pub and restaurant' whose two halves have distinct identities (and separate entrances). Inside the pub the look is very modern: an open-plan bar with terracotta floor tiles, pale walls, and an olive-green, zinc-topped bar counter. Drinkers are welcome but most of the tables are laid for eating. Italian and French influences dominate the menu, as in a starter of crab and spring onion risotto, and main courses of baked cod on Puy lentils with wild mushrooms, or duck confit with cassoulet and Dijon mustard glaze. There are a few more esoteric items like Thai chicken Caesar salad, and traditional favourites such as battered cod with chips, pea purée and tartare sauce. At lunchtime there are also hot toasted baguettes with fillings like Cajun beef with caramelised onion and mature Cheddar. The separate restaurant menu is in similar vein, but with higher prices. Six house wines are available in three glass sizes, or by the bottle from £11.95. The full list runs to around two dozen bottles ranging from the fairly humble to the somewhat grand. Bass, M&B Brew XI and Old Speckled Hen are the real ales. SAMPLE DISHES: kidneys, bacon and field mushrooms on toast £5.95/£9.95; roast local pheasant on parsnip confit with pancetta £12.95; vanilla and amaretti pannacotta with butterscotch syrup £4.95.

Licensee Anthony Day (freehouse)
Open *12 to 3, 5.30 to 11, Sun 12 to 10.30; bar food all week 12 to 2.30, Mon to Sat 6.30 to 9.30; restaurant all week 12 to 2.30, Tue to Sat 6.30 to 9.30; closed 25 Dec*
Details *Children welcome   Car park   Wheelchair access (also WC)   Garden and patio*
No smoking in dining room   Background music   No dogs   Amex, MasterCard, Switch, Visa

▲ *indicates where a pub offers accommodation. At the end of the entry information is given on the number of rooms available and a price range, indicating the cost of a single room or single occupancy to that for a room with two people sharing.*

▲ Spread Eagle

Church Road, Barton Bendish PE33 9DP   TEL: (01366) 347995
pub signposted off A1122 between Swaffham and Downham Market

Even for Norfolk, the Spread Eagle is in a quiet setting, down a no-through road next to the church in a tiny, attractive village. As you enter the pub, a small bar to the left is the place where drinkers congregate – Greene King IPA is one of the ales on draught – while a small yellow-painted bar to the right and, beyond it, another, larger split-level room, also with a beamed ceiling, are set for eating. The list of around half a dozen 'light lunches', as well as enterprising sandwiches, will keep people happy, with a salad of mushrooms, bacon, tomatoes and a poached egg, or local duck breast in orange sauce with fondant potatoes. The full carte is no less interesting, with a soup – potato with smoked haddock, say, or carrot and onion – alongside something like king prawns with avocado purée, crispy bacon and leaves to start, followed by pan-fried chicken breast with wild mushroom sauce, or haunch of venison with apple purée and red wine sauce. Fish is well handled, from 'expertly seared' sea bass and halibut with lemon butter sauce and crushed potatoes to black sea bream with a curried mussel velouté, and desserts are well reported: a slice of rich chocolate marquise with chocolate-lined blobs of crème anglaise, or 'a classic rendition' of sticky toffee pudding. Just two wines are sold by the glass, although the full list runs to over 30 reasonably priced bottles. SAMPLE DISHES: goats' cheese tart with sweet-and-sour onion marmalade and aubergine purée £5.25; seared hake with Pernod sauce, buttered cucumber and new potatoes £13; lemon posset with thyme-flavoured shortbread £5.

Licensees Marjorie and Jessica Ives (freehouse)
Open Wed to Sun 12 to 3, Tue to Sun 6.30 to 11 (10.30 Sun); bar food and restaurant Wed to Sun 12 to 2.30, Wed to Sat 7 to 9.30
Details Children welcome   Car park   Garden   No smoking in 1 restaurant   Occasional background music   No dogs   Delta, MasterCard, Switch, Visa   Accommodation: 3 rooms, B&B £36 to £50 (double room)

Three Horseshoes ✿

Batcombe BA4 6HE   TEL: (01749) 850359
off A359 between Bruton and Frome, 3m N of Bruton

Bring a good map for navigating the lanes and come in daylight, so as to spot Batcombe church tower. The church pinpoints the pub alongside, with its neat grey-stone façade and at the back a terrace and play area. The long, low-ceilinged main bar, warm terracotta walls hung with paintings of flowers and Mediterranean landscapes (for sale), has an inglenook with a wood-burning stove. Beers are Butcombe's, or Mine Beer from Blindmans Brewery in nearby Leighton, and there's Thatchers cider. The dining room, a converted barn, has sporting paintings on exposed stone walls, cream woodwork and exuberant artificial flora. The menu includes the day's specials (many involving fresh fish from Brixham). One diner chose pan-fried scallops with coriander and spring onion ('generous, straightforward…, relying on very good, fresh ingredients and accurate timing'), but an alternative might be marinated palm hearts, wild mushrooms and broad beans with rémoulade dressing. Fairly elaborate main dishes could include casserole of venison, smoked bacon and mushrooms with red wine, or perhaps fried sea bass on pak choi and fried noodles with sweet chilli sauce. Crème brûlée with morello and black cherries to finish, maybe, or Madeira, pineapple and treacle sponge. An international selection of 40-odd wines includes eight by the glass (with house basics £11 per bottle and the bulk of the list between £15 and £20) and is supplemented by a dozen pricier 'celebration' wines, mostly from France. SAMPLE DISHES: leek and potato soup £3.75; lamb chump on spring onion mash with wild mushroom and rosemary sauce £13; terrine of cider apple, mango and raspberry sorbet £4.25.

Licensee David Benson (freehouse)
Open *12 to 3, 6.30 to 11, Sun 12 to 3, 7 to 10.30; bar food and restaurant 12 to 2 (2.30 Sun), 7 to 9.30 (10 Fri and Sat, 9 Sun); closed 25 Dec, evening 26 Dec*
Details *Children welcome   Car park   Wheelchair access (also WC)   Garden and patio No smoking in dining room   No music   Dogs welcome in bar   Delta, MasterCard, Switch, Visa*

BATH   Bath & N.E. Somerset   map 2

Hop Pole ✿ [NEW ENTRY]

7 Albion Buildings, Upper Bristol Road, Bath BA1 3AR   TEL: (01225) 446327

Just outside Bath's centre, opposite Royal Victoria Park, the Hop Pole is slightly back from the busy A431. Inside, it's not road noise you notice but the charming, unassuming, relaxed atmosphere and the tongue-and-groove woodwork that distinguishes Bath Ales' pubs. That brewery's Gem, SPA and Barnstormer are dispensed in slender, elegant glasses, along with seasonal ales and, now and again, the occasional brew Rare Hare. There is also a weekly-changing guest (from Butcombe, perhaps, or the Belgian Affligen), Westons organic cider, and bottled Continentals like Hoegaarden. The simpler lunchtime menu runs from ploughman's and (pork and leek) sausage and mash to confit duck leg with red wine sauce, with Sunday bringing 'delicious, succulent, tender' pot-roast lamb or roast beef and Yorkshire pud. A children's menu involves chips, but the pasta is fresh and the eggs organic. Evenings offer starters like eggs Benedict with smoked haddock and crispy pancetta, or spicy mussel soup, followed by, say, oxtail with bubble and squeak and red wine sauce, or a risotto of wild mushrooms and Jerusalem artichokes. Among puds could be a Baileys dark chocolate mousse, 'light in texture but rich in flavour', or apple and rhubarb crumble with ice cream. Of 13 wines (all under £15), six come by the glass. SAMPLE DISHES: smoked pigeon breast on haggis with pancetta £5; grilled trout with toasted almonds £9; Amaretto pannacotta with pistachio ice cream £4.

Licensee Elaine Dennehy (Bath Ales)
Open *winter 12 to 3, 5 to 11; summer 12 to 11 (10.30 Sun); bar food and restaurant all week 12 to 2.30 (3 Sun), Tue to Sun 6 to 9*
Details *Children welcome in eating areas   Wheelchair access (not WC)   Garden   No-smoking area in bar, no smoking in dining room   Background and occasional live music   Dogs welcome in garden only   MasterCard, Switch, Visa*

Ring O' Bells   NEW ENTRY   map 2
10 Widcombe Parade, Bath BA2 4JT   TEL: (01225) 448870
Widcombe Parade is just SE of railway station, on S side of River Avon

Tucked away in a parade of restaurants and shops, this small hostelry has no traditional pub sign but can be identified by a giant metal ring with six large bells dangling from it. Inside, things aren't so traditional either, and the small, open-plan space has a definite bistro bent. Bright and cheerful Mediterranean colours (yellow walls and a blue tongue-and-groove bar counter lined with stools), pale pine furniture and jazz music further enhance a contemporary slant. The short menu steps out in line too, with simple, fresh, well-priced modern bistro fare: perhaps roast saffron-marinated breast of pheasant with sweet potato and black olive mash, or ribeye steak with pink and green peppercorn butter. The fish of the day – perhaps whole baked sea bass with citrus butter – is chalked on a blackboard, and the set-price two-course lunch is good value at £7.95. Finish with steamed pudding with pear and ginger. Beers change regularly but might include Gem Bitter from Bath Ales, and there are five wines by the glass plus decent coffee. SAMPLE DISHES: parcel of feta, figs and almonds with basil oil £5; poached guinea fowl with winter vegetables and salsa verde £9; apple and cinnamon tarte Tatin £4.

Licensee Joe Lucas (Philip George)
Open Mon 5 to 11, Tue to Sat 12 to 11, Sun 12 to 6; bar food Tue to Sun 12 to 2.30, Mon to Sat 6 to 10
Details Children welcome   Background music   No dogs   MasterCard, Switch, Visa

Salamander 🍺   NEW ENTRY
3 John Street, Bath BA1 2JL   TEL: (01225) 428889

This eighteenth-century backstreet pub in the centre of the city has, like the Hop Pole (see entry), recently come under the ownership of Bath Ales, a small regional pub group. According to a local fan, the group deserves encouragement for the way it has taken some previously unremarkable pubs and given them real character, while avoiding theme-pub clichés. The décor is in a timeless, traditional style with a contemporary edge, featuring orangey-terracotta walls, dark wood panelling, bare floorboards and various pubby artefacts. Among the principal attractions are the fine draught real ales from the Bath Ales brewery, which are supplemented by a couple of guest beers – perhaps Butcombe Bitter and Broadstone Charter Ale. There is also draught organic cider and an excellent selection of bottled beers. Bar food is interesting without being too ambitious. As well as a few pub staples like fish and chips (albeit in herb and beer batter), the menu offers snacks like grilled goats' cheese crostini, chips topped with vegetarian chilli and cheese, and various sandwiches, including hot roast pork with apple sauce and crackling. The separate restaurant menu offers more sophisticated main dishes like pan-fried pork tenderloin with prawns and lemon cream sauce, and seared sea bass fillet with red onion, sun-dried tomatoes and olives and a basil oil dressing. A short wine list gives a reasonable choice of bottles, opening with house French at £11. Five wines are available by the glass. SAMPLE DISHES: warm chicken salad with spicy coleslaw £4.50; shredded duck, spring onion and cucumber tortilla wrap with soy sauce £4; bangers and mustard mash with onion gravy £6.25.

Licensee Malcolm Follain (Bath Ales)
Open 12 to 11, Sun 12 to 10.30; bar food Tue to Sun 12 to 2.30 (3 Sun), Tue to Sat 6.30 to 9.30, restaurant Tue to Sat 6.30 to 9.30, Sun 12 to 3
Details Children welcome in restaurant   No-smoking area in bar, no smoking in restaurant   Live or background music   Guide dogs only   Delta, MasterCard, Switch, Visa

BEELEY   Derbyshire   map 9

Devonshire Arms

Beeley DE4 2NR   TEL: (01629) 733259
WEBSITE: www.devonshirearmsbeeley.co.uk
off B6102, 5m N of Matlock

Attractively set in the centre of the village, at the southern end of Chatsworth Park, this stone pub was built in 1726 as three separate cottages that were converted into a coaching inn in 1747 to serve the traffic on the Bakewell to Matlock run. A warren of little rooms is found within, with masses of dark beams and timbers, scrubbed-wood furniture, thick stone walls and roaring log fires. Food is served throughout the day, seven days a week, taking in chicken ballotine with red onion marmalade, duck and fig terrine, and auld alliance (a pâté of blue and cream cheeses soaked in whisky), followed by deep-fried battered haddock with tartare sauce, beef and horseradish suet pudding, and fillet steak topped with haggis with a creamy Drambuie sauce. Friday night is fish night, with a wide choice running from butterfly king prawns with a spicy dip to whole trout stuffed with spinach and almonds; and on Sunday morning 'Victorian breakfast' is served (booking essential), inclusive of Buck's Fizz and good cooked choice. Cask ales are Black Sheep Best Bitter and Special Ale, as well as Theakston Old Peculier and Marston's Pedigree, and the wine list is short but serviceable, with house wines sold by the glass. SAMPLE DISHES: asparagus soup £3; haggis, neeps and tatties £6.75; mandarin cheesecake £3.

Licensee John Grosvenor (freehouse)
Open 11 to 11, Sun 12 to 10.30 (Victorian breakfast available 10 to 12); bar food and restaurant 12 to 9.30; closed 25 Dec
Details Children welcome   Car park   Wheelchair access (not WC)   Patio   No-smoking area in bar, no smoking in restaurant   No music   Guide dogs only   Amex, Delta, MasterCard, Switch, Visa

BEETHAM   Cumbria   map 8

▲ Wheatsheaf

Beetham LA7 7AL   TEL: (015395) 62123
just off A6, 5m N of Carnforth

Unusual half-timbered corner bay windows are the most striking aspect of this three-storey, sixteenth-century pub by the river and opposite the church in a quiet village. Inside, the taproom, with its convivial hubbub, is the place to head to for a drink: perhaps a pint of Jennings Bitter, Cumberland Ale, or whatever guest ale happens to be on. People eating should make for the lounge bar, which has something of the feel of a country-house drawing room, with its dark-coloured walls, curtained windows and fresh flowers. In between these two rooms is the hotel reception area with a small bar, an impressive wooden staircase leading up to the bedrooms – and a parrot in a cage. Orders are taken at the tables in the lounge, although the same menu is served throughout. Modern ideas with a global scope are what to expect: crab and salmon fishcakes with Thai spices and sweet-and-sour dipping sauce to start, followed by chicken breast stuffed with smoked cheese, wrapped in pancetta and served with a roasted red pepper and balsamic infusion. Alternatively, under the 'Something Simple' heading on the menu are more traditional fillet steak with chips, oven-baked salmon steak with salad, and braised lamb shank on creamed mash with a red wine and redcurrant gravy. Around a dozen wines are available by the glass. SAMPLE DISHES: chicken liver and red wine pâté with Cumberland sauce £4.75; fillets of lemon sole wrapped around a prawn and salmon farce glazed with bisque sauce £13; lemon tart £4.50.

Licensees Kathryn and Mark Chambers (freehouse)
Open *winter 11.30 to 2.30, 5.30 to 11, Sun 12 to 2.30, 6.30 to 10.30, summer 11 to 11, Sun 12 to 3, 7 to 10.30; bar food and restaurant 12 to 2, 6 to 9; closed evening 25 Dec*
Details *Children welcome in family room and restaurant   Car park   Wheelchair access (also WC) Garden   No smoking in eating areas   Background music   Dogs welcome in taproom   Delta, MasterCard, Switch, Visa   Accommodation: 6 rooms, B&B £40 to £85*

BENTWORTH   **Hampshire**   **map 2**

Sun 🍺

Sun Hill, Bentworth GU34 5JT   TEL: (01420) 562338
off A339, 3m NW of Alton

Bentworth used to have a Moon, and still has a Star, as well as the Sun. The last is an attractive country pub on a narrow lane just south of the village. What was once a pair of seventeenth-century cottages is now a riot of summer colour, thanks to tubs and hanging baskets, and has wooden picnic tables in front. Inside, the three interconnecting rooms have low beams and prints and maps on the walls, while settles and open fires add to the homely feel. Draught ales come from Hampshire brewers (Cheriton Pots Ale, Ringwood Best), surrounding counties (Badger Tanglefoot, Stonehenge Pigswill), and further afield (Bass, Courage Directors), plus regularly changing guests, and a couple by the glass from a simple, short wine list. The food – served throughout the pub and advertised on blackboards – is a long roll call of honest (and home-made) country cooking. That means hearty soups or pâté to start, then a range of casseroles and pies, or maybe cheesy haddock bake, or a minted lamb steak ('tender, well-timed, generous portion') with chips. Comforting puddings include treacle tart, and date crumble. SAMPLE DISHES: marinated chicken wings £3; salmon in white wine sauce £9; chocolate fridge cake £3.25.

Licensee Mary Holmes (freehouse)
Open *12 to 3, 6 to 11, Sun 12 to 10.30; bar food 12 to 2, 7 to 9.30*
Details *Children welcome in family room   Car park   Garden   No music   Dogs welcome   Delta, MasterCard, Switch, Visa*

Cricketers Arms

Berwick BN26 6SP   TEL: (01323) 870469
WEBSITE: www.cricketersberwick.co.uk
just off A27 Lewes to Polegate road

A small, mature garden at the front of this attractive flint-faced building, with
its red-tiled roof and cottagey windows, is a pleasant place for fine-weather
eating. Inside, the cricket theme is enthusiastically pursued, with cricket bats
on the beams and walls, and with pictures of the sport going back to the nineteenth century. The large public bar, with its beamed ceilings, robust pine
tables, quarry-tiled floors and log fires, manages to be both 'pubby' and smart
at the same time. There is also a family room, plus another small cosy room
with a fireplace, though no separately designated dining room. The short
printed bar menu, available all day at weekends, is supplemented by blackboard specials, which might include soup, a vegetarian dish and a curry.
Otherwise, the kitchen concentrates on such stalwarts as butterfly prawns
with a cocktail sauce, or garlic mushrooms to start, and main courses of home-
baked ham with a free-range egg and chunky chips, steaks and filled jacket
potatoes. This is a Harveys of Lewes pub, and the brewery's Best Bitter and
seasonal brews are served straight from the cask. Wines of the month are
chalked on a blackboard, and around a dozen are served by the glass. SAMPLE
DISHES: smoked salmon pâté £5.25; battered cod with chips £7.25; sticky toffee
pudding £3.50.

Licensee Peter Brown (Harveys)
Open *summer Mon to Sat 11 to 11, Sun 12 to 10; winter Mon to Fri 11 to 3, 6 to 11, Sat 11 to
11, Sun 12 to 10; bar food Mon to Fri 12 to 2.15, 6.30 to 9, Sat and Sun and all week June, July and
Aug 12 to 9; closed 25 Dec*
Details *No children under 14 in bar   Car park   Wheelchair access (not WC)   Garden   No music
Dogs welcome   MasterCard, Switch, Visa*

▲ Red Lion   NEW ENTRY

Old Reigate Road, Betchworth RH3 7DS   TEL: (01737) 843336
off A25, 3m E of Dorking

The Red Lion is close to being the archetypal English country pub, occupying
a semi-rural position with a cricket pitch behind it. Inside, expect a traditional
pub décor of banquettes and brown Windsor chairs, dark-red patterned
carpets, and a clientele of widely varying ages. Lunchtime 'hot meals', as the
menu describes them, take in pork stroganoff, beef, Guinness and mushroom
pie, and moules marinière, as well as the usual ploughman's, filled baguettes
and jacket potatoes. The dinner menu tends to favour old-fashioned dishes
like prawn cocktail, and steak and mushroom pie, but makes room for a few
more modern ideas, such as seared tuna steak on chilli and thyme couscous
with pesto, or Thai green vegetable and sweet potato curry. Prices on the 20-
strong wine list start at £11.95 and mostly keep below £20. Six are available by
the glass. Real ales include Shepherd Neame Spitfire, Greene King IPA and

Fuller's London Pride. SAMPLE DISHES: mushrooms 'Neptune' (filled with goats' cheese and crabmeat) £4.75; calf's liver and bacon with onion gravy £12; spotted dick £3.50.

Licensees Alan Podemsky and Tony Wolbrom (Punch Taverns)
Open 11 to 11, Sun 12 to 10.30; bar food 12 to 3, restaurant Mon to Sat 6 to 9, Sun 12 to 9
Details *Children welcome   Car park   Wheelchair access (not WC)   Garden and patio*
No-smoking area in bar, no smoking in restaurant   Occasional live or background music   No dogs
Amex, Delta, MasterCard, Switch, Visa   Accommodation: 6 rooms, B&B £75 to £85

BIDDENDEN   Kent   map 3

Three Chimneys 🍺 🍇

Hareplain Road, Biddenden TN27 8LW   TEL: (01580) 291472
on A262, 2m W of Biddenden

Step down from the front door of this old two-storey pub into a tiny bar area, where there's an open fire, and on into a series of interlinked rooms with endearingly mismatched furniture and a predominantly ochre colour scheme. Blackboard menus are transported to the table for closer perusal, and might offer starters such as garlic and thyme bruschetta topped with sun-dried tomato and black olive tapénade, or fishcakes with tartare sauce, and main courses of pan-fried fillets of sea bass on a chowder of spicy roasted sweet potatoes, coconut and coriander, or loin of lamb in a Parmesan and herb crust with lyonnaise potatoes. You might opt to finish with a pancake filled with caramelised bananas served with rum and raisin ice cream, or strawberry and vanilla crème brûlée. The choice for real beer fans encompasses Adnams Best Bitter, Shepherd Neame Spitfire Premium Ale and Master Brew and other seasonal ales – all drawn straight from the casks behind the bar. An appetising house selection of eight wines available in bottle or by the glass includes Sandhurst Vineyards from Kent. The main wine list offers lots of flavour for under £15 from the southern hemisphere and plenty from France, but little of that is so readily affordable. To complete the premium drinking, there is an extensive collection of malt whiskies and, naturally enough, Biddenden cider. At the back is a beer garden, with a stylish courtyard at the front, to the right of the building. SAMPLE DISHES: baked field mushrooms topped with caramelised red onions and grilled goats' cheese £5.50; pan-fried king scallops on chorizo, bacon and spring onion mash £17; sticky toffee pudding with dairy cream £4.

Licensee Craig Smith (freehouse)
Open *11 to 2.30, 6 (7 Sun) to 11; bar food and restaurant 12 to 1.50, 6.30 to 9.45 (9 Sun)*
Details *Children welcome in eating areas   Car park   Wheelchair access (not WC)   Garden and patio   No music   Dogs welcome   Delta, MasterCard, Switch, Visa*

▲ *indicates where a pub offers accommodation. At the end of the entry information is given on the number of rooms available and a price range, indicating the cost of a single room or single occupancy to that for a room with two people sharing.*

BIRCHOVER   Derbyshire   **map 5**

Druid Inn

Main Street, Birchover DE4 2BL   TEL: (01629) 650302
WEBSITE: www.druidinnbirchover.co.uk
from A6 2m SE of Bakewell turn S on B5056; Birchover signposted on left after 2m

This pub was built in 1846 against the bracken and tree-clad background of
Rowtor Rocks, and the thick coat of creeper that has since swathed one side
evokes the nineteenth-century taste for the picturesque. The building
contains a series of rooms on different levels, ranging from the small, beamed
and quaintly traditional, warmed by open fires, to a pair of formal dining
rooms with tablecloths and flowers on the tables. Outside, a sheltered terrace
makes a pleasant place to sup Marston's Pedigree from nearby Mansfield, as
well as guest beers in summer (there is also a large range of whiskies, and from
a concise and kindly priced list three house wines come by the glass). This is
very much a food pub, though, and a huge blackboard menu shows influences
from Matlock to Bangkok and back again. Starters could include spicy lamb
meatballs or port and Stilton pâté, while mains range from plaice and smoked
salmon in a sauce of brandy, chives, spring onions and cream, or a Derbyshire
beef and vegetable stew with herb dumplings, to chicken tikka masala or mae
hong son (pork, chicken and prawns in a chilli broth with rice). Vegetarians
have an excellent choice, including spinach and mushroom cannelloni, and
five-bean casserole. Puddings extend to apple and marzipan torte, and
summer pudding. SAMPLE DISHES: hot and spicy pork spare ribs £6; pot-roast
pheasant with root vegetables £13; bitter chocolate and orange tart £3.50.

Licensee Brian Bunce (freehouse)
Open *Tue to Sun 12 to 2.30, 7 to 9.30/10 (11 summer); bar food and restaurant Tue to Sun 12 to
1.45, 7 to 8.30 (9 summer)*
Details *Children welcome   Car park   Wheelchair access (not WC)   Patio   No-smoking area in bar,
no smoking in dining room   Background music   Dogs welcome in taproom   Amex, Delta, Diners,
MasterCard, Switch, Visa*

BIRCH VALE   Derbyshire   **map 8**

▲ Waltzing Weasel

New Mills Road, Birch Vale SK22 1BT   TEL: (01663) 743402
WEBSITE: www.w-weasel.co.uk
4½m E of Stockport, turn NE off A6 on to A6015; Birch Vale is 2m on

The Waltzing Weasel may be only just outside the Manchester conurbation,
but it is a country inn in feel and setting. The view across the terrace and
garden to Lantern Pike will lift the spirits – so, too, will the absence of games
machines and mobile phones (switch yours off, if you have one). Both bar and
restaurant menus have desserts in common, among them hot apple tartlet and
cream, or brandy-snap basket with ice cream and fruit. The bar menu offers
starters like chicken liver pâté or scallops in basil and prosciutto, with seafood
tart or vegetable crêpe, or an exotic casserole. On Sundays there's roast beef
and Yorkshire pudding too. The restaurant's two- or three-course set meals,
not available in the bar though some of the dishes might be, could start with

sardine tapénade or cheese and onion soufflé, and then go on to fish of the day (brill, Arctic char and sole are possibilities), abacchio alla Romana for lamb lovers, or game in season. Marston's Best Bitter and Kelham Island Gold are on handpump. The short wine list includes a few smart bottles, with half a dozen by the glass. SAMPLE DISHES: torta peperonata £5.75; Peak pie (with meat, game and red wine) £9.95; treacle tart £4.75.

Licensee Michael Atkinson (freehouse)
Open 12 to 3, 5.30 to 11; bar food 12 to 2, 7 to 9.30 (9 Sun); restaurant 12 to 2, 7 to 9 (8.30 Sun)
Details Children welcome   Car park   Wheelchair access (not WC)   Garden and patio
No smoking in dining room   Occasional live music   Dogs welcome   Amex, Delta, MasterCard, Switch, Visa   Accommodation: 8 rooms, B&B £45 to £105

BISHOP'S CASTLE   Shropshire   map 5

▲ Three Tuns 🍺

Salop Street, Bishop's Castle SY9 5BW   TEL: (01588) 638797
WEBSITE: www.thethreetunsinn.co.uk
off B4385, just off A488, 8m NW of Craven Arms

BREW PUB

On a steep hillside in the centre of town, the Three Tuns consists of a court-yard of buildings that includes a formidably tall brewery, which was undergoing extensive renovation at the time the Guide was going to press but was due to be back in operation soon. In the meantime, the fine cask and bottled beers produced here and served in the pub (and a few other outlets) – including XXX Bitter, Sexton, Offa's Ale, Clerics Cure, and the seasonal Old Scrooge – were being brewed temporarily to their specification by the Shrewsbury brewery Salopian. In the pub is a public bar and a sparsely furnished dining area with a long bar counter, fat black ceiling beams, plain wooden furniture including settles, and candles dripping in bottles. Choose from the blackboard menus, order at the bar and your food will be brought to your table. The style of cooking is as unpretentious and uncluttered as the surroundings, offering dishes such as a soup – fish, perhaps, or tomato and basil – with organic bread, or smoked chicken and melon salad with raspberry vinaigrette, followed by tasty and tender beef in ale with herby mash and vegetables, or salmon fillet with lemon butter. Finish with raspberry meringue, or sticky toffee pudding. Four wines are served by the glass. SAMPLE DISHES: a platter of smoked fish with garlic mayonnaise £4.25; lamb shank in red wine, rosemary and redcurrant gravy £11.50; pear and almond tart £4.

Licensees Janet Cross and Janet Wainwright (freehouse)
Open Mon to Thur 12 to 3.30, 5 to 11 (11.30 summer), Fri to Sun 12 to 11.30 (10.30 Sun); bar food and restaurant Tue to Sun 12 to 2.30, all week 7 to 9.30; closed 25 Dec, Mon lunch and Sun evening winter
Details Children welcome   Car park   Wheelchair access (not WC)   Patio   No smoking in restaurant   Occasional live music   Dogs in snug bar only   Delta, Diners, MasterCard, Switch, Visa

Feedback on pubs in the Guide, and recommendations for new ones, are very welcome.

Eagle & Child 🍺

Malt Kiln Lane, Bispham Green L40 3SG   TEL: (01257) 462297
*from M6 junction 27, take A5209 over Parbold Hill, right on B5246, fourth left signposted
Bispham Green; pub is ½m on right*

The bowling green at the back of this white-painted pub, set in an out-of-the-way village, is a popular attraction in summer. Inside are two rustic bar areas, with coal fires, hop-garlanded beams, plenty of prints on the walls and stone or hessian-covered floors. The standard menu is mostly staple pub fare, such as chicken liver parfait, followed by grilled gammon with pineapple, or sausage and mash. Most interesting is the daily specials board, where the kitchen's inventive streak is given full rein. Expect dishes like a starter of red mullet with sautéed potato, or sardines stuffed with coriander and garlic, then beef balti, or seared tuna with spicy ratatouille. Desserts can be equally creative: lemongrass brûlée, or champagne cheesecake, for example. An impressive five ever-changing guest ales, from independent breweries like Jennings and Hart, join regulars Thwaites Bitter and Moorhouses Black Cat on handpump, and there is a large selection of malt whiskies. House wines are listed on a board above the bar, and the full list has nearly 30 bottles, with half a dozen by the glass. SAMPLE DISHES: tomato and roast pepper soup £3.50; roast suckling pig with candied shallots and chestnuts £8.50; pecan and gingerbread pudding £3.75.

Licensee Monica Evans (freehouse)
Open *12 to 3, 5.30 to 11, Sun 12 to 10.30; bar food 12 to 2, 6 to 8.30 (9 Fri and Sat), Sun 12 to
8.30; closed evening 25 Dec*
Details *Children welcome in family room   Car park   Wheelchair access (not WC)   Garden
No-smoking area in bar   Background music   No dogs   MasterCard, Switch, Visa*

Blackboys Inn

Lewes Road, Blackboys TN22 5LG   TEL: (01825) 890283
on B2192, 3m E of Uckfield

The village name probably has to do with charcoal-burning: for centuries this area produced charcoal for the iron foundries at Buxted and Heathfield. Ironworking hereabouts died out in the 1800s, but the pub that quenched the workers' thirsts survives, set slightly back from the main road and peering out of small, high-set, mullioned windows. Inside there are original beams, a convivial atmosphere, and helpfully friendly (mostly young) staff. There are two bars and a games room, plus a series of interconnecting rooms mainly for dining (food is listed on a carte, a bar snack menu and a blackboard above the bar for the specials). This is a Harveys house, so there's Harveys Sussex Best Bitter and Pale Ale, plus seasonal ales, on tap, along with eight wines by the glass. The wine list broadens the range of decent-value drinking and adds a few high-priced trophy bottles and older vintages. Bar snacks cover the jacket potato/ploughman's/burger/steak spectrum, plus sausage and mash, and perhaps Thai red chicken curry. Restaurant dishes are more elaborate but still substantial. Starters might include pancetta-wrapped scallops with citrus vinaigrette, or confit of duck with hoisin dressing, then sturdy paella, char-grilled tournedos with Madeira sauce, or vegetarian lasagne. Finish with prof-iteroles, or soft-fruit crème brûlée. SAMPLE DISHES: tartare of tuna with wasabi coleslaw £7; whole grilled sea bass with salsa verde £15; banoffi pie £3.50.

Licensees Edward and Claire Molesworth (Harveys of Lewes)
Open 11 to 3, 5 (6 Sat) to 11, Sun 12 to 3, 7 to 10.30; bar food and restaurant all week 12 to 2.15, Mon to Sat 6.30 (7 restaurant) to 9.30; closed 25 Dec, 1 Jan
Details Children welcome in snug and dining room   Car park   Garden and patio   No smoking in dining room   Occasional music   No dogs in dining room   Delta, MasterCard, Switch, Visa

BLACKHAM   East Sussex   map 3
Sussex Oak
Blackham TN3 9UA   TEL: (01892) 740273
WEBSITE: www.sussex-oak.co.uk
on A264 about 5m W of Royal Tunbridge Wells

A log fire in winter is a welcoming sight at this Shepherd Neame pub on a long curve of the A264. Hop garlands decorate the bar, and there are copper hunt-ing horns and Guinness-inspired pictures. Across the hall is a warm-looking restaurant with pine tables and chairs. Although separate menus operate in the bar and the Acorn Flambé restaurant, you can pick and mix. As its name suggests, the latter specialises in that technique of finishing dishes: suprême of salmon cooked with garlic, limes and cream and flambé with gin, perhaps, or fillet steak flambé with brandy in a rich peppercorn sauce. Crêpes suzette are inevitably among desserts, while starters range from a plate of smoked salmon to vegetable samosa. From the short bar menu you might choose avocado and bacon salad, followed by ham, egg and chips, or Stilton and mushroom omelette – not forgetting the signature dish of chicken in a nutty masala sauce with basmati rice – and then Baileys ice cream. A selection of Shepherd Neame ales is on draught, and three or four wines are served by the glass. SAMPLE DISHES: goats' cheese on a garlic and herb croûton with raspberry coulis £4.75; goose breast glazed with honey and Cointreau with orange sauce £17.50; blackcurrant cheesecake £3.75.

Licensees Maeve and Vijay Shukla (Shepherd Neame)
Open 11 to 3, 6 to 11, Sun 12 to 4, 6.30 to 10.30; bar food and restaurant (exc Sun evening) 11 to 3, 6.30 to 9.30
Details Children welcome in eating areas   Car park   Garden   No smoking in restaurant   Background music   Dogs welcome   Delta, MasterCard, Switch, Visa

BLACKMORE END   Essex   map 3
Bull
Blackmore End CM7 4DD   TEL: (01371) 851037
between A1017 and B1053, 6m N of Braintree

This somewhat plain-looking traditional village pub is surrounded by rolling fields in the heart of Constable country. Inside, horse brasses adorn the beams and standing timbers, and there's an impressive brick chimney breast.

Straightforward pub food is the order of the day, including a wide selection of hot or cold sandwiches, such as minute steak. The smarter dining area has its own, more ambitious menu, though this is available throughout the pub: start perhaps with wild mushrooms and tiger prawns in a creamy wine and garlic sauce, followed by fillet steak on dauphinois potatoes topped with a croûton layered with pâté, and finish with spotted dick. A good choice of real ales extends to Greene King IPA, Adnams Bitter, Fuller's London Pride, Marston's Pedigree and Old Speckled Hen, and half a dozen wines are available by the glass. SAMPLE DISHES: home-made chicken liver and port pâté £5.50; fillet of sole stuffed with king scallops in a cream sauce £12.95; sticky toffee and banana pudding £4.50.

Licensee Sydney Morris (freehouse)
Open Mon to Fri 12 to 3, 6 to 11, Sat 12 to 2.30, 6.30 to 11.30, Sun 12 to 3.30, 7 to 10.30; bar food and restaurant Tue to Sat 12 to 2.30, 7 to 10
Details Children welcome in eating areas   Car park   Wheelchair access (also WC)   Garden   Occasional live music   No dogs   Delta, MasterCard, Switch, Visa

BLAKENEY   Norfolk   **map 6**

▲ White Horse Hotel ❦
4 High Street, Blakeney NR25 7AL   TEL: (01263) 740574
WEBSITE: www.blakeneywhitehorse.co.uk
off A149, 5m W of Holt

Located on the narrow High Street, just a few yards from the quayside, this seventeenth-century former coaching inn is Blakeney's oldest hotel. Inside, the well-maintained bar is decorated with works by local artists depicting nearby scenes, with many for sale. As befits the coastal location, fish features prominently on the bar menu: wholetail Whitby scampi, local mussels, Thai-style crab cakes, and poached smoked haddock and mustard mash are typical offerings. Meat eaters might choose steak and ale pie, or sausages and mash with braised cabbage, and lunchers looking for a lighter bite will find sandwiches available. The menu in the restaurant, which is in a converted stable block overlooking the walled garden and courtyard, has more ambitious offerings of, perhaps, smoked eel fillet on celeriac rémoulade with pancetta, followed by chargrilled venison medallions on quince purée and blackberry sauce. Beers from Adnams and Woodforde's are on tap, and ten wines from a round-the-world list of around 40 are sold by the glass (with additional specials chalked up on a blackboard). Wine prices are reasonable and the list is pegged resolutely below the £20 mark except for three or four French classics and the champagne – and even then it offers a tasty budget alternative from Touraine. There's a good a sprinkling of half-bottles too. SAMPLE DISHES: cockle chowder £4; haddock and prawn pie £7; treacle tart £3.50.

Licensees Daniel Goff and Simon Scillitoe (Daniel Rees)
Open 11 to 3, 6 to 11, Sun 12 to 3, 7 to 10.30; bar food 12 to 2 (to around 2.30 summer), 6 to 9; restaurant Tue to Sun 7 to 9; closed 2 weeks mid-Jan
Details Children welcome in family room   Car park   Wheelchair access (not WC)   Garden and patio   No smoking in restaurant   Occasional music   No dogs   Amex, Delta, MasterCard, Switch, Visa   Accommodation: 10 rooms, B&B £30 to £90

BLEDINGTON   Gloucestershire   map 5

▲ Kings Head 🍺
The Green, Bledington OX7 6XQ   TEL: (01608) 658365
WEBSITE: www.kingsheadinn.net
on B4450 4m SE of Stow-on-the-Wold

Once a cider house, this sixteenth-century building is set back from the green beside a brook in a timeless Cotswold village of mellow stone cottages. Within is a low-ceilinged, dimly lit, beamed bar with rough stone walls and a large inglenook where a log fire burns. You can eat either in here or in the restaurant, an appealing space with a flagstone floor and solid oak furniture. Some bright, modern ideas show up on the menu, with starters of Thai beef salad with noodles, or grilled scallops with sweet chilli sauce, and main courses of fishcakes with tomato and rocket salad and salsa verde, or free-range chicken breast with chorizo and Parmentier potatoes. More traditional favourites aren't neglected, however, with potted shrimps, followed perhaps by steak stewed in ale served with mash and braised cabbage, then sticky toffee pudding. Hook Norton Best Bitter is a permanent fixture on handpump, joined by guest ales from brewers like Adnams, Archers and Shepherd Neame. The six house wines sold by the glass offer a fair range of modern flavours, but the list has its heart in the traditional regions of France. SAMPLE DISHES: home-cured gravad lax with honey and mustard dressing £5.50; medallions of pork fillet with braised fennel, sweet potato mash and mustard cream sauce £11.50; bread-and-butter pudding £4.

Licensees Archie and Nicola Orr-Ewing (freehouse)
Open *11 to 2.30, 6 to 11, Sun 12 to 3, 6.30 to 10.30; bar food and restaurant 12 to 2, 7 to 9.30 (9 winter); closed 25 and 26 Dec*
Details *Children welcome in family room and restaurant   Car park   Garden and patio*
No smoking in restaurant   Occasional live or background music   Dogs welcome exc in restaurant
Amex, Delta, MasterCard, Switch, Visa   Accommodation: 12 rooms, B&B £50 to £85

BLEDLOW   Buckinghamshire   map 3

Lions of Bledlow 🍺
Church End, Bledlow HP27 9PE   TEL: (01844) 343345
off B4009, 2m SW of Princes Risborough; take West Lane, not Bledlow Ridge turning

Once in the village, look for the pub's name on a prominent signpost, which points you down a long single-track road, at the very end of which, on a bit of a rise, sits the Lions, a sprawled white building with a bit of a green in front. In summer, picnic benches in the garden and on the green make al fresco eating an appealing possibility; otherwise sit in the low-beamed bar, which has a real pubby feel due in part to the horse brasses and glass tankards about the place, or in the slightly smarter restaurant, where tables are adorned with fresh flowers. One compact menu is available throughout, offering snacks (baguettes, salads, ploughman's) and straightforward dishes along the lines of chicken liver pâté, gammon steak with chips, or chicken and mushroom pie, with oriental king prawns in filo with Cajun dip one of the more unusual items. Daily blackboard specials boost the number of options, among them perhaps pork fillet in creamy mushroom sauce, followed by crème brûlée, and another board is dedicated to a handful of vegetarian dishes. There's a children's menu of the fish fingers sort, or an extra plate will cheerfully be provided for children to share an adult's order. As well as a line-up of Marston's Pedigree, Wadworth 6X, Brakspear Bitter and Courage Best, there is a guest ale, usually from a local brewery such as Vale. Wines are a concise selection, the majority under £12, and eight are available by the glass. SAMPLE DISHES: minestrone soup £3; duck in plum sauce £8.50; apricot crumble £4.

Licensee Mark McKeown (freehouse)
Open 11.30 to 3, 6 to 11, Sun 12 to 4, 7 to 10.30; bar food and restaurant 12 to 2.30, 7 to 9.30
Details Children welcome   Car park   Garden and patio   No smoking in restaurant   No music
Dogs welcome   Amex, Delta, Diners, MasterCard, Switch, Visa

BOOTHSDALE   Cheshire   map 7

Boot Inn

Boothsdale, Willington CW6 0NH   TEL: (01829) 751375
coming from Chester on A54, turn right to Oscroft Willington, then left at T-junction, then second right up Boothsdale to pub; from Knutsford on A556, turn left to Kelsall Willington, then second left up Quarry Lane, then left at end, then first left up Boothsdale to pub

---

Backed by wooded hills, on a narrow one-track lane, this mellow brick and sandstone building has a wonderful aspect. The interior is on different levels, a reminder that several cottages have been knocked together to create the pub, with low ceilings and beams remaining from its origins in the early nineteenth century. A central wood-burning stove in the main bar area, with a few benches and tables around its wall, a snug with a black-leaded range and old pews, another room with colour-washed walls and an open log fire, and a light and airy conservatory restaurant with doors to the garden: all create a friendly, lived-in atmosphere. Interesting sandwiches and baguettes are served in the bar – ham, tomato and mozzarella, for instance – where you can also order from the restaurant menu or choose something from the specials board. Black pudding with crispy bacon and onions on creamy mustard sauce, or smoked chicken with apple and walnut salad are typical of the wide choice of starters. Main courses take in the traditional – steak, kidney and ale pie, or Cumberland sausage in rich onion gravy with a large plate of chips – as well as more enterprising dishes: game and turkey pie, 'mouthwateringly good' trout fillets and prawns baked with mushrooms in a light cheese sauce, or baked chicken fillet stuffed with herbs and garlic cream cheese, wrapped in Parma ham and accompanied by tomato sauce. Vegetarians are particularly well looked after, and to finish there's something familiar like lemon tart or sherry trifle. Tetley Bitter, Timothy Taylor Landlord and Bass are among the ales on tap, plus perhaps a brew from local Weetwood Ales. The short, fairly priced wine list includes four tasty house wines by the small or large glass, and malt whisky fans will find thirty to choose from. The pub has produced a leaflet describing six circular walks from the pub, in an area known locally as Little Switzerland. SAMPLE DISHES: kidneys pan-fried with cracked black pepper and paprika served with red wine sauce £5.75; fillet of Scotch salmon poached with herbs £8.50; apple pie £4.

Licensee Mike Gollings (Pubmaster)
Open Mon to Fri 11 to 3, 6 to 11, Sat, Sun and bank hols 11 to 11; bar food and restaurant
Mon to Fri 11 to 2.30, 6 to 9.30, Sat, Sun and bank hols 11 to 9.30; closed 25 Dec
Details Children welcome in snug and restaurant   Car park   Garden and patio   No smoking in
restaurant   No music   No dogs   Amex, Delta, Diners, MasterCard, Switch, Visa

BORASTON   Shropshire   map 5

▲ Peacock Inn

Worcester Road, Boraston WR15 8LL   TEL: (01584) 810506
WEBSITE: www.thepeacockinn.com
on A456, 1¼m E of Tenbury Wells

Oak beams and panelling convey the impression of great age at the Peacock, a
large, white-painted roadside pub in an isolated position looking over fields in
the Teme Valley, and indeed the building dates from the fourteenth century.
An open fire, hop bines and embroideries of peacocks add character to the
series of rooms, while flower-filled hanging baskets and tubs brighten up the
paved patio, with its trestle tables, to the front. Most of the space is given over
to eating, and the same menus are served throughout, with the addition of
sandwiches at lunchtimes. On offer might be crab cakes with spicy mango
chutney, or chicken liver parfait, followed by fillet of pork with apples and a
caraway seed sauce, teriyaki-style salmon on noodles, or a pasta: perhaps tagliatelle with Mediterranean vegetables and a walnut and ricotta paste.
Lunchtime and early-evening specials are a good deal, and among desserts
might be bread-and-butter pudding with custard, or raspberry cheesecake.
Real ales include Hook Norton Old Hooky and Hobsons Best Bitter, and six
house wines are sold by the glass or bottle, the rest of the list selected with a
keen eye for quality to tempt those willing to spend over £20 or even £30 a
bottle. SAMPLE DISHES: smoked salmon timbale with broccoli mousse and
balsamic dressing £6.50; green Thai curry of tiger prawns and chicken with
jasmine rice £9; sticky toffee pudding £4.50.

Licensees James and Alice Vidler (freehouse)
Open 11 to 3, 6 to 11 (10.30 Sun); bar food and restaurant 12 to 2.15, 6.30 to 9.15
Details Children welcome in eating areas   Car park   Wheelchair access (not WC)   Garden and
patio   No-smoking area in bar, no smoking in restaurant   Background music   Dogs welcome in bar
Delta, MasterCard, Switch, Visa   Accommodation: 3 rooms, B&B £45 to £70

BOROUGHBRIDGE   North Yorkshire   map 8

▲ Black Bull   NEW ENTRY

6 St James Square, Boroughbridge YO51 9AR   TEL: (01423) 322413
on B6265, ½m from A1(M) junction 48

The Black Bull is one of several coaching inns that populate the historical
market town of Boroughbridge. To call it ancient is no understatement: its
origins predate the battle of 1322 between Edward II and the Duke of
Lancaster that happened nearby, and although the present building is more
recent it still has thick stone walls, plenty of old beams and a huge fireplace. A
printed menu of bar snacks blends traditional and modern ideas, pitching pork

and chive sausage on a potato pancake against chicken satay, while more substantial dishes run from Asian-spiced chargrilled swordfish steak to beef braised in a rich ale gravy served in a giant Yorkshire pudding with creamy mash. Choice is extended with a blackboard of seasonal specials and fish dishes. The separate restaurant menu, also available in the bar, is a little more upmarket, offering dishes like lamb cutlets with crushed rosemary and garlic potatoes. Regular beers John Smith's Bitter and Black Sheep Best Bitter are joined by a varying guest ale. The wine list offers more than 30 bottles, priced from around £8, plus eight or so by the glass. SAMPLE DISHES: smoked mackerel fillet on warm potato and beetroot salad £5; roast loin of pork with sweet apple and Calvados compote £11.75; orange chocolate bavarois £3.

Licensee Mr A.E. Burgess (freehouse)

Open 11 to 11, Sun 12 to 10.30; bar food and restaurant 12 to 2 (2.30 Sun), 6 to 9 (9.30 Fri and Sat)

Details Children welcome   Car park   Wheelchair access (also WC)   No-smoking area in bar, no smoking in restaurant   Occasional background music   Dogs welcome   Delta, Diners, MasterCard, Switch, Visa   Accommodation: 6 rooms, B&B £30 to £56

BOSCASTLE   Cornwall   map 1

▲ Napoleon 🍺 | NEW ENTRY |

High Street, Boscastle PL35 0BD   TEL: (01840) 250204
pub signposted from B3263 at top of village (don't go down to the harbour)

'A really superb village pub,' was one reporter's verdict on this old coaching inn at the heart of this ancient coastal village. Among its attractions are three beer gardens and two well-appointed bars ('public' and 'officers') decorated with Boscastle memorabilia and warmed by open fires. New licensees arrived towards the end of 2002, bringing with them a good deal of enthusiasm and a love of real ales, which is reflected in the 'staggering' array of regular and seasonal beers from the St Austell brewery, tapped direct from the barrel, and 'local rough cider' is also poured straight from the barrel. Wine drinkers have less to get excited about, with only two sold by the glass. Menus – a small printed list and a full blackboard – have a no-nonsense appeal, offering various pies, steaks, stews and so on, plus whatever fish might have been landed. Creamy fish pie with a smooth mash topping was enjoyed at inspection, while both mushroom soup for starters and treacle tart to finish have been praised for their authentic home-made flavour. Boney's Bistro, the separate restaurant, is open for dinner, offering a fish-orientated menu of dishes like grilled brill with herb butter, or tuna steak with a mango and lime salsa. SAMPLE DISHES: home-made soup with herb scones £3.50; beef and mushroom Napoleon £7.25; bread-and-butter pudding £2.95.

Licensees Liam and Jacquie Flynn (St Austell Brewery)

Open 10.30 to 11; bar food 12 to 2, 6.30 to 9, restaurant 6.30 to 9

Details Children welcome in restaurant   Car park   Wheelchair access (not WC)   Garden and patio   No-smoking area in bar   Live or background music   Dogs welcome   Amex, Delta, Diners, MasterCard, Switch, Visa   Accommodation: 3 rooms, B&B £20 to £45

BOTTLESFORD   Wiltshire   map 2

Seven Stars 🍴 🍇

Bottlesford SN9 6LU   TEL: (01672) 851325

off A345 at mini-roundabout at North Newnton; follow signs for Woodborough then Bottlesford

Head west from Pewsey for three miles and you reach this pretty, brick and
thatch pub in nine-acre grounds. The rambling interior has lots of wood:
some burning on open fires, some carved on panelling and doors, plus
benches, settles and lots of dining tables. Philippe Cheminade – chef/patron as
much landlord – brings a French sensibility not just to food and drink but also
to putting customers at their ease. Among bar snacks, croque-monsieur and
aubergines provençale line up with sandwiches, salads and ploughman's
lunches, while the restaurant menu, changed daily and also available in the
bar, specialises in game in winter and fish in summer. There's fish soup with
croûtons and rouille, or home-made chicken liver paté (even smoked salmon
salade niçoise) to start. Then summer may offer crab mayonnaise, blue shark,
or skate wing, while winter warms with jugged hare, fried venison liver with
wild mushrooms, or roast best end of lamb. There's a good French cheeseboard as an alternative to puddings like tarte Tatin. To drink, there's Badger
Dorset Best, Fuller's London Pride and Wadworth 6X, alongside local organic
cider, a French-led wine list and a range of vintage Armagnacs. Eight house
wines at £10.25 a bottle (£1.90 or £2.95 per small or medium glass) include
unusual grape varieties like Vermentino and Mauzac to offer a better-than-
average choice of flavours. Some quite serious French bottles command
appropriate prices, but with plenty of good stuff from all around the world at
under £20 there's no need to overreach. SAMPLE DISHES: French onion soup
£3.75; whole Dover sole meunière £15.75; forest fruits crème brûlée £4.

Licensees Philippe and Kate Cheminade (freehouse)
Open *Tue to Sat 12 to 3, 6 to 11, Sun 12 to 3; bar food and restaurant Tue to Sat 12 to 2,
7 to 9.30, Sun 12 to 2*
Details *Children welcome in dining room   Car park   Wheelchair access (not WC)   Garden and
patio   No smoking in 1 dining room   Background music   Dogs by arrangement   Delta, MasterCard,
Switch, Visa*

BOUGH BEECH   Kent   map 3

Wheatsheaf   NEW ENTRY

Hever Road, Bough Beech TN8 7NU   TEL: (01732) 700254

off B2027 between Edenbridge and Tonbridge

Local tradition has it that the Wheatsheaf was originally a hunting lodge for
Henry V. This typical Wealden building has also been a smithy in its lifetime
and has been an alehouse on and off since the eighteenth century. Inside, its
antiquity is evident in such features as a patch of original wattle-and-daub wall
dated 1607. Walls are adorned with exotic hunting trophies and unusual musical instruments, while food is listed on a huge blackboard. 'Good, honest,
value for money with no frills' is what to expect. An inspector enjoyed parsnip
soup that was 'true to the vegetable' and 'satisfying' beef goulash. Choice
might run to smoked salmon with a crusty roll, beef and vegetable curry, local

pork and herb sausages with mash, or macaroni cheese with smoked haddock. Finish perhaps with apricot tart, or syrup sponge pudding. A good choice of real ales includes Fuller's London Pride, Shepherd Neame Master Brew Bitter and Harveys Sussex Best, while among the three house wines, all offered by the glass as well as by the bottle (£11.50), is a dry white from nearby Chiddingstone vineyard. SAMPLE DISHES: garlic mushrooms on ciabatta with balsamic vinegar and pesto £6; lamb's liver with bacon, black pudding and mash £11; toffee and date pudding £4.25.

Licensee Elizabeth Currie (freehouse)
Open 11 to 11 (10.30 Sun); bar food 12 to 10
Details Children welcome Car park Wheelchair access (also WC) Garden Live music Dogs welcome MasterCard, Switch, Visa

BRAMDEAN   **Hampshire**   map 2

Fox Inn

Bramdean SO24 0LP   TEL: (01962) 771363
on A272 Winchester to Petersfield road, 3m SE of New Alresford

There is literally a certain amount of history attached to this 400-year-old pub beside the main road: a bracket on an outside wall bears a carving of the Prince of Wales' feathers, in honour of the day in 1780 when the future George IV looked in for a pint and a wad. The interior has since been comfortably modernised on an open plan, and terracotta walls, open fires, attractive lamps and good tables in the dining area, all contribute to a relaxed and civilised atmosphere. On tap are Greene King Abbot and Ruddles County ales, and there are some 30 modestly priced wines on the list, with seven by the glass. Daily-changing blackboard menus are notable for the interesting sauces that accompany the dishes and for a strong contingent of fish dishes. On offer might be avocado, melon, smoked chicken and crispy bacon salad, or kiln-roasted smoked salmon with a dill sauce, followed perhaps by a whole grilled lemon or Dover sole, or a chicken suprême with Parma ham and Boursin sauce. Among the home-made puddings are crumbles, pies and two-nut chocolate torte. Service is friendly and efficient. SAMPLE DISHES: fried scallops and bacon £7; home-made steak and kidney pie £10; fresh fruit cheesecake £4.25.

Licensees Jane and Ian Inder (Greene King)
Open 11 to 3, 6.30 (6 summer) to 11, Sun 12 to 3, 7 to 10.30; bar food 12 to 2, 7 to 9
Details No children Car park Wheelchair access (not WC) Garden and patio No-smoking area in bar No music Amex, Delta, MasterCard, Switch, Visa

BRAMFIELD   **Suffolk**   map 6

Queen's Head

The Street, Bramfield IP19 9HT   TEL: (01986) 784214
off A144, 3m S of Halesworth

Beams, huge fireplaces, a bar with a vaulted ceiling, and scrubbed pine tables are what you will find at this village-centre pub, with a garden (plenty of seats) overlooked by the thatched church. Half of it is non-smoking, and all of it is free of music. It has no restaurant, but the landlord, doubling as chef, describes it as 'very much a dining pub', and many of the ingredients are organic. Soups, served with organic bread, are well reported, from tasty celery and lovage to cockle and bacon chowder, and among other starters might be smoked salmon pâté with cucumber sauce, or mushrooms baked in cream and garlic. Stir-fried vegetables accompany main courses of perhaps minced lamb and tomato pancake, 'excellent' seafood crumble or whole sea bass with a tangy pepper and onion dressing. Vegetarians are given a decent choice – a filo parcel of goats' cheese, sun-blushed tomatoes, olives and garlic, for instance – and among puddings might be apple crumble with custard, or chocolate and brandy pot. On draught are Adnams Bitter and Broadside, plus Crones organic cider. Around twenty-five wines include nine organics, and eight wines are offered by the glass. SAMPLE DISHES: grilled dates wrapped in bacon on a mild mustard sauce £5; steak, kidney and Adnams ale pie with a short-crust pastry lid £8; home-made honey and ginger ice cream £3.75.

Licensees Amanda and Mark Corcoran (Adnams)
Open 11.45 to 2.30, 6.30 to 11, Sun 12 to 3, 7 to 10.30; bar food 12 to 2, 6.30 (7 Sun) to 10 (9 Sun); closed 26 Dec
Details Children welcome   Car park   Wheelchair access (not WC)   Garden and patio
No smoking in 2 rooms   No music   Dogs welcome on a lead   Amex, Delta, MasterCard, Switch, Visa

BRAMPFORD SPEKE   Devon   map 1

Agricultural Inn   NEW ENTRY
Brampford Speke EX5 5DP   TEL: (01392) 841591
WEBSITE: www.theagriculturalinn.co.uk
from A377 Exeter to Crediton, take first right turn after Cowley Bridge roundabout

Narrow, often muddy lanes lead to this aptly named big, brown pub facing a cobbled courtyard in the centre of the village. The sign depicts a farmer ploughing with horses, and there are bucolic prints dotted around the dimly lit, beamed bar; there's also a no-smoking restaurant upstairs, although you can eat anywhere. Baguettes and light dishes like seafood fishcakes with lemon and herb mayonnaise, ham with egg and chips, and roasted vegetable risotto show up on the standard menu, but most customers home in on the black-board of main-course specials such as liver and bacon with mash, and roast fillet of sea bass on minted bean purée with fennel and dill cream, following on with a dessert such as Baileys cheesecake. In the winter there's a real fire and mulled wine to drink, while in summer you can refresh yourself with local cider. Handpumps dispense Adnams Broadside as well as Speke Easy Ale brewed specially for the pub, and there's a short list of everyday wines from £2.50 a glass, £9.75 a bottle. SAMPLE DISHES: king prawns in garlic and cream sauce £5.50; beef casseroled in red wine with bacon and baby onions £8; rich chocolate truffle cake £3.25.

Licensees Allan and Fern Ferns (freehouse)
Open 11 to 3, 6 (7 Mon in Winter) to 11, Sun 12 to 3, 7 to 10.30; bar food Tue to Sat and bank hol Mon 12 to 2, 6.30 to 9, Sun 12 to 2, 7 to 9; restaurant Wed to Sat 6.30 to 9; closed Mon lunchtime in winter, 25 Dec
Details Children welcome   Car park   Patio   No smoking in restaurant   Background music   Guide dogs only   Amex, Delta, Diners, MasterCard, Switch, Visa

BRANCASTER STAITHE   **Norfolk**   **map 6**

▲ White Horse ❦

Main Road, Brancaster Staithe PE31 8BW   TEL: (01485) 210262
WEBSITE: www.whitehorsebrancaster.co.uk

Extensions to the White Horse have resulted in its doubling in size, giving the
formerly uninspiring façade a completely new look and adding a new dining
area to the existing conservatory restaurant. The views from here – across tidal
marshland to the coast and Scolt Head Island beyond – remain as magnificent
as ever, with a sun deck in use in summer. The bar area at the front doesn't
have the view but is attractively decorated in a smart, modern style, with pine
furniture and pale yellow walls hung with old photographs of the area. The
menu also has an up-to-date feel, with things like a salad of red mullet with
chorizo, rocket and red onions, and roast chicken breast with pancetta and
wild mushroom risotto. Equally, more traditional dishes are also to be found,
from chargrilled lamb steak with roast potatoes to deep-fried cod with chips.
Local mussels, cooked in a cream and white wine sauce, are a seasonal treat,
and smoked salmon and crab, also both local, turn up among starters too. The
same menu is available in the bar, which has a list of sandwiches as well, and
there's a separate children's menu. Beers are from East Anglian brewers
Greene King and Adnams, and Woodeford's cider is on draught. The 50-
strong wine list offers excellent choices across the price spectrum. It opens
with 15 interesting wines by the glass and strides on confidently through well-
known and less established territories from Duboeuf's reliable Beaujolais to
Canadian Pinot Gris from Mission Hill. The Owners' Reserve Selection is a
little treasure trove of rarer and more expensive wines. SAMPLE DISHES: baked
fillet of black bream with Vietnamese pickled coleslaw £5.50; pan-fried ox
liver with pancetta and herb mash £11; coffee cheesecake £4.

Licensees Cliff Nye and Kevin Nobes (freehouse)
Open 11 to 11, Sun 12 to 10.30; bar food and restaurant 12 to 2.30, 6.45 to 9.15; closed evening
25 Dec (exc for residents)
Details Children welcome   Car park   Wheelchair access (also WC)   Patio   No smoking in dining
room   Occasional live or background music   Dogs welcome   Amex, Delta, Diners, MasterCard,
Switch, Visa   Accommodation: 15 rooms, B&B £48 to £116

BRANSCOMBE   **Devon**   **map 2**

▲ Masons Arms 🍺

Branscombe EX12 3DJ   TEL: (01297) 680300
WEBSITE: www.masonsarms.co.uk
off A3052, 5m E of Sidmouth

A mile from the coast between Sidmouth and Beer, Branscombe has a pub at
each end. This one – a long stone building with tiled roof and creeper-clad front
– is fronted by tables sitting under beehive-shaped thatched sunshades, reminiscent of Hobbiton, and by an encouraging inn sign proclaiming 'Here ye toil
not'. Inside, exposed stone walls, open fireplaces and beamed ceilings are all
present. Beer is serious here (they have a three-day beer festival each summer),
and – supplementing Otter Bitter, Otter Ale and draught Bass – the ever-

changing array of guests could include anything from Adnams Broadside to Young's Winter Warmer, plus Addlestone and Lyme Bay's Jack Rat ciders. The wine list offers 46 table wines with 14 by the glass. Ploughman's and sandwiches are available at lunch only, but the bar menu also offers crab bisque or devilled lambs' kidneys and flambé mushrooms to start, followed by cod and chips or délice of salmon on couscous, pot-roast pheasant or sausage and mash. Desserts range from spiced plum crumble to tian of strawberries and nougatine. The restaurant, now in a separate building, offers a £25 prix fixe which might run from smoked duck, via a seafood cassoulet, to pineapple and mango pavlova. SAMPLE DISHES: sea trout, scallop and lemongrass parfait £5.50; pan-fried duck breast with summer berry sauce £14; chocolate truffle cake £4.

Licensees Mark Thompson, Murray Inglis and Tim Manktelow-Gray (freehouse)
Open Mon to Fri 11 to 3, 6 to 11 (11 to 11 summer), Sat, Sun 11 to 11; bar food and restaurant 12 to 2 (2.15 Sun), 7 to 9
Details Children welcome exc in restaurant   Car park   Wheelchair access (also WC) from restaurant Patio   No-smoking area in bar, no smoking in dining room   Occasional live music   Dogs welcome in some rooms   Delta, MasterCard, Switch, Visa   Accommodation: 24 rooms, B&B £28 to £150

BRASSINGTON   Derbyshire   map 5

Ye Olde Gate Inne
Well Street, Brassington DE4 4HJ   TEL: (01629) 540448
just off B3035 Ashbourne to Wirksworth road, 4m W of Wirksworth

Reached via lonely roads with nothing but hills on either side, this early-seventeenth-century small stone pub is at the southern edge of the Peak District. Oak beams, flagstone floors, copper bedpans, brasses, rush-seated chairs and black-leaded ranges add to the atmosphere within, and the panelled dining room, with a window overlooking the large garden, is a light and pleasant room. Some of the blackboard menu is as traditional as crab pâté, followed by beef braised in ale, or rack of lamb, while influences from further afield show up in a selection of antipasti, then Thai green chicken curry. In the summer there are barbecues in the garden – steaks, chicken piri-piri, swordfish – while a choice of sponge puddings are among desserts along with perhaps rhubarb and ginger crumble. Marston's Pedigree and guest ales are on handpump, and four wines are served by the glass. SAMPLE DISHES: Parma ham with melon £5.50; balti king prawns £13.50; lemon sponge pudding £3.25.

Licensee Paul Scott Burlinson (Wolverhampton & Dudley)
Open Tue to Sat and bank hol Mon 12 to 2.30 (3 Sat), 6 to 11, Sun 12 to 3, 7 to 10.30; bar food Tue to Thur and bank hol Mon 12 to 1.45, 7 to 8.45, Fri to Sun 12 to 2, 7 to 9
Details No children under 10   Car park   Wheelchair access (also WC)   Garden   No smoking in restaurant   No music   Dogs welcome   Delta, MasterCard, Switch, Visa

---

Which? Online subscribers will find The Which? Pub Guide *online, along with other Which? guides and magazines, at* www.which.net. *Check the website for how to become a subscriber.*

Malt Shovel 🍺

Brearton HG3 3BX   TEL: (01423) 862929
off A61 and B6165, 2m E of Ripley

Brearton is a tiny hamlet, little more than a cluster of old stone cottages, hidden away down a country lane. At the very end of the lane you will find this sixteenth-century inn, which despite its remote location can get very busy. Its popularity is due in part to its charming old-world atmosphere – provided by bottle-glass windows, a log fire and 'more beams than you can shake a stick at' – but food and drink are the main attractions. The menu, chalked up on a blackboard, shows an eclectic approach. A typical day's offerings might take in roast belly pork with crackling and apple sauce, poached salmon with dill and cucumber sauce, and chargrilled tuna with warm potato salad and a lemon and caper dressing. There are also sandwiches, perhaps of thickly sliced tender ham with a generous mixed salad accompaniment. A couple of dozen wines are listed with enthusiastic tasting notes; prices are very reasonable and all are available by the glass (175 or 250ml). And for beer drinkers, a 'grand selection' of five regional ales are on draught – usually Black Sheep Best Bitter, Daleside Nightjar and Theakston Best plus two guests from eminent local microbreweries such as Durham and Rooster's. SAMPLE DISHES: liver, bacon and black pudding with mash and red wine gravy £7; pan-fried sea bass with herb butter £9; banana cheesecake with toffee sauce £3.

Licensee Leslie V. Mitchell (freehouse)
Open *Tue to Sun 12 to 2.30, 6.45 to 11 (10.30 Sun); bar food Tue to Sun 12 to 2, Tue to Sat 7 to 9; closed 25 and 26 Dec*
Details *Children welcome   Car park   Wheelchair access (not WC)   Garden and patio No-smoking area in bar   No music   Dogs welcome on a lead   No cards*

White Horse ✪ | NEW ENTRY |

High Street, Bridge CT4 5LA   TEL: (01227) 830249
take A2050 S from Canterbury and continue into Bridge; pub in centre of village

The White Horse is a sixteenth-century coaching inn at the heart of the quiet village of Bridge, just outside the historic city of Canterbury. Painted white and decked out with colourful hanging baskets, it looks every inch the archetypal English country pub, complete with an attractive shaded beer garden behind. The well-groomed main bar has a traditional look too, with beamed ceilings and a large brick hearth with a log fire. Chef Ben Walton's blackboard menus are divided into salads, starters and main courses, offering a broad range of dishes but keeping it all admirably simple: from herb omelette with tomato and rocket salad, or moules marinière with fries, to chicken breast roasted with garlic and lemon and served on couscous with a sage jus. Seasonal ingredients are to the fore, most of them from local suppliers. So, in May, you may find Kentish asparagus featuring plentifully, perhaps in a salad with fennel and red pepper coulis. Finish with vanilla crème brûlée with mango or choose a selection from the fine cheese list. Portions are generous and prices are notably low for this quality of cooking, and to the rear of the pub is the separate restaurant, with its own more luxurious, upmarket menu. Despite the focus on food, this remains the kind of pub where locals can call in for a drink. If they do, they will find Shepherd Neame Masterbrew and three guest ales which might include Fuller's London Pride, Old Speckled Hen and Greene King IPA. There is also a short but decent wine list arranged by country. Australian Semillon Chardonnay opens the list at £10. SAMPLE DISHES: spicy crab cakes with carrot, spring onion and mint salad £6.50; half or whole Dover sole with herbs and new potatoes £8/£15.50; blood orange mousse with raspberry coulis £4.

Licensee Alan Walton (Enterprise Inns)
Open 11 to 3, 6 to 11, Sun 12 to 4; bar food all week 12 to 2.30, Tue to Sat 6.30 to 9.30, restaurant Wed to Sun 12 to 2.30, Tue to Sat 6.30 to 9.30
Details Children welcome Car park Garden No smoking in eating areas Occasional background music Dogs welcome in bar Delta, MasterCard, Switch, Visa

BRIGHTWELL BALDWIN   Oxfordshire   map 2

Lord Nelson   NEW ENTRY

Brightwell Baldwin OX9 5NP   TEL: (01491) 612497
off B480, 5m SW of M40 junction 6

Slap opposite the church is this white-painted eighteenth-century brick building with its red-tiled roof; the gables at each end joined by a lean-to verandah that fronts the rear give it a distinctive appearance. In 1905 the squire and the parson complained, and the pub closed; however, after years as first a shop and then a house, it finally reopened in the 1970s. At the rear a pleasant green garden offers both sun and shade. Inside, low-ceilinged rooms are decorated in pale terracotta; they include a comfortable main bar with a fire, where they serve Brakspear brews and Fuller's London Pride as well as wines from across the world (and from £10 to £50 a bottle), with four by the glass. Several menus and blackboards offer a wide food choice. You could start with the likes of rabbit and bacon terrine, or Thai-style crab cakes with a chilli dip, to be followed by, say, half a crisp-skinned roast duck with classic orange sauce and pommes Anna, a whole roast sea bass, or wild mushroom lasagne and salad. Desserts, traditional and rich, include a chocolate marquise, and a bread-and-butter pudding – or farmhouse cheeses with biscuits. SAMPLE DISHES: fried chicken livers with smoked bacon and salad £6.50; chilli prawns and rice £15; fresh berry meringue £5.

Licensees Carole and Roger Shippey (freehouse)
Open 11 to 3, 6 to 11, Sun 12 to 3, 7 to 10.30; bar food and restaurant 12 to 2.30, 6 to 10.30, Sun 12 to 2.30, 7 to 10
Details Car park Wheelchair access (also WC) Garden No-smoking area Background music Dogs welcome Delta, MasterCard, Switch, Visa

BRIMFIELD   Herefordshire   **map 5**

▲ Roebuck Inn 🏅 🍇

Brimfield SY8 4NE   TEL: (01584) 711230
WEBSITE: www.theroebuckinn.com
just off A49 Leominster to Ludlow road, 4m W of Tenbury Wells

This cream-painted brick building changed hands in April 2003, but new
licensee Peter Jenkins continues to offer similarly modern food. There are a
couple of areas where drinkers might make themselves comfortable, but it is
mostly devoted to eating. The bar areas are traditional, with shiny dark
panelling on the walls and tables set for diners, while the spacious dining room
is a modern space: blond parquet floor, deep orange walls and blue tablecloths.
Everything is made in the kitchen, from bread to petits fours, and the
frequently changing menus are available throughout the pub. They offer
plenty of interest with, among starters, 'beautifully fresh' pan-fried scallops
with thyme-braised lentils and smoked paprika butter sauce, or beef spring
rolls with Szechuan dipping sauce. Then consider pink-roast rack of lamb on
garlic and shallot confit with a red wine and rosemary sauce, or free-range
chicken breast with an unusual sauce of smoked bacon, roast garlic and
caramelised shallots. Daily specials might include game – perhaps boned
partridge stuffed with parsnips – and fish – simply grilled Dover sole, say. A
selection of notable farmhouse cheeses makes a good alternative to puddings
of glazed citrus tart, or white chocolate and raspberry cheesecake. Real ales
stocked are Parish Bitter and Wonderful from the local Wood Brewery, plus
Tetley Bitter. Around 40 wines are split into seven categories, from 'apéritifs'
to 'big reds', with a few suggestions for matching them to the menu along the
way. Six come by the glass and there is plenty under £15 in this interesting
selection that culminates, not in a predictable French classic, but in an exciting
Primitivo from southern Italy called Prima Mano. SAMPLE DISHES: spicy crab
filo parcels with tomato sauce £5.50; fillet of wild venison on honey-roast figs
with a malt whisky sauce £16; pear and ginger sponge pudding with custard
£4.50.

Licensee Peter Jenkins (freehouse)
Open 11.30 to 3, 6.30 to 11, Sun 12 to 3, 7 to 10.30; bar food and restaurant 12 to 2.15, 7 to
9.30; closed 25 and 26 Dec
Details *Children welcome in bar eating area and restaurant   Car park   Wheelchair access (not WC)
Patio   No smoking in restaurant   No music   Dogs welcome in snug bar   Delta, MasterCard, Switch,
Visa   Accommodation: 3 rooms, B&B £45 to £70*

BRINKWORTH   Wiltshire   **map 2**

Three Crowns 🍇

Brinkworth SN15 5AF   TEL: (01666) 510366
WEBSITE: www.threecrowns.co.uk
on B4042 Malmesbury to Wootton Bassett road

This has been the Three Crowns since 1801, and was probably a pub under
some other name before that. A stone building with an ivy-clad brick extension on one side and a huge conservatory dining room at the back, it lies handy

for Swindon and for the M4. There is no pre-booking, the menu is on black-boards, and there are no starters (main courses aren't stingy, though), but a lunchtime snack menu does offer filled rolls, jacket potatoes and ploughman's lunches. The conservatory offerings change daily but include the traditional (steaks, rack of lamb, veal and mushroom pie, seafood pie) and the exotic (assiette of griddled kangaroo, venison and ostrich, perhaps, or marinated crocodile on noodles with a Thai-style sauce). Sweets take in banoffi pie, fruits of the forest meringue, and hot peppered pineapple (sautéed, flambéed in Kahlùa, served with Tia Maria ice cream). Archers Best Bitter, Castle Eden Bitter, Fuller's London Pride, and Wadworth 6X quench the thirst, and a helpfully annotated list of mostly Old World wines includes 12 by the glass. There's something for all pockets, and a few treats for connoisseurs, such as Robert Arnoux's Vosne-Romanée. SAMPLE DISHES: jacket potato with Mexican spiced sausages £7; tuna en croûte £15.25; cherry Bakewell tart £5.

Licensee Anthony Windle (Windle Pub Co Ltd)
Open 11 to 3, 6 to 11, Sun 12 to 5, 6 to 10.30; bar food 12 to 2, 6 to 9.30; closed 25 and 26 Dec
Details Children welcome   Car park   Wheelchair access (also WC)   Garden and patio
No smoking in dining room   Occasional background music   Dogs welcome in bar   Amex, Delta, Diners, MasterCard, Switch, Visa

BRISTOL   Bristol   map 2

Clifton Sausage   NEW ENTRY

9 Portland Road, Clifton, Bristol BS8 4JA   TEL: (0117) 973 1192

On a corner of a quiet road just back from Clifton's main shopping streets, this self-styled bar and restaurant is a light, bright and uncluttered space: wooden floors, chunky blond-wood furniture, contemporary artwork, and a colour scheme of bright oatmeal blending with exposed-stone walls. The dining area, down a few steps, has a tiled sandstone floor and sky-blue and warm yellow walls. A blackboard lists the specials and around half a dozen types of sausage: pork with Stilton and port, wild boar with apple and sage, even ostrich and fennel. Otherwise, mainstream British food is what to expect, from Cornish crab to toad-in-the-hole, smoked haddock fishcake with parsley and lemon sauce, or roast Quantock duck breast with parsnip and carrot mash and honey and rosemary gravy. The odd exception might break the rule – chargrilled scallops with black pudding, a potato pancake and thyme oil, say – but traditional roasts are the norm on Sundays, with puddings taking in rhubarb and pear crumble, and steamed sticky walnut sponge with whisky custard. Bristol brewers Smiles and Butcombe are the suppliers of real ales, and a decent number of wines is served by the glass. SAMPLE DISHES: cockles and mussels in Stowford Press cider, parsley, cream and shallots £5.50; lamb, mint and apricot sausages with champ and shallot gravy £8.50; chocolate bread-and-butter pudding with white chocolate and Baileys ice cream £4.50.

Licensee Peter Austin (freehouse)
Open Tue to Sun 11 to 11; bar food and restaurant Tue to Sun 11 to 2.30, 6 to 10.30
Details Children welcome   Wheelchair access   Patio   No smoking in restaurant   Background music   No dogs   Amex, Delta, MasterCard, Switch, Visa

Spring Gardens   NEW ENTRY

188 Hotwell Road, Hotwells, Bristol BS8 4RP   TEL: (0117) 927 7112

On a busy road in the redeveloped docks area of Bristol, Spring Gardens is an unassuming building, with a name and outward appearance that for one reader suggested Chinese restaurant more than pub. The open-plan interior has dark wood furniture, leather sofas and dark parquet flooring, and candles in the evening give an almost bistro feel, but there is a reassuringly pubby bar counter, and the upstairs room has pool and table football. The short menu is written up on a blackboard next to the bar. Starters/snacks are soup or salads (Caesar or tomato and mozzarella, for example), while main courses are things like whole lemon sole, lamb moussaka, mussels in white wine, garlic and shallots, and various casseroles and curries, which change weekly. These have included aromatic lamb with star anise, coconut, lemon and lime, enjoyed by our inspector for its tender meat and subtle, well-balanced flavours. Finish perhaps with poached pears or profiteroles. Beers are Bass and Fuller's London Pride and there is a limited selection of wines. Note that booking is essential for Sunday lunch. SAMPLE DISHES: crunchy green salad with bacon and croûtons £4.50; pan-fried duck breast with honey glaze £10.50; lemon brûlée £3.

Licensees Anna Henderson and Lionel Seigneur (Heritage Pubs Co)
Open 12 to 11 (10.30 Sun); bar food Mon to Fri 12 to 2, Mon to Sat 7.30 to 9.30, Sun 12 to 4
Details Children welcome   Wheelchair access (not WC)   Garden and patio   Occasional
background music; jukebox   Dogs welcome   Delta, MasterCard, Switch, Visa

BROADHEMBURY   Devon   map 2

Drewe Arms 🏆 🍺

Broadhembury EX14 3NF   TEL: (01404) 841267   FISH
off A373, 5m NW of Honiton

Among the thatched and whitewashed cottages of Broadhembury, next to the grey-stone church, is a smart custard-coloured building where the food focuses almost entirely on fish. Strange, then, that Broadhembury is not a salt-caked fishing port but a village embedded in east Devon's agricultural hinterland. However, the décor is rather fishy – including an eel-trap along with the piscine prints – so you know what to expect as soon as you enter. What is local, though, is the beer: the Otter Brewery's range, which comes from six miles away at Luppitt, along with Bollhayes cider. Ichthyophagy is first apparent in the bar's open sandwiches (half have fishy toppings), then in the blackboard menus, which offer carnivores perhaps only rack of lamb or fillet of beef and a couple of meaty starters. Otherwise the carte and the prix fixe consist of simply treated fish from home waters in nearly every conceivable form, from Cullen skink, gravad lax, and stir-fried langoustines to John Dory with chilli and beans, seared salmon with samphire, sole (lemon and Dover), mullet, and skate wings. The somewhat chaotic appearance of the wine list belies a fairly priced selection chosen to suit the cuisine; eight wines come by the glass. SAMPLE DISHES: venison carpaccio £6.50; brill fillet with horseradish hollandaise £11.50; St-Emilion chocolate £5.

Licensees Kerstin and Nigel Burge (freehouse)
Open all week 11 to 3, Mon to Sat 6 to 11; bar food and restaurant 12 to 2, 7 to 9.15; closed 25 and 31 Dec
Details Children welcome in eating areas   Car park   Wheelchair access (also WC)   Garden
No smoking in dining room   No music   Dogs by arrangement   Delta, MasterCard, Switch, Visa

---

BROME   **Suffolk**   **map 6**

▲ Cornwallis 🍇

Brome IP23 8AJ   TEL: (01379) 870326
WEBSITE: www.thecornwallis.com
at junction of A140 and B1077, midway between Norwich and Ipswich

---

Huge gates opening on to a long tree-lined drive are the first indication that this is a rather grand country hotel, restaurant and bar. Built in 1561 as the dower house to Brome Hall, the building stands in 20 acres of parkland, not far from the attractive town of Eye. Beams, stripped-wood tables and a glassed-over well (said to be 60 feet deep) are the principal features of the comfortable bar, and there is some rather serious cooking going on, as befits the surroundings. 'Quick Bites' might include an open sandwich of Parma ham, black pudding and truffled scrambled eggs, and starters take in sesame seared tuna with Japanese coleslaw and risotto of mussels and leeks with squash salsa. Innovation shines through main courses of monkfish sag aloo with spiced cardamom broth or a vegetarian alternative of leek and gorgonzola cannelloni with buttered red chard and a basil piquant, and there may also be more prosaic-sounding steak and kidney pudding. End with coconut panna-cotta, or apple and walnut trifle with Calvados custard. The separate restaurant, on the side of the building overlooking the topiary garden, has its own set-price menu along the lines of mussel soup with parsley risotto, followed by coriander beef fillet with spiced rice. A glass of wine is a serious proposition here, with 27 options listed in a separate booklet. The long main list is bursting with fine wines and enthusiastic tasting notes. Prices are reasonable considering the high quality, but the choice thins out considerably below £15. St Peter's Best Bitter and Adnams Best and Broadside are on handpump. SAMPLE DISHES: cream of asparagus soup with samphire and lemon salad £5.50; crab and chilli fishcake with seaweed £10.50; treacle toffee brûlée £4.25.

Licensees Edinburgh and London Inns (freehouse)
Open 11 to 11 (10.30 Sun); bar food 11 to 9.45, restaurant 12.30 to 1.45, 6.30 to 9.45
Details Children welcome   Car park   Wheelchair access (also WC)   Garden   No-smoking area in bar, no smoking in restaurant   Background music   No dogs   Delta, MasterCard, Switch, Visa
Accommodation: 16 rooms, B&B £87.50 to £155

After the main section of the Guide is the 'Round-up' section listing additional pubs where food may not be the main focus but which are well worth a visit for, perhaps, their inviting ambience, fine beers, a stunning setting, special history or other attribute. Reports on these entries are most welcome.

▲ Lamb at Buckland 🍷 🍇

Lamb Lane, Buckland SN7 8QN TEL: (01367) 870484
off A420, midway between Faringdon and Kingston Bagpuize

Beams, typical pub furniture and a bar plastered with postcards sent in by regulars give this eighteenth-century Cotswold-stone building a village pub feel. Given the pub's name, it comes as no surprise to find sheep as a decorative theme throughout. The dining room is a different, more refined world of restful blue and yellow, with starched table linen and upholstered chairs. The menu, the same throughout the pub, changes with the seasons. Snacks range from scrambled eggs with smoked salmon and prawns, or baked goats' cheese with bacon and salad, to tagliatelle carbonara. A full meal might start with Mediterranean fish soup and proceed to a main course of baked sea bass with Pernod sauce, roast breast of Lunesdale duckling with an apple and Calvados sauce, or roast saddle of hare on a bed of root vegetables, and finish with raspberry roulade. Ingredients are first class and are handled by the kitchen with skill. Six interesting and good-quality house wines start at £12.95 and are available by the glass, as are a small number from the more expensive main list, which majors on traditional French wines, but dips more than a toe in the warmer waters of the New World. Plenty of half-bottles are on offer too. The ales on draught are from Hook Norton. SAMPLE DISHES: sautéed lambs' kidneys with mushrooms £5.95; warm Cajun-spiced roast monkfish and prawn salad £18.95; steamed chocolate sponge with chocolate sauce £4.50.

Licensee Paul Barnard (freehouse)
Open Tue to Sun 11 to 3, Tue to Sat 5.15 to 11; bar food and restaurant Tue to Sun 12 to 2 (3 Sun), Tue to Sat 6.30 to 9.30 (10 Fri and Sat); closed 25 and 26 Dec
Details Children welcome Car park Wheelchair access (not WC) Garden and patio No smoking in restaurant Live or background music No dogs Delta, MasterCard, Switch, Visa Accommodation: 1 room, D, B&B £90 to £145

Dysart Arms

Bowes Gate Road, Bunbury CW6 9PH TEL: (01829) 260183
off A51, 5m NW of Nantwich

The Dysart Arms is opposite the church of St Boniface, parts of which date from the fourteenth century and which contains a collection of carved alabaster and stone effigies that are worth a peek. The Dysart Arms pub itself is a red-brick building with a large garden and, within, exposed-brick walls, stone floors and an interesting collection of artefacts scattered around; towards the back is a more formal carpeted dining area. Food is listed on both blackboard and printed menus, with orders taken at the bar. Salmon and smoked haddock fishcakes are mightily proportioned and served with lemon mayonnaise, and the soup of the day might be something a little out of the ordinary, such as parsnip and apple. Grilled fillet steak comes with oyster mushrooms and roast potatoes, bangers and mash, using sausages from a local butcher, come highly recommended, and those in the mood to branch out could go for seared salmon with five-spice rice and mustard sauce on tagliatelle with Thai curry sauce, while vegetarians could try perhaps spicy vegetable and potato cakes with a tomato and mint relish, or baked field mushrooms stuffed with lentils on ratatouille. A range of fine farmhouse cheeses and Mövenpick ice creams and sorbets supplement desserts such as baked sponge cake with apple and sultana sauce, or Eve's pudding with custard. Timothy Taylor Landlord, Weetwood Eastgate and Thwaites Lancaster Bomber are among the beers on handpump, and the continually changing guest beers are always worth investigating too. With around a dozen wines by the glass from a fairly compact list, this is clearly a place in which the casual drinker will feel as much at home as the diner. SAMPLE DISHES: black pudding and Stilton rissole with piccalilli £4.50; Bunbury bangers with mash and onion gravy £7.95; chocolate crème brûlée with shortbread biscuit £3.95.

Licensee Darren Snell (Brunning & Price Ltd)
Open 11.30 to 11, Sun 12 to 10.30; bar food Mon to Fri 12 to 2.15, 6 to 9.30, Sat 12 to 9.30, Sun 12 to 9
Details No children under 10 after 6pm   Car park   Wheelchair access (also WC)   Garden and patio   No-smoking area in dining room   Occasional background and live music   Dogs welcome in bar   Amex, Delta, MasterCard, Switch, Visa

BURLTON   Shropshire   map 7

▲ Burlton Inn 🍺

Burlton SY4 5TB   TEL: (01939) 270284
WEBSITE: www.burltoninn.co.uk
on A528, 9m N of Shrewsbury

While open log fires create a cosy, welcoming atmosphere on a winter's night, the Burlton comes into its own in summer, when the front is awash with tubs and hanging baskets of colourful flowers, with plenty more in the garden. Flowers brighten up the stylish interior of this eighteenth-century pub too, with its warm colour-coordinated décor of deep pink complementing the soft red-brick walls. Refurbishment is planned as we go to press, however, including moving the kitchen and greater demarcation between eating and drinking. The same menu is offered throughout, and food is served at tables decorated by more flowers and candles. Bar snacks are ciabatta rolls, ploughman's and jacket potatoes, while more adventurous dishes from the main menu could see some interesting combinations of flavours, as in a starter of crab cakes with a lemon salad and a sweet chilli sauce, or a main course of fillets of sea bass on glazed crab mash with salsa verde. More conventional are smoked chicken Caesar salad, or grilled green-lipped mussels topped with pesto, followed by steak, kidney and beer pie, breadcrumbed plaice fillet with chips, roasted duck breast glazed with honey and plum with a Madeira jus, and steaks, from a local butcher. A blackboard of daily specials extends what's on offer, and the list of imaginative puddings is also displayed on a board. Banks's Bitter is the regular ale, supplemented by frequently changing guests like Greene King Abbot Ale, Shepherd Neame Spitfire and Everards Tiger Best. The list of 20-plus modestly priced wines is unusual in not including a single bottle (except champagne) from France. Around half a dozen are sold by the glass.

SAMPLE DISHES: caramelised red onion and grilled goats' cheese tartlet with thyme £5.50; chicken breast in a balsamic, orange and rosemary sauce with rice £11; pear and cinnamon crumble £4.25.

Licensee Gerald Bean (freehouse)
Open 11 to 3, 6 to 11, Sun 12 to 3.30, 7 to 10.30; bar food 12 to 2 (only snack menu Mon lunchtime), 6.30 to 9.45; closed bank hol Mon lunchtime, 25 and 26 Dec, 1 Jan
Details No children   Car park   Wheelchair access (also WC)   Garden and patio   No music
Guide dogs only   MasterCard, Switch, Visa   Accommodation: 6 rooms, B&B £45 to £80

BURNHAM MARKET   Norfolk   map 6

▲ Hoste Arms 🌼 🏆
The Green, Burnham Market PE31 8HD   TEL: (01328) 738777
on B1155, 5m W of Wells-next-the-Sea

This Georgian manor house, standing on the green, is one of the largest properties in the village, and its bright lemon-yellow walls make it hard to miss. The front entrance leads directly into the spacious main bar, which has retained much of its original rustic character. Food is not served in here, only in the wood-panelled restaurant, and owing to the pub's long-standing reputation it is a good idea to book if you wish to eat. Assuming you get a table, your next dilemma is what to choose from the long menu that wouldn't look out of place in a city brasserie instead of a country inn. You could start simply with half a dozen Burnham Creek oysters, or go for something more ambitious like pan-seared scallops with coriander and hazelnut butter. Main courses show similarly broad scope, with at least half a dozen each of fish and meat choices, plus salads, rice and pasta. Baked halibut with a tapénade crust and truffled creamed potatoes is typical, as is garlic- and thyme-roasted partridge with wild mushrooms and onion confit. A dozen dessert options might feature apple and ginger crumble, and glazed lemon tart. The wine choice is broad, too, with just enough budget bottles to balance the classier numbers running all the way up to Château Pétrus and Opus One. It's an international selection arranged by style, with an abbreviated list of the cheaper bottles at the front, including a dozen in three sizes of glass. Real ales are from local brewery Woodforde's – Nelson's Revenge and Wherry Best Bitter – and other breweries like Adnams and Bateman. SAMPLE DISHES: salmon and chilli fishcake with sautéed pak choi £6; baked duck breast with celeriac and truffle dauphinois £14.25; pears poached in mulled wine with Chantilly cream £5.

Licensees Paul Whittome, Chris Bensley and Stephen Franklin (freehouse)
Open 11 to 11, Sun 12 to 10.30; restaurant 12 to 2, 7 to 9
Details Children welcome in restaurant   Car park   Wheelchair access (also WC)   Garden
No smoking in restaurant   No music   Dogs welcome   Delta, MasterCard, Switch, Visa
Accommodation: 36 rooms, B&B £71 to £200

The Guide always appreciates hearing about changes of licensee.

▲ Lord Nelson

Creake Road, Burnham Market PE31 8EN   TEL: (01328) 738321

One very good reason for the popularity of this Lord Nelson (not to be confused with another pub so named in neighbouring Burnham Thorpe – see entry, Round-ups) lies in the cooking talents of chef and co-licensee Paula Ayres, who formerly worked at *Good Food Guide*-featured Fishes' restaurant in the village. Another is the 'very pleasant, helpful and friendly service'. A large public bar caters for those who just want to have a drink, while diners can eat in the lounge, which is decked out with Nelson memorabilia, or in the small restaurant at the back. In good weather the patio or beer garden are a draw. The standard bar menu includes traditional offerings such as cod in beer batter, lasagne and filled baguettes, but more interest lies in the restaurant menu, also available in the bar. There you might find starters of scallop and prawn au gratin, or home-made crab soup, and then pork medallions with apricot and brandy cream, or monkfish with garlic and onion. Choose white chocolate terrine with mixed berry coulis to finish. Real ales are Greene King IPA, Courage Directors and Fuller's London Pride, while the short wine list includes five by the glass. SAMPLE DISHES: curried parsnip, Stilton and leek soup £3.75; salmon fishcakes with crab sauce £9; sticky toffee pudding with toffee and pecan sauce £4.

Licensees Richard and Paula Ayres (Unique Pub Company)
Open 11 to 3, 6 (6.30 winter) to 11, Sun 12 to 3, 6.30 to 10.30; bar food 12 to 2.15, 6.30 to 9.30, restaurant 12 to 2.15, 6 (6.30 winter) to 9.30; open all day for food for 6 weeks in summer and bank hols
Details Children welcome in eating areas   Car park   Wheelchair access (also WC)   Garden and patio   No smoking in dining room   Occasional live music; jukebox   Dogs welcome   MasterCard, Switch, Visa   Accommodation: 4 rooms, B&B £40 to £80

BURNSALL   **North Yorkshire**   **map 8**

▲ Red Lion 🍇

Burnsall BD23 6BU   TEL: (01756) 720204
WEBSITE: www.redlion.co.uk
on B6160 N of Bolton Bridge

Next to the five-span bridge over the River Wharfe in this unspoilt Dales village, the Red Lion is a warm (both in terms of atmosphere and welcome), cosy and rambling country inn. Fashioned from a terraced row of old stone cottages, it has a low-ceilinged bar with a real fire and a congregation of stuffed foxes and deer. Beyond the bar is a separate, more formal restaurant with linen-covered tables. Several menus are in operation, all available throughout, from a light-lunch listing of cold items, such as sandwiches and salads, to an ambitious carte. The latter might offer a choice among starters (also available as main courses) of smoked haddock, chickpeas and pak choi topped with a free-range poached egg, or roast calf's liver with pancetta, sage and celeriac purée, followed by something like ribeye steak with béarnaise and chips, or chicken marinated in lemon and chillies served with a spicy tomato sauce. Vegetarian options may run to twice-baked goats' cheese soufflé with sweet-and-sour aubergine and courgette, while among the specials may be loin of cod with celeriac mash and a tomato and courgette chutney, and seasonal game: perhaps pheasant breast wrapped in smoked bacon served with a confit of the leg, or sautéed breast of wood pigeon with wild mushrooms and rösti. Sunday lunch (restaurant only) is a traditional affair, and desserts could take in treacle tart with candied lemon, or rice pudding, or you could opt for a selection of cheeses that celebrates Yorkshire's (and Ireland's) finest. On handpump are well-kept beers from Theakston, along with Old Speckled Hen and Timothy Taylor Best Bitter. The restaurant wine list is available in the bar on request; otherwise, the bar list is a slate of a dozen-plus wines, virtually all also sold in three sizes of glass. SAMPLE DISHES: carpaccio of beef on rocket salad £5.50; roast grouse with game chips, bread sauce and redcurrant compote £15; white chocolate and croissant bread-and-butter pudding £5.50.

Licensee Elizabeth Grayshon (freehouse)
Open 11 to 11.30, Sun 12 to 10.30; bar food 12 to 2.30, 6 to 9.30; restaurant 12 to 2.30, 7 to 9.30
Details Children welcome   Car park   Wheelchair access (not WC)   Garden and patio
No-smoking area in bar, no smoking in dining room   No music   Dogs welcome   Amex, Delta, Diners, MasterCard, Switch, Visa   Accommodation: 11 rooms, B&B £53.50 to £130

BURPHAM   West Sussex   map 3

George and Dragon
Burpham BN18 9RR   TEL: (01903) 883131
2½m up single-track, no-through road signposted Warningcamp off A27, 1m E of Arundel

This seriously rural pub is in some pretty Downs scenery and backs on to vast green fields. Within are black beams in very low ceilings, with a cosy bar area and a 'posh bourgeois' restaurant. Bar and restaurant menus are quite separate and rather different in style, the former a lot simpler than the latter, although this doesn't mean that dishes are any less interesting or ambitious. Starters range from warm smoked duck and bacon salad with balsamic dressing to a 'good-value, generous dish' of layered Selsey crab, prawns and avocado, and main courses from whole sea bass with lemon and thyme to minted rump of lamb with red onion marmalade. Game is served in season – perhaps breast of guinea fowl stuffed with Brie in a tomato and basil sauce – and among puddings might be vanilla pannacotta, or chocolate mousse. Baguettes, sandwiches and jacket potatoes are also possibilities. The restaurant menu is a set-price affair dealing in tarte Tatin of caramelised shallots with quail and sautéed foie gras in a tarragon jus, followed by pan-fried saddle of roe deer with spiced red cabbage and juniper and redcurrant jus. Harveys Sussex Best Bitter, Fuller's London Pride and Arundel Classic are on draught, and four house wines, from Chile, are served in two sizes of glass. SAMPLE DISHES: tiger prawns sautéed with garlic £6.50; partridge wrapped in bacon with cranberry and ginger sauce £9.50; crème brûlée £4.50.

Licensees James Rose and Kate Holle (freehouse)
Open 11 to 2.30, 6 to 11, Sun 12 to 3, 7 to 10.30; bar food all week 12 to 2 (2.30 Sun), Mon to Sat 7 to 9.30, restaurant Tue to Sat 7.15 to 9.30, Sun 12 to 2.30; closed Sun evenings Oct to Apr
Details No children   Car park   Wheelchair access (not WC)   Patio   Background music   No dogs
Amex, Delta, Diners, MasterCard, Switch, Visa

BUXHALL   Suffolk   map 6

Buxhall Crown [NEW ENTRY]

Mill Road, Buxhall IP14 3DW   TEL: (01449) 736521
from Stowmarket take B1115 towards Sudbury and turn right for Buxhall in Great Finborough

A tucked-away but popular and upmarket country pub, the Buxhall Crown draws the crowds with its classy and wide-ranging food that, while displaying imagination, hasn't forgotten typical pub classics. A warm welcome is assured, with open fires in both bars and a comfortable restaurant decked out with botanical prints and photographs of local scenes. The lengthy blackboard menu could deliver a modish goats' cheese and red onion filo tart, or more traditional beef and Guinness pie with a thyme suet pastry crust. Bar snacks along the lines of garlic bread with tapénade, plus light bites and sandwiches, bolster the repertoire. Six ales change on a regular basis, but could see the Earl Soham Brewery's Albert Ale or Fuller's London Pride on handpump, while the wine list, strong in the New World and listed by style, is all available by the glass. Outside is a patio to the front and a lawn to the side, both set with tables. SAMPLE DISHES: duck liver parfait with black cherry and onion jam £4.50; fillet of sea bass on a bed of spinach with roasted cherry tomatoes and balsamic dressing £13; rhubarb crème brûlée £4.75.

Licensee Trevor Golton (freehouse)
Open 11 to 3, 6.30 to 11, Sun 11 to 3; bar food 11 to 3, 6 to 11, Sun 11 to 3
Details Children welcome   Car park   Wheelchair access   Garden   No smoking in restaurant
Background music   No dogs   Delta, MasterCard, Switch, Visa

BYLAND ABBEY   North Yorkshire   map 9

▲ Abbey Inn 🍇

Byland Abbey YO61 4BD   TEL: (01347) 868204
WEBSITE: www.bylandabbeyinn.com
off A170, between Thirsk and Helmsley, 2m W of Ampleforth

Reached along twisting, undulating roads, this ivy-covered Georgian inn is in a rural, isolated spot just over the road from the ruins of Byland Abbey, which are dramatically floodlit at night. The bar counter is tucked under a flight of stairs, and the atmosphere is more that of a restaurant than a pub, with candlelit tables set for eating, although fireplaces, a miscellany of antique-shop jumble and smartly framed paintings on the walls give character to the place. The cooking shows evidence of inventiveness, with a broadly European-based menu that runs from roasted pancetta-wrapped monkfish with broad bean purée to breast of chicken with a sun-dried tomato and pesto dressing. Duck and fig terrine, or grilled scallops with Gruyère could start a meal, and something like Amaretto ice cream in a brandy-snap, or crème caramel could round things off. Sandwiches and salads are also options, and the specials board might feature smoked venison with raspberry dressing, seared salmon fillet with tomato and coriander butter, or Stilton and leek pie. The wine list may not seem so thrilling at first glance, but look closer and you will find over 20 wines by the glass – from the house selection at £2.90 to an Old Vine Shiraz at £4.90 – goodies from South Africa and a 'Fine French' selection. Black Sheep

Best and Tetley Bitter are on draught. SAMPLE DISHES: tomato, celery and apple soup £3.50; pan-fried medallions of pork fillet with honey and tarragon sauce and carrot and swede mash £9.25; chocolate and hazelnut torte with vanilla ice cream £4.50.

Licensees Jane and Martin Nordli (freehouse)
Open *12 to 3, 6.30 to 11; bar food 12 to 2 (3 Sun), 6.30 to 9; closed Sun evening and Mon lunchtime (exc bank hols)*
Details *Children welcome   Car park   Wheelchair access (also WC)   Garden   No smoking in 2 rooms   Background music   No dogs   Delta, MasterCard, Switch, Visa   Accommodation: 3 rooms, B&B £60 to £120*

CALVER   Derbyshire   map 8

▲ Chequers Inn |NEW ENTRY|

Froggatt Edge, Calver S32 3ZJ   TEL: (01433) 630231
WEBSITE: www.chequers-froggatt.com
on B6054, off A623 6m N of Bakewell

There are impressive views over the woodlands of Froggatt Edge from the pretty, elevated garden behind this smartly appointed, sixteenth-century roadside inn. Inside, it has been modernised to provide a more contemporary feel, although there are still plenty of homely touches in the shape of cottagey furniture and country prints. The owners and staff run the place with friendly efficiency. A standard menu offers old favourites like local sausages with buttered mash and shallot gravy alongside grilled fillet of salmon with Mediterranean vegetables and a prawn and vermouth sauce, while daily specials might feature a starter of smoked duck with caramelised kumquats and redcurrant dressing, and a main course of red mullet with ratatouille and tomato and basil sauce. Finish with mixed berry crème brûlée or renowned Bakewell pudding. Charles Wells Bombardier and Greene King IPA are on handpump, and there are eight house wines from £2.50 a glass, £10.50 a bottle. This is a useful base for walking the Peaks or visiting heritage hot spots like Chatsworth House and Haddon Hall. SAMPLE DISHES: tiger prawns in garlic butter £5.25; saddle of rabbit with creamed leeks and red wine jus £13; blackcurrant cheesecake £4.

Licensees Jonathan and Joanne Tindall (freehouse)
Open *Mon to Fri 12 to 3, 6 to 11, Sat 12 to 11, Sun 12 to 10.30; bar food Mon to Fri 12 to 2, 6 to 9.30, Sat 12 to 9.30, Sun 12 to 9*
Details *Children welcome   Car park   Garden and patio   No-smoking area   Background music   No dogs   Amex, Delta, MasterCard, Switch, Visa   Accommodation: 5 rooms, B&B £45 to £65*

CARTERWAY HEADS   Northumberland   map 10

▲ Manor House Inn ✿

Carterway Heads, Shotley Bridge DH8 9LX   TEL: (01207) 255268
on A68, 3m W of Consett

Dating from the mid-eighteenth century, this long, two-storey building is on a busy main road, but the back overlooks the Pennine foothills and Derwent

Reservoir. Beams and panelling are features inside, with a collection of jugs hanging overhead, and the atmosphere is friendly and welcoming. Theakston Best, Courage Directors and Wells Bombardier Premium Bitter are among the real ales on offer, along with guest ales; there is also Weston's scrumpy as well as over 70 malt whiskies for the connoisseur. The kitchen draws inspiration from far afield, producing dishes ranging from king prawns with sweet-and-sour sauce to beef goulash via sausage with black pudding and bubble and squeak. Start with an interesting soup – perhaps blue cheese and onion – crab and salmon cakes with curry cream, or locally smoked kippers. There's a separate sandwich menu, and among desserts might be sticky toffee pudding, or choose local cheeses. 'Very good, excellent value,' summed up a reporter. Ten wines are available by the glass from an interesting globetrotting list of 50 or so. SAMPLE DISHES: crayfish and mushroom crêpes with cherry tomatoes and Gruyère £4.50; trio of lamb cutlets with port and cranberry jus and garlic and rosemary mash £13; banoffi pie £3.50.

Licensees Chris and Moira Brown (freehouse)
Open 11 to 11; bar food and restaurant Mon to Thur 12 to 2.30, 7 to 9.30, Fri to Sun and bank hols 12 to 9.30; closed evening 25 Dec
Details Children welcome in lounge and restaurant   Car park   Garden and patio   No smoking in restaurant   Background music in bar and lounge   Dogs welcome   Amex, MasterCard, Switch, Visa
Accommodation: 4 rooms, B&B £33 to £65

CARTHORPE   **North Yorkshire**   map 9

Fox and Hounds

Carthorpe DL8 2LG   TEL: (01845) 567433
off A1, 4m SE of Bedale

This place attracts the locals, but – since Carthorpe is only a mile from the A1 – it makes a very pleasant stop for knowing long-distance travellers too. The cosy interior has a very homely feel, with its stone fireplaces and the blue and white plates and jugs hanging on the walls. Young staff are attentive and pleasant, but expect delays at busy times. Menus, common to bar and restaurant, include midweek set lunches and dinners (Tuesday to Thursday), set Sunday lunches (half-price for children aged 11 and under), a carte, and blackboard specials. Mainly traditional dishes take in a fresh crab tartlet, steamed game pudding with parsley mash, roast rack of lamb, and rolled lemon sole fillets stuffed with salmon and prawns. Sunday lunch main courses are roasts (beef, pork, lamb or turkey, all with appropriate trimmings), steak and kidney pie, or a salmon steak with hollandaise sauce. Sweets range from delicate (sorbet-filled meringue) to dangerous-sounding (tipsy trifle). On draught are Black Sheep Best Bitter and Worthington Bitter. The wine list offers a reasonably priced range of modern fruity wines (the majority are from the New World). Any wine can be sold by the glass, and only one bottle exceeds £20. Choices are available by region, and careful notes and a style guide assist decision-making. SAMPLE DISHES: smoked chicken and mango salad £4.75; pheasant breast with pear and thyme stuffing and red wine sauce £9.95; apple and cinnamon flan with ice cream £3.75.

Licensee Howard Fitzgerald (freehouse)
Open Tue to Sun 12 to 2.30, 7 to 11; bar food and restaurant 12 to 2, 7 to 10; closed first week Jan
Details Children welcome   Car park   Wheelchair access (also WC)   No smoking in dining room
Background music   No dogs   Delta, MasterCard, Switch, Visa

CARTMEL FELL   Cumbria   map 8

▲ Masons Arms 🍺

Strawberry Bank, Cartmel Fell LA11 6NW   TEL: (015395) 68486
going N on A5074 turn left at sign for Bowland Bridge, then 1m up hill

Beware if you are visiting this pub after dark – it is hard enough to find in daylight, and signposts could be improved. But persevere, because it is worth the effort. New owners took over in the spring of 2002, which unfortunately meant the end of the Strawberry Bank Brewery, but its output has been replaced with a fine selection of other real ales, including local Hawkshead Bitter, Black Sheep and Timothy Taylor Landlord. There is also an astonishing range of international bottled beers, including many Belgian Trappist beers. The pub has much else to recommend it, not least the cosily rustic beamed, flagstoned bar, with its large black range keeping the place warm in winter. A blackboard by the bar counter lists the daily food specials, which might include feta and black olive salad, or chicken Caesar salad among starters, with varied and imaginative main courses ranging from leek and Stilton lasagne to chicken jalfrezi with pilau rice, chutney and naan bread. The regular menu offers further options such as steamed chicken breast with tomato and pesto, or pork chop with black pudding and grain mustard sauce. For non-beer drinkers, there is a list of 20 wines, prices starting at £9.95. All six house wines are sold by the glass. SAMPLE DISHES: chicken liver and spinach rarebit £4.75; half a roast Norfolk duck with raspberry sauce £9; rhubarb crumble £3.50.

Licensees Helen Parker and Andrew McLean (Strawberry Bank Ltd)
Open 11.30 to 11, Sun 12 to 10.30; bar food and restaurant 12 to 2 (3 summer), 6 to 9
Details Children welcome in family room   Car park   Patio   No smoking in restaurant   Occasional background music   No dogs   MasterCard, Switch, Visa   Accommodation: 4 rooms, B&B £100 to £120 (double room)

CASTERTON   Cumbria   map 8

▲ Pheasant Inn

Casterton, nr Kirkby Lonsdale LA6 2RX   TEL: (015242) 71230
WEBSITE: www.pheasantinn.co.uk
on A683, 1m N of junction with A65

The Pheasant, dating from the eighteenth century, faces Casterton's village green, although this is more of a hamlet than a village, set on the edge of the Lune Valley beneath the fells. Although the area is popular with walkers, the location feels remote and rural. Whitewashed without, the pub has a large bar at the front with a horseshoe-shaped bar counter forming a kind of peninsula and dividing the room into two parts. Posters and a motley collection of prints hang on pale-coloured Anaglypta-covered walls, and there's an open fire. There's a separate restaurant, but the same menu is served throughout. Blackboards herald the day's specials, and despite the setting what's on offer has a metropolitan, modern feel. Loch Fyne salmon is smoked over lemongrass and spices, and a pancake is filled with shredded duck and asparagus and accompanied by a port and honey sauce. Grilled salmon on a potato and courgette cake with a langoustine and smoked salmon sauce is typical of main courses, while something more traditional might show up on the printed menu: local Cumberland sausage with apple and sultana chutney, or beef, steak and ale pie. Theakston Best Bitter and Cool Cask, plus Dent Aviator and Black Sheep, are on draught. Over a dozen wines by the glass from £2.60 to £3.95 are listed on blackboards and cover a good range of styles. There's plenty more on the wine list, including some very tasty stuff from South Africa. SAMPLE DISHES: langoustines with garlic dressing and salad £6; shoulder of Lunesdale lamb with minted gravy £10; rhubarb and ginger crumble £3.95.

Licensees Mel and May Mackie (freehouse)
Open 11 to 3, 6 to 11; bar food 12 to 2, 6.30 to 9 (9.30 Fri and Sat); restaurant Tue to Sun 12 to 2, 6.30 to 9 (9.30 Fri and Sat); closed 25 and 26 Dec
Details Children welcome   Car park   Wheelchair access (also WC)   Garden and patio
No-smoking area in bar, no smoking in restaurant   Background music   Dogs welcome   Delta,
Diners, MasterCard, Switch, Visa   Accommodation: 10 rooms, B&B £40 to £76

CASTLE ACRE   Norfolk   map 6

▲ Ostrich Inn
Stocks Green, Castle Acre PE32 2AE   TEL: (01760) 755398
just off A1065 Swaffham to Fakenham road, 4m N of Swaffham

The Ostrich Inn, dating from the sixteenth century, overlooks the tree-lined green in the centre of this small, quaint village, which is known for its ancient stone arch. Enter directly into the main bar area, which is as well maintained as the exterior and has as its major feature an inglenook housing black iron cooking pots; a large hall-type room is up a few steps beyond at the back. Pizzas are made on the premises and blackboards above the bar advertise daily specials. As well as salads, sandwiches and such stalwarts as beef and ale pie and gammon with chips, there may be some fairly unusual and imaginative dishes, such as Lancashire black pudding casserole, smoked chicken breast with pilau rice, vegi-mince burritos, and lamb shank tagine. Desserts also include some exotic choices, like shamali (a semolina biscuit cake of almonds and cinnamon) as well as more traditional sticky toffee pudding, or treacle roly-poly. Greene King ales are on handpump to wash it all down, alongside five wines by the glass. Castle Acre has the remains of a twelfth-century priory and a thirteenth-century castle. SAMPLE DISHES: vegetable samosa £4.50; stuffed chicken leg risotto £5; apple strudel with custard £2.50.

Licensee Raymond Wakelen (Greene King)
Open Mon to Thur 12 to 3, 7 to 11, Fri to Sun 12 to 5, 7 to 11; bar food 12 to 2, 7 to 10; no food 25 and 26 Dec
Details Children welcome in eating area   Car park   Wheelchair access (not WC)   Garden and patio   No smoking in eating area   Live or background music   Dogs welcome on a lead   Amex, Delta, MasterCard, Switch, Visa   Accommodation: 2 rooms, B&B £15 to £30

Nags Head Inn

Hill Top, Castle Donington DE74 2PR   TEL: (01332) 850652
4m from M1 junction 24, on B6540, at S end of Castle Donington

The Nags Head is a modest-looking whitewashed pub on the southern edge
of Castle Donington, close to the motor-racing circuit. But don't be put off by
outward appearances or you might miss out on a pub with a very agreeable
atmosphere and some fine food. The menu – chalked up on a blackboard, the
same for bar and restaurant – takes an appealing modern European approach,
and results on the plate show commendable skill and superior ingredients, as
in an inspector's 'tender and flaky' rare tuna steak with roast peppers. Other
options might include smoked cod kedgeree, sea bass with wild mushroom
cream, and beef fillet in Cajun spices with tsatsiki dressing. Desserts are more
traditionally British in nature: bread-and-butter pudding, for example. Snack
dishes, such as beef stir-fry with rice, and a range of sandwiches and baguettes
are served at lunchtime and early evening (5.30 to 7pm). Beers are Marston's
Pedigree, Banks's Mild and Mansfield Bitter. The wine list offers around 30
good-value bottles, with a changing house selection sold by the glass. SAMPLE
DISHES: tuna and salmon pancakes £6.50; braised pheasant with bubble and
squeak £14.25; treacle oat tart £3.75.

Licensee Ian Davison (Wolverhampton & Dudley)
Open 12 to 2.30, 5.30 to 11, Sun 12 to 2.30, 7 to 10.30; bar food and restaurant Mon to Sat
12 to 2, 6.30 to 9.15; closed 26 Dec to 2 Jan
Details No children   Car park   Wheelchair access (not WC)   Garden and patio   No smoking in
restaurant   No music   Dogs welcome in bar only   Amex, Delta, MasterCard, Switch, Visa

Caunton Beck   NEW ENTRY

Main Street, Caunton NG23 6AB   TEL: (01636) 636793
in village, just off A616 5m NW of Newark-on-Trent

Dating from the sixteenth century, this stone pub next to the village church
has had a face-lift. Now, the bar has ceiling beams and floorboards of light-
coloured wood, farmhouse-style tables, and walls painted ochre and sand,
with comfort provided by a warming brick fireplace, curtains at the windows
and various prints. In addition, there's a more traditional carpeted restaurant,
open to the bar, with cottage-style furniture. The same menu, backed up by
blackboard specials, applies in both areas. A jumble of culinary styles sees
Thai-style mussel curry with coconut milk and coriander alongside chicken
satay brochette with lime pickle yoghurt among starters, and main courses of
osso buco on a bed of saffron and pea risotto, and Chinese-marinated duck
breast with wilted pak choi, bean sprouts and noodles. Those with less adventurous palates could start with potted shrimps, go on to herb-crusted pork
cutlet with champ and mustard jus, and finish with dark chocolate and raspberry mousse with chocolate sauce. Breakfast is also served. Ruddles Best
Bitter, Springhead Bitter and Broadstone Best Bitter are on draught, and more
than 30 wines are sold by the glass from a list of over 50 bottles.

SAMPLE DISHES: carrot and coriander soup £4.50; pan-fried fillet of salmon £13.50; vanilla pannacotta £4.75.

Licensees Toby Hope and Julie Allwood (freehouse)
Open *Mon to Sat 8am to midnight, Sun 12 to 11.30; bar food and restaurant 8am to midnight*
Details *Children welcome   Car park   Wheelchair access (also WC)   Garden and patio*
No smoking in restaurant   No music   Dogs welcome exc in restaurant   Amex, Delta, Diners,
MasterCard, Switch, Visa

CAVENDISH   Suffolk   map 6

Bull

High Street, Cavendish CO10 8AX   TEL: (01787) 280245
on A1092 through village

Dating in part from the sixteenth century, this ivy-covered pub stands on the broad main road through the 'pleasantly quiet and sleepy' town of Cavendish. The open-plan main bar is roughly divided into various areas for eating and drinking, and the atmosphere is relaxed throughout, though the main dining area has a slightly more formal appearance than the rest. Menus offer a mix of old favourites and a few 'mildly fashionable' ideas. Salmon and prawn cocktail among starters is definitely from the traditional camp, as are deep-fried scampi, and liver and bacon from main-course choices. But options may extend to sea bass with ginger and spring onion, or Barnsley chop with minted gravy. Hot baguettes have a good choice of fillings, and desserts range from chocolate sponge with chocolate sauce to vodka-soaked forest fruits layered with meringue and ice cream. Southwold Bitter and Broadside are the regular real ales on offer at this Adnams pub, and there may also be a seasonal guest ale. Six wines are available by the glass. SAMPLE DISHES: deep-fried Brie with red onion marmalade £5; tagliatelle verde with salmon and prawns in a white wine and cream sauce £9; lemon and ginger crunch £3.25.

Licensee D.F. Hare (Adnams)
Open *11 to 3, 6 to 11, Sun 12 to 10.30; bar food and restaurant Tue to Sun 12 to 2 (4 Sun),*
6.30 to 9
Details *Children welcome   Car park   Garden and patio   Wheelchair access (not WC)*
Background music   Dogs welcome in bar area   Amex, Delta, MasterCard, Switch, Visa

CHADLINGTON   Oxfordshire   map 5

Tite Inn 🍺

Mill End, Chadlington OX7 3NY   TEL: (01608) 676475
WEBSITE: www.titeinn.com
off A361, 2½m S of Chipping Norton

Halfway down a tiny valley, this small, stone-built inn is in a pleasingly rustic setting, with a little-used lane running past, across which a public footpath leads to meadows and woodland. It has a family-run feeling, and neither the barely audible background music nor the ghost of an unidentified woman detract from the ambience of a friendly, peaceful hostelry with fast and efficient service from the landlord and landlady. Real ale fans will be glad to find on handpump Charles Wells Bombardier and two guests (often from local breweries) in addition to the Tite Inn Bitter brewed by Robinson's. A cider, usually from Biddenden, is on draught too. The evening menu offers a good choice, with starters ranging from Parma ham with melon to mixed seafood salad, and main courses taking in perhaps lambs' kidneys braised in red wine, boeuf bourguignonne, and salmon fishcake with hollandaise. Lighter dishes are served at lunchtimes: expect the likes of home-baked ham with salad, bobotie, goujons of lemon sole with tartare sauce, and Brazil nut roast with tomato sauce. Desserts – among them posh bread-and-butter pudding, and meringue glacé with toffee sauce – are, like everything else, made on the premises. Around half a dozen wines are sold by the glass on a French-biased, constantly changing blackboard list of close to 20 bottles. SAMPLE DISHES: chicken liver pâté £4.50; caramelised onion and goats' cheese tart with salad £9; coconut tart £3.50.

Licensees Michael and Susan Willis (freehouse)
Open Tue to Sat and bank hol Mon 12 to 2.30, Tue to Sat 6.30 to 11, Sun 12 to 2.30, 7 to 10.30; bar food and restaurant Tue to Sun and bank hol Mon 12 to 2, Tue to Sun 6.45 to 9; closed 25 and 26 Dec
Details Children welcome   Car park   Wheelchair access (also WC)   Garden   No smoking in dining room   Occasional background music   Dogs welcome   Delta, MasterCard, Switch, Visa

CHADWICK END   West Midlands   map 5

Orange Tree   NEW ENTRY
Warwick Road, Chadwick End B93 0BN   TEL: (01564) 785364
on A4141 on outskirts of village

This old pub has been thoroughly and stylishly revamped into one of today's new breed of modern, brasserie-style establishments. The large main room is given over to eating, but smaller areas are set aside for just sitting and drinking too. Earthy colours, coir matting, subdued lighting, low ceilings and beams, and bare-wood tables and chairs all create the mood, while huge niches in the walls are filled with neatly piled logs for the open fires. The modern repertoire matches the décor, with a trendy nod to the Mediterranean and beyond; the menu is ambitiously long but laid out in a simple, sectioned style. Crowd-pleasing dishes span the likes of tuna carpaccio with ginger and wasabi to butternut squash, pine-nut and feta risotto, or rack of lamb with saffron pota-toes, chorizo and broad beans to Siciliana pizza or Caesar salad. Beers roll out with Tetley Bitter and Greene King Abbot Ale and IPA, and four wines are served by the glass. Paul Hales is also the licensee at the Crabmill in Preston Bagot (see entry). SAMPLE DISHES: red onion and tomato tarte Tatin with rocket £5; ribeye steak with burnt tomato salsa and fries £13; chocolate panna-cotta £4.95.

Licensee Paul Hales (freehouse)
Open 11 to 11; bar food and restaurant Mon to Sat 12 to 2.30, 6 to 9.30, Sun 12 to 4.30
Details Children welcome   Car park   Garden   Background music   Dogs welcome   Amex, Delta, MasterCard, Switch, Visa

A list of pubs serving exceptional draft beers is at the front of the book.

CHALGROVE   Oxfordshire   map 2

Red Lion Inn

115 High Street, Chalgrove OX44 7SS   TEL: (01865) 890625
just S of B480, 4 miles NW of Watlington

The Lion feels unfussy and uncluttered, and warm and welcoming with it; parts are supposed to date from the eleventh century. The back garden has a children's play area (children's portions on the menu, too), while inside the main room has well-spaced tables, a beamed ceiling and fireplaces at both ends. Restaurant and bar food are imaginatively European with an Asian undertone (though the menu is more restricted on Mondays and at Tuesday lunchtimes). Start with soup, or smoked salmon, or chargrilled haggis, then try partridge braised with oranges or cloves, or Thai green chicken curry with noodles or rice (or, if feeling traditional, beef and dumplings). Puds take in crème brûlée and treacle pudding and custard. A variety of sandwiches and warm open baguettes is also available. Adnams Bitter and Fuller's London Pride are joined by Fuller's seasonal beers and guest brews from the likes of Timothy Taylor Landlord. From a wide-ranging list of 20-odd wines seven are served by the glass (and a footnote invites enquiry about further 'different and special' bottles). Note that parking is across the street. SAMPLE DISHES: crab cakes with red onion tartare sauce £5; chicken cassoulet with cured meats £11.50; banana Paris-Brest with warm Mars Bar sauce £4.

Licensees Jonathan and Maggi Hewitt (freehouse)
Open *12 to 3, 6 to 11, Sun 12 to 3, 7 to 10.30; bar food and restaurant all week 12 to 2, Mon to Sat 7 to 9 (9.30 Fri and Sat); closed a day between Christmas and New Year*
Details *Children welcome in eating areas   Car park   Wheelchair access (also WC)   Garden and patio   No smoking in dining room   Occasional live or background music   Dogs welcome on a lead Amex, MasterCard, Switch, Visa*

CHAPEL AMBLE   Cornwall   map 1

Maltsters Arms 🍺

Chapel Amble PL27 6EU   TEL: (01208) 812473
off A39, 2m N of Wadebridge

The Maltsters Arms is the archetypical picture-postcard village pub, its smartly painted exterior enlivened by lots of floral tubs and baskets and with outdoor seating on a sunny paved area. The interior has been done out in pale green and cream, with prints and farming implements on the walls, and polished woodwork and gleaming brassware reflecting the light from the roaring log fire. The restaurant menu, also served in the bar, always features daily-changing fish main courses – perhaps grilled fillet of halibut with lemon and olive butter – with other options extending perhaps to steaks, goats' cheese salad, and duck breast stir-fried with peppers, garlic, chilli and soy sauce. Ploughman's with West Country cheeses are other possibilities, and a wide range of locally made ice creams crops up among desserts. Sharp's Maltsters, specially brewed for the pub, heads up the real ales, and Sharp's Eden Ale is also kept, along with Greene King Abbot Ale and Bass. Nearly 20 wines are sold by the glass. SAMPLE DISHES: Japanese-style prawns with a sesame, chilli and ginger dressing £7; grilled John Dory topped with cockles with a chilli and lemongrass sauce £16; bread-and-butter pudding with whisky £4.

Licensees Shelley Harris and Robert White (freehouse)
Open 12 to 3 (2.30 winter), 6 to 11; bar food and restaurant 12 to 2 (1.45 winter), 6.15 to 9.30 (9 winter); closed Sun evenings and Mon winter
Details Children welcome Car park Patio No smoking in restaurant Background music Dogs welcome MasterCard, Switch, Visa

CHAPPEL Essex   map 6

Swan Inn   FISH
Chappel CO6 2DD   TEL: (01787) 222353
take Great Tey turning off A1124 at Wakes Colne and cross River Colne to reach pub

The garden behind the car park of this rambling old pub is dominated by a spectacular high viaduct stretching across the Colne Valley, and the river itself runs past the pub. Enter via a small, covered, cobbled courtyard, which is used for al fresco dining. The main bar is heavily beamed, with standing timbers, dark wooden furniture and burgundy-coloured banquettes and stools, and the 'olde worlde' feel is enhanced by a large inglenook where a log fire burns on cold days. On handpump are Greene King IPA and Abbot Ale, plus a guest, and three house wines are offered by the glass from a short list. Bar snacks along the lines of ploughman's, sandwiches, and sausages and chips are served at lunchtimes, but the pub's speciality of fish is the highlight of the restaurant menu, also available in the bar. The proprietors have their own fish supply business, bringing in daily deliveries from Billingsgate and Lowestoft. Simple treatments make the most of fine ingredients: whole grilled sea bass, for example, along with fried or grilled plaice or haddock fillets. Starters take in prawns wrapped in smoked salmon, smoked trout, and scallops grilled with bacon, and among main-course grills (meat is bought fresh at Smithfield) are prime fillet steaks with a variety of sauces, pan-fried chicken breast with a creamy mushroom sauce, and calf's liver with bacon. At the rear of the garden is a well-equipped children's play area. SAMPLE DISHES: moules marinière £7; poached oak-smoked haddock fillets £9.50; home-made desserts £3.25.

Licensee T.L.F. Martin (freehouse)
Open Mon to Fri 11 to 3, 6 to 11, Sat 11 to 11, Sun 12 to 10.30; bar food 12 to 2.30 (3 Sun), 7 to 10.30 (10 Sun); restaurant 12 to 2.30, 7 to 10 (9.30 Sun); no food served 25 and 26 Dec
Details Children welcome in bar eating area and dining room Car park Wheelchair access (not WC) Garden and patio No smoking in lounge and dining room Background music Dogs welcome on a lead Amex, Delta, MasterCard, Switch, Visa

CHARLBURY Oxfordshire   map 5

▲ Bull Inn
Sheep Street, Charlbury OX7 3RR   TEL: (01608) 810689
on B4026, 6 miles SE of Chipping Norton

The Bull is a sixteenth-century hostelry built of Cotswold stone. Outside is a small paved seating area, while inside old ceiling beams festooned with hops, honey-coloured bare stone walls, and subdued lighting from candles and wall lamps create a 'very pleasant and civilised' atmosphere. As an added bonus, service is 'friendly, polite and willing'. Food is listed on a blackboard: it's all fairly straightforward stuff but makes a good impression thanks to the 'rather good' raw materials and generous portions. Start with something snacky like hummus and warm pitta bread with olives and pickled chillies, or perhaps chicken liver pâté with onion chutney, then move on to main courses such as Thai red fish curry with jasmine rice and sweet chilli dipping sauce, or Toulouse sausage on mash with a casserole of haricot beans, herbs and tomatoes. Half a dozen or so dessert options might include tarte Tatin, or hazelnut meringue with raspberries and cream. Beers are from Greene King and Hook Norton, while the wine list opens with seven house selections at £10.95 a bottle, all available by the glass. SAMPLE DISHES: mussels in white wine with onions, cream and garlic £6; roast breast of guinea fowl with Puy lentils and chorizo £11.75; rich dark chocolate and Cointreau mousse £4.50.

Licensee Roy Flynn (freehouse)
Open Tue to Sun 12 to 2.30 (3 Sun), Tue to Sat 7 to 11.30; bar food Tue to Sun 12 to 2, Tue to Sat 7 to 9 (9.30 Fri and Sat); restaurant Tue to Fri and Sun 12 to 2, Tue to Sat 7 to 9 (9.30 Fri and Sat); closed 25 and 26 Dec, 1 Jan
Details Children over 5 welcome   Car park   Wheelchair access (not WC)   Patio   No-smoking area, no smoking in restaurant   Occasional live or background music   Guide dogs only   MasterCard, Switch, Visa   Accommodation: 3 rooms, B&B £58.50 to £77

CHARLTON   West Sussex   map 3

▲ The Fox Goes Free 🍺
Charlton PO18 0HU   TEL: (01243) 811461
off A286 Chichester to Midhurst road, 1m E of Singleton

The name seems to celebrate The Fox's transition from a tied house to a free-house – but the pub was there for four hundred years before that, and its flint walls, peg-tiled roof and small-paned windows give it a cottagey charm that may explain why they held the first Women's Institute meeting in England here in 1915. The two bars – each with settles, chairs, a good fire and a 'fuggy, cosy' atmosphere (plus live music on Wednesdays) – offer Ballard's Best Bitter, Fuller's London Pride and Ringwood Fortyniner, along with Addlestone cider. Food is ordered from a long blackboard menu in one of the bars, then brought to one of the two dining rooms. You can go for just ham, egg and chips, or you might kick off with a generous starter – say, fresh marinated anchovy salad – before moving on to a venison steak, or spicy haddock and salmon fishcakes with Thai dressing ('two tennis balls, appetisingly golden brown, on a kitchen garden of salad'). To finish there could be crème brûlée – or follow one devil-may-care diner and try the Baileys cheesecake ('hang-the-cholesterol-now-I-shan't-want-any-dinner'). No wine list was available to us at the time of going to press, but we are told that house wines start at £10 and eight wines are served by the glass. SAMPLE DISHES: king prawns and garlic butter £6; steak and kidney pie £8; chocolate, orange and Cointreau pot £4.

Licensee Oliver Ligertwood (freehouse)
Open Mon to Fri 11 to 3, 5.30 to 11, Sat 11 to 11, Sun 12 to 10.30; bar food and restaurant
12 to 2.30, 6.30 to 10.30 (12 to 10.30 Sat and Sun)
Details Children welcome in eating areas   Car park   Wheelchair access (not WC)   Garden and
patio   No smoking in 1 dining room   Live or background music   Dogs welcome exc in dining room
Delta, MasterCard, Switch, Visa   Accommodation: 4 rooms, B&B £40 to £60

CHARSFIELD   Suffolk   map 6

Three Horseshoes   NEW ENTRY
The Street, Charsfield IP13 7PY   TEL: (01473) 737330
in centre of village, approx 2½m W of Wickham Market

There's a Laurel and Hardy theme to the décor here, with lots of pictures and
innumerable figurines throughout the place. Well, it makes an interesting
change from the usual collection of horse brasses and old farming implements. Other themes include regular monthly curry nights and days devoted
to other cuisines, such as Italian. Even without these additions, the menu is
large, with regular options on the printed list supplemented with a host of
daily specials and fish dishes. Nothing in the kitchen's repertoire will chal-
lenge the unadventurous, but moussaka with Greek salad has been
commended as 'the genuine article', while lasagne with salad and garlic bread
was deemed successful by an inspector. Among starters, soup of the day might
be leek and potato, while half a dozen dessert options typically feature things
like banoffi pie and fruit crumbles. Portions, reporters tell us, are enormous.
Adnams Bitter and Broadside should keep real ale fans content, while seven
wines are served by the glass from a list of around 20. SAMPLE DISHES: lamb
hotpot £7; chargrilled steak topped with creamy garlic king prawns £12.50;
raspberry trifle £3.

Licensee Paul Read (freehouse)
Open Mon to Fri 12 to 3, 6 to 11, Sat and Sun 12 to 11 (10.30 Sun); bar food Tue to Sat 12 to
2.30, 6 to 9, Sun 12 to 3, 7 to 9
Details Children welcome   Car park   Wheelchair access (not WC)   Garden and patio
No smoking in dining room   Occasional live or background music   Dogs welcome in bar only   Delta,
MasterCard, Switch,Visa

CHENIES   Buckinghamshire   map 3

Red Lion 🍺
Chenies WD3 6ED   TEL: (01923) 282722
off A404, between Chorleywood and Little Chalfont

Backing on to fields at the edge of the village, the Red Lion is a cheery, popular
place with a relaxed atmosphere. The beamed dining area is reached through
the main bar, and a separate room contains just one table for when only inti-
macy will do. This is a beer specialist's pub. The jewel in the crown among the
range is Lion Pride, brewed especially for the inn by the Rebellion Brewery of
Marlow, and it may be joined by Best Bitter from the local Vale Brewery,
Wadworth 6X plus another ale from Rebellion. Food is ordered at the bar, and
the printed menu is augmented by daily specials on the blackboard. Cold

snacks and jacket potatoes will satisfy lighter appetites, while those in the market for three courses might choose starters of perhaps haggis-filled mushrooms topped with grilled cheese with a tomato and balsamic sauce, or mixed seafood with ratatouille. Then it might be one of the pies – lamb in shortcrust pastry, perhaps – chicken and mango curry with rice, or fillets of red mullet on a bed of pea guacamole with a wine and horseradish cream, finishing with strawberry and white chocolate cheesecake, or peach and basil brûlée. Ten wines are sold by the glass. SAMPLE DISHES: prawns and mushrooms in garlic butter and cream sauce £5.50; jambalaya £10; apple and raspberry pie £2.75.

Licensee Mike Norris (freehouse)
Open 11 to 2.30, 5.30 to 11, Sun 12 to 3, 6.30 to 10.30; bar food 12 to 2, 7 to 10 (9.30 Sun); closed 25 Dec
Details No children Car park Wheelchair access (also WC) Patio No smoking in 1 room No music Dogs welcome Amex, Delta, Diners, MasterCard, Switch, Visa

CHERITON   Hampshire   map 2

▲ Flower Pots Inn 🍺

Cheriton SO24 0QQ   TEL: (01962) 771318
4m S of New Alresford, off B3046 in Cheriton

BREW PUB

Cheriton is a delightful village, with a green and the clear waters of the River Itchen running through. The Flower Pots, a red-brick building, at one time a farmhouse, is in a slightly elevated spot off the road on its fringes. That this is a beer-focused pub should come as no surprise, for across the car park is the Cheriton Brewhouse in what used to be a barn. Highly rated Pots Ale, Cheriton Best Bitter, Diggers Gold and Turkey's Delight (the strongest of the lot) are poured direct from casks behind the bar. To enable drinkers to concentrate fully on the superb ales, food is kept simple: hotpots (beef stew, for instance), sandwiches (toasted or plain), massive baps (filled with things like ribeye steak with onions, or prawns), jacket potatoes and various ploughman's are the standard offerings, with a couple of daily specials: a soup, or spicy bean hotpot with crusty bread, say. 'There is no truck with puddings here,' noted a reporter who admired the 'simplicity-done-well route' taken by the kitchen, and who enjoyed the 'unpretentious, cheery and friendly atmosphere' as well as a couple of pints. The setting is as uncomplicated as the food, with a quarry-tiled floor, a log fire and an assortment of wooden tables and chairs in the bar, where there's a covered well, and another fire and a mixture of armchairs and small tables in the lounge. Three wines are available by the glass. SAMPLE DISHES: cheesy garlic bread £3; jacket potato with bacon and mushrooms £5.25; Cajun chicken with basmati rice £5.50.

Licensees J.M. and P.M. Bartlett (freehouse)
Open 12 to 2.30, 6 to 11, Sun 12 to 3, 7 to 10.30; bar food (exc Sun and bank hol evenings) 12 to 2, 7 to 9
Details No children Car park Wheelchair access (not WC) Garden Occasional live music Dogs welcome on a lead No cards Accommodation: 4 rooms, B&B £40 to £60

The Guide always appreciates hearing about changes of licensee.

Albion 🍺 | NEW ENTRY

Park Street, Chester CH1 1RN   TEL: (01244) 340345
WEBSITE: www.albioninnchester.co.uk
best reached on foot from city walls between Eastgate and the Groves; a flight of steps off the
walls from the Watchtower is virtually opposite the pub

The Albion is a modest-looking but very lively street-corner pub, standing in
the shadow of the famous walls of this historical city. It is of early-twentieth-
century vintage, with plenty of Great War memorabilia and other artefacts
giving the place an authentic period feel. The bar menu is dubbed 'Trench
Rations', but the cooking is somewhat more modern and stylish than that
suggests (though portions are indeed generous): lamb's liver with smoked
bacon and onions in a rich cider gravy, goats' cheese and pesto ravioli with
tomato and chilli sauce, and even vegetarian haggis, for example. There are
also sandwiches and hot filled rolls, and a specials board offers further choice,
perhaps in the shape of beef Madras curry, or pasta with Stilton and black olive
sauce. As well as the good pub grub, there is a superb selection of real ales: the
regular trio of Timothy Taylor Landlord, Banks's Bitter and Jennings Bitter
are supplemented by a regularly changing guest, often a local or seasonal brew.
The small selection of wines eschews France completely, looking instead to
the New World for inspiration, and there is also a choice of up to 20 malt
whiskies. Note that the pub is often closed on race days. SAMPLE DISHES:
Staffordshire oatcakes with black pudding and sliced potato £6.75; boiled
gammon with parsley sauce, pease pudding, creamed potatoes and vegetables
£6.75; lemon cheesecake with lime coulis and cream £3.25.

Licensee Michael Edward Mercer (Inn Partnership)
Open Mon to Fri 11.30 to 3, 5 to 11, Sat 11.30 to 3, 6 to 11, Sun 12 to 2.30, 7 to 10.30; bar
food Mon to Fri 12 to 1.45, 5 to 8, Sat and Sun 12 to 2, 7 to 8.30 (8 Sun); restaurant Mon to Fri
5 to 8, Sat 6 to 8.30, Sun 7 to 8 (all opening and food times subject to change and customers are
advised to check by phone)
Details No children   No smoking in restaurant   Occasional live music   Dogs welcome   No cards

Old Harkers Arms 🍺 | NEW ENTRY

1 Russell Street, Boughton, Chester CH3 5AL   TEL: (01244) 344525

Parking nearby may be difficult, but a marvellous range of beers from a forest
of handpumps warrants walking along City Road and down the steps to the
towpath. This trendy ground-floor pub in a nicely converted warehouse
(same owners as the Grosvenor Arms, Aldford, Dysart Arms, Bunbury, the
Hare, Langton Green, Pant-yr-Ochain, Gresford – see entries) attracts the
crowds but can accommodate them. The brick and cast-iron interior, largely
open-plan, has tall windows and much old wood (board floor, doors reused
for bar counters, recycled port cases on the ceiling), plus framed pictures,
documents, cartoons, on cream walls. The busy, sociable buzz is fuelled by
ever-changing local, regional and other brews from, say, Thwaites, Phoenix,
Caledonian, Moorhouses (Volcano) and Weetwood (Ambush Ale), plus

Inch's Stonehouse cider, all superbly kept. Malt whiskies come by the dozen too, and some 15 wines by the glass from a short list supplemented by black-boards are all commendably sold by the glass, £2 to £3.60. To eat, there are starters like mushroom and ginger soup, or steamed mussels with cream and pink peppercorn sauce ('30-plus mussels, huge hunks of herb bread, a bucket-load of sauce ... very, very tasty'). Mains move from steakburger, egg and chips – via chickpea, chilli and coriander cakes and red onion salad – to salmon marinated in ginger, orange and soy with stir-fried vegetables, while sweets include profiteroles and sorbets. SAMPLE DISHES: fried halloumi with lime and caper vinaigrette £4.50; crispy roast duck breast, parsnip purée and cranberry gravy £9.75; chocolate bread-and-butter pudding with vanilla ice cream £4.

Licensee Catryn Devaney and Barbie Hill (Brunning & Price Ltd)
Open 11.30 to 11, Sun 12 to 10.30; bar food Mon to Fri 12 to 2.30, Mon to Thur 5 to 9.30, Sat and Sun 12 to 9.30
Details Children welcome in bar eating area   Wheelchair access (also WC)   No-smoking area No music   No dogs   Amex, Delta, MasterCard, Switch, Visa

---

CHICHELEY   Buckinghamshire   map 6

Chester Arms   NEW ENTRY

Bedford Road, Chicheley MK16 9JE   TEL: (01234) 391214
on A422, 4m from M1 junction 14

If you can't face the M1 services at Newport Pagnell, here's a welcoming refuge. The Chester Arms is everything you could want from a traditional English country pub: a welcoming atmosphere, straightforward, well-cooked food, and surroundings of low ceilings, plenty of pine, brass lamps and patterned carpets. Fish and seafood are delivered daily, and meat and poultry are supplied by a local butcher. Dishes respect the quality of produce: perhaps simply grilled whole sea bass or Dover sole, and prime Aberdeen Angus rump, sirloin or fillet with a choice of sauce chasseur, au poivre or garlic butter. Alternatively, you could start with smoked duck salad with plum sauce, or Arbroath smokies, and go on to chargrilled lamb chops, or steak and kidney pie, and finish with a traditional, comforting pudding: perhaps treacle tart, or chocolate truffle cake. Greene King IPA and Ruddles County are on hand-pump, while wine drinkers can choose from a reasonably priced list, starting at £10.40, with eight available by the glass. SAMPLE DISHES: avocado and smoked chicken salad £4.75; duck breast with orange sauce £11.75; banana cheesecake £3.25.

Licensee Phil Hale (Greene King)
Open Mon to Sat 11 to 3, 5.30 to 11, Sun 11 to 3; bar food and restaurant Tue to Sat 12 to 2, 6.30 to 9.30, Sun 12 to 2
Details Children welcome in restaurant   Car park   Wheelchair access (also WC)   Garden No-smoking area in bar, no smoking in restaurant   Background music   No dogs   Amex, Delta, MasterCard, Switch, Visa

---

🐾 🐾 *indicates a pub serving food on a par with 'seriously good' restaurants, where the cooking achieves consistent high quality.*

▲ Compasses Inn

Chicksgrove SP3 6NB   TEL: (01722) 714318
turn off A30 2m W of Fovant towards Chicksgrove and follow signs for Compasses Inn

This sixteenth-century, thatched inn is reached along narrow lanes in rolling countryside. The interior gives the impression that nothing much has changed in decades, with part-panelled walls, low ceilings, fat black beams, dim lighting, farming implements all over the walls, and even an upright piano and a stuffed owl in a glass case. The menu is on blackboards, with additional daily specials written on the canopy of a wood-burning stove in the inglenook. You might begin with mussels cooked with bacon in cream, garlic and white wine, or a salad of avocado, sun-dried tomatoes, pine nuts and goats' cheese. Follow with perhaps steak and kidney pie, poussin roasted with rosemary, garlic, apricots and onions, or flash-fried salmon fillet with lemon and ginger. Rolls, salads and jacket potatoes appear on the menu at lunchtimes, and desserts range from peach syllabub to bread-and-butter pudding. On draught are Chicksgrove Churl, brewed for the pub by Wadworth, whose 6X is also kept, along with Ringwood Best Bitter and Bass. All six house wines are sold by the glass, the full list numbering around two dozen. SAMPLE DISHES: smoked chicken and bacon salad with pesto and lemon £5.45; grilled turbot with beurre blanc £13; caramelised banana tart £4.

Licensee Alan Stoneham (freehouse)
Open *Tue to Sun 12 to 3, 6 to 11 (10.30 Sun); bar food Tue to Sun 12 to 2, Tue to Sat 7 to 9*
Details *Children welcome   Car park   Garden and patio   No music   Dogs welcome   Amex, Delta, Diners, MasterCard, Switch, Visa   Accommodation: 4 rooms, B&B £40 to £65*

Six Bells

Chiddingly BN8 6HE   TEL: (01825) 872227
off A22 Uckfield to Eastbourne road at Golden Cross service station

Next to the church in a tiny village, the Six Bells is exactly what to expect of a country pub dating from the eighteenth century, with brick floors, low beamed ceilings, real fires and nooks and crannies. The cooking will delight traditionalists, if what they want is French onion soup, spare ribs in BBQ sauce, shepherd's pie, and cannelloni. Jacket potatoes are other possibilities, and vegetarians get a good deal, from cauliflower cheese to lentil, leek and mushroom loaf, and you can finish with a steamed pudding or banana split. Courage Directors and Harveys Sussex Best Bitter are on draught along with a guest ale. SAMPLE DISHES: garlic prawns £5; hock of ham, French bread and beans £7; raspberry pavlova £2.75.

Licensees Paul Newman and Emma Bannister (freehouse)
Open *Mon to Fri 11 to 3, 6 to 11 (12 Fri), Sat 11 to 12, Sun 11 to 10.30; bar food Mon to Fri 12 to 2.30, 6 to 10.30, Sat and Sun 12 to 10.30*
Details *No children   Car park   Garden and patio   Live music   Dogs welcome   Delta, MasterCard, Switch, Visa*

Griffins Head

Chillenden CT3 IPS   TEL: (01304) 840325
from A2 take Nonnington turn-off; pub is 1m past Nonnington on left-hand side

Hidden in the east Kent countryside halfway between Canterbury and Deal, this medieval farmhouse has exposed beams and timbers, low ceilings, inglenooks and flagged floors. It only acquired a licence in the eighteenth century, but the atmosphere is 'quintessential English pub'. The main bar has a welcoming log fire, like the adjoining attractive dining room (whose popularity may make booking advisable). A blackboard lists daily dishes, with the meat and fish coming from local suppliers, as does game in season. Soups are flavoursome and satisfying, and a whole plaice stuffed with shrimps vies with half a pheasant in red wine and redcurrant sauce, or huge pork or Barnsley chops. Accompanying vegetables are fresh and tasty, the sautéed potatoes earning particular praise. Although we cannot comment on wines, as the list was not available to us at the time of going to press, since this is a Shepherd Neame pub, real ale aficionados will be happy to find that brewery's range on offer. SAMPLE DISHES: warm goats' cheese and bacon salad £4.25; steak and ale pie with seasonal vegetables £9; baked rum bananas with demerara sugar £3.50.

Licensee Mark Jeremy Copestake (Shepherd Neame)
Open 11 to 11, Sun 11 to 4.30 (later in summer); bar food and restaurant 12 to 2, 7 to 9.30, Sun 12 to 2
Details No children   Car park   Garden and patio   No music   Dogs welcome on a lead exc in restaurant   Amex, Delta, MasterCard, Switch, Visa

Sir Charles Napier 🏵 🏵 🍇

Sprigg's Alley, Chinnor OX39 4BX   TEL: (01494) 483011
from M40 junction 6 take B4009 to Chinnor; at mini-roundabout in Chinnor turn right and continue up hill for 2m to Sprigg's Alley

The eccentricities at this cross between a pub and a restaurant start with the décor, which includes giant terracotta pots, unusual sculptures (all for sale) inside and in the extensive garden, plus quirky objects such as the weighted frying pan used as a doorstop. Unmatching old tables and chairs, too, contribute to the relaxed atmosphere, which sometimes encourages customers to linger until sunset. Service is pleasant and unrushed despite crowds of people, especially for Sunday lunch. The menus, served throughout, manage to combine the traditional with the classical, taking in skate wing with caper sauce, braised shank of lamb with mash and rosemary, and ribeye of beef with roast potatoes and veal jus. Game is featured in season – perhaps roast grouse with rösti and blackberries – and brandade of cod, or Roquefort soufflé may show up among starters. Generous portions may rule out desserts of perhaps pear and almond tart with vanilla ice cream, or cappuccino crème brûlée. The exquisite wine list never puts a foot wrong, featuring both classics from Bordeaux, Burgundy and the Rhône – many of them in mature vintages – and New World rising stars, such as South Africa's much-lauded

Boekenhoutskloof. However, with only around a half-dozen bottles under £15 and the majority climbing steeply upwards from £20, a deep breath may be needed (but will be rewarded). There is a good selection of half-bottles, however, and around eight wines are sold by the glass. Wadworth 6X and IPA come straight from the barrel. Note there is a 12.5 per cent suggested service charge. SAMPLE DISHES: pheasant boudin blanc with creamed leeks £5.75; cod with creamed white beans and Jerusalem artichoke £10.50; orange and Grand Marnier soufflé with chocolate chip cookie ice cream £6.75.

Licensee Julie Griffiths (freehouse)
Open Tue to Sun 12 to 3 (6 Sun), Tue to Sat 6.30 to 12; bar food and restaurant Tue to Sat 12 to 2.30, 7 to 10, Sun 12 to 3.30; closed 25 and 26 Dec
Details Children welcome at L, no children under 7 at D   Car park   Wheelchair access (not WC) Garden and patio   No-smoking areas   Background music   No dogs   Amex, Delta, Diners, MasterCard, Switch, Visa

CHOLMONDELEY   Cheshire   map 5

▲ Cholmondeley Arms
Cholmondeley SY14 8BT   TEL: (01829) 720300
WEBSITE: www.cholmondeleyarms.co.uk
on A49, 5½m N of Whitchurch

The village school until 1982, the Cholmondeley (pronounced 'chumley') Arms was converted into a pub in 1988. Grand old cast-iron radiators and, on a gallery above the bar, school desks and a blackboard and easel are reminders of the building's original function, and the playground is now the car park. Farm kitchens, gentlemen's clubs, chapels and sewing rooms seem to have been raided to provide a range of seats and wooden tables within the large open-plan interior, where soaring arches hung with drapes separate the three areas. Despite huge windows and high ceilings, the place has a homely feel, with pastel-washed brick walls hung with oil portraits, wildlife and military paintings, a stag's head and a huge coat of arms above an open log fire. Marston's Pedigree, Banks's Bitter and Adnams Bitter are on handpump, and seven wines are sold by the glass from a global list of around 30 bottles. Printed menus backed up by blackboard specials offer a lot of interest in the shape of smoked trout and watercress roulade, or hot crab pâté to start, followed by fillets of sea bass on samphire, Gressingham duck breast with redcurrant sauce and parsnip mash, or seasonal game: perhaps 'beautifully tender' roast local partridge in porcini mushroom sauce. Omelettes, stuffed pancakes, and sandwiches are available lunchtimes, and something like chocolate and banana split, or spotted dick, will round things off nicely. On two sides of the cross-shaped red-brick building are lawns with picnic tables; Cholmondeley Castle, a Gothic pile, and its gardens are nearby. SAMPLE DISHES: baked prawns in sour cream and garlic £4.75; oxtail braised in red wine £9.25; iced Grand Marnier soufflé £4.25.

Licensees Guy and Carolyn Ross-Lowe (freehouse)
Open 11 to 3, 6.30 to 11; bar food 12 to 2.15, 6.30 to 10
Details Children welcome   Car park   Wheelchair access (also WC)   Garden   Occasional background music   Dogs welcome   Delta, MasterCard, Switch, Visa   Accommodation: 6 rooms, B&B £50 to £65

CLAVERING   Essex   map 3

▲ Cricketers

Clavering CB11 4QT   TEL: (01799) 550442
WEBSITE: www.thecricketers.co.uk
on B1038 between Buntingford and Newport, 6m SW of Saffron Walden

Behind a white roadside picket fence and some picnic tables crouches a slate-roofed white building whose exterior disguises its sixteenth-century origins. Inside, though, there are beams in the bar, exposed-brick walls, and in winter the brass ornaments wink in the light from a roaring fire: a cosy, pleasant and unpretentious setting for ales from Adnams and Tetley. As befits Jamie Oliver's culinary cradle, no-nonsense food shows touches of his Italianate style, as in bar menu starters of thin-sliced seared venison loin with wild rocket, or a warm salad of avocado, pancetta, pine nuts and croûtons with walnut oil vinaigrette. Menu mains – supplemented by a blackboard that changes every session – are homelier but faintly exotified (saddle of rabbit with a vegetable farci, or pink, perfectly textured pigeon breasts with artichoke bottoms and a sweetish juniper sauce), although old-fashioned roasts appear regularly, and fish features prominently, notably on Tuesdays. The restaurant's prix fixe could include roast gammon loin, or roast halibut fillet in leek, mussel and curry sauce. Among desserts might be one diner's best-ever sticky toffee pudding ('enough for four'): light, moist, in a lake of fudge sauce. Ten wines come by the glass from a list of about 50, very few of which exceed £20. SAMPLE DISHES: chicken satay with orange and sesame seed salad £6; king scallops and prawns with sliced potato and linguine £16; sticky toffee pudding with home-made rum and raisin ice cream and caramel sauce £5.

Licensee Trevor Oliver (freehouse)
Open 10.30 to 11; bar food and restaurant 12 to 2, 7 to 10; closed 25 and 26 Dec
Details Children welcome in eating areas and family room   Car park   Wheelchair access (not WC)
Garden and patio   No-smoking area in bar, no smoking in dining room   Background music   No dogs
Amex, MasterCard, Switch, Visa   Accommodation: 8 rooms, B&B £70 to £100

CLAYHIDON   Devon   map 2

Merry Harriers   NEW ENTRY

Forches Corner, Clayhidon EX15 3TR   TEL: (01823) 421270
off B3170, 6m SW of Taunton at Forches Corner, 2m NE of Clayhidon village

In the beautiful Blackdown Hills, the Merry Harriers is a cream-painted and dark-timbered roadside pub. The main bar has a cosy, homely feel and a warming log stove, and the friendly licensees are a welcoming presence and ensure that the place has a relaxed atmosphere. Locally sourced produce and fresh fish from Brixham feature strongly throughout the menu, though the kitchen takes its ideas from far and wide. Starters of green-lipped mussels with pesto, and deep-fried tortillas stuffed with pork and ginger might be followed by griddled scallops with lemon butter, pork and port casserole, goats' cheese and pine-nut ravioli, or venison steak with sloe berry and gin sauce. To finish, there might be crème brûlée, or warm figs in rum syrup. A changing selection of good local real ales might include well-kept Otter Ale. There is also

Bollhayes cider and apple juice. The brief wine list focuses on bin-ends and as a result offers good value for money. Ten wines are served by the glass from £2.50. SAMPLE DISHES: grilled goats' cheese with poppy seeds and raspberry dressing £4; confit of Quantock duck on onion marmalade £13.50; griottine cherries in Kirsch with ice cream £4.

Licensees Barry and Christine Kift (freehouse)
Open Tue to Sat 12 to 3, 7 to 11, Sun 12 to 3; bar food and restaurant Tue to Sat 12 to 2, 7 to 9, Sun 12 to 2
Details No children   Car park   Wheelchair access (not WC)   Garden and patio   No-smoking area in bar, no smoking in restaurant   No music   Dogs welcome on a lead   Delta, MasterCard, Switch, Visa

CLIFFORD'S MESNE   Gloucestershire   map 5

▲ Yew Tree 🏵

May Hill, Clifford's Mesne GL18 1JS   TEL: (01531) 820719
WEBSITE: www.theyewtreeinn.co.uk
off B4222/4216, 4m SE of M50 junction 3

Perched above Clifford's Mesne, on the north slope of May Hill, the Yew Tree has a splendid view north over the Leadon valley to the Malvern Hills. The building began as a sixteenth-century cider press, though you wouldn't know that from the sprawling, modern-looking brick façade softened by colourful hanging baskets and window boxes round the patio. Inside, signs of antiquity are visible, like the ceiling beams in the restaurant area and the spacious L-shaped bar with its cheerfully patterned carpet. Here you can sup Shepherd Neame Spitfire, Wye Valley Butty Bach, and Fuller's London Pride, along with oak-conditioned ciders. Food – from bar snacks to gourmet dinners – is listed on blackboards in the bar and on the restaurant menu (which you can eat from in the bar). Among starters, you may find spinach and broccoli soup, tagliatelle of crayfish with champagne dill cream, or duck and quail eggs with smoked sausage. Mains could include a fillet of Cornish sea bass, or belly of Old Spot pork braised with cider, onion and lentils, while desserts extend from apple crumble with Calvados custard to mango and hazelnut parfait with blackcurrant coulis. A house selection of a dozen or so wines by the glass is complemented by a pricier wine list made up mostly of smart European bottles and some better-value options from Chile. SAMPLE DISHES: courgette risotto with sun-dried tomato and basil £5; braised leg and roast breast of pheasant with claret sauce £13.75; lemon tart with prune and Armagnac ice cream £4.75.

Licensee Paul Hackett (freehouse)
Open Tue to Sun 12 to 2.30 (3 summer), 6.30 to 11; bar food and restaurant 12 to 3, 6.30 to 10
Details Children welcome   Car park   Wheelchair access (not WC)   Garden and patio
No-smoking area in bar, no smoking in dining room   Occasional background music   Dogs welcome
Delta, Diners, MasterCard, Switch, Visa   Accommodation: 2 rooms, B&B £40 to £75

A list of pubs with better-than-average wines, well chosen and decently priced, is at the front of the book.

CLIPSHAM   Rutland   map 6

Olive Branch 🍷 🍇

Main Street, Clipsham LE15 7SH   TEL: (01780) 410355
1½m off A1 at Ram Jam Inn junction, 8m N of Stamford

This is a low stone building on a bend at the western edge of the hamlet of Clipsham. Outside there's a lawn and a gravel patio with trestle tables, while the interior is a quirky but relaxed mix of sisal matting, tiled floors, wooden tables and chairs, pews, pale pastel walls, log fires and lamplight. The beers, largely local, come from Grainstore Brewery (Olive Oil), Fenland Brewery, Oakham Ales or Brewster's, plus Adnams, and Sheppy's farmhouse cider. Surrounding the long bar, blackboards draw attention to food, cigars and bin-ends and special purchases of wines. The wine selection here and on the printed list is outstanding both for quality and value, and manageably brief. It is enthusiastic without being snobbish, taking in clarets from some of the best vintages of the last 30 years on the one hand and offering a simple guide to wine styles on the other. Ten wines can be had by the glass. More boards offer soups, hot sandwiches and a two- or three-course set lunch. The printed carte encompasses the homely (cauliflower cheese with smoked bacon, or fish, chips and mushy peas), the exotic (spicy chorizo ribollita soup, or tandoori-style monkfish with jasmine rice) and the somewhat sinful (crab salad with pink grapefruit, avocado and feta, or game casserole with herb mash and dumpling). Among the puds might be quince and mascarpone tart with a raspberry sorbet, and chocolate roulade with Chantilly cream. SAMPLE DISHES: game terrine with blackberry compote £6.25; smoked salmon tagliatelle with sour cream and dill £9.25; fruit crumble with cinnamon ice cream £5.

Licensee Marcus Welford (freehouse)
Open 12 to 3, 6 to 11, Sun 12 to 3; bar food and restaurant Mon to Sat 12 to 2, 7 to 9.30, Sun 12 to 3
Details Children welcome in bar eating area   Car park   Wheelchair access (also WC)   Garden and patio   No-smoking areas   Occasional background or live music   Dogs welcome   Delta, MasterCard, Switch, Visa

COCKWOOD   Devon   map 1

Anchor Inn 🍺 🍇

Cockwood EX6 8RA   TEL: (01626) 890203
WEBSITE: www.anchorinncockwood.com
off A379, on W side of River Exe estuary opposite Exmouth

FISH

This sixteenth-century pub has three things in spades: location, atmosphere and service. (Hence, of course, it can get very busy, so booking is advisable.) It's right on the harbour's edge, and eastward, over the moored boats, there's a panoramic view of the Exe estuary from its verandah tables. The low-ceilinged, beamed interior feels relaxed and welcoming, helped by lovely old lamps hung on the beams, and staff are friendly, smiley and helpful. Beer drinkers can sample Bass, Fuller's London Pride, Wadworth 6X, and Greene King Abbot Ale and Old Speckled Hen, while oenophiles get a list of around 30 wines at very good prices – eight to ten of them by the glass – plus blackboard specials and a 'reserve list' of 300 more with lots of old vintages (quite a few are too old but there are some gems worth prising out). The lengthy menu emphasises both seafood and themes and variations (5 types of fishcake, 4 of sausage, 8 variations on oysters, 14 on scallops, 30 on mussels, 12 on treacle tart). The bar menu offers dishes like Stilton-topped garlic mushrooms, or battered squid rings to start, with smoked haddock steam pudding, faggots and peas, steak and wassail pie, or cauliflower cheese to follow. The restaurant menu (available in the bar too) adds fried zip-back prawns, or smoked salmon to start, then trawlerman's gumbo pot, half a pheasant, or a scallop-stuffed fillet steak. Sweets run to spotted dick, bread-and-butter pudding, or all those treacle tarts. SAMPLE DISHES: avocado with prawn and crab £5; oysters rolled in plaice fillets with mussel sauce £12.50; treacle tart with walnuts £3.75.

Licensees Terry Morgan and Alison Sanders (Heavitree Brewery)
Open 11 to 11, Sun 12 to 10.30; bar food and restaurant 12 to 3, 6.30 to 10, Sun 12 to 2.30, 6.30 to 9.30; closed 25 Dec evening, no food all day
Details Children welcome in bar eating area   Car park   Wheelchair access (also WC)   Patio
No smoking in dining room   Background music   Dogs welcome exc in restaurant   Amex, Delta, Diners, MasterCard, Switch, Visa

COLDHARBOUR   Surrey   map 3

▲ Plough Inn 🍺   BREW PUB
Coldharbour RH5 6HD   TEL: (01306) 711793
4m S of Dorking, signposted Leith Hill and Coldharbour

It's surprising (to non-residents) how rural bits of Surrey can be. Here, four miles from the A25, yet amid woodland and heath, and near the National Trust's Leith Hill (one of the best viewpoints in the South-East) stands a colour-washed Georgian-looking pub with built-in brewery. The Leith Hill Brewery supplies the Plough with Crooked Furrow Bitter ('good stuff' mumbled one enthusiast) and Tallywhacker Porter, and these sit alongside guest ales, Timothy Taylor Landlord and Shepherd Neame Spitfire. Inside, there are beams and white plaster, but not the folksy over-busyness that many pubs succumb to – and in an old barn outside the main building there's a large family room. Food, listed on blackboards, focuses on doing simple dishes well, with starters like smoked salmon and mackerel pâté, or tomato and mozzarella salad with red onions. Main dishes may include pork and leek sausages ('lots of herby flavour') and mash, or 'succulent, tender' beef bourguignonne with 'lots of rich tomato flavour' and particularly fresh and well-timed vegetables. There's a short children's menu too. Sweets take in rice pudding with plum preserve, and banoffi pie. House wine starts at £9.90, and nine offerings are available by the glass from £2.60. SAMPLE DISHES: prawn cocktail £5; poached haddock, poached egg, mash and vegetables £10; blackberry and apple crumble and custard £4.50.

Licensees Richard and Anna Abrehart (freehouse)
Open 11.30 to 3, 6 to 11, Sun 12 to 10.30; bar food and restaurant 12 to 3, 7 to 9.30, Sun 12 to 9.30
Details Children welcome in family room   Car park   Wheelchair access (also WC)   Garden
No smoking in dining room   Occasional background and live music   Dogs on leads only
MasterCard, Switch, Visa   Accommodation: 6 rooms, B&B £55 to £95

▲ Bell Inn

3 Far Lane, Coleby LN5 0AH   TEL: (01522) 810240
on A607 from Grantham to Lincoln, take second left after Boothby Graffoe

In a village just south of Lincoln, the Bell is an attractive yellow-washed former cottage with a brick-red pantiled roof, and, inside, a decorative theme of red carpets and plush red upholstery on dark wooden furniture. Though the feel is old-fashioned, the approach to food is serious and modern, as one glance at the restaurant menu (also served in the bar) will reveal – an extensive and varied list with something for everyone. Typical are braised lamb shoulder with carrot and parsnip purée and braised red cabbage, braised blade of beef on olive oil mash topped with hollandaise, and crispy duck breast on Chinese-style vegetables with soft noodles. Those with a lighter appetite could opt for eggs Benedict, or corned beef hash, and both starter and main-course portions are offered of such things as spaghetti carbonara, and deep-fried fishcakes on parsley and saffron sauce. Sandwiches and tapas are available in the bar, and among desserts might be sticky toffee pudding or for the more adventurous jelly bean crème brûlée with Mars Bar fritter and Turkish delight ice cream. Draught Bass, Bateman XB and Tetley Bitter are on tap for beer drinkers; for wine there's a choice of four by the glass or a list of 30 bottles, mostly from France. Prices are good and half a dozen also come in half-bottles. SAMPLE DISHES: asparagus with hollandaise £5; pan-fried calf's liver with bubble and squeak and a confit of tomatoes, onions and rosemary £10; baked Alaska for two £8.50.

Licensees Troy Jeffrey and Robert Chamberlain (Pubmaster)
Open *11.30 to 2.30, 5.30 to 11, Sun 12 to 10.30; bar food and restaurant Mon to Sat 11.30 to 2.30, 5.30 to 9 (9.30 Fri and Sat), Sun 12 to 8*
Details *Children welcome in eating areas   Car park   Wheelchair access (not WC)   Patio No smoking in 1 eating area   Background music   Dogs welcome in bar   Delta, MasterCard, Switch, Visa   Accommodation: 3 rooms, room only £34.50*

▲ New Inn 🍇

Coleford EX17 5BZ   TEL: (01363) 84242
WEBSITE: www.reallyreal-group.com
off A377 Exeter to Barnstaple road, 4m W of Crediton

The rambling, characterful interior of this thirteenth-century whitewashed inn has heavy beams, open log fires and sturdy old furniture, and a convivial and relaxing atmosphere. Those wanting something light could opt for bar snacks of ploughman's, baguettes or perhaps an omelette and chips, while those after something more substantial should head for the spacious restaurant, in an extension created from some old barns, with its imaginative menu (also served in the bar). You might choose fish soup, smoked chicken and orange salad, or king prawns in Thai butter to start, followed by pan-fried fillet of salmon niçoise on a bed of vegetables, honey-glazed confit of duck with Cumberland jus, or pork tenderloin with bubble and squeak. Vegetarian

dishes get a decent showing, and to round things off there might be vanilla
crème brûlée, profiteroles with chocolate sauce, or fruit crumble. Otter Ale,
Badger Best and guest ales are on draught, and half a dozen wines are sold by
the glass. The list of around 50 reds and whites organised by grape variety efficiently covers a wide range of flavours with plenty of options under £15 and a
good showing of half-bottles. At the rear is a streamside patio with tables and
chairs – a peaceful spot in this charming thatched village. SAMPLE DISHES: duck
and orange pâté with onion marmalade £4.50; roasted lamb shank with roasted
root vegetables £10.25; mousse au chocolat with rum £4.25.

Licensee Paul Butt (freehouse)
Open 12 to 2.30, 6 to 11, Sun 12 to 2.30, 7 to 10.30; bar food and restaurant 12 to 2, 7 to 10
Details Children welcome   Car park   Wheelchair access (not WC)   Garden   No smoking in
dining room   Background music   No dogs in restaurant   Amex, Delta, Diners, MasterCard, Switch,
Visa   Accommodation: 6 rooms, B&B £55 to £80

COLESHILL   Buckinghamshire   map 3

▲ Red Lion
Village Road, Coleshill HP7 0LN   TEL: (01494) 727020
*village signposted off A355 S of Amersham; once in village go past sign for school; pub
opposite church*

Set back from the road, this white-painted pebbledash building with a profusion of windows looks more like an imposing private residence than a pub,
although the picnic tables at the front are a bit of a giveaway. Inside, the walls
are painted a cheery yellow; above the bar are lots of photographs and plaques
to do with local matters, and village events are announced on notices in the
entrance porch. There is no restaurant, just a few tables in the bar, which can
be reserved. The printed menu lists jacket potatoes, salads, sandwiches and
snacks like buck rarebit, but the real business is chalked up on blackboards:
perhaps starters of a soup, or smoked haddock fishcakes, followed by 'tender'
lamb chops with mint sauce and redcurrant jelly, fish pie, braised oxtail, or, in
summer, cold poached salmon with prawn mayonnaise and salad. Finish with
something like a sponge pudding, or chocolate roulade. Greene King IPA and
Fuller's London Pride are the regular beers, with Rebellion IPA and
Smuggler, Archers Village Bitter or Vale Brewery's Wychert Ale among the
guests. Just three wines are sold by the glass. SAMPLE DISHES: scrambled egg
with smoked salmon £6.50; beef casserole with dumplings £7; brioche and
marmalade pudding £3.25.

Licensees Christine and John Ullman (Innspired Pubs & Taverns)
Open Mon to Fri 11 to 3.30, 5.30 to 11, Sat 11 to 11, Sun 12 to 5, 7 to 10.30; bar food (exc Sun
evening) 12 to 2.15, 7 to 9
Details Children welcome   Car park   Garden and patio   Occasional live music   Dogs welcome on
a lead   No cards   Accommodation: 2 rooms, B&B £20 to £45

All entries are indexed at the back of the book.

COLLINGHAM   Nottinghamshire   map 5

King's Head

6 High Street, Collingham NG23 7LA   TEL: (01636) 892341
on A1133 N of Newark-on-Trent

Despite an open fire, the décor here is cool and airy, with white walls, terra-cotta-coloured tiled floors and a brushed aluminium bar counter giving a contemporary and minimalist feel. Although real ales and lunchtime baguettes and sandwiches are served at the bar, eating is the main business, and the restaurant menu is also served in the bar. Chef/owner Jamie Matts has had plenty of experience at well-respected restaurants, and his menu offers a wide range of dishes, from traditional English to oriental. Old-fashioned pub staples, such as chargrilled ribeye steak with peppercorn sauce, or goujons of plaice, contrast with inventive modern dishes like baked chicken breast stuffed with king prawns wrapped in smoked salmon. Desserts of bread-and-butter pudding and 'wonderfully light' raspberry crème brûlée have been especially commended. Themed evenings – Chinese, say – and a monthly food and drink quiz with its own menu are added attractions. For beer drinkers, regular Timothy Taylor Landlord and Adnams Bitter are supplemented by a guest ale like Springhead Roaring Meg or Adnams Broadside. Half a dozen wines are sold by the glass, and the short, annotated wine list approaches 20 bottles. Breakfast, morning coffee and cakes are served between 9.30 and noon. SAMPLE DISHES: smoked seafood mousse with a horseradish and chive cream sauce £5; fillet of cod rarebit with mustard sauce and tomato and basil mash £11; chocolate and pecan pie £3.25.

Licensee Jamie Matts (freehouse)
Open *Mon to Fri 12 to 2, 6 to 11, Sat 11 to 11, Sun 12 to 6; bar food and restaurant Mon to Fri 12 to 2, 6 to 9, Sat 12 to 9, Sun 12 to 4.30*
Details *Children welcome   Car park   Wheelchair access (not WC)   Garden   No smoking in dining room   Occasional live and background music   No dogs   Delta, MasterCard, Switch, Visa*

COLSTON BASSETT   Nottinghamshire   map 5

▲ Martins Arms ✿ 🍺

School Lane, Colston Bassett NG12 3FD   TEL: (01949) 81361
off A46 Leicester to Newark road, 4m S of Bingham

This eighteenth-century village inn close to a market cross (a National Trust monument) boasts an exemplary collection of ales: Black Sheep Best Bitter, Bateman XB, Adnams Bitter, Timothy Taylor Landlord, Marston's Pedigree and Greene King IPA are all handpumped at the bar. The food here is highly regarded too. The lunchtime bar menu ranges from a choice of ploughman's (one with Stilton from the village) and sandwiches to cod fishcake with rocket salad, or penne with smoked chicken, roasted peppers, olives and spinach, while in the evening you can expect ham hock with pease pudding, confit of duck leg, or daube of beef with horseradish mash. There is no shortage of choice on the ambitious menu that serves both the comfortable bar and the antique-furnished restaurant, and the scope of the cooking is wide, with a warm salad of pheasant with honey-soused vegetables, or mussels baked with Gruyère and breadcrumbs preceding main courses of Tuscan-style calf's liver with watercress mash, honey-roast duck hotpot with root vegetables, or beef and horseradish pie. Puddings maintain interest with the likes of iced tiramisù, or apple and raisin crumble with custard. The wine list peps up a classic French selection with some well-chosen New World bottles. Prices are reasonable, starting at £12.50, and the tasting notes offer good guidance as to style. Six wines are sold by the glass. SAMPLE DISHES: chargrilled squid with panzanella salad and aubergine £7.50; cumin-roast loin of lamb with sautéed sweet potato and aubergine confit £17; banana bread-and-butter pudding with sticky toffee sauce £5.50.

Licensees Lynne Strafford Bryan and Salvatore Inguanta (freehouse)
Open 12 to 3, 6 to 11, Sun 12 to 3, 6.30 to 10.30; bar food 12 to 2, 6 to 10 (6.30 to 9 Sun); restaurant 12 to 1.30, 6 to 10; closed evening 25 Dec
Details Children welcome in family room and restaurant Car park Wheelchair access (also WC) Garden No smoking in snug and restaurant No music No dogs Amex, MasterCard, Switch, Visa Accommodation: 2 rooms, B&B £35 to £65

COLTISHALL Norfolk map 6

▲ King's Head NEW ENTRY
26 Wroxham Road, Coltishall NR12 7EA TEL: (01603) 737426

Back in the seventeenth century the customers must have been wherrymen (the white van-drivers of their day) on the River Bure, which dawdles past just yards from this cream-painted pub. Nowadays Broads tourists sail the river, but it's still relaxing to watch them over the rim of a glass of Adnams Bitter or Marston's Pedigree. These one orders from the counter in the corner of the rectangular bar, with its large polished wood tables (and monster pike, safely in a glass case), while scanning the dishes on the blackboard above the fire-place. The bar menu deals in dishes like sausage and mash, smoked salmon on tagliatelle with wine and cream sauce, or Thai green chicken curry. An à la carte menu available both in the bar evenings and in the non-smoking restaurant offers, say, a 'thick, creamy and delicious' vegetable soup, fried herring roes, or ravioli of rabbit with wild mushrooms. Main courses include saddle of venison, or skate wing and chorizo with butter beans (plus, of course, Sunday lunch roasts). Finish with peach clafoutis and double peach ice cream, or orange and Cointreau sponge with Cointreau custard. A diverse (illustrated) wine list provides eight by the glass and a sprinkling of half-bottles. SAMPLE DISHES: fried duck livers and bacon £5.25; fried lemon sole, chips and tartare sauce £7; vanilla crème brûlée £4.25.

Licensee Kevin Gardner (freehouse)
Open 11 to 3, 6 to 11, Sun 12 to 10.30; bar food Mon to Sat 12 to 2, Sun to Thur 6 to 7; restaurant all week 7 to 9
Details Children welcome in bar eating area Car park Patio No smoking in dining room Background music No dogs Delta, MasterCard, Switch, Visa Accommodation: 4 rooms, B&B £25 to £55

▲ Wyvill Arms   NEW ENTRY

Constable Burton DL8 5LH   TEL: (01677) 450581
on A684, 3½m E of Leyburn

Close to the famous gardens of Constable Burton Hall, this large ivy-clad roadside inn has its own attractive gardens, lovingly restored from their sorry state when the current owners took over in 1999. They have also done a good job on the seventeenth-century building, restoring the large main bar to a smart if somewhat old-fashioned style with old photos and watercolours covering the walls, and an attractively rustic-looking stone fireplace. Landlord Nigel Stevens is a friendly presence in the bar, and seriously enthusiastic about his food: one visitor arriving at lunchtime had a bowl containing chunks of freshly roast suckling pig waved under his nose with the entreaty, 'Here, try some of this, it's wonderful' – it was, too! Menus offer huge choice, with 'old favourites' like steak and onion pie, or lasagne, as well as more sophisticated main courses such as roast duck with mash, roasted shallots, cranberry compote and Drambuie sauce, or pan-fried sea bream with creamy vanilla butter and mussel sauce. The short bar lunch menu is a little out of the ordinary; smoked salmon and scrambled eggs is a popular option. To drink, there are Theakston Best, John Smith's and Black Sheep Bitter, and up to a dozen wines by the glass from the diverse list of forty-odd bins. SAMPLE DISHES: roast mussels in lemon and ginger sauce with scallop ravioli £5.75; pan-fried salmon with spinach and tarragon butter sauce £9.95; bread-and-butter pudding £3.95.

Licensee Nigel Stevens (freehouse)
Open 11.30 to 3, 6 to 11, Sun 12 to 3, 7 to 10.30; bar food and restaurant 12 to 2 (2.30 summer), 6.30 to 9
Details Children welcome   Car park   Wheelchair access (also WC)   Garden and patio
No smoking in dining room   Occasional live or background music; jukebox   Dogs on leads welcome in bar only   Amex, Delta, MasterCard, Switch, Visa   Accommodation: 4 rooms, B&B £34 to £56

▲ Trengilly Wartha Inn 🍷 🍇

Nancenoy, Constantine TR11 5RP   TEL: (01326) 340332
WEBSITE: www.trengilly.co.uk
off A394 Falmouth to Helston road, between Constantine and Gweek

In a small hamlet in an Area of Outstanding Natural Beauty, the Trengilly Wartha is approached via a very minor road on a steep hill. But despite its remote location, the car park may well be full to overflowing. Inside are pubby bars with settles in seating stalls and old beams lined with beer mats, plus a separate restaurant. Even in the bar, the choice on the menu is wide. Care is taken in the preparation and execution of such dishes as local feta cheese in a salad with beans and cherry tomatoes, or leek and cheese soufflé, and, from among the specials, ham hock slowly braised with a stout and honey glaze, or roast pork loin with an apricot, mustard and cider sauce. Fish might include monkfish fillet in a tomato and basil sauce, or fillet of salmon with herb butter, and gratin of butternut squash with tomatoes and goats' cheese may be among vegetarian choices. Highly rated ploughman's and local smoked ham are available at lunchtimes, served with home-made chutneys (some on sale) and bread. The restaurant menu offers such treats as seared local scallops served on ratatouille, followed by roast loin of Cornish venison on a celeriac potato cake layered with a walnut stuffing with redcurrant sauce. Well-kept ales from the cask include Sharp's Cornish Coaster and others from Skinner and Cotleigh. There are 50 malt whiskies and authentic flavoured Cornish meads, and the wine list, running to around 220 bottles and with a selection of up to 20 available by the glass (two sizes), is highly individual. How many other pubs offer a glass of Austrian Pinot Blanc at the bar? Bottle prices are very good value and all the wines are also available at retail price from the pub's own wine business, Cochonnet Wines. SAMPLE DISHES: mackerel and cheese pot with toast £5; grilled sea bass fillets with pistachio butter £15.25; chocolate and Cointreau crème brûlée £3.50.

Licensees Michael Maguire and Nigel Logan (freehouse)
Open 11 to 3, 6.30 to 11, Sun 11 to 3, 7 to 10.30; bar food 12 to 2.15 (2 Sun), 6.30 (7 Sun) to 9.30; restaurant 7.30 to 9.30; no food served 25 Dec, restaurant closed 31 Dec
Details Children welcome   Car park   Garden   No-smoking area in bar, no smoking in dining room   Occasional background music   Dogs welcome exc in dining room   Amex, Delta, Diners, MasterCard, Switch, Visa   Accommodation: 8 rooms, B&B £48 to £95

CORNWORTHY   Devon   map I

Hunters Lodge Inn   NEW ENTRY

Cornworthy TQ9 7ES   TEL: (01803) 732204
WEBSITE: www.hunterslodgeinn.com
follow signs for Cornworthy from A381 about 4m S of Totnes

'Very much at the centre of village life', the Hunters Lodge is a friendly, welcoming and unpretentious freehouse where one might well rub shoulders with the church bell-ringers 'enjoying their regular pint and chips after the weekly practice', while enjoying fresh, locally sourced food cooked to order. Beamed ceilings, a log fire, old village photographs and dark-wood furniture create a cosy, traditional atmosphere. The inn specialises in fish and shellfish (from the market at Plymouth), and a blackboard displays the day's offerings, from scallops, or king prawns (in garlic butter or Thai sauce) to pan-fried whole sea bass, or seared salmon in citrus sauce. The printed menu rolls out favourites like Totnes sausages with mash and gravy, steak and kidney pie, and more racy Moroccan-style lamb casserole. Comfort puddings hit the apple and blackberry crumble and chocolate torte trail, and there's a separate children's menu too. Local Teignworthy Reel Ale is the regular on handpump along with a couple of guests, while a global list of over 50 wines (14 by the glass), plus old country wines and more than 40 malt whiskies, provide substantial alternatives. SAMPLE DISHES: smoked salmon and prawn parcels £5.25; monkfish and scallops in Thai sauce £14; bread-and-butter pudding £3.50.

Licensees Roger and Elizabeth Little (freehouse)
Open 11 to 2.30, 6.30 to 11, Sun 12 to 3, 7 to 10.30; bar food 12 to 2, 6.45 to 9
Details Children welcome Car park Wheelchair access (not WC) Garden and patio
No smoking in eating area Live or background music Dogs welcome Delta, MasterCard, Switch,
Visa

CORSCOMBE Dorset   map 2

▲ Fox Inn ☺ ❦

Corscombe DT2 0NS TEL: (01935) 891330   **FISH**
WEBSITE: www.fox-inn.co.uk
off A356, 6m SE of Crewkerne

In an isolated spot, on a junction of two narrow, winding roads and with a
brook close by, the Fox is a long, custard-coloured stone building with a
thatched roof, its façade graced by a shrub border and climbing plants. The
traditional interior has stone floors, pine furniture, beams a-plenty and
blue-check tablecloths, plus assorted country prints, some stuffed owls, and,
unsurprisingly, a fox's head. New owners in the summer of 2003 have kept
things very much the same, and chef George Marsh remains in the kitchen,
joined by Sue Wheeler. The 'little bar', the stables, the conservatory and country kitchen dining room offer a choice of settings for diners, who can also eat
in the bar. Here the restaurant's long menu is supplemented by blackboards
listing daily specials, with fish a mainstay: halibut, prawn and sweetcorn
chowder makes an unusual starter, and to follow there may be 'beautifully
timed' pan-seared fillet of salmon with creamed spinach, sea bass roasted with
rosemary and sea salt, or monkfish tandoori with raita. But meat eaters are not
neglected: witness warm salad of pigeon breast with bacon, and main course of
fillet of local venison with celeriac purée and a rich game sauce. More homely,
and sometimes classic, influences appear in mushroom risotto with Parmesan,
grilled plaice with parsley butter, and loin of lamb with rosemary gravy and
mustard mash, with perhaps bread-and-butter pudding or a fruit crumble to
finish. Exmoor Ale, Fuller's London Pride and Stowford Press cider are regularly served, and the carefully chosen wine list offers something from nearly
everywhere at very reasonable prices. A separate fine wine listing includes
some New World goodies (also modestly priced), and there's a decent number
of half-bottles plus five house wines by the glass. Tasting notes are helpful aids
to choice. SAMPLE DISHES: smoked salmon salad with garlic and anchovy
mayonnaise £7; whole roast sea bream with sweet potato mash and teriyaki
and sesame-seed dressing £17; lemon crème brûlée £3.50.

Licensees Clive Webb and Margaret Hannell (freehouse)
Open 12 to 3, 7 to 11, Sun 12 to 4, 7 to 10.30; bar food and restaurant 12 to 2, 7 to 9 (9.30 Fri
and Sat)
Details Children welcome Car park Wheelchair access (not WC) Garden No smoking in
restaurant Occasional live music No dogs Amex, Delta, MasterCard, Switch, Visa
Accommodation: 4 rooms, B&B £55 to £100

Cross Keys ✿   NEW ENTRY

Lyes Green, Corsley BA12 7PB   TEL: (01373) 832406
take right turn at Chapmanslade off A3098 from Frome

When Devizes brewery Wadworth took over the Cross Keys in the spring of
2001 it was not known as a food venue. The crowds that now regularly fill the
place are testament to the success of the complete transformation wrought by
tenants Frank and Kate Green – the pub now sports a contemporary-looking
dining area, decorated in warm colours and with fat candles on bare wooden
tables. Frank's past experience working at *The Good Food Guide*-listed Old
Vicarage in Worfield shows in a stylish monthly-changing menu: spiced
pumpkin and coriander soup, pan-fried chicken livers with black pudding and
bacon, or a salad of seared smoked salmon with 'meltingly luscious' scallops
and basil dressing to start, followed by main courses such as roast monkfish
with a potato and pea fritter and fish gravy, or honey-roast breast of duck with
Thai-spiced butternut squash and a 'smooth, warm and absolutely delicious'
oriental sauce. The results on the plate more than live up to expectations –
first-class ingredients, properly made sauces and plenty of technical skill are all
apparent. But though the food is undoubtedly the star attraction, there is no
danger of this place losing its identity as a pub – drinkers will appreciate the
separate quarry-tiled bar where a real log fire provides warmth, traditional pub
games such as bar billiards, cribbage and skittles are played, and live jazz is a
regular fixture. They will also enjoy the Wadworth 6X and IPA that are served
along with seasonal brews and a regularly changing guest ale. Six wines from
the short list are available by the glass and prices are very reasonable. SAMPLE
DISHES: duck leg confit with butter-bean purée and sage gravy £6; lamb leg
steak with roast root vegetables and pearl barley broth £12.50; glazed rice
pudding with spiced apricot compote £4.50.

Licensee Francis James Green (Wadworth)
Open *12 to 3, 6.30 to 11, Sun 12 to 4, 7 to 10.30; bar food and restaurant (exc Sun evening)
12 to 2.30, 7 to 9.30; closed evening 25 Dec and 26 Dec*
Details *Children welcome   Car park   Garden   No smoking in 1 room   Live or background music
Dogs welcome in bar   Amex, Delta, Diners, MasterCard, Switch, Visa*

▲ Dove Inn 🍺

Corton BA12 0SZ   TEL: (01985) 850109
WEBSITE: www.thedove.co.uk
off A36, 5m from Warminster

Tucked away among lovely countryside in the Wylye Valley, this pretty,
much-extended dining pub is well worth seeking out. Dating from the mid-
nineteenth century, the inn is attractively set in a secluded courtyard in a small
village. Inside, the atmosphere is unpretentious and welcoming, with the
balance of old (exposed-brick walls, flagstone floors) and new (spotlights,
laminate flooring) well judged. Beer drinkers appreciate the decent selection

of real ales that might include Butcombe Bitter, Fuller's London Pride and GFB from the local Hop Back Brewery, while the menus manage to combine the traditional with the more exotic. Starters might take in prawn cocktail, as well as Chinese-style crispy duck with hoisin sauce, and main courses might run to calf's liver with roasted shallots and a light red wine jus, and half a char-grilled corn-fed chicken marinated in olive oil, garlic and herbs in a smoky barbecue sauce. Steaks with a choice of sauces are other possibilities, and for vegetarians there could be spinach, mushroom, onion and herb pancakes in a rich cream sauce. Around ten wines are available by the glass. SAMPLE DISHES: chicken liver and foie gras parfait laced with cognac £6.25; beef stroganoff with rice £14.75; cheese and biscuits £4.75.

Licensee William Harrison-Allan (freehouse)
Open 12 to 3, 6.30 to 11, Sun 12 to 4, 7 to 10.30; bar food and restaurant 12 to 2.30, 7 to 9.30 (9 Sun); closed evening 25 Dec
Details Children welcome Car park Wheelchair access (also WC) Garden No smoking in conservatory Occasional background music Dogs welcome exc in restaurant Delta, MasterCard, Switch, Visa Accommodation: 5 rooms, B&B £49.50 to £90.

COTHERSTONE   Co Durham   map 10

▲ Fox & Hounds   NEW ENTRY

Cotherstone DL12 9PF   TEL: (01833) 650241
on B6277, 3m NW of Barnard Castle

Fantastic views over the Pennines make nearby Percymire Rock a popular spot with walkers. They will also find this comfortable village local a welcoming venue, as will anyone else who appreciates decent beers and tasty food. The white-painted slate-roofed building by the sloping green is run by an amiable young landlord. Sketches of wild animals on the walls, old kettles in recesses in the thick stone walls and stone bottles on the floor provide a decorative theme in the 'comfortable, easy-going' main bar. Blackboard lunch menus offer a limited but varied selection of straightforward dishes made largely with local produce: Wensleydale cheese and hazelnut pâté with crusty bread, hot sirloin steak sandwich with onion relish, or the 'fox lair salad' comprising prawns, chicken and Cotherstone cheese with new potatoes, for example. Evening menus are a little more elaborate, ranging from roast rack of Teesdale lamb with cranberry, port and orange to baked cod provençale. Beers from Hambleton brewery are offered alongside Black Sheep Best Bitter, and there is a list of around two dozen wines, the majority under £15, with seven by the glass. SAMPLE DISHES: pan-fried scallops in lemon and parsley butter £5; pan-fried pork tenderloin in Marsala and mushroom cream £10; rich fruitcake with Cotherstone cheese £3.50.

Licensees Ian and Nichola Swinburn (freehouse)
Open 12 to 2 (2.30 summer), 7 to 11 (10.30 Sun); bar food and restaurant 12 to 2, 7 to 9 (9.30 Fri and Sat summer); closed 25 and 26 Dec
Details Children welcome in family room and restaurant Car park Wheelchair access (also WC) Patio No smoking in restaurant No music Guide dogs only Delta, MasterCard, Switch, Visa Accommodation: 3 rooms, B&B £42.50 to £65

COTTESMORE   **Rutland**   map 6

Sun Inn   NEW ENTRY

25 Main Street, Cottesmore LE15 7DH   TEL: (01572) 812321
on B668, 4m NE of Oakham

In the centre of the village, but set well back from the road running through, this white-painted and thatched seventeenth-century pub is an attractive building, complete with hanging baskets and an old yew. Within are beamed low ceilings, country-style furniture, open fires and an abundance of china suns. The kitchen takes a global approach to its cooking, turning out baked piri-piri cod steak in mushroom cream sauce, and spicy Caribbean-style chicken breast with rice. From closer to home comes farmhouse duck and pork terrine with preserved fruits, followed by 'excellent' pink and tender seared wood pigeon breasts with smoked ham and celery on a rich, dark and 'fabulous' apricot and port jus, with that quintessentially British dessert – bread-and-butter pudding – to finish. On draught are Adnams Bitter, Everards Tiger Best and Marston's Pedigree, and a couple of wines are sold by the glass, the full list running to 14 bottles starting at £9.50. SAMPLE DISHES: king prawns in garlic and lemon butter £5.75; roast duck breast with a fig and Grand Marnier sauce £10.50; sticky toffee pudding with Marsala cream £3.50.

Licensee David Johnson (Everards)
Open *Tue to Sat 11.30 to 2.30, 6.30 to 11, Sun 12 to 3, 7 to 10.30; bar food and restaurant Tue to Sun 12 (12.30 Sun) to 2, Tue to Sat 7 to 9*
Details *No children   Car park   Garden and patio   No smoking in restaurant   Background music Dogs welcome   Delta, MasterCard, Switch, Visa*

COWDEN   **Kent**   map 3

Fountain Inn   NEW ENTRY

Cowden TN8 7JG   TEL: (01342) 850528
from A264 take B2026 towards Edenbridge; Cowden is first left

An unpretentious, part-red-brick, part-tile-hung country local at the heart of the picture-postcard village of Cowden, the Fountain still retains its separate entrance doors to public and lounge bars. The former is heavy with dark beams and the flicker of a fruit machine, while the lounge has just four veneered tables accompanied by wooden chairs and a busy red carpet. What it may lack in modern-day refinement it certainly makes up for in genuine, workaday friendliness. Food reflects the atmosphere, with uncomplicated, honest dishes and ambition that's sensibly limited. While the compact hand-written menu could feature chargrilled ribeye steak with rocket mash, or local sausages with cheesy mash and onion gravy, small blackboards list lighter offerings such as sautéed mushrooms on toast as well as such main courses as monkfish and smoked bacon salad with sweet balsamic dressing. Drinkers are catered for with Harveys Sussex Pale and Best, plus a guest beer per month, while the ten-strong wine list features two wines of the month by the glass. SAMPLE DISHES: smoked salmon salad with salsa verde £6; fillet of beef with crushed new potatoes and a balsamic and smoked bacon jus £15; lemon tart £4.50.

Licensees John and Maria E'Vanson (Harveys)
Open *11.30 to 3, 6 to 11.30, Sun 12 to 10.30; bar food Tue to Sun 11.30 to 3, Tue to Sat 6 to 11.30*
Details *Children welcome   Car park   Garden   Background and occasional live music   Dogs welcome   Delta, MasterCard, Switch, Visa*

COXWOLD   North Yorkshire   **map 9**

▲ Fauconberg Arms

Coxwold YO61 4AD   TEL: (01347) 868214
WEBSITE: www.fauconbergarms.co.uk
off A19 7m S of Thirsk; pub on main street in middle of village

Built of local stone, the Fauconberg Arms is halfway up the broad main street of this attractive, sprawling, rural village. The interior is dominated, in season, by an enormous wood-burning fire, around which is a collection of brass, and oak furniture, of various ages, stands on part-flagstoned floors under the beamed ceiling. The bar offers luxurious sandwiches and baguettes at lunchtimes; otherwise there might be potted Whitby crab, or smoked salmon and prawn mousse, followed by braised lamb shank with parsnip mash and rosemary gravy, or chicken breast with mushroom and sherry sauce. The restaurant, with a large oak dresser, runs from the front to the back of the building. The menu in here (also available in the bar) deals in the likes of foie gras and leek terrine with beetroot jelly, or a salad of seared smoked scallops, and main courses of roast duck breast with Lindisfarne mead jus, and monkfish with crispy pancetta and tomato dressing. Potted cheese with home-made chutney and oatcakes is an alternative to desserts of hot chocolate fondant, or brandied peach cobbler with custard. Sunday lunch brings on traditional roasts with all the trimmings. Guest ales from Black Sheep, Cropton and Daleside make an appearance, mainly in summer, alongside regular John Smith's Bitter and Theakston Best Bitter. Four wines are sold by the glass. SAMPLE DISHES: smoked chicken with curried mayonnaise and melon £5; roast fillet of pork on mustard mash with a red wine jus £9.50; chocolate and orange parfait £4.50.

Licensee Julie Gough (freehouse)
Open *11 to 3 (2.30 winter), 6 (6.30 winter) to 11, Sun 12 to 3, 7 to 10.30; bar food 12 to 2.30, 6.30 to 8.30, restaurant Wed to Sat 7 to 9.30, Sun 12 to 2.30*
Details *Children welcome   Car park   Patio   No smoking in restaurant   Background music   Dogs welcome exc in restaurant   MasterCard, Switch, Visa   Accommodation: 4 rooms, B&B £35 to £60*

Red Cat 🍇   [NEW ENTRY]

8 Red Cat Lane, Crank WA11 8RU   TEL: (01744) 882422
follows signs for Crank from junction of A580 and A570

From the patio of this late-Victorian pub there are views across cornfields and
acres of cabbages and sprouts to nearby Billinge Hill – the highest point in
Merseyside. Leaded windows are the order of the day, and much of the interior still has the feel of a dyed-in-the-wool village boozer, although the
kitchen is clearly in tune with today's trends. Bypass the standard bar menu
and go straight to the lengthy specials board, where ambitious modern dishes,
such as oyster fritters with chilli and sesame oil, or Goosnargh chicken with
Spanish black pudding, girolles and white wine jus, are the order of the day.
Both fish and seasonal game have pleased reporters, whether it be seared king
scallops with Parma ham and rocket dressing, or wood pigeon on a bed of
parsnip purée with a porcini and red wine sauce. Theakston Best Bitter, Old
Speckled Hen and Timothy Taylor Landlord are on draught, but the real star
of the drinks show is the wine list. The tempting 'house' list of two dozen
bottles, accompanied by blackboards of bin-ends and specials (including a
good clutch of half-bottles), will keep the majority of wine drinkers more than
happy. But that's just the start: the full slate is a monumental tome running to
some 500 bins with a strong contingent of Bordeaux and Burgundies and
some top Italian and Californian names. Prices are very good value whether
you are in the market for a fruity Chilean Chardonnay for less than a tenner or
some very serious mature claret. SAMPLE DISHES: salmon and parsley fishcakes
with tartare sauce £5; roast suckling pig with apple, sage and onion sauce £11;
banana filo parcel with banana ice cream and Galliano sauce £4.

Licensee Ian Martin (Pubmaster)
Open *12 to 11, Sun 12 to 10.30; bar food and restaurant Wed to Sat 12 to 2, 6 to 9.30, Sun 12
to 8*
Details *Children welcome   Car park   Wheelchair access (also WC)   Patio   No smoking in
restaurant   Occasional background music   Guide dogs only   Delta, MasterCard, Switch, Visa*

▲ Durham Ox 😋   [NEW ENTRY]

Westway, Crayke YO61 4TE   TEL: (01347) 821506
WEBSITE: www.thedurhamox.com
off A19, 2m from Easingwold

In a small, quiet village with views over the Vale of York, the Ox is a plain-looking building from the front, blending in with the houses around it. Inside,
however, it looks very smart. The bar is divided into two areas, one smaller
room with traditional pub furniture, bare floorboards and a log fire, the other
much larger with flagstone flooring, a huge inglenook at one end and tables laid
for dining; walls throughout are painted terracotta and sea green, and the overall effect is modern and stylish. Also making a favourable impact are the menus
– this is definitely not typical pub grub, but upmarket modern country cook-

ing: for example, roast breast of duck with butternut squash and spinach, fondant potato and honey and sesame sauce, roast rump of lamb with a ragoût of vegetables and roast garlic sauce, or baked queenie scallops in garlic butter with Gruyère and aged Cheddar. If you visit at lunchtime, there are also sandwiches with fillings like BLT, or Brie, bacon, lettuce and tomato, on ciabatta or baguette, served with chips, coleslaw and salad. A decent selection of real ales includes Wells Bombardier and Theakston Old Peculier, and the wine list is good but prices are high for the quality. However, nine wines under £15 (also available by the glass) make a reasonable enough spread of budget options. SAMPLE DISHES: pan-seared baby squid with Thai spices and dipping sauce £5.25; roast pork loin with crispy crackling stuffed with apricots and whisky marmalade £13; banana fritters with vanilla ice cream and toffee sauce £6.

Licensee Michael Ibbotson (freehouse)
Open 12 to 3, 6 to 11.30, Sun 12 to 10.30; bar food and restaurant 12 to 2.30 (3 Sun), 6 to 9.30 (8.30 Sun); closed 25 Dec
Details Children welcome in bar eating area before 9pm   Car park   Wheelchair access (not WC) Garden and patio   No smoking in restaurant   Occasional live music   No dogs   Amex, Delta, MasterCard, Switch, Visa   Accommodation: 8 rooms, B&B £60 to £160

CRAZIES HILL   Berkshire   map 3

Horns

Crazies Hill RG10 8LY   TEL: (01189) 401416
off A4 at Kiln Green, 3m N of Twyford

A brick and timber building, the Horns was a hunting lodge in Tudor times. The cosy, low-ceilinged bar leads to an eighteenth-century barn, now the restaurant, with scrubbed pine tables and chairs on its quarry-tiled floor. Dried flowers hang from the beams, and eponymous stags' horns are mounted on the walls. On the menu is a wide selection of first and main courses, ranging from soup, such as pea and ham, and a warm salad of Stilton, bacon, avocado and mushrooms, to pan-fried calf's liver with black pudding and red wine gravy, and slow-roast shoulder of lamb with mint and basil gravy. Fresh fish is a strength too – perhaps rosemary-stuffed whole sea bass with tomato and ginger sauce, or smoked haddock on a bed of spinach with a lightly poached egg – while desserts are of the old school: bread-and-butter pudding, treacle tart, or chocolate mousse with Cointreau. Beers are from Brakspear, and eight wines are sold by the glass from a short but varied list. SAMPLE DISHES: asparagus and lemon soup £4.25; chicken breast wrapped in smoked bacon with blue cheese sauce £12; apple and cinnamon pie £4.25.

Licensee Andy Hearn (Brakspear)
Open Mon to Fri 11.30 to 2.30, 6 to 11, Sat 11.30 to 3, 6 to 11, Sun 12 to 5; bar food and restaurant Mon to Sat 12 to 2 (2.30 Sat), 7 to 9.30, Sun 12 to 4; closed 25 Dec
Details Children welcome in family room and eating areas lunchtime only   Car park   Wheelchair access (also WC)   Garden   No smoking in restaurant   No music   Dogs welcome on a lead in bar area   Delta, MasterCard, Switch, Visa

CRONDALL　Hampshire　　　　　　　　　　map 3

Hampshire Arms ❀ ⎸NEW ENTRY⎸

Pankridge Street, Crondall GU10 5QU　TEL: (01252) 850418
WEBSITE: www.thehampshirearms.co.uk
*from M3 junction 5 take A287 towards Farnham; turn left opposite petrol station and continue
approx 3m*

This 250-year-old white-painted building with picnic tables outside doesn't
look anything out of the ordinary, but this is a pub with ambition. The main
bar area has a traditional look, with dark hop-garlanded beams, log fires and
candles and green linen napkins on tables, while the dining room to the rear is
a little more dressed up. Printed menus and daily blackboard specials make a
sophisticated impression, which is not dispelled when the food arrives.
Striking presentation of dishes illustrates the level of ambition, and there is
often a lot happening on the plate: take, for example, monkfish poached in
saffron sauce and served on a coconut and lemongrass risotto with lightly
curried prawn sauce, or poached chicken on open ravioli of baby leek, asparagus and mushroom in leek velouté. Lunch is simpler (and less expensive),
with blackboard menus offering the likes of soups, steak and kidney pie, and
liver and bacon. This is a Greene King pub, so expect Abbot Ale and IPA, plus
a guest beer. The wide-ranging international wine list has good choice in the
£10 to £15 bracket but nothing cheaper, though there are up to a dozen wines
by the glass. SAMPLE DISHES: wild mushroom gâteau with crispy bacon dressing £5.75; loin of pork on apple and sage tarte Tatin with Stilton mash,
caraway-scented cabbage and cider sauce £16.25; sticky date pudding with
hazelnut and white chocolate ice cream and toffee sauce £5.25.

Licensee Paul Morgan (Greene King)
Open *Mon to Fri 11 to 3.30, 5.30 to 11, Sat 11 to 11, Sun 12 to 10.30; bar food and restaurant
Tue to Sun 12 to 2 (3.30 Sun), Mon to Sat 6.30 to 9*
Details *Children welcome　Car park　Wheelchair access (also WC)　Garden and patio
No smoking in dining room　Occasional live or background music　Dogs welcome but only guide dogs
in dining room　Delta, MasterCard, Switch, Visa*

CROSLAND HILL　West Yorkshire　　　　　　　map 8

Sands House

Blackmoorfoot Road, Crosland Hill HD4 7AE　TEL: (01484) 654478
off A62, 2m SW of Huddersfield town centre

It's a busy place, filled with drinkers in the bar and relaxed parties of every sort
in the animated dining areas. The keynote is robust, hearty food, but that
doesn't exclude some imaginative touches on the menu. Start perhaps with
potted cheese rolled in walnuts, or chilli meatballs with tomato and garlic
sauce, and continue with gammon steak, venison medallions on caramelised
onions with blue cheese butter, or a vegetarian dish such as oriental spring roll
with black-bean sauce. Those with old-fashioned Yorkshire appetites may be
able to cope with rice pudding, or chocolate and orange tart. It's a pleasant
place, and not quite what might be expected on the outskirts of Huddersfield,

where town and moorland meet. The pub is owned by the Unique Pub Company, a name to some extent justified by the collection of clocks inside, and veteran traffic lights, telephone boxes and the like in the children's play area outside. Old Speckled Hen, Boddingtons Bitter, John Smith's, Tetley Bitter and a guest ale are all available. SAMPLE DISHES: 'Po Boy' sandwich (hot beef, fried onions and American mustard on French bread) £2.50; sea bass on salad with sweet pepper salsa £7.25; lemon and walnut meringue £2.75.

Licensee Bob Buckley (Unique Pub Company)
Open Mon to Sat 11.30 to 11, Sun 12 to 10.30; bar food and restaurant 11.30 to 9.30
Details Children welcome in bar eating area   Car park   Garden   No smoking in dining room
Background music   No dogs   Amex, Delta, Diners, MasterCard, Switch, Visa

---

CROSTHWAITE   Cumbria   map 8

▲ Punch Bowl Inn ✿ ✿
Crosthwaite LA8 8HR   TEL: (015395) 68237
WEBSITE: www.punchbowl.fsnet.co.uk
off A5074, 3m S of Windermere

Despite the emphasis on food, this seventeenth-century inn, with its low ceilings, beams and log fires, remains a traditional pub at heart, serving, in an informal setting with lots of atmosphere, Coniston Bluebird Bitter and XB and Old Speckled Hen. Cooking, too, maintains the balance between the quality you would expect from a top chef (Steven Doherty was formerly head chef at London's Le Gavroche) and the lack of pretension you would hope for in a pub; excellent local ingredients also help. Lunchtime menus feature straightforward dishes such as pumpkin and fennel soup, followed by Toulouse sausage on mash with Puy lentils, with apple, cider and Calvados granita to finish. The style is equally down to earth on dinner menus, though wider influences appear along with occasional dishes from the classical French repertoire. Starters might be tuna niçoise, or baked goats' cheese on a filo base served with a salad of warm new potatoes, sweetcorn and green beans, while main courses run to rabbit confit with boned and rolled saddle in a wild mushroom and red wine sauce, or pan-fried fillet of sea bass on minted couscous and sweet pepper sauce. Puddings in the shape of sorbets, and poached fruits with lavender and honey ice cream come highly praised. With 20 wines by the glass to choose from on the succinct and imaginative wine list, with the same number by the litre and half-litre, diners will find ample choice for matching wine with food. Eating on the patio, with views over the Lyth Valley, is pleasant in warm weather. SAMPLE DISHES: pea and ham soup £2.75; roasted chump of Cumbrian lamb sliced on mustard mash with red wine and thyme sauce £14; mango and raspberry sorbet £4.

Licensee Marjorie Doherty (freehouse)
Open 11 to 11, Sun 12 to 10.30; bar food and restaurant 12 to 2, 6 to 9; no food Sun evening;
closed Mon (exc bank hol Mon lunchtime), 1 week Nov, 1 week Dec, 1 week Jan, 1 week June
Details Children welcome   Car park   Patio   No smoking in restaurant   No music   Guide dogs
only   MasterCard, Switch, Visa   Accommodation: 3 rooms, B&B £37.50 to £60

CROUCH   Kent   map 3

Chequers Inn   NEW ENTRY

Basted Lane, Crouch TN15 8PZ   TEL: (01732) 884829
1m S of A25 at Borough Green

Crouch is a 'delightful' hamlet surrounded by undulating hills populated by
grazing sheep, orchards and oast houses. At its centre is the Chequers, a
conventional-looking pub from the outside, with an internal décor of lime-
coloured walls, a light wooden floor and 3-D paintings. Bar food has forthright appeal: steak sandwich, penne with chorizo and spicy tomato sauce, and
moules marinière plus various hot or cold sandwiches, a selection of salads,
and for dessert there might be Grand Marnier crème brûlée. Restaurant
menus are more elaborate: pan-fried scallops with rocket, crème fraîche and
sweet chilli sauce among starters, with perhaps spiced monkfish tails with sag
aloo and pakora broccoli, and apple and coriander relish among main courses.
Harveys Sussex Best Bitter is the one real ale on offer, and a handful of wines
is served by the large or small glass, with the full list running to around 30
reasonably priced bottles; house wines are £9.95 and £11.50. Note that bar
food may not be available on Friday and Saturday evenings. SAMPLE DISHES:
Greek salad £5.50; bangers and mash £8; banoffi pie £4.25.

Licensees Nicola and Damian Kay (freehouse)
Open *Tue to Sun 12 to 3 (4 Sun), Tue to Sat 6.30 to 11; bar food and restaurant Tue to Sun 12 to
2.30, Tue to Sat 6.30 to 9*
Details *Children welcome   Car park   Wheelchair access (not WC)   Garden and patio
Background music   Dogs welcome exc in restaurant   MasterCard, Switch, Visa*

CUDDINGTON   Buckinghamshire   map 2

Crown

Aylesbury Road, Cuddington HP18 0BB   TEL: (01844) 292222
WEBSITE: www.thecrowncuddington.co.uk
off A418, 4½m W of Aylesbury

This thatched and whitewashed pub sits on a corner site in a picturesque
village just off the Aylesbury to Oxford road. The front of the building houses
the clearly popular bar area, where (this being a Fuller's house) there is
London Pride on draught alongside the brewery's seasonal Summer Ale or
Jack Frost, plus guests such as Adnams Bitter. Three interconnecting dining
rooms behind have tiled or wooden floors, mirrors and prints on the walls,
and candles and low-level lighting that creates an intimate atmosphere. The
printed menu is supplemented by a blackboard listing all the puddings and
offering daily specials (a couple of starters and a couple of main dishes). You
could start with a fishcake with smoked paprika aïoli, or a field mushroom and
spinach risotto, then plump for chicken breast in Thai broth with noodles and
oriental vegetables, or (if you don't fancy beef, Guinness and mushroom
casserole) smoked haddock with a Welsh rarebit topping and tomato and basil
salad. The wine list of 20-odd bottles from £11 to £30 includes seven sold by

the glass. SAMPLE DISHES: black pudding with sweet red cabbage £5.50; pavé of salmon on tagliatelle with red pepper coulis and basil £11.50; rhubarb crumble £4.50.

Licensee David Berry (Fuller's)
Open 12 to 3, 6 to 11, Sun 12 to 3, 7 to 10.30; bar food and restaurant 12 to 2, 6.30 to 9.30, Sun 12 to 3, 6 to 10
Details Children welcome   Car park   Wheelchair access (also WC)   Garden and patio
No-smoking area in dining room   Background music   Guide dogs only   Delta, MasterCard, Switch, Visa

CULMSTOCK   Devon   map 2

▲ Culm Valley Inn   NEW ENTRY
Culmstock EX15 3JJ   TEL: (01884) 840354
about 2m off A38 W of Wellington

This traditional village freehouse on the edge of the Blackdown Hills, an Area of Outstanding Natural Beauty, not only serves honest, freshly cooked food but offers up to six real ales straight from the barrel and all 40-odd bottles on the wine list are available by the glass (from £2.50). Richard and Lucy Hartley bought the old pub in December 2001 and have set about revitalising it. Organic produce is used 'where and when it is practical', with much sourced locally: hand-dived scallops from Lyme Bay (served with a pomegranate and molasses dressing), Ladram Bay crab, and line-caught sea bass (perhaps cooked with rosemary and garlic). Despite a leaning towards seafood, carnivores are well catered for via game – perhaps venison with chestnuts and wild mushrooms – or Balinese-style free-range pork. Traditional desserts include home-made ice creams and could showcase apple, apricot and almond pudding, or treacle tart. Local breweries account for many of the real ales dispensed, among them Cotleigh, Otter, O'Hanlon's, Oakhill and Branscombe Vale. SAMPLE DISHES: chicken liver, brandy and mushroom parfait £5 to £9; fillet of brill with quince aïoli £12 to £16; chocolate and pecan tart £3.50.

Licensees Richard and Lucy Hartley (freehouse)
Open 12 to 3, 6 to 11, Sun 12 to 10.30; bar food and restaurant all week 12 to 2, Mon to Sat 7 to 9; closed 25 Dec; may open all day in good weather in summer
Details Children welcome   Car park   Wheelchair access (not WC)   Garden   Occasional live music
Dogs welcome   No cards   Accommodation: 3 rooms, B&B £30 to £65

DACRE BANKS   North Yorkshire   map 8

▲ Royal Oak   NEW ENTRY
Oak Lane, Dacre Banks HG3 4EN   TEL: (01423) 780200
WEBSITE: www.theroyaloak.uk.com
from B6165 Ripley to Pateley Bridge road, turn S on to B6165 at Summerbridge; pub is ½m on left

This creeper-covered three-storey inn has sat beside an oak by the village green since 1752. There's now a terrace and a pétanque piste in front, an old coach house (now restaurant) alongside, and another terrace and a small garden behind, with views across the Nidd towards Brimham Rocks. Inside, one bar serves several beamed rooms (one has a pool table, another a cheerful wood fire), dispensing 'very well-kept' beers from local brewers, such as Rudgate, Viking and Yorkshire Dales bitter, and Old Dacre Ale (specially brewed for the Royal Oak). Accompany these with sandwiches, hot filled baguettes or jacket potatoes; alternatively you can tackle a 'proper' meal – starting perhaps with 'thick, wholesome' pea and leek broth, fried Dover sole in lobster and brandy sauce, or pork, chilli and mint spring rolls with spicy Chinese dip. Upper Nidderdale is good sheep country, so roast rack of local lamb in a port and passion-fruit sauce should make a satisfying main dish, but there's plenty for fish-fanciers (black sea bream fillet, maybe, in a red pesto and prawn sauce), and vegetarians are not forgotten. Sweets, on a blackboard, might include treacle sponge, a pavlova, or home-made ice creams. Wines, mostly non-French and under £20, start with five house wines (also available by the glass) at £10. SAMPLE DISHES: black pudding in whole-grain mustard and whisky sauce £5; fried venison steak with wine, juniper and mushroom sauce £13; bread-and-butter pudding £3.50.

Licensee Stephen Cock (freehouse)
Open 11.30 to 3, 5 to 11, Sun 12 to 3, 7 to 10.30; bar food 12 to 2, 6.30 to 9, Sun 12 to 2.30, 7 to 9; closed 25 Dec
Details Children welcome in bar eating area   Car park   Wheelchair access (also WC)   Garden and patio   No-smoking area in bar, no smoking in dining room   Background music   Guide dogs only
Delta, MasterCard, Switch, Visa   Accommodation: 3 rooms, B&B £30 to £60

DARGATE   Kent   map 3

Dove ☺

Plum Pudding Lane, Dargate ME13 9HB   TEL: (01227) 751360
signposted off A299, 4m SW of Whitstable

Dargate is a pretty village quite handy for the A2 just west of Canterbury, and the Dove overlooks the junction at its centre. It is a solid-looking late-Victorian pub with window boxes at the front and a beer garden to the rear full of flowering shrubs. Inside, it is unfussy, with bare floorboards, stout wooden furniture, and photographs of Dargate past and present. This being a Shepherd Neame house, there's Master Brew on tap, and the wine list includes some eight by the glass. The food here has a slightly Jekyll and Hyde quality. The lunch menu goes in for classy snacks in the £5 to £7 bracket, like croque-monsieur, or salt-cod with chorizo and flageolets. In the evening, though, menu and prices move up a gear, though the surroundings do not change. Many lunchtime dishes figure among the starters, along with Puy lentil and confit duck soup or baked cep and Bayonne ham tart. Mains may include a roast fillet of wild sea bass on tapénade-flavoured new potatoes, or Scotch beef fillet with roast salsify and wild mushrooms. Puddings include orange and passion-fruit crème brûlée, baked chocolate pudding, and cherry clafoutis. SAMPLE DISHES: pan-fried crevettes with pickled ginger and herbs £7; whole grilled royal bream with shallot, tarragon and garlic dressing £14.75; apple and almond tart £4.75.

Licensees Nigel and Bridget Morris (Shepherd Neame)
Open Tue to Sat 11.30 to 3, 6 to 11.30, Sun 12 to 3, 7 to 11; bar food Tue to Sun 12 to 2, Wed
to Sat 7 to 9
Details *Children welcome   Car park   Garden and patio   No music   Dogs welcome   MasterCard,
Switch, Visa*

DIDMARTON   Gloucestershire   map 2

▲ Kings Arms Inn 🍺
The Street, Didmarton GL9 1DT   TEL: (01454) 238245
on A433 SW of Tetbury

On the edge of the Badminton Estate, this seventeenth-century Cotswolds
coaching inn has two bar areas, with a décor of green wood panelling, cream
walls, sporting prints and garlands of hops to go with the old beams and stone
fireplace. The inn is clearly a popular hub of local life, and the lovingly tended
garden, with lawns, dry-stone walls, apple trees, and a boules pitch, simply
adds to its attractions. The restaurant menu, also available in the bar, offers
varied and interesting choice, typically taking in smoked goose, roasted artichoke and celeriac salad, and smoked haddock, cod and chive fishcakes with a
warm tomato and basil dressing, followed by saddle of lamb stuffed with feta,
cashews and mint, and baked sea trout coated in fennel seeds, lemon and herbs
served with horseradish bubble and squeak. Game might include whole
braised partridge with bacon, red wine, baby onions and herbs, accompanied
by rösti, and a risotto of mushrooms, Gruyère and roasted garlic with parsnip
chips might be among vegetarian options. A blackboard of specials extends the
range even further, and baguettes are served in the bar. Though this is principally a dining pub, beers are a strong suit: four real ales are on offer at a time,
regular Uley and Badger Best Bitters being supplemented by fortnightly-
changing guests. No wine list was available to the Guide at the time of going to
press, but the pub tells us that seven wines come by the glass from a 50-strong
list, starting at £10.95 per bottle. SAMPLE DISHES: marinated spicy charred
squid with Thai salad and noodles £5.25; braised oxtail with root vegetables
and barley served with thyme dumplings £13; chocolate mousse with hazelnut
praline £4.50.

Licensees Nigel and Jane Worrall (freehouse)
Open 12 to 2.30, 6 to 11, Sun 12 to 2.30, 7 to 10.30; bar food and restaurant 12 to 2, 7 to 9.30;
open 11am to 1pm 25 Dec (no food)
Details *Children welcome in eating areas   Car park   Garden   No smoking in restaurant
Occasional live music   Dogs welcome on a lead in bar   Delta, MasterCard, Switch, Visa
Accommodation: 4 rooms, B&B £45 to £80*

---

*Licensing hours and bar food times are based on information supplied by each
establishment and are correct at the time of going to press. It is advisable to check
these, however, before making a lengthy journey as they are often subject to change,
especially in winter months.*

DODDISCOMBSLEIGH Devon map 1

▲ Nobody Inn 🌟 🍺 🍇

Doddiscombsleigh EX6 7PS TEL: (01647) 252394
WEBSITE: www.nobodyinn.co.uk
3m W of A38, Haldon Racecourse exit

'Good atmosphere and good service and beers' are just some of the draws at
this beautifully set inn which has its origins in the sixteenth century. The
operation embraces a serious wine business too, and the 800-strong list is
probably unrivalled by any other in the Guide. It is most definitely the best
value list, with very modest mark-ups on the retail prices to drink 'inn'.
Quality is high across the board and, if browsing through 70 pages of wines
seems overwhelming, a lucky dip should turn up something good – as should
the 20-odd wines offered by the glass. Some 240 whiskies of various descriptions are kept, too. Beer lovers will find fine cask-conditioned ales such as the
proprietary Nobody's Bitter from Branscombe Vale, and Doom Bar Bitter
from Sharp's in Cornwall; there's also Brimblecombe Farm cider. The place
itself is thatched, low, white and beamed, complete with dark interiors full of
'lots of quiet corners for romantic trysts'. Bar food takes in starters such as
Nobody soup, or duck liver pâté, and main courses of steak and kidney suet
pudding, or venison steak braised with red wine and rosemary, with sticky
toffee pudding providing a traditional finish – or opt for a selection of one of
the 40 local cheeses. Vegetarians are well treated with, perhaps, chard, spinach
and red Leicester tart with roasted tomatoes, and seafood aficionados might
choose creamy mussel and cider linguine. A separate restaurant menu (not
available in the bar) offers a few more elaborate dishes, such as quail stuffed
with rice and apricots and served with a fig and apricot sauce. SAMPLE DISHES:
spiced lamb meatballs with red and green pepper sauce £4; breast of chicken in
white wine and tarragon sauce £8; apricot sponge pudding £4.

Licensee Nick Borst-Smith (freehouse)
Open *12 to 2.30, 7 (6 summer) to 11, Sun 12 to 3, 7 to 10.30; bar food 12 to 2, 7 to 10;
restaurant Tue to Sat 7 to 9.30; closed 25, 26 and 31 Dec and 1 Jan*
Details *No children Car park Patio No smoking in restaurant No music Guide dogs only
Amex, Delta, MasterCard, Switch, Visa Accommodation: 7 rooms, B&B £23 to £70*

DOLTON Devon map 1

▲ Union Inn 🍺

Fore Street, Dolton EX19 8QH TEL: (01805) 804633
*from A377 Exeter to Barnstaple road going N, turn left on to A3124 towards Winkleigh; after
approx 5m turn sharply left on to B3217 signposted Dolton; inn on right just before village
centre*

Originally built as a Devon longhouse of traditional cob construction, the
Union became a hotel around 200 years ago and is now a popular dining pub.
The interior is as home from home as you could wish for, with a squashy old
chesterfield, cushioned window seats, oak settles and sturdy wooden tables.
An enterprising slate of real ales is on offer, such as two from St Austell (Hicks
Special Draught and Tribute), Sharp's Doom Bar Bitter, Clearwater Cavalier,

and Freebooter and Mainbrace from the Jollyboat Brewery in Bideford. Wine drinkers will be cheered by a succinct but very serviceable list that favours Australia and Chile, and includes four half-bottles plus five or six wines by the glass. Bar snacks (charged £1 extra if eaten in the restaurant) such as spinach and feta pie, beer-battered fish and chips, and local sausages served with bubble and squeak supplement an à la carte menu and blackboard specials. On the former is, among other things, a good choice of steaks and vegetarian dishes, while specials might offer yellow pea and ham soup, followed by noisettes of lamb with rowanberry and red wine sauce, or mixed grilled fish. One couple had special praise for half a lobster in Pernod and herbs, and Gressingham duck breast with spicy lentils. Desserts of raspberry and chocolate tart, summer pudding, and lemon filo tart have all had the thumbs up too. Readers who have stayed overnight at the pub have praised the comfort, good breakfasts and good value. SAMPLE DISHES: potato, tomato and lovage soup £2.50; leg of lamb pan-fried in rosemary and garlic £9; rum pot £3.25.

Licensee Ian Fisher (freehouse)
Open *Thur to Tue 12 to 2.30, 6 to 11, Sun 12 to 2.30, 7 to 10.30; bar food 12 to 2, 7 to 9, restaurant Mon to Sat 6 to 11, Sun 12 to 2.30; closed first 3 weeks Feb*
Details *Children welcome in eating areas   Car park   Wheelchair access (not WC)   Garden No smoking in restaurant   No music   Dogs welcome   Delta, MasterCard, Switch, Visa Accommodation: 3 rooms, B&B £50 to £65*

DOWNHAM   **Lancashire**   map 8

Assheton Arms
Downham BB7 4BJ   TEL: (01200) 441227
WEBSITE: www.assheton-arms.co.uk
3m NE of Clitheroe; turn off A59 for Chatburn, then follow sign to Downham

If Downham seems subliminally familiar, you could have seen it from your armchair; it's one of the villages where road signs and aerials are banned, and TV companies film 'Gad Sir' dramas with men in tight breeches and women with downcast eyes. Actually, it's more hamlet than village – not much more than church, pub, post office and phone box (they try to keep that out of shot!). The pub sits on a rise opposite the church. Outside are tables for summer drinking; inside is a rambling, low-ceilinged bar with horse brasses and copper pots on the walls, solid oak tables and wing-back settles. Boddingtons Bitter, Marston's Pedigree and Guinness are on the pumps (and they have Hoegaarden), while a cheap and cheerful list of some 20 tasty wines includes seven by the glass. A six-page menu (including sections on sandwiches and children's dishes) is supplemented by an impressive blackboard selection. Fish is well represented, from starters of oysters, scallops, potted shrimps, piri-piri prawns or bradan rost, to main dishes involving whole red mullet or Dover sole, or poached salmon fillet or halibut steak. For vegetarians, there's Stilton pâté, and cauliflower and mushroom provençale, among others, and for carnivores, venison casserole, all manner of steaks, and a formidable mixed grill. Puds run the gamut from spotted dick and custard, via banoffi meringue roulade, to tiramisù. SAMPLE DISHES: ham and vegetable broth £3; chicken cordon bleu £8; crêpes suzette with vanilla ice cream £3.50.

Licensees David and Wendy Busby (Enterprise Inns)
Open 12 to 3, 7 to 11, Sun summer 12 to 11; bar food 12 to 2, 7 to 10, Sun winter 12 to 2.30, 7 to 10, summer 12 to 10; closed first week Jan
Details Children welcome   Car park   Wheelchair access (also WC)   Patio   No-smoking area in bar   Background music   Well-behaved dogs welcome   Amex, Delta, MasterCard, Switch, Visa

---

DREWSTEIGNTON   Devon   map 1

▲ Drewe Arms

Drewsteignton EX6 6QN   TEL: (01647) 281224
2m S of A30, 8m W of Exeter

Drewsteignton is an attractive village high above the wooded slopes of the Teign Valley just within the boundary of the Dartmoor National Park, and this thatched old pub is tucked away next to the church. It was run for 75 years by Mabel Mudge, who retired as Britain's longest-serving landlady in 1996 at the age of 99. Colin and Janice Sparks ensure that Mabel's influence lives on, in the small restaurant that bears her name and retains her old cooking range, as well as the original dresser and cupboards. The menus are all on daily-changing blackboards, with the kitchen using as much local produce as possible and giving a modern slant to traditional old favourites: mixed cheese terrine with Cumberland sauce, for instance, followed by sausages on bubble and squeak with apple and cider chutney, braised lamb shank in a rich red wine and orange sauce, or pan-seared scallops with lardons and pesto dressing. Puddings deal in riches such as pan-fried spotted dick with crème anglaise and clotted cream, and steamed chocolate, pear and ginger pudding with chocolate sauce. Sandwiches and ploughman's are prepared at lunchtime, and some evenings are themed: Tuesday is steak night, for instance. Real ales include Bass and Gale's HSB, and also on draught is local farm cider. The National Trust's Castle Drogo, which looks medieval but was built in the early twentieth century, is nearby. SAMPLE DISHES: Gorgonzola and caramelised walnut salad £5; honey-roast ham hock on spinach mash with parsley sauce £10; lemon cheesecake with blackcurrant coulis £4.

Licensees Colin and Janice Sparks (Whitbread)
Open 11 to 3 (2.30 winter), 6 to 11, Sun 12 to 3, 7 to 10.30; bar food and restaurant 12 to 2.30, 6.30 to 9.30
Details Children welcome in eating areas   Wheelchair access (also WC)   Garden and patio
No smoking in restaurant   No music   Dogs welcome in bar   Delta, MasterCard, Switch, Visa
Accommodation: 3 rooms, B&B £60 (double room)

DUNSTAN   Northumberland   map 10

▲ Cottage Inn   `NEW ENTRY`

Dunstan NE66 3SZ   TEL: (01665) 576658
WEBSITE: www.cottageinnhotel.co.uk
from Alnwick take coast road towards Craster

Kippers 'n' custard might be an inventive way to settle in at this inn set in its own large gardens – a dish of flaked Craster kippers in a savoury custard with capers, gherkins and shallots appears as a starter here. More conventional but no less interesting are pigeon pie (pigeon breast in cream, horseradish and leeks with a Parmesan puff pastry lid), and 'Border mushrooms' (stuffed with haggis and deep-fried). The rest of the menu includes some good vegetarian choices, such as crêpes with spinach and cheese sauce, and plenty of meat and fish options: 'porter's pie' (game and steak in Guinness), Madras beef curry, and grilled tuna steak with lime butter, for example, plus a fair range of sandwiches and jacket potatoes. Real ales might include local Wylam Bitter or Belhaven Best, while the short wine list features four house wines at £8.55 plus ten 'specials' at £9.75 a bottle, £2.55 a glass. Dining is spread over several areas, all with an 'ultra-traditional' feel, with lots of beams, wood panelling, leaded glass and brick fireplaces – as well as the bar, covered patio, and no-smoking conservatory, there is the Harry Hotspur restaurant, which is decorated with murals depicting the local hero. SAMPLE DISHES: crab pot soup £4.50; minted roast lamb with Yorkshire pudding and roast potatoes £9; Lindisfarne gâteau (sponge layered with honey, mead and cream) £3.25.

Licensee Zoe Finlay (freehouse)
Open 11 to 11; bar food and restaurant 12 to 2.30, 6 (7 Sun) to 9.30
Details Children welcome   Car park   Wheelchair access (also WC)   Garden and patio
No smoking in conservatory and restaurant after 9   Live or background music; jukebox   Guide dogs only   Delta, MasterCard, Switch, Visa   Accommodation: 10 rooms, B&B £25 to £69

EARLS COLNE   Essex   map 3

Carved Angel | NEW ENTRY |

Upper Holt Street, Earls Colne CO6 2PG   TEL: (01787) 222330
WEBSITE: www.carvedangel.com
on A1124 between Halstead and Colchester

This fifteenth-century inn in an unspoilt village has an 'unflashy but quietly appealing' presence. Inside, there is little sign of the pub's antiquity, save for some old ceiling timbers. Instead, the décor is comfortable, clean and contemporary, and the atmosphere is relaxed but smart. As is the modern way, this is not really an establishment aimed at drinkers – the clientele on a Sunday lunchtime is likely to be mostly couples and families. That said, real ale fans will be satisfied with the choice of Greene King IPA, Adnams Bitter and Mighty Oak's Simply the Best. Food is listed on blackboards opposite the bar, and the choice is plentiful: start with something simple like a deep bowl of sweet potato and red pepper soup with good granary bread, or something more ambitious like pan-fried pigeon breast on a potato cake with red wine jus. Main courses also span a wide range, from roast duck breast or calf's liver, both served on creamy mash, to monkfish with griddled vegetables and a light tarragon sauce. The short, French-dominated wine list is not the cheapest around, offering limited choice under £15, although blackboards list better-value options, and there are around half a dozen by the glass. SAMPLE DISHES: pavé of salmon on wild rocket with lemon and ginger oil £6.50; roast ribeye of beef with Yorkshire pudding and roast potatoes £12; vanilla pannacotta with mint jelly and raspberry sauce £4.

Licensees Michael and Melissa Deckers (freehouse)
Open 11.30 to 3, 6.30 to 11, Sun 12 to 3, 6.30 to 10.30; bar food 12 to 2 (2.30 Sun), 7 to 9 (10 Fri and Sat)
Details Children welcome   Car park   Wheelchair access (not WC)   Garden   No-smoking area in bar   Background music   Guide dogs only   Delta, MasterCard, Switch, Visa

EASINGTON　　Buckinghamshire　　　　　　　　　　　　　　map 2

▲ Mole and Chicken

Easington HP18 9EY　TEL: (01844) 208387
WEBSITE: www.moleandchicken.co.uk
off B4011, 1m N of Long Crendon on Chilton road

'Restaurant and bed & breakfast' proclaims the Mole and Chicken's leaflet, but this is nonetheless a pub, with high chairs at the bar, where you can sup hand-pulled Vale Best Bitter and Fuller's London Pride; alternatively, take advantage of any corner of the pleasantly informal open-plan interior, or perhaps take drinks into the terraced garden, with its expansive views over the Buckinghamshire/Oxfordshire countryside. Candlelight adds appropriately to the atmosphere of the dimly lit bar, with its beams, wood-burning fireplace and flagstone floor. The menus have a touch of the East about them in a starter of creamed chilli mussels, and a main course of Thai prawn curry on saffron rice. Otherwise, tradition shows up in carrot and coriander soup, or duck pâté, and then 'an excellent dish' of a slow-cooked half-shoulder of lamb with a rosemary, honey and garlic sauce, or chargrilled steak with chips. Vegetarian, fish and pasta dishes are offered on specials boards. Over 30 malt whiskies are available, and both Old and New Worlds are represented on the short wine list, with a decent choice by the glass. SAMPLE DISHES: roast mushroom stuffed with spinach and cheese £6; roast rack of pork ribs in barbecue sauce £10; tiramisù £5.

Licensee Shane Ellis (freehouse)
Open *12 to 2.30, 6 to 11, Sun 12 to 10.30; bar food 12 to 2, 7 to 9.30*
Details *Children welcome　Car park　Wheelchair access (not WC)　Garden　Background music
No dogs　Amex, Delta, MasterCard, Switch, Visa　Accommodation: 5 rooms, B&B £50 to £65*

EAST CHILTINGTON　　East Sussex　　　　　　　　　　　　map 3

Jolly Sportsman 🌼 🌼 🍺 🍇

Chapel Lane, East Chiltington BN7 3BA　TEL: (01273) 890400
on B2116 E of Plumpton turn N signposted East Chiltington, continue approx 1½m then first left (pub is signposted)

Even in a hamlet, the Jolly Sportsman is rather set apart. A large, tall building, it's hung with tiles and custard-coloured weatherboarding and has sage-green window frames. Bare floorboards and walls painted pink and green, and a cacophony of contented customers, create an atmosphere that is more modern bistro than pubby. Although having just a pint – one of a constantly changing range of ales generally from microbreweries – is a possibility in the bar, most people come here to eat, and judging by reporters' comments it's easy to see why. 'A really lovely, simple but beautifully made, fresh' salad of mackerel, fennel, anchovies and red peppers kicked off an inspector's dinner, and a main course of pink-roast haunch of venison with port and juniper sauce, dauphinois potatoes, red cabbage and curly kale 'made a superbly fresh and interesting impression'. Alternatives might be spicy crab and mayonnaise with watercress, or fennel soup, and then baked red mullet with garlic and parsley butter, or roast pheasant breast with a mixture of wild mushrooms. The kitchen's straightforward approach to raw ingredients, producing clear, strong flavours, is evident in puddings too: baked Bramley apple with vanilla ice cream, say, or tropical fruit sorbet. The presentation of dishes is unusually attractive, and complimentary olives and bread have come in for praise. A set-price two- or three-course lunch is served from Tuesday to Saturday. The wine list confidently achieves excellence at all levels, without laying on any pretensions. Eight wines by the glass (in three sizes) give a sample of the range on offer rather than sticking with the budget basics; the selection of half-bottles is extensive; and the full list of over 100 wines will leave you spoilt for choice whatever your budget or preferences. The large garden and attractive new covered terrace are al fresco options. SAMPLE DISHES: smoked haddock and bacon salad £6; roast partridge with Puy lentils £13.75; chocolate tart with crème fraîche £5.75.

Licensees Bruce and Gwyneth Wass (freehouse)
Open Tue to Sat and bank hol Mon 12 to 2.30, Tue to Sat 6 to 11, Sun 12 to 4; bar food and restaurant Tue to Sat and bank hol Mon 12.30 to 2, Tue to Sat 7 to 9.30 (10 Fri and Sat), Sun 12.15 to 3; closed 4 days Christmas
Details Children welcome   Car park   Wheelchair access (also WC)   Garden and patio
No smoking in restaurant   No music   Dogs welcome   Delta, MasterCard, Switch, Visa

EAST DEAN   East Sussex   map 3

Tiger Inn 🏵

The Green, East Dean BN20 0DA   TEL: (01323) 423209
off A269 Seaford to Eastbourne road, 4m W of Eastbourne

At the centre of the village in a kind of dip, the Tiger Inn holds pride of place on the pretty green, and note that outside tables fill up fast on warm days, though there is still plenty of room on the green itself. The endearingly oddball interior has low ceilings, lots of panelling, glass cases containing stuffed birds and even a fox, and a coal-effect gas fire. Around 12 wines by the glass, with 40-odd by the bottle, provide plenty of choice to accompany such dishes as feta salad, or a plate of smoked salmon, followed by red Thai pork curry, or mushroom stroganoff, and then rich chocolate roulade, or sticky pecan pie. Fresh fish is sourced each day from Hastings, and smoked seafood comes from a local smokery. On days when they are very busy – often Sundays in summer and bank holidays – they do only cold food (ploughman's, sandwiches and salads). Harveys Sussex Best Bitter, Adnams Bitter and Brakspear Bitter are on handpump. SAMPLE DISHES: smoked chicken breast salad £8; tuna fishcakes £8; lemon tart £3.50.

Licensee Nick Denyer (freehouse)
Open Mon to Fri 11 to 3, 6 to 11, Sat 11 to 11, Sun 12 to 10.30; bar food Mon to Sat 12 to 2, 6.30 to 9 (9.30 Fri and Sat), Sun 12 to 2, 6 to 8
Details No children   Car park   Patio   No music   No cards

The Guide is totally independent, accepts no free hospitality, carries no advertising and makes no charge for inclusion.

EAST END   **Hampshire**   **map 2**

East End Arms ☻

Main Road, East End SO41 5SY   TEL: (01590) 626223
off B3054, 2m E of Lymington; follow signs for Isle of Wight ferry and continue 2m

The drive to this charming pub is through some particularly photogenic parts
of the New Forest, with wild ponies another attraction. The garden is popular
for al fresco eating in summer, and, within, sturdy tables, attractive prints,
inviting furnishings and an open fire enhance the sense of home comforts.
The local microbrewery is Ringwood, and its Fortyniner and Best Bitter are
on offer here, along with a guest ale. So, too, is Thatcher's cider and a short,
serviceable wine list, with four house wines available by the glass. The cooking
is generally highly praised, and seems proficient across the range. The bar
blackboard announces a range of freshly baked baguettes and a steak of the day
along with such things as chicken and ham pie, lamb's liver and bacon, and
whole grilled Dover sole with lemon butter, with perhaps bread-and-butter
pudding, or upside-down crumble among desserts. Fish is a strength of the
restaurant menu, from a casserole with saffron and arborio rice to flounder
with grilled asparagus and tomatoes in red wine. Otherwise, there might be
pan-roast spatchcock poussin with a sticky garlic and herb sauce, or slow-roast
suckling pig with celeriac mash, preceded by perhaps grilled Cornish sardines
with sweet chilli sauce. SAMPLE DISHES: free-range eggs baked with chives and
Gorgonzola £4; smoked haddock and mussel casserole £7; Bakewell tart £4.50.

Licensees P.J. and J.L. Sykes and J. Willcock (freehouse)
Open *11.30 to 3, 6 to 11, Sun 12 to 9; bar food and restaurant Tue to Sun 12 to 2, Tue to Sat
7 to 9; 25 Dec drinks only 11.30 to 2, closed 1 Jan*
Details *Children welcome   Car park   Wheelchair access (not WC)   Garden   Background and
occasional live music   Dogs welcome in bar   Delta, MasterCard, Switch, Visa*

EASTGATE   **Norfolk**   **map 6**

Ratcatchers Inn   NEW ENTRY

Easton Way, Eastgate NR10 4HA   TEL: (01603) 871430
10m NW of Norwich off B1149 Holt road, 1m SE of Cawston

The Ratcatchers is a popular country inn on the edge of the village. Off the
bar, there's a conservatory in one direction and a dining room in the other,
with the same menu served throughout, food being very much the thing here.
The standard printed menu features the usual pub stalwarts, but the blackboard strikes out with more adventure: perhaps duck breast with crushed
black pepper and a caramelised orange and honey sauce, grilled salmon fillet
on creamed spinach, or roasted barracuda with tiger prawns and garlic butter
and a white wine and coriander sauce. There are more familiar dishes too –
perhaps a pot of mussels steamed in white wine and garlic – but pies are the
speciality, including steak and kidney, game, beef and chicken. A good choice
of wines includes seven by the glass, and Adnams Bitter, Hancock's
Ratcatchers and Worthington's 1774 are on draught. SAMPLE DISHES: goats'
cheese roulade £5; liver and bacon in red wine £8; raspberry crème brûlée £4.

Licensee Peter McCarter (freehouse)
Open Mon to Fri 11.45 to 3, 6 to 11, Sat 11.45 to 10, Sun 11.45 to 9; bar food and restaurant
Mon to Fri 12 to 2, 6 to 10, Sat 12 to 10, Sun 12 to 9
Details Children welcome   Car park   Wheelchair access (not WC)   Garden   No smoking in
restaurant and conservatory   Background music   No dogs   Delta, MasterCard, Switch, Visa

EAST HADDON   Northamptonshire   map 5

▲ Red Lion Hotel   NEW ENTRY

Main Street, East Haddon NN6 8BU   TEL: (01604) 770223
WEBSITE: www.redlionhoteleasthaddon.co.uk
off A428, 8m NW of Northampton

The Red Lion is an attractive thatched stone inn-cum-restaurant-cum-hotel
in the centre of this small village. It has a 'sedate country vibe', and the bar has
a 'cosy, homely, cottagey' feel, with dark beams and red-upholstered furniture
set off by floral cushions and curtains, and décor in the line of country-themed
pictures, crockery and horse brasses. Bar menus stick mainly to an old-fashioned country cooking style: pheasant casserole in port sauce, and rabbit
cobbler in cream, thyme and white wine are typical. There are also pasta
dishes, cold buffet platters and sandwiches, and to finish there might be egg
custard tart or blueberry cheesecake. A blackboard lists daily specials, such as
baked avocado filled with bacon and cheese rarebit, while the restaurant
menus go in for more complex dishes like grilled goats' cheese on pear and
vanilla purée, and beef fillet medallions on parsnip rösti. Wells Eagle and
Bombardier and Adnams Broadside are among the real ales on offer, and there
is a short but respectable and fairly priced wine list with house wines at £12
and half a dozen by the glass. SAMPLE DISHES: seafood mousse with herb oil
dressing and brown bread £7; pot-roast lamb shank on root vegetables £13;
Bakewell tart £4.

Licensee Ian Kennedy (Charles Wells)
Open 11 to 2.30, 6 to 11, Sun 12 to 2.30, 7 to 10.30; bar food and restaurant all week 12 to 2,
Mon to Sat 7 to 9.30; closed 25 Dec
Details Children welcome in eating areas   Car park   Wheelchair access (also WC)   Garden and
patio   No smoking in restaurant   Background music   No dogs   Amex, Delta, Diners, MasterCard,
Switch, Visa   Accommodation: 5 rooms, B&B £60 to £75

EAST LANGTON   Leicestershire   map 5

▲ Bell Inn 🍺

Main Street, East Langton LE16 7TW   TEL: (01858) 545278   BREW PUB
WEBSITE: www.thebellinn.co.uk
just off B6047, 4m N of Market Harborough

'An unpretentious, popular, country local' is how one reporter described this
whitewashed sixteenth-century village inn. Nowadays, it's best known for the
Langton Brewery housed in outbuildings next to the pub, where Caudle
Bitter, Bowler Strong Ale and Boxer Heavyweight are produced: these are
kept in fine order in the dark-beamed bar, alongside ales from Greene King.
On the food front, plenty of international classics make their appearance, from
chicken balti and stir-fried duck breast on a bed of noodles to minted lamb

casserole and 'sausages of the season'. Start with, say, spinach and feta samosas and round things off with something homely like baked jam and sultana roly-poly. Sunday lunch is a sell-out carvery with two sittings (booking recommended). A list of around twenty workaday wines includes six by the very small (125ml) or very large (250ml) glass. SAMPLE DISHES: warm pigeon and potato salad £5; fish pie £9.75; sticky toffee pudding £3.50.

Licensee Alistair Chapman (freehouse)
Open 11.30 to 2.30, 7 to 11, Sun 12 to 3, 7 to 10.30; bar food Mon to Sat 12 to 2, 7.15 to 9.30, Sun 12 and 2 (2 sittings), 7.15 to 9.30; closed 25 Dec
Details Children welcome   Car park   Wheelchair access (not WC)   Garden   No smoking in eating area   No music   Dogs welcome   Delta, Diners, MasterCard, Switch, Visa   Accommodation: 2 rooms, B&B £39.50 to £60

EAST LAVANT   West Sussex   map 3

▲ Royal Oak   NEW ENTRY
Pook Lane, East Lavant PO18 0AX   TEL: (01243) 527434
WEBSITE: www.sussexlive.co.uk/royaloakinn

'What a lucky find while out cycling in the South Downs. A stone's throw (downhill) from Goodwood horse track,' enthused one reporter after a visit to this 'cosy pub with designer touches'. The current owners have added a touch of sophistication to what was once a one-room local boozer: a new extension has been tacked on, and customers can sip aperitifs on sofas by the bar, although real ales include Ballard's, Hall & Woodhouse Badger and Sussex Bitter. The food has been described as 'upscale': details such as 'smart butter', olives and excellent bread imported from France are impressive, and there are obvious restaurant overtones, particularly among starters (risotto of asparagus and sun-blush tomatoes with truffle oil and Parmesan, or crispy duck salad with honey, sesame, ginger and alfalfa, for instance). Main courses strike a more robust, traditional note: fillet of cod in beer batter, Sussex sausages with mash, steak and chips, and a decent plateful of home-cooked ham with a free-range egg and bubble and squeak. At lunchtime you can also get a few light dishes, including smoked salmon with scrambled eggs. Wine starts at £9.95 (£3 per glass) but the list doesn't really get into gear until it passes the £15 mark – whereupon it accelerates rapidly towards a selection of top-class French classics, albeit in fairly young vintages. SAMPLE DISHES: Cajun-spiced chicken spring roll with mango dressing £6; roast pork fillet, Savoy cabbage and bacon confit, rösti and Calvados sauce £13.50; lemon tart with raspberry sauce £5.

Licensee Nick Sutherland (freehouse)
Open 12 to 11; bar food and restaurant 12 to 3, 6 to 9.30
Details Children welcome   Car park   Wheelchair access (also WC)   Garden and patio   No music   Guide dogs only   Amex, Delta, Diners, MasterCard, Switch, Visa   Accommodation: 6 rooms, B&B £50 to £150

If a pub has notified us that it has a website, this is listed in the entry. Details shown on these websites have not been checked for accuracy by the Guide.

EASTON   Hampshire   map 2

Chestnut Horse   NEW ENTRY

Avington Park Lane, Easton SO21 1EG   TEL: (01962) 779257
off B3047, 3m NE of Winchester

In a picturesque Itchen Valley village of thatched houses, this attractive old pub has bags of character in its series of cosy interconnecting rooms (five, to be precise). Tankards, teapots and even chamber pots hang from the dark-boarded ceiling in the bar rooms, with their roaring fires and log baskets; walls throughout are hung with a cornucopia of pictures, mirrors and crockery, with a stuffed fish above one fireplace, and every shelf, nook and cranny is filled with bric-à-brac. The place can get busy, which is understandable given the popularity of the set-price (£9.95 for two courses) lunchtime and early-evening menu: among other things, avocado and bacon salad with balsamic dressing, followed by a salmon fishcake on a bed of spinach. Sandwiches and ploughman's are also available at lunchtime, while the full menu is a list of old favourites like smoked mackerel pâté, ham and eggs, calf's liver with crispy bacon, and sticky toffee pudding. Look to the blackboard specials for the likes of Dorset crab, rack of English lamb roasted in a herb crust with rosemary and thyme sauce, Thai chicken curry, or baked fillets of sea bream with sweet chilli sauce. The pub's own locally brewed Chestnut Horse Bitter is on draught along with Courage Best and Fuller's London Pride, and around half a dozen wines are served by the glass. SAMPLE DISHES: sardines grilled with garlic butter and lemon juice £5; pan-fried fillet steak topped with foie gras with a veal and Madeira jus £16; summer pudding £4.50.

Licensees John and Jocelyn Holland (freehouse)
Open *11 to 3.30, 5.30 to 11, Sun 12 to 6 (10.30 summer); bar food and restaurant 12 to 2.30, 6.30 to 9.30, Sun 12 to 4.30 (8.30 summer)*
Details *Children welcome   Car park   Wheelchair access (not WC)   Garden and patio*
No smoking in restaurant   Occasional background music   Dogs welcome   Delta, MasterCard, Switch, Visa

EAST TYTHERLEY   Hampshire   map 2

▲ Star Inn

East Tytherley SO51 0LW   TEL: (01794) 340225
WEBSITE: **www.starinn-uk.com**
off B3084 Romsey road, N of Lockerley

This sixteenth-century brick pub is on the western edge of the Test valley, seven miles north of Romsey and not far from the Mottisfont Abbey rose gardens. It stands on a quiet lane overlooking the village cricket pitch, and idle customers can watch from its terrace (energetic ones can play skittles in the skittle alley). Inside, the comfortable, welcoming main bar has low beams and an open fireplace and serves Gales HSB and Ringwood Best. The nub of the pub is the carpeted dining room, furnished in traditional style with dark wood furniture and plush banquettes. The bar menu (sandwiches, toasted focaccia or jacket potatoes with fillings/stuffings from cheese to steak and mushrooms) and the blackboard menu both apply in restaurant and dining room. Besides the usual steaks, the latter covers the plain (prawn cocktail, battered cod and chips), the fancy (mille-feuille of pheasant, pigeon and venison with forestière potatoes), the oo-er exotic (wild mushroom linguine with truffle oil and coriander) and a bit of each (black pudding risotto with foie gras). Among the sweets are steamed treacle pud and custard, and warm chocolate tart with white chocolate and hazelnut ice cream. Of the 30-odd wines listed, the ten house wines are available by the glass; prices start at £9.50 a bottle (£2.50 a glass). SAMPLE DISHES: smoked venison with warm pickled vegetables £6; baked salmon with saffron-scented mussels £12.50; pannacotta with ginger and lime syrup £4.25.

Licensees Paul and Sarah Bingham (freehouse)
Open *Tue to Sat 11 to 2.30, 6 to 11, Sun 12 to 2, 7 to 10.30; bar food and restaurant 12 to 2, 7 to 9 (9.30 Fri and Sat); closed Mon, evening 25 Dec and all day 26 Dec*
Details *Children welcome   Car park   Wheelchair access (also WC)   Garden and patio No smoking in dining room   Occasional live music   Dogs welcome exc in bedrooms   Delta, MasterCard, Switch, Visa   Accommodation: 3 rooms, B&B £45 to £80*

EAST WITTON   North Yorkshire   map 8

▲ Blue Lion 🏵 🏵 🍇

East Witton DL8 4SN   TEL: (01969) 624273
WEBSITE: www.thebluelion.co.uk
on A6108 Masham to Leyburn road, 2m SE of Middleham

East Witton is a well-kept Dales village with a strongly rural feel and sturdy-looking limestone houses, beyond which hills rise into the distance. Set on the broad main road through the village is the Blue Lion, a long-fronted eighteenth-century coaching inn. The front door leads directly into a warm, snug, flagstone-floored bar with a convivial and welcoming atmosphere. Star of the show is the food, something for which the Blue Lion has built up a well-deserved reputation. On one wall, above a huge fireplace, is a vast blackboard menu, and though the range is wide – perhaps 20 main-course choices – dishes are scrubbed off and replaced as they become unavailable, suggesting that turnover is high enough to maintain freshness. There's something to suit all appetites and tastes: simple pasta dishes like spaghetti carbonara, traditional favourites of the steak and kidney pudding variety, hearty French country cooking, such as cassoulet of pork ribs, pancetta, duck, Toulouse sausage and mash, and some fairly upmarket creations: roast fillet of monkfish wrapped in Parma ham with bacon, mushrooms, shallots and whole-grain mustard sauce, for example. An inspector praised the honest simplicity of it all, impressed with the quality of ingredients and skilled cooking of flash-roasted lamb chump with garlic mash and flageolet beans. Interesting seasonal side vegetables are worthy of special mention, particularly braised spiced red cabbage. The separate restaurant has its own menu in similar vein. There's a respectable line-up of local real ales from Black Sheep and Theakston, but this is trumped by the wine selection. A dozen wines come by bottle, glass or a just-right-for-a-meal-for-two half-litre, and this is a flavoursome and good-value selection. The main list serves up classics with a bit of age and fresh modern flavours from around the world, with serious bottles in both categories. SAMPLE DISHES: warm salad of crab and ginger fritters £5.25; pan-seared pork fillet with honey-glazed apple and sarladaise potatoes £13; raspberry crème brûlée £5.25.

Licensees Paul and Helen Klein (freehouse)
Open 11 to 11, Sun 12 to 10.30; bar food and restaurant 12 to 2, 7 to 9.15; restaurant closed 25 Dec
Details Children welcome   Car park   Wheelchair access (also WC)   Garden   No music   Dogs welcome   Delta, MasterCard, Switch, Visa   Accommodation: 12 rooms, B&B £53.50 to £89

EAST WOODLANDS   Somerset   map 2

Horse & Groom 🍺

East Woodlands BA11 5LY   TEL: (01373) 462802
off A361, 2m S of Frome

Known as the Jockey to its regulars, the Horse & Groom is rurally located at the edge of woodlands surrounding the Longleat estate. On the front lawn are tables among pollarded limes, hanging baskets and tubs of flowers, with more tables in the secluded garden to the side. Inside the seventeenth-century building are stone-flagged floors, two inglenooks, one with a wood-burning stove, stripped pine furniture and a light conservatory-style restaurant. The menus in here might start off with cream of celery soup with Stilton scones, or asparagus, cheese and egg tartlet, and go on to main courses of Aylesbury duck breast with parsnip purée and redcurrant gravy, or breaded pork fillet in wild mushroom sauce. The bar menu lists baguettes and ploughman's and goes through to Yorkshire pudding with sausages in onion gravy, battered cod fillet with chips, and roasted vegetable filo tart. Round things off with raspberry cranachan, or white chocolate pannacotta with crushed strawberries. Butcombe Bitter, Branscombe Vale Branoc, Wadworth 6X and Henry's Original IPA, and McMullen Original AK are on handpump, and Stowford Press cider is also stocked. Half a dozen wines come by two sizes of glass from a modestly priced list approaching 30 bottles. SAMPLE DISHES: spicy Thai fishcakes £4.75; lamb's liver with bacon in onion gravy £7; tropical fruit pavlova £4.

Licensee Kathy Barrett (freehouse)
Open Tue to Sat 11.30 to 2.30, Mon to Sat 6.30 to 11, Sun 12 to 3, 7 to 11; bar food and restaurant Tue to Sun 12 to 2, Tue to Sat 6.30 to 9
Details Children welcome in eating areas   Car park   Wheelchair access (also WC)   Garden   No smoking in restaurant and lounge   Occasional live music   Dogs welcome exc in restaurant   Delta, MasterCard, Switch, Visa

---

EGLINGHAM   Northumberland   map 10

Tankerville Arms

Eglingham NE66 2TX   TEL: (01665) 578444
on B6346, 6m N of Alnwick

The Tankerville Arms stands in the middle of an appealing village full of grey-stone cottages. It's attractively decorated inside and divided into three areas: snug, main bar, with a log fire, and dining area. The printed menu holds plenty of interest, from starters of roasted tomato and basil soup, or melon and tiger prawns in a mild curried coriander mayonnaise, to main courses of

Cullen skink made with locally oak-smoked haddock, or game pie. Sandwiches and salads (smoked duck with roasted vegetables, for example) are also listed, and the choice is broadened even further by a few blackboard specials, among them perhaps prawn and dill fishcake accompanied by roasted scallops and a Thai sauce, or baked breast of guinea fowl on a confit of parsnips and red onions with mustard sauce. The fine line-up of real ales includes Black Sheep Best Bitter, Mordue Five Bridge Bitter and Timothy Taylor Landlord. A handful of wines is sold by the glass, with the short, annotated list opening at £11.45 for South African Sauvignon Blanc. SAMPLE DISHES: sautéed lambs' kidneys on baked onions with port gravy £5; grill of guinea fowl, venison, wild boar sausage, pigeon, wild mushrooms and black pudding £13; chocolate roulade with hot chocolate sauce £4.

Licensee John Blackmore (freehouse)
Open 11 to 2, 6.30 (7 winter Sun to Thur) to 11; bar food and restaurant 12 to 2, 6.30 to 9; closed Mon lunchtimes Jan and Feb; no food 25 Dec and Mon Jan and Feb
Details Children welcome Car park Wheelchair access (also WC) Garden No smoking in restaurant Occasional background music Guide dogs only Amex, Delta, Diners, MasterCard, Switch, Visa

ELKESLEY Nottinghamshire   map 9

Robin Hood Inn [NEW ENTRY]
High Street, Elkesley DN22 8AJ   TEL: (01777) 838259
on A1, 5m SE of Worksop

This custard-coloured pub at the centre of the village has what one visitor described as a 'homely and very pubby' feel, and a bright décor that makes a feature of nostalgic advertising posters. Food-wise, plenty of choice is offered – as well as the long menu, which features eight starters, nine main courses and a selection of 'light bites', there is a good-value midweek set-price menu and a blackboard of daily specials. Among starters you are likely to find chicken liver parfait alongside salmon and cod fishcake with steamed spinach and lemon butter sauce, while main courses take in everything from fried haddock with chips, mushy peas and tartare sauce to beef bourguignonne. The great virtue of the cooking is the honest endeavour behind it: it all has the wholesome feel of proper home cooking. Beers are Marston's Pedigree, Flowers IPA and Boddingtons Bitter, and the wine list runs to around a dozen reasonably priced bottles (from £9.50), of which six come by the glass. SAMPLE DISHES: crab and avocado with lemon and basil oil £6.25; pan-fried chicken breast with mushrooms in a Dijon mustard, white wine and cream sauce £9; chocolate nemesis £4.

Licensee Alan Draper (Enterprise Inns)
Open 11.30 to 3, 6.30 to 11, Sun 12 to 3, 7 to 10.30; bar food and restaurant all week 12 to 2, Mon to Sat 6.30 to 9; closed evening 25 Dec
Details Children welcome Car park Wheelchair access (also WC) Garden No-smoking area in bar, no smoking in restaurant Occasional live or background music Dogs welcome Amex, Delta, MasterCard, Switch, Visa

Woolpack
The Green, Elstead GU8 6HD   TEL: (01252) 703106
on B3001 Milford to Farnham road, 4m W of Godalming

The Woolpack is a substantial L-shaped, part-tile-hung building by a small
green in an attractive North Downs village. The interior is mainly brown with
touches of maroon, and there are local knick-knacks and pictures, and wool-
making paraphernalia. The long menu, written on blackboards, can take time
to absorb. The style can be described as modern eclectic, with hummus with
pitta bread, New Zealand green-lip mussels in herb and garlic butter, and
smoked trout pâté among the starters. Mains take in ostrich steak in a creamy
sauce of pesto, honey and mustard, lamb curry, and chicken tikka with rice.
More homely notions are sausages with garlic mash and onion gravy, or steak
and kidney pie. Desserts along the lines of Yorkshire curd tart are displayed in
a glass cabinet. Shepherd Neame Best Bitter and Greene King Abbot Ale are
dispensed straight from the cask, and around 10 wines come by the glass.
SAMPLE DISHES: deep-fried whitebait with tartare sauce £5; smoked cod, prawn
and egg pie £8.75; trifle with apricots and brandy £3.50.

Licensees S.A. Askew and K.E.W. Macready (Punch)
Open *Mon to Fri 11 to 3, 5.30 to 11, Sat 11 to 11, Sun 12 to 10.30; bar food and restaurant
12 to 2, 7 to 9.45 (9 Sun); no food 25 Dec; closed 26 Dec*
Details *Children welcome in family room and restaurant   Car park   Wheelchair access (also WC)
Garden   No smoking in restaurant   Occasional live music   Dogs welcome exc in restaurant   Delta,
MasterCard, Switch, Visa*

Three Horseshoes 🍺
Elsted GU29 0JY   TEL: (01730) 825746
3m S of A272, 3m W of Midhurst

This white-fronted building covered in climbing roses sits on the north slope
of the South Downs with a large garden in front and views over the Rother
valley. The rooms are quite small but redolent of the pub's sixteenth-century
origins: walls of bare red brick with wooden studwork and dadoes, wooden
floors, ancient pews and settles and an ancient brick and stone fireplace. True
to its Old England atmosphere, this is a 'beef and beer' establishment – the
beer including Cheriton Pots Ale, Ballard's Best Bitter, Timothy Taylor
Landlord and Hop Back Summer Lightning (wines are basic, though, and
only a red and two whites come by the glass). On blackboards might be steak,
kidney and Murphy's pie, braised lamb with apples and apricots, whole grilled
plaice, or the fillet of local venison that a reporter found 'quite outstanding:
clearly well hung, super texture and hugely tasty'. Or try roast red pepper with
basil, garlic and anchovies, or an asparagus and feta salad (huge). Among
puddings are treacle tart, and raspberry and hazelnut meringue. SAMPLE
DISHES: home-made asparagus soup £4; mixed fish pie £10; chocolate truffle
torte £4.50.

Licensee Sue Beavis (freehouse)
Open 11 to 2.30, 6 to 11, Sun 12 to 3, 7 to 10.30; bar food and restaurant 12 to 2, 7 to 9
Details Children welcome   Car park   Garden   No smoking in dining room   No music   Dogs
welcome in bar   Delta, MasterCard, Switch, Visa

ELTERWATER   Cumbria   map 8

▲ Britannia Inn 🍺

Elterwater LA22 9HP   TEL: (015394) 37210
WEBSITE: www.britinn.co.uk
off A593, 3m W of Ambleside

Even on a cold winter's day the small bars of this Lakeland gem might be
packed with walkers. Indeed, it is so popular that customers often spill out on
to the village green. The Langdale Valley is prime walking country, and where
better to quench a thirst than here? Jennings Bitter, Coniston Bluebird and
Dent Aviator are the top-notch local brews on handpump, supplemented by
two guest ales. For those who prefer grape to grain, there are around twenty-
five wines, three served by the glass, plus six country wines from Lindisfarne.
Food is a mixture of traditional English pub grub and more adventurous fare:
steak and mushroom pie, or Cumberland sausage with mash, might appear
alongside rabbit casserole, or grilled red bream on red and yellow pepper
sauces. Starters take in a soup – perhaps pea and ham – a fisherman's platter of
gravad lax, rollmop herring and prawns, and garlic mushrooms, while desserts
run from chocolate cheesecake on a crunchy ginger base to diplomat's
pudding. The pub itself is an attractive whitewashed building in typical
Lakeland style, decked out with flower boxes and hanging baskets. Inside, the
bars have log fires and low oak beams, but the tables and chairs on the patio in
front have the best views of the wonderful scenery. SAMPLE DISHES: potted
Morecambe Bay shrimps £4; bacon-wrapped chicken breast stuffed with
cream cheese and chives on a leek and mushroom sauce £10; summer fruit
crumble with custard £3.75.

Licensees Clare Woodhead and Chris Jones (freehouse)
Open 11 to 11, Sun 12 to 10.30; bar food and restaurant 12 to 2.30, 6.30 to 9.30
Details Children welcome   Car park   Wheelchair access (not WC)   Patio   No smoking in hallway,
restaurant or residents' lounge   No music   Dogs welcome exc in restaurant   Amex, Delta,
MasterCard, Switch, Visa   Accommodation: 9 rooms, B&B £58 to £92

ELTON   Cambridgeshire   map 6

Black Horse

14 Overend, Elton PE8 6RU   TEL: (01832) 280240
just off A605 2m W of A1

Open log fires, antique furnishings and interesting artefacts, such as old
Bakelite telephones and Underwood typewriters, characterise the interior of
this small seventeenth-century rustic inn, and the rear garden overlooks the
village church and open countryside. The menu offers plenty of choice,
perhaps including goose breast with a sweet ratatouille chutney, game pie, or
rack of venison with fruits of the forest compote. Fish is a strong suit, from
plainly grilled fillet of plaice with lemon butter to loin of swordfish with a

white wine, garlic and chive dressing, via Thai-style seafood with noodles. Draught Bass is the regular ale, while others might be Caledonian Deuchars IPA, Everards Tiger Best or Nethergate Suffolk County. A dozen wines are served in two sizes of glass from a list of 30-plus bottles. SAMPLE DISHES: chef's home-made pâté £5; pan-fried duck breast with a sultana and shallot sauce £15; maple and pecan cheesecake £4.

Licensee John Clennell (freehouse)
Open 12 to 3 (5 Sun), 6 to 11; bar food all week 12 to 2.30 (3 Sun), Mon to Sat 6 to 9.30
Details Children welcome   Car park   Garden and patio   No smoking in 1 room   No music   Dogs welcome   Amex, Delta, MasterCard, Switch, Visa

EMPINGHAM   Rutland   map 6

▲ White Horse   NEW ENTRY

Main Street, Empingham LE15 8PS   TEL: (01780) 460221
WEBSITE: www.the-white-horse.co.uk
on A606 midway between Oakham and Stamford

This traditional rural stone-built inn – dating from the seventeenth century and originally a courthouse – enjoys an enviable situation close to the dam on Rutland Water. No wonder the area is popular with anglers and watersports enthusiasts – guests at the White Horse can store their catch in the deepfreeze and make use of the drying room. The inn's charms extend to a welcoming bar with a low, beamed ceiling, exposed-stone pillars and a large central log fire. There is also an extensive menu that takes in everything from rosemary-baked lamb chops with a minty leek, button onion and mushroom gravy to smoked pork steaks with Boursin cheese and a spicy chorizo and cream sauce, as well as simpler items like local bangers and mash with onion gravy, or Irish mussels in white wine, shallots and herb cream, and a couple of more exotic dishes, such as Thai-style dim sum. Daily blackboard specials extend the choice further. Real ales include Old Speckled Hen and locally brewed Grainstore Cooking Bitter. Six of the two dozen or so varied and good-value wines are available by the glass. SAMPLE DISHES: crispy vegetable spring rolls with sweet-and-sour dip £4.25; venison medallions with creamy pepper sauce £10.25; lemon chiffon pie £4.

Licensee Roger Bourne (Unique Pub Company)
Open 7.30am to 11 (10.30 Sun); bar food and restaurant 12 to 2.15, 7 to 9.45 (9.30 Sun)
Details Children welcome   Car park   Wheelchair access (also WC)   Garden   No smoking in restaurant   Background music   No dogs   Amex, Delta, Diners, MasterCard, Switch, Visa
Accommodation: 14 rooms, B&B £50 to £80

EWEN   Gloucestershire   map 2

▲ Wild Duck Inn

Drakes Island, Ewen GL7 6BY   TEL: (01285) 770310
off A429 Cirencester to Malmesbury road, 3m SW of Cirencester

Built of mellow Cotswold stone, with its origins in the fifteenth century, the Wild Duck Inn is a linked group of buildings with a central clock tower. The well-tended garden, with a manicured lawn, matches the characterful interior, which has flagstone floors, beams, open fireplaces, and old pictures and hunting trophies – including ducks – on the walls. The single printed menu, available throughout, changes between lunch and dinner, although there's some crossover between them. Main courses range from roast duck breast on a goose liver croûte with a rich sauce of red wine, orange and brandy, or Thai-style mussel broth with noodles and bean sprouts, to fillet of red bream poached in seafood laksa. Alternatively, chargrilled steaks with the usual trimmings, and beer-battered fish with chips and tartare sauce are also found, as are starters of game terrine with port and raspberry jelly, and a selection of Italian meats and cheeses with bread, while old-school desserts like sticky toffee pudding might be joined by something more exotic like warm lime and coconut cake with toffee sauce and blood orange ice cream. Among a good line-up of real ales are Theakston XB and Old Peculier, Smiles Best, house brew Duck Pond Bitter, Old Speckled Hen and Courage Directors. Around 25 wines are served by the glass. SAMPLE DISHES: prawn and Gruyère bake with toast and roast garlic butter £6; baked chicken with wild mushrooms in a creamy oregano sauce with garlic potatoes and olives £11; warm pear and almond tart with vanilla sauce and chocolate ice cream £4.25.

Licensee Dino Mussell (freehouse)
Open 11 to 11, Sun 11 to 10.30; bar food and restaurant 12 to 2 (2.30 Sun), 6.30 to 10
Details Children welcome Car park Wheelchair access (also WC) Garden and patio Live or background music Dogs welcome Amex, Delta, MasterCard, Switch, Visa Accommodation: 11 rooms, B&B £60 to £100

EXFORD Somerset   map 1

▲ Crown Hotel
Park Street, Exford TA24 7PP   TEL: (01643) 831554
WEBSITE: www.crownhotelexmoor.co.uk
on B3224, 12m SW of Minehead

This hotel seems grand for tiny Exford, but it began in the seventeenth century as a coaching halt on the only east–west road through Exmoor. It looks younger, though, for expansion has topped two white and plastered storeys with a jettied, tile-hung second floor of zigzag gables, creating an almost inter-war look. The bar (with its own entrance) has a comfortably lived-in feel, a hunting theme (fox masks and deer hooves on the walls) and Exmoor Ale, Fox and Gold, plus Clearwater Crown on the pumps (Red C cider too). Enjoyable and interesting bar food includes starters that are also available as main courses: maybe a luscious confit corn-fed chicken leg with spiced lentils, providing stimulating flavour contrasts, or a blue cheese rarebit with mixed leaves. A specials board offers mains like venison sausage and mash to supplement such menu offerings as tagliatelle with wild mushroom and asparagus sauce, or lamb shank with braised red cabbage, or possibly a generous salmon fillet on classically made pesto covering a well-flavoured, crumbly lemon and thyme couscous. Afterwards try ginger and lemongrass brûlée, or Bakewell tart. Seven wines (five French, two Australian) come by the glass from a list of three dozen that starts at £11.75 and includes ten half-bottles. The hotel's restaurant serves a gourmet five-/six-course, no-choice prix fixe menu. SAMPLE DISHES: smoked salmon and scrambled egg £5; pan-roasted poussin and potato rissoles £7.50; profiteroles with butterscotch sauce £3.50.

Licensee Hugo Jeune (freehouse)
Open *winter Mon to Fri 11 to 2.30, 6 to 11, Sat and Sun 11 to 11; summer all week 11 to 11; bar food and restaurant 12 to 2, 7 to 9.30*
Details *Children welcome in bar eating area   Car park   Wheelchair access (also WC)   Garden No smoking in dining room   Background music   Dogs welcome   Amex, Delta, MasterCard, Switch, Visa   Accommodation: 17 rooms, B&B £47.50 to £57.50*

FADMOOR   **North Yorkshire**   map 9

Plough

Main Street, Fadmoor YO62 7HY   TEL: (01751) 431515
about 2m N of Kirkbymoorside, off A170

On the edge of the North York Moors National Park, Fadmoor is a small village of stone houses, with the Plough on the corner of its triangular green. Inside are low ceiling beams, old paraffin lamps, now electric, and a wood-burning range. The carpeted lounge is comfortable and homely, while the dining room is a tad more formal. The menus offer a generous choice at both lunchtime and dinner: perhaps smoked venison with rocket, spinach and endive salad and bramble dressing, or goujons of haddock with lemon and dill mayonnaise to start, and main courses of salmon fishcakes, beef Wellington, or roast pheasant with bacon-braised barley and whisky cream sauce. What the menu rightly describes as 'firm favourites' include deep-fried battered haddock with tartare sauce, griddled rump steak, and steak and kidney pudding. On draught is Black Sheep Bitter, plus a guest in summer. All six house wines are sold by the glass, and there are a further twenty or so bottles to choose from. SAMPLE DISHES: duck and mango spring roll with a sweet chilli and ginger dip £4.75; pan-seared wild salmon on wilted lettuce and cucumber salad with tomato and butter sauce £11.50; dark and white chocolate marble cheesecake £4.25.

Licensee Neil Nicholson (Holf Leisure)
Open *12 to 2.30, 6.30 (7 Sun) to 11.30; bar food and restaurant 12 to 1.45 (2 Sun), 6.30 to 8.45 (8.30 Sun); closed 25 and 26 Dec, 1 Jan*
Details *Children welcome   Car park   Garden and patio   No smoking in restaurant   Occasional background music   No dogs   Delta, MasterCard, Switch, Visa*

FARNHAM   **Dorset**   map 2

▲ Museum Inn 🏵 🏵 🍇   [NEW ENTRY]

Farnham DT11 8DE   TEL: (01725) 516261
WEBSITE: www.museuminn.co.uk
off A354, 9m NE of Blandford Forum

This striking, solid-stone building (seventeenth century with Victorian additions) was originally used to provide sustenance and accommodation for the nearby museum – hence the name. Recently, the place has been given a sympathetic makeover, although the pub itself still has plenty of character and quirky touches: beige-coloured flagstones everywhere, bare wooden tables, even a stuffed fox curled up in a disused bread oven. 'All quite designer and stylish', despite the smoke and the noise that reflects the popularity of the place. A bevy of 'bright and breezy and ever-so-friendly' young girls cope well with the crowds. The bar menu – which is the main attraction – sets out its stall in no uncertain terms: roast scallops are given the oriental treatment with lemongrass, chilli, spring onions and noodles, while main courses span every-thing from breast of wood pigeon on 'gorgeous' mash with assorted mush-rooms, baby artichoke hearts and caramelised button onions, or fettucine of sea bass with lemon butter sauce, to daube of beef, and shepherd's pie with crushed potatoes, pancetta and Parmesan crisps. There is also plenty going on when it comes to desserts: mango mousse has been embellished with pistachio nuts, a scoop of blood orange sorbet and swirls of raspberry coulis. At lunchtime you can also get upmarket sandwiches. Some similar dishes are also served in the Shed Restaurant (note the limited opening times), where the repertoire extends to a terrine of pressed ham knuckle, guinea fowl and mush-rooms, and roast halibut with potato purée, Parma ham and parsnips. A fine selection of ales includes Ringwood Best, Exmoor Gold and Hop Back Summer Lightning, and Thatcher's cider is on draught. Eight house wines are served by the glass from £3.10 (better value by the bottle at £10.95), and the full restaurant list has plenty of good drinking at fair prices, with France the mainstay. A selection of vintage ports, all from very good years, might tempt well-heeled diners. SAMPLE DISHES: wild mushroom and rocket soup £4.25; roast fillet of cod with creamed potatoes, parsnips and lobster sauce £14; chocolate crème brûlée with apricot sorbet £5.25.

Licensees Mark Stephenson and Vicky Elliot (freehouse)
Open 12 to 3, 6 to 10.30, Sun 12 to 3, 7 to 10.30; bar food 12 to 2 (3 Sun), 7 to 9.30 (9 Sun); restaurant Sun 12 to 3, Fri and Sat 7 to 9.30; closed 25 Dec, evenings 26 and 31 Dec
Details No children under 14   Car park   Wheelchair access (also WC)   Garden   No smoking in restaurant   No music   Dogs welcome on a lead   Delta, MasterCard, Switch, Visa   Accommodation: 8 rooms, B&B £65 to £120

FAVERSHAM   Kent   map 3

Albion

29 Front Brents, Faversham ME13 7DH   TEL: (01795) 591411
WEBSITE: www.albiontavern.com
on Faversham Creek, near town centre; from Shepherd Neame brewery take Bridge Road across creek and follow road round to right; pub car park is 150yds on right

Standing on a tree-lined towpath overlooking a creek, this converted pair of white weatherboarded cottages dates from 1750, and shows its age in the gnarled and twisted beams in the cosy main bar. Printed menus demonstrate a preference for fairly simple, mostly traditional tastes such as garlic mush-rooms with crusty bread, or terrine of wild boar, port and redcurrants with plum and apple chutney among starters, followed by main courses of pan-fried calf's liver with crispy pancetta and sage, or local sausages on mash with red onion and thyme jus. Blackboard specials are slightly more ambitious, as in a trio of sea bass, salmon and scallops with chilli and sesame dressing, or chicken with Jack Daniels and hickory sauce and chargrilled pineapple. Beers come from the Shepherd Neame brewery, which is so close that it can be seen from the front windows of the pub, and Master Brew, Spitfire and a seasonal beer such as Early Bird might be on draught. There's a short wine list with four by the glass. SAMPLE DISHES: goats' cheese and basil tart £5; skate wing in parsley and lemon butter £13; pecan and maple cheesecake £4.

Licensee Mrs J.A. Kent (Shepherd Neame)
Open 11 to 3, 7 to 11, Sun 12 to 3, 7 to 10.30, summer 11 to 11; bar food 12 to 2, 7 to 9 (9.30 Fri and Sat)
Details Children welcome   Car park   Wheelchair access (also WC)   Garden   No-smoking area
Background music   Dogs welcome on a lead   Amex, Delta, MasterCard, Switch, Visa

FAWLEY   **Buckinghamshire**   **map 2**

▲ Walnut Tree
Fawley RG9 6JE   TEL: (01491) 638360
6m W of Marlow on A4155, turn N on single-track road signposted Fawley; turn right at T-junction; pub a few hundred yards on left

The single-track road climbs through woodland for about a mile (seems longer when you're behind a tractor). Eventually you reach this 1950s, partly red-brick building with the odd Land Rover parked in front and picnic tables at the side giving a fine view over the Thames valley almost 400 feet below. Inside there's a comfortable and relaxed feel to the restaurant, conservatory and two bars, where they serve Brakspear brews. Bar and restaurant menus differ but overlap, and one can eat from either anywhere in the pub. In the bar some 20 dishes are inscribed on a blackboard, and chef/co-licensee Graham Turner varies the selection every couple of months. Over and above baguettes (never on Sunday) and steaks, the dishes are ambitious and executed with imagination and skill. A starter of four plump and very fresh scallops with oriental salad, enhanced by a 'brilliant' dressing, has been much enjoyed. An avocado, warm chicken and smoked bacon salad intermingled interesting textures and flavours (and again came with an intriguing dressing), while a generous piece of nicely timed grilled salmon came on pappardelle with an intense tomato sauce. Puds run from lightweight crème brûlée to a hulking (but heavenly) portion of light-textured marmalade and whisky bread-and-butter pudding with custard, while the wine list of around 30 bottles is mainly rooted in the Old World, but allows the New a brief look-in too. Eight house wines start at £11.95 and are also available by the glass. SAMPLE DISHES: Pan-fried Portobello mushroom on toasted brioche served with grilled marinated goats' cheese £7; pan-fried calf's liver, mustard mashed potato with smoked bacon and red wine jus £13; chocolate tart with raspberry crème fraîche £5.

Licensees Sean and Tina Mayberry and Graham Turner (Brakspear)
Open 12 to 3, 7 to 9.30, Sun 12 to 4; bar food and restaurant 12 to 2.45, 7 to 9, Sun 12 to 4
Details Children welcome if eating   Car park   Wheelchair access (also WC)   Garden and patio
No smoking in dining room and conservatory   Background or occasional live music   Dogs welcome in bar area   Amex, Delta, Diners, MasterCard, Switch, Visa   Accommodation: 1 room, B&B £45 to £65

Forest Inn

Cuckstool Lane, Fence BB12 9PA   TEL: (01282) 613641
WEBSITE: www.forestinn.co.uk
take Brierfield turning off A6068 outside Fence

Although close to Nelson, this sturdy-looking stone building stands on its own on a country lane surrounded by fields and sheep. Inside, the décor of the spacious, open-plan bar and conservatory has a modern look: think beech tables and halogen lamps. Various eating options are offered. As well as the full menu, there is a range of interesting sandwiches and salads at lunchtime, and black-boards list daily specials. Starters of black pudding in bacon and mushroom sauce, or a trio of smoked salmon terrines are typical of the kitchen's approach. Main courses are in similar vein, ranging from poached salmon salad, or fillet of hake with chips and a poached egg, to confit of duckling with cranberry sauce and sautéed potatoes, or tenderloin of pork with caramelised apples and a shallot and red wine sauce. Theakston and Black Sheep Best Bitter are on hand-pump, along with a guest ale. A short wine list covers the world effectively, with most under £15 and 12 available by the glass from £1.55 to £3.95. SAMPLE DISHES: king prawns wrapped in bacon with soured cream sauce £5; breast of Barbary duck glazed with lime and kiwi fruit served with sautéed potatoes and vegetables £10.50; bread-and-butter pudding with custard £4.

Licensee Clive W. Seedall (freehouse)
Open *12 to 11 (10.30 Sun); bar food and restaurant Mon to Sat 12 to 2.30, 5.30 to 9.30,*
Sun 12 to 9
Details *Children welcome   Car park   Garden and patio   No smoking in restaurant   Background*
music   No dogs   Amex, Delta, MasterCard, Switch, Visa

King William IV

High Street, Fenstanton PE28 9JF   TEL: (01480) 462467
off A14, 6m SE of Huntingdon

The often overloaded A14 luckily loops around Fenstanton. So the village where Capability Brown spent his declining years keeps to itself its seventeenth-century jewels: the lovely little brick-built lock-up with a clock on the roof, and this brick and whitewash terraced pub with kohl-rimmed windows. Take the left-hand door, and you're in the bar, with its brick and studwork counter and low, beamed ceiling, a cheerful red carpet picking up the glow from the brick fireplace at one end. Here there is Greene King Abbot Ale and IPA, plus a guest – maybe Hook Norton Old Hooky or Bateman XXXB. The other end of the building has two dining rooms, the main one low-ceilinged and cosy, with scrubbed wood tables and standing studwork; behind is a lighter, more modern room with large windows. Two blackboards (one for fish specials) complement printed menus and offer, say, a generous pile of moules marinière to start, or baked field mushrooms stuffed with Brie and walnuts. Main dishes cover steaks (including venison), crispy duck leg on ginger stir-fried vegetables, or maybe a whole grilled black bream with lemon butter (Sunday lunch brings a choice of five different roasts). Sweets include tarte au citron and sticky toffee pudding. Ten wines come in litre or half-litre carafes as well as bottles or glasses, with another ten by the bottle, all at friendly prices. SAMPLE DISHES: chicken satay £5.50; roast loin of monkfish with lobster sauce £14; chocolate and rum truffle cake £4.50.

Licensee Mrs D.T. Amps (Greene King)
Open 11 to 3.30, 6 to 11, Sun 12 to 10.30; bar food and restaurant Mon to Sat 12 to 2.15, 7 to 9.45, Sun 12 to 3.30
Details Children welcome in eating areas   Car park   Wheelchair access (not WC)   Patio   No smoking in dining room   Background and live music   Dogs welcome in bar only   MasterCard, Switch, Visa

FERNHURST   **West Sussex**   **map 3**

King's Arms 😺 🍺
Midhurst Road, Fernhurst GU27 3HA   TEL: (01428) 652005
on A286, 1m S of Fernhurst on sharp bend

On a main road, but in the middle of nowhere, this compact 300-year-old inn reminded one reporter of a converted farmhouse rather than a pub. Nowadays, in the hands of Michael and Annabel Hirst, it is a place with aspirations – most of which relate to the output of the kitchen. On the one hand there's a menu designated 'Comfort Food' (or, as an inspector redefined it, 'bar-type food at a price'): expect smoked salmon with scrambled eggs on toast, corned beef hash with a fried egg, beer-battered cod with hand-cut chips and so forth. Most of Michael Hirst's gastro-energies are channelled into the main menu, which moves rapidly into the world of cosmopolitan modern cooking: roast quail is served as a starter with buttered cabbage and a grape and bacon sauce, pan-fried fillet of sea bass is accompanied by creamed spinach and a tomato and dill beurre blanc. Results can be impressive: whole roast partridge on sweet potato rösti with thyme jus has been described as a 'high-quality dish'. Desserts are pretty arty: bitter chocolate tart with Kahlùa syrup has been appreciated; likewise pear, sultana and cinnamon strudel with vanilla and Calvados sabayon. Any doubts that this is still a pub should be quelled by the five real ales on handpump: King's Arms Bitter, brewed by Ventnor Brewery, Ringwood Best, and Yankee from Rooster's in North Yorkshire are just three examples from a regularly changing list; there's also genuine Dublin-brewed Guinness on tap. The no-smoking room at the back has a strong oenological theme, with labels, cartoons, corkscrews and much more on display. The wine list is mostly French, with plenty of half-bottles and eight offered by the glass (from £2.50). The 'odds and ends' page is a changing selection of older vintages of classic wines. SAMPLE DISHES: seared king scallops with a warm salad of crispy prosciutto and cherry tomatoes £6.50; roast rack of lamb with red onion tarte Tatin and rosemary and redcurrant jus £13.75; baked white chocolate cheesecake £4.75.

Licensees Michael and Annabel Hirst (freehouse)
Open 11.30 to 3, 5.30 (6.30 Sat) to 11, Sun 12 to 3; bar food and restaurant all week 12 to 2.30, Mon to Sat 7 to 9.30; closed first 10 days Jan
Details Children welcome in eating areas exc under-14s after 7pm   Car park   Garden   No smoking in 1 room   No music   Dogs welcome in bar   Delta, MasterCard, Switch, Visa

▲ General Tarleton ✿

Boroughbridge Road, Ferrensby HG5 0PZ   TEL: (01423) 340284
WEBSITE: www.generaltarleton.co.uk
off A6065, 3m N of Knaresborough

The General Tarleton, a former coaching inn dating from the eighteenth century, stands in open country at the edge of the village. Although more a restaurant-with-rooms than a pub, with a wing converted to provide accommodation and a restaurant spread over two floors with its own set-price menu, eating and drinking options are flexible, and the beamed bar/brasserie has an informal, pubby feel. The atmosphere in here is relaxed, helped along by a log-burning fireplace and cosy alcoves, and it is still possible to drop in just for a sandwich (lunchtimes only) and a pint – beers come from Yorkshire brewers Timothy Taylor and Black Sheep – but it will be hard to resist the menu of ambitious modern brasserie fare. Typical options have included starters of a warm salad of duck confit with bacon, black pudding and chorizo, and pappardelle with porcini, thyme and tomatoes, and main courses of roast rump of lamb on grilled vegetables and rocket, and chargrilled yellow-fin tuna with butter-bean and truffle purée and crispy onions. Finish with chocolate brownie with chocolate fudge sauce, sticky toffee pudding, or a selection of English farmhouse cheeses. The impressive wine list is arranged by grape variety and style, with a healthy mix of quality names from Old World and New and a dozen by the glass (£2.20 to £3.90). The own-label house wines at £12.95 are the only budget bottles on the list. SAMPLE DISHES: queenie scallops grilled with garlic butter, Gruyère and Cheddar £6; pan-seared calf's liver with creamed potatoes, braised baby gems and a red wine and shallot glaze £13.25; brandy-snap basket filled with vanilla ice cream and chocolate sauce £3.75.

Licensee John Topham (freehouse)
Open *12 to 3, 6 to 11 (10.30 Sun); bar food 12 to 2.15 (2.30 Sun), 6 to 9.30 (10 Sat, 8.30 Sun); restaurant Sun 12 to 2.30, Mon to Sat 6 to 9.30 (10 Sat)*
Details *Children welcome   Car park   Wheelchair access (not WC)   Garden   No-smoking area in bar, no smoking in restaurant   Occasional live or background music   Dogs welcome   Amex, Delta, MasterCard, Switch, Visa   Accommodation: 14 rooms, B&B £74.95 to £84.90*

Whalebone Inn [NEW ENTRY]

Chapel Road, Fingringhoe CO5 7BG   TEL: (01206) 729307
off B1025 Colchester to West Mersea road

Next to the village green and pond, the Whalebone has a garden with wide views over the river valley it overlooks. The place is furnished with light oak tables on bare floorboards, and an open log fire burns in winter. The menu is chalked up on a large board adjacent to the bar, where Greene King IPA and Old Speckled Hen are among the real ales on draught. Start with crisp crab pasties, leek, potato and celery soup, or sautéed chicken livers with walnuts on crispbread with a herb salad, and go on to properly cooked skate wing with black butter and capers accompanied by al dente vegetables, lamb and apricot tagine with couscous, or traditional steak and kidney pie. Rice pudding with apricot compote, or apple pie with custard might be among the familiar puddings. Around half a dozen wines are served by the glass. SAMPLE DISHES: mussels in a white wine, garlic, cream and parsley broth £4.75; lamb's liver and bacon in Madeira sauce with mash £9.50; brown sugar meringues with whipped cream £4.

Licensee Mrs V.K. Steed (freehouse)
Open 10 to 3, 5.30 to 11 (all day Sat and Sun summer); bar food 12 to 2.30, 6.30 to 9.30 (all day Sat and Sun summer)
Details Children welcome in family room   Car park   Garden   No smoking in family room
Occasional background music   Dogs welcome on a lead   Amex, MasterCard, Switch, Visa

FLETCHING   East Sussex   map 3

▲ Griffin Inn ✿ 🍺 🍇

Fletching TN22 3SS   TEL: (01825) 722890
WEBSITE: www.thegriffininn.co.uk
off A272, between Maresfield and Newick, 3m NW of Uckfield

Between the Weald and the South Downs, in the Ouse valley, Fletching has existed since Saxon times. The eleventh century brought a Norman church, and the sixteenth the half-timbered houses in the High Street as well as the Griffin, whose part-brick, part-plaster façade has three doors, each with a tiled canopy above. Behind, a two-acre garden offers adults fine-weather relaxation and children trees to climb and imaginary jungles to explore. In the beamed, wood-panelled bar there are local ales: Harveys Sussex Best Bitter, Rother Valley Level Best and Horsham Best Bitter, along with Badger Tanglefoot from Dorset, and a dozen assorted wines by the glass. The daily-changing bar menu and blackboards run to, say, runner bean and ham hock soup to start, or chicken and Cashel Blue terrine, or maybe Grilled lemon-scented sardines with tomato sauce. Follow that with veal meatballs on tagliatelle with tomato salsa, roast local mackerel with fennel and cider sauce, or a fennel, tomato and Taleggio tarte Tatin. Then try squeezing in sticky toffee pudding, or iced white chocolate and orange mousse. The restaurant moves up a gear, offering roast chicken and spring onion laksa, or crab ravioli, then pancetta-wrapped roast pigeon on grilled polenta, or maybe bouillabaisse; among the desserts are pink pannacotta with plum compote, or glazed orange and sweet potato tart. The wine list, similarly, shifts up to cruising speed here, with a slick selection that is mostly over £20. Both bar and restaurant offer both wine lists. SAMPLE DISHES: seared chicken livers with slow-roast tomatoes on toasted crostini £5.50; chargrilled tuna with salade niçoise £11.50; raspberry fool £5.

Licensees Nigel and James Pullan, and John Gatti (freehouse)
Open 12 to 3, 6 to 11 (7 to 10.30 Sun); bar food and restaurant 12 to 2.30, 7 to 9.30 (9 Sun); closed 25 Dec, restaurant closed Sun evening winter
Details Children welcome   Car park   Wheelchair access (also WC)   Garden and patio
Occasional live music   Dogs welcome exc in restaurant   Amex, Delta, Diners, MasterCard, Switch, Visa   Accommodation: 8 rooms, B&B £50 to £120

FONTHILL GIFFORD   **Wiltshire**   **map 2**

▲ Beckford Arms

Fonthill Gifford SP3 6PX   TEL: (01747) 870385
take minor road off B3089 at Fonthill Bishop and follow signs to Fonthill Gifford

Originating in the eighteenth century, this stone-built inn on a quiet country road has an attractive garden – ideal for balmy summer days. Within is an airy conservatory and lots of dark wood, prints and a log fire in the bar and eating areas. The cooking style varies from the traditional – honey-baked ham with free-range eggs and fries, for instance – to more exotic dishes of Asian-style fishcakes with a sweet chilli dip, or Thai green chicken curry with fragrant rice. Starters are equally broad-ranging, taking in salt-and-pepper squid with pineapple and chilli relish, and gravad lax with wild rocket, and one of the puddings might be treacle sponge. Greene King Abbot Ale and Timothy Taylor Landlord are among the real ales, and all seven house wines are served by the glass from £2.60. SAMPLE DISHES: Cashel Blue fritters with basil mayonnaise £5; Gressingham duck breast with butternut squash purée and blackberry sauce £12; white chocolate and orange crème brûlée £4.

Licensees Karen and Eddie Costello (freehouse)
Open *12 to 11 (10.30 Sun); bar food 12 to 2, 7 to 9; closed 25 Dec*
Details *Children welcome in family room   Car park   Garden   Occasional background music   Dogs welcome   Delta, MasterCard, Switch, Visa   Accommodation: 8 rooms, B&B £40 to £85*

FORD   **Buckinghamshire**   **map 3**

▲ Dinton Hermit

Water Lane, Ford HP17 8XH   TEL: (01296) 747473
off A418, 4m SW of Aylesbury

Dinton was the birthplace of John Bigg, clerk to one of the regicides who sentenced Charles I to execution. After the Restoration Bigg became a hermit and until his death in 1696 lived in splendid squalor in a cave (one shoe survives in an Oxford museum). The pub named after him is an extended brick cottage in the hamlet next door to Dinton. At the time of going to press, it was closed for refurbishment that will include, among other things, an extension to accommodate rooms for B&B. Real ales on tap include Morrells Oxford Blue, and Fuller's London Pride. A short, interesting wine list, starting at £15, has eight by the glass. Lunchtime begins with dishes like home-made soup (the tomato is commended), or six nicely cooked, filo-wrapped prawns with a sweet chilli dip, followed perhaps by a generous helping of well-timed calf's liver and bacon with mash and onion gravy, or a smoked salmon niçoise salad (there's roast beef, lamb or chicken on Sundays). Evenings might bring a warm salad of black pudding and smoked bacon beneath a poached egg, and fancier mains like monkfish swathed in pancetta and laid on spinach under a lemon butter sauce. Sweets could include raspberry brûlée, or strawberry champagne gâteau. SAMPLE DISHES: Cajun chicken salad £7; bacon-wrapped chicken suprême with Cheddar sauce £9; chocolate rum pot £4.50.

Licensees John and Debbie Collinswood (freehouse)
Open *Tue to Sat 12 to 2, 6 to 11, Sun 12 to 3; bar food Tue to Sat 12 to 2, 6 to 9, Sun 12 to 3; closed 25 Dec*
Details *Children welcome   Car park   Garden and patio   Background music   Dogs welcome exc in restaurant   Amex, Delta, MasterCard, Switch, Visa   Accommodation: 13 rooms; prices on application*

FORDHAM   **Cambridgeshire**   **map 6**

White Pheasant

21 Market Street, Fordham CB7 5LQ   TEL: (01638) 720414
on A142, 5m N of Newmarket

Set back a little from the main road, this large, white-painted seventeenth-century inn is easy to miss: look for the turning to Burwell. Inside, the light, airy main bar's atmosphere mixes traditional pub and relaxed restaurant – walls hung with prints and bric-à-brac, background music, tables laid for food. To drink, there's Hobson's Choice from City of Cambridge Brewery, or Woodforde's Wherry and Admiral's Reserve, and the 25-bin wine list offers 12 by the glass and keeps under £20 (ten more 'fine' wines go higher). Interested, attentive service by busy girls in Britney-Spears-as-waitress outfits complements generous portions and fresh ingredients. Choose from bar snacks (sandwiches/salads/sausage and mash) or a menu that doesn't overlook vegetarians and gluten-allergics, plus blackboard specials, offering maybe duck and pistachio pâté, or very large, fresh tiger prawns marinated in ginger and garlic, 'grilled to the right point' and served with an avocado and cream cheese galette. Pork escalope with bleu d'Auvergne and celeriac and apple mash could follow, or large, juicy sea bass fillets, well timed, on crushed new potatoes and creamed leeks. If puds are feasible, sticky toffee pudding is rich and plentifully sauced. SAMPLE DISHES: smoked chicken Caesar salad £5; pheasant, partridge, pigeon and rabbit pie £11; chocolate brownies and cherry sauce £4.25.

Licensee Elizabeth Meads (freehouse)
Open *12 to 3, 6 to 11, Sun 12 to 3, 7 to 10.30; bar food and restaurant Mon to Sat 12 to 2.30, 6 to 9.30, Sun 12 to 2.30, 7 to 9*
Details *Children welcome   Car park   Garden   No-smoking areas   Background music   Guide dogs only   Amex, Delta, MasterCard, Switch, Visa*

FORDWICH   **Kent**   **map 3**

Fordwich Arms

King Street, Fordwich CT2 0DB   TEL: (01227) 710444
off A28, 3m NE of Canterbury

The Fordwich Arms has a solid look to it, built in brick in mock-Tudor style opposite the tiny half-timbered, sixteenth-century town hall. Inside, the one large bar area is dominated by a central counter, and there are log-burning fireplaces at either end of the room. The place is well kept and attractively decorated, with floral wallpaper, dried flowers and a collection of knick-knacks, and friendly staff set a cheerful tone. There is also a separate restaurant. A profusion of ploughman's are served in the bar; otherwise the menu here is similar to the one in the restaurant. The cooking style shows a wide range of modern, international influences, starters encompassing deep-fried anchovies on a red onion and tomato salad, and field mushrooms topped with Stilton and leeks, mains taking in Sheppey lamb and mint sausages on mustard mash, grilled plaice with lime, coriander and chilli butter, and, in season, perhaps roast pheasant with creamy brandy sauce. Finish with something indulgent like chocolate cheesecake with Baileys ice cream, or fruits of the forest pavlova roulade. Beers include Shepherd Neame Master Brew Bitter, Flowers Original and Wadworth 6X, and 10 wines are sold by the glass. SAMPLE DISHES: smoked salmon, smoked trout and cream cheese gâteau £5.25; lamb stew with dumplings £9; iced rum and raisin bombe £3.50.

Licensees Mr and Mrs Sean O'Donnell (Enterprise Inns)
Open 11 to 11, Sun 12 to 3, 7 to 10.30; bar food and restaurant (exc Sun evening) 12 to 2.30 (2 Sun), 6.30 to 9.30
Details Children welcome in restaurant Car park Wheelchair access (also WC) Garden and patio No smoking in restaurant Occasional background music Dogs welcome exc in restaurant Delta, MasterCard, Switch, Visa

FORTON Lancashire   map 8

Bay Horse Inn 😋
Bay Horse, Forton LA2 0HR TEL: (01524) 791204
WEBSITE: www.bayhorseinn.com
from M6 junction 33 take A6 towards Preston; take second left-hand turn; pub is on right

Tables outside and flower-filled window boxes create an inviting air at this black and white pub at a sharp bend in the road. Inside, a separate room for dining is laid up a little more ornately than the rest, but this is essentially a pleasantly attractive, no-frills rural pub. Orders are taken at the bar, and the food on offer may raise some eyebrows if you're expecting standard pub fare. A terrine of chicken, Stilton and Italian ham with chutney, a seafood platter, and smoked duck breast with carrot rémoulade crop up among first courses. After that, the choice extends from braised shank of lamb with mustard mash and an ale and thyme sauce to fish dishes such as grilled lemon sole with dill butter. If you've left a spare corner for a pudding, try chocolate marquise with Baileys ice cream, or crème brûlée. Draught ales include Moorhouses Pendle Witches Brew, Thwaites Lancaster Bomber, Ridleys Rumpus and Adnams Fisherman. Around 10 wines are served by the glass from a list approaching 30 bottles. SAMPLE DISHES: dressed crab with mustard mayonnaise £6.75; roast halibut with potato purée and red chard and rocket salad with red wine dressing £15; bread-and-butter pudding with whisky, nutmeg and walnut ice cream £4.25.

Licensee Craig Wilkinson (Creation Foods)
Open Tue to Sat 12 to 2, 6.30 to 11, Sun 12 to 4, 8 to 10.30; bar food Tue to Sat 12 to 1.30, 7 to 9.15, Sun 12 to 3.45
Details Children welcome in eating areas Car park Wheelchair access (not WC) Garden and patio No smoking in dining areas Background music No dogs Amex, Delta, MasterCard, Switch, Visa

FOTHERINGHAY   Northamptonshire   map 6

Falcon Inn 🏆 🏆 🍇

Fotheringhay PE8 5HZ   TEL: (01832) 226254
WEBSITE: www.huntsbridge.com
off A605, 4m NE of Oundle

Fotheringhay, a quiet village, is where Mary Queen of Scots was executed, and the monarch is depicted in prints on the walls of this pretty country pub. Windsor chairs, fresh flowers, discreet soft colours and properly laid tables lend an air of modern comfort, and the main dining area is in a handsome conservatory extension. Ray Smikle cooks with an eye on developing round-the-world fashions without resorting to over-elaboration, delivering duck spring rolls ('more like filled cornucopias' was the opinion of one reporter) with Asian coleslaw and a sweet-and-sour dressing, pavé of lamb with creamed cannellini beans and salsa verde, and spiced pork chop with harissa aïoli, sautéed potatoes, prunes, apples, bacon and pearl onions. Fish might be fillet of salmon marinated in chilli, lime and soy served with mixed greens and baby vegetables, and desserts take in caramelised lemon tart with cherry compote, and sticky toffee pudding. In common with the other pubs in the Huntsbridge Group (see the entries for the Old Bridge at Huntington, the Pheasant at Keyston and the Three Horseshoes at Madingley), you can eat as much or as little as you want: a blackboard lists snacks, and other possibilities are a bowl of soup – cauliflower, or white onion, sage and cider, say – or something like herby sausages with mash. And, like those other pubs, it lays on wine with panache. A dozen or more wines by the glass from £2.95 to £6 are complemented by a good range of sherries and dessert wines. The main list of around 100 bins is arranged by style and divided into 'under £20' and 'top class' sections with useful, knowledgeable notes. If it's beer you've come for, choose one of the changing guest ales, something from perhaps Adnams or Greene King; Stowford Press cider is on draught too. SAMPLE DISHES: goats' cheese and roasted red onion tart £4.75; chicken breast roasted with lemon and herbs accompanied by roasted peppers, red onions, chorizo, new potatoes and tomatoes with cream cheese £13.50; passion-fruit cheesecake £5.50.

Licensees Ray Smikle and John Hoskins (freehouse)
Open 11.30 to 3.30, 6 to 11, Sun 12 to 3, 7 to 10.30; bar food and restaurant 12 to 2.15, 6.30 to 9.15, Sun 12 to 2.15, 7 to 9
Details Children welcome   Car park   Wheelchair access (also WC)   Garden and patio
No smoking in conservatory   No music   Dogs welcome in 1 room   Amex, Delta, Diners, MasterCard, Switch, Visa

FOWLMERE   Cambridgeshire   map 6

Chequers

High Street, Fowlmere SG8 7SR   TEL: (01763) 208369
off B1368, between A10 and A505, 5m NE of Royston

If you are bemused by the sign outside this sixteenth-century pub, the answer lies in the fact that Fowlmere airfield was a base for pilots from both world wars: the blue chequers on one side represent No. 19 Squadron RAF, the red on the other signify the 339th USAF Fighter Group. Nowadays, it's still a thriving local haunt, warmed by a huge log-burning inglenook. On the food front, you can browse the laminated menu or consider the blackboard: either way, there is plenty to think about. Typically elaborate offerings might include haggis, faggots and black pudding with herbed Puy lentils, pink peppercorns and 'picked' parsley before, perhaps, grilled escolar (aka Spanish mackerel) with shrimp and lobster sauce served with olive oil mash and mange-tout. To finish, Irish farmhouse cheeses might be a better bet than complex desserts such as pan-fried bananas with Muscavado sugar and Tia Maria, served with vanilla ice cream and sprinkled with chocolate shavings. Adnams Bitter and a guest ale are on draught, but it would be a shame to miss out on the freshly squeezed orange juice or the enticing selection of 30 malt whiskies. Seven house wines are under £12 and also available by the glass. Otherwise the wine list has a French bias and favours pricey bottles, although there are some canny choices under £20, such as Côtes du Rhône-Villages from Domaine de la Renjarde for £16.50. SAMPLE DISHES: creamed lovage and vegetable soup £3.50; braised steak with beer and onions, wilted spinach, bubble and squeak and roast orange chicory £9.75; hot date sponge with sticky toffee sauce £4.25.

Licensees N.S. and P. Rushton (freehouse)
Open 12 to 2.30, 6 to 11, Sun 12 to 3, 7 to 10.30; bar food and restaurant 12 to 2, 7 to 10, Sun 12 to 3, 7 to 9.30; closed 25 Dec
Details Children welcome   Car park   Wheelchair access (not WC)   Garden and patio
No smoking in restaurant   No music   No dogs   Amex, Delta, Diners, MasterCard, Switch, Visa

---

FRAMPTON MANSELL   **Gloucestershire**   **map 2**

White Horse 🌣 🍇   NEW ENTRY

Cirencester Road, Frampton Mansell GL6 8HZ   TEL: (01285) 760960
on A419, about 7m W of Cirencester, at junction with road to Frampton Mansell

---

This old stone pub was derelict when Emma and Shaun Davis (formerly of the Hare & Hounds, Foss Cross) took over in 2001. But they have thoroughly revamped it to create a stylish pub-restaurant, with the emphasis more on 'restaurant' than 'pub'. A fittingly ambitious modern British menu offers starters of squid with mixed leaves and lime dressing, or confit duck leg with sautéed potatoes, chorizo and balsamic. Main courses range from ribeye steak with black pepper sauce to skate wing with Chinese cabbage and watercress butter sauce, while desserts are sophisticated-sounding creations like raspberry and elderflower jelly with clotted cream. There is no real distinction between bar and restaurant, but a separate lunchtime bar menu, written on a blackboard and available throughout, lists simpler dishes along the lines of home-glazed ham with egg and chips, or a salad of chicken, bacon and avocado, plus a selection of filled baguettes. Although food is the main business, drinkers are encouraged – to that end, the bar area is furnished with a large sofa and comfortable chairs where you can relax while enjoying a pint of Uley Bitter, Hook Norton Best or perhaps Arkells Summer Ale in season. If you prefer wine, there is a choice of six by the glass, representing each of the styles used to arrange the list of around 40 bottles. It's an interesting mix and quality is good with prices starting at £10.95 and almost all under £20. SAMPLE

DISHES: curried parsnip soup £3.50; roast partridge with caramelised baby apples and redcurrant jus £12.50; sticky toffee pudding with butterscotch sauce and cream £4.25.

Licensees Emma and Shaun Davis (freehouse)
Open 11 to 3, 6 to 11; bar food 12 to 2.30 (3 Sun), restaurant 12 to 2.30 (3 Sun), 7 to 9.45; closed Sun evening, 24 and 25 Dec
Details Children welcome in eating areas   Car park   Garden   No music   Dogs welcome MasterCard, Switch, Visa

FRITHSDEN   Hertfordshire   map 3

Alford Arms   NEW ENTRY
Frithsden HP1 3DD   TEL: (01442) 864480
turn left at Water End off A4146, head towards Frithsden and Nettleden. Turn left at junction, next right, pub is 100yds on right

A traditional cream-painted country pub, with lanes and fields around, at the entrance to the small village of Frithsden, the Alford Arms is home to a class act, delivering a cut above pub food. Part of the interior is devoted to drinkers and browsers, and the rest to a cosy, intimate and countrified dining room. Chintz curtains, warm coral-coloured walls hung with prints and large pewter pans, soft lighting and plenty of old wooden furniture create a relaxed, unstuffy mood. The menus show a creative and serious approach, with an appealing modern repertoire utilising sound ingredients, accurate cooking and stylish presentation, backed by efficient and youthful service. Start with the likes of oak-smoked bacon on bubble and squeak with hollandaise sauce and a poached egg, and move on to rump of lamb on artichoke mash with tomato and olive compote, or perhaps confit belly of pork on mash with sage and cider jus. There's a short global wine list, with five by the glass, and Tetley Bitter, Flowers Original, Marston's Pedigree and Brakspear Bitter are on handpump. SAMPLE DISHES: sautéed chicken livers on toasted brioche with rocket £5.75; pan-fried sea bream on crushed new potatoes with watercress sauce £13; rhubarb, elderflower and saffron crumble £4.75.

Licensees David and Becky Salisbury (freehouse)
Open 11 to 11, Sun 12 to 10.30; bar food 12 to 2.30, 7 to 10, Sun 12 to 3, 7 to 9.30
Details Children welcome   Car park   Wheelchair access   Patio   Background music   Dogs welcome in bar only   Amex, Delta, MasterCard, Switch, Visa

FRODSHAM   Cheshire   map 7

Netherton Hall   NEW ENTRY
Chester Road, Frodsham WA6 6UL   TEL: (01928) 732342
on A56 Warrington to Chester road, on the SW edge of Frodsham

Although beside a main road, with the M56 only half a mile away, Netherton Hall looks up to the steep, wooded slope of Frodsham Hill and feels surprisingly secluded. A former yeoman farmhouse, it looks out of small-paned windows, through the ivy and creeper that clothe its Cheshire brick, over landscaped gardens that include shrubberies and a fish pond. It describes itself as a restaurant/bar, but there is a good pubby feel to the open-plan layout, which creates several 'rooms' around the cheerful brick and tile bar at the centre, and well-kept beers include Greene King (IPA, Abbot), Timothy Taylor (Landlord, seasonal Ram Tam) and Jennings Cumberland Bitter, so drinkers are well catered for. Bar snacks include omelettes, pasties and eccentricities (Wensleydale and strawberry jam sandwich, spam fritters), but a serious meal might start with tomato and basil soup with English gin, or smoked salmon and crayfish. A grilled Dover sole stuffed with king prawns might follow, or a generous bowlful of wild duck and pheasant casserole with rich, dark gravy; vegetarians might pick a whole roast Camembert with black-pepper and strawberry salad. Sweets encompass lemon soufflé in a brandy-snap basket, and Bakewell tart and custard. Of the 20-some wines listed, from £8.80, 20 come by the glass. SAMPLE DISHES: roast Mediterranean vegetable bruschetta £4; pot-roast shoulder of lamb on fried cabbage mash £12; Mars Bar cheesecake £4.50.

Licensee H. Sharter (Punch Group)
Open 12 to 11, Sun 12 to 10.30; bar food and restaurant 12 to 2.30, 6 to 9
Details No children   Car park   Wheelchair access (not WC)   Garden and patio   No-smoking area in bar, no smoking in dining room   Background music   No dogs   Amex, Delta, MasterCard, Switch, Visa

---

FULBECK   **Lincolnshire**   **map 6**

▲ Hare & Hounds | NEW ENTRY |

The Green, Fulbeck NG32 3JJ   TEL: (01400) 272090
on A607 halfway between Grantham and Lincoln

'An absolute gem' was one reporter's summary of this Grade II listed free-house, dating from 1648 and charmingly situated in an attractive village of old stone houses, overlooking the village green. Inside, it has a traditional feel, with requisite beams and fireplaces, and the friendly and welcoming owners ensure a relaxed and informal mood. The menus read well in a traditional kind of way and offer plenty of choice, kicking off with a range of filled baguettes and jacket potatoes. For those after a more substantial meal, starters are things like breaded mushrooms with garlic mayo, and smoked haddock fishcake with sweet chilli dip, while main courses include curried chicken breast with rice, and omelettes with a choice of fillings. 'House specialities' feature steak and Stilton pie, sautéed chicken and mushrooms in champagne sauce, and sirloin steak marinated in a balsamic reduction, while among desserts is 'David's Speciality' – a concoction of meringue, ice cream, rum-soaked raisins and hot butterscotch sauce. Vegetable crumble, or boeuf bourguignonne might be among the blackboard specials, while the restaurant has its own more upmar-ket menu: confit duck salad with cucumber and plum sauce, and sea bass on fragrant Thai-style noodles are typical. The short version of the wine list in the bar covers the basics – 18 wines from £8.95 to £15.95, with seven by the glass – but the restaurant list has a few more tricks up its sleeve, particularly for fans of full-bodied reds, and all these wines are available in the bar too. Beers are also well represented, featuring XB from Lincolnshire brewer Bateman, as well as Fuller's London Pride and others. SAMPLE DISHES: deep-fried Brie with red pepper jam £4.25; pot-roast shank of lamb in mint gravy £10; Baileys cheesecake £4.

Licensees David and Alison Nicholas (freehouse)
Open 12 to 2.30 (2 winter), 6 to 11, Sun 12 to 2.30, 7 to 11; bar food and restaurant 12 to 2,
6 to 10; open 12 to 11 Sat and Sun Apr to Oct
Details Children welcome Car park Wheelchair access (not WC) Garden and patio
No-smoking area in bar, no smoking in restaurant Background music Dogs welcome exc in
restaurant MasterCard, Switch, Visa Accommodation: 8 rooms, B&B £30 to £50

GALPHAY   **North Yorkshire**   **map 8**

Galphay Arms ✸   NEW ENTRY

Galphay HG4 3NJ   TEL: (01765) 650133
of B6265, 4½m W of Ripon

Although close to Ripon, Galphay feels miles from anywhere. Its pub, parts of
which date from around 1800, is a neat, compact stone building rescued from
a run-down state. New owners put a great deal of effort into the renovation,
and according to a seasoned inspector the results are impressive. Enter into a
reception area with leather armchairs and a blazing log fire, then move to the
main bar area, comfortably furnished and panelled with dark wood. Beyond is
the dining area, done out in pale green and with well-spaced pine tables.
Simple sandwiches and snacks are served in the bar, but the main menu offers
plenty of options for those seeking a full and leisurely meal, and the cooking is
refreshingly simple and unpretentious. Among starters might be wild mushrooms and devilled kidneys on hot buttered toast, or whitebait with lemon and
fried parsley, while ten or so main-course choices typically take in poussin
with herbs and braised aubergine, glazed lamb shank with buttered cabbage,
or roast pork loin with bay leaves and Puy lentils. First-class raw materials give
simple dishes a strong impact. Beers are Black Sheep Bitter and John Smith's
Cask Ale, and there are six wines by the glass from a list of around 45 bottles,
mostly under £20. SAMPLE DISHES: warm shredded lamb with mint and pomegranate £5; spiced breast of chicken with wild apricots £9.50; iced lemon
mousse £3.50.

Licensees Robert and Samantha MacArthur (freehouse)
Open Wed to Mon 12 to 3, 6.30 to 11; bar food Wed to Mon 12 to 2, 6.30 to 10
Details Children welcome Car park Occasional live music No dogs Amex, Delta, Diners,
MasterCard, Switch, Visa

GEDNEY DYKE   **Lincolnshire**   **map 6**

Chequers

Main Street, Gedney Dyke PE12 0AJ   TEL: (01406) 362666
WEBSITE: www.chequerspub.co.uk
just off B1359, from Gedney roundabout on A17, 3m E of Holbeach

It's wildfowl country round here, and if you stray off the roads you could find
yourself in the marshes. Safer perhaps to stick close to the Chequers, white-
walled and roofed with orange pantiles, which stands solid under the vast
fenland sky. Outside there's a garden where you can eat and drink in sun or
shade come summer; in winter seek the open fire in the low-beamed bar.
Food is important here, and you may choose to eat in the bar, in a separate

dining room or in a conservatory extension. On the menu and blackboards fresh fish from Grimsby features strongly, along with rare-breed meat, and vegetarians are not forgotten either. You could start with baked goats' cheese, or crab bisque, then move on to suprême of guinea fowl in Gruyère and mushroom sauce with wild rice, or a herb-crumbed fillet of pike. Sweets are mainly old favourites: banoffi pie and Chantilly cream, or fresh fruit Pavlova. Real ales are Elgood's Black Dog Mild, from Wisbech, and Adnams Best Bitter and Greene King Abbot Ale. Ten wines by the glass head up a list that offers a sound international choice at very good prices. SAMPLE DISHES: bang-bang chicken £5.50; 6-oz fillet of Lincoln red beef with peppercorn sauce £14; lemon and caraway crème brûlée £4.

Licensees Simon and Linda Rattray (freehouse)
Open 12 to 2, 7 to 11 (10.30 Sun); bar food and restaurant 12 to 2, 7 to 9; closed Mon evenings winter
Details Children welcome   Car park   Wheelchair access (also WC)   Garden and patio
No smoking in 1 dining room   Background music   No dogs   Amex, Diners, MasterCard, Switch, Visa

GODMANCHESTER   Cambridgeshire   map 6

Exhibition   NEW ENTRY

London Road, Godmanchester PE29 2HZ   TEL: (01480) 459134
along A1198 towards Wood Green, take first right to Godmanchester and pub is 300yds on right

Not only are the food and ale good and the welcome friendly here, but the Exhibition is in a picture-perfect village, with a number of timber-framed old buildings, surrounded by lovely countryside. This is an attractive old building too, and, although the interior has been extensively renovated, the beams and shape of the old house can still be seen. The main bar holds the real surprise, though, with its re-created shop frontages along the outside wall (a post office, gallery, stores), and, with its stone-flagged floors, there's the distinct impression that you're sitting in a Victorian street. Several blackboard menus provide a wide range of choice and interest for all appetites and tastes: perhaps Roquefort and walnut Welsh rarebit on tomato bread with pesto to start, followed by haunch of wild boar with grain mustard cream sauce and sautéed vegetables, with chocolate, walnut and pecan tart with cappuccino ice cream to finish. Greene King IPA and Fuller's London Pride, plus a changing guest beer, and eight wines by the glass all stack up to provide worthy accompaniments. SAMPLE DISHES: chicken, port and olive terrine £4.75; medallions of beef in a red wine and shallot jus with dauphinois potatoes £12.50; summer fruits pudding and green apple sorbet £4.

Licensee J.W. Middlemiss (Unique)
Open Mon to Thur 11.30 to 3.30, 5.30 to 11.30, Fri and Sat 11.30 to 11.30, Sun 12 to 10.30;
bar food and restaurant 12 to 2.15, 6.30 to 9.45, Sun 12.30 to 3, 6.30 to 9.30
Details Children welcome in restaurant   Car park   Wheelchair access   Garden   No smoking in restaurant   Background and occasional live music   No dogs   Amex, Delta, Diners, MasterCard, Switch, Visa

Green Man

The Street, Gosfield CO9 1TP   TEL: (01787) 472746
on A1017, 4m NE of Braintree

This is a low-rise, old-looking building with pink-washed walls standing on the main road. To the left of the entrance is the small public bar, with a dining room beyond; to the right the often crowded lounge bar is part of a series of low-ceilinged rooms knocked together into an open-plan area with quiet corners. This is a Greene King pub, so their IPA and Abbot Ale are on tap, along with 30-plus wines (including 11 by the glass). At lunchtime a long trestle table groans under a magnificent cold buffet that includes a poached salmon, a turkey and joints of roast beef (both rare and well done), plus salads and pickles; one reporter chose pork and ham (both 'excellent') with chips that 'were the best I've had in years'. Blackboards list other dishes (these are available in the evening too). You could begin with home-made pâté and toast, or crab cakes in sweet-and-sour sauce, before tackling half a roast duck in orange and red wine sauce or a whole lemon sole. Then, should you still have room, there might be triple chocolate bombe. SAMPLE DISHES: king prawns wrapped in filo pastry £4.25; lamb casserole with herb dumpling £7.75; apricot and ginger charlotte £3.50.

Licensee Janet Harrington (Greene King)
Open 11 to 3, 6.15 to 11, Sun 12 to 3, 7 to 10.30; bar food (exc Sun evening) 12 to 2, 6.45 to 9
Details Children welcome   Car park   Wheelchair access (not WC)   Garden and patio
No smoking in dining room   Jukebox   Dogs welcome in bar   Delta, MasterCard, Switch, Visa

Green Cross Inn

Station Road, Goudhurst TN17 1HA   TEL: (01580) 211200
WEBSITE: www.greencrossinn.co.uk
on A262, 3m E of A21 and 1m from village of Goudhurst

FISH

This double-fronted building, of mellow brick with a rather splendid central porch, is at the foot of Goudhurst hill about a mile from the village itself. Open fires, beams and pleasant staff are all part of the appeal, but the main attraction is some first-class food. The bar menu ranges from avocado with prawns to spaghetti con vongole, and chicken couscous. The restaurant menu, also served in the bar, is more extensive and also has a Mediterranean slant, with aubergine parmigiano, paella, and duck cassoulet all showing up. Fish is a speciality: maybe moules marinière, or queen scallops with tagliatelle and a vermouth and tarragon cream sauce to start, followed by grilled Dover sole, sea bass baked with spring onions, ginger, soy sauce and white wine, or freshly dressed crab with salad and new potatoes. Pheasant may make an appearance among meat options, its breast and leg braised and served with wild mushroom sauce and pearl barley, alongside fillet steak. Beers are a decent range from Harveys, Shepherd Neame and local independent brewer Larkins. House selections start at £9 on the list of around 50 wines – mostly traditional French but with a few New World bottles at good prices. Six are available by the glass. SAMPLE DISHES: soft herring roe on hot buttered toast £4; tiger prawns piri-piri with saffron rice £13; steamed golden syrup pudding with custard £4.25.

Licensees Eleuterio and Caroline Lizzi (freehouse)
Open 11 to 3, 6 to 11; bar food and restaurant 12 to 2.30, 7 to 10; closed Sun evenings winter
Details Children welcome   Car park   Garden   No smoking in restaurant   Occasional background music   Dogs welcome   MasterCard, Switch, Visa

GRASMERE   Cumbria   map 10

▲ Travellers Rest
Grasmere LA23 9RR   TEL: (015394) 35604
WEBSITE: www.lakedistrictinns.co.uk
on A591 Keswick road, ½m N of Grasmere

Like its sibling the King's Head, six miles up the road at Thirlspot (see entry), this is a low, terraced building beside the Lake District's main through route, its whitewashed rectilinearity contrasting with the organic shapes and the greens and browns and grey-blues of the landscape around. In the sixteenth century it catered to coaches making the long climb out of Windermere on the road to Keswick; today it meets the needs of Lakeland tourists and walkers – so successfully that food can be slow in coming at busy times, despite the touch-screen ordering system at the bar. Here Jennings Bitter, Cumberland Ale and Sneck Lifter are on handpump, along with guest ales, and a wine list, starting at £10.50 and staying under £17, that offers four by the glass. The menu and specials are mainly sure-fire favourites like spicy coated mushrooms, or moules marinière, among the starters, and steak au poivre, Cumberland sausage and mash, or chargrilled tuna niçoise for mains. Puds include sticky date and caramel pudding and apricot and raspberry roulade. There's also a children's menu (lots of chips). SAMPLE DISHES: coriander crab cakes £6; baked salmon suprême £9; pear and chocolate tart £4.

Licensee Derek Sweeney (freehouse)
Open 11 to 11, Sun 12 to 10.30; bar food and restaurant winter 12 to 3, 5 to 9.30, summer 12 to 9.30
Details Children welcome   Car park   Wheelchair access (not WC)   Garden   No smoking in dining room   Background music   Dogs welcome   Delta, MasterCard, Switch, Visa   Accommodation: 8 rooms, B&B £35 to £84

GREAT HINTON   Wiltshire   map 2

Linnet   NEW ENTRY
Great Hinton BA14 6BU   TEL: (01380) 870354
just S of A361, about 2m E of Trowbridge

While it still looks like a village pub, the emphasis is firmly on dining at this pub-cum-restaurant, which underwent complete refurbishment in 2002. The menus offer a widely varied range of dishes, light lunches typically taking in everything from baked pork and cider dumplings to roasted onion, sweet potato and Parmesan tart, and warm focaccia filled with chicken and avocado, or flaked duck and curried onion marmalade. Among starters on the main menu might be Thai-style marinated salmon with cucumber salsa and soya dressing alongside crab in lime and ginger crème fraîche with balsamic dressing, while mains could be as traditional as Parma ham-wrapped pork fillet with prune stuffing and wild mushroom sauce, or as up to date as chicken marinated in lime and chilli yoghurt with roasted red pepper couscous and coriander sauce. Home-made bread and ice creams are strong points. This is a Wadworth house, offering 6X and IPA for real ale drinkers, while for wine fans there are eight by the glass. SAMPLE DISHES: trout and cod fishcake with lemon tartare cream £5; braised lamb shank with haricot bean and mint casserole £12.50; toffee and pecan brownie with chocolate sauce £5.

Licensee Jonathan Furby (Wadworth)
Open Tue to Sat 11 to 2.30, 6 to 11, Sun 11 to 2.30, 7 to 10.30; bar food and restaurant Tue to Sun 12 to 2, 6.30 to 9 (9.30 Fri and Sat); closed 25 and 26 Dec, 1 Jan
Details Children welcome   Car park   Wheelchair access (also WC)   Patio   No smoking in restaurant   Occasional background music   Dogs welcome in bar only   Amex, Delta, Diners, MasterCard, Switch, Visa

GREAT TEW   Oxfordshire   map 5

▲ Falkland Arms 🍺

Great Tew OX7 4DB   TEL: (01608) 683653
WEBSITE: www.falklandarms.org.uk
off B4022, 5m E of Chipping Norton

Part thatched and part creeper-covered, the Cotswold-stone Falkland Arms seems unchanged since it was first built in the sixteenth century, and Great Tew appears to have been bypassed by time too. The interiors have been superbly preserved, with oak beams and settles, flagstone floors, an inglenook, and wooden shutters at the windows, and a vast collection of jugs and vessels hangs from the ceiling of the bar. Another great strength of the place is its commitment to real ales and ciders, with around half a dozen normally on handpump including regulars Wadworth 6X and IPA plus guest ales; Inch's Harvest dry cider is on draught too. In addition, there are 15 conventional wines, plus about the same number of traditional English country wines. The cooking keeps things nice and simple, in harmony with the surroundings, offering jacket potatoes, baguettes and such one-plate meals as cottage pie, or mushroom and herb stroganoff at lunchtime, and a more extensive daily-changing evening range. That might deliver carrot and coriander soup, or smoked trout salad to start, followed by roast duck breast salad with red wine dressing, or flat-cap mushrooms stuffed with chickpeas and vegetables served on a sweet tomato compote. Finish with apple tart with chocolate ice cream, or chocolate crème brûlée with vanilla ice cream. Staff have been described as friendly and chatty. The pub takes it name from the Falkland family, which inherited the manor of Great Tew in the early seventeenth century and which subsequently gave its name to a group of islands in the South Atlantic. SAMPLE DISHES: pâté with chutney and toast £4; grilled sea bass served on a salad with new potatoes £9.25; sticky toffee pudding £4.25.

Licensee Paul Barlow-Heal (Wadworth)
Open Mon to Fri 11.30 to 2.30, 6 to 11, Sat 11.30 to 3, 6 to 11 (11.30 to 11 summer), Sun 12 to 3, 7 to 10.30 (12 to 10.30 summer); bar food 12 to 2; restaurant Mon to Sat 7 to 8; closed evenings 25, 26 Dec and 1 Jan
Details Children welcome in dining room at lunchtime   Wheelchair access (not WC)   Garden and patio   No smoking in dining room   Live music Sun evening   Dogs welcome on a lead   Amex, Delta, MasterCard, Switch, Visa   Accommodation: 5 rooms, B&B £50 to £80

GREAT WHITTINGTON   Northumberland   map 10

Queens Head Inn ☼

Great Whittington NE19 2HP   TEL: (01434) 672267
from A68 4m N of Corbridge turn E on B6318 at Stagshaw roundabout, then left to village

Although it dates from 1615, this stone building in a charming, out-of-the-way village overlooking lovely countryside has been added to over the years and now has a large dining extension. While the pub is given over mainly to eating, it stocks Queens Head and Hambleton Bitters. The alternative to the main menu at lunchtime is a set-price two-course meal (three courses on Sundays), which might take in soup of the day – perhaps tomato and basil – or chicken liver and bacon pâté with Cumberland sauce, followed by roast loin of pork with an apple and herb jus, or steak and ale pie. The restaurant menu – also available in the bar – is a compendium of sophisticated modern ideas, from 'delicious' ravioli filled with seafood mousse glazed with cheese and shellfish sauce, or a salad of smoked chicken, mango and nuts with a white wine and mustard dressing, to pan-fried chicken breast on garlic rösti with braised leeks, pancetta and Gruyère and a roast garlic jus, or pork tenderloin on orange and onion marmalade with black pudding fritters and a cider and sage jus. Vegetarians can choose from roast vegetable kebabs on spicy noodles with a sweet-and-sour sauce, or vegetable strudel, and among the chef's specials may be sirloin steak with king prawn and mushroom kebab and herb and garlic butter. Three wines come by the glass from a list of about two dozen that has a good range from the New World. SAMPLE DISHES: chicken and leek soup £4.50; seared fillet of lamb with a pear and redcurrant tartlet and port and thyme jus £18; iced nougatine with fruit coulis £4.50.

Licensee Ian Scott (freehouse)
Open Tue to Sat and bank hol Mon 12 to 2.30, 6 to 11, Sun 12 to 2.30; bar food and restaurant Tue to Sat and bank hol Mon 12 to 2, 6.30 to 9, Sun 12 to 2
Details Children welcome in eating areas   Car park   Wheelchair access (also WC)   No smoking in restaurant   No music   Guide dogs only   Delta, MasterCard, Switch, Visa

GREAT WOLFORD   Warwickshire   map 5

▲ Fox & Hounds Inn ▮

Great Wolford CV36 5NQ   TEL: (01608) 674220
off A44, 3m NE of Moreton-in-Marsh

'It's small, it's cosy, it's very nicely subtly lit,' runs a favourable report from one who knows this slightly classy Cotswolds pub built around a gravel courtyard. Ancient shiny flagstones, beams garlanded with dried hops and a great hearth give the place an unashamedly 'rural gentry atmosphere'. The current licensee has done little to change its virtues, one of which is a splendid collection of draught beers, which always features weekly guest brews: perhaps Hook Norton Best Bitter, North Cotswold Genesis and Wye Valley Bitter. The pub also boasts 180 different whiskies, and wines include six by the glass from a list of about two dozen. If food is what you're after, consider the blackboards. Cheese turns up regularly in many dishes: Oxford Blue crumbled into cream of celeriac soup, Old Worcester used as a topping with spinach for field mushroom rarebit. Elsewhere, contemporary ideas (pan-fried pigeon breasts with black pudding and fresh orange, fillet of red mullet on warm new potato and rocket salad with tapénade dressing) rub shoulders with old-style comfort food (home-baked ham on bubble and squeak with parsley sauce). Desserts inhabit the traditional world of treacle tart and rhubarb fool. At lunchtime (Tuesday to Saturday) you can also get sandwiches and baguettes. Service struck one reporter as 'beyond compare'. SAMPLE DISHES: wild smoked salmon with lime mayonnaise £6.25; chargrilled venison on roasted root vegetables with a chocolate and redcurrant sauce £12.50; white chocolate and basil crème brûlée £4.25.

Licensee Wendy Veale (freehouse)
Open Tue to Sat 12 to 2.30, 6 to 11, Sun 12 to 3, 6 to 10.30; bar food Tue to Sun 12 to 2, Tue to Sat 6.30 to 9; phone to check bank hol Mon opening times
Details Children welcome in eating area   Car park   Wheelchair access (also WC)   Patio
No-smoking area   Background music   Dogs welcome   Delta, MasterCard, Switch, Visa
Accommodation: 4 rooms, B&B £35 to £60

GREAT YELDHAM   Essex   map 6

White Hart 🌸 🍇
Poole Street, Great Yeldham CO9 4HJ   TEL: (01787) 237250
on A604 between Haverhill and Halstead, 6m NW of Halstead

The setting is an almost monolithic half-timbered Tudor house, dating from 1505, with a red-tiled roof and yellow-ochre walls. It makes an imposing location for this premier-league pub/restaurant. Through the door is a roomy and elegant bar with well-spaced armchairs and an atmosphere of wellbeing and traditional creature comforts (including a log fire in winter). To one side is a slightly more formal restaurant complete with polished floorboards, antique tables and two enormous inglenooks at either end. You can choose to eat where you like. The 'light menu' (available for lunch and dinner) promises a selection of farmhouse cheeses from Jeroboam's, steak sandwiches with fries and mustard, and, say, cod and chips, while the full works is a wide-ranging assortment of dishes spanning everything from calf's liver on buttered leeks and lentils to breast of chicken on a crispy onion and potato cake with buttered spinach and thyme jus. Fish is particularly well handled: an inspection meal yielded 'imaginative' seared scallops on a pak choi and oyster mushroom stir-fry with sweet 'peppadew' sauce, and 'judiciously cooked' roast cod on a chickpea, plum tomato and onion compote. The kitchen also takes account of the seasons: in December you might find grilled goats' cheese with spiced figs, red onions and walnuts, then steamed venison and onion pudding with buttered mash, root vegetables and hisbi cabbage, followed by traditional sherry trifle. Adnams is the house bitter, although there are always guest ales, plus six Belgian bottled beers and oak-matured scrumpy. The outstanding list of 80 wines arranged by style is a joy to choose from, whatever your budget. Thirteen come by the glass from £1.95 to £3.95 and the full selection will get wine lovers' pulses racing with Old World stars like Olivier Leflaive, Verget and Domaine du Vieux Télégraphe set against Californian upstarts Qupé, Bonny Doon and Ridge – but there's good stuff under £15 too. An impressive range of champagnes opens proceedings and sweet wine fans are well catered for come dessert time. SAMPLE DISHES: crispy bacon and black pudding salad topped with a soft-poached egg £5.25; herb-crusted skate on a roasted pepper, French bean and tomato sauté with grain mustard and parsley butter £14; chocolate and pecan nut tart with crème fraîche £5.75.

Licensee John Dicken (freehouse)
Open 11 to 11, Sun 12 to 10.30; bar food 12 to 9.30; restaurant 12 to 2, 6.30 to 9.30
Details Children welcome   Car park   Wheelchair access (also WC)   Garden and patio
No smoking in restaurant   Background music   Guide dogs only   Amex, Delta, Diners, MasterCard,
Switch, Visa

GRETA BRIDGE   Co Durham   map 10

▲ Morritt Arms 🍇

Greta Bridge DL12 9SE   TEL: (01833) 627232
WEBSITE: www.themorritt.co.uk
off A66, 6m E of Bowes

On a cul-de-sac off the A66 and approached over a graceful, high-arched bridge over the river Greta, the Morritt Arms is a classically Georgian building, part of its mellow limestone façade covered with Virginia creeper, with an elegant pillared porch. Inside, the walls of the Dickens Bar, so called because the author reputedly stayed here in 1839, are covered with murals depicting Pickwickian characters. A large curving wooden bar takes up one end of the room, while a stuffed black bear guards the other end; in between are an open fire, a mongrel selection of chairs, settles and Britannia tables and a shelf of pewter mugs and teapots. The hotel also has comfortable beamed lounges, a brightly decorated bistro and a separate panelled restaurant. The bar menu offers an interesting mix: although starters are limited – tomato and mozzarella salad among them – main courses encompass pan-fried chicken breast with mushroom and white wine sauce, steak and mushroom pie, steaks with the usual trimmings, and seafood tagliatelle. Granary baguettes, ploughman's and a platter of cold meats are also on offer, and sticky toffee pudding might be one of the desserts. Real ales come in the form of Timothy Taylor Landlord, Jennings Cumberland Ale and Black Sheep Best Bitter. Ten wines come by the glass from a 150-strong list arranged by grape variety and then by region – and there's plenty of choice whichever way you choose to look at it. SAMPLE DISHES: chicken liver parfait £4; braised lamb shank with root vegetables £8; bread-and-butter pudding £3.75.

Licensee Barbara-Anne Johnson (freehouse)
Open 11 to 11, Sun 12 to 10.30; bar food 12 to 5 (3 Sun), 6 to 9.30 (9 Sun), restaurant 12 to 2,
7 to 9 (8.30 Sun)
Details Children welcome   Car park   Wheelchair access (also WC)   Garden and patio
No-smoking area in bar, no smoking in restaurant   Occasional live music   Dogs welcome exc in
eating areas   Amex, Delta, MasterCard, Switch, Visa   Accommodation: 23 rooms, B&B £59.50 to
£106.50

▲ Black Horse Inn

Grimsthorpe PE10 0LY   TEL: (01778) 591247
on A151, between A1 and A15, 4m NW of Bourne

In the shadow of Grimsthorpe Castle across the road, the Black Horse was built as a coaching inn in 1717. Inside, the bar has a white-painted beamed ceiling, a wood-block floor, two fires, and polished wooden furniture and pews with burgundy-coloured upholstery. Brasses, antlers over a fire, wall and table lamps and books and games all help to create a warm and comfortable atmosphere. To the back are two dining areas, although the same menu is served throughout. This offers plenty of choice, starters ranging from sautéed lambs' kidneys with wild mushrooms in Madeira sauce to a warm tart of tomato and mozzarella with basil and mixed-leaf salad, and main courses typically including medallions of pork fillet with baked apple, red cabbage and honey and balsamic sauce, and smoked haddock with bubble and squeak and fish velouté. Desserts are equally tempting: perhaps woodland fruit cheesecake with mango coulis, or mulled wine fruit pudding with custard. The house beers are Black Horse Bitter and Grimsthorpe Bitter, brewed for the pub by the Oldershaw Brewery in Grantham. Although we were unable to see a full wine list for this edition, at inspection it was noted that there is a short list in the bar, with 16 bottles from £11.95 and six wines by the glass. SAMPLE DISHES: smoked salmon with pickled cucumber, crème fraîche and lumpfish roe £6.25; glazed duck breast with buttered Savoy cabbage, rösti and port jus £13; baked apple with pecan nuts, cinnamon and custard £4.25.

Licensees Brian and Elaine Rey (freehouse)
Open *11.30 to 2.30, 6.30 to 11, Sun 12 to 3, 7 to 10.30; bar food and restaurant 12 to 2,*
7 to 9.30 (9 Sun)
Details *Children welcome   Car park   Garden and patio   No smoking in restaurant   Occasional*
background music   No dogs   Amex, Delta, MasterCard, Switch, Visa   Accommodation: 6 rooms,
B&B £50 to £95

▲ Halzephron Inn

Gunwalloe TR12 7QB   TEL: (01326) 240406
from A3083 4m S of Helston take small lane towards Church Cove

The name means 'hell's cliffs', appropriately enough for the setting on a headland of the Lizard peninsula with dramatic views over Mount Spey to be found a short distance from the pub. It is an atmospheric 500-year-old building with low beamed ceilings in the bar and lots of cosy corners, a warm welcome from landlady Angela Thomas, and a convivial crowd of drinkers and diners – both camps are equally at home here. Separate menus operate for lunch and dinner, the former taking a slightly simpler approach with things like sautéed mushrooms, goats' cheese on garlic bread, crab or prawn salad and various sandwiches, plus daily specials such as smoked mackerel pâté, followed by spicy cinnamon lamb with chilli and apricot couscous. Some of these dishes might also feature on the evening menu, along with savoury filled pancakes, steaks, and creative specials like 'outstanding' tomato and fennel soup, pan-fried pigeon breasts with poached pears, and caramelised Barbary duck on rösti with butternut squash purée and sweet cherry sauce. Desserts are along the lines of raspberry pavlova and banana split. Real ales are from Cornish brewery Sharp's, plus an organic ale, Halzephron Gold. Six house wines at £11.50, also available by the glass, open a list of around 40 reasonably priced bottles. SAMPLE DISHES: shredded pheasant and cabbage soup £4; smoked haddock with a poached egg, spinach, sautéed potatoes and mustard sauce £13; meringues with Cornish clotted cream £4.25.

Licensee Angela Thomas (freehouse)
Open 11 to 2.30, 6 (6.30 winter) to 11, Sun 12 to 2.30, 6 (6.30 winter) to 11; bar food and restaurant 12 to 2, 7 to 9 (6.30 to 9.30 July and Aug); closed 25 Dec
Details Children welcome in family room   Car park   Garden and patio   No smoking in restaurant Occasional live music   No dogs   Amex, Delta, MasterCard, Switch, Visa   Accommodation: 2 rooms, B&B £44 to £78

HALFWAY BRIDGE   West Sussex   map 3

▲ Halfway Bridge Inn 🍺

Halfway Bridge GU28 9BP   TEL: (01798) 861281
WEBSITE: www.thesussexpub.co.uk
on A272, midway between Midhurst and Petworth, just S of Lodsworth

The exterior of the Halfway Bridge might be unprepossessing, but the interior has oodles of character. The two dining areas and long bar have no fewer than five fireplaces, one an old iron range, and people appreciate the cosy and simple décor, with wooden tables of all shapes and sizes blending skilfully with the wooden floors, and dried hops and the occasional flag in a corner providing some of the props. The blackboard menu is supplemented by daily specials, and at lunchtime sandwiches – BLT, say – are available, along with lighter meals that can also be taken as starters: fish soup with rouille and croûtons, or crab and risotto cakes, for instance. Main courses are things like duck confit with sautéed potatoes and root vegetable mash, chicken jambalaya, or venison casseroled in red wine served with red cabbage and mash. Chocolate bread-and-butter pudding might be among desserts. Well-kept Gale's HSB, Fuller's London Pride and Cheriton Pots Ale are the regular real ales, and a guest ale changes regularly. Five wines are sold by the glass. The bedrooms are in a converted barn. SAMPLE DISHES: grilled tiger prawns £8.50; steamed local game pudding £10; pears poached in port with cinnamon ice cream £4.

Licensees Simon and James Hawkins (freehouse)
Open 11 to 3, 6 to 11, Sun 12 to 3, 7 to 10.30; bar food and restaurant 12 to 2 (2.30 Sat and Sun), 7 to 10; closed 25 Dec
Details No children   Car park   Garden and patio   No smoking in 1 eating area   No music   Dogs welcome on a lead in bar   Delta, MasterCard, Switch, Visa   Accommodation: 8 rooms, B&B £45 to £100

The Guide is totally independent, accepts no free hospitality, carries no advertising and makes no charge for inclusion.

▲ Shibden Mill Inn ✿ NEW ENTRY

Shibden Mill Fold, Shibden, Halifax HX3 7UL   TEL: (01422) 365840
WEBSITE: www.shibdenmillinn.com
off A58 Halifax to Leeds road

A small valley over the hill from Halifax, with the Shibden Brook running by the front, gives this old whitewashed inn an inviting setting. The low-beamed interior has a cosy, relaxed atmosphere, and décor is smart but traditional, with rich colours, antique furniture, open fires and walls decked with pictures and memorabilia. Though it has a 'real inn' feel, most of the space is given over to dining. Expect good, sound cooking and some fresh ideas – among starters might be forest mushrooms on toasted brioche with parsley sauce and onion rings, or pea broth with a duck confit spring roll, while main courses have included slow-cooked belly pork with creamed cabbage and mash, smoked haddock fillet with sweetcorn and potato pancake, and grilled marinated vegetable pizza with herbs and truffle oil. Finish with something like caramel rice pudding with roast pear, or raspberry jam tart with red wine syrup and clotted cream ice cream. A good choice of real ales includes John Smith's and their own Shibden Mill Inn ale plus a couple of guests, perhaps Timothy Taylor Landlord, while the wine list focuses on good-value everyday drinking (much from the Antipodes and South America), opening with half a dozen bottles at £9.90. Twelve wines come by the glass. SAMPLE DISHES: spaghetti with roast quail, Parma ham and parsley dressing £5.25; daube of beef with roast potato and root vegetables cooked in duck fat £14.50; banana queen of puddings £4.25.

Licensee Glen Pearson (freehouse)
Open *Mon to Fri 12 to 2.30, 5.30 to 11, Sat 12 to 11, Sun 12 to 10.30; bar food 12 to 2, 6 to 9.30, Sun 12 to 7.30; closed evenings 25 Dec, 26 Dec and 1 Jan*
Details *Children welcome   Car park   Wheelchair access (also WC)   Garden and patio Background music   No dogs   Amex, MasterCard, Switch, Visa   Accommodation: 12 rooms, B&B £65 to £115*

▲ Stag & Huntsman Inn 🍺

Hambleden RG9 6RP   TEL: (01491) 571227
off A4155 Henley to Marlow road, 1m from Mill End

Brick and flint define the look of Hambleden, and this cheerful country pub is totally in keeping with its surroundings. Inside, it is all nooks and crannies, although the place is divided up into three areas: a bar at the front used mainly for drinking, to one side a dining area prettily set with green cloths, and a lounge warmed by a log fire in winter. One menu runs throughout. The main board features things like chicken liver pâté, garlic mushrooms, and chicken fajitas as well as ploughman's and giant Yorkshire pudding filled with 'a stew of the day'. A separate board of specials might list sweet-and-sour pork, pizzas, and seasonal game (venison steak in rosemary jus has been pronounced 'excel-

lent'). Fruit crumbles top the bill to finish. Real ales are taken seriously in this
free house, with regulars including Brakspear Bitter and Wadworth 6X backed
up by guests from Buckinghamshire breweries Rebellion and Vale and – from
further afield – Adnams. Thatcher's cider is also on tap, and three house wines
at £2.50 a glass or £9.75 a bottle kick off a short but flavoursome list. SAMPLE
DISHES: warm salad of Parma ham and roasted shallots £5.25; salmon fishcakes
with chips £8.50; bread-and-butter pudding £4.

Licensee Andy Stokes (freehouse)
Open 11 to 2.30 (3 Sat), 6 to 11, Sun 12 to 3, 7 to 10.30; bar food and restaurant all week 12 to
2, Mon to Sat 7 to 9.30; closed 25 Dec, evenings 26 Dec and 1 Jan
Details Children welcome in eating areas   Car park   Garden   Background music   Dogs welcome
in bar   Delta, MasterCard, Switch, Visa   Accommodation: 3 rooms, B&B £58 to £68

HAMSTEAD MARSHALL   Berkshire   map 2

▲ White Hart

Kintbury Road, Hamstead Marshall RG20 0HW   TEL: (01488) 658201
WEBSITE: www.thewhitehart-inn.co.uk
off A4, 4½m W of Newbury

Dark wooden beams and standing timbers, a central brick fireplace open on
two sides, traditional pub furniture, a red patterned carpet and yellow-
coloured walls hung with country scenes: all sound familiar enough for a
sixteenth-century coaching inn in a Berkshire village. So the all-Italian menu
and Italian staff might come as a bit of a surprise. Though pasta dishes like
spaghetti bolognese are among the items on the printed menu, the blackboard
specials take in many more interesting options: alici con peperonata (marinated anchovies with roast sweet peppers), or butternut squash and leek soup
to start, followed by involtini di pesce (fillet of plaice stuffed with prawns and
leeks poached in white wine, cream and saffron), roast loin of pork stuffed
with herbs in a good, rich gravy, or warm insalata di pollo. Boundary-crossing
raspberry crème brûlée might stand out among tiramisù and cassata on the list
of puddings, with two interlopers (from California and France) appearing on
the otherwise exclusively Italian wine list. Three wines are sold by the glass,
and Wadworth 6X and Hook Norton Best Bitter are on draught. SAMPLE
DISHES: deep-fried whitebait with black olive tartare sauce £5.50; fillet of sea
bass pan-fried with cherry tomatoes, capers and herbs £14.50; torta della
nonna (pine-nut tart with vanilla ice cream) £5.50.

Licensee Nicola Aromando (freehouse)
Open Mon to Sat 12 to 2.30, 6 to 11; bar food and restaurant Mon to Sat 12 to 2, 6.30 to 9
Details Children welcome in eating areas   Car park   Wheelchair access (not WC)   Garden and
patio   No smoking in restaurant   Background music   No dogs   MasterCard, Visa   Accommodation:
6 rooms, B&B £60 to £90

---

*Directions have been included where deemed necessary, but if in doubt about a
pub's location – especially if heading to a rural location – it is advisable to phone
and check.*

HANDLEY   Cheshire   map 7

Calveley Arms   [NEW ENTRY]

Whitchurch Road, Handley CH3 9DT   TEL: (01829) 770619
WEBSITE: www.calveleyarms.co.uk
off A41, 6m S of Chester

One reporter thought this 'just the sort of place to take future in-laws to make a good impression'. From the 'architecturally pleasing' old inn, on clear days, you can look across the Dee plain to the North Wales mountains. Outside is a sheltered beer garden, much used in summer, with a boules pitch and barbecue, while in the beamy but light and airy interior the décor includes oddities like a pair of wooden skis and a section of trawler netting complete with floats. Menus are oddly bound in covers from old children's annuals and agricultural supplies catalogues, while daily specials are chalked on a board. 'Friday night is fish night', but fish features all through the week too. You might consider monkfish with a 'marvellous' bacon, cream and garlic sauce, or silver dorade with cherry tomatoes, onions and white wine; alternatively, try Chinese-style shredded duck, or saddle of Cheshire venison with red wine and redcurrant jus. Otherwise, expect salads, pastas and pub classics like hot avocado with Stilton, followed by, perhaps, treacle tart. Two-course Sunday roasts look fair value at £9. Four real ales, including Theakston Black Bull and Mild, are on draught, and there are around two dozen workaday wines from £9.25, half a dozen by the glass. SAMPLE DISHES: Stilton and Boddingtons soup £2.50; pan-seared king scallops with garlic butter £11.25; bread-and-butter pudding £3.25.

Licensee Simon Grant Wilson (Enterprise Inns)
Open *12 to 3, 6 to 11, Sun 12 to 3, 7 to 10.30, closed evening 25 Dec; bar food 12 to 2.15, 6 to 9.30, Sun 12 to 2.30, 7 to 9*
Details *Car park   Wheelchair access (also WC)   Garden   Background music   Dogs welcome by arrangement   MasterCard, Switch, Visa*

HAROME   North Yorkshire   map 9

▲ Star Inn ♔ ♔ ✿

Harome YO62 5JE   TEL: (01439) 770397
off A170, 3m SE of Helmsley

What was the byre at one end of this fourteenth-century cruck-framed long-house is now the restaurant, and the original parlour and dairy are now the bar. The endearingly lopsided, part-thatched, whitewashed building of some character is in a charming, diminutive village way off the beaten track. Good cheer prevails within, helped by surroundings of low beams, open fires and pews, as does some seriously accomplished cooking, which can be enjoyed in the restaurant, with its bare wooden tables and spindle-backed chairs, or in the main bar. (Note that bookings are not taken in the bar but are advisable for the restaurant.) Dishes such as a starter of braised rabbit faggot with bubble and squeak and wild mushroom gravy, breast of Goosnargh duck with a crisp liver croûton and stewed damson juices, followed by caramelised lemon tart with raspberry sauce are typical of the kitchen's imaginative and skilfully cooked output. Lunchtime sandwiches and buns – Norfolk prawns with whisky marie-rose sauce, marinated tomatoes and basil – and a 'posh ploughman's' consisting of a selection of cold meats and British cheeses with chutney and pickles are no less appealing, and bangers and mash with onion gravy may make an appearance too. Fish and other specialities are chalked up on a board, and seasonal game may crop up in a main course of pan-fried steak of local roe deer with deep-fried Blue Wensleydale beignet with poached quince and raisin syrup. Desserts are no less inventive, among them perhaps rich dark chocolate cake with satsuma sorbet and fresh cherries, or date and walnut pudding accompanied by nutmeg ice cream. Real ales include Black Sheep Special, Theakston Best Bitter, and John Smith's Cask Bitter plus a brew from Cropton Brewery near Pickering, and home-made concoctions like rhubarb schnapps and strawberry gin are also on offer. An interesting selection of nine house wines is available by the glass from £3 to £4.50. The main wine list of around 80 bins has no truck with budget bottles, but concentrates on high quality with equal success in both France and the New World. SAMPLE DISHES: white crabmeat with a little lobster salad, celeriac coleslaw and cucumber dressing £7.50; fillet of North Sea turbot with braised fennel and dill and lobster hollandaise £16; baked banana tart with dandelion and burdock sherbet and stewed raisin syrup £5.

Licensees Andrew and Jacquie Pern (freehouse)
Open Tue to Sat 11.30 to 3, 6.15 to 11, Sun 12 to 11; bar food and restaurant Tue to Sat 11.30 to 2, 6.30 to 9.30, Sun 12 to 6; closed 2 weeks Jan
Details Children welcome Car park Garden No smoking in restaurant Occasional background music No dogs Delta, MasterCard, Switch, Visa Accommodation: 11 rooms, B&B £90 to £195

HARTSHEAD   West Yorkshire   map 8

Gray Ox   NEW ENTRY

15 Hartshead Lane, Hartshead WF15 8AL   TEL: (01274) 872845
From M62 junction 25, take A644 for Dewsbury, then A62 for Leeds, turn left onto B6119, then take three first lefts, and the pub is on the left

The hamlet of Hartshead is hidden in a patch of West Yorkshire countryside between Brighouse and Batley, within striking distance of the M62. Inside this refurbished stone-built hostelry bare floorboards, old fireplaces and beer barrels over the bar give a traditional feel, and service is 'down-to-earth'. Food is only served at lunchtime, but there's plenty to choose from on the printed menu and specials boards. You might begin with, say, lemon prawn salad, or shellfish pistou soup, before tackling a mighty lamb shank with hot black pepper and garlic gravy, a kangaroo rump steak or a herb-crusted salmon fillet with basil and tomato sauce. Finish with a home-made dessert such as tiramisù or bread-and-butter pudding, or else Yorkshire farm cheeses. Sunday lunch (served until 7.30pm) has included ample platefuls of roast beef, Yorkshire pudding and enough vegetables to feed an army, and one correspondent reckoned that the sandwiches were 'some of the best I've had anywhere'. Real ales are from Timothy Taylor and the Black Sheep Brewery, and there are half a dozen wines by the glass. SAMPLE DISHES: home-made mussel and prawn chowder £5.50; salmon baked with asparagus and prawns with tomato and basil sauce £12.75; chocolate and Baileys cheesecake £4.25.

Licensee Wayne Ryan (freehouse)
Open Mon to Fri 12 to 3, 6 to 11, Sat 12 to 11, Sun 12 to 10.30; bar food 12 to 2, 6 to 9 (Sun 12 to 7.30)
Details *Children welcome   Car park   Wheelchair access (not WC)   Garden and patio*
No smoking in dining room   Background music   No dogs   MasterCard, Switch, Visa

HASELBURY PLUCKNETT   Somerset   map 2

Haselbury Inn
North Street, Haselbury Plucknett TA18 7RJ   TEL: (01460) 72488
off A30, 2m NE of Crewkerne

The inn is a large, tall building of rough grey stone on the main road running through the village. The interior manages to be both spacious and cosy, with deep sofas and chairs around a welcoming log fire, with a restaurant to the rear with generously spaced tables, floral curtains, a pine dresser, and two cart-wheels hanging from the ceiling supporting fringed lampshades. The kitchen goes to a great deal of trouble to source top-quality local ingredients – even the butter comes from a farm just down the road – and fish, listed on a blackboard, is something of a speciality: Lyme Bay crab, grilled local flounder, grilled plaice fillet with a rich lobster sauce garnished with prawns, or poached salmon suprême with watercress sauce, depending on availability. The style might be described as 'country fayre', but this translates into such dishes as coarse pork and leek pâté with home-made tomato chutney, followed by roast rack of lamb on cheesy bubble and squeak with a tangle of deep-fried vegetables and a light redcurrant jus (all the flavours described as 'a match for each other'), with a finale of chocolate mousse layered with mango on a base of amaretti soaked in a strawberry liqueur. The restaurant menu is also available in the bar, which has its own snack menu of things like ploughman's. On draught are Palmer IPA and Otter Ale, with Budweiser also on draught. There is a good selection of wines by the glass and prices are very consumer-friendly on the list of over 50 wines. SAMPLE DISHES: a pot of Lyme Bay crab topped with baked Cheddar £4.25; seared fillet of hake with garlic-roasted Mediterranean vegetables and a smooth tomato sauce £12; orange pannacotta £3.50.

Licensee Pat Howard (freehouse)
Open Tue to Sat 10.30 to 2.30, 6.30 to 11, Sun 12 to 3, 6.30 to 10.30; bar food and restaurant 12 to 2 (3 Sun), 6.45 to 9.30
Details *Children welcome   Car park   Wheelchair access (not WC)   Garden and patio*
No smoking in restaurant   Background music   No dogs   Amex, Delta, MasterCard, Switch, Visa

HASSOP   Derbyshire   map 9

Eyre Arms
Hassop DE45 1NS   TEL: (01629) 640390
on B6001, 2m N of Bakewell

The back windows of this neat little stone-built building covered in Virginia creeper overlook an attractive garden with tables, and the pub's location makes it a good place from which to explore the southern Peak District. There is no restaurant, but the long bar menu takes in main dishes such as sliced duckling with orange and Grand Marnier sauce, or venison pie, while an Indian influ-ence appears in chicken korma with rice and mango chutney. Fish, steaks and pasta are other headings on the menu, and there are six interesting options for vegetarians, including aubergine and mushroom lasagne. Blackboard specials point up more interest, from tomato and basil soup to rabbit pie, or fillet of lemon sole bonne femme. Even popular dishes such as breaded plaice with chips are properly cooked and attractively presented. Sandwiches, plough-man's and jacket potatoes are also available at lunchtime, and puddings include, appropriately, Bakewell pudding as well as things like warm choco-late, pear and almond tart. On handpump are Black Sheep Special Ale, Marston's Pedigree, and John Smith's Bitter, and half a dozen wines are sold by the glass. SAMPLE DISHES: deep-fried whitebait £5.25; leg of lamb stuffed with apricots and honey marinated in red wine £9.75; mille-feuille with rasp-berries, peaches and cream £3.25.

Licensee Lynne Smith (freehouse)
Open 11 to 3, 7 (6.30 summer) to 11; bar food 12 to 2, 6.30 to 9
Details Children welcome in eating area   Car park   Wheelchair access (also WC)   Garden   No-smoking area in bar, no smoking in eating area   Occasional background music   No dogs   Delta, Diners, MasterCard, Switch, Visa

HATHERSAGE   Derbyshire   map 9

▲ Plough Inn   NEW ENTRY
Leadmill Bridge, Hathersage S32 1BA   TEL: (01433) 650319
WEBSITE: www.theploughinn-hathersage.com
on B6001, 1m S of Hathersage

This handsome converted sixteenth-century corn mill is the sort of place that inspires its customers to write poetry. No wonder: it is set in its own grounds by the River Derwent deep in the Peak District National Park, and offers a warm welcome, comfortable surroundings and good-value food. It is divided into a convivial open-plan, split-level bar and a cottagey restaurant. In the latter you might go for slow-cooked oriental duck leg with parsnip and ginger purée and tamarind glaze, followed by wild boar meatballs with creamed rose-mary polenta, tomato and caper sauce and grilled fontina cheese. Bar meals (not served in the restaurant in the evening) are more down to earth: a hearty portion of tender sautéed lamb's liver and bacon on creamy mash with good onion gravy, for example, or you might be tempted by the home-made pie of the day. Desserts have featured some pretty unusual ideas, such as Drambuie tart with Stilton ice cream, which a reporter considered 'excellent'. Theakston Best and Old Peculier are top of the real ale billing, with a supporting cast of two regularly changing guests, while the wine list, organised by style, runs to around 40 bottles, with six house wines starting at £11.50 plus a 'connoisseur's collection' that still stays beneath £30. Eight wines are served by the glass. Guest accommodation, in separate buildings across the cobbled courtyard, is stylish, luxurious and well equipped. SAMPLE DISHES: mille-feuille of wood-land mushrooms with tarragon and Madeira cream £5.25; lamb tagine with chickpeas, apricots and couscous £15; cappuccino crème brûlée £3.50.

Licensee Bob Emery (freehouse)
Open 11 to 11, Sun 12 to 10.30; bar food and restaurant Mon to Fri 11.30 to 2.30, 6.30 to 9.30,
Sat 11.30 to 9.30, Sun 12 to 9; closed 25 Dec
Details Children welcome exc in restaurant evenings   Car park   Wheelchair access (not WC)
Garden   No smoking in restaurant   Background music   No dogs   MasterCard, Switch, Visa
Accommodation: 5 rooms, B&B £49.50 to £99.50

HAWKLEY   Hampshire   map 2

Hawkley Inn 🍺

Pococks Lane, Hawkley GU33 6NE   TEL: (01730) 827205
off A325, 2½m N of Petersfield

Hidden away down country lanes, this unpretentious pub, with a verandah at
the front, is well worth seeking out. Two rooms on either side of the bar are
furnished with cottagey tables and chairs and warmed by open fires in winter.
A huge mouse's head hovers menacingly above one fireplace, and a well-trodden carpet emphasises that this is an honest meeting place with no airs and
graces. Wines are not a main feature here (only two are offered), but beers are
a good collection that change frequently; among them might be Ballard's
Trotton Bitter and Nyewood Gold, brewed in nearby Petersfield, Cottage
Golden Arrow and Alton's Pride, from the Triple fff Brewing Company – and
for cider drinkers there's the pub's own Swamp Donkey. A generous, robust
wedge of bacon, Brie and mushroom tart, and spaghetti with pesto, aubergine
and red peppers have been among dishes praised by reporters, or you might
choose crab and sweetcorn chowder, followed by pork and cider sausages with
onion gravy and mash, or lamb casseroled with aubergine and tomatoes. Rolls
and ploughman's are also listed on the blackboards, together with familiar
desserts like apple strudel, and the evenings see the addition of perhaps rump
steak, or grilled duck breast in green peppercorn sauce. Despite its rural location, the pub can get packed. SAMPLE DISHES: bacon and mushroom soup
£4.50; pork and Swamp Donkey cider sausages with onion gravy and mash
£8.25; apple pie £3.50.

Licensee A. Stringer (freehouse)
Open 12 to 2.30 (3 Sat), 6 to 11, Sun 12 to 3, 7 to 10.30; bar food 12 to 2, 7 to 9.30, Sun 12 to 2
Details Children welcome   Wheelchair access (not WC)   Patio   No-smoking area in bar
Background music; occasional live music   Dogs welcome   MasterCard, Visa

HAWKSHEAD   Cumbria   map 8

▲ Queen's Head Hotel

Main Street, Hawkshead LA22 0NS   TEL: (015394) 36271
WEBSITE: www.queensheadhotel.co.uk
on B5285, 4m S of Ambleside

In the middle of the higgledy-piggledy village, the Queen's Head is as much
an eating pub as a drinking one. Rough black beams cross the low ceilings,
walls and bar counters are handsomely panelled, and pictures and decorative
brass and china are well chosen to make the bar and separate restaurant attractive and worthy of the solid black and white exterior. The menus are

interchangeable between restaurant and bar. Main courses can be as traditional as Westmorland pie or as exotic as Thai chicken curry. Start with a soup – flavourful courgette and sage, for instance – or braised leg of guinea fowl on an aubergine croûton with spicy fig chutney, and go on to salmon and lobster cakes with a lemon and caper dressing, or a triple-decker toastie of fell-bred lamb with onion and mint sauce. White chocolate and Baileys cheesecake with coffee bean sauce makes a satisfying pudding. A Robinson's pub, the Queen's Head stocks the brewery's Frederics, Hartleys XB and Cumbria Way. Around a dozen wines are sold by the glass. SAMPLE DISHES: broad bean and crispy pancetta crostini with a radicchio and mint dressing £4.50; pan-fried venison sliced over celeriac mash with a red wine and juniper dressing £14; mocha pannacotta with caramel and rum sauce £4.25.

Licensee Anthony Merrick (Robinson's)
Open 11 to 11, Sun 12 to 10.30; bar food and restaurant 12 to 2.30, 6.15 to 9.30
Details Children welcome   Wheelchair access (not WC)   No-smoking area in bar, no smoking in restaurant   Background music   No dogs   Delta, MasterCard, Switch, Visa   Accommodation: 14 rooms, B&B £40 to £90

HAYDON BRIDGE   Northumberland   map 10

General Havelock Inn 😕 🍺
9 Ratcliffe Road, Haydon Bridge NE47 6ER   TEL: (01434) 684376
on S side of A69, 6m W of Hexham, 100yds from junction with B6319

The Thompson family are welcoming hosts at this long-serving 200-year-old roadside inn: he cooks, while wife and mother serve and help behind the bar. At the front is the main bar, while further back – in a converted barn – is a 'most attractive' room with the bonus of views over the South Tyne ('best seen at midday'). The main menu is a regularly changing, fixed-price affair that might kick off with soup (wild mushroom has been well received) or vegetable terrine, before splendid roast pheasant ('high without being over-powering') served with a faggot made from the leg meat. Cheeses (many from the North Country) make a pleasing alternative to desserts such as pear feuil-leté. Alternatively, stay with the bar menu, which offers heartier stuff in the shape of Cullen skink, Cumberland sausage, or chicken, leek and Cheddar pie followed by, say, egg custard with shortbread and prune compote. Beer drinkers will find a forthright contingent of locally brewed ales including, perhaps, Yates Fever Pitch, Big Lamp Bitter and Geordie Pride from the Mordue Brewery in Shiremoor. Those with a taste for the grape will find a satisfyingly fruity, if less adventurous, selection. The list of 20 sound bottles stays mostly below £15, with wines by the glass starting at £1.95 and five half-bottles. SAMPLE DISHES: cheese croquettes with tomato dip £3.75; beef, Guinness and wild mushroom stew £6; chocolate, rum and raisin crème brûlée £4.25.

Licensee Gary Thompson (freehouse)
Open Tue to Sat 12 to 2.30, 7 to 11, Sun 12 to 2.30, 8 to 10.30; bar food and restaurant Tue to Sun 12 to 2, Tue to Sat 7 to 9
Details Children welcome   Wheelchair access (also WC)   Garden and patio   No smoking in dining room   Occasional live music   Dogs welcome   Delta, MasterCard, Switch, Visa

HAYFIELD Derbyshire map 9

▲ Sportsman

Kinder Road, Hayfield SK22 2LE TEL: (01663) 741565
from centre of Hayfield (off A624 Glossop to Chapel-en-le-Frith road) follow camp site signs; pub is ½m on left

Beside an unclassified dead-end road heading into the high hills behind Hayfield is what might once have been a terrace of cottages but is now a characterful pub. It takes a bit of finding, so in the wintertime locals quietly enjoy its log fire and small warren of cosy seating areas with prints, lanterns and guns on the walls. Then spring brings the walkers on to Kinder Scout once more, and incomers arrive to share the Thwaites beer – Bitter and Lancaster Bomber, plus a third that changes sporadically – and the twenty or more single malts behind the bar (there's also a brief wine list that includes four served by the glass). Thirst slaked, they can refuel from a menu that starts with ploughman's, filled baguettes and club sandwiches, then moves on to a brunch or a farmhouse grill, steaks, lamb cutlets and Cumberland sausages. After that the blackboard kicks in with mushrooms in garlic butter, or chicken and brandy pâté, followed by casseroled pork chops, grilled fresh plaice, or a vegetable bourguignonne with herby dumplings. Puds like blackcurrant and apple crumble, or hot chocolate fudge cake, may take some walking off, for portions are not mean here. SAMPLE DISHES: leek, onion and potato soup £4.75; Thai-style chicken fillets £9.75; apricot and almond tart £4.75.

Licensee John Dunbar (Thwaites)
Open *all week (exc Mon lunchtime) 12 to 3, 7 to 11; bar food (exc Sun evening, Mon lunchtime) 12 to 2, 7 to 9; closed 25 Dec*
Details *Children welcome Garden and patio Background music Dogs welcome exc in bedrooms Amex, Delta, MasterCard, Switch, Visa Accommodation: 6 rooms, B&B £30 to £50*

HAYTOR VALE Devon map 1

▲ Rock Inn 🍇

Haytor Vale TQ13 9XP TEL: (01364) 661305
WEBSITE: www.rock-inn.co.uk
turn off A38 at Bovey Tracey on to A382; after 2m join B3387 to Haytor, then left at phone box

Its covered entrance and a stone trough are testimony to the days when the Rock was a coaching inn on the road from Widecombe in the Moor to Newton Abbot. A series of several small rooms, the largest one the main bar, create a cosy, warm and friendly atmosphere, reinforced by a smart patterned carpet, dark wood tables and chairs, welcoming fires and glowing lighting. Food is the main preoccupation here, with lunchtime sandwiches and dishes of chicken liver pâté, followed by steak and kidney suet pudding, or chicken curry, replaced by an ambitious set-price and à la carte menu in the evening. A couple were well pleased with a meal that started with gravad lax with lemon and mustard dressing, and a 'lovely' warm salad of thinly sliced Brie and pears with roasted hazelnut dressing, and went on to 'excellent' chargrilled rump steak with a creamy, rich peppercorn sauce, and 'equally good' rack of lamb with red wine jus. Vegetables are well reported, and chunky but crisp chips are said to be 'truly wonderful'. Fish, from Brixham, might include pan-fried John Dory with rosemary beurre blanc, and desserts tend to be rich, from raspberry crème brûlée to sticky toffee pudding with pecan sauce. Dartmoor Best is the real ale stocked, along with Bass. The wine list puts serious French offerings up front, but beyond these are more affordable bottles and a good global range that includes the delicious Nativa organic wines from Carmen in Chile. Six come by the glass. SAMPLE DISHES: mussels in chilli, lemon and parsley £6; shank of lamb on braised red cabbage with mint jus £14; bread-and-butter pudding with custard £4.25.

Licensee Christopher Graves (freehouse)
Open 11 to 11 (10.30 winter); bar food and restaurant 12 to 2.30 (3 Sun), 6.30 to 9; closed 25 Dec, evening 26 Dec
Details Children welcome   Car park   Wheelchair access (not WC)   Garden and patio
No-smoking area in bar, no smoking in restaurant   No music   No dogs   Amex, Delta, Diners, MasterCard, Switch, Visa   Accommodation: 9 rooms, B&B £60 to £95.50

HEDLEY ON THE HILL   Northumberland   map 10

Feathers Inn 🍺
Hedley on the Hill NE43 7SW   TEL: (01661) 843607
from New Ridley, signposted from B6309 N of Consett, follow sign for Hedley on the Hill

This solid, stone-built pub in the middle of the village has wonderful views from its hillside location. In the small bars (there is no restaurant) log fires burn brightly in winter, creating a welcoming and comfortable atmosphere. The blackboard menu, which changes twice a week, always includes vegetarian dishes, perhaps leek and sweet potato hotpot with goats' cheese and a Parmesan pastry crust. Among tempting starters might be mushroom and celery soup, prawn salad with a Thai dressing, and hummus and tsatsiki with olives and pitta bread. Cumberland sausage with onions braised in cider, chicken with fennel, orange and rosemary, and seafood pancake may show up among main courses, with desserts of ginger pudding with ginger wine sauce, or citrus cream posset with shortbread. Note during the week food is served in the evening only. Regular ales Workie Ticket from Mordue and Boddingtons Bitter are joined by frequently changing guests from local breweries: perhaps Hadrian & Border Vallum Bitter, or Northumberland Kitty Brewster. Wines by the glass are limited, but there's an interesting choice by the bottle. SAMPLE DISHES: Greek salad £4; Moroccan lamb casserole with spices and apricots £7.50; rich chocolate pudding £3.25.

Licensee Marina Atkinson (freehouse)
Open Mon to Fri 6 to 11, Sat and bank hols 12 to 3, 6 to 11, Sun 12 to 3, 7 to 10.30; bar food (exc Mon evening) 12 to 2.30, 7 to 9; open bank hol lunchtime
Details Children welcome before 9pm   Car park   Wheelchair access (also WC)   Occasional live music   Dogs welcome on a lead   Switch

Report forms are at the back of the book; write a letter if you prefer; or email your pub report to whichpubguide@which.net.

HEMINGFORD GREY   Cambridgeshire   map 6

Cock 🍺   NEW ENTRY

47 High Street, Hemingford Grey PE28 9BJ   TEL: (01480) 463609
follow signs for Hemingford Grey from A14 just W of Huntingdon

From the outside, this looks for all the world like a 'charming, traditional village inn' with a yellow-washed exterior and signs of recent refurbishment. First impressions are confirmed if you venture into the public bar (which has its own entrance), where you'll see locals and beer fans quaffing pints of real ale from East Anglian breweries, including Nethergate IPA, Elgood's Black Dog Mild and Adnams Bitter. But there's more. A summery restaurant, with a small reception desk, has polished light wood floors and numerous depictions of proud cockerels on the walls, and waiting staff who are genuinely eager and keen to please. The main menu is a sensibly shortish affair that shows French and Italian leanings without neglecting British classics. Here you might find anything from heart-warming pumpkin soup, or venison carpaccio with wild rocket and lemon dressing, to roast partridge with Savoy cabbage and chest-nuts. In addition, blackboards advertise the pub's real specialities: fish and sausages. Devotees of seafood might go for roast cod with lime and sea salt, while the range of bangers extends to half a dozen varieties. The cheeseboard is loyal to the British Isles; otherwise there are desserts such as syllabub and sticky toffee pudding. Light lunches are good value (you can also get sand-wiches), and Sunday lunch features meat from rare breeds, such as Long Horn beef and British Lop pork. Wine drinkers are well served by a selection of a dozen wines by the glass and colourful wine list that covers most bases with plenty of choice under £15. As the Guide goes to press, we hear that the team have also taken over the Crown at Horningsea, near Cambridge. SAMPLE DISHES: game terrine with chutney £5; slow-braised lamb shank with pumpkin and rosemary purée £12; chocolate and coffee terrine with whisky anglaise £4.

Licensees Oliver Thain and Richard Bradley (freehouse)
Open Mon 12 to 2.30, 7 to 9.30, Tue to Sat 11.30 to 3, 6 to 11, Sun 12 to 4, 6.30 to 10.30; restaurant all week 12 to 2.30, Mon to Sat 7 to 9.30; no food 25 Dec
Details Children welcome in restaurant   Car park   Wheelchair access (not WC)   Garden
No smoking in restaurant   Occasional live music   Dogs welcome in bar   Delta, MasterCard, Switch, Visa

HETTON   North Yorkshire   map 8

▲ Angel Inn 🏆 🏆 🍇

Hetton BD23 6LT   TEL: (01756) 730263
WEBSITE: www.angelhetton.co.uk
off B6265, 5m N of Skipton

Hetton sits in a saddle of the ridge separating Airedale and Wharfedale, just off the road from Skipton to Grassington – which makes the Angel both rural and easily accessible. It's a terrace building of local stone with window boxes and some climbers on the front. Inside are beams, nooks and crannies, log fires and architectural inconsistencies that reflect rebuildings and extensions over centuries. There's Timothy Taylor Landlord to sup, plus Black Sheep and

Worthington Bitters, along with a range of malt whiskies (including an own-label single malt out of Glen Grant). However, like its stable mate the General Tarleton at Ferrensby (see entry), the Angel is best known for food and wine. There's a bar/brasserie menu (plus specials board), or try the restaurant (on Monday to Saturday evenings only, or Sunday lunch; booking advisable). Bar food subsumes provençale fish soup with aïoli, or beef carpaccio, and mains from (pork and chive) sausages and mash, via fried silver mullet with tagliolini and spinach, to roast chicken breast on wild mushroom risotto. Sweets might be Hetton mess (crushed meringue, strawberries, yoghurt and raspberry coulis) or Baileys bread-and-butter pudding. The restaurant amplifies such dishes with, say, seared tuna on niçoise salad, chargrilled venison topside, and poached figs with vanilla ice cream. The list of over 150 wines has strength in depth when it comes to classic regions like Bordeaux and Burgundy, and the Italian selection is good too. Bargain hunters will have a tough time of it, however – the house white and red are the only wines under £15 – but can still drink well from the 17-strong by-the-glass selection or the impressive collection of half-bottles. Some wines are available for off-licence case sales. SAMPLE DISHES: crispy duck salad £6; chargrilled pork chop with Tuscan grilled vegetables £8.25; pot au chocolat with chocolate chip cookies £4.75.

Licensees Denis Watkins and John Topham (freehouse)
Open Sun to Fri 12 to 3, 6 to 10 (10.30 summer), Sat 12 to 3, 6 to 11.30; bar food 12 to 2,
6 to 9 (8.30 Sun); restaurant Mon to Sat 6 to 9, Sun 12 to 2; closed 25 Dec
Details Children welcome in bar eating area   Car park   Wheelchair access (not WC)   Patio
No smoking in snug and lounge bar and part of dining room   No music   No dogs   Amex, Diners,
MasterCard, Switch, Visa   Accommodation: 5 studio suites, B&B £100 to £160

HEXHAM   Northumberland   map 10

Dipton Mill 🍺
Dipton Mill Road, Hexham NE46 1YA   TEL: (01434) 606577
2m due S of Hexham, beyond Hexham racecourse

This takes some finding but repays the effort. Truly a country pub, it is over the ridge south of Hexham, among trees beside the West Dipton Burn (which used to drive the mill and now runs through the garden). The small-fronted, grey-stone building dates from about 1700 and has 'kohl-rimmed' windows with white glazing bars, a coat of creeper, and a slate roof. The cosy bar – beams, wood panelling, red-trimmed seats – has log fires, no music and Hexamshire beers. From a brewery two miles away run by licensee Geoff Brooker, these are Shire Bitter, Devil's Elbow, Devil's Water (named after a local stream), Whapweasel, and a Christmas special: Old Humbug. There's also Old Rosie cider, and all 11 of the good-value wines are served by the glass. Food is itemised on a blackboard. Pick a ploughman's, and you'll have to choose between ten cheeses (only Stilton and Cheddar come from further away than Barnard Castle), or try the home-made soups. Mains include crab salad, pork fillet with apple, orange and ginger, or ratatouille with couscous. Bread-and-butter pudding or triple chocolate cheesecake might be a course too far for some. SAMPLE DISHES: roast red pepper, tomato and orange soup £2; lamb steak in wine and mustard sauce £6.25; syrup sponge and custard £1.75.

Licensee Geoff Brooker (freehouse)
Open 12 to 2.30, 6 to 11, Sun 12 to 4, 7 to 10.30; bar food 12 to 2.30, 6.30 to 8.30;
closed 25 Dec
Details Children welcome   Wheelchair access (also WC)   Garden and patio   No music   No cards

HEYDON   Cambridgeshire   map 6

King William IV   NEW ENTRY
Heydon SG8 8PN   TEL: (01763) 838773
take B1039 towards Royston, turn right at Great Chishall, follow road to Heydon, pub on right-
hand side past animal sanctuary

A black and white timber-effect country inn, the William IV is just the place
for those 'keen to visit a hostelry with character'. Inside is far more rambling,
cosy and atmospheric than the exterior might suggest. Scrubbed-wood floorboards, oak beams and open fires are joined by an extensive collection of rustic
implements (milk churns, copper kettles, cowbells and so on) that line every
conceivable surface. The menu is a lengthy affair with the occasional wink to
the modish, and an admirable list of vegetarian options (including perhaps
wild mushroom and feta cannelloni served on spinach and glazed with
pecorino, or sweet chestnut potato cakes with a mustard sauce). Among
starters may be 'classic' prawn cocktail, or lobster and crab Thai fishcakes with
an 'oriental jam', while mains could range from confit leg of duck served with
spring onion mash and a ginger and coriander jus, to traditional bangers 'n'
mash with rich onion gravy. Chargrilled steaks, plus lunchtime baguettes and
jacket potatoes, and familiar, comforting desserts of sticky toffee pudding
complete the picture. For beer drinkers, City of Cambridge Hobson's Choice,
Adnams Bitter, Fuller's London Pride and Greene King IPA are all regulars,
while a 30-strong list of wines offers eight by the glass. SAMPLE DISHES: crispy
whitebait with tartare sauce and granary bread £6.25; braised lamb shank with
vegetable confit served with a roasted garlic and red wine jus £12.75; apple
lattice pie with clotted cream £5.25.

Licensee Elizabeth Nicholls (freehouse)
Open 12 to 2.30, 6 to 11, Sun 12 to 3, 7 to 10.30; bar food and restaurant 12 to 2, 6.30 to 10,
Sun 12 to 2.30, 7 to 9.30
Details Children welcome   Car park   Wheelchair access (also WC)   Garden   No-smoking area in
bar, no smoking in restaurant   Background music   No dogs   Delta, MasterCard, Switch, Visa

HEYTESBURY   Wiltshire   map 2

▲ Angel
High Street, Heytesbury BA12 0ED   TEL: (01985) 840330
WEBSITE: www.angelheytesbury.co.uk
just off A36, 2m E of Warminster

In a quiet rural village on the edge of Salisbury Plain, the Angel as it stands
today is the result of eighteenth-century renovations. A comfortable lounge, a
log fire in winter, with a courtyard for use in summer, 'good, helpful staff' and
well-spaced tables in the restaurant all add up to create a comfortable and
welcoming atmosphere. The board in the bar announces such dishes as local

ham with a free-range egg and chunky chips, a trio of game sausages on chive mash with onion gravy, and lamb shank, and the restaurant's seasonal menu is on offer in here as well. Starters include chicken and game terrine wrapped in bacon with Cumberland sauce, and baked goats' cheese rolled in herbs and breadcrumbs served with sun-blush tomato chutney and pine nuts. Among main dishes might be whole baked Wylye Valley trout stuffed with prawns and herbs in a brown butter sauce, peppered venison with blueberry jus on fondant potatoes with parsnip crisps, and double-baked cheese, walnut and spinach soufflé topped with chives. Farmhouse cheeses supplement desserts along the lines of apple and cinnamon crème brûlée, or pears poached in mulled wine with chocolate sauce. Real ales are Ringwood Best Bitter and guest ales like Ringwood Boondoggle or XXXX Porter and Marston's Pedigree. A fair number of familiar high-street names put in an appearance on the list of two dozen wines. Four house wines are served by the glass or for between £11.50 and £13.25 a bottle, and all but one of the rest come in at between £15 and £20. SAMPLE DISHES: queen scallop and Jerusalem artichoke salad with hazelnut dressing £7; fillet of Wiltshire pork stuffed with pistachios and apricots with vanilla dauphinois £11; chocolate tart with cinnamon ice cream £5.

Licensees J.G. Giddings and B.H. Rossiter (freehouse)
Open 11.30 to 11, Sun 12 to 10.30; bar food and restaurant 12 to 2.30 (2 Sun), 7 to 9.30 (9 Sun); open 12 to 2 25 Dec (restaurant closed)
Details Children welcome   Car park   Wheelchair access (also WC)   Patio   No smoking in restaurant   Background music   Dogs welcome exc in restaurant   Delta, MasterCard, Switch, Visa Accommodation: 8 rooms, B&B £50 to £90

HIGHER BURWARDSLEY   Cheshire   map 7

▲ Pheasant Inn
Higher Burwardsley CH3 9PF   TEL: (01829) 770434
off A41 6m SE of Chester, signposted Tattenhall and Burwardsley

The Pheasant, tucked away in a remote setting with enviable views extending as far as North Wales, consists of old sandstone and half-timbered cottages built around a courtyard. The rather stark, open-plan interior is split into distinct areas by the generous use of sandstone-block pillars and timber-framed dividers, all beneath a heavily timbered ceiling. The furniture is mostly of wood, and an island log fire is a feature at one end, with an old range in an inglenook in a rear room. The printed menu, available throughout, is long and varied enough to accommodate all tastes. Among starters might be shellfish terrine – layers of scallops and lobster in a herb dressing – tuna tartare, and grilled black pudding on a bed of braised red cabbage with shallot sauce, and main courses could run from lamb shank on bubble and squeak with a rich red wine gravy, to roast monkfish with smoked ham risotto and chervil beurre blanc. The full range of Weetwood ales are on draught, and all six house wines are served by the glass. Those awesome views can be enjoyed from the patio and garden, where a seaside-style pay telescope has been installed for those wanting close-ups. SAMPLE DISHES: pan-fried pigeon breast and frisée leaf salad £5.75; pan-roast red mullet fillet with sage beignets, steamed fennel and sauce vierge £11.25; caramelised lime tart with chilli and ginger ice cream £5.

Licensee Simon McLoughlin (freehouse)
Open 12 to 11, Sun 12 to 10.30; bar food Mon to Sat 12 to 2.30, 6.30 to 9.30, Sun 12 to 5, 6.30 to 8.30
Details *Children welcome   Car park   Wheelchair access (also WC)   Garden and patio   No-smoking area   Background music   No dogs   Amex, Delta, Diners, MasterCard, Switch, Visa   Accommodation: 10 rooms, B&B £55 to £80*

HINDON   Wiltshire   map 2

▲ Angel Inn ✿

High Street, Hindon SP3 6DJ   TEL: (01747) 820696
WEBSITE: www.theangelhindon.fslife.co.uk
1m from A350 between Warminster and Shaftesbury

This Georgian coaching inn has reverted to its original name, which it held for over 250 years until it was changed some years ago to the Grosvenor Arms. Changes in the décor have also taken place, with the two main bar areas now with a red colour scheme to offset the flagstone floor, while the restaurant, once the stables, is notable for its collection of large black and white photographs of the locality. Log fires create a warm, welcoming atmosphere in winter, and in summer the flowery garden comes into its own, with tables and chairs for al fresco dining. The same menus are served throughout, and flexibility means you can choose something from the list of 'starters, main-course-size starters and lighter meals' or go for the full three-course monty. Among the former are roasted sausages with mash and onion gravy, and chargrilled ciabatta sandwiches, alongside pan-fried scallops with pea purée and mint dressing, or twice-baked cauliflower and Cheddar soufflé. Main courses pick up all sorts of up-to-the-minute ideas to produce grilled smoked haddock with sautéed potatoes, pancetta and a Guinness and mustard seed dressing, or medallions of monkfish braised with tomatoes, olives, chorizo, artichokes and gremolata, although something as traditional as pan-fried calf's liver with leek mash, crispy bacon and mustard sauce could also put in an appearance. Plum tarte Tatin with pear and cinnamon sorbet, or tiramisù are the sort of puddings to expect. Wadworth 6X and Henry's Original IPA, Bass and Adnams Bitter are on draught, and an imaginative wine list, strongest in France and the New World, has around a dozen by the glass from £2.55 (£10 a bottle). SAMPLE DISHES: sardines grilled with oregano, lemon and garlic £6; wild rabbit casseroled with fennel, turnips and blackeye beans in a cider and mustard cream £13; prune and Armagnac parfait with vanilla and tea syrup £4.75.

Licensees Penny Simpson and Bill Laret (freehouse)
Open *summer 11 to 11, winter 11 to 3, 6 to 11; bar food and restaurant all week 12 to 3, Mon to Sat 7 to 9; closed 26 Dec*
Details *Children welcome in bar eating area   Car park   Wheelchair access (not WC)   Garden   No smoking in restaurant   No music   Dogs welcome exc in restaurant   Delta, MasterCard, Switch, Visa   Accommodation: 7 rooms, B&B £55 to £90*

NEW ENTRY   *indicates that the pub was not a main entry in the previous edition.*

HINTON CHARTERHOUSE   Bath & N.E. Somerset   map 2

▲ Rose & Crown   [NEW ENTRY]
High Street, Hinton Charterhouse BA2 7SN   TEL: (01225) 722153
on B3110 6m S of Bath

'This pub reminds you of the virtues of simple food, well cooked.' To seek it
out take the B-road from Bath towards Woolverton, and at the second crossroads in Hinton Charterhouse you'll find a solid-stone building with a pantiled
roof and (from the front, at least) the sort of strictly symmetrical façade one
associates with doll's houses. The immaculate interior has attractive wood
panelling and red carpets, a splendid fireplace (and fire) and old photos and
sporting prints on the walls. The beers are Butcombe and Bass (and there's a
short wine list, including five house wines by the glass). The menu – not yards
long, but nicely varied – may start with home-made soup, or Greek salad,
before moving on to chicken curry, braised partridge, or a rich red wine and
mushroom sauce rendering braised steak tender enough to part with a fork.
Fish alternatives could include a darne of salmon with dill and white wine
sauce, or succulent, really fresh cod in a 'definitely crispy and almost entirely
grease-free' golden batter: 'the very best plain home cooking'. Fruits of the
forest meringue, or sultana pudding with lemon might follow. SAMPLE DISHES:
prawn cocktail £4; steak and ale pie £8; fruits of the forest meringue £3.

Licensees Paul and Rosemary Harris (freehouse)
Open *11 to 2.30, 5.30 to 11, Sun 12 to 3, 7 to 10.30; bar food and restaurant 11 to 2, 6 (7 Sun)
to 9.30*
Details *Children welcome in eating areas   Car park   Wheelchair access (also WC)   Garden and
patio   No smoking in dining room   No music   No dogs   Delta, MasterCard, Switch, Visa
Accommodation: 4 rooms, B&B £45 to £65*

HOGNASTON   Derbyshire   map 5

▲ Red Lion ✿
Main Street, Hognaston DE6 1PR   TEL: (01335) 370396
WEBSITE: www.lionrouge.com
off A5035 between Ashbourne and Wirksworth

The unassuming whitewashed exterior of the Red Lion, in a quiet village close
to Carsington Reservoir, hides a real gem within. The large L-shaped stepped-
level area around the bar is laid with quarry tiles, floorboards and rugs and
warmed by log fires. The white walls, some brick, are hung with old prints,
oils, watercolours and photographs, and there's even a grandfather clock, with
a mixture of farmhouse tables, chairs and settles under the beamed ceiling.
The menu, served throughout the pub, is chalked up on blackboards and
offers much of interest. Start with Chinese five-spice pork with rice, pancetta
and mozzarella salad, or 'excellent-flavoured' garlic mushrooms topped with
melting Cheddar on a bed of salad. Main courses run from ribeye steak with a
red wine and shallot sauce, through an 'excellent' seafood platter (crevettes,
green-lipped mussels, prawns and salmon fishcakes), to lamb and apricot
tagine with couscous, or cod kebabs coated in Thai ginger with strawberry and
pepper mayonnaise. Desserts also take their inspiration from near and far,

from summer pudding to French apple tart and tiramisù. Service has been described as 'faultless' and the atmosphere is warm, welcoming and buzzy. Marston's Pedigree, Old Speckled Hen and Bass are on draught, and the wine list is short and to the point, encompassing a trio of South African house wines available by the glass (£2.75), with another five each of reds and whites and three champagnes. SAMPLE DISHES: celery and cider soup £4; smoked haddock and spring onion fishcakes with salad and lemon coulis £10; chocolate and orange truffle £4.25.

Licensee Philip Price (freehouse)
Open 12 to 3, 6 (7 Sun) to 11; bar food and restaurant Tue to Sun 12 to 2 (2.15 Sat and Sun), Mon to Sat 6.30 to 9; closed 25 Dec
Details Children welcome in restaurant   Car park   Wheelchair access (also WC)   Patio
No smoking in restaurant   Occasional live or background music   Dogs welcome exc weekend evenings   Amex, Delta, MasterCard, Switch, Visa   Accommodation: 3 rooms, B&B £45 to £75

HOLCOMBE   Somerset   map 2

▲ Ring O' Roses   NEW ENTRY

Stratton Road, Holcombe BA3 1EB   TEL: (01761) 232478
WEBSITE: www.ringoroses.co.uk
from Stratton-on-the-Fosse, on A367, follow signpost for Holcombe; pub is to the left after cross-roads, before the village

---

The nursery rhyme from which this sixteenth-century former farmhouse takes its name refers to the plague that once devastated the village of Holcombe. Nursery rhyme fans should also note that the nearby villages of Kilmersdon and Mells are reputedly the respective homes of Jack and Jill and Jack Horner. Such whimsy aside, this is a serious-minded country hotel that takes a grown-up view of relaxation and comfort, with newspapers to read by the log fire in the oak-panelled bar and a peaceful garden overlooking Downside Abbey. Dining is restricted to the bar at lunchtime and the restaurant in the evening. The style of the latter is ambitious, with starters such as baked quail stuffed with chicken and tarragon mousse on a warm pear coulis, and main courses of slow-roast English lamb shank with honey on rosemary-scented vegetables. Bar food is simpler fare, such as prawn and smoked salmon cocktail, deep-fried cod with chips, or pan-fried minted lamb steak with new potatoes, as well as a range of salads, sandwiches, ploughman's and filled tortilla wraps. Otter and Blind Man's Breweries supply the real ales, and there is also an excellent range of bottled ciders. The wine list is a compilation of around thirty bottles, starting with six house wines at £9.50, or £3.35 a large glass. SAMPLE DISHES: duck breast salad with garlic croûtons and toasted pine nuts £6.50; trio of farmhouse sausages on mustard and leek mash with onion gravy £6; apricot Bakewell tart £4.

Licensee Richard Rushton (freehouse)
Open Mon to Fri 11.30 to 11, Sat 11 to 2.30, 6.30 to 11, Sun 12 to 2.30, 7 to 10.30; bar food Mon to Sat 12 to 1.45, restaurant Mon to Sat 12 to 2, 7 to 9.30 (8.30 Sun)
Details Children welcome in restaurant   Car park   Wheelchair access (also WC)   Garden
No smoking in restaurant   Background music   Dogs welcome in bar only   Delta, MasterCard, Switch, Visa   Accommodation: 8 rooms, B&B £65 to £95

Red Lion Inn 🅦 NEW ENTRY

Main Street, Hollington DE6 3AG   TEL: (01335) 360241
Hollington signposted off A52 7m NW of Derby

Most of this whitewashed village inn, with an attractive garden, has been
turned over to dining, although an area to the side of the recently extended bar
is set aside for drinking and bar food. Cottagey tables and chairs, walls either
white or red and hung with prints, fresh flowers on the tables and a warm and
cosy atmosphere all add to the allure. But it's the sophisticated and adventurous cooking that packs people in. The wide-ranging menu runs from cream of
fennel and Pernod soup, or ham hock terrine with spiced peach chutney, to
main courses of osso buco with root vegetables and herb dumplings, or
chicken fillet wrapped in smoked bacon on a tomato and chive coulis. Fish
appears in the form of bouillabaisse, or halibut fillet on wilted spinach with
chive butter sauce, and in season there might be pan-fried breast of pheasant
in steamed Savoy cabbage with parsnip purée. Puddings are no less satisfying,
among them perhaps chocolate and hazelnut meringue roulade. A two-course
set lunch is on offer at lunchtimes as well as the main blackboard menu, which
on Sundays is accompanied by two roasts. Marston's Bitter and Pedigree and
Banks's Mansfield Dark Mild are on draught, and a short printed wine list is
supplemented by a blackboard of more special bottles like Ch. Talbot 1969.
Around nine wines come by the glass. SAMPLE DISHES: chorizo and Parmesan
risotto £4.50; fillet steak in port and wild mushroom jus £15; espresso crème
brûlée and chocolate shortbread £4.

Licensee Robin Hunter (Pyramid)
Open 12 to 3, 6 to 11; bar food and restaurant Tue to Sun 12 to 2.30 (3 Sun), 6.30 to 9 (9.30
Sat)
Details Children welcome   Car park   Wheelchair access (also WC)   Garden and patio
No smoking in restaurant   Live or background music   Dogs welcome   MasterCard, Switch, Visa

Bell and Cross 🅦 NEW ENTRY

Holy Cross DY9 9QL   TEL: (01562) 730319
off A491, SE of West Hagley

Roger Narbett has been a well-known figure on the Midlands restaurant scene
for many years, and his latest venture is this tall, mustard-coloured pub.
Inside, the walls are crammed with prints, photographs and framed portraits,
and the pretty pink, no-smoking restaurant has some pleasing touches, such as
jars of preserves on the windowsill and little terracotta pots with miniature
trees on the tables. The day-to-day cooking is handled by Paul Mohan, and
there's plenty of ambition at work here – witness warm spinach and ricotta tart
with roasted balsamic tomatoes, or glazed belly of Lincolnshire pork with
roasted apple, fondant potato, white-bean cassoulet and sage jus. Simpler
dishes, however, are also on offer: whole Cornish sole with lemon and herb
butter, for example. Desserts might include anything from treacle tart and
locally made ice creams to red fruit pavlova with Chantilly cream. At

lunchtime you can also get 'sarnies' and 'light bites'. Greene King Abbot Ale, Banks's Mild and Marston's Pedigree are among the beers on draught, and the short list of around 30 wines includes some decent stuff, with four by the glass. SAMPLE DISHES: Peking crispy duck salad £5.75; pot-roast chicken breast with Savoy cabbage, peas and spicy sausage £10.75; 'devilish' chocolate charlotte with blackcurrant sorbet £4.50.

Licensee Jo Narbett (Enterprise Inns)
Open 12 to 3, 6 to 11, Sun 12 to 3.30, 7 to 10.30; bar food and restaurant 12 to 2 (2.30 Sun), 6.30 to 9 (9.30 Fri and Sat); closed 25 Dec, 2 Jan, evenings 26 and 31 Dec, 1 Jan
Details Children welcome   Car park   Wheelchair access (not WC)   Garden and patio
No smoking in restaurant   Background music   Dogs welcome in bar   MasterCard, Switch, Visa

HOLY ISLAND   Northumberland   map 10

▲ Crown and Anchor Hotel   NEW ENTRY

Market Place, Holy Island TD15 2RX   TEL: (01289) 389215
WEBSITE: www.crownandanchorinn.fsnet.co.uk

Often referred to as Lindisfarne, Holy Island comes complete with Tudor castle (National Trust), ruined priory, and, for those making a modern-day pilgrimage, the Crown and Anchor, set on the edge of the village, for agreeable sustenance. A tidal island, it's reached by a causeway which is impassable some two hours before high tide and three hours after (tide tables are displayed at the causeway or phone ahead to avoid disappointment). The Crown and Anchor itself is a welcoming hotel and freehouse frequented by locals and visitors to the area alike. Blackboards in the small bar and in the restaurant list wines and specials of the day. David Foxton's menus are 'always interesting' and 'in the evenings quite enterprising', stepping out with modish dishes such as a warm salad of wood pigeon, osso buco, confit of duck with orange cream, potatoes, baby carrots and courgette bake, or perhaps a 'tasty and light' ham, tomato and egg pie. Raspberry crème brûlée could head up desserts. For beer drinkers there's Caledonian Deuchars IPA, and wine lovers can choose from over ten wines by the glass. SAMPLE DISHES: spring rolls of duck confit with red onion salsa £5; local venison casseroled with redcurrants £10.50; passion-fruit cheesecake £4.50.

Licensee David Foxton (freehouse)
Open 11 to 11, Sun 12 to 10.30; bar food 12 to 2.30; restaurant Wed to Sun 6,30 to 8.30; closed Mon, Tue and 3pm to 6pm other days winter
Details Children welcome in restaurant   Wheelchair access (not WC)   Garden   No smoking in restaurant   Background music   No dogs   Delta, MasterCard, Switch, Visa   Accommodation: 3 rooms, B&B £60 to £70

All details are as accurate as possible at the time of going to press, but pubs often change hands and it is wise to check beforehand by telephone anything that is particularly important to you.

▲ Cheshire Cheese Inn

Edale Road, Hope S33 6ZF   TEL: (01433) 620381
on A625 between Chapel-en-le-Frith and Hathersage; leave Hope by the unclassified road to
Edale; pub is on left after ½m

Dating from the sixteenth century, this small, stone-built pub is in a village at the heart of the Peak District National Park, with Castleton and its caverns, the Ladybower and Derwent Reservoirs, and wild open moorland all within easy reach. It's a traditional, unspoilt hostelry, with three rooms on different levels, including a small bar with a log fire, beams and heavy cottage-style furniture and lots of old prints and maps on the walls. Walkers can quench their thirst with a pint of one of the good line-up of hand-pulled real ales, among them Hartington Bitter from Whim Ales near Buxton, Black Sheep Best Bitter, Wentworth Pale Ale and Timothy Taylor Landlord, and satisfy their hunger with something from the printed menu or the blackboard of specials. You could start with a generous bowl of wholesome chicken and mushroom soup, or grilled black pudding with mustard sauce, and go on to a hearty pie – perhaps steak, or pork, apricot and cider – or more modish grilled cod in lime and ginger butter, and end with spotted dick, or, more appropriately, Bakewell tart. Vegetarians get a good deal, and committed carnivores could opt for the 'mammoth mixed grill' served with chips, peas and a fried egg. Around a dozen wines are served by the glass, with bottle prices starting at £7.50. Service has been described as 'excellent' even under pressure from the crowds who gather here. SAMPLE DISHES: prawn cocktail £4; grilled tuna steak in garlic and tomato sauce £9; chocolate fudge cake £3.50.

Licensees David and Anthea Helliwell (freehouse)
Open *Mon to Fri 12 to 3, 6.30 to 11, Sat 12 to 11, Sun 12 to 4, 6.30 to 10.30; bar food 12 to 2*
(2.30 Sat and Sun), 6.30 to 9
Details *Children welcome in eating areas   Car park   Wheelchair access (not WC)   Patio*
No smoking in eating areas   Background music   Dogs welcome exc in eating areas   Amex, Delta,
MasterCard, Switch, Visa   Accommodation: 1 room, B&B £65 (double room)

▲ Crown Inn

Hopton Wafers DY14 0NB   TEL: (01299) 270372
WEBSITE: www.crownathopton.co.uk
on A4117, 2m W of Cleobury Mortimer

The Crown, its façade thickly encrusted with vine, is set at right angles to the road, with a paved terrace at the front containing picnic tables and parasols, then a steep drop to the car park with another steep drop to the lawned gardens that run down to a stream. Its decorative style is traditional, with exposed timbers in bar, restaurant and bedrooms. The Rent Room bar is so called because this was where stewards once collected rents from tenant farmers, while the restaurant takes the name of Poacher's. All menus are available throughout, and a notable feature is the size of the portions. Blackboards list

the bar menu: perhaps a 'thoroughly enjoyable' starter of pan-seared pigeon
breasts with smoked bacon and balsamic-dressed leaves, followed by seared
king scallops on a bed of couscous with a strawberry and balsamic reduction.
Alongside these might be coq au vin, or pan-fried fillets of sea bass on wilted
spinach with avocado salsa. Four real ales are usually stocked, among them
Timothy Taylor Landlord and Hobson's Best, plus always a guest. A laminated sheet of wines by glass and bottle is presented to pub diners, though we
understand an 80-bottle list is also available; unfortunately, the Guide had not
received either before going to press and so cannot comment on their content.
SAMPLE DISHES: home-cured gravad lax £5.50; pan-fried medallions of monkfish £13.50; poached spiced pear in red wine sauce £4.50.

Licensee Howard Hill-Lines (freehouse)

Open 12 to 3, 6 to 11 (10.30 Sun); bar food 12 to 2.30, 6.30 to 9.30 (9 Sun); restaurant Tue to
Sat 7 to 9.30 (9 Sun)

Details Children welcome in bar eating area; no children under 7 in restaurant   Car park   Garden
and patio   No smoking in eating areas   Background music   No dogs in eating areas   Amex, Delta,
MasterCard, Switch, Visa   Accommodation: 7 rooms, B&B £47.50 to £75

HORNDON ON THE HILL   Essex   map 3

▲ Bell Inn 🎭 🍺 🍇

High Road, Horndon on the Hill SS17 8LD   TEL: (01375) 642463
WEBSITE: www.bell-inn.co.uk
off M25 junctions 30 and 31, signposted Thurrock, Lakeside; take A13, then B1007 to Horndon

Despite its 500-year history, the Bell looks quite an unassuming place from
the outside. Within, though, atmosphere is generated by flagstone floors,
standing timbers, a collection of foundry memorabilia, a longcase clock and
normally a bustle of people. Those who come in for just a drink use the front
bar, while the back bar next to the restaurant is where those wishing to eat may
settle (note that bar tables are not bookable). The modern and imaginative
restaurant menu, also served in the bar, may present a starter such as ravioli of
skate and smoked salmon with a fig, caper and honey dressing before main
courses of braised brisket of beef with pak choi and apricot sauce, a risotto of
haggis with celeriac and caper purée, or honey- and pepper-glazed chicken
with mustard leaf and basil. Additional touches, such as stylish presentation,
add to the feeling that this is a well-run operation that knows what it's doing.
Sandwiches are available in the bar along with such dishes as pot-roast lamb
shank with mint jus, or smoked haddock fishcakes with hollandaise. A dozen
or so wines are offered by the glass from an irreverent house list. The main
wine list runs to some serious aged Bordeaux and Burgundy but is sprinkled
with good choices from around the world at fair prices. All wines are also
available to buy at take-away prices. Real ale buffs can choose Greene King
IPA or Abbot Ale, Bass, Crouch Vale Brewers Gold or Mighty Oak
Burntwood Bitter. SAMPLE DISHES: seared tuna-stuffed squid with pomegranate salsa £6.25; grilled salmon with celeriac chips, basil and caper sauce £13.50;
glazed banana and lemon tart with liquorice ice cream £5.

Licensee J.S.B. Vereker (freehouse)
Open *Mon to Fri 11 to 2.30, 5.30 to 11, Sat 11 to 3, 6 to 11, Sun 12 to 4, 7 to 10.30; bar food and restaurant 12 to 1.45 (2.15 Sun), 6.30 (7 Sun) to 9.45*
Details *Children welcome in eating areas   Car park   Wheelchair access (also WC)   Patio No smoking in restaurant   No music   Dogs welcome in bar on a lead   Amex, Delta, MasterCard, Switch, Visa   Accommodation: 15 rooms, room only £50 to £85*

HORRINGER   Suffolk   map 6

Beehive

The Street, Horringer IP29 5SN   TEL: (01284) 735260
on A143, 3m SW of Bury St Edmunds

This well-kept and welcoming brick and flint pub is easily found on the main road through the village – look for the beehive on the front lawn. Enter through the rear, past the small leafy beer garden, into a network of small rooms decorated in a simple, cottagey style, with hessian flooring and a mix of traditional pictures and old photographs. Though the atmosphere is informal, this is by no means a basic boozer – people do come just for a drink (Greene King IPA or the guest ale, or perhaps one of the eight wines by the glass), but the food is the main draw. Blackboards list the dishes of the day, typically featuring coarse Suffolk country pâté and mussel chowder among starters, while main courses might take in roast monkfish fillet in hot sweet-and-sour sauce alongside ribeye steak au poivre. There is also a selection of lighter dishes, such as baked pasta with three-cheese sauce, or toasted salt-beef sandwich, and you might finish your meal with ginger crème brûlée. Horringer is an attractive village, and local places of interest include Ickworth House (NT). SAMPLE DISHES: gravad lax with mustard and dill sauce £6; seared tuna with sauce vierge £12; Bakewell tart £4.

Licensee Gary Kingshott (Greene King)
Open *11.30 to 2.30, 7 to 11, Sun 12 to 2.30, 7 to 10.30; bar food (exc Sun evening) 12 to 2, 7 to 9.30*
Details *Children welcome   Car park   Wheelchair access (not WC)   Garden   No music   No dogs Delta, MasterCard, Switch, Visa*

HORSEBRIDGE   Hampshire   map 2

John of Gaunt 🍺

Horsebridge SO20 6PU   TEL: (01794) 388394
1m off A3057, 8m W of Winchester

The name of this rural, nineteenth-century brick-built pub in the Test Valley is a reference to the deer park in the area owned by John of Gaunt, son of Edward III. With a terrace to one side and bench seating at the front, it is a popular stop for cyclists and walkers (the Test Way long-distance path passes by a mere 100 yards away), who doubtless appreciate the unfussy country interior of dark wooden furniture and open fires. Well-kept real ales are a strong point: on draught might be Palmers IPA, Ringwood Best Bitter and Fortyniner, and Itchen Valley Fagin's. In addition, there's Thatcher's cider and half a dozen wines by the glass. The cooking is as devoid of unnecessary frills as the surroundings, with starters of a soup – perhaps curried parsnip – prawn cocktail, or deep-fried whitebait, followed by steak and Stilton pie, or a roast half-shoulder of lamb. Trout and salmon from the Test feature in season, as do game: braised pheasant, or venison casseroled in red wine. Apple and blackberry crumble and pears mulled in red wine might be fruity options at dessert stage, with perhaps sticky toffee pudding for the sweeter of tooth. SAMPLE DISHES: leek and potato soup £2.75; roast partridge £7.50; bread-and-butter pudding £3.

Licensee Graham Atkins (freehouse)
Open 11 to 3, 6 to 11, Sun 12 to 3, 7 to 10.30; bar food 12 to 2, 7 to 9.30
Details Children welcome   Car park   Garden and patio   Background music   Dogs welcome
No cards

HORSTEAD   Norfolk   map 6

Recruiting Sergeant 🍺 NEW ENTRY

Norwich Road, Horstead NR12 7EP   TEL: (01603) 737077
on B1150 Norwich to North Walsham road, 7m N of Norwich

A little back from the road through the village sits this long, white building with a rather Cape Dutch-looking porch and two tiny dormers in its red-tiled roof. Inside, the main bar extends the length of the building, the I-shaped counter separating the front from the quieter back section that opens on to the garden behind. Logically, the walls are hung with military prints, and the mostly East Anglian beers include Queen's Shilling (brewed for the pub by Courage), Adnams Bitter and Broadside, Greene King Abbot Ale, Woodforde's Wherry or Nelson's Revenge. Of the 20-some wines listed 13 are available by the glass. The food is listed on a carte, but this is supplemented by daily printed morning and evening menus of specials (notably fresh fish) – to save customers peering at blackboards in the middle distance. Typical starters might be jellied eels and granary bread, home-made duck spring rolls with hoisin, or perfectly seared Scottish scallops on mixed leaves, with crispy chorizo strips for contrast. Dual-priced salads (Caesar, niçoise) make starters or mains, and vegetarian options include a mushroom, onion and smoked-cheese suet pudding. Or perhaps roast saddle of venison might tempt, or crisp-skinned, moist-fleshed fillets of wild sea bass with Mediterranean roast vegetables and basil. A raspberry crème brûlée and shortbread could round things off. Staff are 'really friendly and chatty'. SAMPLE DISHES: Dutch-style pea soup £3.25; grilled Lowestoft plaice £9; steamed chocolate and Baileys pudding £3.25.

Licensee Matthew John Colchester (freehouse)
Open 11 to 11, Sun 12 to 10.30; bar food and restaurant 12 to 2, 6.30 to 9 (6.30 to 9.30 Thur to Sat); closed for food 25 Dec
Details Children welcome   Car park   Wheelchair access (also WC)   Garden and patio
No-smoking area in bar, no smoking in dining room   Background music   Dogs welcome on a lead
Delta, MasterCard, Switch, Visa

▲ Knife & Cleaver 🍇

The Grove, Houghton Conquest MK45 3LA   TEL: (01234) 740387
WEBSITE: www.knifeandcleaver.com
between A6 and B530, 5m S of Bedford

While the swinging sign outside might proclaim 'restaurant-with-rooms', this much-extended village local still has an unmistakable bar, with large fireplaces at opposite ends of the room, wood-panelled walls, a squishy leather sofa and comfortable chairs around a variety of wooden and copper-topped tables. Bateman XB and Bass are on draught, with Stowford Press for cider drinkers, and the bar menu is an appealing mix of pub favourites and more unusual offerings. Interesting filled baguettes and ciabattas, as well as ploughman's, are there for those after just a snack, and among starters might be smoked haddock chowder with cheesy croûtons, a salad of shrimps, melon and farm-house cheese, and duck rillettes with pimento chutney and toasted onion bread. Steak and mushroom pudding, crisply braised belly pork with sage and red onion risotto and soy gravy, and salmon and shrimp fishcake with a shrimp and tarragon beurre blanc show the range of main courses, and desserts could well include that old favourite of sticky toffee pudding. Fish is the main thrust of the restaurant menu – perhaps whole grilled Dover sole with chive and caviar butter, or braised fillets of gilt-edged bream with bacon, baby onions and olives – although something like medallions of venison with carrot and celery confit and red wine jus might make an appearance among meat dishes. Wines come on two lists – the first offering around 30 by the glass or 50cl carafe, the second a full restaurant list that sweeps happily from £11 basics to expensive French classics and is grouped by style. To the rear of the property is a courtyard and garden. SAMPLE DISHES: flat bread with smoked trout and mackerel and horseradish dressing £6; spicy chicken risotto with Parmesan crisps £6.50; apple and almond tart £3.50.

Licensee David and Pauline Loom (freehouse)
Open *all week (exc Sun evening) 12 to 2.30, 7 to 11; bar food 12 to 2.30, 7 to 9.30 (no bar food served when restaurant is busy, usually Sat evening and Sun lunchtime: best to phone weekends); restaurant (exc Sat lunchtime) 12 to 2.30, 7 to 9.30; closed 27 to 30 Dec*
Details *Children welcome in eating areas   Car park   Wheelchair access (not WC)   Garden No smoking in restaurant   Background music   No dogs   Amex, Delta, Diners, MasterCard, Switch, Visa   Accommodation: 9 rooms, B&B £53 to £78*

▲ George Inn

Kirk Gill, Hubberholme BD23 5JE   TEL: (01756) 760223
WEBSITE: www.thegeorge-inn.co.uk
off B6160 near Buckden, 17m N of Skipton

WATERSIDE

In the thirteenth century the steep country of Langstrothdale Chase was a hunting ground for the Percys, Dukes of Northumberland. Nowadays many walkers come to this whitewashed and stone-slated pub beside the fledgling Wharfe. Its two bars have low beams, flagstone floors and bare stone walls, and there's a comforting fire. Rain-soaked hats and gloves dry on radiators while their owners refuel with Black Sheep Special Ale and Tetley Bitter on draught, plus guest beers such as Thwaites Best Bitter and Jennings Cocker Hoop. Hearty lunches take in home-made soups, filled wholemeal rolls, Yorkshire puddings (filled with beef, sausages, or onion gravy) or sirloin steak. The evening menu might offer tomato and halloumi salad, or prawn cocktail, followed by a salmon steak or some Dales lamb chops. Puds, from the blackboard, could include a brandy-snap basket filled with ice cream and fruit. The wine list mostly stays well under £20, its 24 bins covering most of the world, but only house red and white are available by the glass. SAMPLE DISHES: mushrooms filled with bacon and goats' cheese £4.25; lamb shank in red wine gravy £10; apple and raspberry crumble £3.25.

Licensees Terry and Jenny Browne (freehouse)
Open Mon to Fri 11 to 3, 6 to 11, Sun 12 to 3, 6 to 10.30; bar food 12 to 2, 6.30 to 8.45; closed second week Jan to first weekend Feb
Details Car park Wheelchair access (not WC) Garden and patio No music Dogs welcome on a lead Delta, MasterCard, Switch, Visa Accommodation: 6 rooms, B&B £38 to £66

HUNTINGDON Cambridgeshire   map 6

▲ Old Bridge Hotel 🏆 🏆 🍇

1 High Street, Huntingdon PE29 3TQ   TEL: (01480) 424300
WEBSITE: www.huntsbridge.co.uk
off Huntingdon ring road, by river

Follow the one-way system through town and you'll find the Old Bridge perched above the River Ouse (visible from the car park but not from inside). The handsome ivy-clad eighteenth-century hotel is a member of the Huntsbridge Group and follows the same formula successfully applied at its sister establishments (see Three Horseshoes, Madingley; Pheasant Inn, Keyston; and the Falcon, Fotheringhay). This means an approach to eating and drinking that combines the virtues of pubby informality with some seriously good cooking by Martin Lee. Two menus apply, offering a similar style of food: an à la carte for the bar areas, including the spacious and relaxing lounge, and the smaller bar down a wide set of carpeted steps (with two back-to-back sofas, one facing a log fire), and in the informal Terrace Restaurant; in the separate Dining Room there is a three-course set menu for £36. The cooking style is distinctly modern, displaying lots of bright Mediterranean influences, as well as some from further afield, alongside more traditional ideas. This can result in such dishes as seared salmon with cannellini beans and black cabbage appearing on the menu next to braised pork with wok-fried greens, ginger and spring onions, or chargrilled sirloin steak with béarnaise sauce and chips. Game is handled confidently – perhaps 'tender' whole roast partridge with girolles, Savoy cabbage and rösti, or roast loin of venison with apple and potato rösti and celeriac – as is seafood – perhaps a starter of 'near-perfect' seared scallops with cauliflower purée and another purée of sultanas and capers. Sandwiches are an alternative, and among puddings may be pear poached in red wine with vanilla rice pudding. Adnams Best Bitter is the regular real ale; this is accompanied by two guests, one of which may be from a local brewery, such as City of Cambridge, Potton or Elgood's. Wine is a passion here, with 15 by the glass priced from £2.95 to £6 and covering an exciting range of flavours; good sherry is on offer too. The full list of around 300 bottles starts off with an appetising 'under-£20' selection arranged by style, but makes no bones about encouraging customers to spend more on the outstanding range of 'top class' bottles. SAMPLE DISHES: terrine of black pudding, foie gras and ham hock with truffled pease pudding £7.50; shoulder of lamb with cumin potatoes and braised red cabbage £13.50; caramel soufflé with prune and Armagnac ice cream £7.50.

Licensees Martin Lee and John Hoskins (freehouse)
Open 12 to 11, Sun 12 to 10.30; bar food and restaurant 12 to 2.30, 6 to 9.30
Details Children welcome   Car park   Wheelchair access (not WC)   Patio   No smoking in restaurant   Occasional live music   Dogs welcome   Amex, Delta, Diners, MasterCard, Switch, Visa
Accommodation: 24 rooms, B&B £80 to £180

ICKLESHAM   East Sussex   map 3
Queens Head 🍺 [NEW ENTRY]
Parsonage Lane, Icklesham TN36 4BL   TEL: (01424) 814552
just off A259 2m W of Winchelsea

Set on a ridge just inland from the stretch of Sussex coastline between Hastings and Rye, the Queens Head was built in 1632 and has been licensed since 1831. Its compact interlinked rooms around a central bar have an 'olde-worlde' feel, with ceilings at different heights and assorted artefacts, ranging from old-fashioned agricultural tools to an ancient delivery bike, hanging from them. The cooking, described as of the 'plainish, no-frills traditional English' variety, is considered 'very good value for money'. The standard menu lists things like soft herring roes on toast, steaks, ploughman's and curry. More interesting are the blackboard specials, which might include game and red wine casserole, or lamb ratatouille with salad and garlic bread. Desserts are from the banoffi pie and chocolate profiteroles school. Real ales are a strong point: up to six are offered at a time, including something from Harveys, Greene King, Woodforde's and Courage Directors. Wines are not bad either – the short list offers plenty of choice by the glass. Visit on Tuesday evenings for live music. SAMPLE DISHES: prawn fritters with garlic mayonnaise £5; steak, ale and mushroom pie £7.50; chocolate fudge cake £3.25.

Licensees Ian Mitchell and Lee Norcott (freehouse)
Open 11 to 11, Sun 12 to 10.30; bar food Mon to Fri 12 to 2.45, 6.15 to 9.45, Sat and Sun 12 to 9.45; closed evenings 25 and 26 Dec
Details Children welcome   Car park   No-smoking areas   Live or background music   Amex, Delta, Diners, MasterCard, Switch, Visa

ICKLINGHAM   Suffolk   map 6
Red Lion
The Street, Icklingham IP28 6PS   TEL: (01638) 717802
on A1101, 7m NW of Bury St Edmunds

This Lion is a smart beast, thatched and painted white and standing back from the main road behind neat lawns. An oriental rug, large winged armchairs and a huge inglenook create a homely and welcoming impression inside. Bar meals tend to be fairly simple dishes like gammon steak with creamy mustard sauce, or Barnsley chops with shallot butter. More interesting is the à la carte menu, which might offer Norfolk chicken breast with mild curry and mango sauce, or even something really exotic like crocodile tournedos with Thai-style butter. There is also a seasonal game menu, and a blackboard of fish specials provides a further 15 to 20 choices, including Brancaster mussels cooked with cream, garlic, celery and white wine and served in 'puny', 'average' or 'stupendous' portions. This is a Greene King pub with IPA and Abbot Ale on draught, and though wine is not a speciality here it would be a shame to pass up the opportunity to taste country wines made from elderberry or silver birch. SAMPLE DISHES: Norfolk crayfish cocktail £7; pork chops with apple and cider sauce £10.25; sticky toffee pudding £4.50.

Licensee Elizabeth Mason (Greene King)
Open 12 to 3, 6 to 11, Sun 12 to 2.30, 7.15 to 10.30; bar food and restaurant 12 to 2.30, 6 to 10
Details Children welcome   Car park   Wheelchair access (also WC)   Garden   Background music
No dogs   Delta, MasterCard, Switch, Visa

IDDESLEIGH   Devon   map 1

▲ Duke of York 🍺
Iddesleigh EX19 8BG   TEL: (01837) 810253
on B3217, 3m NE of Hatherleigh

The Duke of York was built in the style of an old Devon longhouse with a thatched roof, and a cobbled yard with planted tubs, and old cottages and the church next door provide the perfect village setting. Low ceilings and small rooms, plus a 'roast-an-ox fireplace', as one visitor described it, make for a cosy ambience, and old prints and banknotes decorate parts of the walls, with one wall covered with the extensive menu. Bar food encompasses standards such as shepherd's pie, curry, lasagne, fish and chips, and faggots, mash and peas. A more ambitious fixed-price menu is offered in the separate restaurant area, although food from here can be ordered in the bar and there's also some overlap between the two menus. There, you might opt for 'simply scrumptious' port and Stilton pâté, followed by 'marvellous' grilled fillets of sea bass brushed with dill mustard accompanied by 'perfectly cooked' vegetables, or lamb tagine with couscous. Real ales are a particular strength: Cotleigh Tawny Bitter and Adnams Broadside are joined by guests from West Country breweries Sharp's, Jollyboat and Exe Valley. Ten wines are available by the glass. SAMPLE DISHES: grilled scallops wrapped in smoked bacon £4.50; steak and kidney pudding £8; apple crumble with custard £3.50.

Licensees Jamie Stuart and Pippa Hutchinson (freehouse)
Open 11 to 11, Sun 12 to 11; bar food 11 to 10; restaurant 6.30 to 9.30
Details Children welcome   Garden   Occasional live music   Dogs welcome   MasterCard, Switch,
Visa   Accommodation: 7 rooms, B&B £25 to £50

🍺 indicates a pub serving better-than-average wine, including good choice by bottle and glass.

IGHTHAM   Kent   map 3

Harrow Inn ✿

Common Road, Ightham TN15 9EB   TEL: (01732) 885912
just off A25 Sevenoaks to Borough Green road

Open fires, timbered walls, and candles and fresh flowers on wooden tables
are enticements at this Kentish ragstone pub near the National Trust's
Ightham Mote. But first things are not forgotten: on draught are Greene King
IPA and Abbot Ale along with guests. The restaurant menu, also available in
the bar, gives plenty of choice, from starters of coarse country terrine with
cranberry compote, or wild mushroom vol-au-vent in Noilly Prat sauce, to
main courses of pan-fried blackened fillets of sea bass with Cajun spices and
tomato and red onion salsa, or baked ham in mustard sauce with swede,
parsnip and turnip mash. Bar meals might kick off with a tureen of Tuscan
bean soup and go on to smoked haddock with Welsh rarebit, beef and
Guinness pie, or wild mushroom risotto. Finish with something fruity like
raspberry crème brûlée or rhubarb crumble. Five red and five white wines are
sold by the glass. SAMPLE DISHES: crab and ginger spring roll with sweet chilli
dressing £6; chicken and wild mushroom pie £10; mango cheesecake £4.25.

Licensee John Elton (freehouse)
Open *Tue to Sun 12 to 3, Tue to Sat 6 to 11; bar food and restaurant 12 to 2.15, 6 to 9.30;
closed 1 Jan*
Details *Children welcome in family room   Car park   Wheelchair access (not WC)   Patio
No smoking in restaurant   Background music   No dogs   MasterCard, Switch, Visa*

ILKLEY   West Yorkshire   map 8

Bar T-at 🍺 | NEW ENTRY |

7 Cunliffe Road, Ilkley LS29 9DZ   TEL: (01943) 608888

A stylish wine-cum-beer bar on two levels, Bar T-at (as in the song 'On Ilkley
Moor...': get it? Of course you do) is in the centre of town. The ground-level
bar has a vast array of bottled beers as well as six real ales on handpump,
among them Deuchars IPA, Timothy Taylor Landlord and guests like Black
Sheep Bitter. There's also a fair range of wines, with four by the glass. The
non-smoking dining room is downstairs in the cellar but has an airy feel cour-
tesy of steps and a door to an outside terrace. The kitchen is open to view
through a hatch, and the room is laid out with scrubbed-pine tables. There are
separate lunch and dinner menus, the former offering a good range of snacks
and sandwiches alongside a few main courses. The dinner menu, with a daily
specials board, is a homely affair, delivering 'well-cooked, wholesome' and
'good-value' food. Typical main courses are beef and ale pie, claimed to be 'a
triumph' by one reporter, Toulouse sausages (both meals served with leek
mash), plus the likes of roast salmon or seared tuna and a 20-ounce T-bone
steak ('definitely enough for two'). Starters might feature prawns wrapped in
filo with salsa, and a meal could be rounded off with gingerbread accompanied
by a slice of Wensleydale cheese. SAMPLE DISHES: grilled black pudding on leek
mash served with mustard sauce £4.50; pan-fried pork steaks with red onions,
chilli, garlic and tomatoes £9; baked rice pudding with coconut and ginger £4.

Licensee Simon Wright (Market Town Taverns)
Open 12 to 11 (10.30 Sun); bar food and restaurant 12 to 2.30, 6 to 9 (8 Sun)
Details Children welcome in restaurant Garden No smoking in restaurant No music Dogs
welcome in bar Delta, MasterCard, Switch, Visa

ILMINGTON   Warwickshire   map 5

▲ Howard Arms 🍴 🍺

Lower Green, Ilmington CV36 4LT   TEL: (01608) 682226
WEBSITE: www.howardarms.com
off A3400, 4m NW of Shipston on Stour

The Howard Arms has won plaudits from reporters for being an exceedingly
well-run establishment, with intelligent, chatty and attentive service. The
building itself adds to the charm, tastefully done up with bare old wood and
flagstone floors, 'magnificent' old timbers, and honey-coloured walls spar-
ingly adorned with vintage photographs and portraits. Overall, it makes for a
'particularly pleasant' atmosphere. Food has that classic but modern feel. The
menu is listed on numerous blackboards throughout, and you will find oak-
smoked salmon with a warm potato cake, sour cream and chives alongside
spicy lamb koftas with coriander and yoghurt raita, while main courses take in
fillet of Old Spot pork Wellington with apple, sage and cider sauce, and pan-
fried pigeon breasts with carrot and ginger purée and a rich sherry sauce. Beers
are a fine selection, starring Genesis from the North Cotswold Brewery
alongside Everards Tiger Best and guest ales, which might include Timothy
Taylor Landlord or Adnams Broadside. The accurately self-styled 'small but
interesting selection of some rather nice wines' features a dozen house selections by the small or large glass (from £2.75/£3.85) or by the bottle (from
£10.50). SAMPLE DISHES: fish soup with croûtons, rouille and Gruyère £5;
bacon-wrapped cod fillet with creamed leeks £11.50; apricot and amaretti
trifle with almond biscotti £4.50.

Licensees Rob Greenstock and Martin Devereux (freehouse)
Open 11 to 2, 6 to 11; bar food Mon to Sat 12 to 2, 7 to 9 (9.30 Fri and Sat), Sun 12 to 2.30,
6.30 to 8.30; closed 25 Dec and evening 31 Dec
Details Children welcome in eating areas before 8pm Car park Wheelchair access (not WC)
Garden and patio No smoking in 2 rooms No music No dogs Delta, MasterCard, Switch, Visa
Accommodation: 3 rooms, B&B £52 to £94

INKPEN   Berkshire   map 2

▲ Swan Inn

Lower Green, Inkpen RG17 9DX   TEL: (01488) 668326
WEBSITE: www.theswaninn-organics.co.uk
off A338, 4m SE of Hungerford

Despite being extensively extended, this series of rambling buildings manages
to look all of a piece. The core dates from the seventeenth century, and inside
the open-plan layout are log fires, old beams, polished wooden tables, green
banquettes and black and white photographs on the walls. In the restaurant,
massive standing timbers contrast with formal settings on the pink-clothed

tables. The pub must be unique in that it is owned by organic beef farmers, and most of the other ingredients used in the kitchen are organic too. The restaurant menu (not available in the bar) deals in the likes of pan-fried fillet of turbot and tournedos Rossini, while the blackboard of bar meals offers a generous choice: salmon, cod and smoked haddock fishcake with chips and salad, beef, leek and ale sausages with mash and onion gravy, steaks, and a decent selection for vegetarians, including something like vegetable samosas with rice and hot chilli sauce. Puddings are as traditional as they come, from fruit crumbles with custard to banoffi pie. Beers on draught are Butts Bitter, Hook Norton Best Bitter and Best Mild, and Caledonian Golden Promise Organic Ale. Also on offer are Lambourn Valley cider and a list of organic wines, three of which are served by the glass. SAMPLE DISHES: rump steak with chips and salad £10.50; bread-and-butter pudding £4.25.

Licensees Bernard and Mary Harris (freehouse)
Open Mon to Fri 11 to 2.30, 7 to 11, Sat and Sun 11 to 11 (10.30 Sun; 11 to 2.30, 7 to 11 winter); bar food 12 to 2 (2.30 Sun), 7 to 9.30; restaurant Wed to Sun 12 to 2 (2.30 Sun), Wed to Sat 7 to 9.30; closed 25 and 26 Dec
Details Children welcome   Car park   Wheelchair access (also WC)   Garden and patio
No-smoking areas in bar, no smoking in restaurant   Occasional background music   No dogs   Delta, MasterCard, Switch, Visa   Accommodation: 10 rooms, B&B £40 to £90

IRONBRIDGE   Shropshire   map 5

▲ Malthouse ✿ [NEW ENTRY]
The Wharfage, Ironbridge TF8 7NH   TEL: (01952) 433712
WEBSITE: www.malthousepubs.co.uk
in centre of Ironbridge, 200yds from bridge

Despite being, in the view of one reporter, 'the most unpubby pub I've yet come across', the Malthouse nonetheless remains true to pub ideals. Set on a road that winds its way along the river, it comprises a number of attached but dissimilar buildings around a cobbled courtyard. The bright, spacious Jazz Bar is the part that most resembles a traditional pub, and, as the name suggests, it is also frequently a live music venue. Refreshments-wise, you can enjoy Flowers IPA, Old Speckled Hen and Boddingtons Bitter, or one of a dozen or so wines priced from £9.75, of which six are available by the glass. There is also a simple but cosmopolitan bar menu: among starters are pork rillettes, and chilli and goats' cheese fritters, while main courses range from cheese and bacon burger to Moroccan beef stew and teriyaki chicken. In between are various snacky items like macaroni cheese with red pepper oil, minute steak in a ciabatta with onion and mushrooms, or smoked fish salad with basil aïoli and soda bread. Finish perhaps with chocolate bread-and-butter pudding, or prune and almond tart. The main part of the Malthouse is given over entirely to dining, with an ambitious modern menu of things like braised and roasted pork belly in Chinese five-spice with sweet-and-sour vegetables, and pan-fried salmon fillet on carrot and potato rösti with crab and tomato butter and spinach souf-flé. SAMPLE DISHES: grilled mackerel on tapénade toast with paprika and garlic butter £4.25; Thai fishcakes with tomato and soy sauce, citrus-dressed leaves and fries £7.25; lemon cheesecake £4.

Licensee Alexander Nicoll (Pubmaster)
Open 12 to 11 (10.30 Sun); bar food and restaurant 12 to 2.30, 5.30 to 9; closed 25 Dec
Details Children welcome   Car park   Wheelchair access (not WC)   Patio   No smoking in
restaurant   Live or background music   Dogs welcome   Delta, MasterCard, Switch, Visa
Accommodation: 9 rooms, B&B £55 to £70

ITTERINGHAM   Norfolk   map 6

Walpole Arms 🍇

The Common, Itteringham NR11 7AR   TEL: (01263) 587258
WEBSITE: www.thewalpolearms.co.uk
off B1354, 4m NW of Aylsham

'Thoroughly rural' Itteringham nestles in the shallow Bure valley, ringed by
grand houses: Mannington Hall, Wolterton Park, Blickling Hall. One visitor
found the Walpole Arms 'a real delight, from the big, fat white rooster strut-
ting outside the door to the wonderful atmosphere within' the brick-built
former farmhouse. In the large, comfortable green-carpeted bar, with its low
ceiling and light-coloured oak beams and studs, the brick-fronted counter
serves East Anglian beers: Adnams Bitter and Broadside, and Woodforde's
Walpole specially brewed for the pub, plus guests (maybe from Buffy's and
Wolf) and strong French and Belgian beers. Over the fireplace a blackboard
lists snacks from ale-braised faggots with yellow-pea purée to Scotch wood-
cock, or beautifully cooked, meaty haddock and puttanesca potatoes. There's
more formality across the farmyard in the restaurant in the old cart shed. Here
you'll find Norfolk game terrine, or Lebanese goats' cheese salad, preceding
Morston mussels steamed in cream and wine, or tagine of lamb with couscous
and feta salad; sweets include lemon posset with lemon polenta shortbread, or
gingerbread with roast banana and toffee cream. Blackboards advertise weekly
wine specials and ten good-value house wines spanning a range of styles and
available by the glass, as are a host of sherries, ports and dessert wines. The
printed wine list sticks to a manageable 50-odd bottles, with a fair range under
£20. Ten wines are available in half-bottles. SAMPLE DISHES: crayfish cocktail
£6; roast pork loin, braised lentils and red cabbage £9.25; pavé of chocolate
with brandied orange salad £4.75.

Licensees Richard Bryan and Christian Hodgkinson (freehouse)
Open Mon to Sat 12 to 3, 6 to 11 (summer Sats 12 to 11), Sun 12 to 10.30; bar food and
restaurant 12 to 2 (3 Sun), 7 to 9 (9.30 summer); closed evening 25 Dec
Details Children welcome in bar eating area and restaurant   Car park   Wheelchair access (also
WC)   Garden and patio   No smoking in half of dining room   Background music   Dogs welcome on
a lead   Delta, MasterCard, Switch, Visa

KEIGHLEY   West Yorkshire   map 8

Quarry House Inn

Bingley Road, Lees Moor, Keighley BD21 5QE   TEL: (01535) 642239
off A629, 2m E of Haworth

The A629 climbs south out of Keighley to meet the A6033 at Crossroads; if
you then cut back left along the ridge, you pass this former farmhouse on Lees
Moor. And it is worth it just for the wind in the hair and the view over the

Worth Valley – never mind the pub's own merits (which make booking advisable at weekends). This place has two strings to its bow: decent traditional beer (well-kept Yorkshire brews: Timothy Taylor Best Bitter, Golden Best and Landlord, together with Tetley's Cask Bitter) and decent traditional food. The dining areas have pink-clothed tables and spindle-back chairs, and food is listed on a carte (or the £10 three-course Sunday lunch menu) plus blackboards of daily specials and fresh fish. Chicken liver pâté comes recommended as a starter, or there might be home-made soup, grilled sardines, or dressed crab. Then the usual grills and steaks, plus, say, pork tenderloin in cider cream sauce, or chilli- and garlic-spiced chicken fillets with penne pasta. Fish eaters choose among grilled butterfish or cod, battered haddock, baked grouper, or smoked haddock in cheese and prawn sauce, and vegetarians are not forgotten. Tasty, tender roasts (beef, lamb, pork, chicken) feature at Sunday lunch, and traditional puds include spotted dick, sherry trifle and blackberry and apple pie. Wines, listed on a blackboard, come from both Old and New Worlds, with around ten by the glass. SAMPLE DISHES: black pudding and bacon with spiced fruit chutney £4; fillet steak with port and Stilton sauce £13.50; sticky toffee pudding £3.

Licensee C.M. Smith (freehouse)
Open 12 to 3, 7 to 12; bar food and restaurant 12 to 2, 7 to 10; closed 25 and 26 Dec, 1 Jan
Details Children welcome   Car park   Wheelchair access   Garden   No smoking in dining room
Background music   Dogs welcome in bar only   Delta, MasterCard, Switch, Visa

KEMPSEY   Worcestershire   map 5

▲ Walter de Cantelupe Inn 🍴 🍺

Main Road, Kempsey WR5 3NA   TEL: (01905) 820572
WEBSITE: www.walterdecantelupeinn.com
on A38, 4m S of Worcester

Kempsey is a village with a past. In the thirteenth century, for example, it played a key role in Simon de Montfort's campaign against Henry III, and the inn is named after one of de Montfort's supporters who was Bishop of Worcester. But that's enough history, for here is a fine example of a modern dining pub, which nonetheless remains very much a pub. The décor is artistic – in an unpretentious way – with a 'rather baroque' colour scheme (as in red curtains with a gold fleur-de-lis print) and quirky touches such as a giant antique gramophone. Alongside the honours board for the de Cantelupe Golf Society is another board that makes much more interesting reading: it lists the kitchen's output for the day. Though the cooking style is essentially 'pubby and simple', dishes cover a broad range, from steak and ale pie to braised chicken with prunes, apricots, orange, white wine, garlic and chilli, and the focus is firmly on local ingredients: the 'plate-sized' gammon steak comes with locally laid eggs, the pork and leek sausages are hand-made nearby, and the chutneys and smoked ham that go into the thick-cut sandwiches are produced on the premises. Drinks are a strength as much as the food. Everards Beacon Bitter, Timothy Taylor Landlord and King's Shilling from the local Cannon Royall Brewery are the regulars on the superior list of real ales, backed up by some fine guest beers. Up to half a dozen wines from the short list are available by the glass at any one time. Prices are good, with 11 bottles under £10. SAMPLE DISHES: prawn, red grape, and cream cheese filo parcel on mixed leaves £4.50; slow-cooked spicy lamb shank in tomato sauce with aromatic herbs £9; rhubarb and ginger pavlova £3.50.

Licensee Martin Lloyd-Morris (freehouse)
Open Tue to Sat 12 to 2.30, 6 to 11, Sun 12 to 3, 7 to 10.30; bar food Tue to Sat 12 to 2 (2.30 Sat summer), 6.30 to 9 (10 Fri and Sat), Sun 12 to 3; closed 25 and 26 Dec, 2 weeks late Jan to early Feb
Details Children welcome in eating areas   Car park   Patio   No smoking in restaurant   Occasional live or background music   Dogs welcome on a lead   Amex, Delta, MasterCard, Switch, Visa
Accommodation: 3 rooms, B&B £29 to £70

KEYSOE   Bedfordshire   map 6

Chequers Inn
Pertenhall Road, Brook End, Keysoe MK44 2HR   TEL: (01234) 708678
WEBSITE: www.bigfoot.com/~chequers
on B660, 8m N of Bedford and at N end of Keysoe

The Chequers is at the northern end of Bedfordshire, beside the road from Bedford north to Kimbolton: a cream-washed building with dormer windows peeping out of a steep-pitched clay tile roof. Also in the vernacular style are the low, and for the unwary potentially painful, beams inside, where a series of rooms – one of them a family room – clusters around the central bar. Here Fuller's London Pride and Hook Norton Best Bitter are on handpump, and four wines are served by the glass from a short, generic list. The food repertoire may be fairly traditional, but it is cooked with care and raw materials are good. Besides the sandwiches (plain or toasted), ploughman's lunches, salads and a short children's menu, there are starters like home-made soup or mushrooms in a creamy sauce, and mains like Swedish fish casserole, Stilton-stuffed chicken breast, or several varieties of steak. A blackboard lists daily specials and vegetarian dishes, and there's a separate menu for sweets such as caramel walnut meringue. SAMPLE DISHES: deep-fried Brie with cranberries £3.75; Dublin coddle £6.50; bread-and-butter pudding with Drambuie-soaked raisins £2.75.

Licensee Jeffrey Kearns (freehouse)
Open Mon and Wed to Sat 11.30 to 2.30, 6.30 to 11, Sun 12 to 2.30, 7 to 10.30; bar food and restaurant 12 to 2, 7 to 9.30
Details Children welcome in family room and dining room   Car park   Wheelchair access (also WC) Garden and patio   No-smoking area in bar   Occasional background music   No dogs   MasterCard, Visa

KEYSTON   Cambridgeshire   map 6

Pheasant Inn 😋 😋 🍇
Loop Road, Keyston PE18 0RE   TEL: (01832) 710241
on B663, just S of junction with A14

The Pheasant is a long, thatched pub, with, inside, old beams and a log fire. It shares the same informal approach to eating and drinking as its sister establishments in the Huntsbridge Group, the Three Horseshoes, Madingley, the Old

Bridge, Huntingdon, and the Falcon, Fotheringhay (see entries). This means that one menu is served throughout, both in the more formal dining room and the relaxed lounge, and you can eat as much or as little as you like, from a full three-course meal to a light dish of risoni pasta with wood-roast peppers, garlic and rosemary and a rocket and Parmesan salad. As that dish might suggest, modern themes prevail in the cooking, and no small degree of invention is at work. Honey-glazed confit of duck on Thai-spiced barley risotto with chilli, ginger and wasabi dressing is a typically unusual dish, while heartier fare might extend to glazed pig's trotter stuffed with braised oxtail and mushrooms served with parsnip purée. On slightly more familiar territory are starters of fish soup with rouille, Gruyère and croûtons, or pork terrine with spicy apple chutney, followed by bangers and mash with white onion sauce, or ribeye steak with fat chips. The place confirms its pub credentials with its selection of fine real ales, which includes Adnams Best Bitter alongside three guests, of which regulars come from the local Potton Brewery. As with its sister establishments the wine list here will gladden the heart of any wine lover. The 15 wines by the glass (priced from £2.95 to £6) or selection of aperitif sherries offer plenty to relish while browsing the list of over 100 wines arranged into 'under £20' and 'top class' sections. SAMPLE DISHES: butter-bean soup with prosciutto £4.75; knuckle of Cornish lamb slow-cooked with garlic served on soft polenta with curly kale £13; crème brûlée infused with lime leaves and lemongrass served with strawberry sorbet £6.

Licensees Clive Dixon and John Hoskins (freehouse)
Open 12 to 2.30, 6 to 11; bar food and restaurant 12 to 2, 6.30 to 9.30
Details Children welcome   Car park   Wheelchair access (not WC)   Patio   No smoking in restaurant   No music   Dogs welcome   Amex, Delta, Diners, MasterCard, Switch, Visa

KINGSDON   Somerset   map 2

Kingsdon Inn
Kingsdon TA11 7LG   TEL: (01935) 840543
village signposted off B3151 Ilchester to Street road, just N of A372

Little more than three miles from the A303 weary travellers can seek out this pretty thatched cottage overlooking Kingsdon's playing field. Rambling, low-ceilinged rooms with stone fireplaces are furnished with rustic cushioned wall seats and farmhouse chairs at scrubbed pine tables. The lunchtime menu is simpler and shorter, the evening one longer and more restaurant-like. The former might include home-made soup or deep-fried whitebait, followed by tagliatelle carbonara or roast salmon with lemon and capers. Wild boar, rum and ginger pâté or king prawns with lime and ginger, then ragoût of wild rabbit, or lamb shank tagine might appear on the dinner menu. Treacle tart, or a sticky ginger pudding with ginger ice cream, might round everything off. On draught are Butcombe, Cotleigh Barn Owl and Otter bitters as well as Burrow Hill farmhouse cider. A fair selection of malt whiskies is available, plus seven wines by the glass for £2.70. The wine list of nearly 40 bins (eight of them in halves) is arranged by style and stays mainly under £20. SAMPLE DISHES: salmon rillettes £4.60; oxtail in Guinness £6.50; chocolate truffle torte £3.60.

Licensees Leslie and Anna-Marie Hood (freehouse)
Open 12 to 3, 6.30 to 11, Sun 12 to 3, 7 to 10.30; bar food 12 to 2, 6.30 to 9.30 (9 Sun); closed
25 and 26 Dec, 1 Jan
Details Children welcome in bar eating area; no children under 12 after 8pm   Car park
Wheelchair access (not WC)   Garden   No-smoking area   Background music   No dogs   Delta,
MasterCard, Switch, Visa

KINTBURY   Berkshire   map 2

▲ Dundas Arms ✿ 🍺 🍇

Station Road, Kintbury RG17 9UT   TEL: (01488) 658263
WEBSITE: www.dundasarms.co.uk
1m S of A4, between Newbury and Hungerford

WATERSIDE

The setting – Kennet and Avon Canal one side, River Kennet the other –
might seem to make this white eighteenth-century pub a summer watering
hole, but it has its attractions in the winter too. Inside, the décor is predominantly modern, with some bright splashes of colour, and the public bar has a
green ceiling, wood-panelled dado and cream walls hung with prints. Well-
kept handpumped ales include Barbus Barbus from Butts in Hungerford,
Adnams Bitter, Good Old Boy from West Berkshire at Yattendon, and
Morland Original Bitter. The food (there isn't any on Sundays) mixes old
faithfuls with exotics: starters could include home-potted shrimps with toast,
meze of artichokes, roast peppers and hummus, and fried Thai fishcakes with
(very) chilli sauce. Main dishes may take in fried calf's liver or roast pheasant
breast with bacon gravy, baked cod with chips and peas, or a nicely balanced
and presented dish of seared, lightly smoked salmon with couscous and courgette cream. Among puddings you could find St-Emilion au chocolat, or raspberry crème brûlée. An enterprising wine list starts at £13.50 and has much
under £20. There are a good number of half-bottles too, but only four wines
are sold by the glass. Wine lovers might, however, be tempted to try something from the large collection of French and New World classics – dozens of
exceptional wines at fair prices spanning a wide range of vintages. SAMPLE
DISHES: hot, spicy chicken salad with guacamole £7; venison casserole £10;
prune and Armagnac ice cream £5.

Licensee D.A. Dalzell-Piper (freehouse)
Open Mon to Sat 11 to 3, 6 to 11, Sun 12 to 2.30; bar food Mon to Sat 12 to 2, Tue to Sat 7 to
9; restaurant Tue to Sat 7 to 9; closed 25 and 31 Dec
Details Children welcome in bar eating area   Car park   Patio   No smoking in dining room   No
music   No dogs   Amex, Delta, MasterCard, Switch, Visa   Accommodation: 5 rooms, B&B £70 to £80

KIRKBY LONSDALE   Cumbria   map 8

▲ Snooty Fox Tavern ✿

Main Street, Kirkby Lonsdale LA6 2AH   TEL: (015242) 71308
WEBSITE: www.mortal-man-inns.co.uk

The fox does indeed look somewhat snooty in its depiction on the sign outside
this old white-fronted pub on Kirkby Lonsdale's narrow main street.
Flagstone floors, low ceilings, cream-washed stone walls and huge ancient
beams are the order of the day inside, with a jumble of artefacts, including

stuffed animals and costumes, in the lively, dark-panelled front bar. In here, the standard menu is augmented by a blackboard of specials, normally fish and shellfish: perhaps whole grilled plaice with shrimps and black butter, or a substantial portion of soufflé-like smoked haddock rarebit. Another choice might be two giant-sized crab cakes, or, from the children's menu, a slice of pizza served with chunky chips. The lunchtime bar menu offers light bites and sandwiches, and the restaurant menu, also served in the bar, deals in the likes of smoked chicken won ton, and main courses of pheasant breast with roasted beetroot and celeriac jus, or pan-fried fillet of sea bass with wild and basmati rice and lime beurre blanc, with desserts like sticky toffee pudding with butterscotch sauce, or pears poached in a star anise and black cherry syrup. Among three or four regularly changing ales might be Timothy Taylor Landlord, Theakston Best Bitter, Castle Eden Ale and Black Sheep Best Bitter. The modestly priced wine list is strong in the New World, with eight by the glass. SAMPLE DISHES: seared squid in sweet chilli oil with citrus and sun-dried tomato salad £4.75; steamed huss wrapped in a banana leaf with creamy saffron sauce £10; vanilla crème brûlée £3.75.

Licensee Mandy Jenkins (freehouse)
Open 11 to 11, Sun 12 to 10.30; bar food and restaurant 12 to 2.30, 6.30 to 9.30, Sun 12 to 9
Details Children welcome   Car park   Wheelchair access (not WC)   Garden   No smoking in restaurant   Background music   Dogs welcome   Amex, Delta, MasterCard, Switch, Visa
Accommodation: 9 rooms, B&B £36 to £56

KIRKHAM PRIORY   **North Yorkshire**   **map 9**

Stone Trough Inn 🍺 🍇   NEW ENTRY

Kirkham Priory YO60 7JS   TEL: (01653) 618713
WEBSITE: www.stonetroughinn.co.uk
S of A64, between Scarborough and York, 4m from Castle Howard

The eponymous stone 'trough', which stands at the entrance to the car park of this 'lovely old stone building', was actually the pedestal for a cross erected by a twelfth-century French knight as a monument to his son. As well as the French connection, there is a local influence in the patriotic line-up of first-class Yorkshire beers, including Timothy Taylor Landlord, Black Sheep Bitter and Malton Golden Chance. A series of snug alcoves huddled around a pair of large fireplaces in the low-beamed bar gives the place an 'almost Dickensian feel', while the separate candlelit restaurant has a similarly warm and welcoming atmosphere, making a 'gorgeous' setting in which to enjoy some excellent food. The bar menu strikes an ambitious pose: starters might include lightly curried fishcakes on buttered spinach with saffron velouté, or a salad of marinated provençale vegetables and rocket with a Parmesan tuile, while main courses run from the relatively prosaic pork and herb sausages on bubble and squeak with onion gravy to the positively posh pithiviers of crab, potato and scallions with home-made tomato ketchup. Dessert options might take in iced banana parfait, and lunchtime choices include a range of classy sandwiches (poached salmon and citrus crème fraîche, for example). Restaurant meals are more impressive still, perhaps featuring loin of English lamb stuffed with mushrooms and spinach, or beef fillet on truffle mash with wild mushrooms and red wine sauce. Nine house wines from £9.95 to £10.95 a bottle touch all points of the flavour compass and are also sold by the glass. The main list is strongest in the middle ground, with good producers like Enate from Spain and Saint Clair, the latest New Zealand star. SAMPLE DISHES: ravioli of goats' cheese in a spicy red pepper sauce £5; seared salmon fillet on stir-fried cabbage with spicy oriental sauce £9; pear mousse with Calvados sabayon £4.

Licensees Adam and Sarah Richardson (freehouse)
Open *Tue to Sun and bank hol Mon 12 to 2.30, 6 to 11, Sun 11.45 to 10.30; bar food Tue to Sun and bank hol Mon 12 to 2, 6.30 to 8.30, restaurant Tue to Sat and bank hol Mon 6.45 to 9.30, Sun 12 to 2.15; closed 25 Dec*
Details *Children welcome   Car park   Garden and patio   No smoking in 1 room and restaurant Background music   No dogs   Delta, MasterCard, Switch, Visa*

KIRTLING   Cambridgeshire   map 6

Red Lion
214 The Street, Kirtling CB8 9PD   TEL: (01638) 731976
off B1063, 5m SE of Newmarket

If you have only one pub in your village, you probably would be happy to have this old-fashioned local, where you can find well-kept beers and straightforward food. The small, L-shaped bar is a mixture of old and new, with modern prints and signs alongside a cast-iron range in the fireplace and the original bread oven next to it. To the right of the entrance is a more chintzy restaurant; the same menu is served throughout the pub. The cooking style is mostly traditional, with a few modern ideas, and the long menu has sections devoted to fish, poultry, 'from the grill', specials, and vegetarian dishes. Blackboards add further choice, and there is a three-course Sunday lunch menu. On offer are the likes of avocado with prawns and smoked salmon, or mushrooms with bacon, Stilton and cream, followed by Thai green chicken curry, grilled lamb chops with mint sauce, various steaks, and beef stroganoff. Fish is a strong suit, from deep-fried scampi tails with tartare sauce to seafood provençale, and the specials boards may feature monkfish in a red wine sauce, chicken breast stuffed with crabmeat, or pigeon breast with a port sauce. Sandwiches are served, and the snack menu concentrates on salads and such items as cottage pie and omelettes, with the lengthy dessert menu ranging from strawberry pavlova to lemon soufflé. On draught are beers from Adnams and Everards, along with Young's Special and Marston's Pedigree, and four house wines are sold by the glass from a global list of twenty-plus bottles. The long, low building is at one end of the main road through this sprawling village in horse-racing country close to Newmarket. SAMPLE DISHES: deep-fried whitebait £5; tournedos Rossini £18.50; blackberry and apple crumble £3.50.

Licensees Annette and Michael Rolfe (freehouse)
Open *Tue to Sun 11 to 2.30, 6.30 to 11; bar food and restaurant 12 to 2, 7 to 9.30*
Details *Children welcome in restaurant   Car park   Wheelchair access (also WC)   Garden No smoking in restaurant   Background music   No dogs   Delta, Diners, MasterCard, Switch, Visa*

indicates a pub serving exceptional draught beers.

KNIGHTWICK   Worcestershire   map 5

▲ Talbot 🍺

Knightwick WR6 5PH   TEL: (01886) 821235

BREW PUB

WEBSITE: www.the-talbot.co.uk

8m W of Worcester, just before crossing River Teme, turn N off A44 on to B4197 signposted Martley; pub at bottom of hill

The Talbot is not actually in Knightwick but the other side of both the Teme and the A44. A substantial white-painted structure overlooking the river, it has its own Teme Valley Brewery at the back (supplying ten other pubs as well). The home-produced theme extends to the food too: everything bar the fish is from the garden or from local producers. Bar food is substantial and inventive – game and vegetable soup, or crab blinis to start, say, and then breast of lamb stuffed with olives, or pork and sweet potato pie. The main bar area is open-plan with a wood-burning fire, and it serves This, That, T'other and Wot Ever Next all the year, plus nine more seasonal beers and local cider, perry and apple juice. The restaurant offers a set-price menu that may take in cod chowder or hummus to start, with roast silver eels or oxtail stew to follow, and plum cobbler or local cheeses to finish. An interesting list of some 35 mainly New World wines includes two local wines and 17 by the glass. Those in the area at the right time might do well to look in on the farmers' market held here on the second Sunday of every month. SAMPLE DISHES: fish soup with shallots and rouille £4; belly pork with onions and lentils £12; Alsatian apple tart £4.50.

Licensee Annie Clift (freehouse)

Open 11 to 11, Sun 12 to 10.30; bar food and restaurant 12 to 2, 6.30 to 9, Sun 7 to 9; closed evening 25 Dec

Details Children welcome   Car park   Garden and patio   No smoking in dining room   Jukebox in back bar   Dogs by arrangement   Amex, MasterCard, Switch, Visa   Accommodation: 11 rooms, B&B £38 to £69.50

KNOWL HILL   Berkshire   map 3

▲ Bird in Hand 🍇

Bath Road, Knowl Hill RG10 9UP   TEL: (01628) 826622

WEBSITE: www.birdinhand.co.uk

on A4, 3m NE of Twyford

Bits of this complex are reputedly fourteenth century, but over the years it has expanded considerably into a small hotel set round a courtyard. The bar has a large fireplace equipped with a wood-burner, and both it and the buffet bar feature beams and wood panelling, along with the tartan carpet that runs throughout the building. Here you can enjoy Brakspear Bitter, and London Pride and Chiswick Bitter from Fuller's, and eat starters like cauliflower and swede soup, or a warm goats' cheese salad with avocado, pine nuts and pesto. Then, if you aim to finish with spotted dick and rum custard, perhaps fried brill with a coconut crust might be a better choice than the tournedos of venison with shallots and a very good port sauce that comes with seven different just-cooked vegetables. There are lighter puds, though, like poached pear with mulled wine and ice cream. Full marks go to an innovative wine list that balances a range of fresh modern flavours with some serious bottles and offers wines that benefit from cellaring in an appropriate vintage. Twelve tasty options come by the glass for between £2.95 and £3.75 and there are nine half-bottles. A good selection of sparkling wines includes the delights of Charles Melton's red fizz (£27.50) from Australia, and the dessert wine list has impressive Italian sweeties from Maculan and Isole e Olena. SAMPLE DISHES: smoked halibut with caviar dressing £4.25; braised lamb shank in red wine sauce £10; iced passion-fruit soufflé with brandy-snap £4.

Licensee Caroline Shone (freehouse)
Open 11 to 3, 6 to 11, Sun 12 to 4, 7 to 10.30 (summer Sat and Sun 11 to 11); bar food 12 to 2.30, 6.30 to 10, restaurant 7 to 9.30
Details Children welcome in bar no-smoking area   Car park   Wheelchair access (also WC) Garden and patio   No-smoking area in bar, no smoking in dining room   No music   Dogs welcome Amex, Delta, Diners, MasterCard, Switch, Visa   Accommodation: 15 rooms, B&B £60 to £120

KNOWSTONE   Devon   map 1

Masons Arms Inn

Knowstone EX36 4RY   TEL: (01398) 341231
WEBSITE: www.masonsarmsinn.com
1½m N of A361, midway between South Molton and Tiverton

Enthusiastic and friendly owners have recognised the potential of this thatched, thirteenth-century longhouse while remaining sympathetic to its history, and have invested heavily in all areas to make sure this is a real destination pub for both food and atmosphere. The main bar is in classic style, with heavy black beams, large, rustic pine tables, old settles and a huge inglenook with a roaring log fire. Both the modern dining room extension and a terrace enjoy fine views over Exmoor. The menus offer a wide choice, with starters ranging from crisp-coated goats' cheese with cranberry sauce to a soup – perhaps cream of leek and Stilton – and main courses encompassing lasagne, chargrilled Cajun chicken with sautéed potatoes, breaded whole-tail scampi with tartare sauce, and curried cauliflower and courgette crumble with salad. Ploughman's and baguettes are served at lunchtime too. Cotleigh Tawny Bitter and Exmoor Ale are drawn straight from the barrel, and guest beers also feature. Poundhouse cider is on tap, and two tasty wines are served by the glass, complemented by two or three specials displayed on the bar with prices round their necks. Because of its location in the foothills of Exmoor, in a peaceful hamlet opposite the church, this is a popular venue for walkers. SAMPLE DISHES: battered Thai prawns with ginger mayonnaise £4.50; peppered fillet steak with brandy sauce, chips and salad £14; banana and toffee crème brûlée and clotted cream £3.50.

Licensees Paul and Joanna Stretton-Downes (freehouse)
Open 12 to 3, 6 to 11; bar food and restaurant 12 to 2, 7 to 9; no food Sun evenings Dec to Feb
Details Children welcome in family room   Car park   Garden   Background music   Dogs welcome Delta, MasterCard, Switch, Visa

---

NEW ENTRY   *indicates that the pub was not a main entry in the previous edition.*

▲ Charles Bathurst Inn   NEW ENTRY

Langthwaite DL11 6EN   TEL: (01748) 884567
WEBSITE: www.cbinn.co.uk
Langthwaite signposted off B6270 at Reeth, 10m W of Richmond

Langthwaite, a sprawling rural village of stone cottages in breathtaking
Arkengarthdale, used to be a lead-mining community, and it was the local lead
magnate, Charles Bathurst, who gave his name to this huge old inn. The long
narrow bar has been given a thoroughly modern look, with soothing pale-
green walls and expanses of new pine, including floorboards and furniture. At
one end of the room is a small fireplace and above that a vast gilt-framed
mirror, on which is written the day's menu. The scope of the cooking is wide
enough to take in simple lunchtime snacks of hot sausage baguettes and
straightforward main dishes like roast salmon with noodles and pesto, alongside more ambitious fare such as ballottine of pheasant with pistachio and ham
stuffing, or lamb shank on a lentil and potato cake with juniper jus. Despite
the evidently high level of ambition, the place has an unpretentious and informal feel – walkers are not only welcome but can be provided with packed
lunches and Thermos flasks as well as advice on routes. On the drinks side of
things, there are fine local real ales from Black Sheep and a list of around two
dozen modestly priced wines. All three house wines are sold by the glass.
SAMPLE DISHES: duck liver and pork terrine with Cumberland sauce £4; grilled
sea bass with spinach and garlic and herb butter £10.50; raspberry Eton mess
£3.50.

Licensee Charles Cody (freehouse)
Open *11 (3 Mon to Thur 3 Nov to Jan) to 11, Sun 12 to 10.30; bar food and restaurant 12 to 2,
6.30 to 9*
Details *Children welcome   Car park   Wheelchair access (not WC)   Patio   No smoking in
restaurant   No music   Dogs welcome at quiet periods   Delta, MasterCard, Switch, Visa
Accommodation: 18 rooms, B&B £65 to £90 (double room)*

Hare 🍺

Langton Green TN3 0JA   TEL: (01892) 862419
WEBSITE: www.brunningandprice.co.uk
on A264, 2½m W of Tunbridge Wells

The large village green (cricket played here in summer) gives a good outlook
from the back of the Hare, sited on a corner on the edge of suburban Langton
Green. Oriental rugs on a pine floor immediately tell you that this is not typical country-pub style. That said, the place is festooned with antique memorabilia, from chamber pots and brass kettles to plates, bottles and photographs.
The cooking is as modish as the surroundings would indicate: starters might
be monkfish deep-fried in raspberry batter served with apples, walnuts and
grapes and pepper mayonnaise, or a salad of peach, mascarpone, Parma ham
and pistachios in blackcurrant dressing, while main courses explore such
byways as whole sea bass stuffed with lightly chillied prawns accompanied by

stir-fried vegetables, chicken breast wrapped in bacon with a mushroom and garlic sauce, or an inventive vegetarian option, such as Stilton, celery and walnut tart. More traditional things are done well too: moules marinière, steak with herb butter, or, on Sunday, roast forerib of beef with all the trimmings. Portions are substantial, but if you've room you might finish with wild berry cheesecake with whipped cream, or sticky toffee pudding. Real ales on tap may include Greene King Abbot Ale, IPA and Ruddles Best, Wells Bombardier Premium Bitter, and Everards Tiger Best. On top of those, around 15 wines are sold by the glass from a list that gives roughly equal weight to Europe and the New World. SAMPLE DISHES: oriental duck spring rolls with sweet chilli dipping sauce £5.50; roast half-shoulder of lamb in a herb crust with redcurrant and thyme sauce £12.50; bread-and-butter pudding with orange sauce £4.25.

Licensees Brian-Keeley Whiting and Oliver Slade (Brunning and Price Ltd)
Open 11 to 11, Sun 12 to 10.30; bar food 12 to 9.30 (9 Sun); closed evenings 25 and 31 Dec
Details Children welcome in eating areas Car park Wheelchair access (not WC) Patio
Occasional live or background music Dogs welcome in bar Delta, MasterCard, Switch, Visa

LAPWORTH Warwickshire   map 5

Boot
Old Warwick Road, Lapworth B94 6JU TEL: (01564) 782464
WEBSITE: www.thebootatlapworth.co.uk
off A3400 3½m SE of M42 junction 4

Hints of the tone here are given by a very capacious car park and menus advertising the Solihull Porsche centre. Although in the country, Lapworth lies in the angle of the M40 and M42, between Birmingham, Warwick, Redditch and Coventry, so it is not surprising that the Boot is essentially a big city pub/brasserie, with noise and price levels to match. Nonetheless, the tall red-brick building has gardens at the side and back, and the interior has a ruralising style, with natural colours, rough plaster walls, wooden floors and tables and preserving jars of lemons and garlic heads on sills and chimneypieces. Greene King Old Speckled Hen and Wadworth 6X are on draught, along with John Smith's, and an eclectic list of 36 wines includes ten by the glass. The kitchen uses some good raw materials and some dishes are well timed – like a nicely presented dish of fresh scallops with red pepper mash. Among starters might be gravad lax, home-made soup, or melon, Manchego and Serrano ham; mains could include linguine arrabbiata, battered haddock with sauce gribiche and chips, or a smallish portion of tasty, well-textured roast rack of lamb. Finish with Eton mess, Bakewell tart, or even a Havana cigar. The friendly, relaxed service is assiduous almost to a fault. SAMPLE DISHES: seared squid with sweet chilli and leaves £6; duck confit with white-bean cassoulet £13; carrot cake £5.

Licensee James Elliot (Enterprise Inns)
Open 11 to 11 (10.30 Sun); bar food and restaurant 12 to 2.30, 7 to 10 (9.30 Sun)
Details Children welcome Car park Wheelchair access (not WC) Garden and patio
Background music Dogs welcome exc in dining room Amex, Delta, MasterCard, Switch, Visa

LAVENHAM   Suffolk   map 6

▲ Angel 🍺 🍇

Market Place, Lavenham CO10 9QZ   TEL: (01787) 247388
WEBSITE: www.lavenham.co.uk/angel
on A1141, 6m NE of Sudbury

First licensed in 1420, the Angel is the oldest pub in this splendidly well-preserved medieval town, and it dominates one corner of the marketplace. Its 'picturesque antiquity' is certainly impressive, and reporters also consider it a 'well-run, friendly establishment'. Among its highlights are the beers and wines: the former come from distinguished local brewers Adnams, Greene King and Nethergate; the latter, 30 or so good-quality bottles plus seven house basics by the glass or bottle, are gathered up from around the world. Prices are very reasonable and everything barring one or two French classics is under £20. Opinions on bar food have varied but at its best it is 'jolly decent'. The printed menu changes daily but typically offers starters of cream of parsnip soup, or grilled sardine fillets with pesto, while main-course choices have included steak and ale pie, pork, paprika and haricot-bean casserole, and chicken breast with honey, mustard and tarragon. Finish perhaps with chocolate charlotte, or apricot and passion-fruit syllabub. The atmosphere is provided by a wealth of ancient beams and timbers, and, in the evenings, by candlelight, and guest accommodation is comfortable and attractively furnished. SAMPLE DISHES: duck salad with croûtons, pine nuts and raspberry dressing £5.50; roast rump of lamb with garlic and rosemary £11; tiramisù £3.75.

Licensees Roy Whitworth and John Barry (freehouse)
Open 11 to 11, Sun 12 to 10.30; bar food and restaurant 12 to 2.15, 6.45 to 9.15; closed 25 and 26 Dec
Details Children welcome   Car park   Wheelchair access (not WC)   Garden and patio
No-smoking area in bar, no smoking in restaurant   Occasional background music   Dogs welcome in bar   Amex, Delta, MasterCard, Switch, Visa   Accommodation: 8 rooms, B&B £50 to £75

LAXFIELD   Suffolk   map 6

Kings Head | NEW ENTRY |

Gorams Mill Lane, Laxfield IP13 8DW   TEL: (01986) 798395
on B1117, 6m N of Framlingham

Known famously as 'the Low House', this thatched Tudor inn is secreted down a narrow lane at the bottom of the village, behind the ancient church; outside, the garden scene is 'simply delightful'. It's 'one of those rare and wonderful pubs that retains centuries-old charm to the core', observed a traveller. Inside is a tiny parlour dominated by a massive three-sided, high-backed settle facing an open fire. There's no bar: Adnams beers and guest ales are tapped direct from casks and dispensed through a cubbyhole. No wonder the place is a favourite with film and TV crews wanting to capture the spirit of rural England past. Another room is set up principally for diners, with bell pulls to summon a serving 'wench' or the landlord. Printed menus and blackboard specials suggest that the food 'marches with fashion' – although it doesn't try to be too clever. Honest stuff such as carrot and coriander soup, grilled kippers, or pork sausages with buttery mash and onion gravy share the billing with, say, king prawn and pepper kebab on green Thai dressing, or roast partridge with pear and red wine sauce. Salads, baguettes and plough-man's are also on offer. A handful of wines is available by the glass. SAMPLE DISHES: baked banana and Stilton cream £3.25; home-baked gammon with coarse-grain mustard sauce £8; sherry trifle £3.25.

Licensees W.G. and M. Coleman (Adnams)
Open 12 to 3, 6 to 11, Sun 12 to 3, 7 to 10.30; bar food and restaurant all week 12 to 2, Tue to Sat 7 to 9; closed evening 25 Dec
Details No children   Car park   Garden and patio   Live music Tue 6 to 7   Dogs welcome exc in restaurant   No cards

LEDSHAM   West Yorkshire   map 9

Chequers Inn 🍺 NEW ENTRY

Claypit Lane, Ledsham LS25 5LP   TEL: (01977) 683135
WEBSITE: www.thechequersinn.f9.co.uk
1m W of A1 at junction with A63

A rambling, creeper-clad building in a small village of houses built of distinc-tive yellow stone, the Chequers is a traditional pub serving quality food in Yorkshire portions. Inside is a series of low-beamed rooms with log fires, wooden furniture and settles. Old photographs of the area hang on the walls, and large pottery beer jugs dangle from the beams. Upstairs there's a tradi-tional, red-themed restaurant. The standard menu is bolstered by a list of daily specials, most with rather 'witty' descriptions ('plonked precariously', 'heav-enly dusted', 'cascading'), but beneath the light-heartedness lies some serious cooking. Dishes make use of good-quality ingredients and sound skill to deliver the likes of hearty celery and Stilton soup ('almost a meal in itself'), or shoulder of lamb on spinach mash with tomatoes provençale topped with smoked mozzarella. Homely desserts might include a sticky toffee pudding loaf, or bread-and-butter pudding, while the wine list of some two dozen bottles is supplemented by a couple of wines of the month. On handpump are beers from local Brown Cow Brewery, plus Theakston Best Bitter, John Smith's Bitter plus a guest, and all can be enjoyed in the extensive, sheltered garden. SAMPLE DISHES: roulade of sole and crab with grapes and apples £6; guinea fowl breast with forcemeat stuffing, caramelised plums and a cream, orange and sweet sherry glaze £13; pink grapefruit and ginger cheesecake £4.50.

Licensee Chris Wraith (freehouse)
Open Mon to Sat 11 to 3, 5 to 11; bar food and restaurant 12 to 2.15, 6 to 9
Details Children welcome   Car park   Wheelchair access (not WC)   Garden   No music   No dogs
Amex, Delta, Diners, MasterCard, Switch, Visa

🍺 *indicates a pub serving outstanding bar food, backed up by all-round excellence in other departments, such as service, atmosphere and cleanliness.*

Ship

Levington IP10 0LQ   TEL: (01473) 659573
off A45 to Felixstowe, 6m SE of Ipswich

This prettily thatched and whitewashed pub overlooks the River Orwell at the centre of the village and is next to the church, which has an unusual red-brick tower. Inside, its walls are covered with ships in all sorts of guises – models, pictured on plates, tiles and mugs – and other nautical paraphernalia. Dishes are listed on individual boards hung up on a rack, so that they can be changed and replaced as often as necessary. Starters range from simple platters of mixed breads and olives, through soups (cream of potato, celeriac and apple, for example), to griddled sardines in oregano with garlic mayonnaise. Among main courses, expect a wide choice of meat and fish options, taking in traditional steak and kidney pudding as well as modern dishes along the lines of seared tuna steak with salad and guacamole potatoes. Mussels are a seasonal speciality, served in various ways: baked with tomato, garlic, chorizo and basil, for example. Beers from Adnams and Greene King are on draught, and four house wines are available by the glass from a 20-bottle international list that starts at £9.25. SAMPLE DISHES: stir-fried mussels in sweet Thai chilli sauce with coriander £5; sautéed liver and bacon with Madeira sauce £7; pear and walnut crumble tart £4.

Licensees Mark and Stella Johnson (Pubmaster)
Open *Mon to Sat 11.30 to 2.30, 6 to 11, Sun 12 to 3; bar food Mon to Sat 12 to 2, 6.30 to 9.30, Sun 12 to 2; closed 25 and 26 Dec, 1 Jan*
Details *No children exc in garden/patio   Car park   Garden and patio   No-smoking area in bar No music   No dogs   Delta, MasterCard, Switch, Visa*

▲ Sandpiper Inn 🏆

Market Place, Leyburn DL8 5AT   TEL: (01969) 622206

Two well-maintained and restored stone buildings on Leyburn's marketplace, with gardens to the front and back, have been linked together to make up the Sandpiper, and the place is welcomingly floodlit in the evenings. Corner seats, alcoves and a crackling fire make the place homely, and the cheeriness of the staff adds to the air of conviviality. A separate dining area has around a dozen tables. Lighter options, including sandwiches and such dishes as Caesar salad with smoked salmon, or warm duck leg salad with oriental dressing, may be had at lunchtimes. The dinner menu, served in the bar as well as the restaurant, deals in the sort of food you might find at smart city restaurants, spanning a main-course range from grilled sea bass with celeriac purée and roast garlic to saddle of venison with braised red cabbage and a port jus. Starters are equally varied: caramelised belly pork with braised lentils, or orange salad with smoked salmon, for example. Summer pudding has been praised, and there might be vanilla crème brûlée, or raspberry and almond tart. Black Sheep Best Bitter and Dent Bitter, plus a guest, are real ales on offer, and the wine list of

30-plus bottles is good in France and the New World alike, with around half a dozen sold by the glass. Lovers of malt whiskies have no fewer than a hundred to choose from. Bookings are recommended for a table in the restaurant; otherwise be prepared to get here early. SAMPLE DISHES: roast pumpkin and parsnip soup £4; fillet of beef with garlic potatoes and grilled pancetta £14; chocolate fudge cake with milk chocolate ice cream £4.

Licensees the Harrison family (freehouse)
Open Tue to Sat 11.30 to 3, 6.30 to 11, Sun 12 to 3, 7 to 10.30; bar food 12 to 2.30 (2 Sun); restaurant Tue to Sat 6.30 to 9 (9.30 Fri and Sat), Sun 12 to 2, 7 to 9
Details Children welcome in eating area and restaurant   Car park   Wheelchair access (not WC) Garden and patio   No smoking in restaurant   Background music   Dogs welcome in snug area of bar Delta, MasterCard, Switch, Visa   Accommodation: 2 rooms, B&B £50 to £65

LICKFOLD   West Sussex
map 3

Lickfold Inn ✿ ▯

Lickfold GU28 9EY   TEL: (01798) 861285
off A272 Midhurst to Petworth road, signposted Lodsworth, 4m NE of Midhurst

Lickfold, a string of old and handsome houses along a quiet country road, makes an attractive setting for this timber-framed pub, which has its origins in the fifteenth century. The bar is a spacious, beamed room, warm and full of character, with a huge fireplace, ochre-washed and panelled walls, candles and the odd farming implement dotted about. The dining room is similar in style, with white linen napkins on the tables, while upstairs is a more formal-looking restaurant with good views from the windows. Lunchtimes bring on sandwiches and the 'chef's special' fixed-price menu of two choices at each course: perhaps celeriac soup with truffle oil, then pan-fried chicken with bread sauce and roasted garlic, with cinnamon brûlée to finish. Otherwise, the menu might feature foie gras boudin with lentil and rocket salad, or 'tender and full-flavoured' boneless saddle of rabbit stuffed with duxelles, followed by wild boar and apple sausages with mash and a rich, thick gravy with a kick of mustard, pan-fried grey mullet with couscous and ratatouille, or tagliatelle with roasted tomato and pepper sauce. Real ales are a good selection, among them Ballard's Best Bitter, Hop Back Crop Circle, Young's Bitter and a guest, and six wines come by the glass. Tables in the back garden have good views over open countryside. SAMPLE DISHES: onion tarte Tatin with glazed goats' cheese £7.50; pan-fried fillet of sea bass with confit fennel, basil mash and sun-blushed tomato sauce £11; pineapple and coconut cheesecake £4.75.

Licensees Tim Ashworth and Luke Stockley (freehouse)
Open 11 to 3, 6 to 11, Sun 12 to 3, 7 to 10.30; bar food 12 to 2.15, 7 to 9.30; restaurant Fri and Sat 7 to 9.30, Sun 12 to 2.30
Details Children welcome in bar eating area   Car park   Wheelchair access (also WC)   Garden Background or live music   Dogs welcome   Amex, Delta, MasterCard, Switch, Visa

If a pub has notified us that it has a website, this is listed in the entry. Details shown on these websites have not been checked for accuracy by the Guide.

Star Inn 🍇

The Street, Lidgate CB8 9PP   TEL: (01638) 500275
on B1063, 7m SE of Newmarket

This is a very traditional pub with a great atmosphere and a distinctly original menu. The pink-washed building stands slightly above the road and looks out over open country. Inside, there are three interconnecting rooms (two bars and a non-smoking dining room) and a lively mix of appreciative locals. The main room has an inglenook fireplace, a board floor and a miscellany of prints, including one of the Last Supper. There's a range of Greene King beers on handpump – IPA, Abbot Ale and Old Speckled Hen – and the bottled beers include Estrella Dorada, while four Spanish brandies lurk among the spirits. And the wine list (which offers five by the glass) carries bottles from many Spanish regions (though there is plenty from elsewhere, too, especially in the tempting monthly Old World and New World selections). Catalan landlady Maria Teresa Axon is the key to this Anglo-Iberian counterpoint, which appears even more strongly on the menu – where smoked salmon and avocado is juxtaposed with fabada asturiana (a pork and bean stew). Paella Valenciana from the Mediterranean coast, and scallops Santiago from the Atlantic, line up alongside venison in port, or sirloin steak with Stilton sauce, though sweets like treacle tart and sticky toffee pudding are more uniformly Anglo-Saxon. Aside from the carte, there are two-course lunches for £10.50 (three courses for £14.50 on Sundays). SAMPLE DISHES: Mediterranean fish soup £4.50; wild boar in cranberry sauce £13.50; banoffi pie £4.

Licensees Teresa and Tony Axon (Greene King)
Open 11 to 3, 5 to 11 (Sat 6 to 11, Sun 7 to 11); bar food and restaurant Mon to Sat 12 to 2, 7 to 10, Sun 12 to 2.30
Details Children welcome   Car park   Garden   No smoking in diningroom   Occasional background music   Dogs welcome   Amex, Delta, Diners, MasterCard, Switch, Visa

▲ Arundell Arms 🏆 🍇

Lifton PL16 0AA   TEL: (01566) 784666
WEBSITE: www.arundellarms.com
just off A30, 4m E of Launceston

This 'delightful old building', a former coaching inn dating from the eighteenth century, is on the main street of the classically picturesque village not far from Dartmoor. Although this is first and foremost a hotel with a smart restaurant with its own set-price menus, the bar is a comfortable place in which to linger, its sporting prints on pale walls, elegant curtains and cheerful open fire all creating a welcoming impression. Food is ordered at the bar and delivered to the tables promptly and professionally by smartly uniformed staff. Although the menu kicks off with around half a dozen sandwiches, with about the same number of salads, it's perfectly possible to have a three-course meal without feeling like a poor relation of those in the restaurant. Start with 'lovely' chicken terrine with 'yummy' home-made chutney, white onion soup, or black pudding and bacon risotto. 'They know how to treat fish here all right,' noted a reporter who enjoyed a main course of seared tuna steak with rocket salad. Meat main courses are equally well reported, from 'excellent' chicken breast wrapped in prosciutto to confit of Gressingham duck with a peppercorn sauce and mustard mash. Tarte Tatin with cinnamon ice cream and clotted cream or bread-and-butter pudding with vanilla sauce are what to expect at the end of a meal. No real ales are offered: wine is the thing here. The smart list opens with six good-quality house wines available by the glass for £3.50 to £4.50. France is the main focus, with serious bottles from Bordeaux and Burgundy commanding serious prices. Look further afield – to Italy, Spain or the New World – for tasty bottles under £20, or choose from the large selection of half-bottles. The Arundell Arms has 20 miles of its own water on the Tamar, and the lovely countryside offers ample opportunities for other outdoor pursuits too, from walking to shooting, so bring a Barbour. SAMPLE DISHES: oxtail soup with root vegetables and Madeira £4; deep-fried fritters of sea fish with saffron mayonnaise, salad and chips £12.50; hot chocolate pudding with whipped cream £5.

Licensee Anne Voss-Bark (freehouse)
Open 12 to 2.30, 6 to 11; bar food 12 to 2.30, 6 to 10; restaurant 12.30 to 2, 7.30 to 9.30; closed 25 and 26 Dec
Details Children welcome   Car park   Wheelchair access (also WC)   Garden   No smoking in restaurant   Occasional background music   Dogs welcome   Amex, Delta, Diners, MasterCard, Switch, Visa   Accommodation: 28 rooms, B&B £49.50 to £130

LINCOLN   Lincolnshire   map 9

Wig & Mitre 🌢   [NEW ENTRY]
30–32 Steep Hill, Lincoln LN2 1TL   TEL: (01522) 535190
WEBSITE: www.wigandmitre.com

On a street full of tea rooms and gift shops, the Wig & Mitre occupies two floors of a fourteenth-century building between the castle and cathedral. There's plenty of room, and bare wooden tables and paper napkins signal a sense of informality. Flexibility is the thing here, too: you can eat or drink to suit yourself rather than feel restricted to a set formula. Drop in for breakfast, for a sandwich, for the set lunch (two courses £10), served from noon to 6pm, or for a drink: Ruddles Best Bitter and County are on draught, and the wine list, a long and varied collection of bottles from around the world, reflects the philosophy of the place by offering over 30 by the glass. Alternatively, choose from the main menu, which is available at all times, or from the specials board: cod and prawn chowder, or confit of duck leg on red cabbage with honey dressing, then roast sea bass with creamed potatoes, spinach and crispy leeks, or rack of lamb with pea purée, with perhaps saffron-poached pear with pistachio ice cream to finish. A portion of caviar accompanied by a glass of Latvian vodka or champagne are possibilities for those with cause for celebration. SAMPLE DISHES: layered chicken, bacon and leek terrine with mustard dressing £6.25; guinea fowl with honey-roast parsnips, rosemary potatoes and jus £14; white chocolate cheesecake with Baileys ice cream £4.75.

Licensees Toby and Valerie Hope (freehouse)
Open 8am to midnight, Sun 12 to 11.30; bar food 8am to midnight, Sun 12 to 11.30
Details Children welcome   Wheelchair access (not WC)   No smoking in restaurant   No music
Dogs welcome exc in restaurant   Amex, Delta, Diners, MasterCard, Switch, Visa

LITTLE HAMPDEN   Buckinghamshire   map 3

▲ Rising Sun

Little Hampden HP16 9PS   TEL: (01494) 488393
WEBSITE: www.rising-sun.demon.co.uk
from Great Missenden take road signposted Rignall and Butler's Cross; after 2m take turn
marked 'Little Hampden only'

This 250-year-old inn is high in the Chilterns amid beech woods, at the end of
a single-track lane with passing places. It may look quite ordinary from the
outside, with a few picnic benches on the front terrace, but it could lay claim
to being the Prime Minister's local, since his country residence, Chequers, is
little more than a mile up the road. Plenty of beams, a wood-burning stove, a
brick-built bar and three interconnecting rooms are to be found within, along
with horse brasses and old photographs and prints on the walls. Adnams
Bitter, Brakspear Bitter and Old Speckled Hen are the real ales dispensed, and
12 wines are available by the glass. Food, ordered at the bar, is listed on blackboards. Some innovative and enterprising cooking is going on here, as witness
a menu of starters and snacks that extends from deep-fried vegetable spring
roll with chilli mayonnaise and garlic bread, through pan-fried curried prawns
on a mango and orange salad, to spinach pasta filled with ricotta in a creamy
tomato sauce. These may be followed by chargrilled ribeye steak with a
Guinness and pickled walnut sauce, or breadcrumbed chicken breast stuffed
with avocado and herb cheese in tomato sauce. Fish shows up strongly too, the
range taking in poached fillet of sea bass with a cheese and mushroom sauce,
or Catalan-style baked red snapper. Finish with chocolate and rum cheesecake
with chocolate sauce, or rhubarb and ginger fool. SAMPLE DISHES: mussels in
creamy saffron sauce £6; roast guinea fowl with red wine and black cherry
sauce £9.75; summer pudding with cream £4.25.

Licensee Rory Dawson (freehouse)
Open Tue to Sun 11.30 (12 Sun) to 3, Tue to Sat 6.30 to 10; bar food Tue to Sun 12 to 2, Tue to
Sat 6 to 9
Details Children welcome   Car park   Wheelchair access (also WC)   Garden   No-smoking area in
bar, no smoking in restaurant   Occasional background music   Guide dogs only   Delta, MasterCard,
Switch, Visa   Accommodation: 6 rooms, B&B £35 to £70

LITTLE LANGDALE   Cumbria   map 8

▲ Three Shires Inn

Little Langdale LA22 9NZ   TEL: (015394) 37215
WEBSITE: www.threeshiresinn.co.uk
on unnumbered road to Wrynose Pass from A593 just W of Skelwith Bridge

Built in 1872 near the confluence of Cumberland, Westmorland and
Lancashire, the Three Shires makes the most of its lovely setting with tables
on a patio overlooking a stream. The views are stunning and there is an

absolute sense of remoteness here. But however remote the location may seem, you won't lack for company, even on a wet day in January, in the form of fell walkers and families, who pour in for simple lunches of baguettes, baked potatoes, or dishes such as beef and ale pie. Soups are a feature, too, usually based on one vegetable such as carrot or spinach. In the evenings, a fuller menu may take you from salmon and crab parfait with a dill and caper dressing, or venison and pistachio terrine with home-made chutney, to roasted breast of local duckling on braised cabbage and bacon finished with a port and damson jus, or honey-glazed pork chop with a risotto of apple, sage and apricot. Lakeland ice creams are proudly served, and children get their own menu. Dinner in the restaurant is a set-price deal of four courses, with a main course of perhaps roast loin of pork marinated in fennel and garlic with apple mash and creamy mustard sauce, or roast sea bream topped with a zesty crust on buttered leeks with tarragon butter sauce. Jennings Best Bitter and Cumberland Ale, Hawkshead Best Bitter and the Coniston Brewery's Old Man Ale are the beers on offer. Five house wines from a New Worldy list of around 50 are served by the small and large glass. Prices start at £9.50 per bottle and stay mostly under the £15 mark. The twisty road from Skelwith Bridge warns that extreme caution is needed in poor driving conditions. SAMPLE DISHES: pear and Stilton tart £5; herb-stuffed chicken breast with garlic mash, garlic chips and a mushroom-scented jus £10; banana and walnut sponge with butterscotch sauce £3.75.

Licensee Ian Stephenson (freehouse)
Open *Mon to Thur 11 to 10.30, Fri and Sat 11 to 11, Sun 12 to 10.30; 11 to 3, 7.45 to 10.30 Dec and Jan; 11 to 11 27 Dec and 1 Jan; bar food 12 to 2, 6 to 8.45; limited food evenings Dec and Jan; closed 25 Dec*
Details *Children welcome   Car park   Wheelchair access (not WC)   Garden   No-smoking area in bar, no smoking in restaurant   No music   Dogs welcome in bar   Delta, MasterCard, Switch, Visa Accommodation: 10 rooms, B&B £30 to £96*

LIVERPOOL   Merseyside   map 7

Baltic Fleet 🍺 | NEW ENTRY | BREW PUB

33A Wapping, Liverpool L1 8DQ   TEL: (0151) 709 3116

Just across the water from the Albert Dock, the wedge-shaped Baltic Fleet proves an extremely popular pub, producing 'excellent' food served by 'friendly and helpful' staff. The interior is casually low key and understated, with old fixtures merging with a new lick of paint, while a small inglenook adds character and warmth. The blackboard menus at the bar counter roll out some refreshingly modern ideas, such as creamy ham, pepper and cider soup, or chicken liver, bacon and thyme pâté to start, followed by chicken breast stuffed with shallots and black pudding, wrapped in bacon and served in a creamy mushroom and brandy sauce, or tuna, olive and feta fishcakes with pesto and balsamic-dressed salad. Sunday lunch brings on not just roast beef with all the trimmings but perhaps roast goose too. Portions tend to be generous, so finish with something light like lime sorbet. The pub brews its own ales on the premises, including Wapping Bitter, Baltic Extra and Summer Ale, and there are also Cains Traditional Bitter and Dark Mild, plus a guest. Half a dozen wines are served by the glass. SAMPLE DISHES: mushroom, goats' cheese and spinach soup £3; lamb shank slowly cooked with red wine, vegetables, coriander and cumin served on minted mash £10; chocolate and orange cheesecake £3.

Licensee Simon Holt (freehouse)
Open 11.30 to 11, Sun 12 to 10.30; bar food all week 12 to 2.30 (4 Sun), Wed to Sat 6 to 8.30 (9.30 Fri and Sat)
Details Children welcome in eating area   No smoking in 1 room   Background music   No dogs
Delta, MasterCard, Switch, Visa

Philharmonic   NEW ENTRY

36 Hope Street, Liverpool L1 9BX   TEL: (0151) 707 2837
follow signs for cathedrals; pub is between them

The Phil is a monument of high-Victorian design, with stained glass, plaster-work called 'the Murmur of the Sea' depicting Apollo and two female companions, mosaic, high ceilings, large windows, two fireplaces and a gold-painted frieze. In the early days the restaurant was used by people having a pre-concert meal (the Philharmonic Hall is virtually opposite) while their coachmen waited for them upstairs, and two rooms called Brahms and Liszt are a reminder that musical evenings were held here. Nowadays, a relaxed and informal atmosphere prevails, with friendly and very helpful staff, despite the opulence of the architecture. At least five ales are on cask, including perhaps Orkney Dark Island, Old Speckled Hen, and something from Cains (appro-priate, given that the brewery commissioned the building), and four wines, from California and Australia, are sold by the glass. Sandwiches – chopped steak with mushroom, for instance – jacket potatoes, sausages with mash and onion gravy, chicken in BBQ sauce, and cauliflower cheese, followed by trea-cle sponge with custard, are the sorts of homely dishes that keep the customers happy. The men's lavatories are famous for their original marble fittings, mosaics and copper taps. SAMPLE DISHES: mushroom pepper pot £3.50; 12-ounce ribeye steak £8; chocolate puddle pudding £2.50.

Licensee Marie-Louise Wong (Mitchell and Butler)
Open 12 to 11, Sun 12 to 10.30; bar food Mon to Fri 12 to 6.30, Sat and Sun 12 to 3
Details No children   Wheelchair access (not WC)   No smoking in 1 room   Background music
No dogs   Delta, MasterCard, Switch, Visa

LLANFAIR WATERDINE   **Shropshire**   **map 5**

▲ Waterdine 😺 😺 🍺

Llanfair Waterdine LD7 1TU   TEL: (01547) 528214
WEBSITE: www.the-waterdine.co.uk
4m NW of Knighton, off B4355 Knighton to Newton road, over Teme bridge at Lloyney

Built as a drovers' inn in the sixteenth century, the Waterdine is in a lovely setting in the Teme Valley near Offa's Dyke Path. The selection of beers dispensed in the bar, with its wood-burning stove in an ancient inglenook, takes in Wood Shropshire Lad and Parish Bitter plus various real ales from local microbreweries. In here, you can expect ploughman's, baguettes and such dishes as crab cakes on cucumber with beurre blanc, and grilled rump steak with red wine sauce. The strength of the cooking lies in the fact that everything is freshly made using fine regional ingredients, and the separate restaurant menu (also available in the bar) has some ambitious touches with often unusual but nonetheless successful combinations, from a starter of grilled rabbit fillet on truffle sauce with beetroot mousse to a main course of fillet of turbot poached in red wine sauce with Chinese spices. Finish with an exemplary selection of farmhouse cheeses or something like chocolate soufflé. Eat either in the conservatory, with wonderful views, or the taproom, the oldest part of the building, with its stone floor and beams; there's also a no-smoking lounge that shares the views from the back of the pub. Six wines are sold by the glass from a varied list. SAMPLE DISHES: mulligatawny soup £4.25; fillet of beef in a Stilton and walnut crust with port sauce £15.50; vanilla pannacotta with mango and lime £4.50.

Licensee Ken Adams (freehouse)
Open _12 to 3 (2.30 winter), 7 to 11; bar food 12.15 to 2, 7.15 to 9.30, restaurant 12.15 to 1.30, 7.15 to 9; closed Sun evening, 2 weeks autumn/winter_
Details _Children welcome lunchtimes only   Car park   Garden   No smoking in lounge and restaurant   No music   No dogs   Delta, MasterCard, Switch, Visa   Accommodation: 3 rooms, B&B £50 to £80_

LODERS   Dorset   map 2

▲ Loders Arms
Loders DT6 3SA   TEL: (01308) 422431
off A3066, 2m NE of Bridport

Although only a couple of miles out of Bridport, Loders, a village of thatched stone cottages just downstream of Uploders, is in rural isolation. The village pub has a small bar and eating area, and its décor is plain, getting on for spartan, with paintings for sale everywhere and high shelves of decorative plates. The menu, listed on blackboards, ranges from various filled baguettes and familiar pub staples along the lines of lasagne, chilli and soups to more upmarket options: perhaps a crab and coriander parcel, or field mushrooms stuffed with roasted vegetables topped with goats' cheese, followed by scallops pan-fried in Pernod, herby rack of lamb studded with garlic in a red wine gravy, or chicken and Parmesan bake, with apricot sticky toffee pudding, or treacle tart to finish. The Loders is a Palmers pub, serving Bridport Bitter, IPA and 200 – the brewery itself is in Bridport and holds the distinction of being Britain's only thatched brewery. Six house wines, at £9.25 a bottle, are sold by the glass at £2.40. SAMPLE DISHES: tiger prawns £4.50; venison steak pan-fried in gin £13; bread-and-butter pudding £3.75.

Licensees Jane and Clive Legg (J.C. and R.H. Palmer)
Open _11 to 3, 6 to 11, Sun 12 to 10.30; bar food and restaurant 12 to 2, 7 to 9_
Details _Children welcome in eating areas   Car park   Garden   No smoking in restaurant Background music   Dogs welcome   Amex, Delta, Diners, MasterCard, Switch, Visa   Accommodation: 2 rooms, B&B £30 to £50_

Peat Spade ☺ 🍺

Longstock SO20 6DR   TEL: (01264) 810612
off A3057, 1m N of Stockbridge

The white leaded windows are the most striking feature of this large, tall, red-brick building in the centre of the village. A motley collection of prints, colourful flower paintings, seaside postcards and a huge assortment of tightly packed toby jugs give the décor an individualistic feel, and the atmosphere is said to be 'eminently civilised' even when the place is packed. Although a dining pub, the Peat Spade stocks Hop Back GFB and locally brewed Ringwood Fortyniner as well as guests like organic ales from Brakspear and Fuller's and Thatcher's cider. All the vegetables and meat are organic too, and the pub's declared aim is 'to support the use of seasonal local food and sustainable farming'. This policy, combined with high technical skills, translates into such dishes as 'brilliant, fresh and beautifully timed' Dorset scallops seared with soy and sesame, followed by pink breast of Gressingham duck with a lime and ginger dressing. Other options on the short, interesting menu range from free-range pork and apricot terrine, or Orkney herring fillets in a light mustard marinade, to main courses of Hereford beef casseroled in red wine, or kedgeree, with desserts along the lines of sticky toffee pudding, or rich chocolate roulade. An organic wine from Argentina kicks off the short but carefully selected and fairly priced wine list, with eight sold by the glass. SAMPLE DISHES: squash and almond soup £4.25; bourride of salmon, escolar and mussels £11; lemon cheesecake £4.50.

Licensees Sarah Hinman and Bernard Startup (freehouse)
Open *Tue to Sun 11.30 to 3.30, Tue to Sat 6.30 to 11; bar food Tue to Sun 12 to 2, Tue to Sat 7 to 9*
Details *Children welcome   Car park   Wheelchair access (also WC)   Garden and patio No-smoking area in bar   Occasional background music   Dogs welcome   No cards*

▲ Royal Oak 🍺

Duke Street, Lostwithiel PL22 0AG   TEL: (01208) 872552
off A390, 5m SE of Bodmin

Dating from the thirteenth century, the Royal Oak is just off the main road on quite a steep street. Its neatly whitewashed exterior, with blue paintwork and small-paned windows, makes for a cosy, mellowing aspect. The flagstoned bar is where people come for a chat and a pint: the impressive line-up includes Fuller's London Pride, Marston's Pedigree, Bass and Sharp's Own. The other bar has a low ceiling, old prints on the walls and circular tables and chairs; off this is a large lounge, where most of the eating takes place. The printed menu offers plenty of choice, extended even further by a blackboard of daily specials. You could start with a soup – carrot and coriander, say, or 'absolutely delicious' spicy parsnip – mushrooms stuffed with bacon, garlic and herbs, or a platter of smoked fish. 'The cow pie was a steak and kidney to dream of,' commented a reporter, and among other main courses might be vegetable curry ('excellent flavour, and at least six vegetables including okra'), locally caught plaice with chips and peas, and a choice of steaks. Sandwiches, ploughman's and snacks are served at lunchtime, and pies, crumbles and pavlovas are what to expect on the list of puddings. Around half a dozen wines are sold by the glass. Even at busy times, service is friendly, quick and eager. 'It is exactly what we all dream of having as our local,' summed up an inspector. SAMPLE DISHES: avocado and orange salad £3.75; garlic king prawns with mixed salad and garlic bread £10; cherry pie with clotted cream £3.

Licensees Malcolm and Eileen Hine (freehouse)
Open 11 to 11, Sun 12 to 10.30; bar food 12 to 2, 6.30 to 9.15
Details Children welcome in family room   Car park   Garden and patio   Jukebox   Dogs welcome in public bar   Amex, Delta, Diners, MasterCard, Switch, Visa   Accommodation: 6 rooms, B&B £38 to £70

LOWER ASHTON   Devon

map 1

Manor Inn

Lower Ashton EX6 7QL   TEL: (01647) 252304
off B3193 running N from Kingsteignton, 7m SW of M5 junction 31

This part of the Teign valley is rural yet easily accessible, and, if non-gastronomic excuses are needed, nearby Canonteign Falls are impressive, and Lower Ashton itself is a pretty village of whitewashed longhouses. The real draw, though, is the Manor Inn: a 'super country pub' with lots of atmosphere, great beer and hearty home-made food (plus an attractive enclosed garden for children in summer). Its two bars have a comfortably lived-in feel – fat cat snoozing by the window, warm log fires in winter, and an encyclopaedic collection of beer mats on the wall. 'Reliably excellent' beers are Teignworthy Reel Ale, RCH Pitchfork, Princetown Jail Ale, and the latest of 1,500 (so far) changing guest beers, plus bottled lagers (Budvar, Bitburger, Hoegaarden) and Gray's Farm cider. Eight wines are offered by the small, medium or large glass from a short modern list, with all bottles under £15. For eating, come early; things can slow as latecomers arrive. The menu of sandwiches, spuds and ploughman's, plus soup, steaks and chilli con carne, is reinforced by specials boards offering meat, fish and vegetarian mains. These may include vegetable and nut curry, or Stilton and mushroom bake; grilled lemon sole, or salmon and pasta Mornay; venison sausage in onion and butter sauce, or lamb, leeks and mushrooms cooked in cider, or maybe straightforward lasagne. Portions are 'generous in the extreme', and everything tastes home-made. Desserts run to meringue and warm summer fruits, and chocolate biscuit cake with blackcurrant sorbet. SAMPLE DISHES: home-made celery and lentil soup £2.75; chicken, smoked bacon and red wine casserole £7; treacle tart £3.50.

Licensees Geoff and Clare Mann (freehouse)
Open Tue to Sun 12 to 2 (2.30 Sat and Sun), 6.30 to 11, 7 to 10 Sun; bar food Tue to Sun 12 to 1.30, 7 to 9.30 (9 Sun); closed Mon (exc bank hols)
Details No children   Car park   Garden   No music   Dogs welcome on a lead   Delta, MasterCard, Switch, Visa

▲ Fox Inn 🌣

Lower Oddington GL56 0UR   TEL: (01451) 870555
off A436, E of Stow-on-the-Wold

This creeper-covered pub built, like the rest of the village, of honey-coloured
Cotswold stone had a change of ownership in 2002, but the upheaval doesn't
appear to have had any detrimental effect on the food (the chef is unchanged),
and it remains 'a 'super pub' all round. There's always a buzz in the bar, where
the pub's name is (dis)embodied,in a series of snarling foxes' heads mounted
over the blackened stone hearth. Beyond the simple main bar is a smarter
dining room, but you can eat from the same menu anywhere. The long menu
is mostly conservative in nature, though the cooking is consistently impressive, and raw materials are of a high quality, as in a starter of three 'very fresh'
sautéed tiger prawns in a chilli, coriander and garlic sauce, and a main course
of juniper-crusted medallions of venison with morello cherries and a deeply
flavoured sauce. Choices run to slow-cooked lamb shank with rosemary and
garlic, chicken and leek pie, or salmon fishcakes with hollandaise sauce. To
finish, there may be blueberry crème brûlée, or raspberry parfait with red
berry coulis. Three regular real ales include Hook Norton Best Bitter and
Greene King Abbot Ale, and the guest beer might be Old Speckled Hen. The
wine list runs to nearly 50 wide-ranging bins, of which up to a dozen are available by the glass. SAMPLE DISHES: smoked chicken and leek risotto £5.50;
pesto-crusted cod baked with tomato and fennel £9.75; poached pears with
sticky gingerbread £4.50.

Licensees Ian Mackenzie and James Cathcart (freehouse)
Open 11 to 11, Sun 12 to 10.30; bar food 12 to 2.30, 6.30 to 10 (9.30 Sun); closed 25 Dec
Details Children welcome   Car park   Wheelchair access (not WC)   Garden and patio   No music
No dogs   MasterCard, Switch, Visa   Accommodation: 3 rooms, B&B £58 to £85 (double room)

Ship Inn `NEW ENTRY`

The Square, Low Newton-by-the-Sea NE66 3EL   TEL: (01665) 576262
off B1340, 2m N of Embleton

Tucked away among a cluster of whitewashed cottages in this delightful small
village, with views out over the bay towards Dunstanburgh Castle, the Ship
overlooks the green. Behind there's the Newton Ponds Nature Reserve,
where rare birds can sometimes be seen, and, in front, the National Trust-
owned beach of Newton Point. In summer both beach and pub can be packed,
while winter finds quieter times with walkers, locals and the hardy. Plainly
furnished, with board floors and bare-wood furniture, the small bar offers a
good range of handpumped ales, including regulars from Black Sheep and the
local Wylam Brewery, supported by guest beers like East Street Cream from
the RCH Brewery. The simple, crowd-pleasing lunchtime menu offers
snacks along the lines of soup (parsnip and apple, perhaps), fishcakes with
salad, a crab sandwich, and cheese stottie, while evenings see more elaborate
offerings such as venison cooked in a red wine and peppercorn sauce, and

various fish dishes. Eight wines are available too, with a few by the glass. SAMPLE DISHES: goats' cheese with basil and tomato £4; crab with chilli, ginger and lime served with pasta £10; strawberry cheesecake £4.

Licensee Christine Forsyth (freehouse)
Open 11 to 11, Sun 12 to 10.30 in high season; otherwise open every lunchtime but evenings may vary: customers are advised to phone ahead; bar food 12 to 2.30, 6 to 8 (times may vary)
Details Children welcome   Wheelchair access   No smoking evenings while others eat   Occasional live music   Dogs welcome   No cards

LUND   **East Riding of Yorkshire**   map 9

Wellington Inn 🍷 🌺
19 The Green, Lund YO25 9TE   TEL: (01377) 217294
on B1248 between Beverley and Malton

The Wellington sits on one side of the village green facing the war memorial, and benefits from interior touches such as flagstone floors, open log fires in winter and real beams. The blackboard bar menus deal in the sorts of upmarket dishes you might be surprised to find in a country inn, with oak-roast salmon salad, and an 'excellent' tarte Tatin of red onions and shallots topped with grilled goats' cheese among starters, and main courses such as Thai red fish curry, or top-quality calf's liver with 'delicious' onion gravy and exemplary vegetables. Alternatives could be fish goujons, followed by venison suet pudding, or a faultless rendition of black pudding and mushroom risotto accompanied by a chicken breast. The separate dinner menu in the restaurant might overlap with what's on offer in the bar: perhaps steak, mushroom and Guinness pudding. On handpump are Timothy Taylor Landlord and Dark Mild, Black Sheep Best Bitter and John Smith's Bitter, but the wine list far outstrips this selection. Six come by the glass and drinkers on a budget will find plenty to please the palate at under £15, but prices cruise up gently towards first-class bottles at £40 and above. South Africa is good at all price levels and if you want to splash out perhaps go for the Vergelegen (£39.95): André van Rensburg, the winemaker, says 'the wine is a meal' so you could save on food. European wines include Bordeaux cleverly chosen from less-well-known estates and outstanding red Burgundy from Robert Arnoux. A dozen or so also come in half-bottles. SAMPLE DISHES: smoked duck, mozzarella, tomato and basil salad with garlic and chilli oil £5; lamb tagine with couscous £13; iced toffee and banana parfait £4.25.

Licensees Russell and Sarah Jeffery (freehouse)
Open Tue to Sun 12 to 3, all week 6.30 to 11 (7 to 10.30 Sun); bar food Tue to Sun 12 to 2, Tue to Sat 6.30 to 9; restaurant Tue to Sat 7 to 9
Details Children welcome in eating areas   Car park   Wheelchair access (also WC)   Patio No-smoking area in bar   Background music   No dogs   Delta, MasterCard, Switch, Visa

All details are as accurate as possible at the time of going to press, but pubs often change hands and it is wise to check beforehand by telephone anything that is particularly important to you.

LUSTLEIGH Devon **map 1**

Cleave

Lustleigh TQ13 9TJ TEL: (01647) 277223
off A382, 4m SE of Moretonhampstead

The quiet village of Lustleigh is quite a draw, with its lovely setting in the foothills of Dartmoor, its thirteenth-century church, thatched cottages, village green and this charming fifteenth-century thatched pub. The small front bar has an inglenook with a log-burning stove, thick stone walls, antique settles and patterned red carpet, creating a cosy, comfortable atmosphere, with a family room and further wood-panelled bar at the back with more of a feel of a dining room. The menus are supplemented by blackboard specials that might include chilli con carne with rice, spaghetti bolognese, or braised lamb shank with mint gravy, with blackberry and apple pie, or rhubarb and raspberry crumble among puddings. You could start with vegetable soup, with an 'excellent spicy zing', and go on to roast beef with all the trimmings, or a home-made pasta: 'excellent-quality' ricotta cannelloni with goats' cheese and spinach, for instance. Wadworth 6X, Bass and Otter Ale are usually stocked, and there is Addlestone's cider. All 13 wines are priced by both the bottle and glass. SAMPLE DISHES: chicken liver and brandy pâté £5; poached salmon steak with lemon and tarragon sauce £11; rich chocolate fudge cake £4.

Licensee A. Perring (Heavitree)
Open *11 to 11, winter 11 to 3, 6.30 to 11; bar food 12 to 2, 7 to 9; closed Mon winter*
Details *Children welcome in family room Car park Wheelchair access (not WC) Garden No-smoking area in bar, no smoking in eating area Occasional live music Dogs welcome Delta, MasterCard, Switch, Visa*

LUXBOROUGH Somerset **map 1**

▲ Royal Oak Inn of Luxborough

Luxborough TA23 0SH TEL: (01984) 640319
off A396, 4m S of Dunster; drive through Luxborough eastwards to Kingsbridge

In a narrow cleft of a valley, at the bottom of a steep hill by a stream, this large building of rough, reddish-brown stone is in the heart of the Brendon Hills within Exmoor National Park. The interior consists of a rambling series of rooms with flagged or cobbled floors, low beams and, in the main bar, a large open fireplace; one of the rooms has custard-coloured walls, another is in strong emerald green, and a third is done out in tomato red. The seasonally changing printed menus are supplemented by a blackboard, and there's much to tempt the palate, with an exotic note to some of the dishes. You might begin with game rillettes with fig compote, or a salad of smoked duck with pickled walnuts and port dressing, and go on to roast rack of lamb with redcurrant and thyme sauce, or honey- and soy-glazed duck breast served on noodles with plum sauce. Fish is a strength, from salmon and basil fishcakes to grilled fillet of hake with spinach and crayfish butter, or seared loin of tuna with sweet chilli sauce and crème fraîche. Puddings, listed on a portable board, might include treacle or Bakewell tart, or try some of the good Somerset cheeses. An interesting and commendable selection of draught beers includes Exmoor Gold, Cotleigh Tawny Bitter, and IPA and 200 from Palmer, and there's Rich's farmhouse cider too. Three wines are served by the glass from a list of twenty or so bottles, with prices starting at about £11. SAMPLE DISHES: broccoli and lentil soup £3.75; grilled Dover sole with a lemon and herb butter £15; chocolate terrine £4.

Licensee James Waller (freehouse)
Open 12 to 2.30, 6 to 11, Sun 12 to 2.30, 7 to 10.30; bar food and restaurant 12 to 2, 7 to 9
Details Children welcome in eating areas   Car park   Garden and patio   No smoking in restaurant
Occasional live music   Dogs welcome   Amex, Delta, MasterCard, Switch, Visa   Accommodation:
12 rooms, B&B £55 to £85

LYDDINGTON   Rutland   map 5

▲ Old White Hart
51 Main Street, Lyddington LE15 9LR   TEL: (01572) 821703
off A6003, 2m S of Uppingham

Hats off to the Rutlanders for reclaiming their lovely county, which encapsulates England's rural heart. It's well worth exploring, and Lyddington, overlooking the shallow Welland valley, makes a good refuelling point or, better, a base for the exploration. Local red sandstone and Georgian architecture give this pub a look of understated, foursquare elegance that the attractive garden at the back enhances. Inside it feels like a friendly, comfortable local, with the dark seventeenth-century beams and studs lightened by the open fire and the warmer red tones of the comfortable seating and carpets and exposed-stone walls. In the half-panelled main bar Greene King IPA and Abbot Ale are on draught, along with Timothy Taylor Landlord, and wines include six by the glass. Food (a carte or a lunchtime/early-evening prix fixe) is set out on printed menus supplemented by blackboard specials. Among starters might be fried sardine and herb crostini, or a warm salad of wood pigeon with bacon and chard, followed by roast rack of venison, or a Stilton and mushroom parcel with blue cheese sauce, or perhaps a huge portion of beautiful, fresh and well-timed battered haddock with home-made chips and tartare sauce. Then, if you can't manage jam roly-poly and custard, how about Drambuie crème brûlée? SAMPLE DISHES: duck liver parfait and toasted brioche £5.50; calf's liver and bacon with sage jus £12; chocolate sponge pudding and whisky ice cream £3.75.

Licensee Stuart East (freehouse)
Open 12 to 3, 6.30 to 11, Sun 12 to 3, 7 to 10.30; bar food and restaurant Mon to Sat 12 to 2,
6.30 to 9, Sun 12 to 2.30
Details Car park   Wheelchair access (not WC)   Garden and patio   No smoking in dining room
No music   No dogs   Delta, MasterCard, Switch, Visa   Accommodation: 5 rooms, B&B £50 to £80

See 'How to use the Guide' at the front of the book for an explanation of the symbols used at the tops of entries.

Dartmoor Inn ✿ ✿ 🍇

Lydford EX20 4AY TEL: (01822) 820221
on A386 Tavistock to Okehampton road

Despite being on a main road (it's not actually in the village), the Dartmoor Inn has the quiet atmosphere of a country restaurant and inn rather than that of a local watering hole. The décor reinforces this impression, with garlands of dried flowers among the ceiling beams, needlework samplers and naive prints on the walls, ceramic and wooden animals on the windowsills, and a colour scheme of greens, red and terracotta. Smartly set tables, with white cloths, in the series of small rooms show that food is taken seriously, and despite a tiny bar area dispensing Bass, St Austell Dartmoor Best Bitter and Old Speckled Hen, together with Luscombe organic cider, virtually everyone comes here to eat. The lunchtime bar menu is as enterprising as both the set-price two- or three-course lunch deal and the full carte (available in both the restaurant and the bar), featuring roasted tomato soup with a basil cream, shellfish and leek risotto with Parmesan, and braised ribs of beef with orange peel and herbs. Otherwise, expect to find potted pork with a mustard dressing, or pan-fried crab cake with a scallop fritter and green mayonnaise, followed by oxtail with root vegetables, deep-fried onions and a Madeira sauce, or a mixed grill of sea bass, red mullet and brill with buttered fennel and spices. The wine list favours quality over quantity, with star performers such as Gilles Robin, William Fèvre and Vincent Girardin prominent in the 23-strong main selection. For more down-to-earth drinking eight flavoursome house wines come in under £15 and six of these are available by the glass. The pub is in a lovely spot, with a minuscule secluded patio at the back. Accommodation was being planned as the Guide went to press. SAMPLE DISHES: country terrine with apricot chutney £5; deep-fried fillet of hake in a light saffron batter £10.50; individual pineapple and almond tart with vanilla sauce £5.

Licensee Philip Burgess (freehouse)
Open Tue to Sat 12 to 2.15, 6.30 to 10, Sun 12 to 2.30; bar food Tue to Sun 12 to 2.15, restaurant Tue to Sun 12 to 2.15 (2.30 Sun), Tue to Sat 6.30 to 10; closed bank hols
Details Children welcome exc under-5s Fri and Sat evenings   Car park   Patio   No-smoking area in bar, no smoking in restaurant   Occasional live music   Dogs welcome in bar   Delta, MasterCard, Switch, Visa

▲ White Hart ✿ ✿ 🍇

51 Stockport Road, Lydgate OL4 4JJ TEL: (01457) 872566
on A6050, 3m E of Oldham

High on a hill with views over Oldham, the White Hart is a modern interpretation of the traditional coaching inn, a comfortable, tastefully decorated place with a brasserie downstairs and a restaurant in an extension that also houses accommodation. There is still a bar area where those who wish to come for just a drink can enjoy a pint of Pendle Witches Brew, from the local Moorhouses Brewery, Timothy Taylor Landlord or JW Lees Bitter, but food and wine are the main preoccupations of the place. The brasserie menu features the products of the Saddleworth Sausage Company, based on the premises, which come in inventive varieties, such as chicken and black pudding, lamb and mint, or spicy pork, and are served with various flavoured mashes: red onion and mustard, say, or spring onion and garlic. Otherwise, the style is typically modern and cosmopolitan, ranging from starters of deep-fried filo-wrapped prawns with tomato salsa to main courses along the lines of pan-fried fillet of beef with braised oxtail, or seared fillet of sea trout with a dill potato cake, curried spinach and lemon beurre blanc. To finish, the British farmhouse cheese will keep enthusiasts happy, while others might prefer cherry and almond tart with pistachio ice cream, or apple and blackberry crumble with custard. The hundred-strong wine list opens with a short selection of 'favourites', all under £20 and 10 of them available by the glass. It is a surprise to see serious, old and expensive Bordeaux and Burgundy on the next couple of pages, but the list comes back to earth – all four corners of it – for a round-up of good drinking to suit most pockets, including an impressive range of 20 half-bottles. SAMPLE DISHES: oriental duck spring roll with plum sauce £6.50; braised shoulder of Welsh marshland lamb with rocket mash and sun-dried tomato and basil pesto £14.25; spiced pear sponge with ginger custard £5.

Licensee Charles Brierley (freehouse)
Open 12 to 11 (10.30 Sun); bar food Mon to Sat 12 to 2.30, 6 to 10, Sun 1 to 8, restaurant Sun 1 to 3, Tue to Sat 7 to 10
Details Children welcome in bar eating area   Car park   Wheelchair access (also WC)   Garden
No smoking in restaurant   Background music   Dogs welcome in 1 room   Amex, Delta, MasterCard, Switch, Visa   Accommodation: 12 rooms, B&B £62.50 to £105

MADINGLEY   **Cambridgeshire**   map 6

Three Horseshoes 🍷 🍷 🍇

High Street, Madingley CB3 8AB   TEL: (01954) 210221
WEBSITE: www.huntsbridge.co.uk
off A1303, 2m W of Cambridge, close to M11 junction 13

In the village centre, this turn-of-the-last-century thatched pub is as appealing outside as it is in, and it has a pretty garden, with tables, to the rear. The main space has high stools at a light-oak bar counter, with furniture of the same wood, walls of olive green, stripped floorboards and a gas log-effect fire; there's also a small dining area and a more formal conservatory at the back. Although food is the main business here, with the same menu served throughout, the Three Horseshoes has a pleasantly unstuffy and informal atmosphere. In this respect it is much like its sister establishments in the Huntsbridge Group (see the Pheasant, Keyston, the Old Bridge Hotel, Huntingdon, and the Falcon, Fotheringhay). The cooking is highly individual and lively, working with good-quality ingredients and using plenty of bold, modern flavours in inventive – not to mention colourful – combinations. Although there's no requirement to keep to a three-course format, you could start with ribollita (Tuscan bean and bread soup with black cabbage and vegetables), 'bacon and eggs' (twice-cooked belly of pork with quail's eggs and sauce gribiche), or a salad of fennel, radish, olive and marjoram with feta and aubergine toasts. Main courses are just as likely to make an impact, with the same eclectic influences brought to them: try 'quite perfect' pan-fried halibut with stir-fried pak choi, chilli, tofu, sugar snaps and ginger, or chicken breast stuffed with butter and sage accompanied by a gratin of new potatoes, oyster mushrooms and pancetta plus greens braised with garlic, lemon and olive oil. If dishes can be guilty of 'having gone a flavour too far', as one reporter noted, desserts can be equally busy: for instance, dates poached in vanilla and coffee accompanied by cardamom custard, frozen cappuccino mousse and coffee granita. To cater for the beer drinker, the bar stocks Adnams Bitter plus two guest ales, but wine is where the excitement is. Over a dozen house wines come by the glass (£2.95 to £6) and there's an unusually good selection of sherries and sweet wines by the glass too. The 100 or so bottles on the list are grouped by price and style, and it's a tasty selection chosen with flair wherever you look. SAMPLE DISHES: tataki of cured venison with a salad of artichoke, rocket and pickled red onion £6.75; salmon, scallop and langoustine in chicken stock with ginger, corn, black beans and sugar snaps and a chilli coriander relish £16.75; grilled banana with caramel custard and coconut salad £5.50.

Licensees Richard Stokes and John Hoskins (freehouse)
Open 12 to 2.30, 6 to 11; bar food and restaurant 12 to 2 (2.30 Sun), 6.30 to 9.30; closed Sun evening
Details Children welcome Car park Garden No smoking in restaurant No music Dogs welcome in bar only; no dogs in garden Amex, Delta, Diners, MasterCard, Switch, Visa

MAIDENSGROVE   Oxfordshire   map 2

Five Horseshoes
Maidensgrove RG9 6EX   TEL: (01491) 641282
off B480 and B481, 5m NW of Henley-on-Thames

If the weather's fair you can gaze over the vistas of the Chiltern Hills from the long garden at the back of this seventeenth-century pub in an open field; otherwise there are good views from the cheerful conservatory restaurant with its pine dining tables. This is where the main business occurs, although there is also a classic beamed bar warmed by an open fire in winter. No blackboards, but plenty of options are available, judging by the printed menus on the tables. One-dish Winter Warmers please the lunchtime crowd with mild chicken curry and rice or sausages and mash. There's a fixed-price menu on Fridays, while the full works is an ambitious-sounding repertoire that runs from huntsman's pie (ground venison, creamed potato, crispy bacon and grated Cheddar) to grilled suprême of salmon on a 'futon' of creamed celeriac with a light basil sauce. Reporters have enthused about finely executed oven-baked salmon and sea bass stacked on a prawn and orange risotto, and grilled lamb cutlets with mint on parsley mash that 'looked like a painting'. Desserts are things like 'Freckled Richard' (aka spotted dick) and sticky toffee pudding. The full range of Brakspear real ales is on handpump in this tied house; otherwise there's an international wine list with five champagnes and ten wines by the glass. SAMPLE DISHES: warm tartlet of oyster mushrooms and spinach with a duet of sweet pepper coulis £5.75; grilled fillets of sea bass on mussel and vegetable ravioli with butter sauce £13; chocolate fudge cake with vanilla ice cream £4.25.

Licensees Phil and Jan Hills (Brakspear)
Open 11 to 3 (4 Sat), 6 to 11, Sun 11 to 4, 6 to 10.30; bar food and restaurant 12 to 2 (2.30 Sat, 3 Sun), 6.30 to 9.30; closed Sun evenings winter; open 12 to 2 25 Dec (no food), 12 to 3 26 Dec and 1 Jan (no food)
Details Children welcome   Car park   Wheelchair access (not WC)   Garden and patio
No smoking in restaurant   Occasional live music   Dogs welcome   Amex, Delta, Diners, MasterCard, Switch, Visa

MALPAS   Cornwall   map 1

Heron Inn   NEW ENTRY

Malpas TR1 1SL   TEL: (01872) 272773   **WATERSIDE**
2m S of Truro on the River Fal

In a wonderful setting on a creek, the Heron has great views over the water: early birds in summer should try to grab one of the tables outside. A nautical theme runs throughout the one long bar, which has dining areas at each end, an open fire in one of them; walls have been colour-washed a shade of turquoise-blue, tables and chairs are all light wood, and old beams have been lightened in colour. The menu is more or less a cross-section of traditional pub fare: duck and orange pâté, or deep-fried whitebait with citrus mayon-naise, followed by breaded plaice with mushy peas, or roast ham with fried eggs and chips. On the specials board might be onion soup, cold roast beef with pickles and chips, and cottage pie, while puddings might run to 'very good' chocolate fudge cake with clotted cream. St Austell's beers are on draught, and house wines are served by the glass from an annotated list of 25 bottles. SAMPLE DISHES: moules marinière £7; local venison sausages with mustard mash and onion gravy £6.50; blackberry and apple pie £3.50.

Licensee Calvin Kneebone (St Austell Brewery)
Open 11 to 3, 6 to 11 (10.30 winter), Sun 12 to 3, 7 to 10.30; bar food 12 to 2, 6.30 to 9
Details Children welcome   Car park   Garden   No-smoking area in bar   Occasional background music   No dogs   MasterCard, Switch, Visa

MANCHESTER   Greater Manchester   map 8

Barça   NEW ENTRY

Arches 8 & 9 Catalan Square, Duke Street, Castlefield, Manchester M3 4WD
TEL: (0161) 839 7099
from the A56 turn in to Castlefield opposite Deansgate railway station, follow cobbled road towards Castlefield Arena. Cross bridge and Barça is on the left

'A far cry from the classic grubby city pub', this canalside railway arches conversion in a regenerated part of Manchester goes in for clean, modern design yet still has a pubby feel – as many people come just for a drink as visit to eat. A curved glass frontage gives way to a tile-floored bar area with some leather armchairs and sofas and some plainer wooden furniture. The attractive bar menu of contemporary, globally inspired dishes impressed an inspector, who enjoyed crisp, well-flavoured duck, wrapped Peking-style in pancakes with hoisin sauce, and an 'impressive, solidly meaty' chargrilled lamb burger served in a ciabatta bun and accompanied by 'crisp, thick' fries and a pot of good ketchup. The main restaurant menu, also available in the bar, offers everything from tomato and spinach risotto to vegetarian Thai red curry, with poached smoked haddock on bubble and squeak with a poached egg and lemon sauce somewhere in between. Beers and wines are a disappointingly ordinary selection. SAMPLE DISHES: duck confit salad £5.25; chargrilled ribeye steak with pont neuf potatoes, sautéed mushrooms and grilled tomato £13; lemon and lime tart £4.25.

Licensee John Rawlinson (freehouse)
Open 11 to 12 (2am Fri and Sat); bar food 12 to 6, restaurant Thur to Sat 7 to 11
Details No children   Wheelchair access (also WC)   Garden and patio   Live or background music   No dogs   Amex, Delta, Diners, MasterCard, Switch, Visa

Kro 2 Bar   NEW ENTRY

Oxford House, Oxford Road, Manchester M1 5AE   TEL: (0161) 236 1048
WEBSITE: www.kro.co.uk
between the BBC and the Students' Union

'Kro is a Danish village pub,' trumpets the website, and here on the fringe of the city centre is a modern building with a large patio for outdoor eating and drinking. Glass walls stretch from floor to high ceilings, which have white-painted metal girders and beams, the wooden furniture is of modern design, with some leather-look sofas, and the floor is tiled. Although this is no traditional pub, on draught are John Smith's Magnet, Theakston Cool Cask, Timothy Taylor Landlord and regularly changing guest ales like St Austell Tribute. The bar menu is a list of Danish classics, such as open sandwiches, gravad lax, pork schnitzel, and biksemad (chunks of roast beef sautéed with potatoes and onions topped with a fried egg). More substantial main courses run to pasta, Algerian-style pork escalope, and shredded beef wok-fried with garlic, chilli and coconut on baked courgettes, tomatoes and coriander, while the separate dinner menu in the restaurant deals in fillet of red snapper with lemon and butter sauce, crispy roast duck with sweet-and-sour cherries, and fricadeller. Half a dozen wines are served by the glass from an international list of over 30 bottles. SAMPLE DISHES: marinated herring with Danish rye bread and a shot of aquavit £4.25; chicken breast poached with baby onions, capers and tomatoes £7.25; lemon tart £3.50.

Licensee Mark Ruby (freehouse)
Open Mon to Wed 11am to midnight, Thur to Sat 11am to 2am, Sun 12 to midnight; bar food 11.30 to 7.30, restaurant 6 to 10; closed 25 Dec
Details Children welcome in eating areas   Wheelchair access (also WC)   Patio   No smoking in restaurant   Background music   No dogs   Amex, Delta, Diners, MasterCard, Switch, Visa

▲ Ox   NEW ENTRY

71 Liverpool Road, Castlefield, Manchester M3 4NQ   TEL: (0161) 839 7740

On the one hand, this modern city-centre dining pub competes with some of the city's better restaurants for food quality; on the other, it maintains an informal pubby atmosphere that draws in sociable drinkers as well as diners. Blending contemporary and traditional styles, it feels more like a pub than you might expect, and a large TV screen in the front bar shows football matches –

tables adorned with flowers and candles are thoughtfully positioned so you can watch while you eat (but non-fans will appreciate the no-smoking area to the rear, which is spared this experience). The long and varied menu should cater for most appetites: deep-fried octopus with citrus mayonnaise alongside chicken liver parfait with a grape and red onion chutney for starters; main courses ranging from rack of Welsh lamb with rosemary potatoes to roasted aubergine and sweet potato galette with gazpacho dressing. Specials might feature a protein-rich mixed grill, and side orders could double as hearty snacks: zucchini fritters with chilli dressing, for example, or patatas bravas. Among the range of beers and ciders is Timothy Taylor Landlord, while the reasonably priced wine list offers around ten reds and the same number of whites. SAMPLE DISHES: smoked mackerel and Cheddar fishcakes with Swiss chard and tomato and chilli jam £4.50; chicken piri-piri with spinach and roasted potatoes £9; bread-and-butter pudding £4.

Licensee David Leahy (Rowanstar Pub Co)
Open *11 to 11; bar food Mon to Wed 12 to 3, 5.30 to 10.30, Thur to Sat 12 to 11, Sun 12 to 6, 7 to 9.30*
Details *Children welcome in family room   Wheelchair access (also WC)   Garden   No-smoking area   Background music   No dogs   Delta, MasterCard, Switch, Visa   Accommodation: 9 rooms, room only £44.95 to £59.95 (double room)*

MARKET OVERTON   Rutland   map 6

▲ Black Bull

Market Overton LE15 7PW   TEL: (01572) 767677
off B668 Oakham to Stretton road, 2m N of Cottesmore

FISH

The Black Bull, a stone and part-thatched old inn, occupies a corner site in the centre of the attractive village of stone-coloured buildings. A décor of pinkish walls, red-upholstered banquettes, dark beams, lamps on deep windowsills, a welcoming fire and friendly and hospitable staff all create a warm and cheery atmosphere. Food, listed on a blackboard, is ordered at the bar and brought to the table. Seafood is something of a speciality, running from haddock and chips to perhaps grilled fillet of barramundi with a sweet pepper, spring onion and asparagus dressing, or grilled halibut steak with lemon and lime hollandaise. Five real ales are on draught – Hook Norton, Wells Bombardier Premium Bitter, Greene King IPA, Fuller's London Pride and Adnams Bitter – and a couple of wines are served by the glass. SAMPLE DISHES: duck in Chinese five-spice and plum sauce served with pancakes and spring onions £4.50; lamb steak with Stilton £10; strawberry pavlova £3.50.

Licensees John and Val Owen (freehouse)
Open *12 to 2.30, 6 to 11, Sun 12 to 3, 7 to 10.30; bar food and restaurant 12 to 1.45, 6.30 to 9.45*
Details *Children welcome   Car park   Wheelchair access (not WC)   No smoking in restaurant   Background music   Dogs welcome on a lead   Delta, MasterCard, Switch, Visa   Accommodation: 2 rooms, B&B £30 to £45*

Report forms are at the back of the book; write a letter if you prefer; or email your pub report to whichpubguide@which.net.

MARLDON   Devon   map I

▲ Church House Inn   NEW ENTRY

Village Road, Marldon TQ3 ISL   TEL: (01803) 558279
off A380, 2m NW of Paignton

This large white-painted pub was reputedly built in 1362, and it looks authen-
tically ancient with its church-like windows (though the name comes from
the fact that it is next to the equally old village church). It's a friendly and
welcoming place, with the good vibe of a slick, successful operation, and
draws a mixed crowd, mainly locals, for both drinking and dining – and it's
very popular, so try to arrive early. The L-shaped main bar has dark beams, a
stone fireplace and flagstone floors, while the dining area is done out in a more
contemporary minimalist style – plain white walls adorned with mirrors and
prints. Blackboard menus are the same in both areas, and the style is slightly
more refined than the usual pub grub: smoked chicken and watercress stack
with fresh peach compote among starters, and main courses of pork loin with
sage sauce and a roasted pear, whole lemon sole with asparagus and paprika
butter, or fillet steak topped with a prawn cake and brandy cream jus. Real ales
are an above-average range, including Dartmoor Best, Shepherd Neame
Spitfire and Fuller's London Pride, and all five house wines are served by the
glass. SAMPLE DISHES: filo tart of red onion, tomato, mozzarella and basil
cream £5; slow-cooked lamb shank with rosemary, garlic, orange and red wine
£11.50; bread-and-butter pudding £5.

Licensee Julian Cook (freehouse)
Open Mon to Fri 11.30 to 2.30, 5.30 to 11, Sat 11.30 to 11, Sun 12 to 10.30; bar food and
restaurant 12 to 2 (2.30 Sun), 6.30 to 9.30; closed evenings 25 and 26 Dec
Details Children welcome in eating areas   Car park   Wheelchair access (not WC)   Garden and
patio   No-smoking area in bar, no smoking in restaurant   Occasional background music   Dogs
welcome in bar only   Delta, MasterCard, Switch, Visa   Accommodation: 1 room, B&B £40 to £50

MARSH BENHAM   Berkshire   map 2

Red House ♥

Marsh Benham RG20 8LY   TEL: (01635) 582017
off A4 between Newbury and Hungerford

This thatched red-brick pub (once known as the Water Rat) is in a hamlet a
couple of miles west of Newbury and quite close to the Kennet and Avon
Canal. It's more gastro-pub than watering hole, though real ale drinkers can
still enjoy Fuller's London Pride and Brakspear Bitter. It has a garden outside,
and inside there's a bar-cum-bistro with red-painted walls, and, beyond it, a
distinctly upmarket restaurant. The bistro menu offers two- or three-course
set meals with three starters and three mains to choose from. Of the former,
one might be a soup (say, watercress), another something like smoked mackerel fajitas. Mains range from sausage and mash with onion gravy to smoked
cod on couscous, and sweets are the same as those on the restaurant's à la carte
menu – tarte Tatin with ice cream, maybe, or lemon tart with red fruit coulis
(or English and French cheeses). The French-led wine list opens with four
house selections at £12.95, or £3 a glass, but, while there's enough for drinkers

on a budget, upmarket bottles dominate. SAMPLE DISHES: pink grapefruit and prawn salad; chicken casserole with lardons and button onions; espresso pannacotta: £16.95 for 3 courses or £13.50 for 2 courses.

Licensee Xavier Le-Bellego (freehouse)
Open Tue to Sun 11 to 11 (Sun 11 to 3); bar food and restaurant 12 to 2.15, 7 to 10
Details Children welcome in eating area of bar   Car park   Wheelchair access (also WC)   Garden and patio   No-smoking area in bar, no smoking in dining room   Occasional background music   No dogs   Amex, Delta, MasterCard, Switch, Visa

MARSH GIBBON   Buckinghamshire   map 5

Greyhound Inn

West Edge, Marsh Gibbon OX27 0HA   TEL: (01869) 277365
off A41 Bicester to Aylesbury road, 4m E of Bicester

Bare stone walls, a stone floor and beamed ceilings give character to this village local, where a huge log fire burns in winter. A single U-shaped bar leads round to a carpeted area, which is treated as the restaurant, with heavy-topped tables and dark padded chairs. In this apparently quintessential English setting, it might seem a little incongruous to be offered an exclusively Thai menu (with a take-away option for those in a hurry), but that is where the owners hail from. The cooking proves to be impressive, replete with fresh herbs and spices and everything seemingly cooked to order. You might begin, familiarly enough, with spare ribs, or king prawns tempura, before proceeding to weeping tiger (thin slices of sirloin steak tossed quickly in garlic and coriander), fried chicken in sweet-and-sour sauce, or stir-fried salmon fillet with ginger, black beans, garlic and mushrooms. Choose from a variety of ice creams to finish. Greene King Abbot Ale and IPA and Fuller's London Pride are on handpump, and there are also specialities such as Polish lager and (of course) bottled Thai beers. The house wines are the only ones served by the glass. SAMPLE DISHES: minced prawn won tons £4.25; green chicken curry £7; chocolate truffle torte £2.75.

Licensee Richard Kaim (freehouse)
Open Tue to Sun 12 to 3, 6 (7 Sun) to 11.30; bar food and restaurant 12 to 2.30, 6 (7 Sun) to 9.30
Details Children welcome in eating areas   Car park   Wheelchair access (not WC)   Garden   No smoking in restaurant   No music   No dogs   Delta, MasterCard, Switch, Visa

MARSHSIDE   Kent   map 3

Gate Inn 🍺

Marshside CT3 4EB   TEL: (01227) 860498
between A28 and A299, 3m SE of Herne Bay

Marshside's marsh was the Isle of Thanet's 'moat' (long ago, when Thanet *was* an island), and, still, only four roads and a couple of railways cross it. This cottagey-feeling building has an attractive small garden fringed by a stream at one side. It is clearly a village focal point: not only are there notices about local events, but staff and most of the customers plainly know each other well – and they make visitors welcome, too. Modern, up-to-the-minute gastro-pub this ain't: what you get is well-kept Shepherd Neame beers (Master Brew, Spitfire and Bishop's Finger, plus seasonal brews), along with superior pub grub, generously portioned and sensibly priced. Apart from sandwiches and stuffed spuds with a range of fillings, there are dishes such as omelettes, pasta or spicy hotpots for which one can choose various toppings or fillings; soup, pâté, steaks and mixed grills are on the menu too. For dessert, it's ice creams (including home-made kulfi) or bread and cheese. A short list of six wines is available, all served by the glass. SAMPLE DISHES: garlic mushrooms and bread £3; mega grill £6.50; banana split £2.75.

Licensee Christopher Smith (Shepherd Neame)
Open 11 to 2.30 (3 Sat), 6 to 11, Sun 12 to 4, 7 to 10.30; bar food 12 to 2, 6 to 9, Sun 12 to 2.15, 7 to 9
Details Children welcome in family room   Car park   Wheelchair access (also WC)   Garden   No-smoking area in bar (lunchtime only) and family room   No music   Dogs welcome   No cards

MARTON   **North Yorkshire**   map 9

Appletree ✿   NEW ENTRY
Marton YO62 6RD   TEL: (01751) 431457
WEBSITE: www.appletreeinn.co.uk
Marton signposted on A170 between Kirkbymoorside and Pickering

A small village just outside the North York Moors National Park is the setting for this pub-cum-restaurant. Bare stone walls, beamed ceilings and a large open fire give character to the bar, where you can sample John Smith's Bitter from the cask or one of the regularly changing guest ales: perhaps Wells Eagle IPA, Double Chance from the Malton Brewery, or Hambleton Stud. Candles are the main ornament in the red-walled, carpeted restaurant, with its plain wooden tables and comfortable chairs. This is the setting for some imaginative and accomplished cooking, although you can eat wherever you like. Start with the likes of a salad of chorizo, black pudding and bacon, or game terrine with chutney, and proceed to venison suet pudding with red onion marmalade and a juniper and gin jus, or braised shoulder of lamb with tomato confit. No less successful are fish dishes: smoked haddock brandade with a poached egg, followed by steamed fillet of hake with a red pepper salsa. Light bites – avocado, orange and feta salad, for instance – and sandwiches are possibilities at lunchtime, and desserts run from an exemplary summer pudding to rum baba with glazed pineapple and vanilla ice cream. The broad-ranging wine list of around fifty bottles kicks off with eight house wines by two sizes of glass (£2.60 and £3.50) as well as the bottle (£9.95). SAMPLE DISHES: Thai-spiced fishcakes with oyster sauce £5.50; rump of Marton lamb topped with tapénade wrapped in puff pastry £14; marbled chocolate pyramid filled with Baileys chocolate mousse £4.50.

Licensees Melanie Thornton and Trajan Drew (freehouse)
Open summer 12 to 11, Sun 12 to 10.30; winter 12 to 2.30, 6.30 to 11, Sun 12 to 3, 7 to 10.30; bar food and restaurant 12 to 2 (3 Sun), 6.30 to 9.30 (7 to 9 Sun); closed Sun evenings winter, Tue, 3 weeks Jan
Details Children welcome in bar eating area   Car park   Patio   No smoking in restaurant   Background music   No dogs exc guide dogs   Delta, MasterCard, Switch, Visa

MARTON   Shropshire   map 5

Sun Inn 🏵 🏵 |NEW ENTRY|

Marton SY21 8JP   TEL: (01938) 561211
on B4386, 13m SW of Shrewsbury

In a small hamlet on the border between England and Wales, the Sun Inn is a
large building of sombre grey-brown stone and indeterminate age. It is 'very
much a convivial local boozer', and pool and domino contests are held here,
though the décor makes it look more like a private residence and only the giant
stone hearth in the bar area is visibly old. The kitchen concentrates its efforts
mainly on serving the separate no-smoking restaurant, where the menu offers
a range of simple dishes in a modern European style: perhaps roast red peppers
and tomatoes with air-dried ham, or seared scallops with avocado salad and
basil dressing to start, followed by beef fillet with bacon, baby onions,
caramelised potatoes and roasted root vegetables, or fillet of halibut with herb
mash, slow-cooked fennel, prawns and mustard sauce. Bar food is restricted to
a lunchtime blackboard of no more than half a dozen straightforward dishes:
scampi and chips, grilled salmon with salad and herb mayonnaise, and ham
and mushroom omelette are typical. And yet it left a well-travelled inspector
grasping for superlatives. The praise was earned by 'fresh-tasting' lamb stew
containing lots of chunky vegetables served with 'superb' smooth mashed
potatoes, and slow-roast duck leg with 'luscious' meat and 'very, very crisp'
skin plus an accompaniment of tangy diced apple and balsamic vinegar,
sautéed potatoes and celeriac, and wilted spinach, watercress and rocket.
Equally excellent desserts are unusual both in conception and in presentation:
winberry crème brûlée, for example, served in a coffee cup with an accompaniment of elderflower sorbet in a sherry glass. A pair of house wines at £10.25
a bottle, £2.50 a glass, opens the short but diverse list, and Hobson's Choice
and M&B Mild are the real ales on offer. SAMPLE DISHES: chicken liver terrine
with chutney £3.50; roast pork with roast potatoes and vegetables £5.50; date
pudding with butterscotch sauce and vanilla ice cream £4.50.

Licensee Ian MacCallum (freehouse)
Open *Wed to Sun 12 to 2, all week 7 (6 Thur to Sat) to 11 (10.30 Sun); bar food Wed to Sat 12
to 2, restaurant Wed to Sun 12 to 2, Tue to Sat 6 to 9*
Details *Children welcome   Car park   Wheelchair access (also WC)   Patio   No smoking in
restaurant   Background music   Dogs welcome exc in restaurant   Delta, MasterCard, Switch, Visa*

MAWDESLEY   Lancashire   map 8

Red Lion |NEW ENTRY|

New Street, Mawdesley L40 2QP   TEL: (01704) 822999
Mawdesley signposted from A59 at Rufford

Two stone lions guard the entrance to this thriving 'community pub', with its
flower tubs and hanging baskets outside, a dartboard in the bar and a decent
selection of real sales on handpump, including Timothy Taylor Landlord,
Banks's Original and Theakston Best Bitter. Customers wanting to eat,
however, need to head for the Mediterranean-style conservatory restaurant,

which has its own walled patio. The evening carte offers 'hearty British food, sourced with care': you might begin with pâté with port sauce, or sautéed queen scallops with sweet sherry jus before crispy roast Goosnargh duck with wild mushroom and Madeira sauce, or baked sea bream with white wine and crayfish sauce, then finish off in the old style with apple and rhubarb pie with custard, or rice pudding with home-made raspberry jam. Fixed-price lunchtime and 'early-doors' menus (served before 7.30pm) provide great value for, say, minestrone soup with shaved Parmesan, followed by marinated lamb chops, cooked pink and served with two huge bowls of vegetables. At lunchtime you can also get sandwiches and baguettes in the bar. A decent selection of affordably priced wines from around the world kicks off with four house recommendations (£2.25 a glass, £11 a bottle). SAMPLE DISHES: crab and herb crumble with lemon and dill butter sauce £4; pot-roast shoulder of lamb with garlic and rosemary £11; summer fruit torte with mascarpone £3.25.

Licensee Edward Newton (Enterprise Inns)
Open 11 to 11, Sun 12 to 10.30; bar food Wed to Sat 12 to 2; restaurant Wed to Sat 12 to 2, Wed to Sat 6 to 9 (9.30 Sat), Sun 12 to 8
Details Children welcome   Car park   Wheelchair access (also WC)   Patio   No smoking in restaurant   Occasional live or background music   Dogs welcome in bar   Amex, Delta, MasterCard, Switch, Visa

MELLOR   Greater Manchester   map 8

Oddfellows Arms   NEW ENTRY

73 Moor End Road, Mellor SK6 5PT   TEL: (0161) 449 7826
at Marple Bridge, turn SE off A626, signposted Mellor and New Mills

In the Peak District Mellor sits on a ridge between Marple and New Mills, where Derbyshire, Cheshire and Stockport join. Strung along a climbing lane with superb views of Dark Peak are terraces of gritstone houses, one of which includes the Oddfellows Arms: a stern three-storey building with leaded windows, a small yard in front and its car park in an old quarry across the road. Behind the wooden porch is a spacious, flagged bar-room with carpeted sub-divisions off it (beware a head-banging beam near the counter!). Here well-kept beers are served by friendly staff in a relaxed atmosphere: Adnams Bitter, Marston's Bitter and Pedigree, plus guests such as Gale's Ragged Robin. An extensive and eclectic menu draws eaters from miles around. Mussel chowder, or sautéed chicken livers with artichoke hearts, sherry and spring onions make a good beginning. Then perhaps a Catalan cassoulet of beans, chorizo, bacon, onions and duck, or a lamb rogan josh; roast sea bass with a Thai coconut curry, or Cajun tuna steak, offer alternatives – or good old roast rib of beef, or Cumberland sausages. Portions are generous, though, so you might have to ignore rhubarb and ginger torte, or tiramisù. Most of the thirty-odd Old and New World wines are under £15 – a fair number are under £10 – with a varying selection of eight or nine by the glass. There's plenty of tasty everyday stuff with one or two grander offerings. SAMPLE DISHES: pea and ham soup £2.25; Moroccan lamb casserole £10; apple cheesecake £3.75.

Licensee Robert Cloughley (freehouse)
Open Tue to Sun 12 to 3, 5.30 to 11 (Sun 7 to 10.30); bar food Tue to Sat 12 to 2, 6.30 to 9.30, Sun 12 to 2; closed 25, 26 and 31 Dec, 1 Jan

Details *Children welcome in eating areas   Car park   Wheelchair access (not WC)   Patio*
No smoking in dining room   No music   Dogs welcome   Delta, MasterCard, Switch, Visa

---

MELLOR BROOK   Lancashire   map 8

▲ Feilden's Arms 🏮   NEW ENTRY

Whalley Road, Mellor Brook BB2 7PR   TEL: (01254) 812219
follow signposts for Mellor Brook from A59 between Whalley and Preston

---

'Good quality and high standards without the formality of a restaurant,'
summed up a fan of this smart pub not far from Blackburn. The interior is
divided into eating and drinking areas based around a long bar counter,
although at busy times (such as Sunday lunch) the whole place is given over to
diners. Menus stick to a familiar range of dishes: various pies (steak and ale,
fish, or chicken and leek), sausages and mash, and that old local favourite,
hotpot, which comes with red cabbage. If you are just after a snack, there is
also a choice of sandwiches and hot baguettes, and if restaurant formality is
more your thing there is the conservatory dining room, where a more ambitious menu offers dishes like braised shoulder of lamb with boulangère potatoes and lamb's tongue, or roast loin of venison with celeriac purée, fondant
potatoes and red wine sauce. Four red and four white wines are available by
the glass from a reasonably priced list. Beers are a standard range, including
John Smith's Bitter and Boddingtons Bitter. SAMPLE DISHES: chicken liver
salad with streaky bacon £4.25; fish and chips £7.25; plum crumble with
custard £3.25.

Licensees Nigel Smith and Fred Walker (freehouse)
Open *11.30 to 11 (10.30 Sun); bar food and restaurant 12 to 2.30 (3 Sun), 6 to 9; restaurant
closed Mon*
Details *Children welcome   Car park   Wheelchair access (also WC)   Garden   No smoking in
restaurant   Occasional live or background music   No dogs   Amex, Delta, Diners, MasterCard,
Switch, Visa   Accommodation: 4 rooms, B&B £48 to £96*

MELLS   Somerset   map 2

▲ Talbot Inn

Selwood Street, Mells BA11 3PN   TEL: (01373) 812254
WEBSITE: www.talbotinn.com
3m W of Frome

Mells is a picturesque village hidden in a web of lanes at the eastern end of the
Mendips, west of Frome. Once there, the Talbot is easy to spot: a coaching inn
since the fifteenth century, it is a substantial tile-roofed building in the mellow
local limestone. The large entrance arch, welcomingly cool and crepuscular
on a bright day, leads through the building to a characterful courtyard behind,
with tables, chairs and a pergola wrapped in rampant Russian vine. In the
high-ceilinged public bar beyond – once a tithe barn – a horse-drawn single-
furrow plough hangs above barrels of Butcombe Bitter, Fuller's London Pride
and Smiles; the smaller bar has wood panelling, flagged floor and hunting
prints. If you want to eat, booking ahead seems *de rigueur*. Food, fairly elaborate, favours game, fish, wild mushrooms, herb crusts and sauces. Starters

might include crab soup, or chicken liver parfait, and, supplementing the menu's meat main dishes – like roast chicken or lamb, and steaks – is a hand-written page of specials (mainly fish). Examples are roast cod fillet in parsley and garlic crust with wild mushrooms and a 'good, tangy' lemon chive sauce, or pheasant breast with a smoked bacon and onion rösti and a full-flavoured mustard and tarragon sauce. You could finish with mango crème brûlée, or treacle pudding. Portions are 'huge' (the pheasant was suspected of wearing silicone implants) and service friendly and attentive. SAMPLE DISHES: tomato and mozzarella tartlet £5.25; grilled lemon sole with herbs and tartare sauce £16; tiramisù £4.25.

Licensee Roger Elliott (freehouse)
Open 12 to 2.30, 6.30 to 11, Sun 12 to 3, 7 to 10.30; bar food and restaurant 12 to 2, 7 to 9.30; restaurant closed 25 and 26 Dec, 1 Jan
Details Children welcome in restaurant   Car park   Garden and patio   No smoking in restaurant   Occasional music   Dogs welcome exc in restaurant   Delta, MasterCard, Switch, Visa
Accommodation: 8 rooms, B&B £55 to £75

MELMERBY Cumbria

map 10

Shepherds Inn
Melmerby CA10 1HF   TEL: (01768) 881217
on A686 Penrith to Alston road, 8m NE of Penrith

Overlooking the village green in this charming village on the northern edge of Lakeland, away from the tourist hot spots, the Shepherds Inn is a large, square building of local red sandstone. It has a long-standing reputation in the area, drawing tourists, walkers and cyclists (Melmerby is on the coast-to-coast cycle route) and looks set to maintain standards despite a change of ownership in 2002. An inspector was impressed with the excellent value and equally pleased with the quality of the cooking: a generous rack of meaty spare ribs (from a butcher in Penrith) in home-made barbecue sauce, and haddock in a light, crisp batter both made a favourable impact, as did their accompanying fat, golden chips. The rest of the menu is similarly straightforward in style: half a roast duckling with rich gravy and sautéed potatoes is typical, as are Cumberland sausage hotpot, and chicken korma. Three cheeses with the ploughman's are chosen from a fine selection totalling fourteen, all English, and lunchtimes see the addition of a lighter snack menu. Beers are a decent range headed up by Jennings Cumberland Ale, and a short wine list offers good value, with several bottles under £10 and three wines by the glass. The pub's fair treatment of children has also been commended. SAMPLE DISHES: dill-marinated herrings £4.75; venison casserole with Roquefort dumplings £10; apple pie £3.

Licensees Garry and Marcia Parkin (freehouse)
Open 10.30 to 3, 6 to 11, Sun 12 to 3, 7 to 10.30; bar food Mon to Sat 11.30 to 2.30, 6 to 9 (9.45 Fri and Sat and all week summer), Sun 12 to 2.30, 7 to 9 (9.45 summer); closed 25 Dec, lunchtime 26 Dec
Details Children welcome   Car park   Patio   No-smoking area   Live music; jukebox   Dogs welcome in 1 area of bar   Delta, MasterCard, Switch, Visa

MICKLEHAM   Surrey   map 3

King William IV

Byttom Hill, Mickleham RH5 6EL   TEL: (01372) 372590
going S on A24 about 2m S of Leatherhead, just after roundabout junction with A246 look for
Frascati's restaurant on left; pub is up steep track to right of restaurant

This small pub was built in the late eighteenth century and was extended in
Victorian times before it became an alehouse for Lord Beaverbrook's estate
staff. Blackboards list the usual lunchtime sandwiches, ploughman's and
jacket potatoes, before going on to starters such as crab salad, and main courses
ranging from seafood pie, or Cajun-style rump steak with a red onion and
mango marmalade, to lamb kebab with pilaff rice. Desserts might take in treacle tart with 'excellent' vanilla ice cream, or 'very good' toffee and apple bread-
and-butter pudding. On draught are Adnams Best Bitter, Badger Best Bitter
and Hogs Back TEA. Just two wines are sold by the glass. Set on a hillside, the
pub is reached via steep steps from the road. The pretty garden, on several
levels, has plenty of seats and tables; barbecues are held here in summer.
SAMPLE DISHES: goats' cheese and apple salad £4.50; escalope of turkey with
lemon and coriander cream sauce £9.25; apple and plum crumble £4.

Licensees Chris and Jenny Grist (freehouse)
Open 11 to 3, 6 to 11, Sun 12 to 3, 7 to 10.30; bar food 12 to 2, 7 to 9.30; closed 25
and 31 Dec
Details No children under 12   Garden and patio   Occasional live or background music   No dogs
MasterCard, Switch, Visa

MIDDLEHAM   North Yorkshire   map 8

▲ White Swan Hotel 🍴   NEW ENTRY

Market Place, Middleham DL8 4PE   TEL: (01969) 622093
WEBSITE: www.whiteswanhotel.co.uk
on A6108 2m S of Leyburn

Middleham, in scenic Wensleydale, has one of Richard III's favourite castles,
racing stables, and four pubs in the Market Place – two of them Swans (Black
and White). The smallest, the White Swan (white-painted, three storeys, with
black window surrounds and blue-slate roof), has a low-key air of unpreten-
sion concealing solid worth. The serving counter divides the black-beamed
bar: one side is flag-floored with bar stools and a big inglenook containing a
wood-burner and a table alongside; the other is wooden-floored, with tables,
chairs and floral wallpaper. Wherever you sit, you can sample Black Sheep's
full range (Best Bitter, Special Ale and Riggwelter) and John Smith's cask
brews, all in perfect condition; alternatively, a 20-bin wine list (12 by the glass)
starts at £9.50, and only French bottles breach £20. Food is listed on a menu
card, with specials on a blackboard. Start, perhaps, with onion and white
Wensleydale tart, smoked salmon risotto, or a 'simple, well-executed and
satisfying' crispy duck and bacon salad with spicy plum dressing. Mains
include bangers and mash, beer-battered fish and chips, or grills, alongside
bouillabaisse, polpette in beef and tomato sauce, or venison pie; sweets run
from dark chocolate terrine to iced lemon parfait. It is worth noting that

co-licensee Paul Klein is also the licensee of the Blue Lion two miles down the road at East Witton (see entry). SAMPLE DISHES: moules provençale £5.25; beef and ale pie £9; sticky toffee pudding £3.75.

Licensees Andrew Holmes and Paul Klein (freehouse)
Open 11 to 11, Sun 12 to 10.30; bar food and restaurant 12 to 2.15, 6.15 to 9.15
Details Children welcome in bar eating area   Wheelchair access (not WC)   Garden and patio
No smoking in dining room   No music   Dogs welcome exc in food areas when food is being served
Delta, MasterCard, Switch, Visa   Accommodation: 12 rooms, B&B £47.50 to £79

MIDFORD   Bath & N.E. Somerset   map 2

Hope & Anchor Inn
Midford BA2 7DD   TEL: (01225) 832296
on B3110, 3m S of Bath

A very steep terraced garden, with plenty of good seating and trellises, is wrapped around the back of the Hope & Anchor, an unassuming-looking stone-built pub. It's just as straightforward inside, with an open fire, wood panelling and wooden tables and chairs, with a carpeted oak-beamed restaurant at the back, its tables covered with white cloths. Bar and restaurant menus are interchangeable throughout, except on Friday and Saturday evenings, when the bar menu is off-limits in the restaurant. A selection of tapas makes a popular bar snack, with more substantial dishes extending to a salad of smoked chicken, prawns and avocado with honey dressing, or sirloin steak pan-fried with garlic served with fried potatoes and salad. A tartlet of grilled goats' cheese and provençale vegetables, or herrings marinated in Madeira with potato salad could kick off the restaurant menu, followed by Barbary duck breast with ginger, honey and soy sauce, or chicken satay on rice. Desserts might include baked winter berry flan with vanilla ice cream, or chocolate and Baileys cheesecake. Butcombe Bitter, Caledonian Deuchars IPA and Bass are on draught, and seven wines from a short list come by the glass. SAMPLE DISHES: smoked salmon pot filled with crème fraîche, dill and capers served with cucumber relish £4.75; halibut steak with lemon, capers, garlic and parsley £11.50; plum and almond tart £3.75.

Licensee Richard Smolarek (freehouse)
Open 11.30 to 2.30, 6.30 to 11, Sun 12 to 3, 7 to 10.30; bar food and restaurant 12 to 2, 6.30
(7 Sun) to 9.30; closed 25 and 26 Dec
Details Children welcome   Car park   Wheelchair access (not WC)   Garden   No smoking in
restaurant   Background music   No dogs   Delta, MasterCard, Switch, Visa

MILLBANK   West Yorkshire   map 8

Millbank ✿ ❦
Millbank HX6 3DY   TEL: (01422) 825588
signposted on A58 between Sowerby Bridge and Ripponden

On the side of a steep hill, this old stone-built pub has stunning views over the valley from its decked terrace and beer garden. The much-modernised interior shows stripped-down walls and floors, plus a few nice individual touches, such as church chairs with their prayer-book boxes still attached, some abstract paintings, and a fireplace filled with stone heads and candles. Eating goes on to either side of the small main bar area, and hearty portions are the norm. Visitors appreciate 'first-class ingredients presented without fuss': to start, perhaps a terrine of wood pigeon and ham hock with pea purée, or deep-fried goats' cheese niçoise, followed by belly pork braised in honey and cloves served with turnip dauphinois, or confit of lamb with white-bean purée and sweetbread fritters. Vegetarians might like to try mushroom risotto with spinach purée and glazed button onions, and on the fishy side of things there might be roast sea bass with basil mash, roast aubergine and pipérade. Finish with elderflower and grape jelly ('a delicately flavoured revelation', according to a report), pannacotta with strawberries, or a selection of Yorkshire farm-house cheeses. A good range of bottled beers and English cider supplements the handpumped Timothy Taylor Landlord and Tetley Bitter, along with Stowford Press cider. Don't be fooled by the no-frills presentation of the wine list: the selection is excellent, especially the Italian and South African bottles. Eight wines are offered by the glass, and bottle prices start around £10. SAMPLE DISHES: watercress and potato soup £4; deep-fried cod in beer batter with pea purée and chips £9; hot chocolate fondant cake with pistachio ice cream £4.50.

Licensees Paul and Christine Halsey (freehouse)
Open Tue to Fri and bank hol Mon 12 to 3, 5.30 to 11, Sat and Sun 12 to 11; bar food and restaurant Tue to Thur and bank hol Mon 12 to 2, 5.30 to 9.30, Fri and Sat 12 to 2, 6 to 10, Sun 12 to 3; closed Tue evening, first 2 weeks Oct
Details Children welcome   Wheelchair access (not WC)   Garden and patio   No smoking in dining room   Live or background music   Dogs welcome   Delta, MasterCard, Switch, Visa

MILTON STREET   East Sussex   map 3

Sussex Ox
Milton Street BN26 5RL   TEL: (01323) 870840
off A27, 1m NE of Alfriston

The Ox is tucked away among narrow country lanes, just east of Lewes beneath the South Downs, and its family-friendly Sty restaurant has wonder-ful views of them across a large garden with plenty of equipment for exhaust-ing over-energetic children. Both the Sty and the Front Room Restaurant serve the same menu, which focuses on local ingredients (including fish) and suppliers. Unpretentious (but not unimaginative) dishes include home-made soups, or grilled goats' cheese on roast vegetables, to start, then anything from sausage, egg and chips, or 'Sussex Ox burger', to a venison casserole, or duck breast with home-made plum chutney. Along with the log fire and exposed beams in the bar, there's Harveys Sussex Best Bitter and Hop Back Summer Lightning, supplemented by guest ales that change weekly, and a reasonably diverse wine list includes six by the glass. SAMPLE DISHES: Sussex smokie (haddock) £4.45; steak, ale and mushroom pie £8.25; tarte au citron £3.50.

Licensees Doug and Jeanne Baker, Harry Findlay, and Ashley Walton (freehouse)
Open 11 to 3, 6 to 11, Sun 12 to 8 (summer 12 to 10.30); bar food and restaurant 11 to 2, 6 to 9 (12 to 6 Sun winter)
Details Children welcome in family room and dining room   Car park   Wheelchair access (also WC) Garden   No smoking in family room   Occasional live or background music   Dogs welcome MasterCard, Switch, Visa

MITCHELL   Cornwall   map 1

▲ Plume of Feathers 🍺 [NEW ENTRY]

Mitchell TR8 5AX   TEL: (01872) 510387

A30 from Bodmin take left towards Mitchell, ignore first left, drive past a bus shelter and round bend. Pub is 250yds on left

---

In a small village inland from Newquay, this is considered a 'good summer al fresco pub', thanks to its large garden with a children's play area. Inside, a modern décor in the refurbished open-plan bar and dining areas is in harmony with the original features, such as beams and an inglenook. Separate menus are offered for lunch and dinner, but a simple style prevails at both. At lunchtime, regular choices range from moules marinière to smoked chicken Caesar salad, while blackboard specials might include game pie or Sri Lankan curries. Traditional Cornish cream teas are another attractive option. The evening menu adds a few more substantial main courses to the repertoire, such as duck confit with mash and braised red cabbage, and the blackboard extends the choice with pan-fried monkfish on sun-blush tomato and Parmesan mash. Children fare better than average, being offered home-made meatballs or grilled fish with parsley butter alongside the usual burger and chicken nuggets. Real ales are a superior selection, including beers from local breweries Sharp's, Skinner's and Ring O' Bells, as well as better-known names such as Timothy Taylor Landlord and Old Speckled Hen. The short wine list focuses on value, prices starting at around £10, and three wines are served by the glass. SAMPLE DISHES: tapas with chargrilled bread £4.50; slow-cooked lamb shank with chorizo, chickpea and butter-bean salsa and rosemary oil £9.75; banana sticky toffee pudding with butterscotch sauce £4.25.

Licensees M.F.J. Warner and J.E. Trotter (freehouse)
Open 10.30 to 11 (10.20 Sun); bar food and restaurant 12 to 6, 6 to 10; closed evening 25 Dec
Details Children welcome   Car park   Garden   No smoking in restaurant   Occasional live or background music; jukebox   Dogs welcome exc in restaurant   Delta, MasterCard, Switch, Visa
Accommodation: 5 rooms, B&B £41.25 to £95

MONKS ELEIGH   Suffolk   map 6

Swan Inn 🏵 [NEW ENTRY]

The Street, Monks Eleigh IP7 7AU   TEL: (01449) 741391

on B1115 between Sudbury and Hadleigh

Nigel and Carol Ramsbottom run this village pub as a double act: she works behind the bar while he cooks. There are views on to the main street from the south-facing windows in the bar, which is all light wood and bamboo, with carpeted floors and a modest bar counter. Food is taken seriously here, and menus are listed on blackboards. The theme is global: from the East you might find crispy Peking duck salad with hoisin sauce, cucumber and spring onions, smoked chicken bang-bang, or spicy Thai-style pork in lettuce cups, while Western taste-buds could be stimulated by confit of duck terrine with apricots and onion marmalade, or venison sausages on mash with fried onions. To finish, chocolate-dusted iced whisky parfait has been enjoyable; otherwise opt for apricot and ginger pudding, or classic tiramisù. East Anglian beers from

Adnams and Woodforde's are on draught, and the pub has a creditable list of affordably priced, international wines; eight are offered by the glass from £2.35. SAMPLE DISHES: whole smoked Orford prawns with mayonnaise £4.50; braised lamb knuckle with Puy lentil sauce £11.75; glazed lemon tart £4.

Licensees Carol and Nigel Ramsbottom (freehouse)
Open Wed to Sun 12 to 3, 7 to 11; bar food and restaurant 12 to 2, 7 to 9
Details Children welcome Car park Garden No smoking in restaurant No music No dogs
Delta, MasterCard, Switch, Visa

MORDEN   Dorset   map 2

Cock & Bottle

Morden BH20 7DL   TEL: (01929) 459238
on B3075 between A35 and A31

Parts of this rambling roadside pub, in a quiet village, are 400 years old, although the rear extension is more modern. The main bar is spacious, with an open fireplace, while the eating area has farmhouse chairs, cushioned wall settles, attractive prints and an open log fire; adjoining it is the restaurant, whose French doors lead to the garden – lovely views from here across open fields. The menus, both printed and blackboard, are an appealing blend of pub favourites and more imaginative dishes. Starters might include duck spring roll with a sweet chilli jam, or goujons of chicken coated in coconut accompanied by a mild curry sauce, and among main courses might be steak and mushroom pie, rump of lamb braised in rosemary and redcurrant sauce served on creamy mash, or beef Wellington. Game makes an appearance – perhaps pheasant breast in a cider and apple chestnut sauce – and fish might take the form of sea bass fillets on a bed of stir-fried vegetables drizzled with sweet chilli dressing. The light lunch menu runs from ploughman's to steak sandwich, and there's something like treacle suet pudding among the choices for those who enjoy a pudding. Badger Best and Tanglefoot and King & Barnes Sussex are on tap, and six wines are offered by the glass. SAMPLE DISHES: smoked salmon with warm potato salad and horseradish dressing £5.25; pigeon and wild mushroom pie £9.25; soft chocolate pudding with raspberry cream £4.

Licensee Peter Meadley (Hall & Woodhouse)
Open 11 to 3, 6 to 11, Sun 12 to 3, 7 to 10.30; bar food and restaurant 12 to 2, 6 to 9
Details Children welcome in restaurant Car park Wheelchair access (also WC) Garden
No smoking in restaurant Background music in bar only Dogs welcome Delta, MasterCard,
Switch, Visa

MOULTON   North Yorkshire   map 9

Black Bull Inn ♥ ❦

Moulton DL10 6QJ   TEL: (01325) 377289
1m SE of Scotch Corner

Lucky Teesside, having the Black Bull so close – but travellers on the A1 can also benefit from what is definitely a dining pub. Behind the long, low front is dark panelling, velour-covered bar stools and benches, old prints and caricatures of Victorian politicians on the walls, and a huge stuffed fish. Beers there are Theakston Best Bitter and John Smith's Smooth, but the drinking emphasis is really on wines (although only three come by the glass). Whites are well represented – complementing the strong seafood slant of the cuisine – with excellent selections from the Loire, Germany and above all Burgundy. Red Burgundy and claret also figure large, and prices are very fair all round. Bar snacks (lunchtime only) include oysters (au naturel or grilled), salmon (fresh, smoked, gravad lax and fishcakes) and sea trout, tuna carpaccio and battered cod with pea purée; carnivores get Indonesian beef kebab, and salads of duck and avocado, or black pudding, pancetta and chicken liver. The restaurant – in the conservatory and in a converted Pullman carriage in the garden – offers many of the same dishes, plus bouillabaisse, sautéed squid, and variations on bass, sole, turbot and lobster; meat offerings include fried duck breast in Vin Santo sauce, chateaubriand with béarnaise sauce, roast lamb (loin or rack), or a venison cutlet. Any remaining emptiness can be plugged with chocolate and cherry truffle torte, say, or vanilla bavarois with raspberries. SAMPLE DISHES: smoked salmon pâté £6; seafood pancake thermidor £6.25; coeur à la crème with fruit compote £4.

Licensees A.M.C. and S.C. Pagendam (freehouse)
Open Mon to Sat 12 to 2.30, 6 to 10.30; bar food Mon to Sat 12 to 2, restaurant Mon to Sat 12 to 2, 6.45 to 10.15; closed 23 to 27 Dec
Details No children Car park Wheelchair access (not WC) Garden No music No dogs
Amex, Delta, Diners, MasterCard, Switch, Visa

MUNDFORD Norfolk   map 6

▲ Crown Hotel
Crown Road, Mundford IP26 5HQ TEL: (01842) 878233
pub signposted from A1065 in village

The Crown, whitewashed with dormer windows peeping through a tiled roof, looks over the small village green and, the address being Crown Road, has obviously done so for some time (since about 1650, they say). The Village Bar is beamed and basic, with a pool table and dartboard, while the Squires Bar has a carpet and fresh flowers on small round tables. There is also a first-floor dining room. The menu, which applies throughout, could include starters of local smoked duck breast, fried and served on a salad, or a wild mushroom tartlet, followed by a leek and Gruyère strudel or escalopes of tuna and escolar in a provençale sauce. Beers might include Marston's Pedigree or local brews from Woodforde's (Wherry Best Bitter) and Mundford's own Iceni Brewery. Around 20 good-value wines are listed, including six by the glass. SAMPLE DISHES: wild mushroom tartlet £4.75; beef italienne £11.25; Irish crème brûlée £3.

Licensee Barry Walker (freehouse)
Open 11 to 11, Sun 12 to 10.30; bar food and restaurant 12 to 3, 7 to 10
Details Children welcome Wheelchair access (also WC) Garden and patio No smoking in dining room Jukebox Dogs welcome in bar Amex, Delta, Diners, MasterCard, Switch, Visa
Accommodation: 20 rooms, B&B £37.50 to £59.50

MUNGRISDALE   Cumbria   map 10

▲ Mill Inn

Mungrisdale CA11 0XR   TEL: (017687) 79632
WEBSITE: www.the-millinn.co.uk
from A66 7m E of Keswick, turn N on unclassified road signposted Mungrisdale

The hamlet of Mungrisdale nestles under Blencathra at the edge of roadless
mountain country. The Mill Inn is a long, low building of whitewashed stone
with dark window surrounds and a slate roof; there are tables outside where
fell walkers can plan their next ascent or the inactive can drink in the sumptu-
ous scenery. Inside you will find low ceilings and roughcast white walls. The
bar (which has a millstone mounted on the front of the wooden counter)
serves Jennings Bitter and Cumberland Ale, brewed in Cockermouth, and
'lots of malt whiskies'. The kindly priced wine list splits evenly between New
World and Old, and six of the twenty or so listed come by the glass. The food
uses local ingredients wherever possible. Snacky lunch dishes take in filled
baguettes and potatoes, plus the likes of cod and chips or (of course)
Cumberland sausage, mash and onion gravy. The longer evening menu might
bring a platter of rollmops, sardines and anchovies to start, or sautéed mushrooms with garlic chives and cream, followed perhaps by a ragoût of lamb, or
grilled haddock or trout. Vegetarian options include mixed bean chilli on rice.
Desserts are childhood favourites: sticky toffee pudding, lemon meringue pie
or profiteroles. There is also a separate menu for children. SAMPLE DISHES:
curried egg mayonnaise £3; beef and ale pie £6.50; apple crumble £2.50.

Licensees Jim and Margaret Hodge (freehouse)
Open 12 to 11 (10.30 Sun); bar food and restaurant 12 to 2, 6 to 8.30 (summer 12 to 2.30, 5.30
to 9); closed 25 and 26 Dec
Details Children welcome   Car park   Garden and patio   No smoking in dining room   Background
music   Dogs welcome   Delta, MasterCard, Switch, Visa   Accommodation: 6 rooms, B&B £35 to £55

MUNSLOW   Shropshire.   map 5

▲ Crown 🍺

Munslow SY7 9ET   TEL: (01584) 841205
WEBSITE: www.thecrown.clara.net

Known until recently as the Munslow Inn, this tall white-painted building is
in Corve Dale, an Area of Outstanding Natural Beauty, with pretty, hilly
scenery. Within is a series of small rooms, all on slightly different levels, with
fat ceiling beams hung with garlands of hops. The interesting menus feature
plenty of local produce, from crostini of black pudding and tomato with dry-
cured bacon to a main course of 'excellent, tasty, supple' loin of lamb with
fondant potato and a caper and tarragon cream sauce, or pavé of beef with
creamed cabbage and a ragoût of balsamic lentils and vegetables. Seafood,
often griddled, is well represented too: king scallops with a tomato and spring
onion salsa on rocket pesto, followed by fillet of Shetland salmon with a
creamy saffron and crabmeat sauce. An excellent selection of English cheeses
could round off a meal (and can make a fine lunch dish with chutney, pickles
and home-made rolls), with perhaps iced marzipan parfait with Amaretto-

soaked prunes for dessert eaters. Real ale is a strong suit, with a selection from Holden's range, plus Hobsons Town Crier and a guest from a local brewery. Four wines are served by the glass; prices on the full, French-dominated list start at around £11. SAMPLE DISHES: griddled mackerel on horseradish potatoes with chive dressing £4.50; breast of Gressingham duck with apple chutney and green peppercorn sauce £11.75; orange and Grand Marnier crème brûlée £4.

Licensees Mr and Mrs R. and J. Arnold (freehouse)
Open 12 to 2.30, 7 to 11 (10.30 Sun); bar food 12 to 1.45 (2 Sun), 7 to 8.45; restaurant Fri and Sat 7 to 8.45, Sun 12 to 2
Details Children welcome in eating areas   Car park   Wheelchair access (not WC)   Garden
No smoking in restaurant   Background music   Dogs welcome   Amex, Delta, MasterCard, Switch, Visa   Accommodation: 3 rooms, B&B £35 to £65

MYLOR BRIDGE   Cornwall   map 1

Pandora Inn 🍷
Restronguet Creek, Mylor Bridge TR11 5ST   TEL: (01326) 372678   **WATERSIDE**
off A39 from Truro, take B3292 signposted Penryn, then Mylor Bridge road, and
follow steep road down to Restronguet

Parts of this thatched pub date from the thirteenth century. As much as an attraction as its atmospheric rooms – low ceilings, flagstones, wall alcoves – is its prime waterside position: it stands hard by the water's edge, with an outdoor sitting area overlooking the estuary. At high tide the sea almost comes into the car park, and the pub's name is appropriately of naval origin (the *Pandora* was the ship sent to retrieve the *Bounty*'s mutineers). Some tables are on a pontoon that extends over the water. The standard menu – pork medallions pan-fried with garlic and rosemary in a port sauce, crab thermidor, and sautéed strips of chicken served with wild mushrooms in a brandy and crème fraîche sauce – is supplemented by daily specials listed on a blackboard by the bar. These might include starters of pâté with Cumberland sauce, a salad of avocado, mozzarella and cherry tomatoes, and main courses of red mullet on roasted peppers and olives, and John Dory with grapes. The pub is owned by the St Austell Brewery (licensee John Milan also runs the Rising Sun in St Mawes; see entry), and offers beers from its range, including Tinners Ale, HSD and Tribune, as well as Bass. Eleven house wines are sold by the small or large glass, or for £11 a bottle. The tempting main list offers good drinking at fair prices throughout, with top-class wines in the upper reaches. SAMPLE DISHES: crab and smoked salmon salad £7; Mediterranean fish stew £8.50; chocaholic's delight £5.50.

Licensee R.J. Milan (St Austell)
Open 11 to 11, Sun 12 to 10.30; bar food and restaurant 12 to 3, 6.30 to 9.30
Details Children welcome   Car park   Wheelchair access (also WC)   Patio   No smoking in restaurant   Occasional live music   Dogs welcome   Delta, MasterCard, Switch, Visa

---

Directions have been included where deemed necessary, but if in doubt about a pub's location – especially if heading to a rural location – it is advisable to phone and check.

▲ Egypt Mill Hotel   NEW ENTRY

Nailsworth GL6 0AE   TEL: (01453) 833449
on A46, 4m S of Stroud

Egypt Mill, by the River Frome, is an institution of some antiquity. The
current building was operating as a cloth mill and dye-house in the seventeenth century, succeeding a fourteenth-century corn mill on the site. The
name might thus allude to corn (biblically, via Joseph and Egyptian granaries),
to seventeenth-century lessee Richard 'Pharaoh' Webb, or to dye effluent
turning the Frome into the 'Red Sea'. The mill became a hotel in the mid-
1980s, though its old identity remains apparent (with some of the mill
machinery and drive shafts preserved and open to view), and the honey-
coloured stone walls have been left exposed. There is a printed menu plus
daily fish specials. Among the latter might be salmon fillet with Thai-style
broth, or hake with mushrooms, tomatoes, prawns, capers and nut-brown
butter; meat dishes might include chicken liver parfait with red onion and
chilli jam, followed by pot-roast lamb with roast vegetables, or confit duck leg
with truffle mash and red wine jus. Lunch menus are a little simpler, featuring
snack dishes like toasted English muffin with scrambled egg and smoked
salmon. Real ales come from local brewery Goff's, and there is a list of around
two dozen good-value wines, with 12 available by the glass. SAMPLE DISHES:
deep-fried spicy crab cakes with sweet chilli dressing £5.25; roast tenderloin of
pork with chorizo and sage butter £13; sticky toffee pudding with pecan sauce
and cream £4.50.

Licensee S.R. Webb (freehouse)
Open 11 to 11, Sun 12 to 10.30; bar food 12 to 2 (2.30 Sun), 6.45 to 9.30; closed evening 25 Dec
Details Children welcome   Car park   Garden and patio   No smoking in dining room   Occasional
live or background music   Guide dogs only   Amex, Delta, Diners, MasterCard, Switch, Visa
Accommodation: 17 rooms, B&B £54.50 to £95

Crooked Billet ♥ ▮ ❧

2 Westbrook End, Newton Longville MK17 0DF   TEL: (01908) 373936
WEBSITE: www.thebillet.co.uk
take left turn off B4146 from Leighton Buzzard towards Milton Keynes

A quiet corner of Newton Longville, an old brickworks village on the edge of
Milton Keynes, is the setting of this thatched old pub with a grandly proportioned lawn full of shrubs and flowers, outdoor tables and a brick-built barbecue. The place is still very much a traditional village pub, with lots of beams,
polished wooden tables and pictures on the walls, although to the left as you
enter you will notice two rooms set aside for eating, one tiled and one
carpeted. This restaurant area is open only in the evenings and Sunday
lunchtimes, when a full-dress menu (not available in the bar) of elaborately
inventive cooking comes into play, offering perhaps pan-fried pigeon breast
with foie gras, confit of pigeon and caramelised onion ravioli, or roasted bream
fillet with crushed potatoes and a balsamic reduction. The bar menu, available

only at lunchtime, produces sandwiches; starters such as game and foie gras terrine with apricot chutney, or penne with wild mushroom cream and Parmesan; and main courses of roast salmon with creamed mash and parsley purée, or Tuscan-style slow-roasted pork loin with a cassoulet of white beans and tomatoes. For dessert there might be chocolate and cappuccino mousse with vanilla jelly. John Gilchrist offers every one of the 300-odd wines by the glass, and a number of reporters have enjoyed a selection chosen by him to accompany their meals. The quality is outstanding, with particularly fine selections from Burgundy and Bordeaux, but prices of these are not for the faint-hearted. Beer drinkers are not neglected, with Old Speckled Hen and Wychwood Hobgoblin on handpump. SAMPLE DISHES: ham hock, white-bean, parsley and truffle oil broth £4.75; smoked haddock and bubble and squeak fishcake with maple-cured bacon, a poached egg and hollandaise £8; fig and almond tart with honey, date and port ice cream £5.50.

Licensees John and Emma Gilchrist (Greene King)
Open 12 to 2.30, 5.30 to 11, Sun 12 to 4, 7 to 10.30; bar food Tue to Sat 12 to 2; restaurant Tue to Sat 7 to 10, Sun 12 to 3; closed first 2 weeks Jan
Details Children welcome in restaurant   Car park   Garden   No smoking in restaurant   Occasional live music   No dogs   Amex, Delta, MasterCard, Switch, Visa

NEWTON-ON-THE-MOOR   Northumberland   map 10

▲ Cook and Barker Inn 🏻 🍇
Newton-on-the-Moor NE65 9JY   TEL: (01665) 575234
¼ m W of A1, in middle of village

Set on a hill in the middle of a village just off the A1, this stone inn has views over fields to the North Sea. Enter the beamed main bar area, which has an old-fashioned decorative style; leading off it are the snug bar, the informal dining area and the smart, spacious restaurant, which operates its own menu. If you are eating in the bar, you can expect traditional fare: start perhaps with broccoli and fennel soup, and follow it with steak and onion pie, bread-crumbed fillet of plaice with tartare sauce, or mixed grill, and finish with toffee pecan pie, or lemon and lime cheesecake. The relaxed atmosphere and friendly and efficient service have been appreciated, as has a decent selection of real ales that includes Timothy Taylor Landlord, Fuller's London Pride, Black Sheep Bitter, and Theakston XB. Half a dozen wines are sold by the glass from a well-presented list of around 50 bottles that covers a good range of flavours under £15 and is spiced up by some classy bottles with hefty price tags. SAMPLE DISHES: avocado, chillied prawns and crab salad £5.25; lamb shank with fine beans and lentils £9; chocolate fudge cake £3.

Licensee P. Farmer (freehouse)
Open 11 to 3, 6 to 11, Sun 12 to 3, 6 to 10.30; bar food and restaurant 12 to 2, 6 to 9
Details Children welcome   Car park   Wheelchair access (not WC)   Garden   No-smoking area in bar   Background music   No dogs   Amex, Delta, MasterCard, Switch, Visa   Accommodation: 19 rooms, B&B £37.50 to £65

The Guide always appreciates hearing about changes of licensee.

▲ Bathurst Arms

North Cerney GL7 7BZ   TEL: (01285) 831281

WATERSIDE

on A435, 4m N of Cirencester

The setting of this long, low, pink-washed stone building is all you could ask of a country pub: it's in lovely Cotswolds countryside with a lawned garden, where picnic tables are set under trees, alongside the fast-flowing River Churn. Inside, the main bar area is what you'd expect from its location, with a flagstone and tiled floor, a hop-adorned beamed ceiling, panelled walls, a lot of pewter, brass and china, and two large stone fireplaces. The laminated menu lists 'lunchtime regulars' of salmon fishcakes with parsley sauce, and burger and chips, alongside starters like deep-fried local goats' cheese, sharp and creamy, well matched by red onion marmalade, and main courses of organic sausages with bubble and squeak and onion gravy, and lamb steak marinated in spicy tomato sauce accompanied by roasted vegetables. This is augmented by a blackboard of daily specials: a salad of smoked duck, orange and walnuts, followed perhaps by pan-fried tuna steak with spinach and basil oil, loin of pork with caramelised pineapple, herb-roasted new potatoes and sage sauce, or vegetable korma, and, to finish, lemon and treacle sponge pudding, or prof-iteroles with chocolate sauce. Hook Norton Best Bitter, Bathurst Brew and Cotswolds Way are on handpump. Care and effort have gone into the compil-ation of the wine list, which makes a discernible attempt to offer a variety of flavours at sensible prices. Ten come by the glass from £2.50. SAMPLE DISHES: Thai beef salad with a ginger, lemongrass and spring onion dressing £5; pan-fried calf's liver with smoked bacon, crushed potatoes and onion gravy £9.50; a selection of British cheeses £4.50.

Licensee James Walker (freehouse)
Open 11 to 3, 6 to 11, Sun 12 to 3, 7 to 10.30; bar food and restaurant 12 to 2, 7 to 9 (9.30 Sat and Sun)
Details Children welcome   Car park   Wheelchair access (not WC)   Garden   Background or live music   Dogs welcome   Delta, Diners, MasterCard, Switch, Visa   Accommodation: 5 rooms, B&B £45 to £70

Magnesia Banks   NEW ENTRY

Camden Street, North Shields NE30 1AH   TEL: (0191) 257 4831

A large Victorian building on the upper slopes of the River Tyne not far above the fishing quay, Magnesia Banks is a real community pub, its sociable atmos-phere and large range of ales and food proving a draw. Furnished in traditional style, it retains the building's old ceilings and mahogany bar, while dark walls are covered in advertisements announcing the pub's vibrant programme of attractions (music, quizzes, culinary theme nights, etc.). Among the further seating areas is one with a cosy log fire, while the recently added conservatory acts as a restaurant (and charges ten per cent more). While various snack menus crank up towards more substantial dishes like steak and ale pie, it's the blackboard of daily specials that offers the most interest, declaring lamb as the house speciality (the pub owns its own flock). Lamb steak, cutlets or perhaps Mexican-style lamb might feature, plus the likes of ribeye steak, mushroom stroganoff, grilled sea bass, or blackened salmon. On tap are Mordue Brewery's Workie Ticket and the Durham Brewery's Magnus, plus up to five guest beers, or choose from 20-odd wines, with six by the glass. SAMPLE DISHES: king prawn bruschetta £3.25; marinated lamb steak £8.50; chocolate and raspberry mousse gâteau £3.25.

Licensee Richard Slade (freehouse)
Open *Mon to Thur 11 to 11.30, Fri and Sat 11 to 12, Sun 12 to 10.30; bar food and restaurant 12 to 9.30*
Details *Children welcome   Car park   Wheelchair access   No-smoking area in restaurant Occasional live or background music   No dogs   Amex, Delta, Diners, MasterCard, Switch, Visa*

NORTON   Shropshire   map 5

▲ Hundred House Hotel ☺ 🍺

Bridgnorth Road, Norton TF11 9EE   TEL: (01952) 730353
WEBSITE: www.hundredhouse.co.uk
on A442, 6m S of Telford

Red-brick, dark-panelled or red-painted walls, beamed ceilings, boarded, tiled or carpeted floors, with, throughout, bunches of dried flowers and herbs are the notable features of the three open-plan rooms at this elegant Georgian hotel, with a separate non-smoking room at the back and a lovely flower-filled garden outside. This is a fine, all-round operation, from the enveloping sense of hospitality that the Phillips family has made its own to the fine quality of food and drink. Notwithstanding the fact that there are ten guest rooms, the place has retained its identity as a true village local too. Phillips Heritage Bitter, which is brewed in-house, must be the star of the show, but there are also Highgate Saddlers Celebrated Best Bitter and Mild. Wines are a pedigree globetrotting collection, led by house wines in four styles from a southern French cooperative available by the glass. The menu is enhanced by daily specials, and chef Stuart Phillips has some good ideas. Starters might be a warm tartlet of goats' cheese with shallots, fennel and tomatoes, or pea, ham and mint soup. Main courses bring on breast of Hereford duck with gooseberries and confit of duck and black pudding, fillet of beef with seared calf's liver with mushroom marmalade, or grilled plaice with sorrel beurre blanc. Crowd-pleasing desserts are of the treacle tart, tiramisù and tarte Tatin variety. SAMPLE DISHES: griddled scallops with sweet pepper coulis, bacon and Jerusalem artichoke sandwich and Caesar salad £8; pan-fried breast of guinea fowl with port and brandy parfait and wild mushroom sauce £17; pear trifle with honeyed mascarpone £5.

Licensee Henry Phillips (freehouse)
Open *11 to 11, Sun 12 to 3, 7 to 10.30; bar food and restaurant 12 to 2.15, 6 to 9.15, Sun 12 to 2.30, 7 to 8.45*
Details *Children welcome   Car park   Wheelchair access (also WC)   Garden   No smoking in restaurant   Occasional background music   No dogs   Delta, MasterCard, Switch, Visa Accommodation: 10 rooms, B&B £69 to £150*

NORTON   Wiltshire   map 2

Vine Tree ❀ ❀   [NEW ENTRY]

Foxley Road, Norton SN16 0JP   TEL: (01666) 837654
village signposted off A429 1½m N of M4 junction 17

The Vine Tree is a very tall white-pebbledash building, dating from the
sixteenth century, with bright green window shutters, in a tiny hamlet
surrounded by flat countryside and close to the M4. Inside, a series of small,
linked open-plan areas are decorated with lots of quirky, cluttery artefacts,
prints hang on walls the colour of tomato purée, and tables are set with fat
candles. On the food front, there is no blackboard of daily specials for the
simple reason that the main printed menu changes every day anyway. The
style is direct and down to earth, and makes a far better impression than some
of the ostensibly fancier menus offered in other establishments. Chicken liver
parfait with onion confit, for example, may sound straightforward, but an
inspector found it an exemplary version, with a creamy texture and intense
and fresh flavour, while the confit was 'gorgeous and not too sweet'. Other
choices have included deep-fried buffalo mozzarella with blueberry and
walnut dressing, and smoked salmon and prawns with sauce gribiche, while
typical among main courses are local venison with piquant sauce and wild rice,
pot-roast partridge with a casserole of white beans, and classic boeuf bourguignonne. Finish perhaps with lemon tart with a creamy filling and accompanied by a seriously fruity raspberry sorbet. A regularly changing line-up of real
ales might feature Fuller's London Pride, Donoghue Fiddler's Elbow and St
Austell Tribute. The wine list is short but covers a good range of styles and
prices and includes 15 wines by the glass. SAMPLE DISHES: smoked eel salad
with   sauce   gribiche   £6.50;   venison   and   juniper   suet-crust   pie   with
chanterelles, roast baby onions and carrots £12; pink champagne and wild
strawberry jelly £5.

Licensees Charles Walker and Tiggi Wood (freehouse)
Open 12 to 3, 6 to 11, Sun 12 to 10.30; bar food Mon to Sat 12 to 2 (2.30 Sat), 6 to 9.30,
Sun 12 to 9.30 (12 to 3, 6.30 to 9.30 winter); closed 25 Dec
Details *Children welcome   Car park   Wheelchair access (not WC)   Garden and patio
No-smoking area   Occasional live or background music   Dogs welcome   Amex, Delta, Diners,
MasterCard, Switch, Visa*

NORTON ST PHILIP   Somerset   map 2

▲ George

High Street, Norton St Philip BA3 6LH   TEL: (01373) 834224
WEBSITE: www.thegeorgeinn-nsp.co.uk
on A366 at junction with B3110, 6m S of Bath

This really must be one of the oldest pubs in Britain, having been licensed
continually for more than 600 years. The building (Grade I listed, of course),
continually added to from the fourteenth century to the seventeenth, is a
magnificently atmospheric blend of mellow stone and half-timbering
arranged round a cobbled central courtyard overlooked by a gallery. Inside

there are two bars, one subterranean with flagstone floors and an arched stone ceiling, the other a grand hall, open to the roof and warmed by an open fire. Wadworth beers and light refreshments are served in both. Diners also have the choice of two rooms, and menus are fairly mainstream. You could start with game terrine, dressed crab, or wood pigeon and bacon salad, and follow that with steak and kidney pudding, stuffed bell peppers, or prosciutto-wrapped salmon fillet. Desserts range from fruit crumble and custard to a brandy-snap basket of caramel ice cream. The wine list extends to 20-odd bins, of which six are served by the glass. SAMPLE DISHES: mushroom and Stilton pepper pot £4.50; pork tenderloin with apple and Calvados £14; pineapple and passion-fruit cheesecake £4.

Licensee D.J. Satchell (Wadworth)
Open 11 to 2.30, 5.30 to 11 (Sat 11 to 11; Sun 12 to 2.30, 7 to 10.30); bar food 12 to 2.30, 7 to 9.30 (Sun 9)
Details Children welcome in dining room   Car park   Wheelchair access (also WC)   Garden No smoking in dining room   Background music   Dogs welcome in bedrooms by arrangement   Amex, Delta, MasterCard, Switch, Visa   Accommodation: 8 rooms, B&B £60 to £110

NOSS MAYO   Devon   map 1

Ship Inn   NEW ENTRY
Noss Mayo PL8 1EW   TEL: (01752) 872387
WEBSITE: www.nossmayo.com
from A379 E of Plymouth, turn S on B3186 and follow Noss Mayo signs

WATERSIDE

This white pub sits on a slope at the head of an inlet – so close to the water that high tide makes the car park inaccessible, and customers use the first-floor entrance at the back of the building. Or moor alongside if the boat is under 10 metres and you've booked ahead. Recent renovation has given the interior a modern, light-wood feel and a nautical theme; there is a log fire and plenty of newspapers for leisurely drinkers of Summerskills Tamar, Princeton Dartmoor, Exmoor Gold, or Thatcher's cider (in summer you can also drink in the view from the terrace beside the inlet). Food, in the bar or first-floor eating areas, spans smart sandwiches (chilli chicken with coriander, say) and traditional and modern dishes. One visitor found tomato and basil soup 'to die for', or try baked ratatouille and mozzarella tartlet, or moules marinière from the River Yealm outside the door. Then perhaps lamb shank with rosemary and garlic mash, or a warm salad of sautéed scallops, followed by warm black cherry and almond tart with clotted cream (unless you prefer chocolate crème brûlée). A neat, varied wine list has been put together with evident enthusiasm and is pitched mostly at the £15 to £20 bracket, with eight cheaper options by the glass at around £2. SAMPLE DISHES: smoked salmon, cream cheese and spinach parcel £6.25; pork and leek sausages with black pudding, fried pota-toes and onions £8; spotted dick with custard £4.25.

Licensee Bruce Brunning (freehouse)
Open 11 to 11, Sun 12 to 10.30; bar food 12 to 9
Details Children welcome in non-bar areas before 7pm   Car park   Wheelchair access (also WC) Patio   No smoking upstairs   No music   Dogs welcome downstairs   Delta, MasterCard, Switch, Visa

NOTTINGHAM   Nottinghamshire   map 5

Victoria Hotel 🍺 | NEW ENTRY |

Dovecote Lane, Beeston, Nottingham NG9 1JG   TEL: (0115) 925 4049
3m SW of Nottingham city centre, off A6005 in Beeston; pub is next to railway station

This unpretentious, popular pub is a converted Victorian railway hotel in a
suburb of Nottingham, just a few miles south-west of the city centre. It has 'a
good vibe', with a friendly, lively clientele, a warming fire, racks of newspapers, and live jazz on Monday nights, and is something of a mecca for real ale
fans. Choices in the ever-changing range are listed on a blackboard, typically
including locally brewed Castle Rock Hemlock Best Bitter, Bateman XB,
Caledonian IPA and Bass, along with guests. The daily-changing menus are
also chalked on a blackboard. They offer a tempting range of dishes in a
modern Mediterranean-influenced style, and plenty of interesting vegetarian
options: spanakopita (baked parcels of filo filled with ricotta and spinach on a
tomato and herb coulis), for example, or Roquefort, pistachio and sun-dried
tomato pâté with basil, served with warm toast and salad. There might also be
Lincolnshire sausages and mash with onion gravy, as well as burritos filled
with spicy chilli con carne, topped with cheese, sour cream and paprika, or a
'robust, wholesome and thoroughly enjoyable' Victoria club sandwich filled
with roast turkey, bacon, tomato, mozzarella and tarragon in freshly baked
Italian bread. Yet another blackboard lists the wines, prices for the concise
selection starting at £9 a bottle, £2.30 a glass. SAMPLE DISHES: vegetarian faggots
and mash £7; lamb souvlakia £9; spotted dick with custard £3.

Licensees Neil Kelso and Graham Smith (freehouse)
Open 11 to 11, Sun 12 to 10.30; bar food and restaurant 12 to 8.45 (7.45 Sun)
Details No children   Car park   Wheelchair access (also WC)   Garden and patio   No smoking in
restaurant   Live music   Dogs welcome in bar only   MasterCard, Switch, Visa

NUNNINGTON   North Yorkshire   map 9

Royal Oak

Church Street, Nunnington YO62 5US   TEL: (01439) 748271
off B1257, 2m N of Hovingham, adjacent to church

The Royal Oak is a quaint old pub in a sprawling rural village of attractive
stone houses, with Nunnington Hall (National Trust) worth visiting. Inside
are bare stone walls, beams and standing timbers, and a collection of horse
brasses, stone jugs and various oddments like ploughshares and copper urns
hanging from the beams. On handpump are Tetley Bitter as well as Theakston
Best and Old Peculier, and seven wines are sold by the glass. The cooking is
built around a mainstay of classic pub dishes, such as breaded scampi, ploughman's, and steak and kidney casserole with a herb dumpling, while on the
blackboard may be wild boar sausages with leek and potato mash, or battered
cod. Chips – golden and crisp on the outside, fluffy within – have been
described as 'excellent', and puddings might run to lemon cheesecake with
summer fruit compote. Interesting rolls – goats' cheese and pesto, or Brie,
tomato and basil – are sold at lunchtime. SAMPLE DISHES: spicy mushrooms

with petit pain £5; liver and bacon casserole £8.50; apple and blackberry crumble £4.

Licensee A.K. Simpson (freehouse)
Open *Tue to Sat 12 to 2.30, 6.30 to 11, Sun 12 to 2.30, 7 to 10.30; bar food and restaurant 12 to 2, 6.30 (7 Sun) to 9*
Details *Children welcome in restaurant   Car park   Wheelchair access (also WC)   Garden No smoking in restaurant   No music   No dogs   MasterCard, Switch, Visa*

OAKWOODHILL   Surrey   map 3

Punch Bowl Inn
Oakwoodhill RH5 5PU   TEL: (01306) 627249
off A29 Dorking to Horsham road, 5m NW of Horsham

Dating in part from the fourteenth century, this attractive, double-fronted, tile-hung pub built in the Wealden style is in prime walking country on the edge of the hamlet. In summer you can sit at tables in the front garden and on the patio. The spacious main bar has lots of character, with its polished slate-flagged floor, huge inglenook with a log fire, scrubbed tables, long benches and old photographs of the pub on the walls. The adjoining dining area is low-ceilinged and carpeted, and the whole place is well maintained. Some of the dishes on the blackboard menu show imaginative variations on traditional themes. Prawn and apple cocktail, or hot mozzarella in filo with spicy red wine syrup may be among starters, for instance, with chicken breast in smoked bacon stuffed with asparagus and a creamy white wine and tarragon sauce, or lemon sole wrapped in smoked salmon with watercress sauce among main courses. Otherwise you might find smoked chicken and celery salad, or pâté with redcurrant sauce, followed by lasagne, grilled lamb cutlets with roasted vegetables, or beer-battered haddock with chips and peas. Vegetarians could go for something like sweet-and-sour vegetable stir-fry with rice, and banoffi pie may be one of the puddings. Badger Dorset Best and Tanglefoot are on draught, and three wines are available by the glass, with the full list approaching 20 bottles. SAMPLE DISHES: warm seafood salad £6; Thai green chicken curry with rice £9; banana crumble £4.

Licensees Phillip and Wendy Nisbet (Hall & Woodhouse)
Open *11 to 11, Sun 12 to 10.30; bar food Mon to Thur 12 to 2.15, 6.30 to 9.30, Fri and Sat 12 to 9.30, Sun 12 to 9*
Details *Children welcome in eating areas   Car park   Wheelchair access (not WC)   Garden and patio   No smoking in restaurant   Occasional live music; jukebox   Dogs welcome   MasterCard, Switch, Visa*

▲ *indicates where a pub offers accommodation. At the end of the entry information is given on the number of rooms available and a price range, indicating the cost of a single room or single occupancy to that for a room with two people sharing.*

OARE Kent   map 3

Shipwright's Arms 🍺

Hollowshore, Oare ME13 7TU   TEL: (01795) 590088   WATERSIDE
from A2 just W of Faversham take exit to Oare, then right towards Davington,
left into Ham Road; follow signs across the marshes

This remote inn (so remote that until recently it generated its own electricity)
is easier to reach by water, being next to a boatyard on a creek, protected from
the sea by a dyke. The alternative is a bumpy, narrow road across marshland
that seems to go on for ever. Whatever your transport, the waterside location
merits the journey, and the small, cottagey building, first licensed in 1738, is
itself full of charm. Its warren-like interior, with low ceilings, beams and
standing timbers, is partitioned into cosy areas around a central brick fireplace.
A row of casks stands behind the tiny bar counter, dispensing fine beers from
the local Goacher's Brewery, among them Gold Star Ale and the house beer,
Special. Just two wines are served by the glass. Food is reasonably priced,
straightforward and hearty, with soup to start – perhaps broccoli and Stilton –
followed by main courses of chilli con carne, smoked haddock and spring
onion fishcakes, and shepherd's pie. Ploughman's, sandwiches and jacket
potatoes are also possibilities, and desserts are of the spotted dick and bread-
and-butter pudding variety. Children will appreciate fish fingers and chips on
their own menu as well as the large garden at the rear. SAMPLE DISHES: leek and
potato soup £3.25; chicken in spicy BBQ sauce with rice £6.50; blackcurrant
cheesecake £3.25.

Licensees Derek and Ruth Cole (freehouse)
Open *summer Mon to Fri 11 to 3, 6 to 11, Sat and Sun 11 to 11; winter Mon to Fri 11 to 3,
6 to 11, Sat 11 to 4, 6 to 11, Sun 12 to 4, 6 to 10.30; bar food Wed to Sun 12 to 2.30, Wed to Sat
7 to 9; closed 1 week Oct; may close early on quiet evenings in winter (phone to check)*
Details *Children welcome in family room   Car park   Wheelchair access (also WC)   Garden
No-smoking area in bar   No music   Dogs welcome on a lead   No cards*

OCKLEY Surrey   map 3

Old School House

Stane Street, Ockley RH5 5TH   TEL: (01306) 627430   FISH
on A29 Bognor Regis road, 8m S of Dorking

An old school bell hanging above the door gives a clue to the original function
of this white-painted pub on the busy A29. Dark beams and cream-painted
walls set the tone in the modest bar, although the main business is eating
rather than drinking. The printed menu majors on fish, ranging from
Arbroath smokies with cheese sauce and jumbo scampi in 'seriously crisp'
tempura batter to black bream fillets on crab and coriander risotto. Blackboard
specials broaden the range: Cajun-spiced salmon on red pepper and cabbage
coleslaw with sautéed potatoes has been cooked to a T. To finish, consider the
dessert board, which ranges from poached pear with orange and Campari
sorbet to steamed orange and ginger pudding. More ambitious dishes are
served in the formal surroundings of Bryce's Seafood Restaurant, where you
can expect things like fillets of lemon sole filled with crab and ginger on

creamed spinach with langoustine sauce. A trio of real ales from Gale's brewery satisfies the beer brigade, and wine drinkers should raise a smile at the sight of 14 house wines by the glass at a uniformly reasonable price of £2.95. The list continues with a well-chosen selection of 20 or so more serious bottles from around the world. SAMPLE DISHES: minced lamb kofta £5; seafood lasagne £8.50; meringue nest with wild berry compote and red berry coulis £4.

Licensee Bill Bryce (freehouse)
Open 11 to 3, 6 to 11; bar food and restaurant 12 to 2.30, 6.30 to 9.30; closed Sun evening Nov, Jan and Feb
Details Children welcome   Car park   Wheelchair access (also WC)   Patio   No smoking in restaurant   Occasional background music   Dogs welcome exc in restaurant   Delta, MasterCard, Switch, Visa

ODELL   Bedfordshire   map 6

Bell

Horsefair Lane, Odell MK43 7AU   TEL: (01234) 720254   **WATERSIDE**
off A6, 8m NW of Bedford

This 300-year-old building of honey-coloured stone peers over a triangle of green from under low-browed thatch. At the back the large garden (complete with aviary) runs down to the meandering Great Ouse. Interconnecting rooms ramble around a large bar, and there's a big family room at the back. Log fires and low, beamed ceilings create cosiness in winter, but in summer the garden is the focus. Wherever you choose to sit, this is a Greene King house, so its IPA, Abbot Ale and Ruddles County are on handpump, plus guest beers that change quarterly. Ten wines are served by the glass. Daily specials, chalked up over the bar, are largely Anglophile eating – they include the likes of steak and kidney (and Guinness) pie, liver and bacon, or fish, prawn and leek Mornay – although there may be Indian chicken breast as well. Otherwise, there's a regular selection of deep-fried fish and chicken dishes, along with such standards as sausage and chips. Among the regularly changing desserts might be chocolate gâteau or hot sponge puddings. SAMPLE DISHES: lasagne and chips £4; smoked bacon steaks in Cumberland sauce £8.25; banana split £3.25.

Licensees Derek and Doreen Scott (Greene King)
Open 11 to 2.30, 6 to 11, Sun 12 to 2.30, 7 to 10.30; bar food (exc Sun evening) 12 to 2.30, 7 to 9.30; closed evenings 25 and 26 Dec
Details Children welcome in family room and bar eating area   Car park   Garden and patio   Background music   No dogs   Delta, MasterCard, Switch, Visa

OFFHAM   East Sussex   map 3

Blacksmith's Arms

London Road, Offham BN7 3QD   TEL: (01273) 472971
off A275, 2m N of Lewes

This red-brick building has a large cartwheel on the façade and a verandah sheltering the pavement between it and the road. A note on the pub's menu sensibly advises drivers to turn left on leaving the car park, rather than turning right, across the fast-moving traffic. Inside are two bar areas, separated by a canopied bar counter, with plenty of tables for eating at. And food is the main thing. There are ploughman's, jacket potatoes, and sausage, egg and chips (except on Friday or Saturday nights), but ambition and elaboration mark the main menu (and blackboard specials). You might start with a winter vegetable soup with Stilton-topped croûtons, or smoked salmon with peach and orange salsa, lime dressing and toasted naan. Similar contrasts of flavour, texture and colour appear in mains like breast of guinea fowl in a mulled apricot and plum pot roast, or a generous and nicely timed tuna steak that came with a compote made from fresh pineapple, a 'sweet, spicy and especially creamy' pink Creole sauce, and half a dozen different vegetables. Finish perhaps with apple and cinnamon brûlée, or praline parfait on a sultana flapjack with lemon cream. Real ales are from Harveys of Lewes just down the road, and the wine list offers good flavours at very fair prices, with three house wines by the glass. SAMPLE DISHES: pheasant and guinea fowl pâté £5.50; chicken, mushroom and leek pie £8.25; citrus brioche bread-and-butter pudding with marmalade sauce £4.

Licensee Jean Large (freehouse)
Open *Mon to Sat 11 to 3, 6.30 to 11, Sun 11 to 3; bar food and restaurant 12 to 1.30, 7 to 9; closed 25 and 26 Dec*
Details *No children   Car park   Wheelchair access (also WC)   Garden   No music   Dogs by arrangement in 1 area of bar   Delta, MasterCard, Switch, Visa*

OLDBURY-ON-SEVERN   South Gloucestershire   map 2

Anchor Inn
Church Road, Oldbury-on-Severn BS35 1QA   TEL: (01454) 413331
off B4061, 2m NW of Thornbury

Just beyond a bridge over a small stream, the Anchor is an old inn built of rough stone, with colourful window boxes and hanging baskets and a cheery sign. In the small bar area you will find conventional pub décor, including bare stone walls, while the no-smoking restaurant is more reminiscent of a tea room, with chintzy curtains and fresh flowers on the tables. One printed menu serves both areas – a longish list of mainly traditional dishes such as faggots with onion gravy and roast potatoes, or chicken breast with tarragon, white wine and cream sauce. Steak baguettes and home-baked ham with wholemeal bread and butter are among lighter options, and there is a range of salads based around things like chicken and ham pie, or smoked mackerel fillet. Beers are a respectable selection featuring Butcombe Bitter, Theakston Best Bitter and Old Peculier, while a short wine list includes 12 by the glass. SAMPLE DISHES: sliced smoked chicken with orange and mustard dressing £5.50; moussaka with garlic bread £6.25; raspberry crème brûlée £3.50.

Licensees Michael J. Dowdeswell and Alex de la Torre (freehouse)
Open *Mon to Fri 11.30 to 2.30, 6.30 to 11, Sat 11.30 to 11, Sun 12 to 10.30; bar food and restaurant 11.30 to 2, 6.30 to 9.30, Sun 12 to 3.30, 6.30 to 9.30; closed evenings 25 and 26 Dec*
Details *Children welcome in restaurant   Car park   Wheelchair access (also WC)   Garden No smoking in restaurant   No music   Dogs welcome exc in restaurant   Delta, MasterCard, Switch, Visa*

Star Inn 🍇

Church Street, Old Heathfield TN21 9AH   TEL: (01435) 863570
WEBSITE: www.thebestpubsinsussex.co.uk
off B2203 or B2096, just S of Heathfield

This is a sister establishment to the Horse and Groom a couple of miles away at
Rushlake Green (see entry), with which it shares wine list and licensee Mike
Chappell. It sits close to the church, in a cul-de-sac off the road through the
village: partly creeper-covered and looking over its car park and a nicely kept
garden with tables and sunshades behind. The inside seems more ancient than
the outside (the building began as a fifteenth-century hall house, but was much
adapted later). The bar has low ceilings, dark, worm-eaten beams and plain,
warm-coloured décor; there's a wooden dado, wooden tables and wheel-back
chairs. The lengthy menu (listed on blackboards) uses decent raw materials.
Smoked salmon, white crabmeat and dill pâté makes a nice starter, or there's
seafood chowder, or Caesar salad. Mains meanwhile run from locally caught
fish and chips to a slow-cooked half-shoulder of lamb; one reporter's duck
breast marinated in treacle and Chinese spices then roast and served with a pink
peppercorn sauce on egg noodles proved 'very nicely timed and spiced'.
Desserts could take in strawberry squidgy meringue, or bread-and-butter
pudding and custard. To wash it all down, there's Harveys Sussex Best Bitter,
Shepherd Neame Spitfire and Hop Back Summer Lightning, and six tasty
wines are served by the glass. The wine list offers 30 or so enticing bottles, with
plenty under £15, but if money is no object then a magnum of Château
Margaux from the 'proprietor's private cellar' might suit. The price? A mere
£800. SAMPLE DISHES: mussels provençale £6.50; stuffed suprême of chicken
with balsamic syrup and new potatoes £12; raspberry meringue roulade £5.

Licensees Mike Chappell and Fiona Airey (freehouse)
Open 11.30 to 3, 5.30 to 11, Sun 12 to 3, 7 to 10.30; bar food and restaurant 12 to 2.15 (2.30
Sat and Sun), 7 to 9.30 (9 Sun)
Details Children welcome   Car park   Garden   Background music   Dogs welcome in bar   Delta,
MasterCard, Switch, Visa

▲ Crown & Sandys

Ombersley WR9 0EW   TEL: (01905) 620252
off A449 Worcester to Kidderminster road, 4m W of Droitwich

This Dutch-gabled, white-painted inn stands out among the ancient timber-
framed buildings in the pretty village of Ombersley. Inside, two old bars have
been converted into a single, airy long one, although flagstone flooring, beams
and a good mixture of sturdy furnishings remain, from old settles and pews to
traditional tables and chairs. The dining areas are like modern bistros in style.
Most of the well-assorted clientele come to eat, but drinkers can enjoy a pint
of up to six draught ales, perhaps including Greene King Abbot Ale, Marston's
Pedigree or Sam Powell Original Bitter from the Wood Brewery. The

majority of the 50-odd bottles on the wine list are under £20; 10 are served by the glass. The lunchtime menu lists sandwiches and baguettes with imaginative fillings, while main dishes include steak and kidney braised with red wine and mushrooms, honey-roast ham with egg and chips, and grilled fillet of salmon with a creamy dill and prawn sauce. The emphasis of the lengthy main menu is on fish and seafood, from a starter of pan-fried medallions of tuna with turmeric potatoes, cherry tomatoes, green beans and sun-dried tomato crème fraîche, to whatever fish was available at market: perhaps halibut steak, grilled, poached, or pan-fried, with lemon and thyme butter. Meat dishes are not overlooked, taking in lamb shank on bubble and squeak with a red wine and rosemary jus, or sautéed medallions of pork with a Stilton, apricot and sage sauce. Vegetarians could plump for something like linguine with wild mushrooms, asparagus and spinach in a creamy tarragon sauce, and among puddings may be treacle tart. SAMPLE DISHES: chicken liver and brandy pâté £5; pan-fried monkfish tail with mixed herb butter £14; raspberry and vanilla sponge with Chantilly cream £4.25.

Licensee Richard Everton (freehouse)
Open Mon to Fri 11.30 to 3.30, 5 to 11, Sat 11.30 to 11, Sun 12 to 10.30; bar food and restaurant Mon to Sat 11.30 to 2.30, 6 to 10, Sun 12 to 9
Details Children welcome   Car park   Wheelchair access (also WC)   Garden and patio
No smoking in restaurant   Occasional background music   No dogs   Delta, MasterCard, Switch, Visa
Accommodation: 3 rooms, B&B £55 to £65

Kings Arms

Main Road, Ombersley WR9 0EW   TEL: (01905) 620142
WEBSITE: www.kingsarmsombersley.co.uk

This place was already over 200 years old in 1651, when Charles II looked in after losing the Battle of Worcester. The black and white, timbered façade has the slightly crumpled distinction of such age, and oozes charm; the interior (dark oak beams and wooden floors, of course) is a series of interconnecting rooms with three open fires and several cosy corners. Beers on offer are Marston's Pedigree, Banks's Bitter, Morrells Old Varsity, plus perhaps guest ales like Badger Tanglefoot or Gale's HSB. Frequently changing large printed menus are supplemented by blackboard specials (notably fish). Some starters/snacks, such as pan-fried halloumi with lime and caper dressing, or roast vegetable couscous with harissa dressing, are skittishly fashionable, contrasting with down-to-earth toad-in-the-hole or field mushrooms on toast. Main courses tend to fly a Union flag, with oxtail braised in Guinness, beef Wellington, boiled ham with broad beans, or cauliflower cheese – although there's paella too. Desserts might be chocolate orange bread-and-butter pudding for winter, or a gooseberry crème fraîche tart for summer. A dozen wines come by the glass, from a list of about 30. SAMPLE DISHES: crab pâté with watercress £5.75; seared breast of duck with sour cherry sauce £12.50; summer pudding £4.25.

Licensees D. Pendry and J. Willmott (freehouse)
Open 11 to 3, 5.30 to 11, Sun 12 to 10.30; bar food 12 to 2.15, 6 to 10, Sun 12 to 9.30; closed 25 Dec
Details *Children welcome   Car park   Wheelchair access (also WC)   Garden and patio*
No-smoking area in bar   Occasional live music   No dogs   Delta, Diners, MasterCard, Switch, Visa

OSMOTHERLEY   North Yorkshire   map 9

Golden Lion 🏵 ｜NEW ENTRY｜
6 West End, Osmotherley DL6 3AA   TEL: (01609) 883526

The pretty village of Osmotherley is the starting point for the Lyke Wake Walk, so you can expect to encounter plenty of people in walking gear mingling with locals at this old stone-built pub overlooking the village green. The main bar is smart but relaxed, with candles on the plain wooden tables, while upstairs is a slightly posher dining room – it even has paper table covers. Menus cater for a wide range of tastes, with 20 or more choices per course. Typical among starters are mussels in wine and cream with shallots, spaghetti with clams, spicy pork ribs, and avocado and bacon salad. Classic pub cooking is what to expect from main courses – burgers, chicken Kiev, or calf's liver with onions, mash and peas – plus a few more unusual ideas like chargrilled poussin with rosemary and garlic. Real ales are Timothy Taylor Landlord, Hambleton Bitter and John Smith's Bitter, and the list of around thirty wines opens with four house selections from £12 a bottle, also available by the glass. SAMPLE DISHES: grilled sardines in olive oil £5.25; coq au vin with mashed potato and peas £10; Middle Eastern orange cake with marmalade cream £3.75.

Licensee C.F. Connelly (freehouse)
Open Mon to Fri 12 to 4, 6 to 11, Sat and Sun 12 to 11; bar food and restaurant 12 to 3.30, 6 to 10.30; closed 25 Dec
Details *Children welcome   Patio   No-smoking area in bar, no smoking in restaurant   Background music   Dogs welcome on a lead   Delta, MasterCard, Switch, Visa*

OVINGTON   Hampshire   map 2

Bush Inn   ｜NEW ENTRY｜
Ovington SO24 0RE   TEL: (01962) 732764
off A31, just W of Alresford

The secret is out: here is a hidden gem of a pub, tucked away down tree-lined country lanes in an unspoilt location by the River Itchen. The mood is relaxed and unpretentious: a series of 'dark and atmospheric' small rooms around a central bar, lit by gas lamps, decorated with stuffed animals, fishing tackle and copper kettles, and warmed by a roaring log fire in winter. And if these features aren't enough of a draw, there is a blackboard menu of appealing modern pub food. Kick off perhaps with Thai-spiced crab cakes with rocket salad and chilli and peanut dressing, then follow with spinach and wild mush-room lasagne, or beef and ale pie – or stick to something simple like roast beef baguette with salad and fries. It all made a favourable impression on an inspector, not least for the stylish presentation of dishes. This goes equally for desserts, such as rum and banana crumble with banana ice cream. Well-kept beers are from the Wadworth brewery's range, including their seasonal brews, and occasionally supplemented by guest ales. The short wine list throws up a couple of welcome surprises in William Fèvre's Chablis and Water Wheel Shiraz from Australia, both of which are available by the glass (along with four others). SAMPLE DISHES: smoked Loch Fyne trout mousse £6.25; pan-fried duck breast with chargrilled marinated vegetables and honey, cider and rosemary sauce £14.50; hot spiced pineapple £4.25.

Licensees Nick and Cath Young (Wadworth)
Open 11 to 3, 6 to 11, Sun 12 to 3, 7 to 10.30; bar food all week 12 to 2, Mon to Sat 7 to 9 (10 weekends summer)
Details Children welcome in family room   Car park   Wheelchair access (also WC)   Garden   No smoking in 2 rooms   No music   Dogs welcome on a lead   Delta, MasterCard, Switch, Visa

OXSPRING   South Yorkshire   map 9

Waggon and Horses   NEW ENTRY

Sheffield Road, Oxspring S36 8YQ   TEL: (01226) 763259
off A629, 1½m SE of Penistone

'Definitely worth knowing about if you are in the area,' was our inspector's verdict on this eighteenth-century stone inn (once a farmhouse) with a wagon wheel beside the door. The Rafters bar is the one to aim for if you want a real old-fashioned pub atmosphere, a game of pool or darts, and a quiet pint – fine Yorkshire ales Black Sheep and Timothy Taylor Landlord are served. The main bar (dark pink carpet, cream-painted stone walls hung with ornamental brass trays and horse brasses) is more orientated towards eating, and a good-value menu of simple, traditional home cooking is offered throughout the day. Start perhaps with chicken liver pâté, or try 'crêpes Alfredo' filled with minced chicken and spinach and covered with a creamy Parmesan sauce. Main courses typically include steak and vegetable pie, deep-fried catch of the day with mushy peas and chips, and chicken rogan josh with rice and garlic bread. Lighter options include jacket potatoes, baguettes and salads. There's a children's menu (on Tuesday nights kids eat it for free!) and prix fixe meals for early evenings and Sunday lunch. All the wines on the short list come in under £12 and four are served by the glass. SAMPLE DISHES: Yorkshire pudding with gravy £3.25; grilled salmon fillet with spinach and béarnaise sauce £9.50; ribeye steak au poivre £10.50.

Licensee Tony Brewis (freehouse)
Open 11 to 11, Sun 12 to 10.30; bar food and restaurant 11 to 9, Sun 12 to 7
Details Children welcome . Car park   Wheelchair access (also WC)   Garden   No-smoking area in bar, no smoking in dining room   Occasional live or background music   Guide dogs only   MasterCard, Switch, Visa

---

Entries are written on the basis of readers' reports, backed up by independent, anonymous inspections. Factual details at the bottom of entries are from questionnaires which the Guide sends to all establishments that feature in the book.

PAXFORD Gloucestershire map 5

▲ Churchill Arms ✿

Paxford GL55 6XH TEL: (01386) 594000
WEBSITE: www.thechurchillarms.com
2m E of Chipping Campden

Paxford is a hamlet of old Cotswold stone and dry-stone walls, with the
Churchill Arms at its centre near the church. The L-shaped interior is open
plan, with bare floorboards, painted panelling: very much a pub, and used as
such by the locals. This is the setting for some sophisticated cooking, the
dishes written on daily-changing blackboards hung on a stone pillar. The
nearest the style gets to traditional pub fare are chicken, ham and leek pie and
sticky toffee pudding, and even fish and chips come with beetroot tartare.
Typical of starters are potato and horseradish soup, and mille-feuille of veal
sweetbreads with creamed mushrooms, Madeira and thyme. Mains could be
'beautifully cooked, exquisitely flavoured' calf's liver with olive oil potatoes
and courgettes, skate wing stuffed with fennel, beetroot and vanilla with
chervil and tomato butter, or blade of beef with sauce soubise. Hook Norton
Best Bitter and two changing guest ales are on handpump, while the wine list
offers around twenty-five bottles, with eight by the glass. SAMPLE DISHES: salt-
and-pepper squid with tomato, gherkins and parsley aïoli £6.75; pan-fried
lambs' kidneys wrapped in bacon with saffron sauce and Parmesan risotto £8;
polenta and almond cake with morello cherries £4.

Licensee Leo Brooke-Little (freehouse)
Open 11.30 to 3, 6 to 11; bar food 12 to 2, 7 to 9
Details Children welcome Wheelchair access (also WC) Garden and patio No music Guide
dogs only Delta, MasterCard, Switch, Visa Accommodation: 4 rooms, B&B £40 to £70

PEMBRIDGE Herefordshire map 5

▲ New Inn

Market Square, Pembridge HR6 9DZ TEL: (01544) 388427
on A44, between Kington and Leominster, 6m E of Kington

Dating in part from the early fourteenth century, this huge, ramshackle, black
and white half-timbered building justifiably claims to be one of the oldest
pubs in the country. The interior is divided into three separate areas – a
convivial main bar, a no-smoking lounge and the restaurant – but the décor is
uniform throughout: walls of exposed stone or painted terracotta, red
patterned carpets, 'chocolate-box' floral watercolours, and subdued lighting
from wall lamps and candles on the tables. The cooking is chiefly traditional in
nature: chicken liver pâté, deep-fried Camembert, Lancashire hotpot, and fish
and chips are all familiar points of reference on the unchanging printed menu.
A reporter was satisfied with a well-cooked sirloin steak with Stilton, port and
cream sauce and its accompaniment of deep-fried potato wedges. Kingdom
Bitter from the Dunn Plowman brewery in Kington represents local interests
among beers; the range also includes Fuller's London Pride and Timothy
Taylor Landlord. There's plenty of inexpensive wine, including four by the

glass. SAMPLE DISHES: avocado and crab salad £6; beef and vegetable casserole with horseradish dumplings £7.75; chocolate and cherry cheesecake £3.

Licensee Jane Elizabeth Melvin (freehouse)
Open 11 to 3 (2.30 winter), 6 to 11; bar food and restaurant 12 to 2, 6.30 to 9; closed first week Feb
Details Children welcome in eating areas   Car park   Patio   No smoking in restaurant   Occasional live music   No dogs   Delta, MasterCard, Switch, Visa   Accommodation: 6 rooms, B&B £20 to £40

PERRY WOOD   Kent   map 3

Rose & Crown 🍺   NEW ENTRY
Perry Wood, nr Selling ME13 9RY   TEL: (01227) 752214
from A251 at Sheldwich, take road for Selling, continue through village and take right turn signposted Perry Wood

A short walk through the woods from this sprawling sixteenth-century inn leads to fine panoramic views of the surrounding countryside. It is also a great way to build up an appetite before returning for a refreshing pint and some decent home cooking. Inside, it looks suitably ancient, with exposed-brick walls, low beamed ceiling and inglenook fireplaces, and a busy cottagey décor featuring corn dollies, ornamental jugs and china animals. One menu serves throughout, mostly straightforward pub grub with a few more unusual ideas. Expect the likes of Moroccan lamb with couscous, sausages and mash, baked stuffed trout and, on Sunday, roast beef with Yorkshire pudding. Try to save room for dessert: a proper old-fashioned baked cheesecake was a big hit at inspection. Real ale fans will be in their element here: four first-class beers are on offer at a time, all served in peak condition. Goacher's Mild, Harveys Sussex Best Bitter and Adnams Southwold are the regulars, joined by a guest ale, perhaps from the Cottage brewery. Wine drinkers are offered four by the glass. On fine days you can eat and drink in the delightful garden, which has a good children's play area and a bat-and-trap pitch. SAMPLE DISHES: steak and mushroom pudding £8; salmon in ginger and pepper £8; raspberry torte £3.

Licensees Richard and Jocelyn Prebble (freehouse)
Open 11 to 3, 6.30 to 11, Sun 11.45 to 3, 7 to 10.30; bar food all week 12 to 2, Mon to Sat 7 to 9.30, restaurant Sat 7 to 9.30, Sun 12 to 2; closed evenings 25 and 26 Dec, 1 Jan
Details Children welcome   Car park   Garden and patio   No smoking in restaurant   Background music   Dogs welcome on a lead   Delta, MasterCard, Switch, Visa

PETER TAVY   Devon   map 1

Peter Tavy Inn 🍷 🍺
Peter Tavy PL19 9NN   TEL: (01822) 810348
off A386, 3m NE of Tavistock

Peter Tavy is a pretty Dartmoor village, and its inn is a long, low whitewashed building that has dark-painted windows, a tiled roof and a relaxing garden for summer enjoyment. Inside are flagged floors, low beams, a homely atmosphere and friendly, helpful service. Real ales are Princetown Jail Ale, Summerskills Tamar, and Fuller's London Pride, plus such guest beers as

Scattor Rock Devonian or Sutton's Dartmoor Pride. Blackboards serve as menus of a cuisine that treats pub food as just a springboard. At lunchtime you can have baguettes or jacket potatoes with a variety of fillings (roast salmon and minted cucumber, for one) or anything from garlic mussels to butternut squash stuffed with sweet-and-sour vegetables, via ham, egg and chips, chicken balti, game casserole with Stilton dumpling, and plaice bonne femme. The evenings bring Brie and bacon tart, or smoked salmon and scallop terrine, then pheasant suprême in lemon, thyme and bacon sauce, or beef medallions with wild mushrooms – or maybe parcels of salmon wrapped in plaice and spinach. Finish with tangy citrus tart with Grand Marnier oranges, or toffee-coated profiteroles. The concise wine list begins with French house wines at £8 (just one still wine costs over £20), and eight come by the glass. SAMPLE DISHES: leek and potato soup £3.25; roast duck breast with cinnamon plum sauce £13; chocolate truffle torte £3.50.

Licensees Graeme and Karen Sim (freehouse)
Open 12 to 2.30 (3 Fri and Sat), 6.30 to 11 (6 to 11 Fri and Sat, 6.30 to10.30 Sun); bar food 12 to 2, 7 to 9; closed 25 and 31 Dec
Details Children welcome in family room   Car park   Wheelchair access (not WC)   Garden and patio   No smoking in dining room   Background music   Dogs welcome   Delta, MasterCard, Switch, Visa

---

PHILLEIGH   Cornwall   map 1

Roseland Inn

Philleigh TR2 5NB   TEL: (01872) 580254
take Philleigh turning off A3078 5m N of St Mawes

Even though it's down a narrow country lane, it can get crowded here, and booking could be a good idea. Look for a white-pebbledash building with a dark slate roof and lots of cars trying to park. It's a friendly place, with two bars and a dining room, very low beamed ceilings and open fires here and there in the winter. Bar snacks such as ploughman's, sandwiches and what the house describes as 'a proper Cornish pasty', as well as a short choice for children, supplement the main menu. This could offer such starters as Cornish smoked haddock topped with Yarg, or a Cornish goats' cheese and basil tart with sun-blush tomatoes; mains might include fillets of bass on sweet potato mash, Philleigh lamb shank with mustard mash, or risotto and mozzarella gâteau with a spinach and cream sauce. There are also organic and Cornish set menus. Daily specials are chalked on a blackboard, as are desserts, which might include chocolate brioche bread pudding. Sharp's Doom Bar Bitter and Cornish Coaster are on handpump, and there's Callestick cider from Penhallow. Six wines are served by the glass. SAMPLE DISHES: smoked local seafood platter £7.50; chicken, leek and tarragon suet pudding £10.50; treacle tart £4.50.

Licensees Colin and Jacquie Phillips (Pubmaster)
Open 11 to 3, 5.30 to 11 (11 to 11 summer); bar food and restaurant 12 to 2, 6 to 9
Details Children welcome   Car park   Wheelchair access (also WC)   Garden   No smoking in dining room   Occasional live music   Dogs welcome   Delta, MasterCard, Switch, Visa

▲ White Swan ❦

Market Place, Pickering YO18 7AA   TEL: (01751) 472288
WEBSITE: www.white-swan.co.uk

Though it is set in the centre of a bustling market town, this sixteenth-century coaching inn is 'blissfully quiet and civilised'. One menu is served in both the relaxed and informal bar, warmed by a log fire in winter, and the smart restaurant; and the choice is generous. Starters range from soup of the day with home-made bread, to foie gras with black pudding, brioche and Sauternes sauce, while main courses might take in dishes as diverse as 'real fish and chips with posh mushy peas' (as the menu describes it), or roast salted belly pork with apple sauce, while desserts run to bread-and-butter pudding with apricot glaze, or cinnamon-roasted fruits with mascarpone. At lunchtime a selection of sandwiches is also available, and Sunday lunch offers – among other things – a selection of traditional roasts. Beers come from Yorkshire breweries: Best and Special from Black Sheep in Masham, and Goldfield from Hambleton of Thirsk, for example. After eight house wines by the glass, the wine list splits into two parts. The first roams the world, finding plenty of good drinking around £20; the second is a specialist and more expensive range of clarets from St-Emilion that reflects the owner's passion for this region. SAMPLE DISHES: potted Whitby crab and lobster with melba toast £6; roast partridge with game chips and bread sauce £16; glazed bramble and apple tart with fresh vanilla custard £5.

Licensee Victor Buchanan (freehouse)
Open 11 to 11, Sun 12 to 10.30; bar food and restaurant 12 to 2, 7 to 9
Details Children welcome exc in 1 bar   Car park   Wheelchair access (also WC)   Garden and patio   No smoking in 1 bar and dining room   No music   Dogs welcome exc in dining room   Amex, Delta, MasterCard, Switch, Visa   Accommodation: 12 rooms, B&B £70 to £150

▲ Nag's Head ❦

Pickhill YO7 4JG   TEL: (01845) 567391
WEBSITE: www.nagsheadpickhill.co.uk
off A1, 5m SE of Leeming

Although much extended, the 200-year-old Nag's Head has the atmosphere of a traditional, well-kept country inn. The tiny village that it stands in the centre of is mentioned in the Domesday Book, and the whole area is steeped in history, with plenty to look at and to visit, and – as the name might indicate – racecourses aplenty in the vicinity. Summer meals may be taken under a handsome verandah at the front, while, inside, diners may head for the smartly appointed dining room, with its library theme, or the comfortable dark-panelled bar, with its green-velour bench seating. Drinkers of real ales will find Hambleton Bitter and Nightmare, John Smith's and Black Sheep Best Bitter and Special Ale on tap, while the range of speciality spirits encompasses a fine collection of malts, cognacs and Armagnacs. Some highly inventive cooking is going on here too. Try prawn and avocado Caesar salad to start with, or perhaps assorted dim sum with sweet chilli and sour dips, before going on to chicken breast stuffed with Camembert and sage wrapped in Parma ham, or pan-fried duck breast marinated in lime, ginger and honey accompanied by crisp-roast leg. More traditional tastes are catered for with broccoli and Stilton soup, deep-fried scampi with chips, and beef, venison and rabbit pie in a crusty topping. Caramelised banana tart with custard, or Yorkshire curd tart with raspberry coulis may be among puddings. Four appetising wines of the month, all available by the glass for £2.95, reflect the high level of interest that has gone into choosing the main list. Around 60 wines cover the world, with plenty to please those on a budget. Enthusiasts will be gratified to see top-class bottles like Cloudy Bay or Montes Alpha Syrah at reasonable prices and wines that need a bit of maturity sold in older vintages. SAMPLE DISHES: crab salad £5; poached king scallops on a bed of spinach with cheese-glazed potato £15; steamed honey sponge with lemon and lime custard sauce £4.

Licensees Raymond and Edward Boynton (freehouse)
Open 11 to 11; bar food and restaurant 12 to 2, 6 to 9.30
Details Children welcome in eating area of bar   Car park   Wheelchair access (also WC)   Garden and patio   No smoking in restaurant   Background music   Dogs welcome   MasterCard, Switch, Visa
Accommodation: 16 rooms, B&B £40 to £90

PILLEY   Hampshire   map 2

Fleur de Lys
Pilley Street, Pilley SO41 5QB   TEL: (01590) 672158
off A337, 1m NW of Lymington

A lengthy roll call of past landlords dating back to 1498 dominates the stone-flagged entrance to this ancient inn, although the thatched building actually dates back to 1096 – making it a strong candidate for the title 'the oldest pub in the New Forest'. The place comprises three interconnecting rooms, with a hotchpotch of bric-à-brac giving it true rustic style. The printed menu deals in steaks, roasts, seasonal game from a local dealer ('medieval casserole' is a stew of pheasant and partridge with bacon, capers, hazelnuts and garlic), and there are a few options for vegetarians; also look for the appetisingly named 'smelly chips' served as a starter. Thursday night is 'Spice Night', and Tuesday is devoted to seafood: rich, creamy fish soup and pan-fried fillet of cod on a garlic croûton with mushroom sauce have been honestly produced. At lunchtime you can also get 'sarnies and stixs' with various fillings. Locally brewed Ringwood is kept in good order, along with Gale's HSB and Fuller's London Pride; the pub also has a globetrotting list of two dozen reasonably priced wines, with 12 house selections from £2.50 a glass, £9.95 a bottle. SAMPLE DISHES: potato skins with cheese and bacon £2.50; half a shoulder of rosemary lamb with minted gravy £11; pear and almond flan £3.75.

Licensees Neil and Lolly Rogers (Enterprise Inns)
Open 11 to 3, 6 to 11, Sun 12 to 3, 7 to 10.30; bar food 12 to 2, 6.30 (7.30 Sun) to 9.30 (9 Sun); closed evenings 25 and 26 Dec
Details Children welcome in family room   Car park   Wheelchair access (not WC)   Garden and patio   No-smoking area in bar   Occasional live or background music   Dogs welcome on a lead Delta, MasterCard, Switch, Visa

PLUCKLEY   Kent   **map 3**

▲ Dering Arms

Station Road, Pluckley TN27 0RR   TEL: (01233) 840371   **FISH**
WEBSITE: www.deringarms.com
off B2077, close to Pluckley railway station

Although it looks much older, the Dering Arms, with its elaborate Dutch gables, was built in the 1840s as a hunting lodge serving the Dering Estate. Unusually, it is an exact replica, on a smaller scale, of the manor house it once served. Enter the central entrance, itself recessed between two protruding wings, and the interior is as imposing as the exterior, although the bar areas are small and traditional: bare wood everywhere, old chairs with wonky leather seats, a haphazard collection of wall decorations, including a stuffed fish, and dim lighting. Starters of avocado grilled with Stilton, pan-fried king prawns tossed in garlic and lemon butter, and chicken livers sautéed with onions, bacon and mushrooms, all of which can also be served with vegetables as main courses, are what to expect on the bar menu. The same starters are served in the candlelit restaurant, where fish is the focus: main courses of perhaps lobster thermidor, or pan-fried fillet of turbot with a 'nicely balanced' prawn and lemon beurre noisette. Roast rack of lamb with red onion sauce and Puy lentils might be there for meat eaters, with something indulgent like rich chestnut, chocolate and brandy cake, served with apricot compote, among desserts. Dering Ale is brewed exclusively for the pub by Goacher's of Maidstone. An extensive wine list is supplemented by a blackboard giving four reds, four whites and champagne by glass or bottle, starting at £9.95. SAMPLE DISHES: provençale fish soup £4.50; tuna steak pan-fried with garlic and lemon butter £13; oranges in caramel with Grand Marnier £4.50.

Licensee James Buss (freehouse)
Open 11.30 to 3.30, 6 to 11, Sun 12 to 3, 7 to 10.30; bar food and restaurant 12 to 2, 7 to 10; closed 26 to 28 Dec
Details Children welcome   Car park   Garden   No music   Dogs welcome   Amex, Delta, Diners, MasterCard, Switch, Visa   Accommodation: 3 rooms, B&B £30 to £42.50

PORTHLEVEN   Cornwall   **map 1**

Ship Inn

Porthleven TR13 9JS   TEL: (01326) 564204   **WATERSIDE**
off B3304, 2m SW of Helston, on W side of harbour

This pub is perched on rocks beside the harbour, with the main bar filling the width of the building (the family room – a fine granite building that was once a smithy – has its own entrance). Service is friendly and efficient. Specials boards change daily and include at least six different fresh fish dishes. Main-menu fish dishes include an all-dancing shellfish platter, a smoked fish platter, fish pie, and local crab claws. Meat eaters can masticate beef or gammon steaks, BBQ chicken, and a bowl of home-made hot chilli beef. Snacks take in a wide range of toasties, crusties, jacket potatoes, ploughman's and salads, while 'Kiddies Meals' at £3 include local bacon, sausages or burgers served with waffles, bread and butter and beans or peas. Baileys cheesecake features among desserts. On draught are Courage Best Bitter, Greene King Abbot Ale, Sharp's Doom Bar Bitter and Eden Ale, plus Addlestone's cloudy cider. As for wine, there are seven reds and seven whites from £7.75, with five by the glass. SAMPLE DISHES: moules marinière £5; crab thermidor £11; hot chocolate fudge cake £4.

Licensee Colin Oakden (freehouse)
Open 11.30 to 3, 6.30 to 11 (summer 11.30 to 11), Sun 12 to 10.30; bar food 12 to 2, 7 to 9; closed 25 Dec
Details Children welcome in family room   Garden   Background music   No smoking in family room Background music   Dogs welcome   Amex, Delta, MasterCard, Switch, Visa

PORTH-Y-WAEN   Shropshire   map 5

Lime Kiln   NEW ENTRY
Porth-y-waen SY10 8LX   TEL: (01691) 831550
on A495, 1m W of Llynclys crossroads with A483

Having made their reputation as restaurateurs in the bright lights of Brighton, Ian and Jane Whyte decided to head north to this out-of-the-way pub in the Shropshire countryside. Their long, narrow garden comes into its own for barbecues and as a 'jeu de boules' strip, while the interior is 'bare bones, uncluttered', with red floor tiles and nicotine-coloured walls. The Whytes aim to please all-comers all the time, which means anything from lunchtime baguettes, cheesy garlic bread and Tex-Mex chilli in a tortilla basket to more upmarket offerings such as pan-seared halloumi cheese on hot-and-sour beet-root, and half a crisply roast duckling with a cherry and brandy sauce, as well as a neatly constructed dish of grilled sea bass fillets with chunky pineapple and lime salsa and crisp, deep-fried noodles. Similarly, desserts span everything from rhubarb crumble to fresh figs filled with caramelised crème fraîche. The minimal wine list is pasted on to bottles on the tables: house Alexis Lichine is £7.75; alternatively, opt for a pint of Fuller's London Pride or Timothy Taylor Landlord. SAMPLE DISHES: chicken liver pâté with spiced apple chutney £3.75; pan-roast Cajun-spiced tuna steak with sweet-and-sour cucumber £9; fruit meringue roulade £3.75.

Licensees Jane and Ian Whyte (freehouse)
Open Tue to Fri 12 to 3, 5.30 to 11, Sat 12 to 11, Sun 12 to 10.30; bar food Tue to Fri 12 to 2, 6 to 9, Sat 12 to 3, 5.30 to 9, Sun 12 to 4
Details Children welcome   Car park   Wheelchair access (not WC)   Garden   No-smoking area Background music   No dogs   Delta, MasterCard, Switch, Visa

POULTON   Gloucestershire   map 2

Falcon Inn ✿ ✿   NEW ENTRY
London Road, Poulton GL7 5HN   TEL: (01285) 850844
on A417, between Cirencester and Fairford

A traditional old white-painted stone pub, the Falcon Inn looks set to put Poulton on the gastronomic map. It's a small and unpretentious place, with low ceilings, beams, a large fireplace guarded by a pair of stone falcons, and a long bar with stools for drinkers; as the Guide went to press refurbishment work was planned which should double the number of tables. The food keeps things simple, with 'uncluttered', 'freshly prepared' dishes, sound presentation (on huge white plates) and utilises top-class raw ingredients (perhaps fresh seafood from New Wave in Fairford and rare-breed meats from Chesterton Farm in Cirencester). The monthly-changing menu, which charts a modern European course, might feature confit of duck leg with orange and watercress salad to start, and mains of pan-fried sea bass with asparagus risotto, or navarin of mutton with spring vegetables. Puddings, again 'very simple, very fresh', might include a clear-flavoured, wobbly coconut cream with mango, lime and pink grapefruit, or rhubarb trifle. The lunch menu consists of sandwiches and main courses of grilled gammon with a fried egg and chips, or wild mushroom risotto with crispy pancetta and Parmesan. Hook Norton Best Bitter and Gem Bitter or Spa Extra, from Bath Ales, are on handpump, while the wine list of 27 bottles complements the food, with each bottle intelligently and often wittily described. All six house selections are available by the glass from £2.50. SAMPLE DISHES: twice-baked cheese soufflé with spicy pear chutney £6; fillet of halibut with mashed potato and wild mushroom sauce £16; chocolate crème brûlée with spiced oranges £5.

Licensees Robin Couling and Jeremy Lockley (freehouse)
Open Mon 7 to 11, Tue to Sat 11 to 3, 7 to 11, Sun 12 to 3, 7 to 10.30; bar food and restaurant Tue to Sun 12 to 2.30, Tue to Sat 7 to 9
Details Children welcome in eating areas   Car park   Wheelchair access (also WC)   Patio
No smoking in restaurant   Background music   Dogs welcome in bar   Delta, MasterCard, Switch, Visa

PRESTON BAGOT   Warwickshire   **map 5**

Crabmill   NEW ENTRY

Preston Bagot B95 5DR   TEL: (01926) 843342
on A4189, about 1½m E of Henley-in-Arden

The sprawling brick building was once a cider mill (a crab is a type of winch used in the cider-making process) and sympathetic refurbishment has made the most of original features – notably the ancient worm-eaten beams – while updating the décor with food- and drink-themed cartoons on the walls, plants in little metal buckets on the tables and assorted furnishings including leather sofas for drinkers to relax on. Food is 'sharp and modern', taking influences from everywhere and anywhere, but mostly Italy. Options on the printed menu include mixed antipasti, and squid with a sesame-spiced crust and sweet chilli dressing, followed by main courses ranging from smoked haddock and salmon fishcake with parsley sauce to Parmesan-crusted chicken breast stuffed with garlic, herbs and bacon. Daily specials feature some more unusual dishes like whole pigeon roasted in ale with sweet potato mash and a roast pear, while desserts are typically along the lines of steamed chocolate and orange sponge with vanilla ice cream and rum balls. Six house wines at £11.50 a bottle (also available by the glass) open a short but varied list, and real ales include Wadworth 6X and Old Speckled Hen. Paul Hales is also the licensee at the Orange Tree in Chadwick End (see entry). SAMPLE DISHES: seared duck livers with smoked bacon and balsamic-dressed leaves £6; swordfish with herb and lemon polenta and oven-dried tomatoes £13; mango semi-freddo £4.75.

Licensee Paul Hales (freehouse)
Open 11 to 11; bar food and restaurant 12 to 2.30 (12.30 to 3.30 Sun), 6.30 to 9.30
Details *Children welcome   Car park   Wheelchair access (not WC)   Garden and patio*
No smoking in restaurant   Background music   Dogs welcome   Amex, MasterCard, Switch, Visa

PRESTON BISSETT   Buckinghamshire   map 5

White Hart
Pound Lane, Preston Bissett MK18 4LX   TEL: (01280) 847969
*off A421, 4m SW of Buckingham; in village, look for turning marked 'The Square', which leads
into Pound Lane*

Picnic tables to the rear of this thatched, black and white seventeenth-century
pub are an added attraction in summer, when there's also an outdoor bar.
Inside, the compact bar is in the middle, with a tiny dining area at the back and
two even tinier bar areas at the front: taller people will need to duck, as the
ceilings are really low. Given that space is at a premium, diners are advised to
book, although the lack of space creates a jolly, friendly atmosphere. The
range of food on offer changes daily. Bar snacks of vegetable spring rolls with
sweet chilli dip, BLT, or burger are joined at lunchtimes by the likes of Thai-
style mussels, a sandwich platter, and mozzarella, strawberry and bresaola
salad and also what the menu describes as 'hearty fare': perhaps 'excellent,
fresh' beer-battered cod with chips and tartare sauce, chicken, avocado and
Cheddar melt, or crispy duck and bacon salad with raspberry vinaigrette and
parsnip chips. Dinner could start with something traditional like duck and
orange pâté, or prawn cocktail, and go on to sirloin steak with a creamy mushroom sauce, or something more unusual, like whole trout with a prawn and
asparagus mousse and king prawns, or baked herb-crumbed chicken breast
with sun-dried tomato and bacon sauce. Puddings end on a high note: a trio of
'excellent-quality' home-made ice creams with hot toffee sauce, or warm
chocolate tart with raspberry coulis and a matching sorbet. Hook Norton Best
Bitter and Fuller's London Pride, along with two guests, are on draught, and
around ten wines are sold by the glass. SAMPLE DISHES: marinated chicken
skewers with peanut sauce £4; breast of Gressingham duck with a raspberry
and red wine jus £10; lemon tart £3.50.

Licensee Richard Arnott (freehouse)
Open *12 to 11; bar food and restaurant Mon to Fri 12 to 2, 6 to 9, Sat and Sun 12 to 9; closed
Mon winter*
Details *Children welcome in restaurant   Car park   Wheelchair access (also WC)   Garden and
patio   No smoking in restaurant   Live or background music   Dogs welcome   MasterCard, Switch,*

---

*After the main section of the Guide is the 'Round-up' section listing additional
pubs where food may not be the main focus but which are well worth a visit for,
perhaps, their inviting ambience, fine beers, a stunning setting, special history or
other attribute. Reports on these entries are most welcome.*

Polecat Inn

170 Wycombe Road, Prestwood HP16 0HJ   TEL: (01494) 862253
on A4128 Great Missenden to High Wycombe road, 2m W of Great Missenden

This yellow-painted inn with an extensive garden behind stands along a busy road lined with tidy, rather nice houses amidst lots of greenery. Pass through the entrance, which has its own little pitched roof, and the first impression is that this is very much a pub devoted to eating. There are tables all over the place, with a choice of printed and blackboard menus to look at. A degree of ambition runs through daily specials such as sautéed venison strips with wild mushroom and whisky sauce, or suprême of chicken filled with basil mousse-line and served on pepper coulis. The main printed menu extends choice further to, for example, starters of Arbroath smokie parcels, or house pâté served with toast and red onion marmalade, followed by monkfish, pancetta and rosemary baked in filo pastry, or beef Wellington. Home-made pies include a venison and rabbit version, and for vegetarians a mushroom and leek one baked in potato pastry. For pudding there might be sherry trifle or chilled hazelnut soufflé with fudge sauce. Lunchers after a light bite are well served too, with a good choice of sandwiches, ploughman's and jacket potatoes. Lovers of real ales will be pleased to find Flowers IPA, Marston's Pedigree, and Wadworth 6X among those on offer, and there is a fair selection of wines by the glass. SAMPLE DISHES: filo tartlet of smoked chicken, roast vegetables and mozzarella £4.75; magret of duck with redcurrant and juniper sauce £11; meringues with cream and caramel sauce £4.

Licensee John Gamble (freehouse)
Open 11.30 to 3, 6 to 11, Sun 12 to 3; bar food 12 to 2, 6.30 to 9; closed evening 24 Dec, all day 25 and 26 Dec, evening 31 Dec, all day 1 Jan
Details Children welcome in bar eating area   Car park   Wheelchair access (also WC)   Garden No smoking in dining room   Background music   Dogs welcome   No cards

Bell ✿🍸

The Square, Ramsbury SN8 2PE   TEL: (01672) 520230
off A4192, 6m E of Marlborough

The whitewashed exterior gives the Bell a distinctive look among the red-brick and flint buildings of the village where an ancient oak once stood (a 20-foot-high tree has replaced the huge rotted stump). The interior is comfortable and modern, with walls hung with monochrome prints of local scenes, some old beams, a wood-burning stove and jute flooring. Although there is a separate, opulently furnished restaurant area, food can also be ordered at the bar, the tone being pleasingly casual throughout. Stylish cutlery, crisp napery and large wine glasses suggest that gastronomy is taken seriously, and so it proves. The main dinner menu might offer an appetiser such as grilled sardines with garlic butter, or an interesting soup – perhaps chicken and mushroom – before such main courses as grilled plaice with parsley cream sauce, fillet of beef with a wild mushroom and red wine jus, or roasted vegetables with Brie and a chilli and soy dressing. If a cheese selection to finish doesn't appeal, the dessert menu might entice you with chocolate and brandy mousse, praline parfait, or caramel crème brûlée. A trio of real ales changes weekly and might well include something from Wadworth, the West Berkshire Brewery or Butts Brewery. The short, upbeat wine list includes six wines by the glass for around £3. SAMPLE DISHES: pan-fried tiger prawns with sweet chilli sauce £7; breast of Barbary duck with orange sauce £16; white chocolate and mango torte £5.

Licensee Stephen Bedford (freehouse)
Open 12 to 3, 6 to 11; bar food and restaurant Tue to Sun 12 to 2, Tue to Sat 7 to 9
Details Children welcome   Car park   Wheelchair access (also WC)   Garden   No smoking in restaurant   Occasional live or background music   Dogs welcome in bar   Amex, Delta, MasterCard, Switch, Visa

---

RAMSDEN   Oxfordshire   **map 5**

▲ Royal Oak 🍺

Ramsden OX7 3AU   TEL: (01993) 868213
take B4022 from Witney, turn right just before Hailey and follow road to village

---

Dating from the seventeenth century, this Cotswold-stone coaching inn is in the centre of the village opposite the church and war memorial. It is a smallish place that has the requisite stone walls, exposed beams and open fires within, plus one or two idiosyncratic touches such as a two-foot-high carved bear. Hook Norton Old Hooky, West Berkshire Good Old Boy, Adnams Broadside and Butts Barbus Barbus lead a great range of real ales, conferring on the place a richly deserved reputation for good beer. There's also Dunkerton's cider, and a wine list that makes some canny selections in Western Europe and the southern hemisphere and offers around a dozen by the glass. Bar food such as steamed steak and mushroom suet pudding, crab and smoked salmon fish-cakes, and steaks are joined at lunchtimes by ploughman's and such dishes as pork and sage sausage with mash and thick onion gravy. This is supplemented by a more ambitious restaurant menu (also served in the bar). Roast red-leg partridge with caramelised apples, garlic potatoes and Calvados sauce, Italian meatballs with spaghetti, and fillet of salmon in a sauce of pink peppercorns, horseradish and whisky on colcannon indicate the broad range of the approach. Finish with one of the desserts listed on a blackboard, perhaps hot chocolate fudge cake. Sympathetic and welcoming staff work to a high standard. SAMPLE DISHES: crispy smoked duck in a Chinese pancake with oyster sauce £5.50; haunch of venison with garlic potatoes and an orange and honey sauce £13.50; steamed treacle sponge pudding and custard £4.

Licensee Jonathan Oldham (freehouse)
Open 11.30 to 3, 6.30 to 11, Sun 12 to 3, 7 to 10.30; bar food and restaurant 11.30 to 2, 7 to 10.30; closed 25 and 26 Dec
Details Children welcome in restaurant   Car park   Wheelchair access (also WC)   Garden and patio   No smoking in restaurant   No music   Dogs welcome   Delta, MasterCard, Switch, Visa
Accommodation: 4 rooms, B&B £35 to £60

RAMSGATE   Kent   map 3

Royal Harbour Brewhouse 🍺 [NEW ENTRY]
98 Harbour Parade, Ramsgate CT11 8LP   TEL: (01843) 594758   **BREW PUB**
WEBSITE: www.ramsgatebrewhouse.com

On the seafront, overlooking the marina, the Royal Harbour Brewhouse looks
and feels more Continental street café than English pub, with its terracotta
walls, a wood-block floor and steel-framed furniture. And in summer the
frontage opens up completely, and tables and chairs are placed on the pavement outside. However, as the name suggests, its attractions include some
top-notch real ales brewed on the premises (the brewery is open to view at the
rear of the main bar): Gadds Nos 3 and 7 (pale ale and bitter) and Dogbolter
winter porter. On top of that, there is a superb list of 80 different Belgian beers
– some draught, some bottled – including names like Leffe, Chimay, Orval
and Kasteel. And there is also a short wine list, of which four are available by
the glass. Another speciality is the home-baked pastries, perhaps iced apple
turnovers, or Danish-style pastries filled with cherry compote. There is also a
short menu of straightforward home cooking: filled baguettes, moules
marinière, shepherd's pie and baked potatoes with various toppings. SAMPLE
DISHES: vegetable soup with wholemeal baguette £2.50; steak with mushrooms £6.50; pastries 70p each.

Licensees Andy Barrett and Eddie Gadd (freehouse)
Open Mon to Thur 10 to 12, Fri and Sat 10 to 1, Sun 12 to 12 (10 to 12 summer); bar food 12 to
7, 7 to 11
Details Children welcome in bar eating area   Wheelchair access (also WC)   Patio   No smoking in
dining room   Occasional live music   Dogs welcome   Amex, Delta, Diners, MasterCard, Switch, Visa

RAMSGILL   North Yorkshire   map 8

▲ Yorke Arms 🎭🎭 🍇
Ramsgill HG3 5RL   TEL: (01423) 755243
WEBSITE: www.yorke-arms.co.uk
take Low Wath road from Pateley Bridge, then 4m to Ramsgill

The Yorke Arms is an impressive creeper-covered building, dating from the
eighteenth century, in a remote village in Nidderdale, near the head of the
Gouthwaite Reservoir, a bird sanctuary. Though it looks rather grand from
the outside, the atmosphere is not at all snooty, and the unspoilt interior is a
warren of charming rooms, with polished flagstone floors, plenty of low oak
beams and open fires. The restaurant at the Yorke Arms is not only good by
the standards of country inns but has become one of the best restaurants in
England since it was taken over by Gerald and Frances Atkins in 1997. Frances
Atkins's cooking is straightforward and unpretentious but also inventive and
highly accomplished: a game sausage with red onion marmalade and potato
and cauliflower salad, for example, might be followed by blanquette of monkfish with dauphinois potatoes, smoked salmon and celery, or fillet of beef with
foie gras, sauce poivrade and landaise potatoes, while dessert options have
included apple and apricot parfait with passion fruit and blueberries. Only the
restaurant menu is served in the evening, but at lunchtime the bar menu

might offer pumpkin soup, a steak, mushroom and tomato sandwich, and such dishes as gratin of scallops, or tuna Caesar salad. Black Sheep Special travels the short distance from the brewery in Masham to keep beer drinkers happy, and there's also Theakston Best Bitter. The 300-strong wine list concentrates on France, with outstanding selections from Bordeaux and Burgundy that will make fascinating reading for those with deep pockets and a passion for fine wine. It's a rather shorter browse with a budget of £20, but there is plenty from the rest of the world that won't break the bank. The eight house wines come in between £13.25 and £15 a bottle and are all available by the glass alongside a further eight from the main list. SAMPLE DISHES: fillet of salt-cod with scallops and citrus salad £7.50; loin of lamb in a parsley crust with Madeira sauce £17.25; strawberry pannacotta with biscotti £5.50.

Licensees Gerald and Frances Atkins (freehouse)
Open 11 to 3, 6 to 11, Sun 12 to 3, 6 to 10.30; bar food 12 to 1.45; restaurant all week 12 to 1.45, Mon to Sat (and residents Sun) 7 to 8.45; closed last week Nov, last week Jan
Details Children welcome in eating area of bar and snug   Car park   Wheelchair access (not WC)   Garden   No smoking in restaurant   Background music   Dogs welcome in bar   Amex, Delta, Diners, MasterCard, Switch, Visa   Accommodation: 14 rooms, D,B&B £95 to £175

REDE   **Suffolk**   map 6

Plough

Rede IP29 4BE   TEL: (01284) 789208
off A143 Bury St Edmunds to Haverhill road

In a quiet village away from main roads, tucked away under trees behind a grassy area, the Plough is a sixteenth-century cottage-type pub with a half-thatched and half-tiled roof. Inside, the separate bar and restaurant areas are characterised by beams, one bearing the legend 'duck or grouse', floors of old red tiles, wood, or red carpets and an open fireplace with a wood-burning stove. Greene King ales are on draught, and a reasonable selection of wines is kept behind the bar with small descriptive labels attached to their necks; around half a dozen are served by the glass. The same menus, combining international dishes with the more traditional, are available wherever you choose to eat. Typical starters might be squid piri-piri, or wild boar pâté, with perhaps bobotie, chilli beef hotpot with garlic bread and salad, kleftiko, or calf's liver on onion mash among main courses. To finish, try bread pudding with whisky butter, or tangerine charlotte. SAMPLE DISHES: tortellini of brown shrimps £6; rabbit in tarragon sauce with mash £10; warm chocolate tart £4.

Licensees Brian and Joyce Desborough (Greene King)
Open 11 to 3, 6.30 to 11, Sun 12 to 3, 7 to 10.30; bar food and restaurant (exc Sun evenings) 12 to 2, 6.30 to 9
Details Children welcome   Car park   Wheelchair access (not WC)   Garden and patio
No smoking in restaurant   Background music   No dogs   Amex, Diners, MasterCard, Switch, Visa

---

Prices of dishes quoted in an entry are based on information supplied by the pub, rounded up to the nearest 25 pence. These prices may have changed since publication and are meant only as a guide.

▲ Peacock Inn

Church Corner, Main Street, Redmile NG13 0GA   TEL: (01949) 842554
S of A52, 6m W of Grantham

Redmile, which sits just a couple of miles from Belvoir Castle, beside the old Grantham Canal, boasts a rather fine church and – in the middle, with tables on its forecourt – this stone-built pub. Within, refurbishment in 2003 has created a new lounge area, and the whole interior has been given a face-lift. Lunchers in search of bar snacks will find sandwiches, burgers and hot baquettes, while the à la carte restaurant menu is available throughout the pub for lunch and dinner. The cooking style combines fashion and tradition to offer, say, deep-fried cheeses with salad and a plum jam, as well as soup of the day with cheese and onion bread. Main courses similarly might range from confit of duck with braised cabbage, crispy bacon and a five-spice jus, to rump steak with chips.You might not get as far as the sticky toffee pudding or lemon torte. Flowers IPA, Timothy Taylor Landlord and Marston's Pedigree are the regular offerings for real ale drinkers, and the wines include those from both Old and New Worlds, with six by the glass. SAMPLE DISHES: cherry tomato tarte Tatin £4.75; escalope of salmon on crushed new potatoes with capers and asparagus £13; double chocolate parfait with vanilla sauce £4.75.

Licensee Stephen Hughes (freehouse)
Open 11 to 11, Sun 12 to 10.30; bar food and restaurant 12 to 2 (3 Sun), 7 to 9
Details Children welcome   Car park   Wheelchair access (also WC)   Garden and patio
No smoking in dining room   Occasional live or background music   Dogs welcome   Amex, Delta,
Diners, MasterCard, Switch, Visa   Accommodation: 9 rooms, B&B £55 to £80

White Swan   NEW ENTRY

25–26 Old Palace Lane, Richmond TW9 1PG   TEL: (020) 8940 0959

The White Swan is only a couple of oars' lengths from the Thames, and, for that matter, the site of the Palace of Richmond, the last vestige of which, the gatehouse, is close by. Sympathetic to its location, the exterior is painted nautical blue and white, with the words 'bar and restaurant' on a sign outside. Stripped floorboards and stonework, a roaring fire and a convivial atmosphere provide welcome appeal. Tables, plus pew-like seating, are tightly packed, and there's a conservatory dining area out back. Sundays see the traditional full-on roast treatment; otherwise start with smoked salmon and granary bread, followed by wild mushroom ravioli with herbed rice, and finish with an 'awesome' banoffi pie with cream. Fuller's London Pride and Old Speckled Hen are on draught, and, for wine drinkers, there are around 25 bottles to choose from, with about half a dozen by the glass. SAMPLE DISHES: Thai crab cakes with lemongrass, coriander, lime and sweet chilli sauce £6.50; chicken breast baked with chorizo and vine tomatoes £12; elderflower sorbet £4.

Licensee Ron Gibbs (freehouse)
Open 11 to 11.30, Sun 12 to 10.30; bar food and restaurant all week 12 to 3, Mon to Sat
6.30 to 10
Details Children welcome   Garden   No smoking in restaurant   Background music   Dogs welcome
exc in restaurant   Delta, MasterCard, Switch, Visa

RIPPONDEN   West Yorkshire   map 8

Old Bridge Inn 🍺 ❀
Priest Lane, Ripponden HX6 4DF   TEL: (01422) 822595
off A58, 6m S of Halifax

From the middle of Ripponden, take the road to Elland, and after a hundred
yards you find the church, this whitewashed inn and the old packhorse bridge
over the River Ryburn cheek by jowl. Inside, coal fires blaze in winter, and the
three split-level rooms (separated by a couple of steps) have oak beams and
oak panelling, while restrained ornamentation avoids the impression that the
owners have just been to a house-clearance sale. Handpumped ales include a
range from Timothy Taylor and Black Sheep Bitter, plus a guest from, say,
Moorhouses or Burton Bridge, besides which there's a range of imported
beers in bottle, plus over twenty single malts. From blackboards you might
choose smoked duck parfait with plum and orange chutney to start with, or a
salmon and dill fishcake with mango and lime dip; a fisherman's pie (haddock,
salmon and vegetables in a creamy sauce under a topping of mash) or a ragù of
hare could follow. Finish with blackcurrant and Cassis meringue, or oatmeal
parkin and ginger sauce. A largely New World wine list stays mostly under £20
and offers 12 by the glass. SAMPLE DISHES: home-made soup with a crusty roll
£3; lamb, aubergine and lentil curry with rice and raita £6.25; rhubarb and
strawberry crumble £3.

Licensee Tim Eaton Walker (freehouse)
Open Mon to Fri 12 to 3, 5.30 to 11, Sat 12 to 11, Sun 12 to 10.30; bar food all week 12 to 2,
Mon to Fri 6 to 9.30
Details Children welcome in bar eating area   Car park   Wheelchair access (not WC)   Patio
No music   No dogs   Delta, MasterCard, Switch, Visa

ROCKBEARE   Devon   map 1

Jack in the Green ❀
London Road, Rockbeare EX5 2EE   TEL: (01404) 822240
WEBSITE: www.jackinthegreen.uk.com
on A30, 3m NE of Exeter

Handily, for those who like unusual forms of transport, the Jack in the Green
is designated as an Exeter Balloons Meeting and Dispersal point. If you are
arriving by more conventional means, note that the pub is on the *old* A30, not
the new road that bypasses the village. Outwardly, this is a plain white
pebbledash building, while the interior décor majors in pubby paraphernalia –
horse brasses, copper pans and hunting prints – and mix-and-match furniture,
including dark blue chesterfield-style sofas by the large red-brick hearth.
Separate menus serve the bar and restaurant, but you can eat from either

wherever you sit. Bar meals, listed on a blackboard, are generally the simpler option, typically including braised faggots with onion marmalade and olive oil mash, or smoked haddock risotto with chive oil and garlic bread. The restaurant menu (fixed price for two or three courses) is more ambitious. Among dishes to receive favourable reports have been 'moist and very fresh' grilled fillets of red mullet with provençale vegetables, and 'very tasty' grilled rump steak garnished with crisp celeriac wafers and served on celeriac mash with a horseradish and whole-grain mustard sauce, which impressed for its fine ingredients and careful cooking. Desserts are the same in the bar and the restaurant: perhaps raspberry and vanilla crème brûlée, or warm rice pudding with fruit compote. Real ale drinkers will be happy with the choice of Otter Ale, Branscombe Vale Bitter and Cotleigh Tawny, while those who prefer wine are well served by a serious list approaching 100 bottles. Plenty are under £15, including eight house selections by the glass or bottle, but there are also some high-priced oddities, such as mature vintages from California. SAMPLE DISHES: curried parsnip and apple soup £3.75; salmon fishcakes with lemon butter sauce £9.25; treacle tart with clotted cream £3.75.

Licensee Paul Parnell (freehouse)
Open 11 to 3, 5.30 to 11, Sun 12 to 10.30; bar food and restaurant Mon to Sat 12 to 2, 6 to 9.30, Sun 12 to 9.30; closed 25 Dec to 3 Jan
Details Children welcome in bar eating area   Car park   Wheelchair access (also WC)   Patio
No-smoking area, no smoking in restaurant   No music   No dogs   MasterCard, Switch, Visa

ROCKBOURNE   Hampshire   map 2

Rose & Thistle

Rockbourne SP6 3NL   TEL: (01725) 518236
WEBSITE: www.roseandthistle.co.uk
off B3078, 3m NW of Fordingbridge

This 'charming, welcoming, friendly and cosy old pub' dates from the sixteenth century and fits in well in this idyllic picture-postcard village of thatched cottages with a stream running through its centre. Its style is somewhat 'upmarket' but with 'bags of informality and pub character', with flagstones, beams, a welcoming fire and a buzzing atmosphere in the bar. The menu in the separate restaurant, with its huge inglenook, tends towards classic ideas such as tomato, orange and basil soup, braised lamb shank, and steak and kidney pie, with steamed syrup pudding to finish. A blackboard lists fish specials, ranging from fish pie with a crumble topping to scampi in tomato and vermouth sauce. The restaurant menu can also be ordered in the bar, which has its own menu of simpler snacky dishes like bacon and mushrooms on toast, Welsh rarebit, and scrambled eggs with smoked salmon and prawns. The cooking shows an admirable level of skill, as in a reporter's good-quality cod fillet with a lemon and black pepper crust, a 'fine, subtle' lemon sauce and a side dish of well-cooked vegetables. Real ales include some prestigious names, such as Fuller's London Pride, Young's Bitter and representatives from the nearby Hop Back brewery. As well as the house wine, the 'Proprietor's Personal Selection' of 11 bottles, at £10.95, are also sold by the glass. Twenty more bottles, mostly French, add a bit of depth to the selection and four are available in halves. SAMPLE DISHES: warm goats' cheese and bacon salad £5; medallions of pork fillet with wild mushroom and Marsala sauce £11; apple and almond crème brûlée £4.25.

Licensee Tim Norfolk (freehouse)
Open 11 to 3, 6 to 11, Sun 12 to 3, 7 to 10.30; bar food and restaurant (exc Sun evening winter) 12 to 2.30, 7 to 9.30
Details Children welcome Car park Wheelchair access (not WC) Garden and patio
No smoking in restaurant No music Dogs welcome exc in restaurant Delta, MasterCard, Switch, Visa

ROMALDKIRK Co Durham   map 10

▲ Rose and Crown 🍸 🍇
Romaldkirk DL12 9EB TEL: (01833) 650213
WEBSITE: www.rose-and-crown.co.uk
on B6277, 6m NW of Barnard Castle

Built in 1733, the Rose and Crown faces one of Romaldkirk's many village greens. Inside, a door in the characterful wood-panelled hallway leads into the bar. An enormous old stone fireplace takes up much of one wall, its heavy charred wooden mantel supporting various knick-knacks, including a stuffed grouse. A grandfather clock ticks away in one corner, and the walls are filled with gin-traps, animal heads, brasses and a range of old photographs. Separate regularly changing menus are offered for lunch and supper, the main difference being that the lunch version also includes baps – smoked chicken with apple and watercress mayonnaise, for instance – and ploughman's. Both offer a long list of starters and main courses, with much of interest: smoked haddock soufflé with parsley cream sauce, or pork rillettes with cranberry and orange relish and toast, followed by deep-fried salmon fishcakes with spinach and chive sauce, or lamb's liver and bacon with black pudding mash and shallot gravy. Finish with pannacotta with stewed apricots, or sherry trifle with toasted almonds. The oak-panelled restaurant operates a fixed-price four-course dinner menu and is also open for Sunday lunch. Beers come from Black Sheep and Theakston. The 10 wines available by the glass (£2.95 to £4.95) are listed on the back of the menu, and they make an excellent flavour-filled selection on their own. The separate wine list adds a further 50-odd arranged by grape variety. SAMPLE DISHES: home-made corned beef with red cabbage £4; grilled sea bass with tomato and fennel broth £11.75; banana and toffee tart £3.50.

Licensees Christopher and Alison Davy (freehouse)
Open 11.30 to 3, 5.30 to 11, Sun 12 to 3, 7 to 10.30; bar food 12 to 1.30, 6.30 to 9.30; restaurant Mon to Sat 7.30 to 9, Sun 12 to 1.30; closed 24 to 26 Dec
Details Children welcome Car park Wheelchair access (also WC) Garden No smoking in restaurant No music Dogs welcome exc in eating areas MasterCard, Switch, Visa
Accommodation: 12 rooms, B&B £70 to £110

Report forms are at the back of the book; write a letter if you prefer; or email your pub report to whichpubguide@which.net.

ROMSEY   Hampshire   map 2

Three Tuns 🏵   NEW ENTRY
58 Middlebridge Street, Romsey SO51 8HL   TEL: (01794) 512639

Among a row of old terraced cottages, the black and white façade of the Three
Tuns shines out like a culinary beacon. Joining the new breed of contemporary gastro-pubs, this new kid on the block has real pedigree, not least in the
presence of chef Billy Reid. A sympathetic, contemporary makeover has revi-
talised the building without loss of character: a flagstone floor, plenty of dark
beams and timbers, wooden furniture, and a roaring log fire create a traditional atmosphere, with modern touches found in its polished light-wood bar
counter, a large vase of flowers and recessed spotlighting. The dining room,
off to one side, has a relaxed and informal feeling. The modern brasserie-style
menu offers light, appealing, well-balanced, well-presented dishes with clear
and restrained flavours: perhaps 'fathom-deep' fish soup with salmon-stuffed
won tons, or pork rillettes, followed by duck confit with rissole potatoes and a
dressing of haricots blancs, or roasted Scottish salmon with a red wine and
shallot jus, and puddings of crème brûlée with mango sorbet, or cherry
Bakewell tart with Armagnac ice cream. The thirty-five-bin wine list (with
four by the glass) befits the food, while handpumped ales are Ringwood Light
Ale and Gale's GB and HSB. SAMPLE DISHES: risotto of pickled shiitake mushrooms and Parmesan £6; fillet of cod with roasted carrots, spinach and chive
cream £11; dried figs poached with star anise and cinnamon with vanilla ice
cream £5.

Licensee Nick Geaney (Enterprise Inns)
Open 11.30 to 11; bar food Mon to Sat 12 to 2.30, restaurant Mon to Sat 12 to 2.30, 6.30 to
9.30 (10 Sat), Sun 12 to 3
Details Children welcome   Car park   Wheelchair access (not WC)   Garden   No smoking in
restaurant   Background music   Dogs welcome in bar only   Amex, Delta, MasterCard, Switch, Visa

ROSEDALE ABBEY   North Yorkshire   map 9

▲ White Horse Farm Inn
Rosedale Abbey YO18 8SE   TEL: (01751) 417239
WEBSITE: www.whitehorsefarmhotel.co.uk
on A170, turn right signposted Wrelton and Rosedale, 3m NW of Pickering

The White Horse is a large, solid-looking hotel on a hillside just above the
village of Rosedale Abbey. Thanks to its elevated position, it enjoys wonderful
panoramic views across a broad valley, and behind it the road climbs steeply
up the spectacular Rosedale Chimney Bank – this is prime walking territory.
Inside, the bar has an old-fashioned look, with dark wood furniture, exposed-
stone walls and black iron chandelier-style light fittings. The bar menu likewise takes a traditional tack: prawn cocktail and garlic baguette are among the
handful of starters, while main courses offer plenty of choice, including deep-
fried Whitby scampi, lasagne, Cajun chicken sizzler, chilli con carne, and a 20-
ounce mixed grill. The separate restaurant has its own menu of things like
spicy chicken kebabs or moules marinière to start, and grilled halibut steak
with parsley sauce or rack of lamb on minted mash with rosemary and red

wine jus to follow. Beers are from Black Sheep and Timothy Taylor Landlord, and around 20 table wines are listed, with two available by the glass. SAMPLE DISHES: duck and orange pâté with onion and apricot relish £5; half a roast chicken with stuffing £6.50; gammon steak with grilled pineapple £10.

Licensees Penny Biglin and Dave Smith (freehouse)
Open summer 12 to 11 (10.30 Sun), winter Mon to Thur 12 to 2.30, 5.30 to 11, Fri and Sat 12 to 11, Sun 12 to 10.30; bar food and restaurant 12 to 2.30, 6.30 to 9; barbecues all day Sun summer
Details Children welcome   Car park   Garden   No smoking in restaurant   Background music
Dogs welcome in 1 room   Amex, Delta, Diners, MasterCard, Switch, Visa   Accommodation:
12 rooms, B&B £32.50 to £88

ROSS-ON-WYE   Herefordshire   map 5

▲ Eagle Inn   NEW ENTRY

23 Broad Street, Ross-on-Wye HR9 7EA   TEL: (01989) 562652

The Eagle is a large, three-storey building on the corner of one of the main roads through Ross-on-Wye. The bar is on the ground floor, with the upstairs restaurant accessed by an iron spiral staircase; each has a similar décor of dark tongue-and-groove half-panelling topped by rows of wine bottles, with bistro chairs and bare floorboards in the bar giving way to a dark-blue carpet and upholstered chairs in the restaurant. The same menu, augmented by black-board specials, applies in both rooms, and on offer are some bright and modern ideas. Mackerel fillets come in crisp breadcrumbs mixed with basil surrounded by a ring of tomato purée, sautéed wood pigeon is accompanied by walnut mash and red wine juices, and aubergine confit shares the plate with seared sea scallops in balsamic dressing. Those wanting to splash out may be gratified to find tournedos Rossini and grilled Scottish lobster on the board; otherwise, main courses take the form of chargrilled chicken with cider and onion sauce, or 'well-hung, tasty' haunch of venison wrapped in bacon with a well-balanced redcurrant and juniper sauce. Jacket potatoes and sandwiches are on the cards for lunch, and puddings are of the sticky toffee and bread-and-butter school. Hook Norton and Wye Valley ales are on draught, and three wines, from a list of around 30 bottles, are sold by the glass. SAMPLE DISHES: mussels, leek and chive soup £3.25; pot-roast shoulder of lamb £10.50; lemon tart £3.95.

Licensee James Arbourne (freehouse)
Open 11 to 11; bar food and restaurant 11 to 6, 6 to 12
Details Children welcome in eating areas   Wheelchair access (also WC)   Garden and patio
No smoking in restaurant   Live or background music   Dogs welcome   Delta, MasterCard, Switch,
Visa   Accommodation: 6 rooms, B&B £21.50 to £55

ROWDE   Wiltshire   map 2

George & Dragon ❀ 🍺 🍇   FISH

High Street, Rowde SN10 2PN   TEL: (01380) 723053

Fish remains the speciality at this roadside pub near Devizes, which looks plain from the outside but is anything but ordinary. Supplementing the main menu is a blackboard that changes daily according to what is delivered from

Cornwall. Dishes run from simple classics like provençale fish soup, or steamed skate with capers and black butter, to modern inventions such as Thai curry of lobster, monkfish and squid. There are also plenty of appealing non-fish dishes on the rest of the menu: gratin of free-range chicken savoyarde on the one hand, immos (lamb cooked in yoghurt with garlic and coriander) on the other. On the drinks side of things, there is Butcombe Bitter on draught plus a strong range of international bottled beers, including Scottish Fraoch Heather Ale, German Erdinger, Chimay Red and Duvel. The list of 70-odd wines is sprinkled with welcome surprises like a 1995 Vouvray from Huët, mature vintage Pol Roger champagne and the South of France's top rosé, Domaine Tempier. Prices start at £10 for the six white and two red house offerings (also sold by the small and large glass for £2.50/£3.35) and range all the way up to £50 with excellent quality at every level. SAMPLE DISHES: organic Glenarm salmon fishcakes with hollandaise £5.50; fried squid with lemon, garlic and parsley £12; marmalade sponge pudding with custard and whisky sauce £4.50.

Licensee Tim Withers (freehouse)
Open 12 to 3, 7 to 11 (10.30 Sun); bar food and restaurant Tue to Sat 12 to 2, 7 to 10; closed 25 Dec, 1 Jan
Details Children welcome in eating areas   Car park   Garden   No smoking in restaurant No music   Dogs welcome in bar   Delta, MasterCard, Switch, Visa

ROYDHOUSE   **West Yorkshire**   **map 8**

▲ Three Acres Inn 🎥

Roydhouse HD8 8LR   TEL: (01484) 602606
WEBSITE: www.3acres.com
off B6116 (from A629), 1m E of Kirkburton

Between Huddersfield and Barnsley, home in on the Emley Moor television mast, which is a quarter of a mile from this inn with its three-acre grounds. There, you might eat, drink, stay the night, and plunder the well-stocked delicatessen before leaving. Inside, the terrace of roadside buildings has been knocked through into a long warren of rooms with a miscellany of decoration – some walls bare stone, others papered – and all is busy bustle. Timothy Taylor Landlord, Marston's Pedigree and Adnams Bitter are stocked, but this is more a dining than a drinking pub. For decades people have been coming from miles around to eat here, so they must have a winning formula. Starters subsume game broth, artichoke soup, potted shrimps, Peking duck, and charcuterie from the delicatessen. Mains run from salmon fishcakes, or jugged hare, to confit of duck leg, or herb-crusted roast cod on a pipérade confit (roast turkey specifically comes 'with all the trimmings', but most dishes include a trimming or three). Sweets include baguette-and-butter pudding, or cranberry and walnut tart with caramel and lime sauce. Some 70 wines – listed in price order, from £12 – cover Old World and New; seven come by the glass, and nearly twenty are available in halves. SAMPLE DISHES: Yorkshire pudding with black pudding compote and sage and onion gravy £5; pot-roast pheasant with pancetta, bay leaves, Barolo and black olives £15; mulled-wine-poached pear with crème fraîche £5.50.

Licensees Neil Truelove and Brian Orme (freehouse)
Open 12 to 3, 6 to 11 (Sun 7 to 10.30); bar food and restaurant 12 to 1.45, 6.30 to 9.45; closed
25 and 31 Dec, 1 Jan
Details Children welcome in bar eating area   Car park   Wheelchair access (not WC)   Patio
Background music   No dogs   Amex, Delta, MasterCard, Switch, Visa   Accommodation: 20 rooms,
B&B £55 to £80

RUDGE   Somerset   map 2

▲ Full Moon
Rudge BA11 2QF   TEL: (01373) 830936
WEBSITE: www.thefullmoon.co.uk
off A36/A361, 5m NE of Frome

Rudge sits in tiny lanes ten miles south of Bath and six north of Longleat.
Overlooking the junction amid stone, brick and flint cottages sits this white-
plaster pub with red-tiled roof and red phone box outside. Within are two
small dining rooms – one white-painted and stone-floored with wing settles,
board tables and riding boots on the mantelpiece, the other with tiled floor,
ruched curtains, wallpaper and chairs – and two bars offering beers from
Butcombe, Abbeydale (Moonshine) and Wadworth (6X), plus Thatcher's
Cheddar Valley dry cider. A short wine list (mostly under £15 a bottle) has six
by the glass; a Romanian dessert wine intrigues. A blackboard of fish dishes
(grilled cod with lemon, prawn and dill sauce has drawn praise) supplements
two menus. The snackier has sandwiches, ploughman's and 'big breakfast',
plus the likes of fish and chips and ham and eggs. The other – notable for
starters expandable into mains and vice versa – changes monthly and may offer
mozzarella and Parma ham parcels, or port-marinated pheasant, pork fillet
with apples and almonds, or a tender, tasty beef ribeye in white wine and
Stilton sauce. Decent, fresh ingredients fairly traditionally cooked produce
generous, satisfying portions (after which puds like peach and apple charlotte,
or banoffi pie, may strain the waistband), and friendly service really does seem
'only too pleased to help'. SAMPLE DISHES: avocado and prawn mousse £6; veal
escalope pan-fried with lemon and cracked pepper £15.25; New Orleans
whiskey pudding £4.

Licensees Pat and Christine Gifford (freehouse)
Open 12 to 11 (10.30 Sun); bar food and restaurant 12 to 2.30 (2 sittings Sun lunchtime carvery,
12 and 2), 7 to 9.30 (9 winter)
Details Children welcome   Car park   Wheelchair access (also WC)   Garden and patio
No smoking in dining room   Occasional background music   Dogs welcome exc in dining areas
Delta, MasterCard, Switch, Visa   Accommodation: 17 rooms, B&B £49.50 to £85

RUSHLAKE GREEN   East Sussex   map 3

Horse and Groom
Rushlake Green TN21 9QE   TEL: (01435) 830320
off B2096, 4m SE of Heathfield

The well-tended garden, with shrubs, topiary, little arches with climbers, and
trestle tables, is a draw at this big pub on the village green. Inside, the beams in
both walls and ceilings seem blacker and thicker than most, the giant hearth is

hung with a row of copper teapots, the carpet has the usual pubby red pattern, and stuffed deer heads and antlers hang on one wall. Green-tinted table mats depicting a vintage photograph of the pub show that the place is geared towards food, reinforced by the large number of blackboard menus. These offer some rewarding modern cookery of the likes of smoked chicken and mango in curried garlic mayonnaise to start, and main courses of Thai-style chicken curry with aromatic coconut rice, salmon fillet baked with herby garlic and tomato purée in filo served on sun-blush tomato and chive sauce, or chicken breast stuffed with mozzarella, garlic and tomatoes in a roasted red pepper sauce. Traditionalists aren't neglected either: avocado with prawns could be followed by deep-fried battered haddock with chips, or pan-fried peppered medallions of Scottish beef with roasted parsnips with melted Stilton and a rich Madeira sauce. Finish with something indulgent, like clementines in Cointreau syrup with Grand Marnier ice cream. Harveys Sussex Best Bitter and Shepherd Neame Master Brew Bitter are on hand-pump, and six wines are available by the glass. SAMPLE DISHES: moules marinière £5.50; home-cooked ham with a free-range egg and chips £7.50; autumn crumble with custard £5.

Licensees Mike and Sue Chappell (freehouse)
Open 11.30 to 3, 5.30 (6 Sat) to 11, Sun 11.30 to 3, 7 to 10.30; bar food and restaurant 12 to 2.30, 7 to 9.30
Details Children welcome Car park Wheelchair access (also WC) Garden Occasional background music Dogs welcome Delta, MasterCard, Switch, Visa

ST MAWES   Cornwall   map 1

▲ Rising Sun 🍇
The Square, St Mawes TR2 5DJ   TEL: (01326) 270233
off A3078, S of Trewithian; or reached by ferry from Falmouth

Close to the harbour in the heart of the delightful small town of St Mawes, this comfortable hotel overlooks the Carrick Roads – just a short ferry ride across the water from Falmouth. Inside, it has an upmarket and cared-for feel, being elegantly and tastefully decorated throughout. The cooking combines the virtues of chef Ann Long's search for the best ingredients with her flair, imagination and experience, although Ann's hands-on involvement is in the restaurant, with its view of the sea. In here, the set-price two- or three-course menu typically offers haggis pasty, or lobster and crab bisque to start, followed by game pudding, seafood casseroled with celery, leeks, fennel and saffron, or fillet steak in creamy sherry sauce. The blackboard menu in the bar is a more straightforward affair, listing perhaps vegetable soup, or cream cheese and herb pâté, and main courses of lasagne, sirloin steak with chips, or hot smokie crumble. Finish with something like a fruit crumble. This St Austell pub regularly serves HSD and Tinners plus a guest ale. Eleven house wines are on offer at £11 a bottle or £2.75 a glass, or you could splash out £6.50 on a glass of Bollinger champagne. Thirty other wines complete a well-rounded list that gathers up some classy bottles from around the world, without charging the earth for them (top of the range is Laroche's Chablis Premier Cru Vaudevay for £33.50). SAMPLE DISHES: duck pâté £4; sausages with bubble and squeak £6; warm ginger cake £4.

Licensee R.J. Milan (St Austell Brewery)
Open 11 to 11, Sun 12 to 10.30; bar food 12 to 2, 6.30 to 9 (all day summer);
restaurant Sun 12 to 2, all week 6.30 to 9
Details Children welcome   Car park   Wheelchair access (also WC)   Patio   No smoking in
restaurant   No music   Dogs welcome   Delta, MasterCard, Switch, Visa   Accommodation: 8 rooms,
B&B £45 to £100

SALT   Staffordshire   map 5

Holly Bush Inn   NEW ENTRY

Salt ST18 0BX   TEL: (01889) 508234
WEBSITE: www.hollybushinn.co.uk
4m N of Stafford, off A51, A518 and B5066

This flower-festooned, thatched and white-painted inn is reputed to be the
second-oldest licensed premises in the country, with a history that goes all the
way back to 1190. Its age is apparent inside, with its dark, heavy beams and
timbers and stone pillars, while its vibrant, buzzy atmosphere shows it to be a
popular place. Simple, unpretentious and good-value food is what to expect
from the regular menus: pan-fried calf's liver, steak and ale pie, and pot-roast
venison are typical. Blackboard specials add further choice, perhaps in the
shape of 'thick and wholesome' spicy lentil soup, braised ham hock with
horseradish sauce, and interesting fish and seafood dishes, such as pan-fried
monkfish with fennel, shallots and morels, or chargrilled red snapper with
Jamaican-spiced tomato chutney. Desserts might feature Bakewell tart with
custard. Boddingtons Bitter, Bass and Marston's Pedigree are the real ales, and
there is a short list of wines priced from £6.95. Several wines are available as
quarter-bottles. SAMPLE DISHES: leek and Stilton sausages with two fried eggs
and chips £6; venison braised in beer with shallots, root vegetables and spiced
dumplings £8.25. banoffi pie £3.25.

Licensee Geoff Holland (freehouse)
Open Mon to Fri 12 to 2.30, 6 to 11, Sat 12 to 11, Sun 12 to 10.30; bar food Mon to Fri 12 to 2,
6 to 9.30, Sat 12 to 9.30, Sun 12 to 9; open all day bank hols
Details Children welcome in bar eating area   Car park   Wheelchair access (also WC)   Garden
and patio   No smoking in eating area   Occasional live music   No dogs   Amex, Delta, MasterCard,
Switch, Visa

SANDY GATE   Devon   map 1

Blue Ball   NEW ENTRY

Sandy Gate, nr Exeter EX2 7JL   TEL: (01392) 873401
off M5 junction 30 follow A3052 towards Clyst St Mary, go round roundabout as if returning to
M5 and before last exit take road on left; pub is 300yds on right

This cream-coloured, thatched food pub shares licensees with the Drewe
Arms, Drewsteignton (see entry). Within spitting distance of the M5 (just
yards south and east of junction 30), it is a better place to refuel humans (if not
cars) than the motorway service area half a mile north. Both bars have mint-
green tongue-and-groove panelling to dado height; one also has a flagged
floor, salmon-pink upper walls, settles, and saws hung over the fireplace, the

other has cream walls and wooden floor, tables and chairs. Beers are well-kept Bass and Gale's HSB, plus a guest such as Wyre Piddle's Piddle in the Hole. Here and in the brighter, more minimalist dining room portions are whopping. The bar menu lists dishes such as smoked haddock on mash, topped with tangy Stilton and a poached egg, or liver and bacon with caramelised onion, mash and seven further vegetables ('phew!') – after which one reporter wished he hadn't bothered with breakfast. The restaurant menu may offer marinated chilli and ginger prawns, or fried pigeon breast with Puy lentils, followed by seared sea bass with chargrilled aubergine and sweet red pepper sauce, or perhaps corn-fed roast chicken with roast fennel and a porcini and truffle sauce. Conclude with home-made bread-and-butter pudding or try the Blue Ball plate of ice creams which includes chilli and ginger flavour. A New-World-accented list of 25 (from £9.75) has 13 wines by the glass. SAMPLE DISHES: caramelised red onion tartlet £6; chicken chasseur £9; dark chocolate and pistachio tart £5.

Licensees Colin and Janice Sparks (Enterprise Inns)
Open *11 to 3, 6 to 11, Sun 12 to 3, 7 to 10.30; bar food 12 to 2.30, 6 (7 Sun) to 9.30*
Details *Children welcome in eating areas   Car park   Wheelchair access (also WC)   Garden and patio   No-smoking area in bar, no smoking in dining room   Background music   No dogs   Delta, MasterCard, Switch, Visa*

SAPPERTON   **Gloucestershire**   **map 2**

Bell at Sapperton 🍷 🍺 🌸   NEW ENTRY

Sapperton GL7 6LE   TEL: (01285) 760298
WEBSITE: **www.foodatthebell.co.uk**
follow signs from A419 midway between Cirencester and Stroud

A beautiful village amid lush, verdant rolling countryside is the setting for this honey-coloured inn, which has quickly established itself on the Cotswold pub-dining scene. Inside, a refined atmosphere is set by single roses on assorted bare wooden tables, cream-plastered or bare stone walls, and lots of open log fires or iron stoves in the many hearths. The menu aims to make a modern impression, typically things like warm merguez sausages with a salad of cannellini beans, lime and coriander, or chargrilled spicy lamb burger with melted cheese, fries and relish. A blackboard of daily specials adds to the already wide choice, and on Sundays there is always a lunchtime roast. Lemon posset with almond biscuits is typical of desserts, or you could go for the first-rate cheeses, which are served in pairs: Vacherin Mont d'Or and Gorgonzola, for example. A two-page wine list is fairly priced, running from the £11.50 house wines to good red Burgundy for £40, with two Rhône reds, Selaks New Zealand Sauvignon Blanc and Villa Caffagio Chianti offering excellent quality in the middle ground. Seven reds and six whites, plus five dessert wines, are available by the glass. Among beers, Uley Old Spot Prize Ale and Hogshead PA and Wickwar Cotswold Way show evidence of the declared partiality for good-quality, locally brewed real ales. SAMPLE DISHES: salad of buffalo mozzarella, nectarines and rocket £5.50; pan-fried monkfish tail with crisp pancetta, tarragon and tomato oil £14.50; apple and sultana crumble with custard £4.75.

Licensees Paul Davidson and Pat Le Jeune (freehouse)
Open 11 to 2.30, 6.30 to 11, Sun 12 to 3, 7 to 10.30; bar food 12 to 2, 7 to 9.30 (9 Sun); closed
25 Dec, evening 26 Dec
Details No children under 10 evenings   Car park   Garden and patio   No-smoking area in bar
No music   Dogs welcome   MasterCard, Switch, Visa

SAWLEY   Lancashire   map 8

Spread Eagle ✿ | NEW ENTRY |

Sawley BB7 4NH   TEL: (01200) 441202   WATERSIDE
WEBSITE: www.the-spreadeagle.co.uk
off A59, 4m NE of Clitheroe

Set on the bank of the River Ribble in a small hamlet at the heart of the Forest
of Bowland, the Spread Eagle is a seventeenth-century inn with a twenty-first-
century outlook. The bar has an inviting 'olde worlde' look, with real coal fires
and a relaxing atmosphere, while the restaurant has Queen Anne-style furniture and enjoys the benefit of picture windows overlooking the river. Bar food
is limited to soups and sandwiches, perhaps filled with smoked salmon or
Lancashire cheese, and real ales are Tetley Bitter and a weekly-changing guest.
Wine drinkers have more choice, with a 50-bin list that offers excellent value
throughout, prices starting at £9.95. The restaurant menu aims to produce
dishes of 'Lancastrian substance' in a European brasserie style, using quality
local produce. Expect the likes of pressed terrine of pork knuckle with spiced
apple and thyme, followed by seared sea bass fillet on buttered crushed potatoes, or flash-roasted venison haunch steak with sweet red cabbage, bay leaf
sauce and date purée. Note that restaurant food is not available in the bar, and
vice versa. SAMPLE DISHES: grilled goats' cheese salad £5.50; roast pork fillet
with black pudding and an apple and cider velouté £10.25; date and ginger
sponge £4.

Licensee Nigel Williams (freehouse)
Open Tue to Sat 12 to 4, 6 to 11, Sun 12 to 4; bar food Tue to Sat 12 to 2, restaurant Tue to Sun
12 to 2, Tue to Sat 6 to 8.45
Details Children welcome   Car park   Wheelchair access (also WC)   No smoking in restaurant
Background music   Guide dogs only   Amex, MasterCard, Switch, Visa

SAWLEY   North Yorkshire   map 9

Sawley Arms

Sawley HG4 3EQ   TEL: (01765) 620642
off B6265 Pateley Bridge to Ripon road, 5m SW of Ripon

A short distance from the World Heritage Site of Fountains Abbey, the Sawley
Arms is virtually opposite the village church close to the green (complete with
old pump). It consists of a range of stone buildings (two cottage apartments
are to let), and within is a series of rooms, with beams, alcoves stuffed with
brass and copper jugs, upholstered benches and chairs, and countless plates
and prints on the walls. The emphasis throughout is on food, with the bar no
more than a wide hatch for ordering both food and drink: John Smith's Bitter,
ales from Theakston, and six wines by the glass. The short, enterprising menu

is augmented by a daily-changing board of specials, among them perhaps a good-sized helping of braised lamb shank in Madeira gravy. Fish is a strength of the starters: smoked Nidderdale trout with horseradish Chantilly cream, say, or a 'very tasty' salmon, celeriac and herb pancake with a cheese glaze. Half a roast duckling with orange and Curaçao sauce, and sautéed corn-fed chicken breast with a creamy mushroom sauce are among main courses. Salads and sandwiches are also on offer. The pub's sizeable windows look across the gravelled car park to well-tended gardens and pasture beyond. SAMPLE DISHES: salmon mousse with toast £5.25; steak pie £9.50; bread-and-butter pudding £4.50.

Licensee Mrs June Hawes (freehouse)
Open 11.30 to 3, 6.30 to 10.30; bar food and restaurant 11.30 to 2.15, 6.30 to 9; closed Sun and Mon evenings, 25 Dec
Details No children Car park Wheelchair access (also WC) Garden No-smoking area in bar, no smoking in restaurant Background music No dogs Delta, MasterCard, Switch, Visa

SEAHOUSES Northumberland map 10

▲ Olde Ship Hotel
9 Main Street, Seahouses NE68 7RD TEL: (01665) 720200
WEBSITE: www.seahouses.co.uk
on B1430, 3m SE of Bamburgh

In the centre of the village, near the harbour, this building, with its broken-coursed stone façade, has been a pub since 1812. That was when corn and lime were shipped out of Seahouses, before it became a big fishing port; today those are memories, though Seahouses is still the starting point for three-mile trips to the Farne Islands (where Grace Darling made her name), with their birds and seals. Still, it does explain the décor of the two bars – walls festooned with fish baskets, oars, figureheads and model fishing boats, and pine floors made of old decking planks. The real ales on tap might include Black Sheep, Marston's Pedigree, Old Speckled Hen, Bass and Theakston Best Bitter, plus many guests. Basic house wines by the glass are complemented by a range of mini-bottles at £2.50 each, and most of the bottles on the short list come in well under £15. On the food front, dinner is a fixed-price three courses and sorbet, while at lunch main dishes are all one price, as are sweets, and starters vary. Among the last, soups (crab, say, or leek and potato) and fish (Craster kippers, or sweet pickled herring) predominate. Then there could be a liver and onion casserole, steak and Guinness pie, or a fish stew (prawns, squid and monkfish), followed by coffee and walnut sponge and custard, or lemon meringue pie. SAMPLE DISHES: chicken liver pâté £3.60; beef stovies £6; plum crumble £2.75.

Licensees Alan and Jean Glen (freehouse)
Open 11 to 11, Sun 12 to 10.30; bar food and restaurant 12 to 2, 7 to 8.30
Details Children welcome by arrangement Car park Wheelchair access (not WC) Garden and patio No smoking in dining room and 1 bar Occasional background music Guide dogs only MasterCard, Switch, Visa Accommodation: 18 rooms, B&B £39 to £92

SEAVIEW   Isle of Wight   map 2

▲ Seaview Hotel ۞
High Street, Seaview PO34 5EX   TEL: (01983) 612711
WEBSITE: www.seaviewhotel.co.uk
on B3340, 2m E of Ryde

Seaview is one of the Isle of Wight's most civilised places, a quiet Victorian
resort between Ryde and Bembridge. In the High Street, which leads down to
the sea wall with its prospect across Spithead to Portsmouth, stands the
Seaview Hotel: a handsome three-storey, double-fronted building of brown
brick. In front, a deck-like terrace has tables, chairs and a flagpole flying the
Union and English flags. The shipboard theme continues in the bars: one
wardroom-like, walls crowded with nautical pictures, the other with tongue-
and-groove deal counter and dado, boarded floor, and creamy walls and ceiling hung with all manner of maritime memorabilia. Here you find Goddard's
Special Bitter (brewed in Ryde) and Greene King Old Speckled Hen, along
with a selection of malt whiskies. The large-print wine list focuses strongly on
claret (impressively listing nine under £20 alongside pricier famous names)
and a range of Burgundies and offers a few half-bottles as well. Just two house
wines are offered by the glass. Bar food (on a menu, supplemented by blackboard) emphasises local ingredients. Try rich brown and white crabmeat
topped with cheese and breadcrumbs and warmed in a ramekin, or courgette,
fennel and tarragon soup; a pork chop with apple bubble and squeak could
follow, or duck, ceps and Gruyère tart; if room remains, there's lemon posset,
or a hot chocolate sponge and cream. The restaurant menu is similar but
longer. SAMPLE DISHES: chicken and sweetcorn chowder £4; smoked haddock
fishcakes with pea purée and caper crème fraîche £10; caramelised rice
pudding with spiced plums £4.

Licensees Nick and Nicky Hayward (freehouse)
Open 11 to 2.30, 6 to 11, Sun 12 to 3, 7 to 10.30; bar food and restaurant 12 to 2, 7 to 9.30;
closed 3 days Christmas
Details *Children welcome in bar eating area   Car park   Wheelchair access (not WC)   Patio*
No smoking in 1 dining room   Occasional background music   Dogs welcome   Amex, Delta, Diners,
MasterCard, Switch, Visa   Accommodation: 16 rooms, B&B £55 to £140

SELLACK   Herefordshire   map 5

Lough Pool Inn ۞ ۞ 🍇
Sellack HR9 6LX   TEL: (01989) 730236
off A49, 3m NW of Ross-on-Wye

A big log fire burns in the bar at this seventeenth-century inn. In here, Wye
Valley Butty Bach, John Smith's Bitter and Theakston Old Peculier are joined
by an extensive choice of ciders and perries from small local producers.
Beyond the bar is the smart-looking, yellow-walled restaurant, with its pine
floorboards, some exposed brick and yellow walls. The menu, served
throughout, ranges from familiar-sounding fish soup and liver and bacon with
crispy onion rings to hare terrine with pistachios and juniper, fillet of brill
with a crab crust and lobster oil, and nine-spiced roast rack of lamb with
tomato and haricot beans. Readers have been full of praise for leek and blue

cheese tart, and haggis fritters with beetroot relish, among starters, and for
main courses of crépinette of lamb with garlicky flageolet beans, and deep-
fried haddock fishcakes with tartare sauce. Game makes an appearance in
season – venison, say, or hare cooked in red wine, bitter orange and chocolate
sauce served with polenta – and cakes and tarts dominate the pudding list,
with perhaps raspberry Eton mess offering a bit more variety. The wine list is
everything a pub wine list should be – concise, well chosen, good value and
full of interesting flavours. It would be perfect if a few more than the basic
four wines were sold by the glass alongside the excellent Larmendier-Bernier
organically grown champagne. The pub is well off the beaten track in lovely
countryside, and there are plenty of picnic tables on the grass outside. SAMPLE
DISHES: twice-baked goats' cheese soufflé £5.75; fillets of sea bass with citrus
and olive sauce £14; warm ginger cake with treacle toffee ice cream £5.

Licensee Stephen Bull (freehouse)
Open 11.30 to 2.30, 6.30 to 11, Sun 12 to 2, 7 to 10.30; bar food and restaurant 12 to 2.15,
7 to 9.30; closed evenings 25 and 26 Dec, Sun evening and all day Mon in winter
Details Children welcome in eating areas   Car park   Wheelchair access (also WC)   Garden
No smoking in restaurant   No music   Dogs welcome   Delta, MasterCard, Switch, Visa

SHALFLEET   Isle of Wight   map 2

New Inn   NEW ENTRY

Main Road, Shalfleet PO30 4NS   TEL: (01983) 531314
WEBSITE: www.thenew-inn.co.uk
on A3054 Newport to Yarmouth road

The A3054 is part of the island's main road circuit, but it's no motorway, and
Shalfleet's narrow street has single-line traffic enforced by traffic lights.
Among the pleasant stone buildings is this eighteenth-century one, painted
cream and with dark green woodwork, on a corner beside the main road.
Several different spaces inside include the main bar with flagged floor, large
fireplace and a wood-topped brick counter, plus a carpeted saloon area with
yellow walls and blue-wood dado, and a tile-floored eating area. A nautical
theme unifies them, with pictures of boats on walls, and charts and models on
ledges and windowsills. Four real ales always include local Ventnor Golden,
plus maybe Goddards Fuggle-Dee-Dum, Greene King IPA, Marston's
Pedigree, or Bass. The printed menu and specials boards emphasise fish (five
of eight starters are fishy – crab and prawn cocktail, and grilled sardines among
them). Apart from old faithful bangers and mash, or steaks, meat main dishes
take in roast half guinea fowl with redcurrant sauce, Stilton-topped gammon
steak, and lamb shank with garlic mash. Fish may include grilled plaice,
lobster salad, or the honey- and ginger-marinated tuna that came with sliced
carrots and courgettes and decorative flourishes aplenty. There are desserts
like spotted dick, and crème brûlée. Ten wines come by the glass, and around
60 by the bottle. SAMPLE DISHES: smoked venison with green fig chutney £5;
hake fillets with lemon and tarragon £10; sherry trifle £3.45.

Licensees Martin Bullock and Mark McDonald (Enterprise Inns)
Open 12 to 3, 6 to 11 (10.30 Sun); bar food 12 to 2.30, 6 to 9.30
Details Children welcome   Car park   Garden   No-smoking area in bar   No music   Dogs welcome
Amex, Delta, Diners, MasterCard, Switch, Visa

▲ Montague Inn

Shepton Montague BA9 8JW   TEL: (01749) 813213
village signposted off A359 between Bruton and Castle Cary

The interior of this white-painted village-centre inn is composed of two
dining areas, one with a giant exposed-stone inglenook and a collection of wall
plates, off a central bar area, and the atmosphere has been described as 'cosy
and unpretentious'. The same menu is served throughout, and what's on offer
is mainly traditional fare along the lines of lamb curry, fillet steak with chips,
pork and apple pie, or fish pie. Starters won't rock any boats either, among
them perhaps king prawns in garlic butter, pâté with caramelised onions, and
mozzarella and tomato salad with sun-dried tomato pesto, with authentic
English desserts like bread-and-butter pudding. Greene King IPA, Butcombe
Gold and Brakspear Bitter are kept, along with over 30 wines, including a
board listing specials and five sold by the glass. SAMPLE DISHES: smoked duck
breast and mango salad with raspberry vinaigrette £7; seafood gratin £10;
lemon and lime crunch £4.

Licensees Julian and Linda Bear (freehouse)
Open *Tue to Sat 11 to 2.30, 6 to 11, Sun 12 to 2.30; bar food and restaurant Tue to Sun 12 to 2,
Tue to Sat 7 to 9*
Details *Children welcome in family room and restaurant   Car park   Garden and patio
No smoking in restaurant   Occasional live music   No dogs   Delta, MasterCard, Switch, Visa
Accommodation: 3 rooms, B&B £60 to £70 (double room)*

▲ Seven Stars Inn   NEW ENTRY

High Street North, Shincliffe DH1 2NU   TEL: (0191) 384 8454
on A177 just S of Durham

If you're feeling fit, you might fancy walking from Durham to this roadside
village pub; alternatively, take the car – but you will need to park in a nearby
side street. This is an 'oldish' place which has been given 'a bit of a lick to bring
it up to date' without going over the top: the lounge bar has wood panels
painted red, and beyond is a dining room done out it green. One menu serves
both areas, and dishes are chalked on boards all around. It's a real mixed bag,
taking in everything from shepherd's pie and smoked haddock tart with
spinach and a poached egg ('decent home-made stuff') to sesame duck salad, a
plate of sausage with Tuscan beans, and Cajun-spiced chump of lamb. You
can also get soup, sandwiches and tortilla wraps in the bar. Desserts are mostly
familiar offerings, ranging from home-produced ice creams and sorbets to
chocolate fudge brownie. North Country ales such as Theakston Best and
Black Sheep Bitter are on draught, and the wine list is an affordable, well-
assembled slate with plenty of decent drinking and eight by the glass (£2.40).
SAMPLE DISHES: Thai crab cakes on tomato salad with coriander dressing £5;
sirloin steak on bacon, leek and mushroom fricassee with red wine jus £14.50;
white chocolate and blueberry brûlée £3.50.

Licensee Louise Swinburne (freehouse)
Open 11 to 11, Sun 12 to 10.30; bar food and restaurant 12 to 2.30, 6 to 9.30 (9 Sun); closed evening 25 Dec
Details Children welcome in eating areas Patio No-smoking area, no smoking in restaurant Background music Dogs welcome in bar Delta, MasterCard, Switch, Visa Accommodation: 8 rooms, B&B £40 to £55

SHIPSTON ON STOUR   Warwickshire   map 5

▲ White Bear

4 High Street, Shipston on Stour CV36 4AJ   TEL: (01608) 661558
WEBSITE: www.whitebearhotel.co.uk
just off A429 Ettington to Moreton-in-Marsh road

The Georgian red-brick façade of the White Bear is easy to spot on the main street of this small and villagey market town. The building itself dates from the sixteenth century, with some exposed-stone walls and ceiling beams to show for it. There's a popular bar, a quieter lounge, its walls packed with prints, and a restaurant at the back with a restrained, calming décor of neutral shades and white-clothed tables. Both restaurant and bar are served by the same menu, which opens with about eight starters, among them perhaps crab fritters with Thai dipping sauce, or sautéed lambs' kidneys on a croûton with crispy bacon. Standard pub staples of steak and Guinness pie might be among main courses, but the repertory is extended by the likes of grilled salmon fillet with saffron risotto and caper and tomato dressing, baked guinea fowl with an orange and vermouth sauce, or chicken breast stuffed with Brie and olives served with a celery and walnut dressing. Bass and Adnams Bitter and Broadside, plus a guest, are on draught, and a reasonably priced dozen wines are served by the glass. SAMPLE DISHES: deep-fried filo prawns with lemon mayonnaise £5.25; minted shoulder of lamb with mash and jus £10; sticky toffee pudding £3.75.

Licensees George Kruszynskyj and Lou Snoxall (Punch Group)
Open 11 to 11, Sun 12 to 10.30; bar food and restaurant 12 to 2 (2.30 Sat and Sun), 6.30 to 9.30 (10 Fri and Sat); no food Sun evening
Details Children welcome Car park Wheelchair access (also WC) Garden Occasional live music; jukebox in bar Dogs welcome MasterCard, Switch, Visa Accommodation: 10 rooms, B&B £30 to £50

SHOCKLACH   Cheshire   map 7

Bull Inn

Shocklach SY14 7BL   TEL: (01829) 250239
off A534 Wrexham to Nantwich road; turn right after crossing River Dee, then 3m to village

---

With so many rural pubs closing down, it is remarkable that one in such an isolated hamlet as Shocklach, just a mile from the Welsh border, should be not merely surviving but thriving. The Bull, which styles itself a 'country bistro', stands at a crossroads, a solid-looking building, mostly several hundred years old but with modern extensions. The atmospheric oldest parts are heavily beamed, though the dining area is in one of the more modern sections. Food options are spread across numerous menus (including one for children), extended further by specials on a blackboard plus another board listing curries.

Bar lunches range from 'hearty' sandwiches (chicken with stuffing and bacon, for example) through filled jacket potatoes to pies (shepherd's, beef in ale). From the carte you might choose a generous-sized breaded pork escalope, 'pan-fried to perfection', served with a 'very tasty' cider and apricot sauce. Start with something like deep-fried Camembert with plum sauce and finish with profiteroles or bread-and-butter budding. Bass, Burtonwood Bitter and Banks's Bitter and Mansfield Cask Ale are the ales on offer, and a dozen or so wines include three house wines by the glass, with prices starting at £6.95. SAMPLE DISHES: devilled whitebait £4; halibut with herb mash and parsley sauce £9; chocolate and strawberry cheesecake £3.

Licensee John Williams (Pyramid Pub Co)
Open Tue to Sat 11.30 to 3, 6.30 to 11, Sun 11.30 to 3, 7 to 10.30; bar food and restaurant Tue to Sun (exc Tue lunchtime) 12 to 2.30, 6.30 to 9.30
Details Children welcome   Car park   Wheelchair access (not WC)   Patio   No smoking in restaurant   Background music   Guide dogs only   MasterCard, Switch, Visa

SINNINGTON   North Yorkshire   map 9

▲ Fox and Hounds ✿

Sinnington YO62 6SQ   TEL: (01751) 431577
WEBSITE: www.thefoxandhoundsinn.co.uk
off A170 between Helmsley and Pickering

The Fox and Hounds is an attractive sandstone building that looks much like the others on this stretch of road through the village. The front door leads into a cosy, low-ceilinged bar area, all neat and well looked after, with lots of little ornamental bits and pieces about the place. The food is a major attraction here, with the same menu served throughout, offering cooking that is somewhat more cosmopolitan than may be expected in such a remote setting: pan-seared king scallops and green-lipped mussels with a Parmesan and dill crust and gazpacho sauce, chicken breast with pesto accompanied by wild mushroom and spinach ravioli and a chunky tomato and thyme sauce, and roast monkfish tail wrapped in pancetta with a sweet pepper coulis and balsamic reduction. There may even be ostrich fillet (served on braised celery and fennel) among the chef's specials, and for dessert try perhaps tiramisù, or saffron and mint crème brûlée with mint ice cream. The pub's position on the edge of the North York Moors, within easy driving distance of both York and the coast, makes it a good base for exploring the area. Black Sheep Special Ale and Camerons Bitter are provided for real ale drinkers, while wine enthusiasts get a concise but varied and fairly priced list opening with half a dozen house selections, all available by the bottle (£11.50) or by the glass (£3). SAMPLE DISHES: steamed mussels in garlic and rosemary sauce topped with crispy bacon £6; beef and potato pie £8; dark chocolate mousse wrapped around raspberry compote on a chocolate biscuit base £4.25.

Licensees Andrew and Catherine Stephens (freehouse)
Open 12 to 2.30, 6 (6.30 winter exc Fri and Sat) to 11, Sun 12 to 2.30, 6.30 to 10.30; bar food and restaurant 12 to 2, 6.30 (7 winter) to 9 (8.30 Sun)
Details Children welcome   Car park   Wheelchair access (also WC)   Garden and patio
No smoking in restaurant   Background music   Dogs welcome exc in restaurant   Amex, MasterCard, Switch, Visa   Accommodation: 10 rooms, B&B £44 to £80

SLAIDBURN Lancashire map 8

▲ Hark to Bounty Inn

Slaidburn BB7 3EP   TEL: (01200) 446246
WEBSITE: www.hark-to-bounty.co.uk
on B6478, 8m N of Clitheroe

Slaidburn is on the edge of the Forest of Bowland – hunting country since it
was a medieval royal forest – and the pub's name recalls a nineteenth-century
hound that protested loudly when the squire interrupted the hunt to stop here
for a drink. But this long, low, solid-looking stone pub has been here since the
thirteenth century, as thick walls and small windows confirm, and the magnificently beamed function room, a courtroom till 1937, still has jury benches
and the judge's box. In the cosy, oak-beamed bar, by the log fire, well-kept
Theakston Best Bitter and Old Peculier are on draught, and many malt
whiskies and three wines come by the glass. Bar food includes sandwiches,
jacket potatoes and baguettes, plus starters like steamed black pudding with
creamy mustard sauce, or a dish of bubbling-hot garlic prawns. Mains include
steak, kidney and Theakston's pie with melt-in-the-mouth shortcrust pastry,
grilled haddock fillet, or leek, mushroom and walnut strudel. The restaurant
offers moules marinière to start, or blue Lancashire cheesecake garnished with
pears in a balsamic vinaigrette, then maybe roast suckling pig loin on braised
red cabbage, or monkfish fillet with herbs and cherry tomatoes. If room
remains, there are meringue nests with apples, rum and raisins stacked on a
biscuit bottom to finish. SAMPLE DISHES: ham-wrapped banana, baked and
topped with melted cheese £4.50; fishcakes in tomato, onion and basil sauce
£6.75; chocolate and hazelnut roulade £3.50.

Licensee Isobel Bristow (freehouse)
Open 11 to 11; bar food Mon to Sat 12 to 2, 6 to 9 (8 Mon to Thur winter), Sun 12 to 2.30, 6 to
8 (12 to 8 summer); restaurant Tue to Sat 12 to 2, 6 to 9 (8 winter), Sun 12 to 2.30
Details Children welcome   Car park   Wheelchair access (not WC)   Garden   No-smoking area in
bar, no smoking in dining room   Occasional live and background music   Dogs welcome exc in eating
areas   Delta, MasterCard, Switch, Visa   Accommodation: 9 rooms, B&B £29.50 to £69.50

SLAPTON Devon map 1

▲ Tower Inn 🍺

Church Road, Slapton TQ7 2PN   TEL: (01548) 580216
off A379, 5m SW of Dartmouth

Built in about 1347 to accommodate the men working on the Collegiate
Chantry of St Mary, the Tower then probably became the college's guest-
house to dispense alms and hospitality to the deserving. Much of the chantry
tower is still standing, and in its shadow sits the atmospheric inn, with benches
in the walled garden overlooking the tower, and an extremely narrow doorway
to squeeze through. Inside, it is all low ceilings, stone walls, pews and open
fires, coming into its own particularly in the evening, when candlelight creates
even more atmosphere. Separate menus operate at lunch and dinner. The
former may feature coriander-crusted salmon with creamed leeks, a trio of
local sausages with mustard mash, and four-cheese linguine. Evenings go a

touch more elaborate, with starters of a tower of crab and prawns, or duck
liver, red onion and Calvados tart with smoked tomato and cumin chutney,
followed by beef fillet in watercress cream topped with horseradish mousse, or
pan-fried John Dory fillets on orange-glazed fennel. Daily specials are chalked
on a board – among them perhaps baked halibut fillet with clams in thyme and
garlic on roast samphire – and the range of favourite puddings might include
lemon or treacle tart. The superb range of real beers extends from Dartmoor
Best Bitter to Tower Ale (supplied by Badger), plus guests such as Exmoor
Gold and Wells Bombardier Premium Bitter. Ciders from Weston's and
Addlestone are available, as is a well-chosen wine list with seven by the glass.
SAMPLE DISHES: locally smoked prawns, mackerel and salmon with dill
mustard sauce £6; roast partridge on celeriac mousse with a rosemary and red
wine sauce £13.25; vanilla crème brûlée with rum-soaked apricots £4.25.

Licensees Josh and Nicola Acfield (freehouse)
Open 12 to 3, 6 to 11, Sun 12 to 3, 7 to 10.30; bar food 12 to 2.30, 7 (6 summer) to 9.30
Details Children welcome in family room   Car park   Wheelchair access (not WC)   Garden
No smoking in eating area   Occasional live or background music   Dogs welcome on a lead
MasterCard, Switch, Visa   Accommodation: 3 rooms, B&B £35 to £50

SMARDEN   Kent   map 3

▲ Chequers Inn
The Street, Smarden TN27 8QA   TEL: (01233) 770217
village is off A274 Maidstone to Tenterden road, signposted just S of Headcorn

The rustic interior of this weatherboarded inn, with its low-beamed ceilings
and flagstoned floors, must look much as it did when the place was built in the
fourteenth century. Food is served in two dining areas, but there is plenty of
room for drinkers, who are offered ales from the Harveys and Adnams
Breweries plus draught Bass and a guest, and a 30-bottle wine list that starts in
France and takes a brisk trot around the world. About half a dozen wines are
served by the glass. The frequently changing menus offer a mostly familiar
range – steak and kidney pie, for example – but less-usual options might
include a starter of duck confit on pea and thyme risotto, followed by baked
cod with Welsh rarebit on bubble and squeak, vegetable moussaka, or roast
chicken with tomato and oregano sauce. Directly behind the pub is a paved
terrace furnished with attractive wrought-iron tables and chairs, and
surrounded by shrubs and flowers in tubs. Beyond this is a beautifully landscaped garden with a large pond and views of the village church, an idyllic
setting for sitting outside on a sunny summer's day. SAMPLE DISHES: seafood
salad £5; calf's liver with red onion marmalade and Madeira sauce £13.50;
lemon crème brûlée £4.

Licensees Lisa and Charles Bullock (freehouse)
Open 11 to 11, Sun 12 to 10.30; bar food and restaurant 11.30 to 2.30 (3 Sun), 6 to 9.30
(10 Sat)
Details Children welcome   Car park   Wheelchair access (not WC)   Garden   No smoking in
restaurant   Occasional background music   Dogs welcome   Delta, MasterCard, Switch, Visa
Accommodation: 4 rooms, B&B £40 to £80

Bottle House Inn

Smart's Hill, Penshurst TN11 8ET   TEL: (01892) 870306
W of B2188, 1m S of Penshurst

This pub hides in rolling country on the ridge south of Penshurst but north of the fledgling Medway, and it's a pretty drive to this 'white-painted, higgledy-piggledy building on a bank' beside a narrow lane. The inside is olde worlde – open fire, low beams, patterned carpet and dark wood tables. The spacious bar has pleasant, chatty, welcoming staff who can offer you brews from Larkins, three miles off in Chiddingstone, or Harveys from Lewes, all of twenty miles away. There are also six wines by the glass on a list that stays mostly under £15 and includes the local Penshurst Müller-Thurgau. Both bar and the restaurant alongside it have the same menu. A nicely coarse-textured Thai fishcake with chilli jam was reckoned 'very enjoyable', the heat of the jam, building up as the dish was eaten, cut by plenty of green herbs – alternatively you could start with wild boar terrine. A spicy BBQ chicken topped with cheese and bacon made a good flavour combination that suited one reporter, while a skinless salmon fillet in basil and pine-nut crust on a green-leaf salad was a 'nice, fresh, light' main dish for another. Among desserts that catch the eye are Drambuie and orange Catalan cream with orange caramel sauce, and treacle and pumpkin tart with custard. SAMPLE DISHES: Vietnamese spring rolls and chilli jam £5; pheasant breast with venison and bacon stuffing en croûte £13; chocolate Armagnac loaf and coffee sauce £5.

Licensees Gordon and Val Meer, and Paul Hammond (freehouse)
Open 11 to 11 (Sun 12 to 10.30); bar food and restaurant 12 to 10 (Sun 12 to 9)
Details *Children welcome in eating areas   Car park   Garden and patio   No smoking in dining room   Background music   Dogs welcome exc in dining room   Delta, MasterCard, Switch, Visa*

▲ Crown Inn

Bridge Road, Snape IP17 1SL   TEL: (01728) 688324
off A1094, on way to Snape Maltings

Dining tables fill most of the open-plan space at this fifteenth-century pub, so there's not too much room to prop up the small bar counter, giving the impression that the Crown is more 'a restaurant with bar than a drinking pub'. A wealth of beams, brick floors, open fires and simple wooden furniture – some old and stripped, others modern varnished pine – set a relaxed, informal tone. The longish, crowd-pleasing blackboard menu rolls out the likes of toasted goats' cheese bruschetta with cranberry chutney and salad, moules marinière, and game pâté to start, while mains could take in traditional steak and kidney pudding, fillet steak with melted Stilton, or roast partridge with bacon and creamy cabbage. Finish with one of the comforting desserts, such as a 'commendable' apple and sultana suet pudding, or 'calorific' banana toffee crumble tart. The wines, approaching 40 bottles and majoring on France, are supplied by Adnams of Southwold, as are the ales. Before you leave, search out what the pub claims is probably the finest example of a double Suffolk settle.

SAMPLE DISHES: king prawns in tempura with chilli dip £7; venison casseroled with juniper and red wine £10.75; crème brûlée £3.75.

Licensee Diane Maylott (Adnams)
Open 12 to 3, 6 to 11, Sun 12 to 3, 7 to 10.30; bar food and restaurant 12 to 2, 7 to 9; closed 25 Dec
Details No children Car park Wheelchair access (also WC) Garden and patio No smoking in restaurant No music No dogs Delta, MasterCard, Switch, Visa Accommodation: 3 rooms, B&B £55 to £65

SNETTISHAM Norfolk

map 6

▲ Rose & Crown

Old Church Road, Snettisham PE31 7LX   TEL: (01485) 541382
WEBSITE: www.roseandcrownsnettisham.co.uk
just off A149, 4m S of Hunstanton

This building opposite the cricket ground looks like a long, white-painted cottage with a climber-grown trellis porch. But it's a 'delightful pub with exceptional food and cheerful, caring staff', and inside it's a lot bigger than it looks, with three bars and three dining rooms, all linked by twisting passages. The bars (one non-smoking) serve Adnams brews, Bass and Greene King IPA – and of thirty-odd wines (half European, half New World) over twenty can be had in 175ml or 250ml glasses. The biggest dining room, a family room, opens on to the walled garden at the back. Lunch and evening menus are supplemented by a blackboard of specials and 'classics' (Caesar salad, or fish and chips with minted mushy peas); lunch menus include sandwiches and focaccias (bacon and egg butty with red pepper ketchup, say, or oriental duck and hoisin wrap). Among starters might be wonderfully fresh Brancaster oysters with frozen lime and tequila Tabasco, 'not that they needed any embellishment', or seared pigeon breast and chorizo salad with beetroot and sage. Mains could span Irish stew, a roast partridge with swede and carrot risotto and Spanish black pudding, and beautifully fried mackerel with rainbow chard and an intriguing coleslaw of fine-sliced fresh fennel. Finish with a chocolate hamburger and mango chips, a palette of sorbets, or Welsh rarebit with plum tomato and Parma ham. SAMPLE DISHES: crunchy Vietnamese duck salad with sweet-and-sour dressing £6; pine-smoked salmon fillet with poached egg, pancetta and watercress £11.50; warm cherry soup, cherry pancakes and clotted cream £4.50.

Licensee Anthony Goodrich (freehouse)
Open 11 to 11, Sun 12 to 10.30; bar food and restaurant 12 to 2 (2.30 summer), 6.30 to 9 (9.30 summer)
Details Children welcome in family room and restaurant Car park Wheelchair access (not WC) Garden No-smoking area in bar, no smoking in dining room No music Dogs welcome Delta, MasterCard, Switch, Visa Accommodation: 11 rooms, B&B £55 to £100

✿ indicates a pub serving outstanding bar food, backed up by all-round excellence in other departments, such as service, atmosphere and cleanliness.

SOUTHAMPTON   Hampshire   **map 2**

White Star Tavern   `NEW ENTRY`

28 Oxford Street, Southampton SO14 3DJ   TEL: (02380) 821990
WEBSITE: www.whitestartavern.co.uk
on corner of Latimer Street and Oxford Street, just N of Queen's Terrace (A33) in S of city

At one time a hotel for ocean-going travellers, this imposing building has been renovated but retains masses of wooden panelling to walls, pillars and ceilings, large windows etched with the White Star logo, and a number of fireplaces. Comfortable modern seating and contemporary lighting (as well as a number of old chandeliers) create a modern bar-bistro atmosphere, while the dining area is similar in both style and ambience. Enterprising bar snacks are along the lines of Welsh rarebit topped with smoked haddock, tempura prawns with sweet chilli dipping sauce, and sandwiches, while some up-to-the-minute ideas shine out of the full menu: scallops and black pudding with orange sauce, or crab, apple, and coriander spring roll with hot-and-sweet sauce to start, and then monkfish with mussels in saffron sauce with a vegetable ragoût, or chicken breast stuffed with lobster accompanied by risotto in a shellfish and lemongrass sauce. Among these might be more familiar starters of chicken Caesar salad, or moules marinière, and main courses of chargrilled ribeye steak with chips and béarnaise, or crispy pork on mash with Savoy cabbage and a port and Stilton sauce. Fuller's London Pride, Bass and Courage Best are on handpump, and eight wines are offered by the glass from a list of forty mainly French and New World bottles. SAMPLE DISHES: wild mushroom and tomato risotto with shaved Parmesan £6; half a chargrilled lobster with thick-cut chips and spicy mayonnaise £17.50; white chocolate bread-and-butter pudding £5.

Licensees Mark Dodd and Yannick Hugoo (freehouse)
Open *summer Tue to Sat 11 to 11, Sun 12 to 10.30, winter Tue to Sat 12 to 3, 5.30 to 11, Sun 12 to 10.30; bar food and restaurant Tue to Sat 12 to 2.30, 6 to 9.30 (10 Fri and Sat), Sun 12 to 9; closed 25 and 26 Dec, 1 Jan*
Details *Children welcome Sat and Sun   Wheelchair access (also WC)   Patio   No-smoking area in restaurant   Background music   No dogs   MasterCard, Switch, Visa*

SOUTH LEIGH   Oxfordshire   **map 2**

▲ Mason Arms

South Leigh OX8 6XN   TEL: (01993) 702485
off A40, 3m SE of Witney

Though the thatched, fifteenth-century pub looks regular enough from the outside, once you are inside, you may think it a little 'idiosyncratic'. It may be a matter of taste, but our inspector enjoyed the quirky décor of Turkish rugs on flagstone floors, 'antique shop' furniture, casually arranged stacks of leather-bound tomes and cigar boxes, rows of dust-covered old wine bottles and 'politically incorrect' pictures. The food has also been favourably reported on, and though the printed menu changes little from year to year – Mr Baxter's potted shrimps, and roast duck with Armagnac and orange sauce remain fixtures – there is a blackboard to ring the changes: beef tomato and fresh anchovy salad among starters, with cottage pie, or roast grouse with bread sauce and game crisps to follow. Though the style is 'dead simple', the cooking is based on top-quality ingredients – which is reflected in prices (note that side dishes of vegetables are charged extra). To finish, there is a selection of desserts or a 'proper' cheeseboard. Burton Ale is offered for beer drinkers, the wine list includes three by the glass, and connoisseurs of single malts and Armagnac are well served, as are fans of Cuban cigars. SAMPLE DISHES: mussels in vermouth and cream £7; thick-cut sirloin steak au poivre £19; cheeseboard £8.

Licensee Gerry Stonhill (freehouse)
Open Tue to Sun 12 to 3.30, Tue to Sat 6.30 to 11; bar food and restaurant Tue to Sat 12 to 2.30, 7.30 to 10.30, Sun 12 to 3
Details No children   Car park   Wheelchair access (not WC)   Patio   No music   No dogs   Amex
Accommodation: 2 rooms, B&B £35 to £65

SOUTHWOLD   Suffolk   map 6

▲ Crown Hotel 🍇   NEW ENTRY

90 High Street, Southwold IP18 6DP   TEL: (01502) 722275
WEBSITE: www.adnams.co.uk

This white-painted Georgian building, on the main shopping street of this attractive seaside town, attempts to be all things to all people: a pub, restaurant and small hotel rolled into one. Owned by local brewers Adnams, the beers (Broadside and Bitter) are 'excellent'. While the extended main bar has a dining note, with stripped-wood tables, wooden chairs and cushioned settles, the back bar still retains a real pub atmosphere. The non-smoking restaurant resides in the old parlour. The bar menu dishes are imaginative and attractively presented, with some arriving on black slates: for example, a tapas starter of chorizo, crab spring roll, salmon belly, and smoked chicken peanut salad with marinated chicken wings. Main courses continue the modish trend, with perhaps seared sea bass paired with saffron risotto and peanut pesto, and baked hoki teamed with a vegetable cheese glaze and sweet potato chips. More familiar, but still with a twist, is pan-fried sirloin steak with mustard mash and sweet-and-sour onions. Desserts go straight down the line: perhaps sultana and mixed-spiced sponge pudding with caramel sauce, or iced chocolate parfait with chocolate sauce. Choose from the monthly selection of around 20 wines by the glass or bottle, or from the full Adnams interest-packed list, full of sensible prices and good choice. SAMPLE DISHES: wild mushroom and feta risotto with herb crème fraîche £5.25; confit duck leg on crushed potatoes with red onions £11; tiramisù with coffee bean syrup £4.50.

Licensee Michael Bartholomew (Adnams)
Open 10 to 11, Sun 12 to 10.30; bar food 12 to 2, 7 to 10; restaurant 12.30 to 1.30, 7.30 to 8.45
Details Children welcome in bar   Car park   Wheelchair access (also WC)   No-smoking area in bar, no smoking in restaurant   No music   Dogs welcome in back bar   Delta, MasterCard, Switch, Visa   Accommodation: 13 rooms, B&B £75 to £150

SOWERBY   West Yorkshire   map 8

Travellers Rest ✿ [NEW ENTRY]

Steep Lane, Sowerby HX6 1PE   TEL: (01422) 832124
off A646, 2m W of Sowerby Bridge

There are spectacular views from this isolated spot on the moors, hidden among steep, winding lanes on Calderdale's southern scarp. Interior décor is also easy on the eye, with a look that makes the most of original features like exposed-stone walls and flagstone floors, but also creates a contemporary feel and gives an impression of no expense spared. The level of ambition is apparent from blackboard menus listing pub grub with a decidedly upmarket twist – home-made steak burger on focaccia with blue cheese dressing and tempura onion rings, for example. Other main courses might be confit Gressingham duck leg with champ, red onion marmalade and redcurrant sauce, or game casserole with thyme and apple dumplings. Starters take in rustic roast red onion filled with home-dried tomatoes, feta, basil, olives and roast red pepper, while original dessert creations feature baked figs with mascarpone, orange, pistachios and hot-cross-bun butter pudding. Landlord and Golden Best from Timothy Taylor are the real ales on draught, and for oenophiles there is a list of two dozen bottles, of which four come by the glass. SAMPLE DISHES: stir-fried salad of king prawns and baby courgettes with ginger, chilli and soy sauce £7; beef fillet on Stilton mash with creamy green peppercorn sauce £17; pink grapefruit mousse with passion-fruit sauce £5.50.

Licensee Caroline Lumley (freehouse)
Open Tue to Fri 5 to 12, Sat and Sun 12 to 12; bar food and restaurant Sat and Sun 12 to 2.30, Tue to Sun 6 to 9.30 (8.30 Sun); open all day bank hols
Details No children   Car park   Wheelchair access (not WC)   Garden and patio   No smoking in dining room   Background music   Dogs welcome   Delta, MasterCard, Switch, Visa

SPARSHOLT   Hampshire   map 2

Plough Inn

Sparsholt SO21 2NW   TEL: (01962) 776353
off B3049 1½m W of Winchester

Just a few miles from Winchester and on the edge of a quiet village, the Plough has seen many extensions and additions in its 200-year history. The spacious bar area and the cosy and convivial front rooms in the original cottage are furnished with sturdy pine tables and chairs to create a rustic and comfortable atmosphere, and attractive prints and farm tools adorn the walls. Booking for dinner is advisable, for this is a very popular place. Blackboard menus offer lunchtime sandwiches and ploughman's and more elaborate restaurant-style dishes, such as smoked chicken, bacon and spring onion salad, or a chicken, prawn and herb sausage on tomato sauce, followed by home-made steak burger with boulangère potatoes, or lamb's liver and bacon with mash and onion gravy. A vegetarian option might be spinach and ricotta tortellini with baby vegetables and pesto, while puddings range from traditional bread-and-butter to chocolate brownie with banana ice cream. Three or four Wadworth ales might include 6X, Henry's Original IPA and JCB, and there's normally a guest ale. Twelve wines, plus champagne, are sold by the glass. The shrub-filled garden, complete with chalet and rural views, is a great spot in summer. SAMPLE DISHES: cauliflower and almond soup £3.75; breast of chicken with avocado and Parma ham in garlicky cream sauce £12; chocolate, orange and brandy terrine £4.

Licensees Richard and Kathryn Crawford (Wadworth)
Open 11 to 3, 6 to 11, Sun 12 to 3, 6 to 10.30; bar food 12 to 2, 6 to 9 (9.30 Fri and Sat); closed 25 Dec
Details Children welcome in eating areas   Car park   Wheelchair access (also WC)   Garden
No-smoking area in bar, no smoking in eating areas   No music   Dogs welcome   Delta, MasterCard, Switch, Visa

STANFORD DINGLEY   Berkshire   map 2

Old Boot Inn

Stanford Dingley RG7 6LT   TEL: (01189) 744292
from M4 junction 12 take A340 N towards Pangbourne, then follow signs to Bradfield, then to Stanford Dingley

Stanford Dingley is a pretty, well-kept village, and this friendly and relaxed inn's garden – extending to over half an acre – is a pleasant spot in summer. The attractive white-painted brick building proclaims its purpose, past and present, with a sign reading 'eighteenth-century free house'. Two bars, with old-fashioned paintings and prints, have wood-burning fires, and beside one is a giant boot holding the fire irons. The restaurant extends into a light and airy non-smoking conservatory, but customers can sit where they want and the blackboard menus are available everywhere. As bar food you might choose steak and kidney pudding, cod in beer batter, or a curry. A more formal restaurant meal might start with Thai fishcakes with chilli salsa, goats' cheese with sesame seeds and red onion marmalade, or duck liver pâté. Main courses might run to pork tenderloin with mushrooms and blueberries, various steaks, and perhaps roast pheasant with a garlic, lemon and parsley sauce and celeriac chips, with puddings of treacle tart, apple pie, or white chocolate cheesecake. Ales on draught are likely to include a couple from West Berkshire Brewery – among them perhaps Good Old Boy – Bass, Brakspear Bitter and a guest like Young's Special, and there is Stowford Press cider. Around ten wines are sold by the glass from a list of thirty-odd bottles. SAMPLE DISHES: prawn stir-fry in a filo basket with a light curry sauce £6.75; loin of veal with sweet peppers and tomatoes £14.50; crème brûlée with pine nuts £4.50.

Licensee John Haley (freehouse)
Open 11 to 3, 6 to 11; bar food and restaurant 12 to 2.15, 7 to 9.30
Details Children welcome   Car park   Wheelchair access (not WC)   Garden and patio
No smoking in conservatory   No music   Dogs welcome exc in restaurant   Delta, MasterCard, Switch, Visa

---

★ ★ *indicates a pub serving food on a par with 'seriously good' restaurants, where the cooking achieves consistent high quality.*

STANTON WICK   Bath & N.E. Somerset   map 2

▲ Carpenters Arms
Stanton Wick BS39 4BX   TEL: (01761) 490202
WEBSITE: www.the-carpenters-arms.co.uk
off A368, ½ m W of junction with A37 Bristol to Shepton Mallet road

The Carpenters Arms seems pretty busy. No wonder, really. Once a row of
miners' cottages, it's a pretty building of mellow local stone, with pantiled roof
and white window frames, sitting in the peaceful Chew valley, yet Bristol and
Bath are just a few miles away. And, what's more, it has the feel of a cosy,
friendly local. Inside, cream/primrose colours set off the bared stone walls,
low beams and wooden panelling. The dining room menu has the likes of
mussels steamed in cider, or Parma ham, mozzarella and figs in a honey vinaigrette; roast duck breast in whisky and orange sauce might follow, or a fillet of
sea bass on gingered onions. The Coopers Parlour menu (supplemented by
blackboards) offers salads, sandwiches, a children's menu, and some of the
dining room dishes plus others – sardines with orange and parsley butter, say,
steak and ale pie, or Thai red fish curry with rice. Sweets range from bread-
and-butter pudding to baked pistachio and chocolate fondant with honeycomb ice cream. Handpumped Butcombe, Bass and Wadworth 6X ales are
supplemented by Natch cider. Ten wines come by the glass for £2.50 to £3.35,
and the short list of bottles includes some more upmarket offerings. SAMPLE
DISHES: smoked salmon and prawn salad £5.50; lamb's liver and bacon with
oyster mushrooms £10; dark chocolate and brandy torte £3.75.

Licensees Simon Pledge, A.M. Jones and T.S.C. Ruthven (freehouse)
Open 11 to 11 (Sun 12 to 10.30); bar food and restaurant 12 to 2, 7 to 10 (Sun evening bar food
7 to 9, restaurant closed); closed evenings 25 and 26 Dec
Details Children welcome in eating areas   Car park   Patio   No smoking in 1 dining room
Occasional live music   Dogs welcome in bar   Amex, Delta, MasterCard, Switch, Visa
Accommodation: 12 rooms, B&B £62 to £84.50

STATHERN   Leicestershire   map 5

Red Lion ☺ ❀
2 Red Lion Street, Stathern LE14 4HS   TEL: (01949) 860868
from A607 halfway between Melton Mowbray and Grantham, turn NW for about 4m

In a village in the Vale of Belvoir, the cream walls and red woodwork of a
rather ordinary exterior conceal an 'out-of-the-way gem'. This Red Lion is
now the stablemate of the Olive Branch at Clipsham (see entry), twenty miles
away. Hence, it is unambiguously a foodie pub, but still pleasingly a pub. The
stone-flagged bar is 'full to the beams with cheery drinkers' consuming
Brewster's VPA (from a few yards away in Penn Lane), Grainstore's Olive Oil
(from faraway Oakham), or more distant guests like Brains SA from Cardiff.
Local sourcing also marks the brasserie-tinged modern British cuisine. Roast
suckling pig from Bidwell Farm, Clipsham, is teamed with parsnip mash and
leeks, while wild mushroom and pearl barley risotto, plus peas and tarragon,
accompany roast Belvoir pheasant. Melton Mowbray pork pie and Cropwell
Bishop Stilton also figure – but so do sea bream (pan-fried, with spiced

couscous and Mediterranean vegetables), Thai-style steamed mussels and clams, and penne with artichoke, capers, tomato and pesto. Puddings include home-made sorbets and ice creams, crème brûlée, and chocolate sponge with hot chocolate sauce. A concise list cherry-picks the wine world's highways and byways for interesting bottles from £11 to £40, with plenty under £15 and eight by the glass. Service is friendly, informal and efficient. SAMPLE DISHES: Caesar salad £4.75; roast loin of fallow buck with red cabbage and fondant potatoes £14.50; apple, apricot and sultana crumble £5.

Licensee Ben Jones (Rutland Inn Company Ltd)
Open *Mon to Fri 12 to 3, 6 to 11, Sat 12 to 11, Sun 12 to 5.30; bar food Mon to Sat 12 to 2, 7 to 9.30, Sun 12 to 3; closed 26 Dec, lunch 31 Dec, 1 Jan*
Details *Children welcome   Car park   Wheelchair access (not WC)   Garden and patio No smoking in dining room   Background music   Dogs welcome in bar only   Delta, MasterCard, Switch, Visa*

STAVERTON   Devon   map 1

▲ Sea Trout Inn

Staverton TQ9 6PA   TEL: (01803) 762274
WEBSITE: www.seatroutinn.com
off A384, 2m N of Totnes

Once called Church House, this white-painted building isn't far from the church, and not much further from the Dart, where a former landlord caught the fish after which he renamed the pub. The patio-style garden has a pond and fountain, while, inside, there are two bars: the poolroom and the rambling lounge bar, which continues the fishy theme with specimens in showcases. Here there are sandwiches, salads and a children's menu, plus dishes such as liver and mushroom pâté, sausage and mash, or poached salmon, with raspberry crème brûlée or West Country cheeses to follow. Ales from the owners, Palmers of Bridport, include IPA, Dorset Gold and 200, and there's farmhouse cider too. The dining room leads into the conservatory restaurant, overlooking the garden. This serves a two- or three-course set-price menu with about four choices per course. This could offer, say, quail's egg, chorizo and black olive salad, roast duck breast on rösti, and strawberry pavlova. Nine of the twenty wines listed can be had by the large or small glass. SAMPLE DISHES: galantine of wild game £5; grilled fillets of red mullet £12; lemon bread-and-butter pudding £4.

Licensees Nick and Nicky Brookland (Palmers)
Open *11 to 3, 6 to 11, Sun 12 to 3, 7 to 10.30; bar food and restaurant 12 to 2, 7 to 9; closed 25 Dec*
Details *Children welcome in dining room   Car park   Wheelchair access (also WC)   Garden and patio   No-smoking area in bar   Occasional jukebox music   Dogs welcome   Amex, Delta, MasterCard, Switch, Visa   Accommodation: 10 rooms, B&B £45 to £74*

Feedback on pubs in the Guide, and recommendations for new ones, are very welcome.

Hamilton Arms
School Lane, Stedham GU29 0NZ   TEL: (01730) 812555
WEBSITE: www.thehamiltonarms.co.uk
off A272, 2m W of Midhurst

It can't be easy to combine an English pub and a Thai restaurant/take-away at the same address and to succeed with both, but it seems to have been done here. The exterior, with a small, flowery terrace for al fresco dining, gives no hint of the ornate interior, where the décor incorporates carved furniture, low tables and stools, displays of Thai handicrafts, and a stall selling oriental food-stuffs. Customers can enjoy the bar's pubby atmosphere, but they have a choice to make. They can sink pints of Ballard's Best, Fuller's London Pride and seasonal guest beers alongside traditionalist dishes like sirloin steak, battered fish or Spanish omelette. Or they can have a bottle of imported Chang beer with their pick of the 19 dishes on the illustrated Thai bar menu – say, roast duck with light sesame sauce, pickled ginger and soya sauce on rice. Other choices range from a platter of 'mixed titbits', via rice or noodle dishes with chicken, beef, pork or prawns and various sauces and accompaniments, to red or green curry and five vegetarian choices. The serious, eclectic list of 28 wines includes only two over £20. SAMPLE DISHES: chicken Kiev £6; fried rice with crabmeat, chicken, eggs and raisins £6.50; fried thick noodles in gravy with pork and broccoli £6.

Licensee Suhail Hussein (freehouse)
Open Tue to Sat and bank hol Mon 11 to 3, 6 to 11, Sun 12 to 4, 7 to 10.30; bar food and restaurant Tue to Sun and bank hol Mon 12 to 2.30, 6 to 10.30 (9.30 Sun)
Details Children welcome in eating areas and games room   Car park   Wheelchair access (also WC)   Garden and patio   No smoking in restaurant   Occasional music   Dogs welcome on a lead in bar area only   Delta, MasterCard, Switch, Visa

▲ Bell Inn
Great North Road, Stilton PE7 3RA   TEL: (01733) 241066
WEBSITE: www.thebellstilton.co.uk
off A1, 6m SW of Peterborough

In the early eighteenth century, this was the birthplace of the cheese, as well as being a coaching inn on the Great North Road. Barely a stone's throw from the modern A1, this building of appropriately creamy-coloured stone still meets the needs of hungry travellers, and is a smart hotel besides. The restaurant is fairly formal and its set menu fairly traditional (smoked haddock risotto, then roast Gressingham duck, say). The beamed Village Bar, with its flagstone floor and open fire, has a pleasant, pubby air and a menu that takes in tomato and shellfish bisque or duck and bean sprout samosas, as well as braised beef and ale stew, or roast cod and creamed potato with mushy pea mint sauce. And, needless to say, that cheese pops up – in soups, sauces and cheesecake as well as on the cheeseboard. The beers on offer are JHB (from the local Oakham Brewery), Marston's Pedigree, Greene King Abbot Ale and

IPA, and Adnams Bitter, and six wines are available by the glass. SAMPLE
DISHES: Stilton and broccoli soup £3.50; lamb's liver and bacon on roast celeriac with thyme jus £9.25; baked Stilton cheesecake £3.50.

Licensees M.J. and L.A. McGivern (freehouse)
Open 12 to 2.30 (3 Sat), 6 to 11, Sun 12 to 3, 7 to 10.30; bar food and restaurant 12 to 2,
6.30 to 9.30, Sun 12 to 2.30, 7 to 9; closed 25 Dec
Details Car park   Garden and patio   No-smoking area in bar, no smoking in restaurant
Background music   No dogs   Amex, Delta, Diners, MasterCard, Switch, Visa   Accommodation:
19 rooms, B&B £72.50 to £109.50

STOCKBRIDGE   Hampshire   map 2

Greyhound 😀 😀   NEW ENTRY

31 High Street, Stockbridge SO20 6EY   TEL: (01264) 810833
village at junction of A30 and A3057 S of Andover

The Test has always attracted game fishermen to the attractive village of
Stockbridge, but now the Greyhound is proving a draw too. The old inn has
been sympathetically converted with style: there's a clubby lounge with
leather sofas and chesterfields, and an open-plan space laid out with simple
wooden furniture and a traditional bar. The lunchtime menu knocks out
simple pub offerings like ploughman's and baguettes, while the short, regularly changing carte moves up through the gears to deliver sophisticated,
accomplished modern cooking. Begin with a freebie amuse-gueule of pressed
foie gras and Armagnac terrine with pear chutney, perhaps, continue with a
starter of seared diver-caught scallops with baby leeks and sauce Jacqueline,
and move on to fillet of beef with herbed potato purée and a port and lentil jus.
Finish in tropical mode with coconut crème brûlée with lime sorbet. The
wine list covers a good range, with the selection by the glass more interesting
than most, and Wadworth 6X and Greene King IPA and Abbot Ale are on
handpump. SAMPLE DISHES: risotto of crab and clams £6.50; pan-fried turbot
with leek and truffle oil gratin and mushroom velouté £16.50; chocolate
fondant with mint and chocolate ice cream £5.50.

Licensee Barry Skarin (Innspired Pubs & Taverns)
Open 12 to 2.30, Mon to Sat 7 to 10.30; bar food 12 to 2.30, restaurant 12 to 2.30, 7 to 10
Details Children welcome   Car park   Wheelchair access (also WC)   Garden   Dogs welcome
Delta, MasterCard, Switch, Visa

STOCKLAND   Devon   map 2

▲ Kings Arms Inn 🍇

Stockland EX14 9BS   TEL: (01404) 881361
WEBSITE: www.kingsarms.net
*signposted from A30 Chard to Honiton road, or from A35 take Shute garage exit W of
Axminster*

This is some six miles north-east of Honiton, between the two main roads on
that side of the town, but Stockland is well signposted. At its centre is this
two-storey thatched building in creamy-coloured render. If the outside does-
n't look especially antique, the inside is Olde English in excelsis: low ceilings

with dark oak beams and windowsills, wooden settles and dadoes, more cream paint and much exposed stonework. The bars serve Exmoor Ale, Otter Ale and O'Hanlon's Port Stout, plus incomers like Webster's Green Label, and there's a long list of malt whiskies. A substantial and eclectic wine list opens with twenty-odd house wines at £10 a bottle and also by the glass. Reporters have had some disappointments here but there are plenty of exciting options from £12.50 up to £50. It's the same food in bar and red-carpeted, non-smoking dining room (dinner is à la carte only): a Monday-to-Friday lunchtime snack menu and a long blackboard mostly listing main ingredients without further detail (e.g. 'fillet of ostrich'). A varied repertoire includes plenty for fish-fanciers and vegetarians; there may be melon, Portuguese sardines, or chicken liver pâté to start, then mushroom stroganoff, king prawn Madras, or breast of Quantock duck (which came with red cabbage, broccoli and carrots, plus a choice of chips or new potatoes, and an orange sauce). Crowd-pleasing puddings range from apple and treacle crumbly to strawberry meringue. SAMPLE DISHES: confit du canard £5; venison pie £9.50; chocolate nut sundae £5.

Licensees Heinz Kiefer and Paul Diviani
Open 12 to 3, 6.30 to 11 (10.30 Sun); bar food and restaurant 12 to 1.45, 6.30 to 9; closed 25 Dec
Details Children welcome in bar eating area and dining room   Car park   Wheelchair access (not WC)   Garden and patio   No smoking in dining room   Live music in bar weekends; background music in dining room   Dogs welcome exc in dining room   Delta, MasterCard, Switch, Visa   Accommodation: 3 rooms, B&B £40 to £60

STODMARSH   Kent   map 3

▲ Red Lion   NEW ENTRY
The Street, Stodmarsh CT3 4BA   TEL: (01227) 721339
follow Stodmarsh signpost from A257 about 2m E of Canterbury

Stodmarsh is a tiny village just outside Canterbury, comprising a handful of houses and a quaint little church. A nearby nature reserve draws its fair share of visitors, but perhaps the star attraction is the village inn. The fifteenth-century building has bags of character – a reflection of its enthusiastic and charming owner, Robert Whigham. Inside is a warren of linked areas around a central island bar, each with its own theme – one plastered with sheet music and with musical instruments hanging from the ceiling, another covered with diagrammatic prints of Victorian kitchenalia. Hop wreaths and all sorts of knick-knacks abound throughout. Food, listed on a huge blackboard, is straightforward country cooking that makes a virtue of fine produce – much of it local – and careful but unfussy preparation. Pheasant and wild rabbit hotpot with claret and field mushrooms is typical, as is pan-fried sole with green capers, salted butter and king prawns. Portions are hearty to say the least – a reporter's 'richly moreish' plateful of roasted pheasant and partridge with smoked bacon provided 'about a week's supply of protein'. The choice of wines includes six by the glass, while first-class real ales are drawn directly from the cask: perhaps Greene King IPA or Flagship Admiral's Bitter. In winter mulled Biddenden cider is served, and other unusual drinking options include fresh figs in vodka and bullshot. SAMPLE DISHES: baked rösti with pan-fried kidneys and sherry £6; maize-fed chicken, leek and cider pie £10; pan-fried pork fillets with a cottage cheese vol-au-vent and cider sauce £13.

Licensee Robert Whigham (freehouse)
Open 11 to 11, Sun 12 to 10.30; bar food all week 12 to 2.30 (3.30 Sun), Mon to Sat 7 to 9.30
Details Children welcome in eating area   Car park   Garden and patio   Live or background music
Dogs welcome   Delta, MasterCard, Switch, Visa   Accommodation: 3 rooms, B&B £30 to £50

STOKE-BY-NAYLAND   Suffolk   map 6

▲ Angel Inn
Polstead Street, Stoke-by-Nayland CO6 4SA   TEL: (01206) 263245
on B1068 8m N of Colchester

For energetic art-lovers this is a good pit stop halfway between Flatford Mill and the Gainsborough Museum in Sudbury, but leisurely lovers of landscape in the round, savouring the glorious summer country of the Stour valley, might pause here too. It's on a crossroads in the centre of the village (hence, hard to miss), though the main entrance is round the back. Inside, the atmosphere is upmarket rustic (rough red-brick walls, brick and tiled floors, polished oak tables), and this clearly appeals, because the bars can get crowded (booking ahead is sensible). With a glass of Adnams Best Bitter (or Greene King Abbot Ale or IPA) in hand, one can consider the daily-changing blackboard beside the bar. Tempting starters might include Roquefort soufflé, a salad of calamares and prawns, or a warm pork terrine that proved to be more a roulade of pork and sage and onion stuffing. Follow with liver and bacon on bubble and squeak, or roast lamb, or maybe grilled lemon sole with salad and chips. Then those with loosenable waistbands might attempt toffee sponge pudding with vanilla sauce and pecan nuts; the fainter-hearted might settle for a brandy-snap basket of poached plums. An interesting and eclectic wine list has over 50 bins and six by the glass. SAMPLE DISHES: smoked chicken Caesar salad £4.75; baked suprême of salmon with roast fennel £10.75; pistachio crème brûlée £4.25.

Licensee Clive Richardson (Horizon Inns)
Open 11 to 2.30, 6 to 11, Sun 12 to 10.30; bar food and restaurant 12 to 2, 6.30 to 9, Sun 12 to 5, 5.30 to 9.30; closed 25 and 26 Dec, 1 Jan
Details Children welcome in family room   Car park   Wheelchair access (also WC)   Patio
No smoking in eating areas   No music   Dogs welcome on patio only   Amex, Delta, MasterCard,
Switch, Visa   Accommodation: 6 rooms, B&B £54.50 to £69.50

STOKE HOLY CROSS   Norfolk   map 6

Wildebeest Arms ✿
82–86 Norwich Road, Stoke Holy Cross NR14 8QJ   TEL: (01508) 492497
off A140 4½m S of Norwich

Close to the site of Venta Icenorum, Boudicca's capital, in this quiet, one-shop-cum-post-office village, the Wildebeest Arms's slightly dowdy exterior conceals its modern credentials from the passing world, the only giveaway being the large car park at the side. The inside is different: all one room with cool, contemporary décor of natural wood and pale yellow walls dotted with African masks and ethnographica. A central bar counter divides drinkers and eaters. The former can expect Adnams Bitter and a guest beer; the latter may peruse a long, varied and interesting wine list with a dozen available by the glass – plus an array of post-prandials from Armagnac and Calvados to sweet Muscats and single malts. The Anglo-Mediterranean menus (prix fixe changes daily, the carte every six to eight weeks) offer starters like Parmesan, orange and beetroot salad, or grilled smoked haddock ('nice chunky and meaty flesh, flaked easily') with sautéed spinach and a delicate cockle cream. Mains might encompass calf's liver with bubble and squeak and warm Parma ham, a sautéed wild mushroom and milanese risotto, or a pesto-baked chicken breast with a white-bean cassoulet – a combination that 'couldn't be faulted'. Desserts subsume orange and vanilla pannacotta with blood orange sorbet, and a raspberry Bakewell tart. SAMPLE DISHES: warm Parma ham and Parmesan salad £6.25; grilled sea bass with tarragon risotto, wilted spinach and sauce vierge £13; roast apple and pistachio with sultanas and clove ice cream £5.25.

Licensees Henry Watt and Sarah Boyd (freehouse)
Open 12 to 3, 6 to 11, Sun 12 to 4, 7 to 11; bar food and restaurant 12 to 2, 7 to 10, Sun 12 to 2.30, 7 to 9.30
Details Children welcome   Car park   Wheelchair access (not WC)   Garden   No smoking in dining area   Background music   No dogs   Delta, MasterCard, Switch, Visa

STOKENHAM   Devon   map I

Tradesman's Arms

Stokenham TQ7 2SZ   TEL: (01548) 580313
off A379 Kingsbridge to Torcross road, 5m E of Kingsbridge

This unpretentious pub opens only in the evenings most days, and at lunchtime only on Sundays. Part thatched and part tiled, it sits comfortably in a terrace of cottages; inside, the beamy bar is simply furnished and cosy with its wood-burning stove. The small, informal dining room and the bar operate the same menu, supplemented by blackboard specials, with traditional roasts at Sunday lunch. Wholesome dishes from fresh local produce will tempt vegetarians, carnivores and especially fish eaters. You might find starters of wild duck pâté, or a tartare of smoked salmon and Puy lentils, followed by grilled hake on orange and lemon sauce, braised venison and butter beans, or an aubergine stuffed with roast peppers, mushroom and more aubergine, then sprinkled with cheesy breadcrumbs and grilled. Desserts range from bread-and-butter pudding with ice cream to iced Grand Marnier soufflé on mango coulis, via fresh strawberry fool. Adnams ales are on handpump, alongside such guests as Exmoor Fox and Gold, and brews from Butcombe and Otter, plus Ruddy Turnstone cider from the Heron Valley. They keep a range of single-malt Scotches, and two Sharpham Vineyard's Devon wines figure in a list of two dozen (all under £20, and 6 come by the glass). SAMPLE DISHES: fresh asparagus with melted butter £3.75; pot-roast quails with rice and apricot stuffing £12.50; apple and walnut pudding with coffee ice cream £3.50.

Licensees John and Elizabeth Sharman (freehouse)
Open Tue to Sat 6.30 to 11, Sun 12 to 3.30; bar food Sun 12 to 1.45, Tue to Sat 6.45 to 9
Details Children welcome in dining room at Sun lunch   Car park   Wheelchair access (not WC)   Garden and patio   No-smoking area in bar, no smoking in dining area   No music   Dogs on a lead welcome in bar   Delta, MasterCard, Switch, Visa

Crooked Billet

Newlands Lane, Stoke Row RG9 5PU   TEL: (01491) 681048
WEBSITE: www.thecrookedbillet.co.uk
off B481 Reading to Nettlebed road, 5m W of Henley-on-Thames

Despite being off the beaten track, this seventeenth-century whitewashed-brick inn is a popular place. Its rustic interior is part of the appeal: beams, an enormous basket of wine-bottle corks by a huge open fire and green candles to match the colour of the banquettes in the main eating area, whose maroon walls are hung with vintage black and white photographs and shelves filled with books. Unusually, there is no bar counter, and pints of Brakspear are brought up from the cellar, where they are drawn direct from the cask. The extensive, eclectic and adventurous weekly-changing menu makes a real change from the usual 'pub grub' without being pretentious about it: starters of warm truffled wild mushroom tartlet with a tomato and broad bean salad, or five pan-fried scallops with Bayonne ham, Parmesan, radicchio and figs might be followed by pink-roast breast and crisp leg of duck in mandarin sauce with noodles, or roast hake with queenies, clams and mussels accompanied by rösti. Vegetarians get their own menu, cheeses are unpasteurised (and local), and desserts are largely old school: trifle, or chocolate and vanilla cheesecake. Luxury ingredients such as lobster, oysters and caviar are common, so it may come as a surprise to find that prices are reasonable, with the set lunch considered especially good value. Around 50 wines, plus champagnes, feature on the wine list, and daily specials add to the variety. A decent number come by the glass. Diverse live music events include jazz, skiffle and boogie-woogie evenings (note that these usually attract a cover charge). SAMPLE DISHES: potted foie gras and chicken liver mousse with onion marmalade £7; roast rump of lamb with Parmesan polenta, broad beans, tomato, olives and pancetta crisps £15.25; rich dark Belgian chocolate mousse with clotted cream and raspberries £5.50.

Licensee Paul Clerehugh (freehouse)
Open Mon to Fri 12 to 3.30, 7 to 11.30, Sat 12 to 11, Sun 12 to 10.30; bar food Mon to Fri 12 to 2.30, 7 to 10, Sat and Sun 12 to 10
Details Children welcome   Car park   Garden   Occasional live or background music   No dogs   MasterCard, Visa

Hare Arms

Stow Bardolph PE34 3HT   TEL: (01366) 382229
WEBSITE: www.theharearms.co.uk
off A10, 2m N of Downham Market

This is a large Georgian pub built of red brick under its creeper cladding and substantial chimneys. At the back there's a garden with peacocks and chickens and a patio. The porch at the front is non-functional, and one enters at the side, through a modern conservatory extension. Doubling as a no-smoking dining area, this leads into a main bar crusted with a startling diversity of bric-à-brac (a sporting theme is discernible in among the advertisements and old brass blowlamps). All this attracts a similar diversity of customers, and it can get very busy here. A long bar menu ranges from sandwiches and jacket potatoes, via the expected steaks (tuna, pork or beef), to bradan rost or Thai chicken curry – besides catering for children and vegetarians (and for Sunday lunch there's roast beef and Yorkshire, too). Puddings are listed on black-boards. The restaurant offers set and à la carte menus that cover the likes of Thai-style tiger prawns or gammon crêpe starters, then slow-cooked lamb shank or Moroccan chicken, plus a dessert trolley. The beers are Greene King's (Abbot, Old Speckled Hen), plus such guests as Hook Norton Old Hooky – and there's Much Marcle Millennium Cider as well. The 25 or so wines are mostly under £20, and seven come by the glass. SAMPLE DISHES: avocado and smoked salmon salad £6.50; tournedos zingara £15; Baileys bread-and-butter pudding £3.25.

Licensees David and Trish McManus (Greene King)
Open 11 to 2.30, 6 to 11, Sun 12 to 2.30, 7 to 10.30; bar food 12 to 2, 7 to 10; restaurant Mon to Sat 7 to 9.30; closed 25 and 26 Dec
Details Children welcome in family room and conservatory   Car park   Wheelchair access (not WC) Garden and patio   No-smoking area in bar, no smoking in conservatory or dining room   No music No dogs   MasterCard, Switch, Visa

---

STOW-ON-THE-WOLD   Gloucestershire   map 5

▲ Eagle and Child

Digbeth Street, Stow-on-the-Wold GL54 1BN   TEL: (01451) 830670
WEBSITE: www.theroyalisthotel.co.uk
at junction of A429, A436 and A424, 8m W of Chipping Norton

The Eagle and Child must be one of the oldest inns in England: it served its first ale as long ago as 947. It now forms the pub arm of the Royalist Hotel, and can be accessed through the hotel reception. A small L-shaped bar and a room with bare stone walls and a flagstone floor have been extended with a conser-vatory dining area for days when it isn't pleasant enough to sit outside. The menu mixes traditional dishes with more contemporary ideas: local sausages with onion gravy and mash, or roast pheasant with stuffing, game chips and bread sauce alongside seared liver with thyme mash, pancetta and onion marmalade, or crab and cod fishcakes with tomato and ginger sauce. You might begin a meal with sautéed prawns and scallops with a sweet chilli and lime salsa, or oxtail faggot with celeriac purée, and finish with banana fritters with toffee sauce, or caramelised fruit pudding. Local Hook Norton Best Bitter, Worthington Bitter and Timothy Taylor Landlord are on tap, and a short and simple wine list includes 12 by the glass from £2.50. SAMPLE DISHES: smoked chicken spring rolls with satay dressing £5; pan-fried sea bass with aubergine caviar and sun-dried tomato and pea risotto £12.25; bread-and-butter pudding with custard £4.

Licensees Alan and Georgina Thompson (freehouse)
Open 11 to 11 (10 Sun); bar food and restaurant 12 to 2.30 (3 Sun), 6 to 10
Details Children welcome   Car park   Wheelchair access (also WC)   Patio   No-smoking area in restaurant   Background music   Dogs welcome   Amex, Delta, MasterCard, Switch, Visa
Accommodation: 8 rooms, B&B £90 (double room) to £170 (suite)

▲ Kings Arms ☼ NEW ENTRY

The Square, Stow-on-the-Wold GL54 IAF   TEL: (01451) 830364
WEBSITE: www.kingsarms-stowonthewold.co.uk

Set on the market square among top-class antique shops, this ancient stone pub – a tall building with mullioned windows – fits in well in this old and prosperous Cotswolds town. It has bags of atmosphere inside, with eating and drinking (and smoking) areas spread over two floors, dimly lit by spotlights and candles, furnished with sofas and Charles Rennie Mackintosh chairs, and decorated with a mix of arty photographs and posters, and hunting and showjumping pictures. This is a pub that wants to remain a pub, with no aspirations to restaurant status, and the daily menu, chalked on a blackboard, reflects that philosophy, listing some very simple-sounding dishes. But the kitchen nonetheless achieves impressive results. As an inspector put it, this is 'clever' rather than highly technical cooking, relying on top-quality raw materials and plenty of rich and bright flavours, using lots of exotic herbs and spices in inventive combinations, such as pea and fennel soup, grilled squid piri-piri, monkfish casseroled with peppers, almonds and saffron, lamb shank with chickpeas, mint and coriander, and grilled marinated venison with caponata, balsamic and chilli. Puddings, surprisingly, are more run-of-the-mill choices, but interesting British cheeses make a tempting alternative way to finish. There is no wine list as such – instead, all bottles are displayed on shelves on an L-shaped wall, with price tags around their necks. Value is fair, with prices starting around £10, and ten wines are available by the glass. Real ales are Greene King IPA and Hook Norton Old Hooky. SAMPLE DISHES: grilled quail with figs £5; roast skate wing with aïoli, new potatoes and purple-sprouting broccoli £10; poached white peach melba £4.50.

Licensees Louise and Peter Robinson (Greene King)
Open II to II, Sun 12 to 10.30; bar food and restaurant 12 to 2.30, 6 to 9.30 (10 Fri and Sat); closed Stow Horse Fair, I week May, I week Oct
Details Children welcome   Car park   Background music   Dogs welcome exc in restaurant   Delta, MasterCard, Switch, Visa   Accommodation: 10 rooms, B&B £60 to £100

STRETTON   Rutland   map 6

Jackson Stops Inn   NEW ENTRY

Rookery Road, Stretton LE15 7RA   TEL: (01780) 410237
on B668, just off A1 about 9m N of Stamford

This long, low, stone-built partly thatched building – now a popular pub/restaurant – dates from 1721, its name reputedly acquired when the property was on the market for so long that it became known by the name on the estate agent's for sale board. Stone fireplaces, exposed stone, quarry-tiled or carpeted floors, pine tables and copper warming pans and farm implements create a warm, convivial atmosphere. The appealing, modish menu might open with seared scallops and black pudding with mash and garlic sauce, while fillet of halibut could be teamed with saffron tagliatelle and baby spinach as a main course. A 'spot-on' spiced apple pannacotta could head up desserts. Simpler bar food, the likes of Brie and bacon on toasted ciabatta, or beer-battered haddock fillet with chips, appears on blackboards. Oakham Ales' JHB and Adnams Bitter are on handpump, while the globetrotting wine list offers ten by the glass from £2.75. SAMPLE DISHES: ham hock and foie gras terrine with mustard dressing £6.25; slow-roast belly pork with black pudding, apple and rösti £9.25; vanilla-roasted figs with mascarpone £4.

Licensee James Trevor (freehouse)
Open 12 to 2.30, 6.30 to 11, Sun 12 to 2.30; bar food and restaurant 12 to 2, 7 to 10, Sun 12 to 2; closed 31 Dec, 1 Jan
Details Children welcome Car park Garden No smoking in 1 room Background music Dogs welcome Delta, MasterCard, Switch, Visa

SUTTON GAULT **Cambridgeshire** map 6

▲ Anchor Inn ☺ ❀

Sutton Gault CB6 2BD   TEL: (01353) 778537
off B1381 Sutton to Earith road, 6m W of Ely

WATERSIDE

The Anchor was built in the mid-seventeenth century as lodgings for the men who were draining the Fens, and it stands in the shelter of the bank of the New Bedford River (named after the earl who commissioned the drainage), a straight, wide canal also known as the Hundred Foot Drain. Inside are pine tables on uneven floors, antique prints, wall-mounted working gas lamps and log fires. Given the pub's remote location, the modern and imaginative menu, with a blackboard of daily specials, might come as a bit of a surprise: a stew of mussels, bacon and Brie with tarragon, or venison carpaccio with beetroot confit and celeriac rémoulade to start, followed by pan-fried king scallops with crispy bacon, sautéed new potatoes, wild mushrooms and an orange cream sauce, or seared wood pigeon breasts with sweet potato mash, lentils, chorizo and roast chicory. Old favourites aren't overlooked either, with smoked haddock fishcakes with mushy peas, wild boar sausages with mash, and roast fillet of salmon with hollandaise all making an appearance, and lemon posset and marmalade-glazed bread-and-butter pudding might be among desserts. Boathouse Bitter and Hobson's Choice from the City of Cambridge Brewery are on draught, along with Thatcher's scrumpy in summer. Eight wines by the glass, priced from £2.90 to £4.45, make a tempting introduction to an inspiring choice of 60 or so bottles, with a dozen also in halves. The options are limited under £15, but prices are not unreasonable for the quality and rarely seen wines like Henschke Louis Semillon or Pinot Noir from Jean Denois are something special. SAMPLE DISHES: avocado and crab gâteau with sweet chilli dressing £7.50; roast wild duck with rösti, Savoy cabbage and bacon with a red wine, sour cherry and redcurrant sauce £13.50; petit pot au chocolat £3.75.

Licensee Robin Moore (freehouse)
Open 12 to 3, 7 to 11 (10.30 Sun); bar food 12 to 2, 7 to 9 (6.30 to 9.30 Sat)
Details Children welcome Car park Wheelchair access (also WC) Patio No smoking in 3 rooms No music Guide dogs only Amex, Delta, MasterCard, Switch, Visa Accommodation: 2 rooms, B&B £50 to £95

Use the maps at the back of the book to plan your trip.

SUTTON LANE ENDS   Cheshire   map 8

▲ Sutton Hall Hotel

Bullocks Lane, Sutton Lane Ends SK11 0HE   TEL: (01260) 253211
1½m S of Macclesfield turn E off A523, signposted Langley; after ½m turn left at Bullocks Lane
crossroads

Not exactly your average pub! Once the local manor, and later a nunnery, this
place has 'a great, original atmosphere'. Set back from the road in parkland
near the Macclesfield Canal, it was built in 1520 and added to later, so it is part
black and white half-timbered and part mellow local sandstone, with a stone-
slate roof. The bar has gleaming copper measures lining a huge old fireplace,
dark-wood panelling, and a suit of armour, while the bar menu is not so old-
fashioned, though it doesn't seek to be cutting edge either. It offers starters
like deep-fried Brie on mango coulis, marinated salmon and sliced melon, or
mushrooms and smoked oysters in sage oil on tagliatelle. A main dish of a
cheese basket filled with 'slightly crisp, perfectly cooked' sautéed leeks with
Gruyère sauce was appreciated by one diner; others praise a kidney-heavy,
rich-gravied steak and kidney pie, its puff pastry topped with smoked oysters
to give 'an unusual piquancy', or 'a veritable slab' of cod in a lovely crisp batter
with masses of mushy peas. Puddings run from fruit sorbets for the virtuous
to profiteroles with chocolate sauce for the uninhibited. Marston's Bitter,
Bass, and Greene King IPA are on draught, plus guests like Mauldon's
seasonal brews, and four wines are served by the glass from an extensive list.
SAMPLE DISHES: French onion soup £3.25; seafood tagliatelle in tomato sauce
£7.25; caramel apple flan £3.50.

Licensee Robert Bradshaw (freehouse)
Open 11 to 11; bar food and restaurant 12 to 2.30 (2 Sun), 7 to 9.45
Details Children welcome in restaurant   Car park   Garden   Background music   Amex, Delta,
Diners, MasterCard, Switch, Visa   Accommodation: 10 rooms, B&B £75 to £90

SUTTON UPON DERWENT   East Riding of Yorkshire   map 9

St Vincent Arms   NEW ENTRY

Sutton upon Derwent YO41 5BN   TEL: (01904) 608349
on B1228, SE of York

'It's impossible to get in at the weekends without three weeks' booking in
advance,' warned a reporter, finding that people drive out from York and the
surrounding area to eat at this popular pub in a pretty little village. A good
range of ales, including Fuller's London Pride and Chiswick Bitter, Timothy
Taylor Landlord, Wells Bombardier Premium Bitter and locally brewed
Yorkshire Terrier, will tempt beer drinkers, but the real draw here is the food.
While the St Vincent continues to fulfil the role of traditional village pub via
its small locals' bar and friendly atmosphere, its other three rooms are devoted
solely to food. Modestly decorated, warm and comfortable, with gas fires and
orderly set-out tables, these rooms manage to maintain an old pub atmosphere
too. An extensive menu of largely traditional fare takes in pan-fried pigeon
breast, or baked goats' cheese to start, while main courses include steak and
kidney pie with 'excellent pastry', fillet steak with Stilton, or 'tender' rack of

lamb with red wine and rosemary sauce. Seafood might appear in the form of moules marinière, haddock and prawn pie, or grilled Dover sole, and puddings are from the school of lemon meringue pie. Around ten wines come by the glass. SAMPLE DISHES: home-made soup of the day £3.50; sirloin steak £11; treacle tart £3.

Licensee Philip Hopwood (freehouse)
Open 11.30 to 3, 6 to 11; bar food and restaurant 12 to 2, 7 to 9.30
Details Children welcome Car park Wheelchair access (not WC) Garden No smoking in restaurant No music Dogs welcome in bar Delta, MasterCard, Switch, Visa

SWALLOWFIELD Berkshire map 2

George & Dragon 😊 NEW ENTRY
Church Road, Swallowfield RG7 1TJ TEL: (0118) 988 4432
Swallowfield signposted on B3349 S of Reading; proceed through village towards Farley Hill

An old cottagey inn beyond the village, 'in the middle of nowhere', as one reporter put it, the George & Dragon is very much a dining pub (booking essential), smart and informal but still offering a welcome to drinkers. A series of rooms, including a conservatory, are decked out with polished-wood tables set for food. Walls are painted a distinctive warm pink, there are low ceilings and beams, a big fireplace, and chatty, friendly and youthful staff. The bar snacks menu is available only at lunchtimes, while the printed carte is backed up by blackboard specials, perhaps a Stilton, red onion and peppered beef salad. Dishes are well constructed, well presented and balanced: witness a dish of honey-glazed duck breast ('tender and first class') with redcurrant sauce and 'well-flavoured' red cabbage. For fish eaters, the carte might feature whole baked sea bass in a Thai-style marinade. Desserts err on the side of familiarity, with the likes of sticky toffee or bread-and-butter puddings, or possibly baked cheesecake with mango sorbet. Fuller's London Pride, Wadworth 6X and Adnams Bitter make an appearance on handpump, while six wines of the week, chalked on a blackboard, are available by the glass. SAMPLE DISHES: Malaysian squid salad with crispy noodles £5.75; cannon of lamb with Moroccan-spiced couscous £15; banana cake with vanilla sorbet £5.

Licensee Paul Daley (freehouse)
Open 12 to 11; bar food and restaurant 12 to 3, 7 to 9.30
Details Children welcome Car park Wheelchair access Garden Background music Dogs welcome Delta, MasterCard, Switch, Visa

SWAN BOTTOM Buckinghamshire map 3

Old Swan
Swan Bottom HP16 9NU TEL: (01494) 837239
off A413, between Great Missenden and Wendover, just N of The Lee

The wavy line of the long tiled roof of this whitewashed building hints at the pub's origins in the sixteenth century, as does a well to the side. Its flagstone-floored interior has a cosy atmosphere, and the sign saying 'duck' hanging from a beam is not the Swan's homage to its relatives but valuable advice on safeguarding your head. It is a rural pub, in a tiny, peaceful hamlet, where locals drink and people come to lunch or dine. The blackboard menu changes twice daily, and lunch dishes such as a salad of avocado, prawns and bacon with tarragon vinaigrette, or moules marinière can also be starters in the evening. More substantial lunch dishes might include steak, kidney and mushroom pie, boeuf bourguignonne, or Irish stew. The dinner menu might offer roast partridge on a bed of spiced red cabbage with roast potatoes, or, given that fish is something of a speciality, roast fillet of cod on a bed of spinach with creamed potato. Blackcurrant crème brûlée is typical of desserts. Adnams Bitter, Brakspear Bitter and Bateman XB are on draught, and Stowford Press cider is kept too. Around half a dozen wines are sold by the glass. SAMPLE DISHES: chargrilled ciabatta with Mediterranean vegetables roasted in olive oil with Parmesan £6.50; medallions of pork fillet with sage on a bed of sweet potato with a cider and mustard sauce £9.50; chocolate roulade with raspberry coulis £3.75.

Licensee Sean Michaelson-Yeates (freehouse)
Open *Mon to Fri 12 to 3, 6 to 11, Sat 12 to 11, Sun 12 to 10.30; bar food and restaurant (exc Sun evening) 12.30 to 2, 6.30 to 9*
Details *Children welcome in eating areas   Car park   Wheelchair access (also WC)   Garden No smoking in restaurant   No music   Dogs welcome in bar   MasterCard, Switch, Visa*

SWANTON MORLEY   Norfolk   map 6

Darby's 🍺

1–2 Elsing Road, Swanton Morley NR20 4NY   TEL: (01362) 637647

Converted into a pub in 1988 from a pair of cottages that originated in the eighteenth century, Darby's is a solid-looking building on a corner in the centre of the village. A narrow corridor leads into a spacious bar, which has a rustic feel created by beams, brick walls and an inglenook with a log fire. Plenty of fish and seafood appear on the menu, done up in a variety of styles: steamed Brancaster mussels with salad, Thai red crab cakes with garlic mayonnaise, or pan-fried sea bass with spinach, for example. There are also plenty of meaty offerings, ranging from a starter of barbecued spare ribs to main courses of chargrilled steaks, chicken and vegetable stir-fry with oyster sauce and Thai-style rice, or venison braised in red wine. Baguettes, vegetarian options and a children's menu are also possibilities. Beers are a fine selection comprising regulars from Adnams, Badger, Woodforde's and Greene King as well as three guest ales. A short list of wines is reasonably priced, and there are three by the glass. In the garden is a children's adventure play area. SAMPLE DISHES: smoked salmon, bacon and Brie salad £5.50; steak and mushroom suet pudding served with vegetables £10; chocolate and orange bread-and-butter pudding £3.50.

Licensees John Carrick and Louise Battle (freehouse)
Open *Mon to Fri 11.30 to 3, 6 to 11, Sat 11.30 to 11, Sun 12 to 10.30; bar food and restaurant Mon to Fri 12 to 2.15, 6.30 to 9.45, Sat 12 to 9.45, Sun 12 to 9.15*
Details *Children welcome   Car park   Wheelchair access (also WC)   Garden   No smoking in family room and restaurant   Occasional live music   Dogs welcome in bar and family room   Delta, MasterCard, Switch, Visa*

SWERFORD   Oxfordshire   map 5

Masons Arms   [NEW ENTRY]

Swerford OX7 4AP   TEL: (01608) 683212
on A361 just outside village

'A London gastro-pub transported out to the Cotswolds' is how one reporter
described this old, brown-stone country inn. Add an attractive, scrubbed-
pine, Tuscan-farmhouse reworking of the old interior (complete with
wooden floors and light beams), modern eclectic cuisine, friendly, efficient
service and an urbane, relaxed atmosphere, and you have the Masons Arms in
a nutshell. At lunchtime there's a choice of baguettes on the blackboard or an
enticing menu that travels the globe for inspiration: perhaps baby squid
tempura with salad, plum sauce and Parmesan shavings, Barbary duck stuffed
with lemon, garlic, lime leaves and ginger, served with rocket and sweet chilli
sauce, or more homely beer-battered fish and chips with tartare sauce. A 30-
strong wine list, with the New World to the fore, offers a handful by the glass,
while, for beer lovers, there are three regularly changing ales from the local
Hook Norton Brewery on tap, including Best Bitter. SAMPLE DISHES: rocket
and roasted pear salad with Roquefort and shaved Parmesan £5.75; sea bass
with lemongrass and lime leaves served with mizuna salad, burnt lemon and
sauce vierge £14; Belgian apple flan £4.25.

Licensee Jeanette Hill-Wickham (freehouse)
Open *Tue to Sat 12 to 3, 7 to 11, Sun 12 to 3; bar food and restaurant Tue to Sat 12 to 3,
7 to 11, Sun 12 to 3*
Details *Children welcome   Car park   Wheelchair access   Garden   No-smoking areas   Occasional
live or background music   Dogs welcome   Amex, Delta, Diners, MasterCard, Switch, Visa*

SWILLAND   Suffolk   map 6

Moon & Mushroom Inn 🍺

High Road, Swilland IP6 9LR   TEL: (01473) 785320
from Ipswich take B1077 N; about ¼ m past Witnesham fork right for Swilland

This place must be the high spot of the village. There's a small terrace at the
front with a couple of tables and a rather larger garden at the back. Inside, the
long, beamed main bar has comfortably cushioned benches, and a separate
'food bar' off it. Perhaps the most notable thing is the beer, all of it very well-
kept, and all from local microbreweries: representing Norfolk, there are
Buffy's Hopleaf and Norwich Terrier, Wolf's Coyote Bitter, and Woodforde's
Wherry and Norfolk Nog, plus Nethergate Umbel Ale from Suffolk. But the
food is satisfying too. There are various varieties of ploughman's, including
collar bacon, and mackerel. Alternatively you could go for a main dish (there
are no starters) served from a hotplate at the bar, after which you help yourself
to the tasty array of fresh vegetables (new/sautéed potatoes, broccoli, cauliflower, red cabbage...). These could include minted lamb, beef nog with
dumplings, or perhaps a salmon fillet in herb sauce, or a cheese and broccoli
bake. Puddings are old favourites like apple crumble, or treacle sponge.
Twelve wines may be had by the glass from a list of eighteen. SAMPLE DISHES:

pâté ploughman's £5; whole partridge in pear chutney £8; bread-and-butter pudding £3.50.

Licensees Clive and Adrienne Goodall
Open Tue to Sat 11 to 2.30, Mon to Sat 6 to 11, Sun 12 to 2.30, 7 to 10.30; bar food Tue to Sat 12 to 2, 6.30 to 8.15
Details No children Car park Wheelchair access (not WC) Garden and patio No smoking in dining room No music Dogs welcome in bar only MasterCard, Switch, Visa

---

TADPOLE BRIDGE   Oxfordshire   map 2

▲ Trout at Tadpole Bridge 🏵 🍇

Tadpole Bridge, Buckland Marsh SN7 8RF   TEL: (01367) 870382   *WATERSIDE*
WEBSITE: www.trout-inn.co.uk
approx 1½m N of A420 Faringdon to Oxford road; follow signs to Buckland Marsh; continue a further ½m beyond Buckland Marsh to river

---

Despite its remote location, this detached stone building with a large garden fronting the Thames can get very busy, with business folk at lunchtime using laptops as well as eating. Stuffed or artificial fish in glass cases and fishing paraphernalia reinforce the pub's name in the yellow-walled interior, with its old timber uprights. Although there's a separate restaurant, you can order from the same menu in the bar. A starter of trout gravad lax with marinated cucumber and drop scones, and a main course of roast rack of lamb with roasted parsnips and haggis sauce show what the kitchen's imagination is capable of producing. Otherwise, look out for cream of watercress soup, or confit of duck leg with honey-roast root vegetables, followed by roast loin of venison with sautéed greens and a fig tart, roast fillet of halibut with kedgeree, linguine with rocket, artichokes, roasted tomatoes and pesto – 'excellent overall flavour,' noted a reporter – or, more prosaically, ham, egg and chips. Less substantial dishes like spicy meatballs with tagliatelle are also possibilities, particularly for those who enjoy a pudding: a 'calorific heap (suet used)' of syrup sponge, for instance, or rich chocolate tart. Two first-class regular real ales – Young's Bitter and Archers Village Bitter – are joined by one or two guest ales such as West Berkshire Full Circle. The wine list is very drinker-friendly, with ten by the glass and all bottles under £25 offered on a 'pay for what you drink' basis. The list opens with a selection of sherries and includes a whole page of Bordeaux in a range of vintages, but there's also plenty of fruity modern drinking and prices are reasonable throughout. Other drinking options include home-made sloe gin, cherry plum vodka and elderflower cordial. The Thames Path, just over Tadpole Bridge, is popular with walkers taking it to Oxford in one direction, Lechlade in the other. SAMPLE DISHES: cured breast of duck with soy, ginger and melon £6; roast breast of chicken wrapped in Parma ham with Puy lentils and chorizo casserole £12; Bramley apple pie £5.

Licensee Christopher J. Green (freehouse)
Open 12 to 2, 7 to 11; bar food and restaurant all week 12 to 2, Mon to Sat 7 to 9; closed Sun evenings exc July and Aug, 25, 26 and 31 Dec, 1 Jan
Details Children welcome Car park Wheelchair access (also WC) Garden No smoking in restaurant Background music Dogs welcome Delta, MasterCard, Switch, Visa Accommodation: 6 rooms, B&B £55 to £80

TARRANT MONKTON   Dorset   map 2

▲ Langton Arms 🍺

Tarrant Monkton DT11 8RX   TEL: (01258) 830225
WEBSITE: www.thelangtonarms.co.uk
on Tarrant Valley thoroughfare, 1¼m S of A354 and 4m NE of Blandford Forum

A seventeenth-century thatched red-brick building beside a church and a ford
in the middle of Hardy country – it even has hollyhocks in the garden! The
Langton Arms meets all the outer stereotypes of a country pub, but it hits the
inner man's gastronomic targets too. In its two bars, with black-beamed ceilings and cream-coloured walls (one has an open fire), the five handpumps
offer a constantly changing selection of real ales, with a brew from Ringwood
and Hop Back Best Bitter from Salisbury permanently available. The bar
menu, starting with baguettes and jacket potatoes, moves on to king prawns in
filo, or deep-fried Brie wedges. Among main-dish offerings are faggots in
onion sauce, braised wild rabbit, and battered fillet of pearl snapper, while
notable desserts are summer pudding or butter toffee waffles with bananas,
cream and maple syrup. The separate restaurant, under head chef Francis
Baumer, has more restricted opening; examples of its weekly-changing menu
are a terrine of salmon, crab and scallops, a saddle of local venison, and a
layered lemon and raspberry mousse to finish. From a list of twenty-odd
European, American and Antipodean wines, eight come by the glass. SAMPLE
DISHES: country farmhouse pâté and toast £4.25; steak and ale pie, chips and
vegetables £7; profiteroles with butterscotch sauce £3.25.

Licensees Barbara and James Coussins (freehouse)
Open 11.30 to 11, Sun 12 to 10.30; bar food 11.30 to 2.30, 6 to 9.30 (Sat and Sun 11.30 to
9.30); restaurant Sun 12 to 2, Wed to Sat 7 to 9
Details Children welcome in family room and dining room   Car park   Wheelchair access (also WC)
Garden   No smoking in dining room   Jukebox   Dogs welcome in locals bar   MasterCard, Switch,
Visa   Accommodation: 6 rooms, B&B £50 to £80

TETBURY   Gloucestershire   map 5

Trouble House 🏵️   NEW ENTRY

Cirencester Road, Tetbury GL8 8SG   TEL: (01666) 502206
WEBSITE: www.troublehouse.co.uk
on A433, 1½m outside Tetbury towards Cirencester

This long, low, cream-washed stone building, dating from the seventeenth
century, is hard alongside the main Tetbury to Cirencester road in the middle
of lovely Cotswolds countryside. The main entrance opens into a proper pub
bar, with big black beams in the low ceiling, butter-yellow walls with terra-
cotta-coloured panelling, log fires at each end of the room, and country-
cottage artefacts. The eating area has a fire too, and a lounge has polished
tables, easy chairs and an attractive stone fireplace and chimney. The same
menu is served throughout. Start with lamb broth with new potatoes and peas,
or 'really super' pan-fried chicken livers with an 'inspired' pistachio and foie
gras butter, before going on to rack of lamb with spicy couscous, or ribeye
steak with béarnaise sauce and chips. Game might be represented by roast

partridge with a creamed lentil and truffle broth, and fish by roasted lemon sole with a potato and bacon cake and creamed Savoy cabbage. Finish with a home-made ice cream or something like panettone bread-and-butter pudding. As the pub is tied to Wadworth, it stocks the range of the brewery's ales. Eight wines are sold by the glass from an international list of around forty bottles, with prices starting at £10.25. SAMPLE DISHES: herb risotto £5.50; braised ox cheek with horseradish mash and roast swedes £13; rice pudding with raspberries £5.

Licensees Michael and Sarah Bedford (Wadworth)
Open *Tue to Sat 11 to 3, 6.30 to 11, Sun 12 to 3, 7 to 10.30; bar food Tue to Sun 12 to 2, Tue to Sat 7 to 9.30; closed 1 week Sept, 25 Dec, 1 Jan, 2 weeks Jan*
Details *Children welcome in eating area   Car park   Wheelchair access (not WC)   Garden No smoking in eating area   Background music   Dogs welcome   Amex, Delta, MasterCard, Switch, Visa*

THELBRIDGE   Devon   map I

▲ Thelbridge Cross Inn
Thelbridge EX17 4SQ   TEL: (01884) 860316
WEBSITE: www.thelbridgexinn.co.uk
off B3137 from Tiverton, before Witheridge, take left fork on to B3042 for 2m

---

This long, two-storey building, smartly painted white behind its climbing foliage, seems quite isolated, although the church and other buildings are within half a mile. Its location in rolling hills gives views on a clear day as far as Dartmoor to the south and Exmoor to the north. The pub dates from the eighteenth century, and although the interior has been opened up it still manages to remain cosy, with a roaring log fire and deep sofas in the main bar area. Decoration is provided by lots of old prints, bank notes, toby jugs and framed 45rpm discs – a reminder that the landlord is the former bass player in the pop group Love Affair. The separate restaurant is in a converted barn, although you can order from the menu in the bar. The carte springs few surprises, with starters of a platter of prawns and smoked fish with horseradish cream, or deep-fried breaded Brie with cranberry sauce, and main courses of breast of guinea fowl stuffed with bacon and mushrooms in Madeira and red wine sauce, or pork dijonnaise. Sandwiches, ploughman's, and main courses of ham, egg and chips, for instance, are what to expect on the bar menu, but the daily specials always include vegetarian dishes: mushroom and tarragon soup, say, followed by nut roast loaf, the latter showing 'plenty of crunchy texture and a skilful blend of flavours'. Otherwise there might be pork curry, steak and kidney pie, or mixed grill, followed by a traditional fruit crumble. Badger Best Bitter, Castle Eden Ale and Bass are on draught, along with Stowford Press cider. A handful of wines is sold by the glass, while the full list runs to around 25 bottles. SAMPLE DISHES: pea and ham soup £3.25; crisp-roast half-duckling in orange sauce £13; treacle tart £3.25.

Licensees W.G. and R.E. Ball (freehouse)
Open *11.30 to 3, 6.30 to 11, Sun 12 to 3, 7 to 10.30; bar food and restaurant 12 to 2.30, 7 to 9.30 (9 winter)*
Details *Children welcome in eating areas   Car park   Garden   No smoking in restaurant Background music   No dogs   Amex, Delta, Diners, MasterCard, Switch, Visa   Accommodation: 7 rooms, B&B £30 to £70*

THIRLSPOT Cumbria   map 10

▲ King's Head [NEW ENTRY]

Thirlspot CA12 4TN   TEL: (017687) 72393
WEBSITE: www.lakedistrictinns.co.uk
on A591, 6m N of Grasmere

The setting for this large roadside inn is quintessentially Lakeland: a broad, flat-bottomed valley below Helvellyn with magnificent, craggy peaks rearing up on either side. Under the same ownership as the Travellers Rest in Grasmere (see entry), it offers a similar package, comprising hotel, smart restaurant and traditional bar – although the atmosphere is not particularly pubby, and serving staff are dressed formally in black and white. Nevertheless, the bar is a pleasant, relaxed environment, its dark red walls adorned with watercolours depicting Lakeland scenes, and it draws crowds for its fine ales and superior cooking. Menus show some emphasis on local produce though the cooking style is fairly cosmopolitan, as in Waberthwaite Cumberland sausage with rustic bean casserole, and Thai-spiced red bream fillets. Among more traditional dishes are deep-fried Whitby scampi, and sirloin steak au poivre, and lighter options include Waberthwaite black pudding with puréed spiced apples and whole-grain mustard gravy. Desserts are sticky-sweet creations like banana and butterscotch pancakes. Real ales include Theakston Best and Old Peculier, top-notch local brew Jennings Bitter and a guest beer, perhaps Coniston Bluebird. The list of around two dozen wines represents fair value and good choice, prices starting at £10.95, and four house wines are available by the glass. SAMPLE DISHES: moules marinière £6; steak and kidney in Jennings ale pie £9; chocolate trio £4.

Licensee Derek Sweeney (freehouse)
Open 11 to 11, Sun 12 to 10.30; bar food winter 12 to 3, 5 to 9.30, summer (Easter to Oct) 12 to 9.30; restaurant 7 to 9
Details Children welcome   Car park   Wheelchair access (not WC)   Garden and patio
No smoking in dining room   Background music   Dogs welcome exc in restaurant   Delta,
MasterCard, Switch, Visa   Accommodation: 17 rooms, B&B £35 to £110

THORNHAM Norfolk   map 6

▲ Lifeboat Inn 🍺 🌿

Ship Lane, Thornham PE36 6LT   TEL: (01485) 512236
WEBSITE: www.lifeboatinn.co.uk
follow A149 from Hunstanton; in Thornham turn left into Straithe Road, then right
into Ship Lane

WATERSIDE

When the tide is out, the view from this sixteenth-century village inn is salt marshes almost as far as the eye can see. It is an atmospheric location, and the Smugglers' Bar aims to re-create as far as possible the original feel of the place, when it really was a haunt of smugglers. The bar menu highlights mussels as the house speciality, cooked in white wine, garlic, cream and parsley. Other options run from chargrilled beefburger topped with bacon and melted cheese to wok-fried Thai-spiced monkfish and mussels with noodles and garlic bread, while daily blackboard specials might feature herb-crusted sea bass on rice with pesto. There are also various ploughman's and filled baguettes plus desserts such as sticky toffee pudding. The fixed-price restaurant menu has a modern feel, as in a warm salad of chorizo and black pudding with a balsamic reduction, followed by spicy couscous with Mediterranean vegetables, or baked crab topped with smoked salmon with saffron cream sauce. A very respectable selection of real ales includes Adnams Bitter, Greene King IPA and local Woodforde's Wherry Best Bitter. Ten wines come by the glass, representing a fair selection from the list of 34, which takes in everything from budget vins de pays to a prestigious Super-Tuscan. Dessert wines include an unusual sweet Pinot Noir from Austrian winemaker Helmut Lang (£6 per glass). SAMPLE DISHES: glazed goats' cheese on tomato and onion salad with red pesto dressing £5.25; Gressingham duck breast with roasted vegetables, noodles and hoisin £13; rhubarb crumble £3.75.

Licensee Charles Coker (freehouse)
Open 11 to 11, Sun 12 to 10.30; bar food 12 to 2.30, 6.30 to 9.30; restaurant 7 to 9.30
Details Children welcome   Car park   Wheelchair access (also WC)   Garden and patio
No smoking in restaurant   No music   Dogs welcome exc in restaurant   Delta, MasterCard, Switch,
Visa   Accommodation: 14 rooms, B&B £56 to £100

THORNTON   West Yorkshire   map 8

Ring O' Bells 🏵 🍇

212 Hill Top Road, Thornton BD13 3QL   TEL: (01274) 832296
WEBSITE: www.theringobells.com
just off B6145, 3m W of Bradford

This is a three-storey building of the honey-coloured stone that hereabouts hides under a grey-grime coating until shot-blasting reveals it. On one end is a single-storey extension, the glazed front part being a conservatory, with the dining room behind. And, for all the proper pubby feel (not to mention the Black Sheep Best Bitter and Special Ale, and John Smith's Directors Bitter), dining is important here – as the series of awards noted on the menus testify. On weekdays two- and three-course set meals supplement the carte. Among starters are Chinese-style ostrich strips, or corned beef and spam fritters, alongside staider soups and smoked haddock fishcakes, while main dishes include a range of meat pies (including an award-winner whose beef is beefed up with whisky and wild mushrooms), plus roast chicken, roast beef, stuffed pork fillet, and lamb in a Greek kleftiko; fish eaters could choose a baked turbot fillet, or a chargrilled swordfish steak with a mango and pineapple salsa. Puds run the gamut from a date and sticky toffee sponge with butterscotch sauce and Baileys ice cream, to lemon tart with crème fraîche and raspberry coulis. The wine list looks a bit fussy and old-fashioned, but it's extensive and reasonably priced with plenty of up-to-date flavours alongside the classics. Half the 100 or so bottles come in under £15 and there are a dozen halves and eight wines by the glass. SAMPLE DISHES: baby Thai shrimp spring rolls with raita crème fraîche £5; chargrilled venison steak with soused cucumber, shallots and a juniper, orange and brandy cream sauce £17; steamed roly-poly and custard £4.

Licensee Ann L. Preston (freehouse)
Open 11.30 to 4, 5.30 to 11 (Sun 6.30 to 10.30); bar food and restaurant 12.30 to 2, 5.30 (6.30 Sat and Sun) to 9.30; closed 25 Dec
Details Children welcome Car park Wheelchair access (also WC) Patio No smoking in dining room Background music No dogs Amex, Delta, MasterCard, Switch, Visa

THORNTON WATLASS   North Yorkshire   map 9

▲ Buck Inn 🍺

Thornton Watlass HG4 4AH   TEL: (01677) 422461
off B6268 midway between Masham and Bedale

Only a matter of minutes from the A1, Thornton Watlass is a pretty village, notable for its eleventh-century church, on the eastern side of the Ure Valley. The Buck Inn, right on the village green, is comfortably furnished in traditional style, and the décor is a mixed bag of foxes' and otters' heads, old bottles and cartoons. 'Masham rarebit', made with local ale and Wensleydale cheese and topped with good bacon, typifies the sort of dishes to expect at lunchtime, along with a good selection of sandwiches and such things as salmon fillet with creamy tarragon sauce, omelettes, lasagne, and steak and kidney pie. In the evening, expect to find tandoori king prawns, or beer-battered mushrooms with dips among starters, and main courses ranging from chickpea and potato curry to stir-fried chicken with black-bean sauce via grilled gammon with eggs, chips and peas. Sunday lunch brings on a traditional roast with Yorkshire pudding. Handpumped real ales are from Yorkshire breweries Black Sheep, Theakston, and John Smith's, plus a guest from a local microbrewery such as Hambleton. There are also about 30 wines, mostly under £15 with just the three house basics by the glass, and a range of more than 40 malt whiskies, including many of the more unusual brands. SAMPLE DISHES: feta, tomato, olive and basil salad £4.25; tagliatelle with scampi, scallops and prawns £10.50; treacle sponge £4.

Licensees Michael and Margaret Fox (freehouse)
Open 11 to 11, Sun 12 to 10.30; bar food and restaurant Mon to Fri 12 to 2, 6 to 9.30, Sat and Sun 12 to 9.30; closed evening 25 Dec
Details Children welcome Car park Garden No smoking in restaurant Live or background music No dogs exc in bedrooms Amex, Delta, Diners, MasterCard, Switch, Visa Accommodation: 7 rooms, B&B £45 to £65

THORPE LANGTON   Leicestershire   map 5

Bakers Arms

Main Street, Thorpe Langton LE16 7TS   TEL: (01858) 545201
off B6047, 5m N of Market Harborough

This is a popular, homely and traditional local providing a friendly atmosphere and honest, reliable country food. First find Thorpe Langton, then look for a yellow-painted, thatched, sixteenth-century pub that's part of a terrace of brick cottages. It looks small, because the frontage is quite narrow, but the building's depth makes it roomy enough inside, and there's a garden behind as well. The bar (which has a cosy little non-smoking snug off it) is quintessential country pub: wooden chairs and tables, stripped-pine dresser, dark beams, red carpet, warm fire and country prints and wall lights on burgundy walls. Draught beers include one on handpump (Tetley's Bitter), and wines include four by the glass. Except at weekends, food is served only in the evenings, and advance booking could be wise. The blackboard menu may begin with scallops, black pudding and orange sauce, or melon, fruits and sorbet, before continuing with chicken stuffed with chorizo and red pepper, or a tartlet of wild mushrooms and spinach topped with goats' cheese. It could also be worth leaving room for either tarte Tatin with Calvados cream, or a basil-scented fruit terrine with lime syrup and shortbread. SAMPLE DISHES: home-made mushroom soup £3.50; confit of lamb with white onion sauce £12; mocha chocolate torte with Tia Maria anglaise £3.75.

Licensee Kate Hubbard (freehouse)
Open Sat and Sun 12 to 2.30, Tue to Sat 6.30 to 11; bar food and restaurant Sat and Sun 12 to 2.30, Mon to Sat 6.30 to 9.30
Details No children   Car park   Wheelchair access (also WC)   Garden   No-smoking area in bar   No music   No dogs   Amex, Delta, MasterCard, Switch, Visa

THORVERTON   Devon   map 1

▲ Thorverton Arms   NEW ENTRY

Thorverton EX5 5NS   TEL: (01392) 860205
off A396, a few miles N of Exeter

Dating from the sixteenth century, the Thorverton Arms is a low, very long building in the centre of the village, its plain façade broken by a row of five windows on each floor and by a central columned porch jutting out. Inside is one long space, with bar seating to one side of the bar counter and the restaurant to the other. Red is the main colour, with a carpet in the bar replaced by a Turkey rug on bare floorboards in the restaurant, where a large gilt-framed mirror hangs over the fireplace. The 'snack menu' may be a bit of a misnomer, as it includes substantial dishes along the lines of a trio of fishcakes (tuna with mozzarella, salmon and prawn, Thai-style crab) with salad and chips, and even eight-ounce sirloin steak with all the usual accompaniments. The main menu is divided into the usual starters and main courses – king prawns in filo with garlic mayonnaise, for instance, followed by medallions of local venison on caramelised red cabbage and onions with braised turnips and rosemary ('some of the most beautiful, well-hung venison ever,' noted an inspector) – with a pudding like 'delicious' creamy rice pudding with raspberry and ginger compote chosen from a movable board. A blackboard also lists the daily specials: perhaps 'spankingly fresh' scallops pan-fried in lime, ginger and chilli butter, followed by breast of pheasant accompanied by vegetable korma curry and rice. Greene King Abbot Ale, Flowers IPA and Bass are on draught, and five wines are available by the glass. SAMPLE DISHES: oak-smoked salmon and prawn salad with balsamic dressing £4.25; pigeon breasts on celeriac mash with deep-fried parsnip shavings and mint dressing £7.50; white chocolate and brandy mousse with raspberries £4.

Licensees D. Ough and C. Lipscompe (Enterprise Inns)
Open 11.30 to 3, 6.30 to 11, Sun 12 to 3, 7 to 10.30; bar food and restaurant 12 to 2, 6.30 to 9.30

Details *Children welcome in eating areas   Car park   Wheelchair access (also WC)   Garden and patio   No-smoking area in bar, no smoking in restaurant   Occasional live or background music   No dogs   Delta, MasterCard, Switch, Visa   Accommodation: 4 rooms, B&B £35 to £45*

TIRRIL   Cumbria   map 10

▲ Queens Head 🍺
Tirril CA10 2JF   TEL: (01768) 863219
WEBSITE: www.queensheadinn.co.uk
on B5320, 2m S of Penrith

BREW PUB

Tirril is a couple of miles from Ullswater, much the same from Penrith and the M6, as well as yards from the River Eamont, so the Queens Head will suit Lakeland tourists, Eden Valley fishermen or even north- or south-bound drivers needing a break from the motorway. As well as its lovely (and convenient) setting, this long, low, eighteenth-century whitewashed building also houses the Tirril Brewery. And, of course, in the various low-beamed bars you will find the brewery's John Bewsher's Best Bitter (Bewsher bought the pub from Wordsworth's nephew in 1827), Thomas Slee's Academy Ale, and Charles Gough's Old Faithful, plus a local guest beer. Besides filled jacket potatoes, baguettes and pittas, the lunchtime bar menu offers tuna fishcakes on a lemon hollandaise, chicken tikka or Cumberland sausage, plus desserts such as toffee apple bread-and-butter pudding. Among choices from the restaurant menu, which is supplemented by specials boards, might be a deep-fried Brie starter, braised shoulder of lamb and hand-made Lake District ice creams or sorbets. The 30-odd wines on the well-spread list are under £20, and ten of them, including a pudding wine, can be had by the glass. SAMPLE DISHES: asparagus and smoked cheese tartlet £3.25; braised lamb shank in orange and apricot sauce £9.75; butterscotch pavlova £3.

Licensees *Chris Tomlinson and Ian Harris (freehouse)*
Open *Mon to Fri 12 to 3, 6 to 11, Sat 12 to 11, Sun 12 to 10.30; bar food and restaurant Mon to Sat 12 to 2, 6 to 9.30, Sun 12 to 2, 7 to 9*
Details *Children welcome   Car park   Patio   No smoking in dining room   Occasional live or background music; jukebox   Dogs welcome   Amex, Delta, MasterCard, Switch, Visa   Accommodation: 7 rooms, B&B £30 to £60*

TITLEY   Herefordshire   map 5

▲ Stagg Inn 🏆 🏆 🍺 🍇
Titley HR5 3RL   TEL: (01544) 230221
WEBSITE: www.thestagg.co.uk
on B4355, NE of Kington

Although the focus is on the restaurant here, the Stagg manages to remain the village inn, with drinkers mixing with diners. And not least of the attractions are the ales dispensed at the bar: Hobsons Best Bitter, Town Crier and Old Henry, plus guests, such as Timothy Taylor Landlord; there's also Dunkerton's organic Black Fox cider and home-made damson and sloe gins. The lower bar area is strong on natural colours, with a wood-burning stove, half-timbered walls and closely set ceiling beams thickly hung with mugs, while a log fire burns in the upper area, reached via a couple of steps. Chef and co-owner Steve Reynolds was trained by the Roux brothers, and he applies his considerable skills to the excellent produce of Herefordshire: organic pork, bacon and sausages come from small local farms, as do duck, free-range poultry, lamb and beef. The cooking style is appealing, sophisticated and modern. A typical day's options might include 'excellent' mussel tart, or smoked chicken and bacon salad with tarragon vinaigrette, followed by Herefordshire beef fillet with red wine and shallot sauce, or chicken breast stuffed with pistachios. Game crops up in season in the shape of perhaps roast grouse with bread sauce, and among fish main courses may be fillet of sea bass with duxelles and herb oil. The bar has a blackboard of lighter meals, such as smoked haddock with mustard mash, beef stroganoff, and pork sausages with onion gravy. Finish with a selection from the board of unpasteurised English and Welsh cheeses, or opt for a dessert such as bread-and-butter pudding with apricot coulis, or banana and caramel meringue. Eight house wines at £2 a glass kick off a reasonably priced list of over 60 bottles, plus around 20 halves. Classic styles and modern favourites are all well represented, along with a few enticing oddballs such as Gary Crittenden's 'i' range of Italian grape varieties from Australia. Dark and rich Pedro Ximénez Viejo Napoleon sherry from Hidalgo is a rare pudding treat not to be missed. SAMPLE DISHES: seared scallops with parsnip purée and black pepper oil £6; Trelough duck breast with elderflower sauce £14; three crème brûlées of vanilla, coffee and cognac £4.50.

Licensees Nicola and Steve Reynolds (freehouse)
Open *Tue to Sat and first May Day bank hol 12 to 3, 6.30 to 11, Sun 12 to 3; bar food (exc Sat evening and Sun) 12 to 2, 6.30 to 10; restaurant Mon to Sat 12 to 2, 6.30 to 10; closed Tue after bank hols, first 2 weeks Nov, 25 and 26 Dec, 1 Jan, 1 week Feb to Mar*
Details *Children welcome   Car park   Garden   No smoking in restaurant   No music   Dogs welcome exc in restaurant   Delta, MasterCard, Switch, Visa   Accommodation: 2 rooms, B&B £40 to £70*

TORCROSS   Devon   map 1

Start Bay Inn
Torcross TQ7 2TQ   TEL: (01548) 580553
FISH
on A379 Dartmouth to Kingsbridge coast road

Dating from the fourteenth century, this thatched inn is right beside the beach at the southern end of the magnificent sweep of Slapton Sands; across the road in the other direction is Slapton Ley, a freshwater lagoon and noted bird reserve. Variously furnished inside with old oak benches, a brick fireplace and black-painted beams, it may not be the most elegant place, but it is the quality of fish that has people flocking here from miles around. Local fishermen work off the beach outside and deliver all kinds of seafood. Depending on what's been caught, there might be sea bass, John Dory, lemon and Dover sole and skate, along with deep-fried cod, plaice, or scampi. Crab, dropped off at the back door by a local crabber, is perennially popular, and smoked mackerel, shell-on prawns, or seafood cocktail could be among other starters, with steaks, gammon, Devon ham, and vegetable curry among non-fish main courses. Snacks and a children's menu are also available, with ploughman's served at lunchtimes, with the likes of chocolate sponge pudding, or a gâteau with clotted cream to finish. Bass, Flowers Original, and Otter Ale are on draught, along with ciders from Addlestone's and Heron Valley, and there is a serviceable international wine list, with seven by the glass. SAMPLE DISHES: giant prawns in garlic butter with salad £4.50; deep-fried haddock with chips £6.25; summer pudding £3.

Licensee Paul Stubbs (Heavitree)

Open 11.30 to 11 (11.30 to 2.30, 6 to 11 winter), Sun 12 to 2.30, 6 to 10.30; bar food 11.30 to 2, 6 to 9.30 (10 summer)

Details Children welcome in family room   Car park   Patio   No-smoking area in bar, no smoking in restaurant   Background music   Dogs welcome   MasterCard, Switch, Visa

---

TREEN   Cornwall   map 1

▲ Gurnard's Head Hotel

Treen, Zennor, nr St Ives TR26 3DE   TEL: (01736) 796928
WEBSITE: www.gurnardshead.fsnet.co.uk
on B3306, 6m SW of St Ives

It's only ten miles as the crow flies from here to Land's End, so rugged moorland and granite cliffs should come as no surprise, but they are spectacular nonetheless. The hotel sits above the rocky promontory of Gurnard's Head and beside the South West Coast Path – a welcoming haven for the wet or weary. There's free live music on Wednesday and Friday nights (no Muzak or fruit machines, though) to enhance the tasty and wholesome food and well-kept beer (Flowers Original and IPA, Boddingtons Bitter, plus guests like Fuller's London Pride and Skinner's Cornish Knocker Ale). The same menus are available in the large bar, where there's a fire, and in the dining room off it. Specials might include parsnip and chestnut soup, or roast partridge with braised red cabbage, while the regular printed menu offers a smoked fish medley of salmon, tuna, halibut and trout with horseradish soured cream, followed by confit of duck with lentil purée and Madeira sauce. Baked figs with hazelnuts, whisky and honey, or old-fashioned rice pudding with jam and clotted cream might need an afternoon to walk off, or there are Cornish and other UK cheeses with biscuits. Five wines are available by the glass, and only one of the 15 bins on the list tops £20. SAMPLE DISHES: garlic-roasted aubergine and red pepper £5; grilled gurnard fillets £11.50; praline meringue with Tia Maria coffee cream £4.

Licensees Ray and Joy Kell (freehouse)

Open 12 to 3, 6 to 11, Sun 12 to 4, 7 to 10.30; bar food and restaurant 12 to 2.15, 6.30 to 9.15, Sun 7 to 9.15

Details Children welcome in family room   Car park   Wheelchair access   Garden and patio   No-smoking area in restaurant and family room   Live music   Dogs welcome in bar only   Amex, MasterCard, Switch, Visa   Accommodation: 6 rooms, B&B £32.50 to £75

▶ indicates a pub serving exceptional draught beers.

TRISCOMBE Somerset   map 2

Blue Ball Inn ❦
Triscombe TA4 3HE   TEL: (01984) 618242
signposted off A358 between Taunton and Minehead

Occupying three huge renovated old barns as well as the original thatched
building, the Blue Ball is now 'the most wonderful open space' on slightly
different levels, all warm-coloured bare wood open to the roofs decorated in
quiet country fashion, with a series of antlers on the ceiling cross-beams,
carved wooden owls, and a stuffed snarling fox. New owners took over as we
went to press, and things are to continue along the same lines. There is no
separate restaurant but the attractive menus are based on largely locally
sourced ingredients. Ploughman's and crusty rolls – warm Stilton with
onion marmalade, say – are options at lunchtimes, alongside perhaps pea
soup, followed by pigeon breasts with a red wine sauce and Bury black
pudding, or whole lemon sole with tartare sauce. The daily-changing dinner
menu might include fillet steak with green peppercorn sauce, or rack of
lamb in a herb crust with port sauce, Indonesian-style braised chicken
with pilau rice, or halibut and langoustine in flat bread with red pepper
salsa. Desserts might take in bread-and-butter pudding, or rich chocolate
tart with caramel ice cream. Four real ales are on handpump. The 130-strong
wine list has plenty of good drinking at very fair prices, from a spot-on New
Zealand selection to some affordable Burgundy. Most wines are also available by the glass. SAMPLE DISHES: tian of Cornish crab £6.50; chicken breast
with Serrano ham and goats' cheese butter £11.50; pear and almond tart
£4.25.

Licensees Peter Alcroft and Sharon Murdoch (freehouse)
Open 12 to 2.30, 7 to 11, Sun 12 to 3, 7 to 10.30; bar food 12 to 1.45, 7 to 9.30
Details Children welcome   Car park   Wheelchair access (also WC)   Garden   No smoking in
eating areas   Background music   Dogs welcome   Delta, MasterCard, Switch, Visa

TROUTBECK Cumbria   map 8

▲ Queens Head Hotel ✲ 🍺
Townhead, Troutbeck LA23 1PW   TEL: (015394) 32174
WEBSITE: www.queensheadhotel.com
at start of Kirkstone Pass, 2½m from junction of A591 and A592

Dating from the seventeenth century, this attractive black and white half-
timbered hostelry in the Troutbeck Valley has unsurpassed views. Within is a
fine bar where the top of a four-poster bed acts as the roof of the bar itself, but
the character doesn't stop there: flagstoned floors, low oak beams in the ceilings, fireplaces, one with a stag's head over it, and lovely old cushioned settles,
one dated 1687, all create a good atmosphere, with, hanging on the walls, some
delightful old photographs of the area. The menus in the bars are the same as
those in the Mayor's Parlour Restaurant, except that tables can be booked in
the latter. On the set-price three-course menu you might find warm potted
prawns cooked in cream and garlic topped with Parmesan, followed by

peppered venison and redcurrant casserole with rice. The dishes on the carte and the daily specials are similarly ambitious, well thought out and accomplished. Typical are an 'excellent' salmon and crab fishcake, or Thai-spiced chicken on coriander risotto with sweet chilli dressing, followed by a generous plateful of 'wonderful' beef cobbler, salmon fillet topped with a pesto and cured salmon crust with a rich butter sauce, or seared calf's liver on creamed celeriac topped with crisp pancetta and a raspberry vinegar-spiked jus. Desserts, along with the daily specials, are listed on blackboards, and at lunchtime baguettes are also on offer. A good choice of real ales – normally four or five at any one time – includes Coniston Bluebird Bitter and Old Man Ale, Boddingtons Bitter, Jennings Cumberland Ale and Cocker Hoop and Black Sheep Special Ale. Wine lovers will find plenty of good-value bottles among the 30 listed. It's a well-chosen global selection and half a dozen house basics are offered by the small or large glass (£2.70 and £3.60 respectively). SAMPLE DISHES: goats' cheese roasted with basil and pistachios wrapped in filo and served on lime- and garlic-dressed leaves £5.25; pan-fried chicken breast with grape and shallot compote and white wine cream £9.50; chocolate and Tia Maria torte with chocolate sauce and cream £3.75.

Licensees Mark Stewardson and Joanne Sherratt (freehouse)
Open 11 to 11, Sun 12 to 10.30; bar food and restaurant 12 to 2, 6.30 to 9; closed 25 Dec
Details Children welcome Car park Wheelchair access (also WC) Patio No-smoking area in bar No music Dogs welcome Delta, MasterCard, Switch, Visa Accommodation: 14 rooms, B&B £47.50 to £95

TRUMPET Herefordshire   map 5

▲ Verzons Country Inn NEW ENTRY

Trumpet HR8 2PZ TEL: (01531) 670381
on A438, 2m W of Ledbury

This smart country hotel, a large Georgian red-brick farmhouse in open country between Ledbury and Hereford, does not look much like a pub from the outside. Inside, however, there is the Hop Bar, which looks the part with its exposed-brick walls, beams and assorted pub-style accoutrements. You will also find decent real ales on tap – Hook Norton Best and Shepherd Neame Spitfire. Lunchtime bar meals range from hearty, rustic dishes of faggots with pea and vinegar purée and crushed potatoes to lighter platters of mixed antipasti or Greek salad. Evening menus are considerably more elaborate. A starter of beetroot carpaccio with goats' cheese and Granny Smith mayonnaise, for example, might be followed by pan-roasted Gressingham duck with spicy risotto, apricot and pear chutney and apricot jus. An inspector thought that it could all do with being a bit simpler but nonetheless felt the cooking was notably 'honest and fresh'. The standard wine list opens with six house wines at £9.75 a bottle, also served in two sizes of glass. SAMPLE DISHES: crisp cured salmon fishcakes with smoked butter and lemon sauce £5.50; pork cutlet with braised butter beans and apple and bacon cider purée £10.50; malted Horlicks and cocoa bavarois £4.50.

ENGLAND

Licensee David Roberts (freehouse)
Open 11 to 11, Sun 12 to 10.30; bar food and restaurant 12 to 2, 7 to 9; closed evenings 25 and 26 Dec
Details Children welcome Car park Wheelchair access (also WC) Garden and patio
No smoking in dining room No music Guide dogs only Amex, Delta, Diners, MasterCard, Switch, Visa Accommodation: 8 rooms, B&B £45 to £88

TUCKENHAY Devon   map 1

▲ Maltsters' Arms 🍺

Bow Creek, Tuckenhay TQ9 7EQ   TEL: (01803) 732350   **WATERSIDE**
WEBSITE: www.tuckenhay.com
off A381, 2½m S of Totnes

Built at a time when Tuckenhay was a bustling port, this remote eighteenth-century inn enjoys a spectacular position overlooking Bow Creek. It is a lively place with plenty of character and a bright, cheerful décor throughout its various bar and dining areas. Standards are high in every department, including the individually styled guest rooms, but perhaps above all in drinks: regular Dartmoor IPA is backed up by top-notch guest ales from local breweries such as Otter and Blackawton, as well as local cider. Wines also show up well, with around 15 by the glass covering a good range of flavours, including the local Sharpham Estate white. The main list is not very informative but has something tempting for all budgets. Food is in an uncomplicated modern vein, and portions are large. One wide-ranging menu serves all areas, offering pan-fried pigeon breasts with chillied sherry and honey among starters, and main courses taking in everything from steak, kidney and mushroom pie to sweet potato and banana curry. Theme nights have included tandoori and tapas, and music and barbecues are regular features of summer evenings. Families should also note that there is a menu of 'real food for children', where instead of chicken nuggets and fish fingers you will find pan-fried chicken breast and grilled plaice. SAMPLE DISHES: flash-fried scallops in orange and Cointreau £6.50; pot-roast partridge in Shag cider, fennel and rowan berries £12.75; blueberry and banana bread-and-butter pudding £4.25.

Licensees Denise and Quentin Thwaites (freehouse)
Open 11 to 11, Sun 12 to 10.30; bar food and restaurant 12 to 3 (4 Sun), 7 to 9.30 (all day July and Aug); open 12 to 2 25 Dec (no food)
Details Children welcome in family room Car park Garden and patio Occasional live music
Dogs welcome Delta, MasterCard, Switch, Visa Accommodation: 7 rooms, B&B £50 to £125

TUNBRIDGE WELLS Kent   map 3

Sankey's [NEW ENTRY]

39 Mount Ephraim, Tunbridge Wells TN4 8AA   TEL: (01892) 511422   **FISH**
WEBSITE: www.sankeys.co.uk
on A26, virtually opposite Kent and Sussex Hospital

In a row of shops just seconds from the common, Sankey's trade is 'wine, ale, oyster bar and garden', according to its menu. Drop down some steps to a small lobby filled with an old-fashioned red telephone box and turn into the bar, where there are lots of tables with pew-type benches, a flagstone floor, a number of enamel advertising signs and mirrors, and doors leading to a terrace. Blackboards list lunchtime baguettes and daily specials: perhaps French onion soup, coq au vin, and skate wing with capers. The main menu concentrates on fish and shellfish: tiger prawns in filo with sweet chilli dip, or moules marinière, followed by 'fresh, crisp and tasty' salmon and cod fish-cakes with 'excellent' chive and dill crème fraîche, 'flavoursome' fish pie, and lobster. Finish with something like toffee pecan pie with whisky cream. Larkins Traditional Ale, brewed in Chiddingstone, is on draught, and around 10 wines are served by the glass from a list of over 30 bottles (all available to take away). SAMPLE DISHES: parfait of duck with onion marmalade £6.50; Loch Duart salmon baked in a basil, garlic and lemon crust served with olive mash £9.50; rich chocolate mousse £4.

Licensee Guy Sankey (freehouse)
Open 10 to 11, Sun 12 to 3, 7 to 10.30; bar food 12 to 2.30, 6 to 10; closed Christmas
Details No children   Garden   No-smoking area in bar   Background music   Dogs welcome
MasterCard, Switch, Visa

TUNSTALL   Lancashire   **map 8**

Lunesdale Arms   NEW ENTRY
Tunstall LA6 2QN   TEL: (015242) 74203
WEBSITE: www.thelunesdale.com
on A683, S of Kirkby Lonsdale

This smart old country hotel stands on the main road through the village. The main bar has been modernised to create an open-plan L-shaped room with the bar counter at its centre. Primrose-yellow walls and a bare wooden floor are lifted by watercolours on the walls. Menus, listed on blackboards, make a show of pointing up the sources of supplies – home-baked bread, meat from local farms and organically grown vegetables and salads – which are used in a straightforward cooking style. Lunch offers light meals of salmon fishcakes, or bacon, tomato and avocado salad, plus a few more substantial dishes, like steak and kidney pie. The choice increases in the evening, adding starters of pâté, or tomato bruschetta with pesto, and main courses of lime and lemongrass chicken with rice, and pork fillet stuffed with basil, tomato and Parmesan and wrapped in Parma ham. Finish perhaps with roasted nectarines with mascarpone cream. Good cask ales come from the Black Sheep Brewery, and there's also a guest. Half a dozen wines are sold by the glass from a list of 20 bottles, prices starting around £10. SAMPLE DISHES: goats' cheese croûte with salad £3.75; haddock goujons with tartare sauce and chips £8; lemon and lime cheesecake £3.75.

Licensees Emma Gillibrand and John Simmons (freehouse)
Open Tue to Sat 11 to 3, 6 to 11, Sun 12 to 3, 6 to 10.30; bar food Tue to Fri 12 to 2, 6 to 9, Sat and Sun 12 to 2.30, 6 to 9; closed 25 and 26 Dec
Details Children welcome   Car park   Wheelchair access (also WC)   Patio   Occasional live or background music   Dogs welcome   Delta, MasterCard, Switch, Visa

Bull and Butcher 🍇

Turville RG9 6QU   TEL: (01491) 638283
WEBSITE: www.bullandbutcher.com
between B480 and B482, 5m N of Henley-on-Thames

If Turville, a quaint village in the Hambleden Valley with outstanding views,
looks familiar, it could be because it provides the setting for TV's *The Vicar of
Dibley*. The small half-timbered inn, next to the thirteenth-century church,
received its first licence in 1617, and within are low beams, old settles and an
inglenook. The pub's approach to food is serious and ambitious, and the
kitchen is not averse to producing some interesting flavour combinations:
cream of roasted sweet pepper and goats' cheese soup laced with basil leaves
and olive oil, or pan-fried queen scallops with lightly peppered strawberries
and balsamic vinegar, followed by main courses of poached salmon fillet with
a tart lime hollandaise and prawn dumplings, or vanilla confit of rabbit with
bitter chocolate Chinese pears and a light port sauce. More conventional
palates will find more to their liking in, perhaps, gravad lax with a light dill
mayonnaise, or roast fillet of beef en croûte with a mushroom, onion and herb
stuffing and Madeira jus. Regular beers are from the Brakspear range, plus
Bateman Dark Mild and a couple of ciders. Wine drinkers should applaud the
policy of offering the whole list of over 30 wines by the 125 or 250ml glass.
From simple vins de pays up to a mature claret at £12.80 for a big glass, there
are Old and New World options to suit all tastes and wallets. The hilltop
windmill opposite is accessible on foot – also by car for those making the effort
after they've eaten. SAMPLE DISHES: smoked chicken, celeriac, toasted walnut
and apple salad with mustard dressing £7; pan-fried raspberry- and rosehip-
smoked Barbary duck breast with a honey and mustard jus on a pepper- and
almond-encrusted galette £15; bitter raspberry posset £5.

Licensee Nicholas Abbott (Brakspear)
Open 11 to 3, 6 (6.30 Sat) to 11, Sun 12 to 5, 7 to 10.30; bar food Mon to Sat 12 to 2.30,
Sun 12 to 4, Wed to Sat 7 to 9.45
Details Children welcome in eating areas   Car park   Garden   No-smoking areas in bar   No music
Dogs welcome   Delta, MasterCard, Switch, Visa

ULLINGSWICK   Herefordshire

Three Crowns Inn 🍴 🍇

Ullingswick HR1 3JQ   TEL: (01432) 820279
WEBSITE: www.threecrownsinn.com
off A465 between Hereford and Bromyard

The front of this small country pub, set back from a lane, is half-timbered and
red brick, and there are a few tables on a patio. Inside are two simply furnished
dining rooms and a small bar, with exposed beams and a wood-burning stove
in an inglenook. This is an upmarket dining pub, and it can get busy. The
straightforward but lively menu, which changes daily, could start with a
cheese and swede soufflé, or duck and foie gras terrine with pease pudding.

Much use is made of produce from local sources, as in chargrilled sirloin of Marches beef with béarnaise sauce, with other main courses of perhaps glazed duck breast with prunes, pommes Anna and red cabbage, or line-caught sea bass with champagne butter sauce and green beans. A blackboard lists a set-price two- or three-course lunch (except Sundays), and puddings are of the crumble and tart variety. Hobsons Best Bitter and Mild are kept, plus a guest from the local Wye Valley Brewery; Stowford Press cider is also available, along with Dunkertons. Six fruity house wines are sold by the glass from a list of around two dozen, but these are the only options below £15 a bottle. However, there is tasty drinking under £20, such as the Regaleali white from Sicily or Prunotto's Barbera d'Asti Fiulot from the north of Italy, and wine fans will find sought-after names in the 'Fine & Distinctive' selection. SAMPLE DISHES: grilled scallops in prosciutto with garlic mash and roasted coral sauce £5.75; roast rack of Marches lamb with white-bean and chorizo cassoulet £13.75; sticky toffee pudding with lime sorbet £4.25.

Licensee Brent Castle (freehouse)
Open Tue to Sat 12 to 3, 7 to 11, Sun 12 to 2.30, 7 to 10.30; bar food 12 to 2 (2.30 Sun), 7 to 9.30 (9 Sun); closed 2 weeks from 24 Dec
Details Children welcome   Car park   Wheelchair access (also WC)   Patio   No-smoking area in bar   No music   No dogs   Delta, MasterCard, Switch, Visa

ULVERSTON   Cumbria   map 8

▲ Bay Horse Hotel 👯 🍇

Canal Foot, Ulverston LA12 9EL   TEL: (01229) 583972
WEBSITE: www.thebayhorsehotel.co.uk
off A590, 8m NE of Barrow-in-Furness, take Canal Foot turn in Ulverston, then next signposted left turn following lane to pub

If your heart sinks as you pass the Glaxo works and its industrial landscape, don't despair – at (literally) the end of the road there's a magnificent view of Cartmel Sands and Morecambe Bay, where the tide sweeps in over the flats to within feet of the pub's verandah. Inside, under low ceilings and black beams, all is 'homely, inviting and cosy. A couple of cats curled up on comfy sofas – a place to relax in.' Bar food (Tuesday to Sunday lunchtimes – in the evenings there's the restaurant) is listed on menus, plus a daily special blackboard. Superior sandwiches, hot and cold, might include smoked salmon on sliced leeks with water chestnuts and crème fraîche (hot), or smoked chicken with curry mayonnaise and toasted coconut (cold). Starters subsume treats like a 'really tasty' sweetcorn lemon and mint soup, or a range of home-made meaty or vegetarian pâtés and terrines. Follow with crab and salmon fishcakes in a white wine and herb cream sauce, or a 'flavoursome' puff pastry pie of tender lamb chunks enhanced by the hotness of ginger and the sharpness of apricot. Orange crème brûlée is commended as a finisher. Real ales could include Everards, Jennings Cumberland Ale, Hydes, and Thwaites Bitter and Thoroughbred. The substantial wine list, focusing mainly on France, Australia and a very well-chosen South African range, has no budget bottles but offers reasonable choice under £20 and temptingly indulgent bottles above. Eight wines are usually available by the glass. SAMPLE DISHES: cheese and herb pâté £6.25; grilled Waberthwaite Cumberland sausage with date chutney and cranberry and apple sauce £9; summer fruits with home-made ice cream £5.75.

Licensee Robert Lyons (freehouse)
Open 11 to 11, Sun 12 to 10.30; bar food Tue to Sun 12 to 2; restaurant Tue to Sun 7.30 for 8 (1 sitting)
Details Car park   Wheelchair access (also WC)   Garden   No smoking in dining room
Background music   Dogs welcome   Amex, Delta, MasterCard, Switch, Visa   Accommodation:
9 rooms, D,B&B £77.50 to £185

Farmers Arms   NEW ENTRY

Market Place, Ulverston LA12 7BA   TEL: (01229) 584469
WEBSITE: www.farmersrestaurant-thelakes.co.uk
on A590, 9m NE of Barrow-in-Furness

Ulverston is one of those unspoilt old country towns where you can still find traditional butcher's shops selling cow heels and tripe. At one end of its cobbled main street is this traditional old pub. The large, open-plan bar is beamed, bare floorboarded and comfortably furnished, and there is also plenty of outdoor seating for fine weather. Supplementing the printed menu, daily specials are listed on a blackboard over a large stone hearth. At lunchtime, choice includes hot and cold sandwiches and filled jacket potatoes, plus 'traditional favourites' like steak and mushroom pie or dishes 'from around the globe' such as spicy Cajun chicken. Dinner menus dispense with the sandwiches but extend starter and main-course choices with things like hot garlic prawns on toast, and chicken curry with rice and poppadoms, while specials might typically include seared salmon fillet on roast Mediterranean vegetables with buttered lime sauce. Finish perhaps with mille-feuille of redcurrants and mango with Chantilly cream. Among draught beers are Timothy Taylor Landlord, Hawkshead Bitter and Hoegaarden, and a regularly changing selection of wines by the glass is listed on a blackboard. SAMPLE DISHES: garlic mushrooms £3.25; gammon 'jamboree' with melted cheese, tomato and mushrooms £7.50; iced sticky toffee parfait with mint and lime syrup £3.25.

Licensee Roger Chattaway (freehouse)
Open 10 to 11, Sun 11 to 10.30; bar food and restaurant 11 to 2.30, 5.30 to 8.30
Details Children welcome in bar eating area   Car park   Wheelchair access (not WC)   Patio
No smoking in dining room   Occasional live or background music   No dogs   MasterCard, Switch,
Visa

UPPER HAMBLETON   Rutland   map 6

▲ Finch's Arms 🏵

Oakham Road, Upper Hambleton LE15 8TL   TEL: (01572) 756575
WEBSITE: www.finchsarms.co.uk
off A606, E of Oakham

In a beautiful spot overlooking Rutland Water, yet in the centre of the tranquil village close to the church, the Finch's Arms is a stone-built, farmhouse-style building with lawns to the rear sweeping down to the lake providing the perfect setting for outdoor refreshments in summer. Inside are two rooms with flagstone floors linked by a wood-panelled bar; each has an open fire, beamed ceilings and ochre-coloured walls. The kitchen takes an eclectic approach, producing crisp Thai fishcakes ('cooked to perfection,' noted a reporter) on sesame noodles, Kerala king prawn curry with tamarind chickpeas and basmati rice, and seared sea bass on ratatouille with crispy polenta, chorizo and a parsley dressing. Starters are equally varied, from pheasant and truffle sausages with bubble and squeak, to 'scrummy' sun-dried tomato and mozzarella tart with pesto, or 'thick and fulsome' tomato and roasted red pepper soup. Finish with something like ginger crème brûlée with warm plum and cinnamon compote. Although this is a serious dining pub, it stocks Greene King Abbot Ale, Grainstore Cooking Bitter and guests, while half a dozen or so wines are sold by the glass. SAMPLE DISHES: black pudding and an apple and potato cake in a lemon and mustard dressing £4.25; corned beef hash with fried eggs, mange-tout and pickled beetroot £8; white chocolate, raspberry and vodka trifle £4.

Licensee Colin Crawford (freehouse)
Open 11 to 11; bar food and restaurant 12 to 2.30, 6 to 9.30 (all day Sun)
Details Children welcome   Car park   Wheelchair access (also WC)   Garden and patio
No smoking in restaurant   Occasional live or background music   No dogs   Delta, MasterCard,
Switch, Visa   Accommodation: 6 rooms, B&B £55 to £75

UPPERMILL   Greater Manchester   **map 8**

Church Inn 🍺   NEW ENTRY   BREW PUB
Church Lane, Uppermill, Saddleworth OL3 6LW   TEL: (01457) 820902

Value and quirkiness go hand in hand here. High above trendy Uppermill, beside the parish hearse-house and across the lane from the fine but smoke-grimed Victorian church, this pub sits on a steep hillside with two storeys at the front, but four to prop it up at the back. Down in those bowels the Saddleworth Brewery produces tasty Hopsmacker and Robyn's Bitter and Shaftbender stout. These – plus guests like McEwan's 80/- or Ruddles County – you can sup among ducks, geese and peacocks in the garden alongside, drinking in the view and watching llamas graze (there's a trekking centre nearby). The open-plan bar has stoves at each end for winter warmth, and decoration bespeaks a morris dancers' haunt: among the plates and brassery on the wall are a girning collar and photos of the Longwood Thump rushcart festival (on August bank holidays). Food comes in gargantuan portions, and vegetarians are well catered for. Menu and blackboards offer borscht or creamy garlic mushrooms, then perhaps a vast, perfectly timed cod fillet with chips and mushy peas, wild boar in red wine sauce, a roast, or one of several suet puddings (lamb and mint, or steak and ale are commended). Maybe only masochists would dare a dessert, but there are things like tiramisù, or banoffi pie. Some 30 wines start at £7.50, and most come by the glass. SAMPLE DISHES: vegetable soup £1.65; mushroom stroganoff £5.25; lemon cheesecake £2.25.

Licensee Julian Taylor (freehouse)
Open 12 to 11, Sun 12 to 10.30; bar food Mon to Fri 12 to 2.30, 5.30 to 9, Sat and Sun 12 to 9
Details Children welcome in eating areas   Car park   Wheelchair access (also WC)   Garden and
patio   No-smoking area in bar   Background music   Dogs welcome on a lead   Amex, Delta, Diners,
MasterCard, Switch, Visa

UPPER ODDINGTON   Gloucestershire   map 5

▲ Horse & Groom   NEW ENTRY
Upper Oddington GL56 0XH   TEL: (01451) 830584
off A436, E of Stow-on-the-Wold

The rough stone exterior of this sixteenth-century pub gives way to a stylish
modern interior decorated with a sea-green and gold colour scheme, though
some original features remain, such as the huge stone hearth and some ancient
flagstones. The menu, too, is a blend of traditional and contemporary ideas,
with starters ranging from prawn and avocado salad to smoked chicken and
mozzarella salad with beetroot and toasted almonds. Main courses are similarly eclectic: chicken chasseur with bacon lardons and sautéed mushrooms,
and peppered pork fillet with Savoy cabbage appear alongside Cajun-spiced
chicken, vegetarian sausages with potato and cheese mash, and poached
gammon with sautéed cabbage and honey and peppercorn sauce. The
Wednesday night special is a variation on a theme of crispy roast duck, and
lunch options include a variety of sandwiches. Hook Norton Best Bitter,
Wadworth 6X and Old Speckled Hen are the real ales on offer, and four wines
are available by the glass from the list of twenty bottles, prices starting at £9.95.
SAMPLE DISHES: asparagus and black pudding salad £4.25; grey mullet
provençale with crushed potatoes and garlic and parsley crust £10.50; red
berry bavarois £4.

Licensee Peter Golding (freehouse)
Open 11 to 11; bar food and restaurant 12 to 2, 7 to 9.30; closed 25 Dec
Details Children welcome   Car park   Garden   No smoking in restaurant   Live music   No dogs
Delta, Diners, MasterCard, Switch, Visa   Accommodation: 7 rooms, B&B £45 to £60

UPPER WOODFORD   Wiltshire   map 2

Bridge   NEW ENTRY
Upper Woodford SP4 6NU   TEL: (01722) 782323
the Woodfords signposted from centre of Amesbury

Where the road crosses the River Avon at Upper Woodford you'll find the
aptly named Bridge, festooned with window boxes and with green shutters.
The open-plan space inside has three linked areas, all with mint-green walls: a
poolroom with a fruit machine, and a bar and dining room both hung with
botanical prints, the latter also with bunches of garlic everywhere ('enough to
ward off a herd of Count Draculas'). The food, pretty much following a traditional path, is simple, unpretentious and honest ('as are the prices'). The
printed menu, backed up by blackboard specials, might deliver grilled scallops
and bacon with a tomato, red onion and coriander salsa, followed by duck
confit with parsley and garlic mash, or deep-fried Cornish cod in Bridge Ale

batter with chips. The compact, global wine list has plenty under £20 and nine by the glass, while on handpump there's Hop Back GFB and guest ales Enterprise Brewery Best, Bridge and Grumpy Cow. SAMPLE DISHES: coarse country pâté with onion confit and toasted brioche £5; peppered rump steak with herb butter and chips £10; sticky toffee pudding with vanilla ice cream £4.

Licensee Andrew Sergeant (Enterprise Inns)
Open 12 to 3, 6 to 11; bar food and restaurant 12 to 2, 6 to 9 (8.30 Sun)
Details Children welcome   Car park   Wheelchair access (not WC)   Garden   Occasional live or background music   Dogs welcome in bar only   Delta, MasterCard, Switch, Visa

UPTON BISHOP   Herefordshire   map 5

Moody Cow at Upton Bishop
Upton Bishop HR9 7TT   TEL: (01989) 780470
WEBSITE: www.moodycow.co.uk
at crossroads of B4224 and B4221, 4m NE of Ross-on-Wye

The flowery patio at this stone-built pub makes a good spot for outdoor eating and drinking in fine weather; inside is a choice of areas for eating: a carpeted bar (where drinkers are also welcomed), the 'Fresco' (an informal wooden-floored dining area), plus a two-level restaurant housed in an attached bar conversion. There's also a snug with its settees, armchairs and open fire for pre- or post-prandial drinks or coffee. Food on offer includes a selection of open sandwiches, plus main courses of perhaps battered cod with chips, a choice of pastas, Moody Cow Pie (steak and kidney with vegetables and potato), bangers and mash, and pork confit. Ales kept are Bass, Hook Norton Best Bitter and Flowers IPA, plus two guests, and a couple of wines are served by the glass. SAMPLE DISHES: fishcakes with tangy tomato salsa £5; pan-fried duck with mixed berry compote £14; Baileys rice pudding £4.75.

Licensee James Lloyd (freehouse)
Open 12 to 2.30, 6.30 to 11 (10.30 Sun); bar food and restaurant 12 to 2, 6.30 to 9.30
Details Children welcome   Car park   Wheelchair access (also WC)   Patio   No smoking in restaurant   Background music   Dogs welcome in bar   Amex, Delta, Diners, MasterCard, Switch, Visa

UPTON SCUDAMORE   Wiltshire   map 2

▲ Angel Inn ✿ ❦
Upton Scudamore BA12 0AG   TEL: (01985) 213225
Upton Scudamore signposted off A350 Warminster to Westbury road

In a tiny village just north of Warminster, the Angel is a neat-looking, white-painted building with a paved patio with good-quality seating and plants in large tubs. The interior is equally spick and span: the high, narrow, light-filled bar area has a boarded floor, terracotta and beige check curtains over French windows and pine tables, while the extensive open-plan restaurant is 'thoroughly civilised', with well-spaced tables, a comfortable seating area with low sofas, books and magazines, and floors on different levels. The lunch and light bites menu is full of interest, running from potted prawns with chilli and papaya, or foie gras and guinea fowl terrine with chutney and walnut bread, to game casserole with bacon dumplings, or smoked haddock risotto with a caper and watercress relish, while the dinner menu brings the flavours of the Mediterranean to deepest Wiltshire: deep-fried salt-cod fritters with rocket, blush tomatoes and balsamic, followed by 'incredibly fresh and tasty' rack of lamb in a spicy crust with a rosemary polenta cake and lamb jus, or aïoli-glazed fillet of salmon with ratatouille and basil cream. Traditionalists may prefer to stick with chicken breast with cep sauce, or chargrilled sirloin steak with chips, and finish with crème caramel. Note a new chef started just as we went to press. A decent array of real ales includes Ushers Best Bitter, Wadworth 6X, Hook Norton Best Bitter and various guests. Modish modern wines like Wither Hills Sauvignon Blanc rub shoulders with Old World counterparts like Vincent Pinard's Sancerre on an upbeat wine list arranged by style. Eight wines come by the glass (£3 or £3.50 for 175ml) and 12 in half-bottles. SAMPLE DISHES: double-baked goats' cheese soufflé with tapénade £4.75; saddle of rabbit stuffed with prunes and Puy lentils with a tarragon and mustard sauce £13.50; Normandy pear tart with vanilla ice cream £4.

Licensees Anthony and Carol Coates (freehouse)
Open 11 to 3, 6 to 11 (10.30 Sun); bar food and restaurant 12 to 2, 7 to 9.30; closed 25 and 26 Dec, 1 Jan
Details Children welcome   Car park   Wheelchair access (not WC)   Garden and patio
No smoking in restaurant   Background music   Dogs welcome exc in restaurant   Delta, MasterCard, Switch, Visa   Accommodation: 10 rooms, B&B £60 to £75

WADHURST   East Sussex   map 3

▲ Best Beech Inn ☻ │ NEW ENTRY │

Mayfield Lane, Wadhurst TN5 6JH   TEL: (01892) 782046
WEBSITE: www.bestbeechinn.com
on B2100, 1m from Wadhurst towards Mark Cross

The Best Beech has been totally transformed by new owners who arrived in summer 2002. It is divided into three areas – a traditional bar for drinking, a bistro and a restaurant – and has a lively but relaxed atmosphere throughout. If you come to eat in the bistro in the evening, expect a menu of contemporary European cooking that is fairly upmarket by pub standards. Tartlet of quails' eggs, spinach and hollandaise, or duck rillettes with toasted brioche and orange essence are typical starters, while main courses might feature pan-roast monkfish with purple potatoes, broad beans and baby leeks with garlic butter, or griddled beef fillet with leek rösti, roast baby onions and button mushrooms. Among desserts, a tarte Tatin with prune and Armagnac ice cream provided one diner with 'a magical combination of flavours and temperatures'. Simpler lunch dishes might include wild mushroom and pea risotto with Parmesan, pan-seared lamb's liver with bacon and mash, and grilled mackerel fillets with melted leeks and buttered mash. Harveys Sussex Best, Adnams and Old Speckled Hen are the regular real ales. There are some 30 varied and reasonably priced wines, starting at £9.95, and seven come by the glass. SAMPLE DISHES: pea and truffle oil risotto £5; roast rump of lamb with parsnip purée, fondant potato and balsamic jus £15; raspberry pannacotta with Irish shortbread and berry compote £5.

Licensees Roger and Jane Felstead (freehouse)
Open *11.30 to 3, 6 to 11, Sun 12 to 3, 7 to 10.30; bar food and restaurant Tue to Sat 12 to 2,*
7 to 9, Sun and Mon 12 to 2
Details *Children over 12 welcome in bar eating area   Car park   Wheelchair access (not WC)*
Garden and patio   No smoking in dining room   Background music   Dogs welcome exc in restaurant
MasterCard, Switch, Visa   Accommodation: 7 rooms, B&B £39.90 to £59.90

WALBERSWICK   Suffolk   map 6

▲ Bell Inn

Ferry Road, Walberswick IP18 6TN   TEL: (01502) 723109
WEBSITE: www.blythweb.co.uk/bellinn
on B1387, off A12, S of Southwold

At the far end of the village, by the green, this upmarket 600-year-old inn is in
a peaceful, rural part of Suffolk just over the Blyth estuary from Southwold,
where Adnams brews it ales – so it is hardly surprising that the full range of the
brewery's beers are on draught here. Low beams, flagstone or uneven brick
floors, open fires, settles and lighting provided by old ships' lanterns are what
you'll find inside, with a room towards the back often busy with families
eating (the beach is a mere walk away). The menu is supported by daily blackboard specials, with fish and seafood in plentiful supply on both, and the
kitchen takes its inspiration from around the world. Options range from traditional steak and kidney pie, or whole grilled plaice, to tenderloin of pork marinated in oyster sauce and ginger accompanied by oriental-style vegetables and
noodles, lamb tagine with couscous, or a kebab of monkfish wrapped in
prosciutto served with lemon vinaigrette and wild rice. Starters likewise could
be as simple as cauliflower soup or as exotic as pan-fried king scallops with
chunky guacamole and crispy bacon. The wine list is an interesting compilation, with seven house wines, from France, Spain and Australia, sold by two
sizes of glass. SAMPLE DISHES: hummus with chilli oil and toasted pine nuts
£4.50; pheasant and partridge casseroled in red wine with pancetta, parsnips,
carrots and Stilton dumplings £8.50; apple and ginger crumble £3.50.

Licensee Susan Ireland-Cutting (Adnams)
Open *summer 11 to 11, Sun 12 to 10.30, winter Mon to Fri 11 to 3, 6 to 11, Sat 11 to 11,*
Sun 12 to 10.30; bar food 12 to 2 (2.30 Sun and bank hols), 6 (7 winter) to 9; restaurant Fri and Sat
6 (7 winter) to 9
Details *Children welcome in family room and eating areas   Car park   Wheelchair access (also WC)*
Garden and patio   No smoking in restaurant   Occasional live or background music   Dogs welcome exc
in restaurant   Delta, MasterCard, Switch, Visa   Accommodation: 6 rooms, B&B £60 to £90

WARHAM ALL SAINTS   Norfolk   map 6

▲ Three Horseshoes 🎦 🍺

Bridge Street, Warham All Saints NR23 1NL   TEL: (01328) 710547
off A149 or B1105, 2m SE of Wells-next-the-Sea

'Wellingtons are welcome,' announces the brochure produced by this long,
two-storey flint and brick inn in the centre of a small village not far from the
North Norfolk Coast Path. You enter a small bar area with a tiled floor and
Victorian fireplace; beyond this is the carpeted dining area, though you can eat

in either. Both are similarly furnished with sturdy old scrubbed pine furniture, and both are similarly decorated with a jumble of old beer advertising paraphernalia, stuffed birds and old cigarette boxes in cases, and even a grandfather clock and old slot machines. Blackboard menus list the daily specials – local crab to start, followed by a pie made with good home-made pastry and generously filled with things like garlic lamb, or rabbit and chicken in rich, tasty gravy. Light lunches from the printed menu take in jacket potatoes and variations on the ploughman's theme, with main courses of steak and kidney pudding, game and wine pie, and fillet of cod in cheese sauce. Beers are another strength: regular Woodforde's Wherry Best Bitter, Greene King IPA, and regularly changing guest ales that might come from local microbreweries, all tapped by gravity feed direct from the barrel. Around half a dozen wines are served by the glass, and the pub also boasts a choice of fruit wines. Bed and breakfast is available in the adjoining Old Post Office. SAMPLE DISHES: Mrs Beeton's potted cheese £4; fisherman's pie £7.50; golden syrup sponge £3.

Licensee Iain Salmon (freehouse)
Open 11.30 to 2.30, 6 to 11, Sun 12 to 3, 6 to 10.30; bar food 12 to 1.45, 6.30 to 8.30; no food 25 and 26 Dec
Details Children welcome in eating areas   Car park   Wheelchair access (also WC)   Garden and patio   No smoking in eating areas   No music   Dogs welcome   No cards   Accommodation: 4 rooms, B&B £24 to £52

WARWICK   Warwickshire   map 5

▲ Rose and Crown   NEW ENTRY
30 Market Place, Warwick CV34 4SH   TEL: (01926) 411117
WEBSITE: www.peachpubs.com

This first offering from the fledgling Peach Pub Company is the sort of place that leaves visitors impressed but confused, not fitting comfortably into any traditional notions of what a pub should be, yet more relaxed and informal than any restaurant. Its look is from the contemporary school of pub design. Two huge picture windows flank the entrance, allowing plenty of light into the simply decorated L-shaped room. Furniture is large wooden tables and chairs for diners, and leather sofas, bar stools and coffee tables for drinkers. Unlike most pubs, this one opens for breakfast, and lunchtime snacks are served until early evening: these include interesting sandwiches (teriyaki salmon with coriander mayo, for example) and tapas-style 'deli plates' with pick-and-mix cheeses, cold meats and assorted posh nibbles. This kind of flexibility is a hallmark of the style: several options are offered as 'either-or' portions, such as Caesar salad, and charred salmon niçoise. Lunchtime main courses are simple, hearty dishes like bacon, eggs and bubble and squeak, seafood chowder, or beef and ale pie, while the evening menu adds a few more choices, such as roast medallions of lamb with crushed squash and new potatoes, or baked hake with crushed new potatoes, rocket and romesco. To finish, there might be sticky syrup tart 'that should have a health warning'. Fuller's London Pride and Timothy Taylor Landlord are among the real ales on offer, and around half a dozen wines are available by the large or small glass from the list of two dozen bottles, prices starting at £10.50. SAMPLE DISHES: Thai mussels £5.50; roast chicken breast with leek, potato and bacon dauphinois £10.50; poached pear with vanilla pannacotta £4.25.

Licensee Hugo McFerran (Peach Pub Co)
Open 11 to 11, Sun 12 to 10.30; bar food 12 to 2.30, 6.30 to 10
Details *Children welcome* *Wheelchair access (also WC)* *Patio* *No music* *Dogs welcome*
Amex, Delta, Diners, MasterCard, Switch, Visa *Accommodation: 5 rooms, B&B £65 to £85*

WATH-IN-NIDDERDALE   North Yorkshire   map 8

▲ Sportsman's Arms 🍷 🍇
Wath-in-Nidderdale HG3 5PP   TEL: (01423) 711306
off B6265, 2m NW of Pateley Bridge

The seventeenth-century Sportsman's Arms is well named: set in Upper Nidderdale, it's surrounded by moors famous for their grouse, it has its own fishing on a stretch of the Nidd, and Gouthwaite Reservoir, with its wild brown trout, is a short walk away. The bar décor reflects this hunting and fishing theme, but the more formal restaurant has white-clothed tables and gleaming silver and glass. Although this is a hotel and restaurant, beer drinkers will find various ales on draught. The wine list works well in both pub and restaurant modes, with ten very drinkable house recommendations under £15 also available by the glass, and a well-rounded international selection of around 150 wines, including some affordable Bordeaux. The restaurant menu is also served in the bar, where a blackboard lists some daily specials: perhaps calf's liver, or sausage and mash. Fish and seafood are strengths and might turn up as a starter of feuilleté of langoustine and asparagus with orange hollandaise, and as a main course of pan-fried local trout with almonds and capers. Otherwise expect rack of venison with wild mushrooms and beetroot in a red wine and garlic cream, or loin of pork in an apple and plum sauce, with summer pudding – the house speciality – among desserts. SAMPLE DISHES: smoked haddock and cod fishcakes with sauce rémoulade £6.50; fillet of local lamb with asparagus and a roasted garlic and tomato jus £14; creamed sago pudding with raspberries £4.

Licensees Ray and Jane Carter (freehouse)
Open 12 to 2, 6.30 to 11; bar food and restaurant 12 to 2, 6.30 to 9; closed 25 Dec
Details *No children* *Car park* *Wheelchair access (not WC)* *Garden* *No smoking in restaurant*
No music *Dogs welcome* *Delta, MasterCard, Switch, Visa* *Accommodation: 13 rooms, B&B £60 to £105*

WATTON-AT-STONE   Hertfordshire   map 3

George & Dragon
High Street, Watton-at-Stone SG14 3TA   TEL: (01920) 830285
WEBSITE: www.georgeanddragon-watton.co.uk
on A602, 5m SE of Stevenage

Two traditional bars and two dining rooms are what you'll find at this characterful, sixteenth-century country pub in an attractive village. Virtually the whole place is given over to eating, and the same menus, both printed and blackboard, are served everywhere. Among first courses or light snacks may be salmon carpaccio with lemongrass, coriander, lemon and lime, 'interesting and tasty' spicy potted chicken with walnuts, and a parfait of duck and chicken liver with cranberry chutney. Main courses include chargrilled steaks, grilled king prawns with garlic butter, and lamb shank slowly roasted with tomatoes, baby onions, mint and red wine. Lighter dishes such as meatballs with rice, burger or salads are also possibilities, and puddings run to tarts, roulades and perhaps something fruity like melon, kiwi, pineapple and grapes in a brandy-snap basket. Greene King IPA and Abbot Ale and a guest are on draught, while fifteen wines are sold by the bottle and six by the glass and carafe. SAMPLE DISHES: timbale of smoked haddock and potato in horseradish and chive dressing £4.75; roast breast of duck on rösti with a mixed pepper, caper and olive salsa £12.75; chocolate and brandy mousse £3.50.

Licensees Jessica and Peter Tatlow (Greene King)
Open Mon to Fri 11 to 3, 6 to 11, Sat 11 to 11, Sun 12 to 3.30, 7 to 10.30; bar food and restaurant (exc Sun evening) 12 to 2, 7 to 10; no food 25, 26 and 31 Dec
Details Children welcome in eating areas before 8.30pm   Car park   Wheelchair access (also WC) Garden and patio   No smoking in restaurant   No music   No dogs   Amex, Diners, MasterCard, Switch, Visa

WENLOCK EDGE   Shropshire   map 5

▲ Wenlock Edge Inn
Hilltop, Wenlock Edge TF13 6DJ   TEL: (01746) 785678
WEBSITE: www.wenlockedgeinn.co.uk
on B4371, 4½m S of Much Wenlock

Despite a change of ownership since the last edition of the Guide, not a lot has changed at this isolated eighteenth-century grey-stone inn, built at one of the highest points of Wenlock Edge – the views across Apedale to Caer Caradoc and the Long Mynd are 'wonderful'. Though the interior décor is somewhat plain by contrast, staff brighten the place up with their relaxed, friendly approach and keep everything running smoothly with a degree of wit and intelligence. The regular menu – mostly along the lines of sautéed mushrooms with garlic and cream, steak and ale pie, and chicken tikka masala – is supplemented by daily specials that might include 'simple, decent and delicious' Bantry Bay mussels in white wine and garlic, or Barbary duck breast on stir-fried bean sprouts with tangy rhubarb and ginger compote. Desserts include pecan pie and sticky toffee pudding. Hobsons Best Bitter and Town Crier are the real ales served. Five of the dozen wines on the list give change from a tenner, and the same number come by the glass. A good range of soft drinks is also offered along with a strong selection of malt whiskies. SAMPLE DISHES: duck liver and Cointreau pâté £4.25; beef stroganoff £10; banoffi pie £3.50.

Licensee Julia Christ (freehouse)
Open 12 to 3 (2.30 winter), 6.30 (7 winter) to 11, Sun 12 to 3, 7 to 11; bar food and restaurant 12 to 2, 7 to 9; closed Mon, Tue lunchtime winter, 24 to 26 Dec, 31 Dec, 1 Jan; no food Mon or Tue winter
Details Children welcome in eating areas   Car park   Garden and patio   No smoking in 1 room and restaurant   No music   Dogs welcome   Delta, MasterCard, Switch, Visa   Accommodation: 3 rooms, B&B £45 to £70

▲ Crown 🍺

Westleton IP17 3AD   TEL: (01728) 648777
WEBSITE: www.westletoncrown.com
on B1125, 8m N of Saxmundham

The Crown dubs itself 'England's oldest working coaching inn', and, indeed, horse-drawn carriage rides start here, lasting anything from 15 minutes to an hour amid attractive countryside. The pub itself is warm and welcoming, with a log fire in the bar and walls practically covered in photographs of local scenes, old implements and so on. All four eating areas – conservatory, parlour, bar and brew room – are served by the same menu, which offers much interest: local venison sausages with parsnip and mustard purée, or wild mushroom risotto with a poached egg to start, and then seared salmon fillet with lemon and caper butter, or rosemary-roasted rump of lamb with rösti, and, to finish, something like lemon tart with passion-fruit sorbet, or home-made ice cream with lime syrup. Lunchtimes bring out a good choice of sandwiches and cold platters like ploughman's and Creole prawn salad. Two guest ales join Greene King IPA and Abbot Ale and St Peter's Organic Best Bitter on handpump, and around half a dozen wines are served by the glass. Westleton is not far from the coast, halfway between Southwold and Aldeburgh, and near Minsmere RSPB Reserve. SAMPLE DISHES: tea-smoked duck salad £5.25; pan-seared corn-fed chicken with pumpkin tagliatelle and chanterelle sauce £15; white chocolate truffle with pear compote £4.

Licensee Richard C. Price (freehouse)
Open 11 to 3, 6 to 11, Sun 12 to 3, 7 to 10.30; bar food and restaurant 12 to 2.15 (2.30 Sat and Sun), 7 to 9.30
Details Children welcome exc in bar   Car park   Wheelchair access (also WC)   Garden
No smoking in 2 rooms   Background music   Dogs welcome in bar   Amex, Delta, Diners,
MasterCard, Visa   Accommodation: 19 rooms, B&B £62.50 to £139

▲ George & Dragon

High Street, West Wycombe HP14 3AB   TEL: (01494) 464414
WEBSITE: www.george-and-dragon.co.uk
on A40, 3m NW of centre of High Wycombe

West Wycombe is a largely sixteenth- to eighteenth-century village owned by the National Trust, and, fittingly, its pub is a well-preserved coaching inn of rough-hewn charm and bustle. One enters off the archway to the old coach-yard to find a homely, old-fashioned, no-nonsense pub. The busy bar serves Adnams Broadside, Charles Wells Bombardier and Courage Best Bitter, plus Normandy farmhouse cider and a range of malt whiskies, and food is ordered here too. Blackboards supplement a menu that is based on tradition but not confined by it. Starters range from venison pâté to chicken satay kebab – three pieces of chicken grilled 'just right' with a little dish of 'interesting and complementary' home-made peanut sauce. Mains, similarly, span the spectrum from steak and kidney pie to chicken tikka masala, via lentil and cider loaf, and a 'satisfying and nicely tender' duck, pigeon and orange pie with subtly flavoured gravy. Desserts like sticky toffee pudding or apple pie are highly rated. Gallic wines (mostly southern French or Loire) start at £9 a bottle, with only one topping £20, and all fifteen of them are available by the glass. (If you take a shine to any, the importer's wine shop is out the back.) SAMPLE DISHES: smoked salmon and mascarpone layer gâteau with dill dip £6; chargrilled salmon steak with rösti £9.50; chocolate mud cake £4.

Licensee Philip Todd (Unique)
Open 11 to 2.30, 5.30 to 11, Sun 12 to 3, 7 to 10.30; bar food 12 to 2 (2.15 Sun), 6 to 9.30; closed 25 Dec
Details Children welcome in family room   Car park   Wheelchair access (not WC)   Garden
No- smoking area in bar   No music   Dogs welcome   Amex, Delta, Diners, MasterCard, Switch, Visa
Accommodation: 11 rooms, B&B £76 to £80; hotel closed 24 Dec to 3 Jan

WHITCHURCH   Hampshire   map 2

Red House Inn ✿
21 London Street, Whitchurch RG28 7LH   TEL: (01256) 895558
on B3400 Basingstoke to Andover road, 7m E of Andover

In many-pubbed Whitchurch it seems wilful to call this sixteenth-century establishment the Red House when its walls are white (even if doors and windows *are* red). Surmount this obstacle, though, and you must then decide which door to enter: one leads to a traditional public bar with real fire and fruit machines, the other to a beamy lounge bar with cottagey upholstered chairs, polished wood tables and matting on the floor. Two local beers are on tap, perhaps Cheriton Pots Ale and Hogs Back TEA, and thoughtfully chosen wines include ten house bottles (six by the glass). Menu and specials list are kept to sensible lengths, and the contemporary repertoire shows ambition and style. Start perhaps with hearty, rather creamy asparagus soup, or with chicken, artichoke and feta ravioli with cep sauce, or a crab and Serrano ham salad. Two paupiettes of brill (well timed, excellently fresh) stuffed with smoked salmon mousseline provided colour and flavour contrasts for one diner, or try cannelloni of aubergine filled with artichoke, mushroom, Brie and lentils. And there's a whole blackboard of steak variations. If you can manage a pud, there's double chocolate pie or berry meringue. SAMPLE DISHES: smoked halibut and red onion tart, roast pepper coulis and quail's eggs £6.25; pork fillet wrapped in Parma ham with sage and red pepper stuffing £11.50; bread-and-butter pudding £3.75.

Licensee Shannon Wells (freehouse)
Open 11.30 to 3, 6 to 11, Sun 12 to 3, 7 to 10.30; bar food and restaurant 12 to 2, 6.30 to 9.30, Sun 12 to 3, 7 to 9.30
Details Car park   Garden and patio   No smoking in dining room   Occasional live music; jukebox
Dogs welcome in bar   MasterCard, Switch, Visa

Food mentioned in the entries is available in the bar, although it may also be possible to eat in a dining room.

WHITEWELL   Lancashire   map 8

▲ Inn at Whitewell 🍇

Whitewell, Forest of Bowland BB7 3AT   TEL: (01200) 448222
off B6243 Clitheroe to Longridge road, 6m NW of Clitheroe

Coal fires, flagged floors, oak beams and a plethora of prints and photographs set the tone in this ever-popular old inn in the picturesque hamlet of Whitewell. On the restaurant menu – not available in the bar – are original dishes such as seared scallops with black pudding, creamed leeks and potato fritters, followed by perhaps roast loin of venison with walnut and thyme rösti, baked figs and sloe-gin sauce, or a vegetarian leek and Stilton tartlet with a salad of crushed tomatoes and rocket. Things are a little more straightforward in the bar, with Cullen skink, or pressed duck and pistachio terrine with peach and ginger chutney, and main courses of Cumberland sausage with champ, deep-fried haddock with chips, or pan-fried medallions of pork with mustard sauce. Sandwiches and salads are served at lunchtimes, and puddings could extend to raspberries and blueberries in lemon-balm jelly with vanilla ice cream. Service is competent and relaxed. Marston's Pedigree and Boddingtons Bitter are on draught. The wine list kicks off with several pages of champagne, Bordeaux and Burgundy, but the short selections from the Rhône and Portugal are more impressive for quality and value and the Italian reds are all top-notch. House wines start at £9.90 and an impressive 15-odd are offered by the glass. Wines are also sold in the Vintners' Shop. SAMPLE DISHES: salad of poached salmon, quail's eggs, asparagus and sauce vierge £5.50; fish pie £8.50; Baileys and chocolate brownie cheesecake with caramelised bananas £3.50.

Licensee Richard Bowman (freehouse)
Open 11 to 3, 6 (7 Sun) to 11; bar food 12 to 2, 7.30 to 9.30; restaurant 7.30 to 9.30
Details Children welcome   Car park   Garden   No music   Dogs welcome   Delta, MasterCard,
Switch, Visa   Accommodation: 17 rooms, B&B £63 to £125

WHITLEY   Wiltshire   map 2

Pear Tree Inn 🍸 🍺 🍇

Top Lane, Whitley SN12 8QX   TEL: (01225) 709131
from Bath take A365 at Box; just after Atworth take left turning signposted to Whitley

Top Lane is aptly named, as it's the most northerly of the three roads running through the village, and this detached old building of rough stone is set back off it, facing a neat lawned area and courtyard. Lots of natural materials and colours have been used in the dimly lit interior, with decoration provided by an assemblage of white-painted gardening implements on one wall and farm and kitchen utensils on others. Areas are set aside for drinkers – on draught are Barnstormer and Gem Bitter from Bath Ales, Oakhill Best Bitter, Heel Stone and Pigswill from Stonehenge Ales, and an ale from Moles Brewery in nearby Melksham – but the modern and interesting menus, the same throughout the pub, pull in diners too. The approach is flexible (starters can be served in main-course portions at lunchtime), and the style ranges from starters of pigeon and foie gras terrine with Bramley jelly, or accurately timed steamed Cornish mussels with white wine and chive cream, to main courses of

Moroccan lamb stew, or confit of duck with celeriac mash, pickled red cabbage and port jus. An inventive streak is evident in such combinations as baked red mullet on a crab and lime risotto with coriander sauce, while traditionalists should be happy with fish soup followed by pan-fried ribeye steak with garlic mushrooms and sautéed potatoes. The home-baked bread has come in for praise, as have the roasted vegetables, and among out-of-the-ordinary puddings might be spicy rice pudding fritters with vanilla-roasted rhubarb. The wine list includes at least eight well-chosen offerings by the glass from £2.95 and, without shouting about it, an impressive line-up of Old and New World names, including Vincent Pinard's Sancerre, Gilles Robin's Crozes-Hermitage and the fashionable Nepenthe wines from Australia. As the Guide went to press, plans were in hand for the addition of eight letting rooms. SAMPLE DISHES: pan-fried pigeon breast with fennel and leek fondue £5.50; braised rump of lamb with celeriac purée and roasted root vegetables £15.50; chocolate baba in Amaretto syrup with pistachio ice cream £4.50.

Licensees Martin and Debbie Still (freehouse)
Open 11 to 3, 6 to 11, Sun 12 to 6, 7 to 10.30; bar food and restaurant 12 to 2, 6.30 to 9.30
(10 Fri and Sat), Sun 12 to 2, 7 to 9; closed 25 and 26 Dec, evening 31 Dec
Details Children welcome in restaurant   Car park   Wheelchair access (also WC)   Garden
No smoking in restaurant   No music   Dogs welcome in bar only   Delta, MasterCard, Switch, Visa

WHITNEY   Herefordshire   map 5

▲ Rhydspence Inn
Whitney HR3 6EU   TEL: (01497) 831262
off A438 Hereford to Brecon road, 4m E of Hay-on-Wye

The two heavily panelled bars are in the Tudor part of this ancient half-timbered hostelry seemingly in the middle of nowhere, though close to bustling Hay-on-Wye. The pub is on an old drovers' route and still attracts passing travellers to this day, who come for the traditional bar and the smart restaurant with views of the Wye Valley. The country-house style of cooking means starters like home-made chicken liver pâté, or Thai prawns, followed by mini-breaded lobster tails, fillet steak with Stilton sauce, or spiced chicken and coconut pilaff, and then perhaps sherry trifle, or blackberry and apple tart. In the restaurant, prime ingredients come to the fore: garlic-studded monkfish, for instance, Welsh lamb cutlets, or local wild boar steak with apple compote and mustard seed and cider sauce. Real ales are from Robinson's and Bass, and Dunkerton cider is also available. The list of about 50 wines, concentrating on Europe with a short selection from the New World, includes a decent number of half-bottles. Four are available by the glass. The pub's spacious gardens look over the Wye Valley, and the stream marks the border between England and Wales. SAMPLE DISHES: baked filo purses filled with goats' cheese, spinach and mushrooms £7; grilled trout with prawn and fennel sauce £10; home-made cranberry and elderflower ice cream £4.

Licensee Peter Glover (freehouse)
Open 11 to 2.30, 7 to 11, Sun 12 to 2, 7 to 10.30; bar food and restaurant 11 to 2, 7 to 9.30;
closed 25 Dec

Details *Children welcome in family room and restaurant   Car park   Garden and patio*
No smoking in restaurant   No music   Guide dogs only   Amex, Delta, Diners, MasterCard, Switch,
Visa   Accommodation: 7 rooms, B&B £32.50 to £75

WHITSTABLE   Kent

map 3

Sportsman ✸

Faversham Road, Seasalter, Whitstable CT5 4BP   TEL: (01227) 273370
take Whitstable exit from A299, go through Whitstable and follow signs for
Seasalter; pub at far end of village

WATERSIDE

This place has been called the Sportsman since 1798 – maybe its patrons were
wildfowlers who diced with death on the tidal flats of the Swale just over the
sea wall. That could also explain why this fadedly elegant white building
surrounded by a glass-roofed verandah sits here, in an isolated spot, looking
down the coast to Whitstable in one direction and over to Sheppey in the
other. Its three spacious rooms are clean, spare and well lit, with chunky
wooden furniture, wooden floors and dado, and cream-painted walls. The
blackboard menu, which changes daily, offers feta, watermelon and pumpkin
seed salad, or Serrano ham with artichokes and Parmesan to start, while main
courses might be steamed sea bass with cockle dressing, or crispy duck with
smoked chilli salsa and sour cream. Alternatively a selection of 'ultra-thin'
pizzas that live up to their description and may be topped simply with fresh
tomato sauce and mozzarella or artichokes are also available. This is a
Shepherd Neame pub (the brewery is only a few miles away) serving their
usual real ales, including seasonals. Six wines are available by the glass from a
list of thirty-plus that starts at £9.95. SAMPLE DISHES: salt-cod bruschetta £6;
braised pork belly stuffed with black pudding and crackling £13; chocolate
mousse cake £5.

Licensees Phil and Steve Harris (Shepherd Neame)
Open *12 to 3, 6 to 11, Sun 12 to 11; bar food and restaurant Tue to Sat 12 to 2, 7 to 9,*
Sun 12 to 2.30
Details *Children welcome everywhere exc front bar   Car park   Wheelchair access (not WC)*
Garden and patio   No smoking in 1 room   Background music   Dogs welcome   Delta, MasterCard,
Switch, Visa

WIDECOMBE IN THE MOOR   Devon

map 1

Old Inn

Widecombe in the Moor TQ13 7TA   TEL: (01364) 621207
from Bovey Tracey take B3387 through Haytor to Widecombe

This Dartmoor village is a fair step from most places, but people come by the
coachload (often literally) – so be warned and *book ahead*, especially for weekend lunches, lest you find no tables free. There's a traditional pub atmosphere
in the warren of small cosy rooms: roaring log fires in winter, flagged floors,
wooden tables and chairs. Quick, efficient and friendly staff are good at coping
with crowds, and children have their own menu and a family room with high
chairs. Thirsts can be quenched with local Teignworthy ales, plus Bass,
Boddingtons Best Bitter, Flowers IPA, and Gray's farmhouse cider. Almost all

wines are under £15, and five come by the glass. As for food – listed on a long menu and a blackboard – brace yourself for *huge* portions ('Next time we'll order one main course between up to six of us!'), though value is good. At busy times, starters – from home-made soup to haggis, neeps and tatties, or from avocado and prawns to whitebait – must be followed by mains. Among these are cottage pie and curries, steaks (8 to 18 ounce) and mixed grills (one massive, one platoon-sized), a barbecued half-chicken on fresh salad 'with lots of fruit in it', battered cod, poached salmon, and mushroom stroganoff. If you can manage dessert, expect the likes of zabaglione trifle, and apple bread-and-butter pudding. SAMPLE DISHES: smoked salmon £5; beef in red wine £7; meringue glacé £3.

Licensees Mr J.C. Haughton and Mr D. Bowden (freehouse)
Open *11 to 2.30, 7 (6.30 summer) to 11, Sun 12 to 3, 7 to 10.30; bar food and restaurant 11 to 2 (12 to 2.30 Sun), 6.30 to 10*
Details *Children welcome exc in public bar   Car park   Wheelchair access (also WC)   Garden and patio   Occasional background music   Dogs welcome   Delta, MasterCard, Switch, Visa (credit card service charge)*

WILMINGTON   East Sussex   map 3

▲ Giants Rest   NEW ENTRY
The Street, Wilmington BN26 5SQ   TEL: (01323) 870207
off A27, 2m W of Polegate

Look for a tall building with a red-brick ground floor, white-painted first floor and bright blue barge boards. The name the Giants Rest is a nice conceit, but the Long Man of Wilmington carved into the chalk down above couldn't squeeze his 240-foot length into any of the beds here, doubles though they be. He couldn't even fit into the bar – two rooms that have been knocked together – with its comfortably worn wooden floors and wooden tables, benches and spindle-back chairs. A pleasant touch, consistent with the friendly and informal atmosphere: each table has a wooden puzzle or game to play while nursing a glass of Harveys Sussex Best Bitter, Timothy Taylor Landlord or Hop Back Summer Lightning. Food, ordered at the bar, comes predominantly from local suppliers. Starters like Stilton and walnut pâté, or melon and prawns, lead on to nice, open-textured hake fishcakes spiced with slices of chilli, fresh ginger and coriander leaves, or perhaps (a long-overdue revival) good old rabbit and bacon pie. Vegetarian choices include a thick, tomato-based African sweet potato, spinach and peanut stew with a rich, nutty flavour. Puds like meringue glacé or treacle tart will fill any remaining chinks. A short wine list starts at £11.75 and offers six by the glass. Wise diners will book in advance. SAMPLE DISHES: bacon and garlic mushrooms £4.50; lamb Madras and basmati rice £9; blackberry crème brûlée £4.

Licensees Adrian and Rebecca Hillman (freehouse)
Open *Mon to Sat 11.30 to 3, 6 to 11, Sun 12 to 3, 6 to 10 (summer Mon to Sat 11.30 to 11, Sun 12 to 10.30); bar food 12 to 2, 6.30 to 9*
Details *Car park   Wheelchair access (not WC)   Garden and patio   No-smoking area in bar Background music   Dogs welcome on a lead   Delta, MasterCard, Switch, Visa   Accommodation: 2 rooms, B&B £40*

WINCHOMBE   Gloucestershire   **map 5**

▲ White Hart   NEW ENTRY

High Street, Winchcombe GL54 5LJ   TEL: (01242) 602359
WEBSITE: www.the-white-hart-inn.com

A pretty town, Winchcombe lies between Cheltenham and Broadway, surrounded by rolling countryside with Sudeley Castle a glamorous neighbour. At its centre is this smart black and white-painted old hotel, a relaxed but fairly upmarket establishment. Unusually in such a traditionally English setting, décor has an Anglo-Swedish feel throughout the main bar's three interlinked areas, with the back room in particular striking a Scandinavian theme: sisal floor coverings, blue and white colour scheme, lots of pale wood. The taproom in converted stables and the main restaurant are more traditional. A Swedish flavour also permeates the menus – open sandwiches of herrings and gravad lax, for example, and 'smorgasbord' platters of cold meats, seafood and salads. But there are also plenty of non-Swedish bar snacks, like goats' cheese with red onion marmalade baked in a pastry case, Spanish omelette, ploughman's, filled baguettes and Caesar salad. Ingredients are high quality (including an inspector's 'best pub roast beef ever'). The main restaurant menu is more ambitious – braised duck in Guinness with potatoes, truffle oil and tomato compote among starters, and perhaps rack of lamb with potato squares, red onion confit, grilled zucchini and garlic and white-bean crème to follow. Real ales are Stanney Bitter, from nearby Stanway brewery, along with Greene King IPA and Wadworth 6X. The wine list is better than most, and prices (generally not too scary) start at £12; six come by the glass. SAMPLE DISHES: crusty baguette with rare roast beef £6; Swedish meatballs in a creamy sauce with lingonberries £9; Baileys and Kahlùa parfait £5.

Licensees Nicole and David Burr (Enterprise Inns)
Open 10 to 11, Sun 11 to 10.30; bar food 10 to 10; restaurant 6 to 10; closed 25 Dec
Details Children welcome   Car park   Patio   No smoking in dining room   Background and occasional live music   Dogs welcome (£10 in accommodation)   Delta, MasterCard, Switch, Visa
Accommodation: 8 rooms, B&B £45 to £105

WINCHESTER   Hampshire   **map 2**

▲ Wykeham Arms 🍴 🍺 🍇   NEW ENTRY

75 Kingsgate Street, Winchester SO23 9PE   TEL: (01962) 853834
S of Cathedral, near Winchester College

Hidden away in the narrow cobbled streets of the oldest part of the city, this 250-year-old gem of a pub is as much of an institution as the famous College and Cathedral, both of which are close by. Behind the unassuming exterior is a maze of rooms of timeless charm, fitted out with old school desks and lined with all manner of memorabilia – tankards, lamps, hats and books, for example – and log fires are always burning. The Hamilton Bar is the spot for drinkers, while the characterful no-smoking Watchmakers Bar is reckoned to be the pick of the eating areas. This is a popular venue, so it is always advisable to book if you want to eat. Lunch is a simple affair, the blackboard menu typically offering spicy tomato soup, salmon and aniseed fishcakes, 'Wyk' cottage pie, and lamb and spinach curry. But the kitchen cranks up a gear for dinner, turning out Thai-marinated pigeon breast on citrus and coriander couscous with hoisin and sesame dressing, and roast rack of Hampshire Downs lamb on celeriac and potato mash with braised leeks and bacon, oyster mushrooms and creamy mustard sauce. To finish, there might be elderflower jelly with pineapple and mango compote. With 22 wines by the glass and plenty of half-bottles, the 70-bin wine list shows a real commitment to pleasing one and all. It takes in a full range of styles, with lots on offer under £20. Real ale drinkers are also well served, with five to choose from, including three from Hampshire brewery Gale's and a changing guest. SAMPLE DISHES: hummus and caramelised red onion salad £9; baked sea bass on spicy mussel bouill-abaisse with cocotte potatoes and crispy prosciutto £14; iced lemon and ginger parfait £4.50.

Licensee Peter Miller (George Gale & Co.)
Open 11 to 11, Sun 12 to 10.30; bar food all week 12 to 3, Mon to Sat 6.30 to 8.45; closed 25 Dec
Details No children Car park Garden and patio No smoking in restaurant No music Dogs welcome in bar only Amex, Delta, Diners, MasterCard, Switch, Visa Accommodation: 14 rooms, B&B £50 to £120

WING Rutland map 6

▲ King's Arms
Top Street, Wing LE15 8SE TEL: (01572) 737634
WEBSITE: www.thekingsarms-wing.co.uk
off A47, 4m SE of Oakham

Wing is famous for its medieval maze, although this comfortable and convivial inn is also a strong contender in the local popularity stakes. Owners Jason Allen and Richard Page took over in summer 2002, and the place seems to be ticking over efficiently. The main part of the building dates from 1649, and the bar retains much of its original character, with beams, a flagstone floor and a roaring log fire in winter; by contrast, the restaurant strikes a more modern note, with its light-wood furniture. There's plenty of exotic and ambitious-sounding stuff on the printed menu, from strips of crocodile in tangy plum sauce, and chargrilled medallions of ostrich with peppercorn sauce, to fillet of halibut on Parmesan mash with oriental spring onions. Blackboard specials provide a few more conventional ideas, like whole Rutland trout stuffed with oranges and mushrooms. Real ales such as Cooking Bitter and Ten Fifty come from the Grainstore Brewing Company in nearby Oakham, and the pub has a workmanlike list of around two dozen wines including a handful of house selections (from £10.95 a bottle) available by the glass. SAMPLE DISHES: gravlax with king prawns and dill crème fraîche £6.50; roast herb-crumbed rack of lamb with honey and lavender jus £12.50; chocolate and hazlenut torte £4.75.

Licensees Jason Allen and Richard Page (freehouse)
Open 12 to 3, 6.30 to 11, Sun 12 to 3, 6.30 to 10.30 (12 to 11 Sat summer, 12 to 10.30 Sun summer); bar food and restaurant 12 to 2, 6.30 to 9
Details Children welcome Car park Garden and patio No smoking in restaurant Background music No dogs Diners, MasterCard, Switch, Visa Accommodation: 8 rooms, B&B £40 to £70

WINGFIELD   Suffolk   map 6
De La Pole Arms 🍺
Church Road, Wingfield IP21 5RA   TEL: (01379) 384545
off B1118 Framlingham to Diss road, just N of Stradbroke

The de la Poles were medieval dukes of Suffolk, but the cream-plastered and
pantiled building opposite the church dates from rather later – the sixteenth
century. The nicely restored interior, in the same restful cream, has mellow
exposed beams and studwork, tiled floors, and stuffed fish and otters on the
walls. On draught are St Peter's Best Bitter, Strong Bitter, and seasonal ales,
plus bottled beers from the St Peter's brewery six miles away. The cuisine
mixes plain and fancy (e.g. beer-battered Lowestoft cod and chunky chips, and
hot-and-sour pickled crevettes). From Tuesday to Friday there's a £10 two-
course lunch; otherwise there are bar and restaurant menus, plus specials,
with fish dishes prominent and large helpings the norm. One couple had a
Stilton and celery soup 'we cannot praise too highly – thick but not glutinous,
flavours perfectly balanced' – but you could try grilled crab instead. Meaty
main dishes include rack of lamb on pommes dauphinoise, or turkey, leek and
pancetta pie, as alternatives to witch (part of the sole family) baked under an
olive/tomato/basil Mediterranean topping, or a grilled salmon steak and sorrel
sauce. Then, space permitting, there's iced lemon bombe with mango sauce,
or stacked Scotch pancakes with brandied apple slices and honey. The list of
30-plus wines (mostly under £20) offers seven by the glass. SAMPLE DISHES:
devilled whitebait £5; blue cheese and walnut tagliatelle £8.50; peach melba
cheesecake £4.

Licensee Sally Prior (St Peter's)
Open *Tue to Thur (summer Mon to Thur) 11 to 3, 6.30 to 11, Fri and Sat 11 to 3, 6 to 11,
Sun 12 to 3; bar food and restaurant all week 12 to 2 (2.30 Sat and Sun), Mon to Sat 7 to 9 (9.30
Fri and Sat)*
Details *Children welcome   Car park   Wheelchair access (also WC)   Patio   No smoking in dining
room   Background music   Dogs welcome in public bar   Delta, MasterCard, Switch, Visa*

WINSFORD   Somerset   map 1
▲ Royal Oak Inn
Winsford TA24 7JE   TEL: (01643) 851455
WEBSITE: www.royaloak-somerset.co.uk
off A396, 5m N of Dulverton

The Royal Oak is a picture-postcard building of neatly clipped thatch above
yellow-painted plaster walls, parts dating from the twelfth century, in a
picturesque village on the edge of Exmoor National Park. The cosy, rather
cramped bar has tongue-and-groove pew-style seating with red and green
tartan cushions, an inglenook, a sage-green patterned carpet, wall lamps in
pairs, and hunting prints. The menu here is adaptable enough to provide
anything from ploughman's or a sandwich to a full three-course meal. Dishes
impress with the 'excellence and freshness' of the ingredients (suppliers are
listed on the menus), from a tian of crayfish, crab and avocado topped with
citrus-dressed leaves, to a main course of braised lamb shank on spring onion

and bacon mash with red wine sauce. White wine and herb risotto finished with cream and Parmesan makes a nod to fashion, while those who enjoy traditional pub fare could go for ribeye steak with chunky chips and all the trimmings, followed by bread-and-butter pudding. The restaurant menu, also served in the bar, is a short list of largely mainstream dishes: terrine of local game, followed by roast rack of English lamb in a herb and mustard crust. The restaurant wine list has around twenty-five bottles, mainly French, while the bar has its own list of nine fairly priced bottles, with a full page of half-bottles and three house wines sold by the glass from £2.75. Ales from Butcombe and Brakspear are on draught. SAMPLE DISHES: king prawns with lemon, garlic, chilli and coriander butter £6.25; half a slow-roast local duckling with orange sauce £10.50; rhubarb crumble £3.25.

Licensee Charles Steven (freehouse)
Open *11 to 2.30, 6 to 11; bar food 12 to 6.30, restaurant 7.30 to 9*
Details *Children welcome in bar eating area   Car park   Wheelchair access (also WC)   Garden and patio   No-smoking area in bar   Background music in restaurant   Dogs welcome   Amex, Diners, MasterCard, Visa   Accommodation: 14 rooms, B&B £89 to £145*

WINTERBOURNE   Berkshire   map 2

Winterbourne Arms   NEW ENTRY
Winterbourne RG20 8BB   TEL: (01635) 248200
WEBSITE: www.winterbournearms.tablesir.com
Winterbourne signposted off B4494 3½m NW of Newbury

The Winterbourne Arms is a cottagey old pub at the heart of this charming, peaceful little village. Old photographs of the village and country prints line the walls of the three interconnecting bar areas, windows have curtains and there are warming fires at colder times of the year. Menus show a modern style, with starters of chargrilled plum tomatoes and asparagus with plum chutney, or warm salad of pan-fried pigeon breasts, and around ten main-course options taking in seared duck breast on sweet potato rösti, roast pork fillet with mustard and tarragon sauce, and baked salmon with tapénade on buttered leeks. At lunchtimes there are a few simpler options, such as scampi and chips, or pork and leek sausages and mash, plus sandwiches and filled ciabattas. Desserts are things like apple pie and custard, or tarte au citron. The wine list opens with house French red and white at £9.95, and most of the rest of the 20 or so bottles are helpfully priced under £15. Ten wines are served by the glass. Beers include Good Old Boy from the local West Berkshire Brewery. SAMPLE DISHES: salmon and cod terrine with mixed-leaf salad and red pepper dressing £6.25; pan-fried chicken breast stuffed with Brie and bacon with rice and tomato sauce £13; chocolate fudge cake £5.

Licensee Claire Owens (freehouse)
Open *Tue to Sun 12 to 3, 6 to 11.30 (10.30 Sun); bar food and restaurant 12 to 2.30, 7 to 9.30; closed Sun evenings winter*
Details *Children welcome in restaurant   Car park   Garden   No smoking in restaurant Background music   Dogs welcome exc in restaurant   Amex, MasterCard, Switch, Visa*

WINTERTON   North Lincolnshire   map 9

George ✿   NEW ENTRY

Market Street, Winterton DN15 9PT   TEL: (01724) 732270
off A1077, 6½m N of Scunthorpe

North of Scunthorpe, the Trent and Ermine Street march in parallel towards
the Humber; between them sits Winterton, in whose marketplace is a neat
Georgian building of grey stone with two white pillars marking the door.
Inside, the welcoming lounge bar has a brick bar counter, wood floor and
beams, while in the tap a stuffed barn owl lurks in a glass case among the
prints, old photographs and golf clubs on the wall. Beers are from Tetley and
Wells (Bombardier). There's no bar food – the blackboard menu is for the
small restaurant upstairs, which John O'Connor has refurbished since arriving in 2001 (after 11 years as restaurant manager at nearby Winteringham
Fields). From the tempting array of starters here pumpkin soup (spiked with
ginger and nutmeg) has stood out, also a delicious seared pigeon breast with
'lovely fresh mash and the richest, deepest red wine sauce'. Fish figure prominently among main courses (viz., turbot and prawn ragoût with fennel and a
lemony risotto), but there's also fried duck breast with damson wine and
cherry jus – or surf'n'turf it with steak and oyster pie and Guinness gravy.
Desserts encompass Amaretto crème brûlée and chocolate bread-and-butter
pudding, and the short, kindly priced wine list has four by the glass. SAMPLE
DISHES: smoked-halibut-topped blinis with pickled cucumber and beetroot
sorbet £4.75; baked marlin roll with bacon, lime and coriander stuffing
£14.50; spiced pear and gooseberry crumble £4.

Licensee John O'Connor (Enterprise Inns)
Open *3 to 11, Sun 12 to 5, 8 to 10.30; restaurant Wed to Sat 7 to 9.30, Sun 12 to 4*
Details *Children welcome in dining-room   Car park   Wheelchair access (also WC)   Garden and
patio   No smoking in dining room   Background music; jukebox   No dogs   No cards*

WINTERTON-ON-SEA   Norfolk   map 6

▲ Fishermans Return 🍺

The Lane, Winterton-on-Sea NR29 4BN   TEL: (01493) 393305
WEBSITE: www.fishermans-return.com
on B1159, 8m N of Great Yarmouth

A paved patio at the front of this two-storey, red-brick and flint old pub makes
an ideal spot to relax in after a stroll across the dunes. Inside is a homely
carpeted lounge furnished with traditional circular pub tables, and a larger bar
adjacent to it with varnished wood-strip-panelled walls and good-sized tables
(sharing may be necessary at peak times). Both have a wood-burning stove,
with local prints and old photographs providing the decoration. A selection of
excellent real ales and ciders is served, including Wherry Best Bitter and
Norfolk Nog from Woodforde's, Broadside and Bitter from Adnams, and Old
Rosie cider. There is also a menu of straightforward pub food – burgers,
omelettes, and toasted sandwiches, for instance – plus a blackboard of home-
cooked specials: perhaps starters of celery and Stilton soup, or hot Winterton
smoked salmon, main courses of seafood lasagne, or pork loin stuffed with

bacon and wild mushrooms, and puddings of spotted dick with custard. A handful of wines is available by the glass from the short, reasonably priced list. With mile after mile of beach nearby, this is a popular place with holidaymakers in summer. SAMPLE DISHES: button mushrooms cooked in oregano, butter and garlic with French bread £3.50; Whitby scampi with tartare sauce £7.50; black cherry cheesecake £3.

Licensees John and Kate Findlay (freehouse)
Open Mon to Fri 11 to 2.30, 6.30 to 11, Sat and Sun 11 to 11; bar food 12 to 2, 6.30 to 9
Details Children welcome in family room and eating area   Car park   Garden and patio
No smoking in family room and 1 eating area   Background music; jukebox   Dogs welcome   Amex, Delta, MasterCard, Switch, Visa   Accommodation: 3 rooms, B&B £45 to £70

WISWELL   Lancashire   map 8

Freemasons Arms
8 Vicarage Fold, Wiswell BB7 9DF   TEL: (01254) 822218
1m off A680 near Whalley

Wiswell is a tiny village at the foot of Pendle Hill in rolling countryside, and this homely pub is 'hidden away' at its centre on an unmade lane. With low ceilings, beams and horse brasses, the interior is divided into two rooms, one set out for dining, the other a bar with copper-topped tables. A straightforward but extensive menu features starters like melon, prawn and avocado salad in a honey and mustard dressing, or baked stuffed tomatoes, and main courses of steak and kidney pie, or roast bacon-wrapped chicken breast stuffed with orange and garlic butter in a creamy white wine sauce. Fish tends to dominate the specials board – spicy Thai-style prawns, say, followed by monkfish wrapped in Parma ham drizzled with tapénade – although pheasant might also appear in season, roasted and accompanied by apple and redcurrant sauces, while desserts might include jam roly-poly, or lemon meringue pie. Real ales come from Jennings and Black Sheep, 80-plus whiskies are available, and there is a list of around 30 wines, of which half a dozen are served by the glass. SAMPLE DISHES: feta, olive and sun-dried tomato salad with pesto £4.50; poached salmon fillet in tarragon sauce with asparagus tips £10; summer pudding £3.

Licensee Pauline Livesey (freehouse)
Open Wed to Sat 12 to 2.30, 6.30 to 11, Sun 12 to 2, 6 to 10.30; bar food and restaurant Wed to Sat 12 to 2, 6.30 to 9.30, Sun 12 to 2, 6 to 9
Details No children   Wheelchair access (not WC)   No smoking in restaurant   Background music   No dogs   Delta, MasterCard, Switch, Visa

WITHYHAM   East Sussex   map 3

Dorset Arms
Withyham TN7 4BD   TEL: (01892) 770278
WEBSITE: www.dorset-arms.co.uk
on B2110 between Hartfield and Groombridge

Withyham is lucky in its pub, and knows it. The L-shaped building, walls tile-hung and then painted white, has been an inn since the eighteenth century, though it started as a farmhouse in the fifteenth – and has wall studs and ceiling beams to prove it. There's a bar menu and a restaurant menu, though (except on Friday and Saturday nights) restaurant customers may eat from the bar menu. This offers ploughman's, jacket potatoes and toasted sandwiches, plus starters like whitebait with brown bread, or home-made pâté and toast, or mains like omelettes, smoked salmon and prawn salad, or rump steak with chips and salad. In addition, a blackboard tempts one to pheasant, partridge, moussaka, prawn curry, and puds from pannacotta to pavlova. This being a Harveys pub, you can wash it all down with Harveys Sussex Best Bitter and Pale Ale, plus seasonal brews; there's also a short, basic European/Australian wine list, including one bin from East Sussex and three by the glass. The restaurant serves a £20 three-course meal, perhaps including Thai-style crab cakes, or melon and fresh fruit cocktail, followed by a baked half-shoulder of lamb with red wine gravy, or griddled fillets of sea bass with hollandaise. Desserts, the same as in the bar, could include banoffi pie, and bread-and-butter pudding. SAMPLE DISHES: half-pint of prawns with dip £3.75; breaded plaice and chips £6; white chocolate cheesecake £4.

Licensees John Pryor and Peter Randall (Harveys of Lewes)
Open Mon to Sat 11 to 3, 6 to 11, Sun 12 to 3, 7 to 10.30; bar food and restaurant all week 12 to 2, Tue to Sat 7.30 to 9
Details Car park Wheelchair access (not WC) Garden and patio No smoking in dining room Background music Dogs welcome in bar Amex, Delta, Diners, MasterCard, Switch, Visa

WITNEY Oxfordshire   map 2

Three Horseshoes 🌸 NEW ENTRY
78 Corn Street, Witney, OX8 7BS   TEL: (01993) 703086
WEBSITE: www.thethreehorseshoes.tablesir.com

On a corner, close to the centre of town, the Three Horseshoes is a traditional-looking pub with two small bar areas at the front and another room to the rear that is set aside for eating. It's not at first glance the sort of place where you would expect to find anything above ordinary pub grub, but the food is considered 'great – and good value'. And while there are plenty of traditional dishes to choose from, such as Cornish moules marinière, fishcakes with parsley sauce and daube of beef with spring onion mash and red wine gravy, chef Lee Groves also cooks more unusual dishes: roast breast and braised leg of Aylesbury duck with caramelised sweet potato and a sweet-and-sour ginger and spring onion glaze, for example, or seared escalope of salmon with lobster, orange and cucumber butter sauce. Baguettes, too, come with interesting fillings like fresh crab and cucumber. This is a Greene King pub, so expect their Abbot Ale and Morland Original Bitter on draught, along with a quarterly changing guest, and four of the 21 wines come by the glass. SAMPLE DISHES: grilled asparagus with orange mousseline and chive oil £5; roast best end of lamb with roast fennel mash, olives, tomato and basil gravy £13.50; caramelised apple crumble with vanilla ice cream £4.25.

Licensee Peter Wheeler (Greene King)
Open Mon to Sat 12 to 2, 6.45 to 11, Sun 12 to 5; bar food Mon to Sat 12 to 2, 6.45 to 9.15, Sun 12 to 4.30
Details Children welcome in eating areas Garden No smoking in dining room Background music No dogs Amex, Delta, MasterCard, Switch, Visa

Three Horseshoes

Wixford B49 6DG   TEL: (01789) 490400

from A46 at Alcester roundabout follow A435 towards Redditch; left on to A422, then left following signs for Wixford

This creeper-covered brick pub in a sprawling village has been the Three Horseshoes since 1811, and even in the 1930s smithing work was still done here alongside innkeeping. These days it has forged a reputation as a dining pub. Warm terracotta colours and an open fire contribute to a bustling but comfortable atmosphere, along with the friendly welcome and quick, efficient service. A printed light lunch menu offers sandwiches, jacket potatoes, ploughman's lunches and the likes of fish and chips; a blackboard lists the main dishes (half-portions available for children, in addition to the children's menu). Steamed mussels with curried cream sauce and naan to start perhaps, or smoked chicken with plum sauce dressing on a green salad; then a roast half-pheasant with blackberry sauce, a grilled plaice fillet with 'duo of peppers' coulis, or a leek and potato terrine with watercress cream sauce. Finish with apple and cinnamon pie with figgy pudding ice cream, or chocolate rum and raisin mousse with Baileys cream. Beers include Wadworth 6X, Marston's Pedigree and Tetley, as well as a guest beer (perhaps Wood's Shropshire Lad, or Pooh Beer from Church End Brewery), while six wines come by the glass from a mainly New World list of 20. SAMPLE DISHES: prawns, tomato, avocado and spring onion bound in crème fraîche £5; braised faggots, mushy peas and gravy £9; ginger sponge with orange custard £4.25.

Licensee Simon Dearden (NCM Leisure)

Open *summer 12 to 3, 6.30 to 11 (10.30 Sun); bar food 12 to 2 (2.30 Sun), 6.30 to 9.30; closed 25 Dec, 1 Jan*

Details *Children welcome   Car park   Wheelchair access (also WC)   Garden and patio No-smoking areas   Occasional live or background music   No dogs   MasterCard, Switch, Visa*

▲ Chequers Inn 🅩 🍇

Kiln Lane, Wooburn Common HP10 0JQ   TEL: (01628) 529575

from M40 junction 2, take A355 S, then first right on minor road; follow signs for Taplow, then Bourne End; pub is on left of road

This place is large, brick-built and seventeenth-century, but (as Eric Morecambe said) not necessarily in that order. It has the look of an old pub much expanded, mainly in the twentieth century, into something more like a small hotel. It lies in the middle of the Chiltern Hundreds, in open country between Beaconsfield and Maidenhead. There is a substantial and pleasant-looking garden for summer drinking, while the smallish bar area inside has an open fire in winter as well as beams, brickwork and board floor. The beers on offer are Greene King IPA, Ruddles County, Abbot Ale and Morland Original. At inspection the blackboard bar menu offered but one starter. Mains, though, may run from chicken curry and rice, via sautéed lambs' kidneys with mustard butter, to mussels with linguine. Wild duck with orange and olive sauce struck one diner as both nicely fresh and mutually complementary in its flavours, while a good-quality grilled lamb steak with rosemary jus came with a selection of well-timed vegetables. A bread-and-butter pudding had some good vanilla ice cream on top, or there might be poached pear with chocolate sauce. The Old World rules on a restaurant wine list peppered with expensive bottles. A blackboard selection of wines by the glass in the bar draws on the cheaper end and is occasionally complemented by a range of bin-ends. SAMPLE DISHES: borlotti bean soup with olive oil and Parmesan £4; mixed game sausages with mash and onion gravy £9; blackberry and apple crumble £4.

Licensee Peter J. Roehrig (freehouse)
Open 10am to 11pm, Sun 10am to 10.30pm; bar food and restaurant 12 to 2.30, 6.30 to 9.30
Details Children welcome   Car park   Wheelchair access (not WC)   Garden and patio
No-smoking area in bar   Background music   Dogs welcome   Amex, Delta, MasterCard, Switch, Visa
Accommodation: 17 rooms, B&B £99.50 to £107.50

WOODHILL Somerset   map 2

▲ Rose and Crown
Woodhill, Stoke St Gregory TA3 6EW   TEL: (01823) 490296
WEBSITE: www.browningpubs.com
between A361 and A378, 8m E of Taunton, via North Curry

A tiny hamlet on the Somerset Levels is the setting of this 300-year-old inn. The décor is bright, if a little dated, and walls are cluttered with old prints, photographs, signs and posters. The bar menu lists a wide range of pub fare, predominantly grills: lambs' kidneys and bacon with tomato and mushrooms, or gammon with pineapple, for example. Fish gets a good showing, from grilled Dover sole to salmon fishcakes with garlic dressing, and vegetarians are offered a decent choice. Sandwiches, salads and snacks – sausage, eggs and chips, for instance – are possibilities at lunchtime. The restaurant menu, which can also be ordered in the bar, is a set-price affair with a number of supplements. Expect king prawns sautéed in garlic butter, or duck liver pâté, followed by rack of lamb with rosemary, or monkfish meunière. Exmoor Ale and Fox plus a guest are on draught along with Thatcher's cider. The wine list is an interesting compilation from around the world, with some good producers at reasonable prices; five are sold by the glass. The flowery patio is popular in summer. SAMPLE DISHES: chorizo, egg mayonnaise and watercress sandwich £3.75; deep-fried plaice stuffed with prawns and mushrooms £7.50; gooseberry and apple crumble £3.

Licensees R.F. and I.M. Browning (freehouse)
Open 12 to 3, 6.30 to 11, Sun 12 to 3, 7 to 10.30; bar food and restaurant 12 to 2, 7 to 9.30; closed evening 25 Dec, 1 Jan
Details Children welcome   Car park   Wheelchair access (not WC)   Garden and patio
No smoking in restaurant   Live or background music   Dogs welcome exc at peak times   Delta, MasterCard, Switch, Visa   Accommodation: 6 rooms, B&B £36.50 to £78

▲ Royal Oak

Wootton Rivers SN8 4NQ   TEL: (01672) 810322
WEBSITE: www.wiltshire-pubs.com
off A346, 3m NE of Pewsey

The Kennet and Avon passes through a lock at the lower end of this picturesque village of thatched buildings. The Royal Oak, which dates from the sixteenth century and once housed a bakery, farrier's and alehouse, is itself thatched and built in the shape of a right angle. Inside is an L-shaped bar/dining room with white walls and dark beams, alongside a spacious public bar. A fine selection of malt whiskies, cognacs and liqueurs lend authority to the range of speciality drinking, which is founded on handpumped Fuller's London Pride plus a choice of guest ales and an imaginative wine list that includes seven by the glass. The kitchen produces some accomplished cooking. Fish is good – maybe whole lemon sole baked with sea salt, or grilled tuna steak with provençale sauce – as are meat dishes that extend from local ham with eggs and chips to steak Rossini via partridge with game sauce. Starters include a good showing of pub favourites, along the lines of prawn cocktail, or chicken liver and brandy pâté, although there may also be potted shrimps, or Thai fishcake with sweet chilli sauce, while puddings indulge with the likes of sherry trifle, or banana and butterscotch sundae. SAMPLE DISHES: deep-fried calamari with tartare sauce £5.25; medallions of venison with apricot stuffing £14.50; green figs with Pernod £4.25.

Licensees Mr and Mrs John C. Jones (freehouse)
Open *10 to 3, 6 to 11; bar food and restaurant 12 to 2.30, 7 to 9.30; closed evening 25 Dec*
Details *Children welcome   Car park   Wheelchair access (also WC)   Patio   No smoking in restaurant   Jukebox in 1 bar   Dogs welcome   Amex, Delta, Diners, MasterCard, Switch, Visa Accommodation: 6 rooms, B&B £30 to £50*

Dog Inn

Main Street, Worfield WV15 5LF   TEL: (01746) 716020
village signposted off A454 NE of Bridgnorth

This pub started life as the Greyhound, before becoming the Davenport Arms; either way everyone called it the Dog, so that's now its proper name. Worfield is some three miles from Bridgnorth on the River Worfe, tucked between the roads to Telford and Wolverhampton. This is a fairly plain redbrick building, with a small garden at the back. Inside, a tiled floor, light pine furnishings and some floral prints on the walls give a neat, clean impression. In the bar there are Wadworth 6X, Courage Best Bitter, Wells Bombardier Premium Bitter and Highgate Dark Mild, and a simple lunchtime snack menu of baguettes, ratatouille cheese, and the like, plus children's dishes (sausages, chicken nuggets, vegeburgers, etc., all with chips and beans, and ice cream with chocolate sauce to follow). The restaurant's lunch menu may offer soup or pâté, then locally made faggots or navarin of rabbit. The evening carte might add seafood hors d'oeuvre, lobster (various ways), kedgeree, or 'blanks and fries' (gammon, broad beans and parsley sauce), banging the drum for local ingredients as it does so. Desserts, such as double chocolate pudding, are listed on a blackboard. Three wines come by the glass from a world-spanning list of 25. SAMPLE DISHES: sardine and tomato pâté £4; duck with port sauce £10.50; black cherry crêpes £3.50.

Licensee Vic Pocock (freehouse)
Open *12 to 2.30, 7 to 11, Sun 12 to 3, 7 to 10.30; bar food 12 to 2, restaurant 12 to 2, 7 to 9.30*
Details *Children welcome   Car park   Wheelchair access (also WC)   Patio   No smoking in dining room   Occasional background music   Dogs by arrangement   Amex, Delta, MasterCard, Switch, Visa*

WRIGHTINGTON   Lancashire   map 8

Mulberry Tree ✿
9 Wrightington Bar, Wrightington WN6 9SE   TEL: (01257) 451400
2m from M6 junction 27, on B5250

This is a gastro-pub, focusing more on food than beer (though Flowers IPA is on offer). After twenty years cooking in the south, including stints with both Roux brothers, Mark Prescott returned to his roots to run his own show in this Victorian pub, and what he puts on the plate seems to be appreciated. The place is informal, with a light, open feel, and has separate menus for bar and dining room (though eaters in the bar can choose from either). From the former you can choose a rather superior sandwich (sirloin steak with red onions and fried egg, say), a classy version of cod and chips, or slow-roast belly pork with ribollita, pancetta and Parmesan crisp – not to mentions starters like roast figs wrapped in Parma ham with Gorgonzola and rocket salad, or nougat glace with raspberry coulis to finish. Some dishes also appear in the dining room, alongside oysters, caviar, or ham hock and foie gras terrine as starters, or mains like chargrilled tuna with curried lentil dressing, or roast duck with green peppercorns and cranberries. Pears poached in mulled wine, or bitter marmalade bread-and-butter pudding round things of (in every way). An interesting, modern list includes four good house wines by the glass. Most bottles are well under £20 but there is a short 'connoisseurs' list' for anyone who feels like pushing the boat out. SAMPLE DISHES: pumpkin soup with Amaretto cream and Parmesan straws £4.50; Irish stew with herb dumplings £10.50; warm, creamy rice pudding with apricots and ice cream £4.50.

Licensees Mark and Annie Prescott (freehouse)
Open *11 to 11 (10.30 Sun); bar food and restaurant 12 to 2, 6 to 9*
Details *Children welcome in bar eating area   Car park   Wheelchair access (not WC)   Patio   No smoking in dining room   Background music   No dogs   Delta, MasterCard, Switch, Visa*

WYMONDHAM   Leicestershire   map 5

Berkeley Arms
Main Street, Wymondham LE14 2AG   TEL: (01572) 787587
off B676 between Melton Mowbray and Colsterworth

In a quiet village surrounded by gently rolling countryside, the Berkeley Arms is a building of yellow stone with a pantiled roof and colourful window boxes to the front. It's fairly rustic and well maintained inside, with beamed ceilings garlanded with dried hops, and plain scrubbed tables in the bar, which shares the same menu as the separate, bay-windowed restaurant, where there's a Victorian-style fireplace and decoration provided by dried flowers and a plethora of empty wine bottles. Lunchtimes see a menu of dishes like smoked salmon and prawns in lemon mayonnaise, followed by oak-smoked bacon with bubble and squeak and a poached egg and hollandaise, and burgers or sausages, while a full carte operates in the evening: mussels dressed with lardons in a 'thick, rich and seriously tasty' creamy white wine sauce with herbs, and main courses of pan-fried chicken breast with a leek and onion sauce, or roast cod fillet with mustard sauce. Expect to finish with something rich and filling, like chocolate and banana bread-and-butter pudding with custard, or sticky toffee pudding. Tetley Bitter, Marston's Pedigree, Greene King IPA and a regularly changing guest beer are supported by a short but varied wine list, with all four house wines sold by the glass at £2.35. SAMPLE DISHES: pâté de campagne with apple and sage dressing and blue cheese bavarois £4.75; roast duck breast with honey and cider sauce and deep-fried leeks £11.25; spotted dick with custard £4.

Licensee Denise Hampson (Pubmaster)
Open 12 to 3, 6 (5.30 Fri) to 11, Sat 12 to 11, Sun 12 to 10.30; bar food and restaurant Tue to Sun (exc Sun evening) 12 to 2 (2.30 Sat and Sun), 7 to 9 (9.30 Fri and Sat)
Details Children welcome   Car park   Wheelchair access (also WC)   Garden   No smoking in restaurant   Background music   No dogs   Amex, Delta, Diners, MasterCard, Switch, Visa

WYTHAM   Oxfordshire   map 2

White Hart 😕   NEW ENTRY
Wytham OX2 8QA   TEL: (01865) 244372
Wytham signposted on north-bound carriageway of A34 (ring road) W of Oxford

Opposite the post office in the chocolate-box village, just a stone's throw from the A34, the old stone-built White Hart is a quintessential gastro-pub that for one visitor 'hit the spot for a stylish environment and food'. Inside is bright, open and full of colour, with a modern bar, warm paintwork, flagstone floors, roaring fire and chunky light-wood furniture; and frequented by a relaxed-looking clientele (more jumpers and conversation than suits and business deals). The menu (bolstered by blackboard specials) steps out in tune with the surroundings to deliver a modern British repertoire backed by 'friendly, patient and considerate' service. Typical of starters are seared scallops with red chard and soy and wasabi dressing, and a platter of antipasti, while mains might see braised lamb shank with sage mash, cannellini beans and rosemary jus pitched alongside confit of duck with sesame pak choi and hoisin sauce. Familiar desserts could be headed by bread-and-butter pudding with vanilla ice cream. Hot filled focaccia sandwiches are also available. Hook Norton Best Bitter and Fuller's London Pride provide sustenance for beer drinkers, while a list of 45 wines offers 12 by the glass. SAMPLE DISHES: smoked chicken, bacon and pine-nut salad with honey dressing £5.50; paella with saffron rice £12; chocolate fondant with amaretti £5.

Licensee David Peevers (freehouse)
Open 12 to 11, Sun 12 to 10.30; bar food and restaurant all week 12 to 2.30, Mon to Sat 7 to 10
Details Children welcome Car park Garden No-smoking areas Occasional live or background
music Dogs welcome exc in restaurant Delta, MasterCard, Switch, Visa

YARMOUTH   Isle of Wight   map 2

King's Head

Quay Street, Yarmouth PO41 0PB   TEL: (01983) 760351
opposite harbour

Yarmouth is an attractive old town with a fort, a pier and lots of yachts bobbing about, and the King's Head (that of Charles I, as depicted on the pub sign) is in a narrow street very near the landing stage of the ferry from Lymington. Inside is a series of open rooms and alcoves, with low ceilings, a few dark beams, half-panelled walls and, in the lounge area, a piano, seafaring prints and a large fireplace; towards the rear is a separate room with pine furniture, dark green walls and another fireplace. Baguettes, ploughman's and sandwiches, such as prawns in marie-rose sauce, are a welcome proposition at lunchtimes. Otherwise, the menu might feature guacamole with tortilla chips, followed by old favourites like steak and ale pie, ham, eggs and chips, steaks and burgers, and then chocolate steamed pudding, or vanilla and chocolate ice cream with chocolate sauce and raspberry coulis. Alternatively, go for something from the weekly-changing specials board: to start, perhaps lobster bisque, or crab au gratin, then Cajun tuna steak with salad, honey-glazed breast of duck, or char-grilled veal T-bone with lemon and sage butter. On draught are Bass, Flowers Original, Boddingtons Bitter and Old Speckled Hen, and the short, well-selected wine list runs to around twenty bottles, with four offered by the glass. SAMPLE DISHES: battered Thai-style prawns with sweet chilli sauce £5; char-grilled pork chops with mustard sauce £9; lemon meringue soufflé £3.25.

Licensees Robert and Michelle Jackson (Enterprise Inns)
Open 11 to 11.30, Sun 12 to 10.30; bar food 12 to 2.30, 6 to 9.30; food served all day in
holiday periods
Details Children welcome in bar eating area Garden No smoking in eating area No music
Dogs welcome exc in eating area Amex, Delta, Diners, MasterCard, Switch, Visa

YATTENDON   Berkshire   map 2

▲ Royal Oak ☺

The Square, Yattendon RG18 0UG   TEL: (01635) 201325
off B4009, 5½m W of Pangbourne

Between junctions 12 and 13 the M4 runs through a patch of pretty, well-wooded upland on the north side of the Pang valley. Tucked in here lies Yattendon, and therein the sturdy red-brick Royal Oak under its coat of creeper. This is more gastro-pub than boozer; true, there are Boddingtons Bitter and Wadworth 6X on handpump, but the wine list is more the focus of attention. It's classy, European-biased and just a bit pricier than you might hope, but there are a few budget bottles to start things off and six come by the glass. But the food is the thing, and you can eat it in bar, brasserie or restaurant (it's the same menu in all three). Start with mussels cooked in coconut, lemongrass, lime leaves, coriander and green chilli, or maybe a salad of artichokes and feta with fried cherry tomatoes, chicory and pine nuts. For mains, try Buckum Farm beef, grilled, on wilted greens with seared foie gras, or pan-roasted halibut on celeriac cream with rösti and roast salsify. Note, though, that vegetables cost extra. Puddings (nay, desserts) run the gamut from orange and lemon soufflé with chocolate ice cream to warm toffee pudding with fromage frais and fudge ice cream. SAMPLE DISHES: watercress soup with bacon pancakes and herb Chantilly £4.25; pork fillet with ceps, cannellini beans and mustard velouté £14.50; apricot and almond clafoutis with pistachio ice cream £5.50.

Licensee Corinne MacRae (freehouse)
Open *11 to 11, Sun 11 to 10.30; bar food and restaurant 12 to 2.30, 7 to 10; closed 1 Jan*
Details *Children welcome   Car park   Wheelchair access (not WC)   Garden   No smoking in dining room   Background music   No dogs   Amex, Delta, Diners, MasterCard, Switch, Visa*
Accommodation: 5 rooms, B&B £95 to £130

Scotland

▲ Applecross Inn

Shore Street, Applecross IV54 8LR   TEL: (01520) 744262
WEBSITE: www.applecross.co.uk
off A896, 18m W of Loch Carron

FISH

The awe-inspiring, if not vertigo-inducing, drive over the single-track road of
Bealach na Ba, Britain's highest mountain pass, brings the intrepid to this
modest inn with wonderful views across the Inner Sound to Raasay and Skye.
Even when bad weather obscures the views, the white-painted inn, which
stands hard by the shore, would make the journey worthwhile. To take in the
atmosphere, head for the long, busy bar, where an elongated dining area
stretching along the front of the building has views over the water. Fish and
seafood, much of it landed locally, are the stars on the daily bar menu. Starters
might take in smoked haddock and mussel chowder, squat lobster in sweet
chilli sauce, or a platter of smoked salmon, with main courses of king scallops
with crispy bacon and garlic butter on rice, battered monkfish with chips and
peas, or pan-fried fillet of salmon with pesto. Among meat options might be
spicy duck salad or local haggis flambé in Drambuie, followed by venison
casserole, or beef stroganoff. Finish perhaps with banana split, or sticky toffee
pudding. Bottled versions of the Isle of Skye Brewery's range are available, as
well as McEwan 80/- and Fraoch Heather Ale, a range of over fifty single
malts, and four wines by the glass from a list of around twenty bottles. SAMPLE
DISHES: prawn cocktail £6; haddock in crispy batter with chips, peas and
tartare sauce £7; hot chocolate fudge cake £3.25.

Licensee Judith Fish (freehouse)
Open 11 to 11.30, Sun 12.30 to 11; bar food 12 to 9, restaurant 7 to 9; closed 25 Dec, 1 Jan
Details Children welcome   Car park   Wheelchair access (also WC)   Garden and patio
No-smoking area in bar, no smoking in restaurant   Occasional live music; jukebox   Dogs welcome
exc in restaurant   Delta, MasterCard, Switch, Visa   Accommodation: 7 rooms, B&B £30 to £70

▲ Loch Melfort Hotel   NEW ENTRY

Arduaine PA34 4XG   TEL: (01852) 200233
WEBSITE: www.lochmelfort.co.uk
on A816, 4m SW of Kilmelford

Glorious views over Asknish Bay to the island of Jura are all part of the appeal of this family-run hotel, set in one of the finest locations on Scotland's west coast. The Skerry Bar/Bistro is a sparsely furnished room with nautical charts on the wall and a large window to make the most of those views. As expected from such a setting, the kitchen makes full use of the best of local fresh produce, especially fish and shellfish (but meats and cheeses too). Loch Etive mussels, Ardencaple oysters, lobster and Islay scallops all find their place. The standard menu is bolstered by daily blackboard specials: perhaps langoustines of 'overwhelming quality' with herby garlic butter, twice-baked Cheddar soufflé, or chicken with Cajun cream. The printed menu runs from an array of sandwiches to the likes of grilled Aberdeen Angus sirloin steak. In the restaurant things crank up a culinary gear with more elaborate offerings. Beers on tap include Theakston Best Bitter and McEwan 80/-, bottled Scottish beers Heatherale, Froach and Fyne are also available, while around twenty wines are listed on boards, two come by the glass. If all this is not enough, the National Trust for Scotland's Arduaine Gardens are next door. SAMPLE DISHES: Morecambe Bay potted shrimps with toast £6; cutlets of Speyside lamb grilled with rosemary in a caper wine gravy £8.50; pear and gingerbread upside-down cake £3.50.

Licensee Nigel Schofield (freehouse)
Open *summer 10.30 to 11, winter 11 to 10.30 (11 Fri and Sat); bar food 12 to 2.30, 6 to 9 (8.30 Jan and Feb), restaurant 7 to 9*
Details *Children welcome   Car park   Wheelchair access (not WC)   Garden   No smoking in restaurant   Background music   Dogs welcome   Amex, Delta, MasterCard, Switch, Visa Accommodation: 26 rooms, B&B £49 to £158*

▲ Harbour Inn

The Square, Bowmore, Isle of Islay PA43 7JR   TEL: (01496) 810330
WEBSITE: www.harbour-inn.com

Hard by the quayside, this sturdy white-painted hotel makes a good base for a stay on Islay, with bird- and wildlife-watching, fishing, walking and visiting distilleries just some of the attractions. Locally produced malt whiskies can be sampled in the bar too, where, at lunchtime, light meals are served as well as in the restaurant with its lovely views over Loch Indall. The proprietors are firm supporters of local ingredients in their cooking, with meat and seasonal game from both hereabouts and from neighbouring Jura the centrepieces. Seafood, too, is celebrated, perhaps in the form of scallops baked in garlic butter, salmon and crab fishcakes with tartare sauce, or oysters from Loch Gruinart. For main course, warm smoked beef, from Bruichladdich (just across the loch), is layered with rösti and surrounded by wild mushroom sauce, honey-glazed roast duck breast is accompanied by plum and ginger sauce on rice, and grilled Islay lamb cutlets come with home-cut chips. To finish, expect dark chocolate tart with white chocolate sauce, or a selection of Scottish farmhouse cheeses. No real ales are served, but eight wines are sold by the glass. SAMPLE DISHES: smoked haddock and saffron soup £4; baked maize-fed chicken breast with fruity couscous £6.75; lemon posset £4.25.

Licensee Scott Chance (freehouse)
Open 11am to 1am; bar food and restaurant 12 to 2.30, 6 to 9; occasionally closed Sun evenings winter
Details Children welcome in restaurant   Wheelchair access (also WC)   No smoking in restaurant   No music   Dogs welcome   Amex, Delta, MasterCard, Switch, Visa   Accommodation: 7 rooms, B&B £55 to £105

BRIG O' TURK   Stirling   map 11

Byre Inn
Brig o' Turk FK17 8HT   TEL: (01877) 376292
on A821 between Callander and Aberfoyle

This tiny whitewashed-stone pub, about 100 yards from the main road, is just outside the Trossachs village of Brig o' Turk ('Bridge of the Wild Boar'), with its stream and woodlands. The interior is simple and uncluttered, with beams, stone walls and the occasional piece of stuffed wildlife. In winter a large fire burns, and in summer tables and chairs out at the front are popular with walkers, cyclists and tourists. The lunchtime menu consists of mainly traditional pub fare along the lines of steak and ale pie, or fried haddock with chips, while evenings see the appearance of more ambitious ideas: chicken and mushroom croustade with mushrooms and leeks, or salmon fillet baked with saffron and prawns served with Pernod cream. Common to both sessions are commendably Scottish dishes: Cullen skink, followed by haggis, neeps and tatties, or grilled Trossachs trout with prawns and a lemon and herb butter. Drinking options include Heather Ale and a reasonably priced wine list (with house wines by the glass). SAMPLE DISHES: Rob Roy haggis with oatcakes £3.50; medallions of venison with juniper and crème Cassis £11; cranachan £3.25.

Licensee Anne Park (freehouse)
Open Mon to Thur 11 to 11, Fri and Sat 11 to 12, Sun 12.30 to 11; bar food and restaurant 11 (12.30 Sun) to 2.30, 6 to 8.30
Details Children welcome   Car park   Wheelchair access (also WC)   Garden   No smoking in restaurant   Background music   No dogs   MasterCard, Switch, Visa

CLACHAN-SEIL   Argyll & Bute   map 11

▲ Tigh-an-Truish
Clachan-Seil, Isle of Seil PA34 4QZ   TEL: (01852) 300242
on B844, 12m S of Oban

Hard by the single-span stone 'Atlantic Bridge' that links the island of Seil to the mainland stands this two-storey, whitewashed pub, the 'House of Trousers' (and thereby hangs a tale!). Its two bar areas are comfy – one being a traditional snug which will suit those with children. A full menu is available from April to October (snack lunches only in the winter), and the cooking, too, is neat but not showy and focuses on local ingredients: satisfying dishes in substantial portions. A heartening soup or moules marinière might precede haddock Mornay, or local prawns with brown bread and salad (meat eaters could go for steak and ale pie, or venison in a pepper, cream and Drambuie sauce); chocolate pudding and Mars Bar sauce will fill any remaining space. Regularly changing guest ales might come from Fyne Ales or McEwan (80/-), among others, and a basic wine list includes a red and two whites by the glass. SAMPLE DISHES: locally caught smoked salmon £4.75; seafood paella £6; sticky toffee pudding £2.25.

Licensee Miranda Brunner (freehouse)
Open 11 to 2.30, 5 to 11 (summer 11 to 11.30), Sun 12 to 11; bar food 12 to 2, 6 to 8.30; closed 25 Dec, 1 Jan
Details Children welcome in family room   Car park   Garden and patio   No smoking in family room   Background music   Dogs welcome   No cards   Accommodation: 2 rooms, room only £45

CRINAN   Argyll & Bute   map 11

▲ Crinan Hotel ☺

Crinan PA31 8SR   TEL: (01546) 830261
WEBSITE: www.crinanhotel.com
take B841 off A816 6m NW of Lochgilphead

WATERSIDE

Crinan is a tiny village at the northernmost point of the Crinan Canal, which links Loch Fyne with the Sound of Jura, and from this waterside hotel, with breathtaking views, boats can be seen negotiating the complex lock system. The bar is an elegant, wood-panelled room with pictures of marine wildlife and a pleasantly relaxed atmosphere. The food in here is perfectly simple, and yet a combination of fine raw materials and care in presentation elevates it out of the ordinary. Locally smoked wild salmon to start, and main courses of organic pork chop with garlic-roast potatoes, buttered greens and meat juices, Loch Etive mussels braised with lemon, thyme and garlic, or pork and leek sausages with grain mustard mash and caramelised red onions are what to expect, with desserts of vanilla pannacotta with poached figs, or pineapple bavarois. A list of carefully chosen wines offers only a pair of wines by the glass, but there are a few half-bottles to consider. Only bottled beers are stocked. The hotel has two separate restaurants – the Westward and Lock 16 – each with its own menu. SAMPLE DISHES: warm salad of Ayrshire bacon, goats' cheese and red onion confit £6; west coast salmon and scallop fishcake with seasonal greens, a poached egg and hollandaise £11; passion-fruit parfait with berries £3.50.

Licensee Nicolas Ryan (freehouse)
Open 11 to 11, Sun 11 to 2.30, 6.30 to 11; bar food 12 to 2.30, 6.30 to 8.30; restaurant 7 to 8.30; closed Christmas and New Year
Details Children welcome in eating areas   Car park   Wheelchair access (also WC)   Patio   No smoking while others eat   Occasional live music   Dogs welcome   MasterCard, Switch, Visa   Accommodation: 20 rooms, D,B&B £130 to £284

DRYMEN Stirling   map 11

Clachan Inn

2 Main Street, Drymen G63 0BP   TEL: (01360) 660824
off A811, 20m W of Stirling

At the top of Drymen's green, the Clachan is a traditional Scottish pub offering a genuine welcome to all-comers. The décor may be somewhat dated,
with horse brasses and Highland scenes on the walls and plain wooden tables,
but the atmosphere is warm and welcoming, and the bar can get crowded.
People walking in the Queen Elizabeth Forest Park appreciate the hearty
portions of such dishes as steak pie, Irish stew and lasagne, while the daily
specials board could feature local salmon and venison. Steaks, which have
their own menu, are something of a speciality too: perhaps fillet with haggis
sauce. Belhaven St Andrew's Ale is among the ales dispensed, and three wines
are available by the glass. SAMPLE DISHES: deep-fried Camembert £4.25; warm
Cajun chicken salad £7.25; hot chocolate fudge cake £3.25.

Licensee Elizabeth Plank (freehouse)
Open 11 to 12, Sun 12.30 to 12; bar food and restaurant 12 to 4, 6 to 10; closed 25 Dec and 1 Jan
Details Children welcome   Wheelchair access (also WC)   Background music   Dogs welcome on a
lead in bar   MasterCard, Switch, Visa

DYSART Fife   map 11

Old Rectory Inn

West Quality Street, Dysart KY1 2TE   TEL: (01592) 651211
off A955 Methil road, N of Kirkcaldy

In a picturesque seaside village just outside Kirkcaldy, a short walk from the
harbour, the Old Rectory was built in 1771 by a merchant. Inside is a bar
dispensing Calders Cream Ale on draught, and there's a good selection of malt
whiskies, but the main attraction here is the restaurant to the rear of the building, although the same menu is served in the bar. A large Yorkshire pudding
filled with chilli con carne, or venison and mushroom casserole might be
lunchtime options, while the long supper menu might start with onion soup
with Parmesan under a pastry lid, or Stilton mousse, and go on to fish stew,
chicken curry, steaks and a decent choice for vegetarians. The monthly-
changing list of chef's recommendations adds to the repertory the likes of
haggis with Drambuie, followed by tiger prawns Madras, or tournedos
Rossini, while the ambitious carte might start with an omelette with lambs'
kidneys and mushrooms braised in Madeira and finish with bread-and-butter
pudding, with a main course of baked fillet of halibut with sweet-and-sour
sauce and stir-fried vegetables. Around half a dozen wines come by the glass.
SAMPLE DISHES: Portuguese fish soup £2.50; roast leg of lamb with mint sauce
£6.50; strawberry melba £2.50.

Licensees Mr and Mrs D. North (freehouse)
Open Tue to Sun 12 to 3, Tue to Sat 7 to 12; bar food and restaurant Tue to Sat 12 to 2, Sun
12.30 to 2.30, Tue to Sat 7 to 9.45; closed 1 week early Jan, 1 week early July, 2 weeks mid-Oct
Details Children welcome in eating areas   Car park   Wheelchair access (not WC)   Garden
No music   Guide dogs only   Amex, Delta, MasterCard, Switch, Visa

EDINBURGH   Edinburgh   map 11

Baillie 🍺   NEW ENTRY

2 St Stephen Street, Edinburgh EH3 5AL   TEL: (0131) 225 4673

A low-ceilinged basement bar with an open fire, a rather smoky atmosphere and small tables, the Baillie has a traditional, friendly local vibe. Lunch draws the crowds (no dinner is served, although breakfast is) with a reasonably priced daily-changing repertoire backed up by a regular menu of more traditional pub fare, ranging from a steak or BLT sandwich to haddock and chips, or ribeye steak with peppercorn and cream sauce. The relatively substantial daily menu has a more modish note, featuring the likes of chicken breast seared in Cajun spices accompanied by a soured cream dip, salad and fries, or meatballs in spicy tomato sauce with pasta. Interesting vegetarian options get a similar treatment: perhaps spicy enchiladas with roasted peppers and onions grilled with mozzarella and topped with soured cream, guacamole and salsa. Sticky toffee pudding is typical of desserts. A range of real ales – Timothy Taylor Landlord, Flowers IPA, McEwan 80/- and Courage Directors, to name a few – and around half a dozen wines by both glass and bottle complete the picture. SAMPLE DISHES: mussels steamed with cream, garlic and white wine £4; shredded chicken wok-fried with vegetables in garlic, coriander and lemon sauce served with noodles £5.75; strawberry tart with ice cream and chocolate sauce £2.

Licensee Vanessa Torquemada (freehouse)
Open 9.30 to 12 (1am Fri and Sat), Sun 12.30 to 12; bar food 11.30 to 5
Details Children welcome before 5pm   Occasional live music   Dogs welcome exc in eating areas
Delta, MasterCard, Switch, Visa

Café Royal 🍺   NEW ENTRY

19 West Register Street, Edinburgh EH2 2AA   TEL: (0131) 556 1884

This is a classic Victorian city-centre pub, just north of Princes Street, with a built-in wow factor. The Circle Bar makes a bold statement with its splendid island counter and flamboyant fixtures and fittings, including an ornate ceiling, intriguing Doulton tiled panels featuring renowned inventors, a fine fireplace and etched glass. There are marble floors, a revolving door and elaborate screens to divide off the similarly ornate Oyster Bar restaurant. After you've feasted your eyes on the architectural extravagances, you might wish to check out a range of ales that includes Caledonian Deuchars IPA, McEwan 80/- and Courage Directors, plus a guest beer or two. There are also ten wines by the glass to choose from and a bar menu to deliberate over. The speciality here is seafood, in particular oysters and mussels. These come in a variety of guises, including oysters Rockefeller (with spinach and hollandaise) and Kilpatrick (with bacon), and mussels with red onions, coriander and chilli, or there's crab and coriander fishcake if you prefer. Apart from the seafood, it's pretty much standard pub fare, from sandwiches to the likes of braised lamb shank, and Cajun chicken breast. Desserts roll out the glazed lemon tart and chocolate fudge cake variety. SAMPLE DISHES: seafood chowder £4; steak and mushroom pie £6.25; sticky toffee pudding £3.

Licensee David Allen (Scottish & Newcastle)
Open Mon to Wed 11 to 11, Thur 11 to 12, Fri and Sat 11 to 1, Sun 12.30 to 11;
bar food Mon to Sat 11 to 10, Sun 12.30 to 10, restaurant 12 to 2 (2.30 Sun), 7 to 10
Details Children welcome in restaurant   Wheelchair access (not WC)   No-smoking area in restaurant   Background music   No dogs   Amex, Delta, Diners, MasterCard, Switch, Visa

Ship on The Shore   NEW ENTRY
24–26 The Shore, Leith, Edinburgh EH6 6QN   TEL: (0131) 555 0409

Located on the popular remodelled shore area of Leith, the aptly named Ship charts a dining-pub course but manages the balancing act between restaurant and bar well. Though displaying the appearance of a traditional bar, with wooden tables, chairs and floors, nautical paraphernalia, 'wee windows' and an island bar, effectively half the space is turned over to dining. Candlelit tables, 'affable staff' and a menu that tacks away from the more cliché pub food draws the crowds. The repertoire – strong on fish – befits the location, ebbing between the likes of seafood chowder, moules marinière and prawn cocktail to avocado and feta salad to start. Mains could feature sea bass done Chinese-style with ginger, or whole sole simply cooked with a lemon butter sauce. Steaks with hollandaise, or perhaps rich pheasant stew, provide sustenance for meat eaters. A decent range of beers includes Deuchars IPA, McEwan 70/- and Caledonian 80/-, and four wines are served by the glass. SAMPLE DISHES: Scottish oysters in lemon and Tabasco sauce £6.95; red mullet tempura with sweet chilli dip £14.95; sticky toffee pudding £4.50.

Licensee Roy West (freehouse)
Open 11 to 11; bar food 12 to 2.30, 6.30 to 9.30, Sun 11 to 2.30
Details No children under 5   Wheelchair access   Background music   No dogs   Delta, MasterCard, Switch, Visa

ELGIN   Moray   map 11

Swish   NEW ENTRY
8–10 Batchon Street, Elgin IV30 1BH   TEL: (01343) 550150

Swish lives up to its name with modern good looks – 'lots of wood, split-level dining and drinking areas' – that offer quite a contrast to Elgin's more traditional boozers. The wide-ranging menu steps out with reasonably familiar offerings: perhaps fillet of smoked haddock with creamed leeks and cherry tomatoes baked in a Cheddar and grain mustard sauce, or beef stroganoff with basmati rice, while fillet, sirloin or rump steaks, with the obligatory onion rings, mushrooms, tomatoes, fries and salad, bolster the repertoire alongside salads of chargrilled chicken Caesar or duck and orange. To start there might be Cullen skink, or chicken liver pâté with Cumberland sauce and oatcakes. John Smith's Bitter and a list of 14 wines, all available by the glass, provide the liquid accompaniments. SAMPLE DISHES: monkfish saladette £3.25; Barnsley lamb chops with thyme mash and rosemary and red wine jus £8; sticky toffee pudding £3.

Licensee Grant Macdonald (freehouse)
Open *Mon and Tue 11 to 5, Wed 11 to 11, Thur 11 to 12.30, Fri and Sat 11 to 12.30;*
bar food Mon and Tue 12 to 3, Wed to Fri 12 to 3, 6 to 9, Sat 12 to 5, 6 to 9
Details *Children welcome   Wheelchair access (also WC)   No-smoking areas   Occasional live or*
background music   No dogs   Amex, Delta, Diners, MasterCard, Switch, Visa

ELIE   Fife   map 11

▲ Ship Inn

The Toft, Elie KY9 1DT   TEL: (01333) 330246

WEBSITE: www.ship-elie.com

on A917, 5m SW of Anstruther

WATERSIDE

The Ship sits on a terrace overlooking the old harbour and is fronted by a beach where its cricket team plays (spectators line the sea wall, and home matches are sponsored by a range of drinks-trade institutions). Winter's open fires give way in summer (weather permitting) to an outdoor barbecue on Sundays, and all week meals in the beer garden supplement those in the year-round indoor restaurant (the same menu applies to both) The interior is simply decorated and furnished, and can be crowded. A shortish menu offers the expected (steak and Guinness pie, bangers and mash), the Caledonian (haggis, finnan haddock) and the outré (king prawn chingri malai, or chicken fillet stuffed with black pudding in a Stilton and apple sauce), plus dishes for vegetarians and children. Fish is well represented: mussels and monkfish, crab and lobster, haddock and chips. Desserts, such as sticky toffee pudding, are on a blackboard. Real ales come from Belhaven and Caledonian (Deuchars IPA and 80/-), and a short wine list stays the right side of £20 and includes two reds and six whites by the glass. SAMPLE DISHES: haggis, neeps and tatties £3.75; monkfish tails with tagliatelle verde £12; lemon pavlova £3.50.

Licensees Richard and Jill Philip (freehouse)
Open *11am to midnight (1am Fri and Sat), Sun 12.30 to midnight; bar food 12 to 2 (12 to 2.30*
summer; 12.30 to 3 Sun), 6 to 9 (9.30 Fri and Sat); closed 25 Dec
Details *Children welcome in family room and eating areas   Wheelchair access (also WC)   Garden*
Occasional live music   Dogs welcome   MasterCard, Switch, Visa   Accommodation: 6 rooms,
B&B £25 to £50

GLASGOW   Glasgow   map 11

Babbity Bowster   `NEW ENTRY`

16–18 Blackfriars Street, Glasgow G1 1PE   TEL: (0141) 552 5055

Built by Robert Adam in the old Merchant City, Babbity Bowster – named after an old Scottish song – has been discreetly restored and offers an authentic Glasgow welcome to locals and tourists alike. Downstairs, the open bar has old-fashioned wooden seats and oilcloth-covered tables, an open fire and newspapers to peruse, while walls are hung with black and white photographs. There's a cosmopolitan, 'non-chichi atmosphere'. A menu of unpretentious, good-value food, bolstered by blackboard specials, runs the gamut of simple panini through authentic Scottish fare (Cullen skink, and haggis, neeps and tatties – there's also a vegetarian version), seafood (mussels in white wine, or

Loch Fyne smoked salmon and oysters) and a brace of French dishes (perhaps duck leg confit, or Toulouse sausage with haricot beans). An upstairs restaurant serves more ambitious meals, while the garden is popular on fine days. Houston Peter's Well and guests like Durham Magus are on handpump, and a dozen wines are sold by the glass. SAMPLE DISHES: soup of the day £2.50; lamb shank £5.50 to £7.50; strawberry cheesecake £2.95.

Licensee John Fraser Laurie (freehouse)
Open 11 to 12, Sun 12.30 to 12; bar food 12 to 10, restaurant Tue to Sat 6.30 to 9.30
Details Children welcome   Car park   Wheelchair access (not WC)   Garden   Occasional live music   Dogs welcome   Amex, Delta, Diners, MasterCard, Switch, Visa

Brel   NEW ENTRY

37–43 Ashton Lane, Glasgow G12 8SJ   TEL: (0141) 342 4966
WEBSITE: www.brelbarrestaurant.com

A 'basic, good-value' kind of place, Brel is close to the university and proves a magnet for lovers of 'Belgian beer, good mussels, merguez and good chips at bargain prices'. A former stable in a mews area flush with pub/restaurants, Brel has been described as 'amusingly basic', with its tiled floors and tables covered in brown-paper sheets and candles. There's a large bar and two dining areas, one a popular conservatory opening on to a grassy bank for sunny days. Frequented mainly by students and the arty, there's a buzzy atmosphere often cranked up by live music. Decent, plain cooking is the style, with simple, freshly cooked dishes that fit the ambience: perhaps robust vegetable soup served with generous amounts of fresh bread, followed by spinach and mushroom omelette with chips, or sausage with spinach mash. The single dish of the day could be salmon with frites and salad, while there's a red and a white house wine by the glass as well as a variety of Belgian beers on draught, De Koninck, Leffe Blanch and Brune, to imbibe, and bottled ones. The pub is named after Belgian poet and songwriter Jacques Brel. SAMPLE DISHES: soup of the day £2; mussels with lemon and spring onion £9.50; Belgian chocolate mousse £3.50.

Licensee Laurie Keith (BB Grand)
Open 10 to 12; bar food 12 to 3, restaurant Mon to Thur 5 to 10, Fri and Sat 5 to 11,
Sun 12 to 11
Details Children welcome in terrace conservatory   Wheelchair access   Garden   Live or background music   Dogs welcome in terrace conservatory   Amex, Delta, Diners, MasterCard, Switch, Visa

Corinthian   NEW ENTRY

191 Ingram Street, Glasgow G1 1DA   TEL: (0141) 552 1101
WEBSITE: www.corinthian.uk.com

Formerly a bank and now a listed building, this 'stunning' city-centre venue is the sort of place that is 'favoured by the chic' and has door staff to greet evening visitors. Inside, the erstwhile banking hall is decked out with baroque Roman motifs – a pleasing change from the contemporary trend towards minimalism, thought one visitor. Bar menus bear little relation to traditional ideas of pub grub. Boudin of chicken and wild mushroom with chilli and lemon is typical among starters, and main-course choices might include lamb cutlet, noisettes and navarin with sautéed onions, purée potatoes and red wine reduction, or baked pavé of salmon with noodles and salmon tartare. Lunchtime options include good-value soup-and-sandwich deals: perhaps carrot, tomato and coriander soup with a crisp half-baguette filled with tuna and mayonnaise. Desserts are original creations like Baileys soufflé pancakes with double chocolate ice cream. Caledonian 80/- is the one real ale offered, and there is a competitively priced wine list, with house Spanish red and white at £10.95 a bottle, £2.75/£3.75 a glass. SAMPLE DISHES: Oban mussel casserole £5.50; breast of Gressingham duck and confit leg with twice-baked potato soufflé, roast parsnips and basil jus £14; iced piña colada parfait with passion-fruit coulis £4.50.

Licensee Colin Drummond (GI Group)
Open *11am to 3am, Sun 12 to 3am; bar food and restaurant Mon to Thur 12 to 9, Fri and Sat 12 to 6, Sun 12 to 9*
Details *Children welcome before 8pm   Wheelchair access (also WC)   Live music   Guide dogs only   Amex, Delta, MasterCard, Switch, Visa*

▲ Rab Ha's   NEW ENTRY

83 Hutcheson Street, Glasgow GI ISH   TEL: (0141) 572 0400

A one-time warehouse, Rab Ha's is a refreshingly traditional pub in the Merchant City, with a friendly atmosphere and full of Glaswegians enjoying hearty food, lively chatter and the bustling atmosphere. It's furnished with unpretentious wooden tables and capacious old chairs, with an old-fashioned bar and a cheery gas fire around which to peruse the pub's newspapers. Rab Ha, the famed 'Glesca Glutton', gives his name to the place, and he would have no doubt approved of the keenly priced and hearty pub fare on offer: leek soup, 'rich' beef and Guinness pie with mash, and 'huge' battered cod with chips 'as thick as your thumb'. More modern tastes could be drawn to Thai red chicken curry with sticky coconut rice, or pasta with salmon and mush-rooms. Simple puddings are along the lines of white chocolate cheesecake or ice cream. More ambitious dishes are available at the separate restaurant: roast monkfish and mussel bouillabaisse, or roast roe deer with honey-roasted parsnips and shallots, mashed potato and a port jus, for example. Beers include draught Budvar and Belhaven, and four wines are served by the glass. SAMPLE DISHES: haggis, neeps and tatties £6; organic beefburger £6; cheese and biscuits £2.95.

Licensee Kerry Tolwart (freehouse)
Open *11 to 12, Sun 12 to 12; bar food 12 to 10, restaurant 5.50 to 10*
Details *Children welcome   Wheelchair access (not WC)   Background music   Dogs welcome exc in restaurant   Amex, Delta, Diners, MasterCard, Switch, Visa   Accommodation: 4 rooms, B&B £50 per room*

Prices of dishes quoted in an entry are based on information supplied by the pub, rounded up to the nearest 25 pence. These prices may have changed since publication and are meant only as a guide.

Ubiquitous Chip ♥ ❧ [NEW ENTRY]

12 Ashton Lane, Glasgow G12 8SJ   TEL: (0141) 334 5007
WEBSITE: www.ubiquitouschip.co.uk

This Glasgow institution, opened by Ronnie Clydesdale in 1971 to champion
Scottish produce and recipes, still packs in the crowds of devotees to its
cobbled mews location in the heart of the West End. There's now a new 'ultra-
popular' Wee Chip, a compact pub where you can quaff a splendid array of
drinks (but no food), and an informal brasserie/bar-style operation. This long
room, laid out with wooden tables, has an original pubby area with small bar,
fire and buzzy bohemian atmosphere. From here one can look down on the
famous Mediterranean-style courtyard overhung with trailing plants and its
more formal downstairs restaurant, which offers more elaborate cuisine. The
menu continues to pay homage to the bountiful Scottish larder with staples
such as vegetarian haggis with neeps 'n' tatties, Ayrshire collar of bacon, basil
mash and Malmsey sauce, or Peeblesshire pheasant, root vegetable and rowan
jelly casserole with boiled potatoes and greens. Upstairs offers an individual
selection of 18 wines by the glass from £2.50, with all but one under £15 a
bottle – and the huge range of bottles on the savvy restaurant list is also available. For beer drinkers there's Caledonian 80/- and Deuchars IPA. SAMPLE
DISHES: Loch Etive mussels marinière £5.75; pan-fried Scotch lamb's liver
with Ayrshire bacon, mashed potatoes and onions in Caledonian 80/- beer
batter £7.25; bread pudding with Muscat and double cream £4.25.

Licensee Ronald Clydesdale (freehouse)
Open 11 to 12, Sun 12 to 11; bar food and restaurant 12 to 11; closed 25 Dec and 1 Jan
Details Children welcome   No music   Dogs welcome   Amex, Delta, Diners, MasterCard, Switch,
Visa

GLENDEVON   Perthshire & Kinross   map 11

▲ Tormaukin Hotel

Glendevon FK14 7JY   TEL: (01259) 781252
WEBSITE: www.tormaukin.co.uk
on A823, 6m SE of Auchterarder

Although seemingly in the middle of nowhere, encircled by the Ochil Hills,
the Tormaukin is clearly a favoured destination, judging by the number of
people who come here. Originating in the eighteenth century as a drovers'
inn, the building has been sympathetically renovated, and much has been
made inside of its stone walls and timbers, with blazing fires warming the
comfortably furnished rooms. The broad-ranging bar menu holds plenty of
interest: prawn cocktail may be found alongside Thai-marinated chicken with
mango and honey dressing among starters, with main courses running from
deep-fried battered haddock fillet with chips and tartare sauce to braised lamb
shank on colcannon, or collops of haunch of venison with a ragoût of tomatoes, bacon, peppers and onions. The alternative eating option is the relaxed
restaurant, which has its own menu of such dishes as Cullen skink, or
Inverawe smoked beef with potato salad in horseradish mayonnaise, followed
by roast saddle of hare with caramelised shallots, or a duo of salmon and

halibut with tomato tagliatelle. Real ales include Timothy Taylor Landlord and a selection from the Harviestoun Brewery in nearby Dollar. A good wine list, strong in France and the New World, has the bonus of a dozen half-bottles. Around eight wines are served by the glass. SAMPLE DISHES: peppered mackerel pâté with beetroot salsa £4.50; oriental-style pork stir-fried with ginger, spring onions and bamboo shoots served with spicy noodles £9.50; rhubarb and ginger crumble with custard £4.50.

Licensee Isodora Simpson (freehouse)
Open 11 to 11; bar food and restaurant Mon to Sat 12 to 2.30, 5.30 to 9.30, Sun 12 to 9.30; closed 1 week Jan
Details Children welcome   Car park   Wheelchair access (also WC)   Patio   No-smoking area   Live or background music   Dogs welcome   Amex, Delta, MasterCard, Switch, Visa   Accommodation: 14 rooms, B&B £53 to £90

INNERLEITHEN   Borders   map 11

▲ Traquair Arms 🍺
Traquair Road, Innerleithen EH44 6PD   TEL: (01896) 830229
off A72, 6m SE of Peebles

This imposing Victorian stone building is set by itself in the picturesque village not far from the main street on the road out to Traquair House, one of the oldest inhabited houses in Scotland. The same menu is offered in both the comfortable restaurant and the bar, with its log fire, medallion-patterned wallpaper and curtains and wooden-topped tables. The menu, an enterprising slate of dishes, is extended by a few daily specials, so the range could run from steak pie through 'excellent' finnan savoury to mussels stewed with chorizo and potatoes or 'delicious' curried spinach, lentil and feta pie. Start with something like deep-fried Brie with cherry sauce, and finish with blueberry syllabub or Rob Roy (vanilla and butterscotch sundae). On handpump are Bear Ale and sometimes others from the eighteenth-century brewery in Traquair House, as well as brews such as the Ghillie and Winter Fire from the local Broughton Ales brewery, plus Calder's 70/- and Cream. House wines are sold in two sizes of glass and by the carafe and half-carafe. SAMPLE DISHES: deep-fried king prawns with barbecue sauce £3.50; pan-fried chicken breast stuffed with haggis with creamy apple sauce £6.25; rhubarb and orange crumble £2.50.

Licensee Dianne Johnson (freehouse)
Open 11 to midnight; bar food and restaurant 12 to 9
Details Children welcome   Car park   Wheelchair access (not WC)   Garden   No smoking in restaurant   Background music   Dogs welcome   Amex, Delta, MasterCard, Switch, Visa   Accommodation: 15 rooms, B&B £35 to £90

🍷 indicates a pub serving better-than-average wine, including good choice by bottle and glass.

▲ Killiecrankie Hotel 🍇 | NEW ENTRY |

Killiecrankie PH16 5LG   TEL: (01796) 473220
WEBSITE: www.killiecrankiehotel.co.uk
off A9, then B8079, 4m N of Pitlochry

Dating from 1840 and originally a dower house, this large, white-painted hotel is set in a beautiful valley, surrounded by trees, with lawns at the front and side and formal gardens behind. Inside, the mahogany-panelled bar and adjoining conservatory offer the traditional range of refreshments, including a good selection of malt whiskies, as well as light lunches and suppers. Typical starters of sweet-cured Orkney herrings, or Stilton and walnut pâté on oatcakes with pear chutney are followed by hot and cold main courses that could include grilled mackerel fillets with sweet pepper, chilli and garlic sauce, or a pan-fried venison steak with onion gravy, vegetables and chips, or chargrilled Thai chicken with lemongrass and ginger. There are upmarket ice creams or apple and cinnamon crumble for dessert. In the evenings the elegant dining room's fairly upmarket prix fixe offers alternatives like smoked salmon and leek strudel, and roast duck breast in date and port sauce. The wine list offers an extensive range of bins from excellent producers around the world, with eight by the glass. There's plenty to choose from under £20 but this is a place where you can also splash out with confidence. SAMPLE DISHES: locally smoked venison, lamb and beef with juniper chutney and salad £6; chargrilled lamb gigot steak marinated in mint and lemon with garlic and peppercorn butter £9; chocolate chip pudding with chocolate sauce and vanilla ice cream £3.95.

Licensee Maillie Waters (freehouse)
Open *Mon to Sat 12.30 to 11, Sun 12.30 to 2.30, 6.30 to 11; bar food 12.30 to 2, 6.30 to 8 (9.30 summer), restaurant 7 to 8.30; closed 3 Jan to 13 Feb*
Details *Children welcome in bar eating area   Car park   Wheelchair access (not WC)   Garden No-smoking area in bar, no smoking in dining room   Background music   No dogs exc in garden Delta, MasterCard, Switch, Visa   Accommodation: 10 rooms, D,B&B £79 to £198*

▲ Cuilfail Hotel

Kilmelford PA34 4XA   TEL: (01852) 200274
WEBSITE: www.cuilfail.co.uk
on A816 at head of Loch Melfort, 12m S of Oban

A creeper-covered stone building, the Cuilfail (Gaelic for 'sheltered corner') is an old drovers' inn in a tiny hamlet at the foot of the Argyll hills, close to the shore of Loch Melfort. Most of the present structure dates from Victorian times, although the building has much older origins. Prime Highland produce is put to good use in the kitchen, and the centrepiece of the Tartan Puffer restaurant is the indoor barbecue, which is used to cook beef, lamb, pork and venison, as well as local fish and seafood. Otherwise, go for something like poached sea bass, preceded by perhaps mussel and bacon kebab in a balsamic dressing, or smoked salmon in a salmon patty parcel, and followed by wild berry pavlova, or chocolate terrine. The same menu is available for those eating in the cheerful bar, where there's an open fire. Beers are an uninspiring selection, although some bottled beers are produced on the bank of Loch Fyne, and wine drinkers have three by the glass to choose from. SAMPLE DISHES: Highland cheese parcel in filo pastry £5; venison marinated in white wine and juniper berries £10; sticky toffee pudding £4.

Licensee David Birrell (freehouse)
Open 11 to 12; bar food 12 to 2.30, 6 to 10, restaurant 6 to 10
Details Children welcome   Car park   Wheelchair access (also WC)   Patio   Occasional live music
Dogs welcome exc in restaurant   Delta, Diners, MasterCard, Switch, Visa   Accommodation: 12 rooms,
B&B £30 to £77

KIPPEN   Stirling   map 11

▲ Cross Keys
Main Street, Kippen FK8 3DN   TEL: (01786) 870293
on B822, 10m W of Stirling

On the main village street, this old inn has a public bar, a family room and a low-ceilinged, beamed restaurant area, all plainly decorated but comfortable, with plain wooden tables and Windsor chairs and a picture of old Kippen on a wall. The same daily-changing menu applies throughout the pub, listing the likes of duck liver pâté, a soup such as spinach and leek, and a parcel of smoked salmon with prawns to start. These may be followed by chicken breast with sweet peppers and white wine, smoked haddock omelette, Stilton and broccoli quiche, or lasagne, all accompanied by fresh vegetables. Sandwiches are available all day. Desserts run from profiteroles or apple crumble to a selection of ice cream or cheese. Belhaven St Andrew's Ale and the ominously named Brooker's Bitter & Twisted from the Harviestoun Brewery are the real ales on offer. Three wines from a list of around twenty-five come by the glass. There's a garden with tables to the rear. SAMPLE DISHES: Arbroath smokie pâté £4; Aberdeen Angus sirloin steak glazed with Stilton and cider £13.75; baked apples with apricots and walnuts £3.75.

Licensee Gordon Scott (freehouse)
Open Mon to Fri 12 to 2.30, 5.30 to 11, Sat and Sun 12 to 12; bar food Mon to Sat 12 to 2,
5.30 to 9, Sun 12 to 9; closed 25 Dec, 1 Jan
Details Children welcome   Car park   Wheelchair access (also WC)   Garden   No smoking in
eating area   Occasional background music   Dogs welcome in bar   MasterCard, Switch, Visa
Accommodation: 2 rooms, B&B £30 to £60

MELROSE   Borders   map 11

▲ Burt's Hotel 🍇
Market Square, Melrose TD6 9PL   TEL: (01896) 822285
WEBSITE: www.burtshotel.co.uk
on A6091, midway between Galashiels and St Boswells

Burt's is a smart white-painted building, dating from the early eighteenth century, on Melrose's attractive marketplace. In summer, when hanging baskets and window boxes add splashes of colour to the front, the garden is a relaxing spot. This is a friendly hotel with a formal restaurant and popular lounge bar with an open fire and traditional décor. The bar menu has a Scottish feel but also shows wider influences, so carpaccio of ostrich with beetroot chutney might appear alongside other starters of 'excellent' parfait of local venison flavoured with orange, cognac and green peppercorns. Main courses are no less imaginative, taking in goujons of chicken coated in coconut served with a Cajun dip, fishcakes (of cod, smoked salmon and prawns) on straw vegetables with herb cream – 'a wonderful combination of flavours and textures,' noted a reporter – or, more traditionally, deep-fried breaded haddock fillet with tartare sauce. Appealing options on the restaurant menu might include prawn mousse in a parcel of smoked salmon, followed by breast of Barbary duck dusted with five-spice. Drinks-wise, this is whisky heaven, with no fewer than 80 single malts on offer. Alternatively, Caledonian 80/- and Deuchars IPA, Fuller's London Pride and Tetley Bitter are served. A tempting selection of house wines starts at £11.95 and is also available by the glass. The main list of about 100 wines concentrates on France and the New World and offers plenty of tasty options under £15 before setting off into more serious territory. Old Vines Chenin Blanc from South Africa at £14.95 is great value. For connoisseurs there is a fine wine list, crowned by the magnificent 1986 Château Cos d'Estournel (£150, if you were wondering). Melrose, on the Tweed and nestling under the Eildon Hills, contains the ruins of the abbey founded by King David I in 1136. SAMPLE DISHES: glazed casserole of smoked salmon, avocado, tomato and orange bound with tarragon cream £4.50; char-grilled medallion of pork on a ragoût of butternut and shallot with green peppercorn sauce £8.25; pear and almond tart with butterscotch sauce and caramel ice cream £4.25.

Licensee Graham Henderson (freehouse)
Open 11 to 2.30, 5 to 11, Sun 12 to 2.30, 6 to 11; bar food and restaurant 12 to 2, 6 to 9.30 (10 Fri and Sat); closed 24 to 26 Dec
Details Children welcome in eating areas   Car park   Wheelchair access (also WC)   Garden and patio   No-smoking area in bar, no smoking in restaurant   No music   Dogs welcome in bar   Amex, Delta, MasterCard, Switch, Visa   Accommodation: 20 rooms, B&B £52 to £98

NETHERLEY   Aberdeenshire   map 11

Lairhillock Inn
Netherley AB39 3QS   TEL: (01569) 730001
on B979, 4m S of Peterculter

Built over 200 years ago on an old drovers' road between Stonehaven and Aberdeen, the Lairhillock is surrounded by nothing but countryside for miles. The centrepiece of the bar and lounge is a charming log fire, and a conservatory with fine views is popular with families. Beer drinkers will appreciate a range that includes Timothy Taylor Landlord, Courage Directors and ales from the Isle of Skye Brewing Company, plus guests. Sixty-five malt whiskies are also available. The bar menu offers an extensive and varied range, from Highland lasagne (venison and pork), or chicken breast stuffed with haggis topped with whisky sauce, to finnan haddock and leek fishcakes, or Aberdeen Angus steaks. The separate menu in the Crynoch Restaurant is based on local produce and combines a classical cooking style with modern ideas, typically offering a salad of locally smoked salmon with crab, spring onions and avocado, followed by grilled fillet of salmon in a Parmesan and black pepper crust with balsamic dressing, or medallions of venison with polenta, wild mushrooms and bacon and port gravy. The lengthy restaurant wine list is a serious tome; a shorter version is offered in the bar, and both house and guest wines are served by the glass. SAMPLE DISHES: broccoli and Stilton soup £2.75; grilled venison and wood pigeon with wild mushroom and red wine sauces £9.25; sticky toffee pudding £3.25.

Licensee Roger Thorne (freehouse)
Open *Mon to Fri 11.30 to 2.30, 5 to 11 (12 Fri), Sat 11 to 12, Sun 11.30 to 11; bar food 12 to 2, 6 to 9.30 (10 Fri and Sat), restaurant Sun 12 to 1.30, Wed to Mon 7 to 9.15; closed 25 and 26 Dec, 1 and 2 Jan*
Details *Children welcome in bar eating area and conservatory   Car park   Wheelchair access (also WC)   Garden   No smoking in restaurant   Background music   Dogs welcome in public bar   Amex, Delta, Diners, MasterCard, Switch, Visa*

PLOCKTON   Highland   map 11

▲ Plockton Inn

Innes Street, Plockton IV52 8TW   TEL: (01599) 544222
WEBSITE: www.plocktoninn.co.uk
off A87, 5m NE of Kyle of Lochalsh

FISH

Select one of the fifty or so malt whiskies and relax in front of a log fire at this pub in a seaside village just a few miles from the main road to Skye, or sample a pint of one of the real ales: Fuller's London Pride, Peter's Well from the Houston Brewing Company, Old Speckled Hen, or Greene King Abbot Ale. The menu pays tribute to the proximity of the sea with generous netfuls of fish and seafood in the restaurant and the bar. Oysters, Plockton prawns, 'very good' gravad lax served simply with some dill and mayonnaise, and Loch Leven mussels steamed in white wine are all among starters, while main courses take in 'lovely' whole grilled Dover sole, fillet of salmon with orange vinaigrette, and Loch Carron scallops with bacon, garlic and cream. Meat eaters are not neglected, with Moroccan lamb casserole, haunch of venison with a red wine and rowanberry sauce, and haggis, neeps and tatties to choose from. The pub has its own fish smokery to the rear of the building, and Scottish cheeses from a local merchant are something of a speciality. The wine list is a compilation of twenty-plus bottles from around the world, with three house wines sold by the glass at £1.95. SAMPLE DISHES: smoked seafood platter £6.25; chicken breast wrapped in sage and bacon stuffed with cream cheese and baked with tomatoes £8.50; chocolate and lime cheesecake £3.50.

Licensee Kenneth J. Gollan (freehouse)
Open *Mon to Fri 11am to 1am, Sat 11am to 12.30am, Sun 11am to 11pm; bar food and restaurant 12 to 2.30, 6 to 9.30*
Details *Children welcome   Car park   Wheelchair access (also WC)   Garden and patio No smoking in restaurant   Live or background music   Dogs welcome   Delta, MasterCard, Switch, Visa   Accommodation: 7 rooms, B&B £37 to £64*

A list of the top-rated pubs for food is at the front of the book.

STRACHUR   **Argyll & Bute**   **map 11**

▲ Creggans Inn 🍇

Strachur PA27 8BX   TEL: (01369) 860279
WEBSITE: www.creggans-inn.co.uk
on A185, to N of village

WATERSIDE

On a clear day you can see for miles across the waters of Loch Fyne from this waterside inn; otherwise sit under the glass roof in the bar and admire the sky. Fish is a good bet, and you can get anything from mussels and locally sourced oysters to Tarbert cod in a 'brilliant light real ale batter'. Meat eaters are not neglected either: steak pie laced with Maverick Ale has been much appreciated; sandwiches are also on offer, as well as a few desserts such as chocolate parfait. In the evening there's a daily-changing, fixed-price restaurant menu taking in, say, smoked salmon and Shetland crab salad with mustard dressing, or breast of chicken studded with thyme served with a tomato and tarragon reduction and Puy lentils, followed by orange pannacotta. Apart from Maverick, you can also sample other Fyne ales, such as Highlander and Piper's Gold. The pub boasts a well-assembled wine list: the full slate runs to around 100 bins majoring on France and the rest of Europe, with a quick round-up from the rest of the world. Six good house wines start at £2.60 a glass or £10.70 a bottle and there is a fair selection under £15 further up the ladder. Some rather good aperitif sherry is hidden away between the dessert wines and the port at the end of the list. SAMPLE DISHES: timbale of haggis, neeps and tatties with whisky chasseur sauce £5; roast fillet of salmon with aïoli and roasted vegetables £7; sticky toffee pudding £3.50.

Licensee Alex Robertson (freehouse)
Open 11 (12 Sun) to 11; bar food 12 to 3, 6 to 9; restaurant 7 to 9; closed 25 and 26 Dec
Details Children welcome   Car park   Wheelchair access (not WC)   Patio   No smoking in restaurant   Jukebox   Dogs welcome in bar   Delta, MasterCard, Switch, Visa   Accommodation: 14 rooms, B&B £47.50 to £135

TROON   **South Ayrshire**   **map 11**

Apple Inn   NEW ENTRY

89 Portland Street, Troon KA10 6QU   TEL: (01292) 318819

A small, bustling, stylish dining pub on the main shopping street in the centre of town, the Apple Inn has been completely refurbished and now has a contemporary, bistro-like persona. The décor is modern and clean, with a stylish wooden bar with tall stools and lots of mirrors on the walls, while the dining area (off to one side) has tightly packed, polished wooden tables and comfortable chairs. The kitchen's repertoire runs on equally modern lines, with blackboard specials (perhaps pan-fried fillet of sea bass with garlic prawns) supporting a printed menu that could well feature a 'substantial and enjoyable' dish of mussels in white wine with garlic and cream, or grilled goats' cheese with apple and tomatoes to start. Peppered Toulouse sausage with Calvados sauce, or casserole of beef bourguignonne with mushrooms, bacon and red wine continue the bistro theme, while desserts might feature an 'excellent' pannacotta with summer fruits. Beers include McEwan 70/-, supported by a dozen or so wines by the glass. SAMPLE DISHES: Caesar salad with smoked salmon, croûtons and Parmesan £4.50; pan-fried sirloin steak with Meaux mustard sauce £13.50; chocolate torte with home-made coconut ice cream £4.

Licensee Bill Costley (freehouse)
Open 9 to 11.30; bar food 12 to 2.30, 5.30 to 9.30
Details Children welcome   Wheelchair access (also WC)   Background music   No dogs   Delta, MasterCard, Switch, Visa

Wales

Nag's Head Inn 🍺

Abercych SA37 0HJ   TEL: (01239) 841200

2m W of Cenarth, where B4332 crosses River Cych

BREW PUB

The Welsh inscription on the pub sign translates as 'Be cunning as a serpent but peaceful as a dove' – though whether that is the house motto or an injunction to customers is not made clear. These days the orange-painted building by the river, having been the village courtroom and a forge, is a proper family pub with its own microbrewery and a very lengthy menu. The home-brewed beer is Old Emrys, and the three weekly-changing guest ales have included Tomos Watkin's Canons Choice and Fuller's London Pride. A wood-burning stove warms the beamed, stone-floored bar, and assorted memorabilia, plus an impressive international collection of bottled beers, adorn walls and shelves. The long menu includes a 'lighter eater' section of smaller portions at reduced prices for the less hungry or dieters. Typical dishes include garlic mushrooms, steak and ale pie (the ale is Old Emrys, of course), and chicken curry with poppadom; among desserts are death by chocolate, and treacle sponge and custard. The wine list is short and simple, around twelve bottles, with three house selections by the glass. SAMPLE DISHES: hot and spicy dragon wings £4; locally dressed crab salad £8; blackcurrant cheesecake £3.

Licensee Steven Jamieson (freehouse)

Open 11.30 to 3, 6 to 11.30 (Sun 11.30 to 11.30); bar food and restaurant 12 to 2, 6 to 9; closed Mon lunchtime winter

Details Children welcome   Car park   Wheelchair access (not WC)   Garden   No smoking in dining room   Occasional background music   Dogs welcome   Delta, MasterCard, Switch, Visa

▲ Penhelig Arms Hotel 🏵 🍇

Aberdovey LL35 0LT   TEL: (01654) 767215

WEBSITE: www.penheligarms.com

on A493 Tywyn to Machynlleth road, opposite Penhelig station

Welsh linguists, of course, know that Aberdovey lies at the mouth of the Dovey, where the coast road turns to follow the river bank upstream. Here, alongside the road, stands this smart three-storey white terrace hotel with deep sash windows and white chimneys poking soldier-like out of a blue-slate roof. The Fisherman's Bar is an unspoilt traditional pub in a self-contained part of the hotel, with slate walls, wood panelling and open fire in winter (on fine summer days you can sit outside by the sea wall relishing the view south across the estuary with your food and drink). Bar food, strong on fish, comes from the kitchen that also serves the hotel's restaurant, so is nearer posh nosh than pub grub. Dishes like cream of fennel soup, or grilled mullet fillets with chilli, ginger and garlic, precede chicken in Burgundy sauce with shallots and mushrooms, or braised lamb shank. Apricot frangipane tart, or chocolate and brandy mousse, make nice notes to end on. On tap you might find Wadworth 6X, Greene King Abbot Ale, Hook Norton Old Hooky, or Brains Reverend James. The wine list runs to over 200 bins and at least as many exclamation marks. But it is worth getting into a lather over: all the world's regions are covered in depth with plenty of famous names, new discoveries, old vintages and half-bottles, all at amazingly good prices whether you care to spend £12 or £40. Two dozen wines come by the glass. SAMPLE DISHES: chicken liver pâté and crostini £4.50; chargrilled tuna with rouille £9; pannacotta with fresh fruit £3.75.

Licensees Robert and Sally Hughes (freehouse)
Open *11 to 3, 6 to 11 (11 to 3.30, 5.30 to 11 summer); bar food 12 to 2.30, 6 to 9.30, restaurant 12 to 2.30, 7 to 9.30; closed 25 and 26 Dec*
Details *Children welcome in bar eating area   Car park   Patio   No-smoking area in bar, no smoking in dining room   No music   Dogs welcome   Delta, MasterCard, Switch, Visa Accommodation: 10 rooms, B&B £35 to £90*

AFON-WEN   Flintshire   map 7

Pwll Gwyn
Denbigh Road, Afon-Wen CH7 5UB   TEL: (01352) 720227
off A541, 10m NW of Mold

Built as a dower house, the black and white beamed Pwll Gwyn became a coaching inn in the early nineteenth century. Inside, collections of bric-à-brac and an inglenook in the bar area, together with friendly service, create a traditional pubby ambience. Although there is a separate restaurant, the same menu is available throughout. Starters vary from baked field mushrooms filled with home-made pâté and topped with smoked bacon and garlic butter to black pudding and potato fritters with a sweet-and-sour sauce, while main dishes may take in lemon pepper cod fillet ('moist inside and good flavour'), or spicy pork balls in curry sauce with rice. Those seeking plainer fare could start with perhaps chicken liver pâté and toast and go on to grilled fillet of plaice with tartare sauce. Finish with something like banana crêpes with vanilla ice cream, or hot chocolate fudge cake. Tetley cask, the regular ale, is joined by two guests, which might include Old Speckled Hen, Fuller's London Pride or Everards Tiger. Five wines are sold by the glass. SAMPLE DISHES: salmon and asparagus terrine £4; honey-roast rack of Welsh lamb with redcurrant sauce £9; bread-and-butter pudding £2.50.

Licensee Andrew Davies (freehouse)
Open *Tue to Sat 12 to 3, 6 to 11, Sun 12 to 4, 6 to 10.30 (may close earlier in quiet months); bar food and restaurant Tue to Sun 12 to 2, 7 (6 Fri to Sun) to 9*
Details *Children welcome in eating areas   Car park   Wheelchair access (also WC)   Garden No smoking in restaurant   Occasional live or background music   No dogs   MasterCard, Switch, Visa*

BEAUMARIS   Isle of Anglesey   map 7

▲ Olde Bulls Head Inn ✹

Castle Street, Beaumaris LL58 8AP   TEL: (01248) 810329

No visit to Beaumaris would be complete without a walk around the castle, established by Edward I in the thirteenth century and now a World Heritage Site. Don't miss the views from the walls over the Menai Strait to Snowdonia. Another attraction is the Olde Bulls Head, where Bass, Worthington and Hancock's HB are pulled in the cosy bar, with its open fire. Adjacent to the bar is a modern conservatory extension that houses the brasserie, where you can eat as much or as little as you like, from a sandwich or a salad to a three-course meal: perhaps potted salmon with chopped pickles, or grilled Bury black pudding with roasted apple and smoked bacon in walnut dressing, followed by beef bourguignonne, or pan-fried fillet of black bream with balsamic tomatoes and a saffron and spring onion cream, and then Eton mess. The separate restaurant has its own set-price menu. A selection of wines can be found on the back of the brasserie menu, with ten available by the glass; the full restaurant list (not available in the brasserie) runs to over 160 bins. SAMPLE DISHES: cured ham terrine with pineapple and apricot chutney £4.50; chargrilled swordfish steak with pea risotto and sauce vierge £10.25; toasted coconut tart with mandarin sorbet £3.75.

Licensee David Robertson (freehouse)
Open 11 to 11, Sun 12 to 10.30; brasserie 12 to 2, 6 to 9, restaurant Mon to Sat 7 to 9.30; closed 25 and 26 Dec, 1 Jan
Details Children welcome   Car park   Wheelchair access (also WC)   No smoking in lounge and restaurant   Occasional background music   No dogs   Amex, Delta, MasterCard, Switch, Visa
Accommodation: 13 rooms, B&B £65 to £97

BETWS-Y-COED   Conwy   map 7

▲ Ty Gwyn Hotel

Betws-y-coed LL24 0SG   TEL: (01690) 710383
WEBSITE: www.tygwynhotel.co.uk
on southern outskirts of village, at intersection of A5 and A470 by Waterloo Bridge

Ty Gwyn means 'white house', so that's what you look for – a slightly straggling, slate-roofed building crouched along the A5, peering over tubs and hanging baskets at the River Conwy on the other side. Built at perhaps the most strategic crossroads in north Wales, this is an old coaching inn, with all the beams and bric-à-brac to match (horse brasses, too). But it is also warm, welcoming and chintzily comfortable – a good place to recharge. The bar has Tetley Bitter and Wells Bombardier on tap, a rotating guest ale, and a straightforward list of European and New World wines includes one red and three white wines by the glass. An unchanging list of bar snacks includes Thai curries, grilled trout and fresh mackerel, plus cottage pie and lasagne, but is buttressed by daily-changing blackboard specials like a pair of large and delicious crab cakes with a sweet chilli sauce, or half a braised pheasant with a sauce of Beaujolais and wild mushrooms. The restaurant menu, also available in the bar, might offer a plentiful, carefully flavoured wild mushroom and pine-nut stroganoff with pilau rice, or one reporter's 'best scallops for a long time, cooked to perfection': six, with a velvety hollandaise and spiced mash. Still got room for a three-chocolate mousse gâteau? SAMPLE DISHES: baked peach stuffed with prawns £4.50; chargrilled sirloin of bison £14; chocolate and raspberry fondant £3.25.

Licensee James Ratcliffe (freehouse)
Open 11 to 11; bar food and restaurant 11.45 to 2, 7 to 8.30 (9 Apr to Oct); in Jan, closed Mon to Wed
Details Children welcome   Car park   Wheelchair access (also WC)   No smoking in dining room
Background music   No dogs   MasterCard, Switch, Visa   Accommodation: 12 rooms, B&B £20 to £90

CAPEL CURIG   Conwy   map 7

▲ Bryn Tyrch Hotel

Capel Curig LL24 0EL   TEL: (01690) 720223   VEGETARIAN
on A5, 5m W of Betwys-y-coed

Inside this old roadside inn, the large bar has loafing areas with big sofas on plank flooring, a number of tables and a welcoming open fire. There's also a lounge area near reception and a small dining area before the main bar, off which is a poolroom and another room for drinking and eating. The hotel takes great pride in its vegetarian and vegan cooking, and among the items on a typical menu might be a starter of vegetable samosa with mango chutney, and main courses of aduki bean and vegetable cottage pie with potato wedges and salad, and aubergine and pepper moussaka topped with ricotta and accompanied by garlic bread. Otherwise the large chalkboard over the fire might offer a pint of shell-on prawns with garlic mayonnaise, followed by pan-fried duck breast with ginger and orange sauce, shepherd's pie with spiced onion and parsnip mash, or smoked haddock, prawn and mushroom pie. Portions are hearty, but lovers of desserts could go for chocolate fruit cake (vegan) or apple crumble. Lunchtimes see a more snacky menu of soup, salads, and Welsh rarebit. Bass, Castle Eden Ale and Flowers IPA lend pedigree to the drinking options, as does the well-chosen wine list of around a dozen bottles, plus three or four house wines also served by the glass. Large windows make the most of the views to Snowdonia, and there's plenty of room outside for al fresco eating and drinking. SAMPLE DISHES: hot goats' cheese, celery, apple and walnut salad with sage dressing £4.25; grilled fillet of salmon with lime butter, new potatoes and salad £9.50; apricot and almond tart £4.

Licensee Rita Davis (freehouse)
Open 12 to 11.30; bar food and restaurant 12 to 9.30; closed Christmas; may close Mon to Thur lunchtimes winter
Details Children welcome   Car park   Garden   No-smoking area in bar, no smoking in restaurant
Occasional background music   No dogs   MasterCard, Switch, Visa   Accommodation: 16 rooms, B&B £33.75 to £49

Directions have been included where deemed necessary, but if in doubt about a pub's location – especially if heading to a rural location – it is advisable to phone and check.

Carew Inn

Carew SA70 8SL   TEL: (01646) 651267
off A477, 4m E of Pembroke

The beamed public bar, with its local prints and dartboard, is where locals
gather for a drink in this stone pub on a corner, the rest of the place given over
to eating. The two ground-floor cosy and old-fashioned dining areas have
coal-effect gas fires, jugs on a high shelf and hunting prints, and there's a separate restaurant on the first floor; the same menu applies throughout. The
'Favourites' section of the menu is just that: steaks, gammon with egg and
pineapple, and pan-fried fillet of plaice among them. The rest is a mixture of
traditional, Continental and Eastern ideas, with starters as diverse as lamb
samosas, prawn cocktail and Thai-style scallops. Main courses continue the
format, taking in chicken, leek and mushroom pie under an enormous puff
pastry lid, ostrich steak with orange and ginger sauce, and sweet-and-sour
pork with rice. Puddings are along the lines of 'quite delicious' lemon cheesecake on a chocolate digestive base, and Bakewell tart. On draught are
Worthington Best Bitter, Brains Rev James and Fuller's London Pride, and
three wines are available by the glass from a short list. The imposing remains
of Carew Castle and a Celtic cross are immediately opposite the pub and a
working tidal mill – the only one in Wales – is nearby; a mile-long, flat, circular walk takes in all three. SAMPLE DISHES: dressed local crab £5; breast of duck
with an orange and Cointreau sauce £12; rice pudding £3.25.

Licensee Mandy Hinchliffe (freehouse)
Open *summer 11 to 11 (10.30 Sun), winter 11 to 2.30, 4.30 to 11 (10.30 Sun); bar food and
restaurant summer 12 to 2.30, 5.30 to 9.30, winter 12 to 2, 6 to 9; closed 25 Dec*
Details *Children welcome in eating areas   Car park   Garden   No smoking in restaurant   Live or
background music   Dogs welcome in public bar only   MasterCard, Switch, Visa*

▲ Clytha Arms 🏵 ▉ 🍇

Clytha NP7 9BW   TEL: (01873) 840206
off old Abergavenny to Raglan road, S of A40, 6m E of Abergavenny

A verandah runs along the front of this converted dower house set at the top of
a wooded hill in rolling countryside in its own lawns and gardens. The rural
style is confirmed in the main bar, which has an old-fashioned wood-burning
stove, pews of stripped wood, and old posters on the walls. In the lively public
bar, locals play darts and other pub games and enjoy excellent beers at the
same time. These include frequently changing guest ales, which join regulars
from Hook Norton, plus Felinfoel Double Dragon and draught Bass; or
there's Old Rosie cider, and a good choice of malts, cognacs and Calvados. In
the restaurant, blackboard specials, mostly fish, shellfish and game, supplement the à la carte and set-price menus, where you could find leek and laverbread rissoles with beetroot chutney, followed by venison in ale with herb
dumplings, and then plum pudding. There are temptations also on the bar
menu, with its sandwiches along with more substantial dishes such as wild

mushroom omelette with garlic and rosemary potatoes, faggots with peas and sautéed potatoes, or crab and avocado salad. The list of about 100 wines, plus a good number of half-bottles, travels the world and caters for all budgets at each destination. Trophy wines like Cloudy Bay and Tignanello top the range but a lot of effort has gone into the under-£15 selection, which even includes two local Welsh wines. It's just £1.90 for a glass of house wine (£10.95 for a bottle) and there are ten good ones to choose from. SAMPLE DISHES: game risotto £6.50; pheasant in Riesling and wild mushroom sauce £15.50; spiced prunes with Sauternes cream £5.

Licensees Andrew and Beverley Canning, and Sarah Canning (freehouse)
Open Mon 6 to 11, Tue to Fri 12 to 3.30, 6 to 11, Sat 12 to 11, Sun 12 to 10.30; bar food and restaurant Tue to Sat (and restaurant Sun) 12.30 to 2.15 (2.30 Sun), Tue to Sat 7 to 9.30; closed 25 Dec
Details Children welcome   Car park   Wheelchair access (not WC)   Garden and patio
No smoking in restaurant   Occasional live music   No dogs   Amex, Delta, Diners, MasterCard, Switch, Visa   Accommodation: 4 rooms, B&B £45 to £90

CRICKHOWELL   Powys   map 4

▲ Bear Hotel 🍷 🌿

High Street, Crickhowell NP8 1BW   TEL: (01873) 810408
WEBSITE: www.bearhotel.co.uk
on A40, 6m NW of Abergavenny

Although it traces its ancestry back to 1432, this three-storey building is dignified and Georgian, white-painted with windows outlined in black. Among the warren of ground-floor rooms is a black-beamed bar where a large fireplace and a nineteenth-century coach timetable recall the inn's former function; here you will find Bass, Hancock's HB, Old Speckled Hen, and Brains Rev James and SA, plus a large selection of malt whiskies. If you prefer wine, there are sixteen by the glass from an annotated list of 40 or so well-priced bottles, largely from the New World. Interesting and versatile food draws the customers, too, with the bar menu offering, *inter alia*, Penclawdd cockles with capers, or carrot and coconut soup, then faggots in onion gravy, or home-cured ox tongue with Madeira sauce and bubble and squeak. Puds include the house special rum and banana bread-and-butter pudding with brown bread ice cream, or vanilla crème brûlée with walnut shortbread. The specials list could add such starters as a salad of oak-smoked duck and sun-dried tomato, or mains like a hotpot of local game cooked with liquorice and gin-soaked sloes. In the evenings food is available in the restaurant too. SAMPLE DISHES: white fish steamed pudding with red pepper coulis £5.50; roast pork with truffle and pistachio stuffing £8.50; marbled chocolate truffle terrine and white chocolate ice cream £4.50.

Licensee Mrs J.L. Hindmarsh (freehouse)
Open 11 to 3, 6 to 11, Sun 12 to 3, 7 to 10.30; bar food 12 to 2, 6.30 to 10, Sun 12 to 2, 7 to 9.30, restaurant 7 to 9.30; closed evening 25 Dec
Details Children welcome in bar eating area   Car park   Wheelchair access (also WC)   Garden and patio   No-smoking area in bar   Occasional background music   Dogs welcome exc in dining room   Amex, MasterCard, Switch, Visa   Accommodation: 36 rooms, B&B £54 to £130

▲ Nantyffin Cider Mill Inn �{ 🍇

Brecon Road, Crickhowell NP8 1SG   TEL: (01873) 810775
WEBSITE: www.cidermill.co.uk
1½m W of Crickhowell at junction of A40 and A479

The Cider Mill has seen some changes: a new wooden floor in the dining room, once the apple store, along with new tables and larger and more comfortable chairs, and the installation of new lighting to brighten up the area. The kitchen remains as passionate about local flavours and good home cooking as ever, with the proprietors' own farm providing much of the organic, free-range meat. This policy may translate into a starter of pot-roast pork with aromatic cabbage, roast peppers and bacon, and main courses of breast of duck with pear and apricot chutney and a rich sauce, or chargrilled lamb steak with a black olive and rosemary dressing and roasted provençale vegetables. Fish and shellfish might appear among the daily specials: perhaps a pancake of cockles, leeks and mussels with chive butter sauce, followed by grilled whole lemon sole with parsley butter, or grilled fillets of red mullet with a rich casserole of potatoes, leeks and saffron. A recent innovation is the Drover Menu, a cheaper set-price deal from Monday to Thursday: for example, Thai fishcakes, followed by home-made Gloucester Old Spot pork sausages with garlic mash and caramelised onion gravy, then apple cobbler. Wadworth, Fuller's, Brains and Tomos Watkin provide the three real ales, and Thatcher's Premium Press and Weston's Old Rosie cider are also on draught. After a rather self-congratulatory introduction the wine list makes good on its promises with an imaginative selection of 50 or so bottles (with four by the glass) plus a page of bin-ends. These and a number of monthly-changing specials (also by the glass) are healthy signs of an ongoing search for interesting wines. At one time a drovers' inn, the sixteenth-century building has lovely views of the Usk and mountains. SAMPLE DISHES: confit duck leg with red onion marmalade and a rich sauce £6; roast monkfish in Parma ham with sautéed spinach, shallots, garlic and linguine and caper and lemon dressing £14; poached pears in mulled wine jelly with raspberry compote £5.

Licensees Sean Gerrard and Glyn Bridgeman (freehouse)
Open 12 to 2.30, 6.30 to 11; bar food and restaurant 12 to 2.15, 6.30 to 9.30; closed Sun evening and Tue Sept to mid-Mar, 1 week Jan
Details Children welcome   Car park   Wheelchair access (also WC)   Garden   No smoking in restaurant   No music   No dogs   Amex, Delta, MasterCard, Switch, Visa   Accommodation: 23 rooms, B&B £40 to £115

CWMDU   Powys   map 4

▲ Farmers Arms

Cwmdu NP8 1RU   TEL: (01874) 730464
WEBSITE: www.thefarmersarms.com
on A479, 4m NW of Crickhowell

The Farmers Arms is a white-painted building of rough stone on a corner in the centre of the village, with a terraced garden to the side. Most of the interior is given over to a large, rather formal and old-fashioned dining area, with red chesterfield-style wall seats and vintage family photographs, although there's a bar with a wood-burning stove and an upright piano. The restaurant menu, also available in the bar, essays some interesting turns and makes resourceful use of local produce. Glamorgan sausages come with a piquant tomato sauce, and pancetta in minestrone soup gives an added dimension to an old favourite. Other starters range from Greek salad to smoked haddock fishcakes with a 'red-hot' sweet chilli sauce. For mains, there might be confit leg and pan-fried breast of duck, served pink, on soy-scented noodles with an elderflower, ginger and blackcurrant sauce, grilled fillet of halibut glazed with lemon and coriander pesto accompanied by a prawn and asparagus sauce, or 'tasty' rack of Brecon lamb brushed with honey and rosemary on a port, balsamic and orange reduction. If main courses seem over-complicated, accompanying vegetables, said to be 'super', are plainly anointed with butter. Handpumped real ales might include Old Speckled Hen, Shepherd Neame Spitfire Premium Ale or Uley Pig's Ear, and the wine list – short and to the point, with four sold by the glass – majors in New World and Spanish bottles. SAMPLE DISHES: chicken, apple and asparagus strudel with tarragon cream £5.25; fillet of Gower sea bass baked with lime and tarragon with tomato and tarragon coulis £13; cappuccino and Tia Maria gâteau £4.25.

Licensees Andrew and Susan Lawrence (freehouse)
Open 12 to 3, 6.30 to 11, Sun 12 to 3, 7 to 10.30; bar food 12 to 2.15 (2.30 Sun), restaurant Tue to Sun 12 to 2.15 (2.30 Sun), 7 to 9.30; closed 2 weeks Oct to Nov, 2 weeks Jan to Feb, phone to check weekday lunchtime openings Oct to Feb
Details Children welcome   Car park   Wheelchair access (not WC)   Garden   No smoking in restaurant   Background music   Dogs welcome in bar area only   Delta, MasterCard, Switch, Visa
Accommodation: 3 rooms, B&B £25 to £55

DRAETHEN   Caerphilly   map 4

Hollybush Inn

Draethen, Lower Machen NP10 8GB   TEL: (01633) 441326
off A468 Newport to Caerphilly road, about 1m from main road; pub is signposted

The terraced garden of this solid-looking building gives fine views of wooded hills and farming country, and a strongly rushing stream running all round it adds to the charm of the setting. Inside, an attractive pub atmosphere is created by lightly beamed ceilings, open stonework, carefully chosen pictures and artefacts, country-style furniture and carpet throughout, plus friendly and helpful staff. The pub draws those wishing to eat as well as locals who've come for a chat and a drink. The menu in the bar, with its open fires, concentrates largely on traditional main courses of ribeye steak with tomato and chips, chicken curry, and loin of pork with a brandy, cream and peppercorn sauce, while the restaurant menu (not available in the bar) might start off with honey-roast confit of duck leg with coriander and hoisin sauce, or deep-fried field mushrooms filled with pâté in a rich tomato and herb sauce, and then proceed to grilled fillets of sea bass on a creamy spring onion risotto drizzled with lobster sauce, or chargrilled duck breast on chive mash with juniper berry jus. Desserts might include trifle, or sticky toffee pudding. The set-price, early-evening 'flyer menu', available to 7.30, is good value. Brains Bitter, plus a guest such as Marston's Pedigree or Fuller's London Price, are the real beers on tap, while wine drinkers can choose from 20, with a handful sold by the glass. SAMPLE DISHES: Welsh goats' cheese baked in puff pastry with pesto dressing £5; pork tenderloin wrapped in bacon with leek and potato dauphinois and Marsala sauce £12.50; chocolate and red berry parfait layered with chocolate sponge £3.50.

Licensees Paul and Tanya Verallo (Punch Taverns)
Open *Mon to Thur 11.30 to 3, 5 to 11, Fri and Sat 11 to 11, Sun 12 to 10.30; bar food 12 to 2.30, 6 to 10, restaurant Mon to Sat 6 to 10, Sun 12 to 2.30; closed evening 26 Dec*
Details *Children welcome   Car park   Wheelchair access (not WC)   Garden and patio No smoking in restaurant   Background music   No dogs   Delta, MasterCard, Switch, Visa*

FELINFACH   Powys   map 4

▲ Felin Fach Griffin ✿   [NEW ENTRY]

Felinfach LD4 4DW   TEL: (01874) 620111
WEBSITE: www.felinfach.com
on A470, 4m N of Brecon

'This is something else!' enthused a reporter, impressed after lunch at this foursquare stone and brick pub set deep in the Powys countryside with nothing but sheep for company. You could take the comment literally: it is not really a pub in the traditional sense – there is no room for standing at the bar with a pint in your hand – although it does have a delightfully cosy, relaxed and informal atmosphere throughout its various rooms, some with bare floorboards, some with flagstones, all with solid beams and several with open log fires. And there are real ales – good Welsh ones at that: Crow Valley Bitter from Cwmbran and Tomos Watkin OSB from Swansea. The emphasis, though, is firmly on the food, with a frequently changing menu somewhat removed from the ploughman's and jacket potatoes clichés. Expect expansive modern cooking, full of bright ideas like steamed mussels with coconut and coriander, or boudin blanc with caramelised apple, beetroot and horseradish. There is room for more traditional options among main courses, such as pan-fried ox liver with creamed mash, smoked bacon and sage butter, but you are just as likely to encounter roasted mackerel with black olives, ratatouille and buttered spinach. Wines number around 50, a large proportion being from the New World, with prices starting at about £11 for the six house wines, which are also served by the glass. SAMPLE DISHES: salmon and leek tart with sun-dried tomato mayonnaise £6; black sea bream with braised leeks, cockles and lemon butter £10.50; orange and Cointreau crème brûlée £5.50.

Licensee Charles Inkin (freehouse)
Open *Mon 6 to 11, Tue to Sun 12 to 3, 6 to 11 (10.30 Sun); bar food Tue to Sun 12.30 to 2.30, all week 7 to 9.30 (10 Fri and Sat, 9 Sun)*
Details *Children welcome   Car park   Wheelchair access (also WC)   Garden and patio Occasional live music   Dogs welcome   MasterCard, Switch, Visa   Accommodation: 7 rooms, B&B £57.50 to £92.50*

The Guide always appreciates hearing about changes of licensee.

GLANWYDDEN   Conwy   map 7

Queen's Head ✪
Glanwydden LL31 9JP   TEL: (01492) 546570   **FISH**
just off B5115 Colwyn Bay to Llandudno road

The front bar of this whitewashed village pub has the feel of a real local, with
its wooden counter, stained-glass panel, flagstone floor and deep lounge seating. The back bar, split by a central coal fire, has red and blue carpeting, stone
walls, and wooden tables set with place mats. The menu changes monthly, and
open sandwiches served at lunchtime are replaced in the evening by steaks and
grills. Despite the unassuming style of the place, food is well above average.
Starting off the menu is a selection of hot and cold starters, such as 'rich and
aromatic' wild mushroom and garlic soup, or avocado with smoked salmon
and prawns. The rest of the menu is divided into pastas and salads, chef's
specials (pot-roast pheasant with orange and cranberry jus, for instance, or
'ultra-pink and juicy' lamb chops on blackberry and port sauce), and vegetarian dishes. Fish, listed separately, is something of a speciality: salmon and
coriander fishcakes, fillet of plaice wrapped in asparagus on tagliatelle with a
'tasty' shellfish sauce, or a kebab of 'sweet and moist' chunks of monkfish with
red onions and black pudding on mustard sauce. The list of home-made
desserts runs to around half a dozen each of hot and cold options: bread-and-
butter pudding among the former, tiramisù among the latter. To drink,
choose from Tetley Bitter, Greene King Abbot Ale, Old Speckled Hen and
Marston's Pedigree, or go for one of the seven wines sold by the glass from a
list of about forty bottles. A self-catering cottage is to let. SAMPLE DISHES:
crispy duck leg on a bed of sticky onions £5; grilled fillet of sea bass on wilted
spinach with sun-dried tomato and dill butter £9.50; black cherry cheesecake
£3.50.

Licensee Robert Cureton (Punch Group)
Open 11.30 to 3, 6 to 11 (10.30 Mon), Sun 11.30 to 11; bar food 11.45 to 2.15, 6 to 9,
Sun 11.45 to 9; closed 25 Dec
Details No children under 7   Car park   Patio   No-smoking area   Background music   Guide dogs
only   Delta, MasterCard, Switch, Visa

GRESFORD   Wrexham   map 7

Pant-yr-Ochain 🍺
Old Wrexham Road, Gresford LL12 8TY   TEL: (01978) 853525
WEBSITE: www.brunningandprice.co.uk
take Gresford turning off A483 Wrexham bypass

In a deserted area of pastureland by a lake, this Dutch-gabled pub is quite as
quirky within as without, boasting a book-lined room as well as hordes of
nostalgic memorabilia, from seaside postcards to vintage advertising posters.
The choice of real ales is very good, with Flowers Original and Timothy
Taylor Landlord joined by guests such as Phoenix Arizona and Weetwood Old
Dog Bitter, and there are around 60 malt whiskies. Drawing inspiration from
diverse corners of the globe, the food, which is ordered at the bar, might take

in duck confit with chilli and spring onion noodles and oriental dressing, or smoked salmon on rösti with horseradish crème fraîche, followed by lamb curry with basmati rice, or fillet of red bream with a tomato and roast garlic dressing. To tempt the sweet of tooth might be Baileys and chocolate bread-and-butter pudding, or Bakewell tart with berry compote. The wine list, arranged by grape variety, has 14 by the glass, with bottle prices starting at about £10 for house wines. SAMPLE DISHES: pear and Stilton salad with rustic croûtons and walnut and parsley dressing £4.50; grilled pork cutlet with black pudding potato and apple and red onion chutney £10; warmed waffle with chocolate fudge sauce and spiced winter fruit ice cream £4.25.

Licensee Lindsey Prole (freehouse)
Open *12 to 11 (10.30 Sun); bar food 12 to 9.30 (9 Sun)*
Details *Children welcome before 6pm   Car park   Wheelchair access (also WC)   Garden and patio   No smoking in 1 room   Occasional live music   No dogs   Amex, Delta, MasterCard, Switch, Visa*

HAY-ON-WYE   **Powys**   **map 4**

▲ Old Black Lion

26 Lion Street, Hay-on-Wye HR3 5AD   TEL: (01497) 820841
WEBSITE: www.oldblacklion.co.uk

This whitewashed seventeenth-century inn (with parts dating from the four-teenth century) is close to what was known as the Lion Gate, one of the origi-nal entrances to the old walled town of Hay-on-Wye. Oliver Cromwell reputedly billeted himself here while the Roundheads besieged Hay Castle, then a Royalist stronghold. Choose to eat in the oak-timbered King Richard (the Lionheart) Bar or the Cromwell Restaurant, which overlooks the garden terrace. In the former you might enjoy fish pie, steak and kidney pudding, Moroccan lamb or creamy chicken and mushroom vol-au-vent. In the restau-rant a more extensive choice takes in starters such as Parma-style Carmarthen ham with poached pear and fig, or confit duck leg with chilli plum sauce. Around three vegetarian choices precede other main courses of perhaps pot-roast partridge in port sauce, whole grilled plaice with herb butter, or beef Wellington. Desserts aim to indulge with the likes of profiteroles, or sticky toffee and date pudding. Dorothy Goodbody's Golden Ale and Old Black Lion Ale, from the Wye Valley Brewery, are the beers on offer, and the commendable wine list delves about in Europe and the New World to produce some tempting bottles. Six are available by the glass. Hay-on-Way claims to be the largest second-hand book centre in the world and also hosts the famous annual literary festival. SAMPLE DISHES: goats' cheese and sun-dried tomato tart £6; herb-crusted rack of Welsh lamb with parsnip mash and rosemary jus £15.50; warm chocolate torte with cherries and cream £4.25.

Licensee Vanessa King (freehouse; Simply Inns Ltd)
Open *11 to 11, Sun 12 to 10.30; bar food and restaurant 12 to 2.30, 6.30 to 9.30; closed 25 and 26 Dec*
Details *Children over 5 welcome in eating areas   Car park   Patio   No smoking in restaurant No music   No dogs   Delta, MasterCard, Switch, Visa   Accommodation: 10 rooms, B&B £42.50 to £100*

LAMPHEY   Pembrokeshire   map 4

▲ Dial Inn

Ridgeway Road, Lamphey SA71 5NU   TEL: (01646) 672426
just off A4139 Tenby to Pembroke road

A cheerful and welcoming atmosphere pervades this village-centre pub, once
the dower house of Lamphey Court. It is near the ruins of the Bishop's Palace,
a large mural of which is above the fireplace in the main room, which has
wood-panelled walls, a gas fire, a glass-doored cupboard full of china,
photographs on the walls and blue and white plates on a shelf. The menu
offers imaginative, sensible variations on such classics as smoked salmon (with
olives and a Welsh Brie), beef fillet (in a creamy whisky sauce), and local
salmon (wrapped in leeks and wafer-thin smoked bacon and pan-fried). The
same menu, as well as daily specials – maybe Lamphey lamb, sea bass or red
snapper – is served throughout. So, too, is the 'And Also' menu of simple pub
food with the accent on quality. Starters include prawn cocktail and soup, with
main courses of salads, Welsh steaks, a curry of the day and vegetarian lasagne.
Welsh cheeses are something of a speciality, and home-made desserts might
include sticky toffee pudding, or Baileys cheesecake. Draught Bass,
Worthington Bitter and a guest ale are offered, along with a concise wine list
and short selections of half- and quarter-bottles. A large modern extension at
the back houses squash courts. SAMPLE DISHES: crab cakes with aïoli £5.25;
Gressingham duck with black cherry sauce £14; hazelnut meringue £4.25.

Licensees Granville and Ruth Hill (freehouse)
Open 11 to 12, Sun 12 to 4, 7 to 11; bar food and restaurant 12 to 2.30, 6 to 9.30
Details *Children welcome   Car park   Wheelchair access (also WC)   Patio   No smoking in
restaurant   Background music   No dogs   Delta, Diners, MasterCard, Switch, Visa   Accommodation:
6 rooms, B&B £25 to £50*

LITTLE HAVEN   Pembrokeshire   map 4

▲ Castle   NEW ENTRY

1 Grove Place, Little Haven SA62 3UF   TEL: (01437) 781445
WEBSITE: www.castlelittlehaven.co.uk
off B4341, 6m W of Haverfordwest

Come through Broad Haven, drop down into Little Haven, and the Castle is
in the central square, opposite the glorious beach of one of Pembrokeshire's
most attractive (and smallest) resorts. A lively and traditional family pub, it has
an informal feel: tables outside, and inside flagged floors and exposed-stone
walls hung with prints of maps, local shipwrecks and advertisements offering
emigrants passage to America. There are two bars (offering Worthington,
Bass, Brains SA, and Tomos Watkin brews), a poolroom and a restaurant that
operates in the evenings. Bar food – on a menu, plus a specials board with
plenty of local fish on it – is fresh and simple: perhaps a starter of creamy
Pembrokeshire goats' cheese piled on slices of beef tomato and grilled, or scallops in white wine. Main dishes include mixed grill, steaks, a home-made pie
of the day (one day's was beef and ale, with plenty of both in it!), or, say, plaice

St Clements, 'large, fresh and juicy with a tart fruity sauce'. Desserts might be crème brûlée, or home-made apple pie. Lunchtime fare is simpler – sandwiches, steak and traditional cawl soup. A concise wine list starts under £8 a bottle and peaks at £15; there are seven by the glass. SAMPLE DISHES: mushrooms stuffed with Camembert £4; pasta with prawns, apple and a cheese topping £7; profiteroles £3.25.

Licensees Mr and Mrs A.M. Whitewright (Celtic Inns)
Open 12 to 2.30, 6 to 11 (11 to 11 summer); bar food 12 to 2, 6.30 to 9, restaurant Thur to Sat (all week summer) 6.30 to 9
Details Children welcome in bar eating area until 9pm   Wheelchair access (also WC)   Patio   No smoking in dining room   Jukebox   Dogs welcome on a lead   Delta, MasterCard, Switch, Visa   Accommodation: 2 rooms, B&B £50 to £60

LLANARMON DYFFRYN CEIRIOG   Wrexham   map 7

▲ West Arms ☙

Llanarmon Dyffryn Ceiriog LL20 7LD   TEL: (01691) 600665
WEBSITE: www.thewestarms.co.uk
off A5 LLangollen to Oswestry road at Chirk, then follow B4500 for 11m

At the confluence of three cattle drovers' tracks in the Ceiriog Valley, the West Arms has been dispensing refreshment and hospitality since the late seventeenth century. Its age explains its low ceilings, slate floors, massive inglenooks and ancient blackened timbers that give the bar its character. The menus in here have some enterprising touches: shoulder of Welsh lamb braised with ginger, honey and cider, grilled Ceiriog trout fillet wrapped in bacon served with a horseradish and chive sauce, locally made sausages with creamed potato, and something like a spinach and ricotta pancake with salad among vegetarian options. A wide choice of sandwiches, toasted or plain, is also available, with a couple of children's main courses. The separate restaurant has its own two- or three-course set-price menu following a more upmarket route, taking in seafood salad with avocado and asparagus in a tomato dressing, followed by 'poacher's platter' (breast of local pheasant, partridge and wood pigeon sliced on herbed rösti with roast chestnuts and claret sauce), with lemon and raspberry tart to finish. Alongside Whitbread Trophy and Stowford Press cider is an extensive wine list that offers affordable examples of traditional classics like claret and Burgundy alongside innovative wines from Spain and Italy and a respectable showing from the New World countries. Only three or four are available by the glass, but there is an impressive spread of half-bottles. SAMPLE DISHES: West Arms pâté £5.50; chicken breast chargrilled with garlic served with bean cassoulet £9.25; vanilla pannacotta £3.75.

Licensee Geoff Leigh-Ford (freehouse)
Open 8am to midnight; bar food 12 to 2, 7 to 9, restaurant all week 7 to 9, Sun 12 to 2
Details Children welcome   Car park   Wheelchair access (also WC)   Garden   No smoking in restaurant   Background music   Dogs welcome exc in restaurant   Delta, MasterCard, Switch, Visa   Accommodation: 15 rooms, B&B £47.50 to £138

LLANDWROG   Gwynedd   map 7

▲ Harp Inn 🍺

Ty'n Llan, Llandwrog LL54 5SY   TEL: (01286) 831071
WEBSITE: www.welcome.to/theharp
off A499, 5m SW of Caernarfon

On the old pilgrims' route from Holywell to Bardsey Island and now on the
cycle path from Holyhead to London, this stone-built hostelry is a favourite
with lovers of the great outdoors: the National Sailing School is nearby, and
energetic types are attracted to the walks and climbs around Snowdonia.
Alternatively, sit in the bar with the locals or try your luck in the games room.
It's a 'comfortable and cheerful haven'. A printed menu offers the likes of
breaded mushrooms, lasagne and lamb's liver, and there is a specials board
promising vegetarian dishes, curries and so on. As a finale, try good old-fashioned apple pie with locally produced Cadwallader's ice cream. During the
summer, a Taste of Wales Menu celebrates specialities like Menai mussels
with cider and leeks, Welsh mackerel rarebit, and lamb steaks with laverbread
and citrus sauce. Up to nine real ales and ciders are kept in pristine condition,
with names from near and far including Bass, Plassey Bitter, Black Sheep and
Wyre Piddle. Added to this are around 30 malt whiskies (including a contingent from Islay). The small selection of wines includes Cariad from Wales and
house basics are served by the glass for £1.95. SAMPLE DISHES: breaded Welsh
goats' cheese with fruit coulis £5; Pembroke fish pie £9; rum and raisin sponge
with rum sauce £3.25.

Licensee Colin Downie (freehouse)
Open Tue to Fri 12 to 2, 6 to 11, Sat 12 to 11, Sun 12 to 3; July and Aug Mon 6 to 11, Tue to Sun
12 to 11; bar food Tue to Sun (exc Sun evenings winter) 12 to 2, 6.30 to 8.30 (9 summer); also open
bank hol Mon 12 to 11
Details Children welcome in eating areas and games room   Car park   Wheelchair access (also WC)
Garden and patio   No smoking in restaurant   Background music   Dogs welcome on a lead in bar
Delta, MasterCard, Switch, Visa   Accommodation: 4 rooms, B&B £25 to £50

LLANFRYNACH   Powys   map 4

White Swan [NEW ENTRY]

Llanfrynach LD3 7BZ   TEL: (01874) 665276
WEBSITE: www.the-white-swan.com
off A40/B4558, 3m SE of Brecon

Hard against the north edge of the Brecon Beacons is Llanfrynach, and there,
opposite the church, a long row of roughly dressed stone cottages has been
run together, painted white (window surrounds black) and given a designer
hanging sign. At the back is a garden and, under a massive pergola, a terrace
divided into little 'rooms' by waist-high box hedges. Go inside, and you find
stone walls (some painted, some exposed), flagged floor, wooden furniture
and bar counter, plus leather sofas, a log fire and some very atmospheric lighting. Here they offer two regularly changing real ales, such as Brains Rev James
and Worthington Bitter, along with a worldwide wine list running from £12 to
£160 that has eight by the glass. Bar snacks begin with home-made soup, or

Welsh cheese rarebit with creamed leeks, and go on to local sausages and mash, or navarin of Welsh lamb with root vegetables. The restaurant's printed menu has similar dishes, plus blackboard fish specials like nice, fresh, fried monkfish served with bacon, crushed (very) potatoes and a saffron cream sauce. Sweets run to orange and syrup steamed pudding and custard, or perhaps iced honey and whisky parfait with chocolate brownies. SAMPLE DISHES: chicken liver and wild mushroom terrine £5.45; spiced beef with noodles and stir-fired vegetables £8; banana bread-and-butter pudding £4.

Licensees Stephen Way and Byron Lloyd (freehouse)
Open Wed to Sun 12 to 3, 7 to 11 (10.30 Sun); bar food and restaurant Wed to Sun 12 to 2 (2.30 Sun), 7 to 9.30 (8.30 Sun); closed 24, 25 and 26 Dec
Details Children welcome Car park Wheelchair access (also WC) Garden and patio No smoking in dining room Background music No dogs MasterCard, Switch, Visa

LLANGATTOCK Powys   map 4

Vine Tree Inn
The Legar, Llangattock NP8 1HG TEL: (01873) 810514
off A40, SW of Crickhowell

WATERSIDE

The Vine Tree's long, narrow interior has horse brasses on beams, dark stone or honey-coloured walls, dark floor tiles, plain wooden furniture and many a snug little alcove. A large blackboard by the bar gives notice that the pub also has a very industrious kitchen. Food is ordered from the bar and then brought to your table, turning up perhaps tuna and tomato salad, or baked egg provençale to start, then venison casseroled in red wine, gammon with parsley sauce, or salmon wrapped in filo with a creamy leek sauce. Portions can be gargantuan, but if you feel you can manage a pudding, then rejoice in the oldfangled likes of a fruit crumble, or profiteroles. Vegetarians might go for a bake, nut roast, pasta or curry. Hancock's HB, Worthington 1744 and Fuller's London Pride are on draught, and just the house wines from the short, red-dominated list are sold by the glass. The pub is made up of a row of linked cottages facing the road. Across the road is the car park, which is right beside the River Usk, crossed here by an ancient bridge leading to Crickhowell on the other side of the river. SAMPLE DISHES: mackerel pâté £3.25; half a roast duckling with game sauce £12; strawberry pavlova £3.

Licensee Andrew S. Lennox (freehouse)
Open 12 to 3, 6 to 11, Sun 12 to 3, 7 to 10.30; bar food and restaurant 12 to 2.30, 6 to 10
Details Children welcome Car park Garden No-smoking area in bar No music No dogs Delta, MasterCard, Switch, Visa

MACHYNLLETH Powys   map 4

▲ Wynnstay Hotel ✿
Maengwyn Street, Machynlleth SY20 8AE TEL: (01654) 702941
WEBSITE: www.wynnstay-hotel.com

Close to the main-road junction in the centre of this ancient market town is a substantial white building with slate roof, dormer windows and a high through-passage to its yard for the stagecoaches from Shrewsbury. Inside, refurbishment has brought clean, bold colours. In the welcoming bars (there's a new stable bar at the back with a pool table) regularly changing ales might include Brains Bitter, Greene King IPA and Timothy Taylor Landlord, as well as Powys-brewed Ralph's cider. In the bar food area, with its low, beamed ceiling and stone fireplace with club fender, Gareth Johns's food focuses on local ingredients (especially fish) just as much as that in the restaurant. Start with soused mackerel, from down the river at Aberdovey, or leek and rocket soup, then try local lamb steaks, or Borth crab salad. Lemon posset, chocolate tart or Welsh cheese and biscuits would round things off nicely. In the evenings, the restaurant – the menu is also available in the bar – chimes in with, say, wild boar pâté to start, or gratin of cockles and mussels from the Gower, followed by roast crown of Llynlloed partridge with red cabbage and foie gras, or wild Dovey salmon with pickled samphire. If you fancy it, there might be bara-brith-and-butter pudding to end on. The Italian-flavoured list of 30-odd bins has a rating of each wine's weight or sweetness to help decisions and includes four house wines from £10.75 that also come by the glass. SAMPLE DISHES: country pork pâté £5; strips of Welsh black beef fillet with pepper sauce £9; nougat glace with forest fruit £4.

Licensees Kathryn Vaughan, Charles Dark and Phil Copeland (freehouse)
Open 11 to 11, Sun 12 to 10.30; bar food 12 to 2, 6.30 to 9, restaurant 7 to 9
Details Children welcome Car park Wheelchair access (also WC) Patio No-smoking area in bar, no smoking in dining room Occasional live or background music Dogs welcome Amex, Delta, Diners, MasterCard, Switch, Visa Accommodation: 23 rooms, B&B £45 to £100

MONKNASH   Vale of Glamorgan   map 4

Plough and Harrow 🍺

Monknash CF71 7QQ   TEL: (01656) 890209
WEBSITE: www.publive.com
off B4265 from Llantwit Major

An ancient, foursquare pub, the Plough and Harrow is on a narrow lane with the sea and coast path in one direction and St Donat's Arts Centre and Atlantic College in the other. Outside is a patch of grass crammed with picnic tables, while inside are two stone-walled bars with tiny windows, flagstone floors, huge wood-burning fireplaces and black beams. The place has a real buzz, thanks to a lively crowd, but outsiders are made to feel just as welcome. The lunchtime menu is full of modern ideas, with salt-and-pepper squid salad, hoisin duck salad, and peppered tuna teriyaki with Thai-style salad all making an appearance. These may be joined by more traditional Welsh faggots, or butcher's sausages, while evenings see the introduction of such main courses as chargrilled fillet of beef with caramelised shallots and tarragon jus. Common to both sessions are puddings of cheesecake, profiteroles and crème brûlée. Beers are the real stars of the show, with seven regulars, including ales from the Wye Valley, Archers and Tomos Watkin breweries, as well as up to nine guests. Old Rosie cider is also served, plus around a dozen wines by the glass. SAMPLE DISHES: Vietnamese-style spring rolls with a plum and soy dipping sauce £6; fillet of cod wrapped in pancetta £10; sticky apple and caramel pudding £4.

Licensee Andrew Davies (freehouse)
Open 12 to 11 (10.30 Sun); bar food 12 to 2, 6 to 9
Details Children welcome in eating areas before 8pm   Car park   Garden and patio   Background and occasional live music   Dogs welcome exc during dining times   MasterCard, Switch, Visa

NANT-Y-DERRY   Monmouthshire   map 2

The Foxhunter 😋 😋 NEW ENTRY
Nant-y-derry NP7 9DN   TEL: (01873) 881101
between A4042 and A40, 6m S of Abergavenny

'They're perfectly happy for people to pop in just for a drink, and people do. It just seems silly when there's such brilliant food on offer,' says an inspector. The Grade II listed former stationmaster's house of rough grey-brown stone looks fairly ordinary outside; inside, though, the open-plan main bar's plain wooden furniture, bare oak floor, white walls and occasional seafood-themed prints give a fresh, uncluttered feel. Menus (changed daily) start with simple, rustically appealing dishes like roast organic tomatoes with crème fraîche and basil, or brochette of pork belly with oysters and sweet chilli sauce. Main courses take a similar line – whether rack of lamb with roast garlic mash and root vegetables, or fried monkfish with cherry tomatoes, rocket and salsa verde. Welsh ribeye with tarragon and shallot butter may appear in other pubs, but rarely so well handled as here: top-class beef perfectly cooked and infused with the flavour of the herb. Likewise, mixed seafood bourride – made with proper shellfish stock and packed with fresh-tasting seafood and chunks of fish – is a very superior version. Desserts are also superb: subtly flavoured vanilla-roasted pineapple flecked with chilli and served with pineapple ice cream was a hit at inspection. There are no draught beers but a few decent English and Italian bottled beers compensate. The wine list of around 60 bins has a handful under £15 but plenty above £30 too; four are available by the glass. SAMPLE DISHES: home-cured gravad lax with pickled cucumber and dill £7; noisette of lamb with French beans and rosemary potatoes £15; banana tart, butterscotch sauce and banana ice cream £6.

Licensee Lisa Tebbutt (freehouse)
Open Tue to Sat 12 to 3, 7 to 12; bar food and restaurant Tue to Sat 12 to 2.30, 7 to 9.30; closed Christmas and 2 weeks Feb
Details Children welcome   Car park   Wheelchair access (also WC)   Garden and patio No smoking in dining room   Background music   Delta, MasterCard, Switch, Visa

PEMBROKE FERRY   Pembrokeshire   map 4

Ferry Inn
Pembroke Ferry SA72 6UD   TEL: (01646) 682947   **WATERSIDE**
off A477 N of Pembroke; turn left at roundabout at S end of Cleddau Bridge

This old-fashioned pub with a coat of creeper sits at the south end of the former ferry crossing over the Cleddau, and almost under the less than lovely bridge that superseded it. Hence, the Ferry Inn, and especially its waterside terrace, enjoys an unrivalled view of the river and everything that moves on it – which explains the quarry-tiled floor and nautical paraphernalia decorating the 'pleasant, homely and unfussy' bar. The beers served include Bass and a weekly guest ale, perhaps Theakston Old Peculier, Shepherd Neame Spitfire or Robyns Bitter. Apart from chicken liver pâté, almost all the starters on the printed menu are fishy (smoked mackerel, and Thai fishcakes among them); spaghetti marinara, chicken korma and grilled gammon with pineapple exemplify main dishes (there are baguettes, salads and vegetarian alternatives too). The dishes that stand out, though, are those on the specials board: mostly fresh, locally caught fish. One reporter felt 'the pub was worth a visit just for the grilled plaice, served plain with a wedge of lemon and home-grown peas – straightforwardly cooked and served, as it should be'. Other possibilities might be sea bream, sea bass, or a mixed grill. Puddings might include lemon brûlée and hot chocolate sponge. Four wines from the short and inexpensive list are offered by the glass. SAMPLE DISHES: French butter crêpe with prawns and haddock in cream, wine and butter sauce £4; sirloin steak, chips and peas £9.50; summer pudding and ice cream £2.95.

Licensee Colin Williams (freehouse)
Open 11.30 to 2.45, 6.30 (7 Mon) to 11, Sun 12 to 2.45, 7 to 10.30; bar food and restaurant 12 to 2, 7 to 10 (9 Sun); closed 25 and 26 Dec
Details Children welcome   Car park   Wheelchair access (also WC)   Patio   No smoking in dining room   Background music   Guide dogs only   Delta, MasterCard, Switch, Visa

PORTHGAIN   Pembrokeshire   map 4

Sloop Inn

Porthgain SA62 5BN   TEL: (01348) 831449
off A487, 4m W of Mathry

WATERSIDE

The Sloop is a long, low building by the harbour in a small village in the Pembrokeshire Coast National Park, a particularly scenic area. Apart from its name and setting, its maritime connections are seen inside in relics salvaged from a ship wrecked off the coast here in the mid-nineteenth century. The sea provides much of the produce used in the kitchen too: starters of moules marinière, or deep-fried whitebait, and main courses of macaroni and seafood bake, or pan-fried dogfish in a creamy caper sauce. Otherwise, there might be game and orange terrine, followed by steak, kidney and mushroom pie, fillet of pork wrapped in sun-dried tomatoes and pancetta, or Welsh black beef steaks. Real ales are Rev James from Brains, Wadworth 6X, Felinfoel Double Dragon Ale and Flowers Original, and three wines are sold by the glass. SAMPLE DISHES: crab cakes with gooseberry sauce £4.25; slow-roast leg of lamb in cranberry and honey sauce £8.25; marbled chocolate parfait with red berry coulis £3.75.

Licensee Matthew Blakiston (freehouse)
Open 11 to 11, Sun 12 to 4, 5.30 to 10.30; bar food and restaurant 12 to 2.30, 6 to 9.30
Details Children welcome   Car park   Patio   No-smoking area in restaurant   Occasional live music; jukebox   No dogs   MasterCard, Switch, Visa

Which? Online subscribers will find The Which? *Pub Guide online, along with other Which? guides and magazines, at* www.which.net. *Check the website for how to become a subscriber.*

Ship Inn 🍺

Red Wharf Bay LL75 8RJ   TEL: (01248) 852568

WATERSIDE

off A5025, 6m N of Menai Bridge

Taking up a row of eighteenth-century cottages, the Ship is in a glorious position overlooking miles of beach and sea. Inside are log fires, beamed ceilings, wheel-back chairs and wall benches around the tables, and the decoration is provided by a profusion of prints and china on the walls along with an old ship's wheel. People wanting to eat may have to wait for a table, although some of the pressure is removed when the separate restaurant is open, and the food is a large part of the Ship's appeal. A wide range of culinary influences produces a modern, eclectic style of cooking: Conwy mussels with leeks, saffron and white wine, and sautéed duck livers on melted goats' cheese with raspberry vinaigrette are typical starters. Main courses vary from the traditional – pink pan-fried venison steak topped with caramelised onions in a rich, well-rendered red wine sauce with red cabbage, for instance – to the more exotic – pan-fried red snapper fillet on a bed of noodles in a chilli sauce, say – while desserts are a mixture of the two: warm rice pudding with an amaretti crust and tamarillo sauce, or sticky toffee pudding with treacle sauce. Ales are from Adnams, Greene King and Tetley's, and there's also Burton Ale plus guests. The pub stocks over 50 malt whiskies and a good range of liqueurs, and half a dozen wines are sold by the glass. SAMPLE DISHES: seafood soup £3.25; baked half-shoulder of Welsh lamb with redcurrants and rosemary £13; tarte Tatin with butterscotch ice cream £3.75.

Licensee Andrew L. Kenneally (freehouse)

Open *summer 11 to 11, Sun 12 to 10.30, winter Mon to Fri 11 to 3, 6.30 to 11, Sat 11 to 11, Sun 12 to 10.30; bar food Mon to Sat 12 to 2.30, 6 to 9.30, Sun 12 to 9, restaurant Fri and Sat and all week summer 6 to 9.30, Sun winter 12 to 9; opening hours vary bank hols and high season*

Details *Children welcome in family room and restaurant   Car park   Wheelchair access (not WC) Garden and patio   No smoking in 2 rooms   Occasional background music   No dogs   Delta, MasterCard, Switch, Visa*

Kinmel Arms

St George LL22 9BP   TEL: (01745) 832207

off A55, 2m SE of Abergele

Although it dates from the seventeenth century, the Kinmel Arms struck one visitor with an impression of a 'spacious, light, sparkly and lively area of space', with plenty of room for everyone: at a stool at the bar, near the fire, on a sofa, on cushioned wicker chairs in the conservatory, or in the eating area. The same menu is available throughout. Open sandwiches and baguettes are served at lunchtimes, but larger appetites might choose a salad of Bury black pudding, caramelised apple, bacon and rocket dressed with a Calvados sauce, or Chinese-style chicken goujons with sweet chilli dressing, and then braised ham hock with creamy mash and a white wine and herb sauce, or Cumberland sausages. Fish is well represented, with even more specials on a Friday: perhaps poached

Conwy plaice with black-bean butter. Beers are a familiar range, with three guest ales changing every six weeks or so, and eight wines are sold by the glass. SAMPLE DISHES: smoked chicken and bacon salad with honey and mustard dressing £4.50; chargrilled tuna steak with salade niçoise £9; apple pie £3.50.

Licensees Lynn Cunnah-Watson and Tim Watson (freehouse)
Open 12 to 3, 7 to 11, Sun 12 to 5.30; bar food 12 to 2, 7 to 9.30, Sun 12 to 4; closed 25 Dec
Details Children welcome in eating area   Car park   Wheelchair access (also WC)   Garden and patio
No-smoking area   Live or background music   Dogs welcome in bar only   Delta, MasterCard, Switch, Visa

ST HILARY   Vale of Glamorgan   map 4

Bush Inn

St Hilary CF71 7DP   TEL: (01446) 772745
WEBSITE: www.downourlocal.com/thebushinn
off A48 Cardiff to Bridgend road, 2m E of Cowbridge

For travellers who stick to the M4 en route for beaches further west, southernmost Wales means spoil heaps on the right, sea and steel works on the left. But the old road from Cardiff to Bridgend opens up a greener, gentler, more rural landscape, where English and Welsh place names intermingle amid a peppering of castles. This pub fits that setting: a long, low building of sandy-coloured stone with a thatched roof, opposite a Norman church in a quiet village. The inside is as sixteenth century as the outside, with exposed beams and stone walls, an inglenook and copper pans on the walls of the three bars and restaurant. Bar food (listed on menu plus specials board) involves well-executed old faithfuls, plus items like parsnip and apple soup, or laverbread and bacon to start. For mains there is fresh fish, grilled or fried (plaice, cod, trout); chicken curry; or a meaty steak and ale pie with rich gravy and 'fluffy baked potato, clearly baked in a real oven'. Grand Marnier crème brûlée is commended, or there's sticky toffee pudding for the sweetest-toothed. The restaurant menu adds some more upmarket ideas, like poached salmon fillet, or boeuf Calvados. Beers are Bass, Old Speckled Hen, Hancock's HB and Worthington Bitter, plus Old Rosie cider. Three house wines, at £8.95, open a varied list of thirty-eight bottles, and four are available by the glass. SAMPLE DISHES: Welsh rarebit £4; baked ham and parsley sauce £6; crème caramel £3.50.

Licensee Sylvia Murphy (Punch Taverns)
Open 11.30 to 11, Sun 12 to 10.30; bar food and restaurant 12 to 2.15, 7 to 9.45 (6 to 9.45 Sat), Sun 12 to 2.15, 6.30 to 8.30; closed evening 25 Dec
Details Children welcome in eating areas   Car park   Wheelchair access (not WC)   Garden and patio   No smoking in dining room   Background music   No dogs   Delta, MasterCard, Switch, Visa

▲ *indicates where a pub offers accommodation. At the end of the entry information is given on the number of rooms available and a price range, indicating the cost of a single room or single occupancy to that for a room with two people sharing.*

SKENFRITH Monmouthshire   map 2

▲ Bell at Skenfrith ☺ ❦ [NEW ENTRY]

Skenfrith NP7 8UH   TEL: (01600) 750235
WEBSITE: www.skenfrith.com
on B4521, between Abergavenny and Ross-on-Wye

Originating in the seventeenth century, this slate-roofed, white-painted pub is right by a hump-backed bridge over the River Monnow, with hills rising steeply behind the building. Refurbishment has given the interior a modern, stylish look, the open-plan area decorated in natural shades, with some vintage photographs and well-spaced furniture. Lunchtimes see a choice of light main courses like locally smoked salmon salad, or Old Spot open sandwich, though more substantial dishes might turn up as braised lamb shank with creamed potato, mange-tout and onion cream sauce. Some starters are common to both lunch and dinner menus – grilled buffalo mozzarella and rosemary focaccia with roasted pepper dressing, or chilled gazpacho soup with herb oil – while main courses might take in Welsh Black sirloin steak with chips and béarnaise sauce, or pork tenderloin with sautéed potatoes, vegetables and a 'baby onion' cream sauce. Desserts run from local ice creams, via Welsh cheeses to bread-and-butter pudding. For drinkers, Freeminer Bitter and Hook Norton Best Bitter are on draught, along with Broome Farm cider. The 100-strong wine list strides confidently from the ordinary world of easy-drinking wines for under £15 (where you'll find nine wines by the glass) to the rarified heights of first-growth claret from the amazing 1989 and 1990 vintages. Prices are on the high side, but the selection is impressive. SAMPLE DISHES: tiger prawns with tomato fondue, lemon and garlic butter £8; pan-fried fillet of beef with beetroot dauphinois baby leeks and red wine sauce £18; apple tart with caramel sauce and ice cream £4.75.

Licensees William and Janet Hutchings (freehouse)
Open *11 to 11, Sun 12 to 10.30; bar food 12 to 2.30, 7 to 9.30; closed Mon Nov to Mar, 2 weeks end Jan to early Feb*
Details *Children welcome   Car park   Wheelchair access (also WC)   Patio   No smoking in eating area   Background music   Dogs welcome   Amex, Delta, MasterCard, Switch, Visa   Accommodation: 8 rooms, B&B £65 to £150*

STACKPOLE Pembrokeshire   map 4

Stackpole Inn

Stackpole SA71 5DF   TEL: (01646) 672324
off B4319, 3m S of Pembroke

Formerly called the Armstrong Arms, this pair of converted seventeenth-century cottages on the National Trust-owned Stackpole Estate, close to the Pembrokeshire Coast Path, changed its name when new owners took over in summer 2002. The menus offer a varied choice, with a mix of traditional and modern ideas. As well as bar snacks – one reporter enjoyed a generously filled smoked salmon and salad baguette served warm with an excellent mayonnaise-style dressing – more substantial meals may begin with starters such as broccoli and Stilton soup, or Thai fishcakes with wok-fried pak choi and chilli oil. Main courses typically take in ribeye of Welsh beef with sautéed potatoes, wild mushrooms and red wine jus, pan-fried sea bass with spiced rice and sauce vierge, and chicken breast stuffed with wild mushrooms and Stilton with white wine and shallot cream sauce. To finish, there might be chocolate tart, or apple pie and custard. Beers include Welsh real ales Brains Rev James and Felinfoel Best Bitter. There is also a list of around 20 wines, with eight house selections priced from £9.60 – four of these are also available by the glass. SAMPLE DISHES: salad of roasted vegetables with garlic and basil dressing £5.75; rump of Welsh lamb in a garlic and herb crust with sautéed potatoes, Mediterranean vegetables and red wine jus £13; blackberry and apple cheesecake £4.50.

Licensees Mr and Mrs R.H. and L.D. Dearling (freehouse)
Open *Mon to Fri 11.30 (12 winter) to 3, 6 (6.30 winter) to 11, Sat 11.30 to 11 (12 to 3, 6.30 to 11 winter), Sun 12 to 3, 7 to 10.30; bar food and restaurant 12 to 2.30, 6 (7 winter) to 9*
Details *Children welcome   Car park   Wheelchair access (also WC)   Garden   No smoking in restaurant   Occasional background music   Dogs welcome in bar only   Delta, MasterCard, Switch, Visa*

TYN-Y-GROES   Conwy   **map 7**

▲ Groes Inn

Tyn-y-Groes LL32 8TN   TEL: (01492) 650545
WEBSITE: www.groesinn.com
4m S of Conwy; from mini-roundabout at Conwy Castle take B5106 towards Trefriw for 2m

---

In summer, this white-painted ancient building is all colourful hanging baskets, tubs and creeper, with benches making the most of breathtaking views eastwards over the Conwy Valley and westwards towards Snowdonia. Inside, the décor is what might be expected from a pub dating from the sixteenth century, with a wood-burning stove in a huge inglenook with a mantel beam hung with pots, low ceilings, beams and brasses, toby jugs, bookshelves behind the optics, and varied prints on the walls. The bar menu is supplemented by a blackboard of specials, while a fixed-price menu is offered in the more formal restaurant, with its old prints and portraits and heavy swagged curtains. The choice in the bar is wide, covering traditional and modern styles, and many of the first-rate ingredients are local: for example, Anglesey gammon (grilled and served with eggs and big chips), sausages (with mash and onion gravy), and roast Welsh black beef served with all the trimmings at Sunday lunch. Typical offerings might include a seafood hors d'oeuvre of 'excellent fresh quality', smoked and fresh salmon and trout with prawns in a creamy tomato mayonnaise, 'simply delicious' poached fillets of Conwy salmon, or crisp-roast duckling with sage and onion stuffing and gravy. Vegetables are said to be outstanding, and puddings maintain the momentum: sharp and refreshing lemon and lime syllabub, for instance, or mixed berry compote with rose petal ice cream. Tetley Bitter and Burton Ale are provided for real beer drinkers, and house wines are served by the glass. SAMPLE DISHES: avocado, smoked chicken and crispy bacon salad £6; fresh and smoked salmon fishcakes with tartare sauce £7.75; almond and amaretti parfait with chocolate sauce £3.75.

Licensee Dawn Humphreys (freehouse)
Open 12 to 3, 6 to 11; bar food and restaurant 12 to 2, 6.30 to 9
Details *Children welcome in eating area of bar   Car park   Wheelchair access (also WC)   Garden and patio   No-smoking area in bar   Occasional live music   No dogs   Amex, Delta, Diners, MasterCard, Switch, Visa   Accommodation: 14 rooms, B&B £68 to £121*

ROUND-UPS

Pubs have all kinds of attractions, and people use them for all kinds of reasons. Those in the Round-up section are a mixed bag, but each has some special quality that makes it well worth visiting.

Some of the pubs listed here are superlative outlets for real ale; others have a fascinating history or architecture. There are hostelries close to public gardens, castles, rivers and canals; lively urban drinking pubs; and plenty of establishments that will appeal to walkers, bird-watchers, climbers and fishermen. Many places are also excellent family venues, and some may offer decent accommodation.

Most of these pubs serve food, although that is not the main reason for their inclusion in the Round-ups. Food is often incidental to the proceedings (especially in some town and city pubs), and a number of places provide only limited snacks, while a few serve no food at all.

Pubs in the Round-up sections are listed on the basis of readers' recommendations, backed up wherever possible – but not always – by inspectors' reports. Further feedback on these places is most welcome.

ENGLAND

ABBOTS BROMLEY

Staffordshire   map 5

Bagot Arms

Bagot Street, Abbots Bromley WS15 3DB
TEL: (01283) 840371

on B5104, 6m S of Uttoxeter

If you suffer sympathetic dehydration while watching the famous Horn Dance (see entry below), look for this white building in Bagot Street. Here Marston's Pedigree and Banks's Mild are on offer, and all eight wines listed come by the glass. Along with baguettes and sandwiches, potato skins or mussels might provide a light snack, and a comprehensive list of pub favourites includes curries, lamb shank, and chicken wrapped in bacon with Stilton sauce.

Open *Mon to Fri 12 to 2.30, 5.15 to 11, Sat 12 to 11, Sun 12 to 10.30*

Goats Head

Abbots Bromley WS15 3BP
TEL: (01283) 840254

Home to the extraordinary Horn Dance – an annual event in which an ancient collection of antlers is paraded around the parish by a motley crew of dancers dressed as mythical characters – Abbots Bromley can also boast this Goats Head. No fancy dress required, though, at this black and white timbered pub, just an appetite for tasty food and a thirst for a pint of Greene King Abbot Ale or Marston's Pedigree, or one of the dozen wines on offer.

Open *12 to 3, 6 to 11*

AINSTABLE

Cumbria   map 10

New Crown

Ainstable CA4 9QQ
TEL: (01768) 896273

take A6 N from M6 junction 41, follow signs to Armathwaite, then 2m to Ainstable

In the Eden Valley, between the walkers' high hills and the fishermen's river, this family-run, white-painted inn makes a pleasant place to pause. Ales on draught include Tetley's, and

guests such as Carlisle State Bitter, Derwent's Teacher's Pet, and Jennings Cumberland Ale. As well as snacks, the menu includes dishes such as gammon steak, Cumberland sausage, or duckling with orange sauce, plus children's 'small bites'. B&B available.

Open *all week 12 to 3, Fri to Sun winter and all week summer 6 to 11*

ALDEBURGH

Suffolk   map 6

Ye Olde Cross Keys Inn

Crabbe Street, Aldeburgh IP15 5BN
TEL: (01728) 452637

on A1094, 6m E of A12

There's more to the Aldeburgh area than music, though a car (and binoculars) help to make the most of it. But you don't need either to enjoy the Cross Keys, its three guest rooms and its Adnams beers. (Adnams are responsible for the wine list, too, from which six come by the glass.) Food is fish-orientated and includes fisherman's pie, moules marinière, scallops in bacon or Dover sole, with bread-and-butter or summer pudding to follow.

Open *11 to 3, 5.30 to 11, Sun 12 to 3, 7 to 10.30 (summer 11 to 11)*

ALMONDSBURY

South Gloucestershire   map 2

Bowl Inn

16 Church Road, Lower Almondsbury
BS32 4DT
TEL: (01454) 612757

on A38, close to M4/M5 interchange

This red-roofed, whitewashed inn perches on the escarpment above the Severn, looking across to the M4 bridge and Wales. Licensed since 1550, it now serves seasonally changing cask ales from, say, Moles Brewery, Melksham, and Bath Ales (Barnstormer), alongside 40 wines (six by the glass). Bar and restaurant menus offer the likes of half-shoulder of lamb in red wine sauce, or salmon fillet with tomato and mussel sauce. Thirteen rooms.

Open *11 to 3, 5 to 11, Sun 12 to 3, 7 to 10.30*

ALSTON

Cumbria   map 10

Turk's Head Inn

Market Place, Alston CA9 3HS
Tel: (01434) 381148
*at junction of A686/A689/B6277, 16m NE
of Penrith*

Just over the watershed from the Eden,
flowing to the Solway, Alston straddles
the steep valley of the still small South
Tyne. This inn, dating from 1611,
looks over the charming and spacious
market square. It offers Boddingtons
Cask, Flowers IPA and Trophy Bitter
on draught, plus guests like Old
Speckled Hen. And there's scampi,
haddock, lamb knuckle in rosemary or
mushroom lasagne to refuel hungry
walkers. Children are welcome.
Open *11 to 3.30, 6.30 to 11, Sun 12 to 3.30,
7 to 10.30; closed eve 25 Dec*

ALVESTON

Warwickshire   map 5

Ferry Inn

Ferry Lane, Alveston CV37 7QX
Tel: (01789) 269883
off B4056, 2m NE of Stratford-upon-Avon

As its name implies, this pub is beside
the meandering Avon, downstream of
tourist-haunted Stratford. It is off main
roads, too, which should enhance
peaceful enjoyment of Adnams Bitter,
Marston's Pedigree, Fuller's London
Pride, or a guest like Hook Norton Old
Hooky. Four of 29 wines come by the
glass, and crowd-pulling food includes
duck and chicken liver pâté, and fried
sea bass in citrus butter sauce.
Open *12 to 3, 6 to 11, Sun 12 to 3*

ANICK

Northumberland   map 10

Rat Inn

Anick NE46 4LN
Tel: (01434) 602814
just N of A69, 1½m NE of Hexham

This was a drovers' inn in the
eighteenth century. 'Rat' once meant a
drunk taken into custody (dissolute
people, drovers!), but the pseudo-
mosaic on the floor shows a rodent.
Beers are Old Speckled Hen, Ruddles

Best and John Smith's, plus guests like
Marston's Pedigree or Mordue's
Radgie Gadgie. All wines come by the
glass, and specials like duck à l'orange,
or tuna steak with tomato, garlic and
basil, supplement the bar food.
Children are welcome throughout the
pub and garden.
Open *11 to 3, 6 to 11, Sun 12 to 3*

APPLEBY

Cumbria   map 10

Tufton Arms

Market Square, Appleby CA16 6XA
Tel: (017683) 51593

In the middle of what was the county
town of Westmorland, this is a 21-
room hotel dating from the
seventeenth century, but revamped in
Victorian style. It has a conservatory
restaurant overlooking a mews
courtyard, and the Victorian Bar serves
Tufton Ale (now brewed by
Boddingtons). There is also an
extensive wine list (165 bins, 16 by the
glass). Food runs to a hotpot of wild
mushrooms followed by local produce
in the form of, perhaps, roast rack of
Cumbrian lamb, or breast of organic
chicken in red wine sauce. Children
are welcome.
Open *11 to 11, Sun 12 to 3, 7 to 10.30*

APPLETON ROEBUCK

North Yorkshire   map 9

Shoulder of Mutton

Chapel Green, Appleton Roebuck
YO23 7DP
Tel: (01904) 744227
*3m E of Tadcaster, off A64 Leeds to
York road; turn S at Colton Lane End*

Travellers along the A64 might well
break their journey with a detour to
this tiny village where this Samuel
Smith's pub overlooks the village
green. Here, Old Brewery Bitter is
drawn straight from the wood, and you
will also find bottled Organic Best Ale,
plus a menu that includes such
modern dishes as aubergine black
pudding tower, and lime coriander
chicken.
Open *11 to 3, 6.30 to 11, Sun 12 to 3,
7 to 10.30*

ASHBURNHAM

East Sussex   map 3

Ash Tree Inn

Brown Bread Street, Ashburnham
TN33 9NX
TEL: (01424) 892104

just off B2204 (off A271), 4m W of Battle

Homely sixteenth-century local tucked
away down narrow country lanes in an
isolated hamlet close to the historic
town of Battle and Ashburnham Park.
Cosy beamed bars with three
inglenook fireplaces, old settles,
exposed brickwork, and evening
candlelight. Expect Harveys Best as
well as Old Speckled Hen on
handpump, and a short selection of
hearty country dishes listed on
blackboards and a printed menu on
Sundays. Children are welcome.

Open *12 to 3, 7 to 11*

ASHBY ST LEDGERS

Northamptonshire   map 5

Olde Coach House Inn

Ashby St Ledgers CV23 8UN
TEL: (01788) 890349

off A361, 4m N of Daventry

This nineteenth-century brick former
farmhouse replaced an older pub that
was knocked down. Its rambling
interior contains both large family
tables and small, intimate dining areas.
Beers are Flowers Original Bitter and
Everards Original, plus five guests, and
eight wines are offered by the glass
from a list of over 35. Eat from bar and
(more ambitious) restaurant menus.
Children are welcome (there is a baby
changing room and a garden play area),
and six rooms are available.

Open *12 to 11 (Jan/Feb 12 to 2.30, 6 to 11),
Sun 12 to 10.30*

ASHLEWORTH

Gloucestershire   map 5

Boat Inn

The Quay, Ashleworth GL19 4HZ
TEL: (01452) 700272

off A417, 6m N of Gloucester

Since at least 1780 this pub on the west
bank of the Severn, near the spot
where the old chain ferry used to cross
it, has been quenching the thirst of

boatmen. Arkell's 3B, RCH Pitchfork
and most probably brews from Wye
Valley, Bath Ales or Cottage Brewing
are on tap – at least five at any time –
plus traditional ciders. The food is
confined to a selection of filled baps,
but in summer services extend to a
coffee house offering drinks and cakes.

Open *11 to 2.30, 7 (6 summer) to 11, Sun 12
to 3, 7 to 10.30; closed Mon and Wed lunchtime
winter, 25 Dec*

ASHPRINGTON

Devon   map 1

Waterman's Arms

Bow Bridge, Ashprington TQ9 7EG
TEL: (01803) 732214

*off A381 Totnes to Kingsbridge road, 2m SE
of Totnes*

In an isolated location by a bridge over
Bow Creek, this picturesque pub has
in its colourful past been variously a
smithy and a brewery. Nowadays it is a
thoroughly modern inn with an
ambitious kitchen, producing dishes
like green-lipped mussels in spicy
Thai-style broth, half a shoulder of
lamb on 'broken' potatoes with
redcurrant sauce, as well as steak and
ale pie, and breaded cod with chips
and peas. Lunch is a simpler affair.
Beers are Wadworth 6X and Bass,
although plans are in the air to extend
the range, and there are eight wines by
the glass.

Open *11 to 11, Sun 12 to 10.30*

ASWARBY

Lincolnshire   map 6

Tally Ho Inn

Aswarby NG34 8SA
TEL: (01529) 455205

*on A15 Peterborough to Lincoln road,
5m S of Sleaford*

A popular stone-built eighteenth-
century pub in an isolated location,
reputedly once a farmhouse. A hunting
theme dominates the décor in the
beamed main bar area, and a convivial
atmosphere prevails. Printed menus
offer soups, baguettes and snacks,
while blackboards list dishes such as
lamb's liver and bacon with red wine
and onion gravy, and gammon steak
with pineapple, as well as a few more

unusual ideas like salmon fillet with peanut and sweet chilli sauce, or red snapper with pepper salsa. A decent selection of beers includes Bass, Bateman XB and Greene King Abbot Ale.
Open *12 to 3, 6 to 11, Sun 12 to 3, 7 to 10.30*

AYOT ST LAWRENCE

Hertfordshire   map 3

Brocket Arms

Ayot St Lawrence AL6 9BT
TEL: (01438) 820250

off B656/B651, 5m NW of Welwyn

This building housed monks in pre-Reformation days. Now it has two cosy, low-beamed bars serving Greene King Abbot Ale and IPA, Fuller's London Pride, Adnams Broadside and Young's IPA, plus such guests as Gale's HSB. Apart from Sunday roasts, lunch menus offer basic pub grub, but more adventurous evening fare might include local game in season. Eight wines come by the glass. There is a large walled garden, and children are welcome. Seven letting rooms.
Open *11 to 11*

BAKEWELL

Derbyshire   map 9

Peacock Hotel

Bridge Street, Bakewell DE45 1DS
TEL: (01629) 812994

This stone-built pub facing the square on Bridge Street hums along very nicely thank you, with standards like Cumberland sausage or deep-fried cod, chips and mushy peas pulling in the lunchtime crowd, while evening menus and specials are more ambitious. Beers extend into real ale territory with guests such as Greene King Abbot Ale, Black Sheep Bitter and Marston's Pedigree. Children are welcome in three of the rooms and the garden.
Open *Mon 10.30 to 11, Tue to Sat 11.30 to 11, Sun 12 to 10.30*

BARBON

Cumbria   map 8

Barbon Inn

Barbon LA6 2LJ
TEL: (01524) 276233

just off A683, 3m N of Kirkby Lonsdale

Seventeenth-century coaches slogged north towards Shap and Penrith, stopping for breath at this peaceful inn. (Now we take the M6, and don't know what we've missed!) Here there is a secluded beer garden, and bar food is available all day – in the evenings the restaurant operates too. Beers include Theakston Best, plus a guest like Dent Aviator or Courage Directors, and three wines (out of 40) come by the glass. Ten guest rooms.
Open *12 to 3, 6 to 11.30*

BARHAM

Suffolk   map 6

Sorrel Horse

Barham IP6 0PG
TEL: (01473) 830327

off A14 at Claydon, 5m N of Ipswich

This pink-washed seventeenth-century building has been an inn since about 1840. It has a spotlessly refurbished and modernised interior with oak beams, an open log fire and a friendly atmosphere. Expect Adnams Bitter, Old Speckled Hen and Boddingtons Bitter, plus competently cooked food, notably the daily blackboard specials. The extensive rear garden with children's play area is a particular attraction, and a converted barn houses eight en suite bedrooms.
Open *Mon to Fri 11 to 3, 5 to 11, Sat 11 to 11, Sun 11 to 10.30*

BARTHOMLEY

Cheshire   map 5

White Lion

Barthomley CW2 5PG
TEL: (01270) 882242

off Alsager road, from M6 junction 16, 4m SE of Crewe

This is a picture-postcard pub: a seventeenth-century black and white timbered building, with thatched roof, diamond-pane windows and a simple, traditional interior. There are quarry-tiled floors with changing levels, heavy (and low!) oak beams, wonky walls, scrubbed tables and benches, crackling log fires, and no piped music. This is a peaceful retreat to enjoy a pint of Burtonwood Bitter or Top Hat, or a guest beer. Simple, good-value lunchtime food.

Open *11.30 to 11 (Thur 5 to 11), Sun 12 to 10.30*

BATH

Bath & N.E. Somerset   map 2

Old Green Tree

12 Green Street, Bath BA1 2JZ
TEL: (01225) 448259

'A lovely old pub that hardly seems to have changed for centuries' was how one fan described this unassuming city-centre hostelry on one of Bath's quainter streets. A 'Dickensian' feel pervades the three tiny wood-panelled rooms. Beer drinkers will appreciate the wonderful array of regularly changing real ales, all in superb condition – typically Otter Ale, Barnstormer from Bath Ales, Wickwar Stout and RCH Pitchfork among them. Food includes traditional things like bangers and mash and shepherd's pie, and some more unusual ideas like roasted vegetable and Brie risotto, and asparagus and smoked Cheddar pancakes.

Open *Mon to Sat 11 to 11, Sun 12 to 10.30*

BEADLAM

North Yorkshire   map 9

White Horse

Main Street, Beadlam YO62 7SU
TEL: (01439) 771500

3m E of Helmsley on A170 towards Scarborough, pub is on left on main road

Originally a coaching inn, although now it would seem rather scaled down, the White Horse is an honest village pub with unprepossessing décor. But the food is in a different league, relying on good-quality fresh ingredients – especially for fish specials such as freshwater trout with almonds and butter. Beers are John Smith's and Theakston.

Open *11 to 3, 6.30 to 11, Sun 12 to 10.30*

BECKLEY

Oxfordshire   map 2

Abingdon Arms

High Street, Beckley OX3 9UU
TEL: (01865) 351311

off B4027, 5m NE of Oxford

Brakspear Bitter and Special along with seasonal ales are on draught at this traditional village pub with open fireplaces and a curious old cider flagon outside the main door, which operates a bell. The menu, under new licensees, is more modern but equally imaginative; among the specials might be braised lamb shank, Vietnamese yellow chicken curry and fish stew (scallops, mussels and salmon) along with steak and bangers and mash. Reports please.

Open *11 to 3, 6 to 11, Sun 12 to 10.30*

BEER

Devon   map 2

Anchor

Beer EX12 3ET
TEL: (01297) 20386

off A3052 Sidmouth to Lyme Regis road, adjacent to Seaton on B3174

Set around its cove, Beer is idyllic. Although its name has nothing to do with brewing (it means 'place by the grove'), the village was connected with strong waters – via smugglers. Was this neat-looking, colour-washed, freshly redecorated pub, overlooking the harbour and beach, involved? At any rate, given the setting, it is no surprise that the menu focuses largely, though not exclusively, on local seafood. Courage Best, Otter and Directors are on draught, and there are 16 wines by the glass.

Open *11 to 11, Sun 12 to 10.30*

BEMBRIDGE

Isle of Wight   map 2

Crab & Lobster

32 Forelands Field Road, Bembridge PO35 5TR
TEL: (01983) 872244

B3395 to Bembridge, right on to Lane End Road, second right in to Egerton Road and at junction follow brown signs

Brown tourist signs are a useful aid in tracking down this waterside pub, which is away from the village centre, right next to the coastguard's station. Inside, it's a large, open-plan space decked out with black and white photos of village and sea life, and decorated plates, making it seem more tea-room than publike. Crabs and lobsters feature on the printed and blackboard menus, whether in sandwiches or more elaborate dishes. You might also find moules marinière, cream of leek and potato soup, and various other pub staples. Beers include Fuggle-Dee-Dum from local brewery Goddard's.

Open *Mon to Fri 11 to 3, 6 to 11, Sat 11 to 11, Sun 12 to 10.30*

BERKSWELL

West Midlands   map 5

Bear Inn

Spencers Lane, Berkswell CV7 7BB
TEL: (01676) 533202

off A452, 6m W of Coventry

Originally the Bear and Ragged Staff (badge of Warwick the King-Maker), this substantial sixteenth-century building has a Crimean cannon outside the door. Food includes bar snacks such as prawns by the pint, and a long menu whose range extends from sausage with bubble and squeak to half a duck with honey and ginger. Theakston Best Bitter and Courage Directors are joined by guest ales like Everards Equinox or Exmoor Gold. All 16 bottles on the wine list are offered by two sizes of glass.

Open *11 to 11, Sun 12 to 10.30*

BERRYNARBOR

Devon   map 1

Ye Olde Globe

Berrynarbor EX34 9SG
TEL: (01271) 882465

off A399, 4m E of Ilfracombe

First licensed in 1675, this converted row of ancient cottages probably dates from about 400 years earlier. The inside is full of antiques and curios. Children enjoy a special menu, the garden and play area, and a large family room with a climbing frame. For adult eaters there's a long list of pub

standards. On tap is St Austell Dartmoor Best Bitter, plus a guest ale. There are ten wines by the glass.

Open *11.30 to 2.30, 7 (6 summer) to 11, Sun 12 to 2.30, 7 to 10.30*

BETCHWORTH

Surrey   map 3

Dolphin

The Street, Betchworth RH3 7DW
TEL: (01737) 842288

off A25, 2m W of Reigate, in centre of Betchworth

This substantial early-seventeenth-century pub is just across the road from a fully functioning blacksmith's forge. It is a Young's house, and so serves their Bitter, Special, and the seasonal Winter Warmer (from October to March), along with 12 wines by the glass. Traditional pub food takes in sausages, steak and mushroom pie, and chicken curry.

Open *11 to 3.30, 5.30 to 11, Sat 11 to 11, Sun 12 to 10.30*

BEWDLEY

Worcestershire   map 5

Little Packhorse

31 High Street, Bewdley DY12 2DH
TEL: (01299) 403762

3m W of Kidderminster

This started as a fifteenth-century transport caff, catering to packmen and carriers. Now, white, with darker-painted windows, it is an atmospheric and oddly eccentric drinkers' pub. The tiny interior is adorned with everything from old clocks and advertising signs to fascinating tools. It serves Greene King IPA on draught and a guest, perhaps Hook Norton or Bombardier. Hearty and traditional food includes Desperate Dan cow (i.e. steak and ale) pie – is that why the Bewdley and District Mountaineering Club meets here?

Open *Mon to Fri 12 to 3, 6 to 11, Sat 12 to 11, Sun 12 to 10.30*

BILBROUGH

North Yorkshire   map 9

Three Hares

Main Street, Bilbrough YO23 3PH
TEL: (01937) 832128

off A64, between Tadcaster and York

Thomas Fairfax, the Parliamentary
general in the Civil War, is buried in
the churchyard in Bilbrough, a village
just on the outskirts of York. The
former coaching inn's proximity to the
city makes it appropriate for the York
Brewery to be one of the suppliers of
the guest ales, the regulars being Black
Sheep Best Bitter and Timothy Taylor
Landlord. Some modish ideas show up
on the daily-changing menu, from
main courses of guinea-fowl sausages
on mash, or duck confit with Puy
lentils and chorizo, to honey and
lemon parfait; there's normally a range
of fish dishes, and there's always a
steak for the die-hards. Ten wines by
the glass.

Open *Tue to Sat 12 to 3, 7 to 11, Sun 12 to 3*

BIRMINGHAM

West Midlands   map 5

Old Joint Stock

4 Temple Row West, Birmingham B2 5NY
TEL: (0121) 200 1892

This Fuller's Ale & Pie House is in
impressive premises. Reasonably grand
on the outside, set on a pretty square
opposite the cathedral, the impact on
entering is immediate: a vast space
dominated by a big domed skylight.
Everything is on a large scale, from
huge windows and imposing
chandeliers to the paintings on the
walls. The usual range of Fuller's beers
is available, and the printed menu is
backed up by daily specials: perhaps
roasted monkfish on rocket mash with
bacon and chive cream.

Open *Mon to Sat 11 to 11*

Prince of Wales

84 Cambridge Street, Birmingham B1 2NP
TEL: (0121) 643 9460

The tower blocks opposite this
Victorian pub do not create the ideal
setting, although it is only a short walk
to the canal and the modern Brindley
Place development of shops,
restaurants and bars. Once inside,
however, the traditional-looking pub
remains delightfully unaffected by the
progress that has surrounded it. Dark-
panelled walls, banquettes and old
sepia photographs set the tone – there
are even some Shakespearean quotes
on the walls to set you thinking. On
tap are Greene King Abbot Ale, Wells
Bombardier, Adnams Broadside,
Brains SA, Marston's Pedigree, Ansells
(bitter and mild) and Tetley, so there is
no shortage of inspiration. Food is
available.

Open *Mon to Sat 12 to 11, Sun 12 to 10.30*

Tap & Spile

10–15 Gas Street, Birmingham B1 2JT
TEL: (0121) 632 5602

This atmospheric canalside pub is
close to Brindley Place and is where to
head if you want a taste of the old
world. Enter at ground level from Gas
Street, or directly from the towpath
below, into a series of rooms with
stripped floors, exposed bricks, and
pictures of how the area looked in its
industrial heyday. Five ales were
available from the eight handpumps
during our visit: Old Speckled Hen,
Adnams Best, Courage Directors, Bass
and Marston's Pedigree. Food from
the long menu is standard hearty pub
food.

Open *all week 12 to 11 (12 Fri and Sat,
10.30 Sun)*

BLAISDON

Gloucestershire   map 5

Red Hart Inn

Blaisdon GL17 0AH
TEL: (01452) 830477

off A4136, 2m from Huntley

An attractive garden is one of the
attractions of this sixteenth-century
pub in a village on the edge of the
Forest of Dean. Another is the good
line-up of real ales, with Hook Norton
Best and Tetley's cask joined by three
guests from local breweries, perhaps
Wickwar, Uley, Bath Ales or Goff's.
The traditional bar menu is supported
by a specials board, and there is a
separate restaurant.

Open *11.30 to 2.30, 6 to 11.30, Sun 12 to 3,
7 to 11*

BLETCHINGLEY

Surrey   map 3

William IV

Little Common Lane, Bletchingley
RH1 4QF
TEL: (01883) 743278

This brick and tile inn is in a leafy
Surrey byway and has an appealing
garden. Built as a pair of cottages in
the nineteenth century, it has now
been converted into one large space
where among the four handpumped
real ales might be Adnams Bitter,
Fuller's London Pride and Harveys
Sussex Best Bitter, and around half a
dozen wines are available by the glass.
Friday is fish day; otherwise expect the
likes of pan-fried fillet steak with a
creamy brandy sauce. Food uses local
produce and is served all day on
Sunday.
Open *12 to 3, 6 to 11, Sun 12 to 10.30*

BLICKLING

Norfolk   map 6

Buckinghamshire Arms

Blickling NR11 6NF
TEL: (01263) 732133
off B1354, from A140, 2m NW of Aylsham

This elegant inn was built in 1693 to
accommodate the servants and horses
of guests visiting Lord Buckingham at
Blickling Hall (NT), by whose gates it
sits. It serves beers from Adnams and
Woodforde's of Woodbastwick, further
down the Bure, and the blackboard
lists unpretentious, well-cooked
dishes, including locally reputed
Betty's steak and kidney pie, and ample
vegetarian options (there is also a
separate evening restaurant menu).
The friendly and attentive service has
been praised. Three en suite rooms
available.
Open *11 to 3, 6 to 11 (open 11 to 11 some days
in summer)*

BODICOTE

Oxfordshire   map 5

Plough

Bodicote OX15 4BZ
TEL: (01295) 262327
just off A4260, 2m S of Banbury

Since 1957 this welcoming, two-
roomed village pub has been presided
over by the Blencowe family, who
have been brewing beer on the
premises since 1982. The range
includes Bitter, No. 9 and Life
Sentence, plus more powerful winter
ales like Triple X and Old English
Porter. Food runs from sandwiches
and filled baguettes to roasts, casseroles
and steaks. Children are welcome in
the eating area only.
Open *11 to 3, 6 to 11, Sun 12 to 3, 7 to 10.30*

BOLLINGTON

Cheshire   map 8

Poachers

Bollington SK10 5RE
TEL: (01625) 572086
*A523 N towards Stockport, turn right B5091
to Bollington, in village turn left Wellington
Road, right Palmerston Street, straight over,
pub 200yds on right*

An attractive pub on the edge of the
Peak District, a short drive from
Macclesfield. The inside hasn't been
tarted up but is welcoming, with a
real fire and a friendly atmosphere.
Most of the clientele are locals.
Menus are generally traditional in
nature – expect the likes of peppered
duck and steaks – but feature decent
home cooking. Vegetarian Kiev in
mushroom sauce impressed a non-
meat eater, and mustard-roasted rump
of local lamb with creamy mash in
rich wine gravy has also been enjoyed.
Timothy Taylor Landlord is the real
ale offered.
Open *Mon 5.30 to 11, Tue to Fri 12 to 2,
5.30 to 11, Sat 12 to 2, 7 to 11, Sun 12 to 2.30,
7 to 10.30*

BOLTER END

Buckinghamshire   map 3

Peacock

Bolter End, Lane End HP14 3LU
TEL: (01494) 881417

on B482 Marlow to Stokenchurch road

The interior of this old-style pub is
rich in character – wooden pews, china
plates, old advertising posters, prints
and photos abound. On draught are
Brakspear Bitter and Fuller's London
Pride, and 12 wines by the glass. For
diners, a few blackboard specials
including lamb shank with red wine
and rosemary supplement the
straightforward printed menu. Reports
please.

Open *12 to 2.30, 6 to 11, Sun 12 to 3*

BOTTOM-OF-THE-OVEN

Cheshire   map 8

Stanley Arms

Bottom-of-the-Oven, Macclesfield Forest
SK11 0AR
TEL: (01260) 252414

*just S of A537, between Buxton and
Macclesfield*

A welcome refuge after an
invigorating walk, this isolated and
beautifully situated pub is close to
Macclesfield Forest, the Peak District
National Park and miles of open
moorland. The rear terrace and garden
afford good views, while the small,
cosy interior with open fires in winter
is the setting for hearty home-made
soups and pies on the traditional pub
menu, or choose from daily specials
and the restaurant à la carte. Marston's
Bitter and Pedigree are on tap, and
children are welcome in the lounge
bar until 7pm.

Open *Mon to Fri 12 to 2.30, 5.30 to 11,
Sat 12 to 11, Sun 12 to 10.30*

BOWNESS-ON-WINDERMERE

Cumbria   map 9

Hole in't Wall

Lowside, Bowness-on-Windermere
LA23 3DH
TEL: (01539) 443488

on A5074, on E shore of Lake Windermere

Good Robinson's ales such as Hartleys
XB and Robinson's Best are served at
this unspoilt tavern, in the old part of
the town, where champion wrestler
Will Longmire was landlord during the
1800s and Charles Dickens visited; it
can get very busy, especially in the
tourist season. Full of interest and
character, with a lively and chatty
atmosphere, the rambling series of
rooms are crammed with artefacts and
curios, including old farming
implements, chamber pots, stuffed
animals and old pictures. Bar food –
perhaps roasted pheasant – is chalked
up on a blackboard.

Open *11 to 11, Sun 12 to 10.30*

BRADFIELD

South Yorkshire   map 8

Strines Inn

Mortimer Road, Bradfield S6 6JE
TEL: (0114) 285 1247

*2m off A57 (not in village), 6m NW of
Sheffield*

Although most of the present building
dates from the mid-sixteenth century,
it originated as a manor house in 1275.
Marston's Pedigree, Banks's Bitter,
Old Speckled Hen and guest ales such
as Kelham Island Pale Rider are on
draught, and four wines are sold by
the glass. The menu features grills,
pies and pasta, plus blackboard
specials. Children will enjoy the play
area in the garden and the visitor-
friendly animals. As well as three
rooms with four-posters,
accommodation includes a family
room and a holiday cottage: the pub is
in the Peak District National Park
overlooking Strines Reservoir
('strines' means 'meeting of the
waters').

Open *winter 10.30 to 3, 5.30 to 11 (10.30
Sun); summer 10.30 to 11 (10.30 Sun)*

BRANCASTER STAITHE

Norfolk   map 6

Jolly Sailors

Main Road, Brancaster Staithe PE31 8BJ
TEL: (01485) 210314

*on A149, between Hunstanton and Wells-
next-the-Sea*

A whitewashed pub on the main road
through the village, the Jolly Sailors
has a pleasant garden and several small,

cosy interconnecting rooms warmed
by real fires. Star attraction is the
selection of draught real ales, which
include local Woodforde's Wherry and
Iceni Fine Soft Day as well as Adnams
Bitter and Whin Hill Norfolk cider.
Wine drinkers are reasonably well
served too. The menus offer simple
pub cooking along the lines of king
prawns in garlic butter, sausages with
mash and onion gravy, and garlic and
rosemary lamb steak, with treacle
sponge or fruits of the forest
cheesecake for dessert.
Open *11 to 11, Sun 12 to 10.30; 25 Dec 12 to
3 (no food); 26 Dec 12 to 6*

BREDON

Worcestershire   map 5

Fox and Hounds
Church Street, Bredon GL20 7LA
Tel: (01684) 772377
*from M5 junction 9, follow signs to
Tewkesbury then take B480 to Bredon*

The large, open-plan bar is geared up
for eating at this village inn – expect
daily fish dishes, game in season, and
Caribbean-style chicken breast with
ham and banana in a mild curry sauce,
or braised lamb shoulder with mint
and rosemary gravy. Should you want
a pint of real ale, there are Banks's,
Marston's Pedigree and Old Speckled
Hen to choose from. Eight wines are
served by the glass.
Open *11 to 3, 6.30 to 11, Sun 12 to 3, 6.30 to
10.30*

BRETFORTON

Worcestershire   map 5

Fleece Inn
The Cross, Bretforton WR11 5SE
Tel: (01386) 831173
on B4035, 4m E of Evesham

This striking black and white building,
with a stone-tiled roof, dates from the
early fourteenth century and was a
farmhouse until 1848 (when it became
an inn), and was bequeathed to the
National Trust in 1977. Rare and
valuable antiques and collections of
pewter and Victorian measures grace
the entirely original interior, divided
into the Brewhouse, the Dugout
(originally the pantry; the coffin-

shaped table was used to prove dough)
and the Pewter Room. This is also a
drinker's paradise, offering Uley Pig's
Ear Strong Beer, Ansells Best Bitter
and Hook Norton Best Bitter plus two
guests and Weston's Old Rosie cider
on draught, and a range of 20 fruit
wines and 12 wines by the glass. An
asparagus auction is held in early
summer and a Morris Dancing festival
in July. The kitchen uses fresh local
produce whenever possible and makes
a point of reviving traditional recipes.
Children are welcome.
Open *Mon to Fri 11 to 3, 6 to 11,
Sat 11 to 11, Sun 12 to 10.30*

BRIGHTON

East Sussex   map 3

Evening Star
55–56 Surrey Street, Brighton BN1 3PB
Tel: (01273) 328931

The Dark Star Brewery Co started off
in this pub close to the station, and
moved the brewing operation to the
Sussex village of Ansty in 2001 to
enable an increase in output. Beer is
the thing – of course – although there
is also free live music (Sundays, more
often than not) and food is currently
served at lunch only between 12 and 3.
The range of Dark Star ales, perhaps
Hophead, Critical Mass, or Landlords
Wit, are joined by such as Everards
Sunchaser, or Crouch Vale Brewers
Gold. The nine handpumps also
include two real ciders or perries.
Open *all week 12 (11.30 Sat) to 11,
Sun 12 to 10.30*

Greys
105 Southover Street, Brighton BN2 2UA
Tel: (01273) 680734

In the Hanover residential district of
the city, the Greys is a Brighton
institution. The corner location looks
unassuming, and inside the part-
flagged, part-boarded floors and
nicotine-coloured walls demonstrate
that the casual, relaxed informality
extends to the décor. Music is as
much a draw as drinks and food, and
the single room gets crowded
(particularly when there are musicians
on the go – Sunday from 8pm and
Monday from 8.30pm). Three real

ales might include Bests from Harveys and Ringwood, and a list of Belgian beers is worth exploring. Food from the French-focused menu is available 12 to 12.30 Tuesday to Sunday and 6 to 9.30 Tuesday through to Saturday.

Open *Mon 5.30 to 11, Tue to Thur 11 to 3.30, 5.30 to 11, Fri and Sat 11 to 11, Sun 12 to 4, 7 to 10.30*

BRINDLE

Lancashire   map 8

Cavendish Arms
Sandy Lane, Brindle PR6 8NG
TEL: (01254) 852912

on B5256 between Leyland and Blackburn
Bar food is served both at lunchtime and in the evening at this seventeenth-century inn, while the separate restaurant is open in the evening (5.30 to 9.30). The pub is in a peaceful village, beside the parish church, just a few miles from the Leeds and Liverpool Canal and the sprawl of Blackburn. The garden and small terrace are popular in summer and make the most of the pub's position. Inside, modern stained glass depicts medieval scenes. Burtonwood ales and a guest – perhaps Caledonian 80/- or Thwaites Lancaster Bomber – are on handpump, and a couple of wines come by the glass.

Open *Mon to Fri 12 to 3, 5 to 11, Sat 12 to 11, Sun 12 to 10.30*

BRISTOL

Bristol   map 2

Brewery Tap
6–10 Colston Street, Bristol BS1 5BD
TEL: (0117) 921 3668

Smiles is the brewery in question, and the works can be glimpsed at the back of this small, well-maintained pub set back from a busy road and opposite the children's hospital. The pub consists of two small rooms, the first with a black and white tiled floor and a tiny panelled bar, the second with a wooden floor and blood-red walls. The latter is non-smoking and contains a modern interpretation of a snug: a boxroom with mirrors and upholstered banquettes. The pub

successfully manages to maintain a traditional feel but has high-quality fixtures and fittings (well-designed solid wooden tables, for example) that create a vibrant environment. It is the ideal venue for sampling the range of Smiles ales. Food consists of soup and sandwiches, steak and kidney pie, beef chilli and tortilla wraps.

Open *11 to 11, Sun 12 to 4, 7 to 10.30*

Cornubia
142 Temple Street, Bristol BS1 6EN
TEL: (0117) 925 4415

The city has grown up around this old pub close to the station surrounded by large office blocks. 'Circa 1775' declares the sign on the wall, and it can't have changed one iota. The bow window is every inch the Old Curiosity Shop, and the interior is as small and basic as can be. The business is ale, as the many beer mats stuck to the walls testify, with four on tap the day of our visit and a list of those coming soon to whet the appetite. Goff's Black Knight, Oakham Old Tosspot, Butts Jester and Crouch Vale are what you might expect to find, plus a short menu should food be required, and a blackboard of malt whiskies. No children.

Open *Mon to Fri 12 to 11, Sat 5.30 to 11 only*

Old Fish Market
59–63 Baldwin Street, Bristol BS1 1QZ
TEL: (0117) 921 1515

The centrally located Old Fish Market is a fine example of a large urban tavern and makes an ideal escape for the reluctant shopper (it is in the main shopping area). The interior has a full checklist of Victoriana: large chandeliers, an impressive carved bar, walls covered in prints and oil paintings, even a handsome tiled lavatory. This Fuller's Ale & Pie House offers a wide range of beers, plus Smiles Best, and a traditional menu of well-prepared pub dishes, including fish pie, liver and bacon, and beer-battered cod with mushy peas. Over a dozen wines are available in two glass sizes.

Open *12 to 11, Sun 12 to 10.30*

BROAD CAMPDEN

Gloucestershire　　map 5

Bakers Arms

Broad Campden GL55 6UR
TEL: (01386) 840515

off B4081, 1m SE of Chipping Campden

At this creeper-streaked Cotswold-stone pub in north Gloucestershire they go in for real ales, five at a time. Generally these are three local and two national beers: perhaps Hook Norton Best, Donnington SBA, Stanway Stanney Bitter, Wells Bombardier and Timothy Taylor Landlord. Sandwiches, ploughman's and smoked haddock bake feature at lunchtimes; otherwise the menu runs to dishes like pan-fried duck, and vegetarians are not forgotten.

Open *Mon to Fri 11.30 to 2.30, 4.45 to 11, Sat 11.30 to 11, Sun 12 to 10.30; summer 11.30 to 11, Sun 12 to 10.30; closed 25 and 26 Dec, eve 31 Dec*

BROADWAY

Worcestershire　　map 5

Crown and Trumpet

Church Street, Broadway WR12 7AE
TEL: (01386) 853202

off High Street (A44), on Snowshill Road

Broadway is a charming village, one of the most popular beauty spots in the Cotswolds. The Crown and Trumpet fits in well, as it was built of local stone in the seventeenth century. On draught are up to five ales, among them Hook Norton Old Hooky, Old Speckled Hen, and Lords-a-Leaping from the Stanway Brewery in Cheltenham, and five wines are served by the glass. Food is in traditional English vein, with pies a speciality of the pub.

Open *Mon to Fri 11 to 3, 5 to 11 (summer 11 to 11 Fri), Sat 11 to 11, Sun 12 to 10.30*

BROCKHAM

Surrey　　map 3

Royal Oak

Brockham Green, Brockham RH3 7JS
TEL: (01737) 843241

just off A25, 2m E of Dorking

The Royal Oak is a popular destination in summer, with a children's play area in the garden and its attractive location on the village green making it ideal for families. Other factors that draw people here are all-day opening at weekends, eight wines by the glass, two ales from Harveys, plus Fuller's London Pride and two guests, and a straightforward bar menu that deals in chilli con carne, Cumberland sausage, steak and kidney pie and so forth, with daily specials on a board.

Open *Mon to Thur 11 to 3, 5.30 to 11, Fri and Sat 11 to 11, Sun 12 to 10.30*

BROOKLAND

Kent　　map 3

Woolpack

Brookland TN29 9TJ
TEL: (01797) 344321

just off A259, 5m W of New Romney

The large beer garden pulls in families to this atmospheric fifteenth-century pub in summer, and in winter the capacious inglenook in the beamed bar is part of the attraction. On draught are Shepherd Neame Master Brew Bitter and Spitfire Premium Ale, and steaks, pies and daily specials, including game in season, are listed on the menus.

Open *Mon to Fri 11 to 3, 6 to 11, Sat 11 to 11, Sun 12 to 10.30*

BROOM

Bedfordshire　　map 6

Cock

23 High Street, Broom SG18 9NA
TEL: (01767) 314411

on B658, 2m SW of Biggleswade

Unusually, the Cock has no bar counter; instead, Greene King ales are stored by the steps leading to the cellar. Three centuries have done little to change the pub's four snug rooms, with log fires, low ceilings and tiled floors. Bar food is along the lines of cottage pie, and steak and mushroom casserole.

Open *Mon to Fri 12 to 3, 6 to 11, Sat 12 to 4, 6 to 11, Sun 12 to 4, 7 to 10.30*

BUCKDEN

North Yorkshire   map 8

Buck Inn

Buckden, Upper Wharfedale BD23 5JA
Tel: (01756) 760228
on B6160, between Kettleworth and West Burton

Picnic tables at the front of this part-creeper-covered grey-stone Georgian coaching inn have lovely views across to the western slopes of Wharfedale, which in summer can get very busy with walkers. The open-plan interior comprises a flagstone bar plus two spacious carpeted areas; above the fireplace is a large buck's head. Food includes haggis and black pudding, a trio of local sausages or medallions of beef fillet, while beers run to Black Sheep and Timothy Taylor Landlord with nine wines by the glass. A new owner arrived in spring 2003; reports please.
Open *11 to 11, Sun 12 to 10.30*

BUCKLERS HARD

Hampshire   map 2

Master Builder's House Hotel

Bucklers Hard SO42 7XB
Tel: (01590) 616253
off B3054, just S of Beaulieu

As its name suggests, this comfortably renovated eighteenth-century hotel was at one time the home of a master shipbuilder. It's on the bank of the Beaulieu River, in a fascinating preserved shipbuilding village, and the beamed and rustic Yachtsman's Bar is popular with boatmen and tourists alike, offering welcome respite from the summer crowds in the village. Courage ales are on tap, and snacks and a limited evening menu operate in the bar. There's a separate upmarket restaurant.
Open *Mon to Sat 11 to 11, Sun 12 to 10.30*

BURCOT

Oxfordshire   map 2

Chequers

Burcot OX14 3DP
Tel: (01865) 407771
on A415, 4½m E of Abingdon

This thatched village pub has a terrace with seating, and inside are beams and an open fire. On draught are Brakspear Bitter and Wychwood Fiddler's Elbow plus a guest ale, perhaps from Hook Norton, and four wines, plus a couple of monthly specials, are served by the glass. Food ranges from standard pub offerings to a number of changing specials.
Open *11 to 2.30, 6 to 11, Sun 12 to 3, 7 to 11*

BURITON

Hampshire   map 2

Five Bells

High Street, Buriton GU31 5RX
Tel: (01730) 263584
off A3, 1m S of Petersfield

The pub gets its name from the bells of the village church. It was built in 1639, and at one time part of the building housed a farrier's. It retains its rambling sequence of rooms, heated by open fires and wood-burning stoves. Badger Best and Tanglefoot, Gribble Inn Fursty Ferret and King & Barnes Sussex are the regular ales on draught, and eight wines are served by the glass. Game is no stranger to the menu, perhaps in the form of game pie or rabbit; otherwise there might be chicken, chipolata and bacon pie, or sea bass, with gardener's pie (similar to shepherd's pie but made with vegetables) among a good choice of vegetarian dishes.
Open *11 to 2.30, 5.30 to 11, Sun 12 to 3, 7 to 10.30*

BURNHAM THORPE

Norfolk   map 6

Lord Nelson

Walsingham Road, Burnham Thorpe
PE31 8HN
Tel: (01328) 738241
off A149/B1155/B1355, 2m S of Burnham Market

A new licensee (who has brought in a new chef) took over this charming old inn, which is hidden away down a maze of country lanes, in summer 2003, and tells the Guide he plans to carry on in much the same vein as his predecessor. Inside, quarry-tiled floors, open fireplaces and old scrubbed pine furniture give it a feel of 'untouched rusticity'. Excellent, imaginative food has been a tradition here, so reports on the new chef's output would be especially welcome. This is a Greene King pub, with Abbot Ale and IPA on offer plus guests such as Woodforde's Wherry and Nelson's Revenge; as there is no bar, all beers are dispensed straight from the cask, and nine wines are served by the glass.

Open *11 to 2.30 (3 summer), 6 to 11, Sun 12 to 3, 6.30 to 10.30*

BUTTERTON

Staffordshire   map 5

Black Lion Inn

Butterton ST13 7SP
TEL: (01538) 304232
just off B5053, 6m E of Leek

Butterton is a small, remote village in the middle of the Peak District, the kind of place that is popular with walkers, and at the centre of the village, opposite the church, is this cottage-like old stone inn. Inside is a maze of small rooms, decorated with brewers' badges and with tankards hanging from the ceiling beams. The regular menu offers things like steak and ale pie, or cod and prawn crumble, while blackboard specials have featured sea bass steak and red snapper with lemon caper sauce. A good selection of real ales might include Everards Tiger, and Theakston Mild and Best.

Open *Tue to Sun 12 to 2.30 (3 Sat and Sun), all week 7 to 11 (10.30 Sun)*

BYWORTH

West Sussex   map 3

Black Horse

Byworth GU28 0HL
TEL: (01798) 342424
off A283, just S of Petworth

A large garden with lovely views over the South Downs is an attraction at this unspoilt, traditional country pub.

The three regularly changing ales may be from the Arundel or Itchen Valley Breweries, and on the daily-changing menu may be crab cakes, roast pheasant with Calvados, and lemon syllabub or chocolate lumpy bumpy.

Open *11 to 11, Sun 12 to 10.30*

Welldiggers Arms

Byworth GU28 0HG
TEL: (01798) 342287

In the same family for decades and 'untouched by fashion', this characterful, rustic-looking pub on a country lane enjoys impressive views of the surrounding South Downs. While the bar is the hub of the place, often thronged with drinkers supping Young's Bitter, there is also an assortment of trestle tables and benches. Fish and game in season are the food specialities, but the blackboard menus may also include hearty things such as 'poacher's pot', oxtail casserole, deep-fried cod, and chicken curry. Prices are somewhat above average for pub food.

Open *Tue to Sat 11 to 3, Sun 12 to 3, Thur to Sat 6 to 11; closed 25 and 26 Dec*

CAMBRIDGE

Cambridgeshire   map 6

Clarendon Arms

35 Clarendon Street, Cambridge CB1 1JX
TEL: (01223) 313937

A cosy, friendly pub within easy reach of the city centre, the Clarendon Arms has a relaxed, unpretentious atmosphere and a welcoming landlord. The tiny bar is L-shaped, with two distinct areas, one for eating, the other for drinking. Hearty lunchtime sandwiches have been recommended, and if you eat from the main menu you can anticipate large portions and rock-bottom prices. Chicken liver pâté, cream of mushroom soup, spicy chilli con carne, and Cajun chicken with roast vegetables are the sorts of things to expect. Real ales are from Greene King. B&B accommodation is available.

Open *11 to 11, Sun 12 to 10.30*

Free Press

7 Prospect Row, Cambridge CB1 1DU
TEL: (01223) 368337

An atmospheric Greene King pub, tucked away down a side street about five minutes from the city centre, with a good choice of drinks and good-value food served in large portions. Blackboard menus typically list spinach and ricotta tortellini, minted lamb shank with mash, fish and chips, and Indian chicken with rice. Walls are covered in assorted bits and pieces ranging from coins and cinema tickets to cricketing memorabilia and old newspaper cuttings. Current newspapers are also provided, and pub games such as dominoes are played here too. Smoking and mobile phones are banned.

Open *12 to 2 (2.30 Sat), 6 to 11, Sun 12 to 2.30, 7 to 10.30*

CARDINGTON

Shropshire   map 5

Royal Oak

Cardington SY6 7JZ
TEL: (01694) 771266

off B4371, 4m E of Church Stretton

Hobsons Best Bitter, Bass and a couple of guests, including perhaps Champflower Ale from the Cottage Brewing Company in Somerset, are on draught at this 500-year-old inn not far from Wenlock Edge. A choice of baguettes is on offer at lunchtimes, while main courses could run to game in season – venison, pheasant in bacon, or pigeon pie – with sea bass among fish dishes.

Open *Tue to Sun and bank hol Mon 12 to 2.30, 7 (6 Fri) to 11 (10.30 Sun)*

CAREY

Herefordshire   map 5

Cottage of Content

Carey HR2 6NG
TEL: (01432) 840242

between A49 and B4224, 6m SE of Hereford

Oak beams, open fires, ancient settles and farmhouse tables in the tiny bars add to the old-world charm of this 500-year-old pub in a remote rural setting near the River Wye. The

standard bar menu is extended by specials, and two vegetarian dishes are always available, and game and fish make an appearance. The Wye Valley and Hook Norton Breweries provide the beers, and around a dozen wines are served by the glass. Two ciders, perry and 40 malt whiskies are also stocked. Note that accommodation is no longer provided.

Open *12 to 3, 7 (6 Sat) to 11, Sun 12 to 3, 7 to 10.30; closed Mon winter*

CASTLE HEDINGHAM

Essex   map 3

Bell

10 St James Street, Castle Hedingham CO9 3EJ
TEL: (01787) 460350

off B1058, 4m NW of Halstead

The Bell was built in the sixteenth century of wattle-and-daub construction, some of which has been uncovered, and the series of linked small rooms inside has retained some of the character of times past. The pub still follows a no-chips policy, instead concentrating on fish: take your pick from calamari, mussels, salmon, sea bass, or swordfish, with barbecued fish every Monday evening. Greene King IPA and Adnams Bitter are joined by two guests – perhaps Old Speckled Hen and something from the Mighty Oak Brewing Company. Live music is a regular feature here.

Open *Mon to Thur and Sat 11.30 to 3.30, 6 to 11, Fri 11.30 to 11, Sun 12 to 3.30, 7 to 10.30*

CAULDON

Staffordshire   map 5

Yew Tree

Cauldon, nr Waterhouses ST10 3EJ
TEL: (01538) 308348

off A523 Leek to Ashbourne road at Waterhouses, 6m NE of Cheadle

'A one-off atmospheric gem,' thought our inspector. Part pub, part museum, it is worth visiting just to witness for yourself the incredible treasure trove of Victorian memorabilia, ranging from penny-farthing bikes to grandfather clocks, plus an assortment of swords, guns and spears hanging from the beams. It is popular with a

regular crowd of drinkers and darts players, who appreciate the well-kept Burton Bridge Bitter. This is not really a diner's pub but bar snacks are available most of the time – pies, sandwiches, salads and so on.
Open *10 to 2.30, 6 to 11, Sun 12 to 3, 7 to 10.30*

CAVENDISH BRIDGE

Leicestershire   map 5
Old Crown
Cavendish Bridge, nr Shardlow DE72 2HL
TEL: (01332) 792392
take A50 from M1 junction 24, turn off for Long Eaton and head for Shardlow
Bass, Marston's Pedigree, Fuller's London Pride, Tower Bitter and Everards Tiger Best are among the real ales on draught at this characterful pub in a tiny village near the River Trent. Food is served at lunchtimes only and might include salmon and prawn platter, followed by lamb in red wine, garlic and rosemary, and ending with a home-made fruit crumble. Five wines by the glass. Two letting rooms available.
Open *11.30 to 3, 5 to 11; bar food 12 to 2 (3.30 Sun); closed eve 25 and 26 Dec and 1 Jan*

CERNE ABBAS

Dorset   map 2
New Inn
14 Long Street, Cerne Abbas DT2 7JF
TEL: (01300) 341274
on A352, 7m N of Dorchester
The New Inn is a popular stopping-off point for visitors to the huge chalk figure of the Cerne Abbas Giant. The sixteenth-century inn, with its own walled orchard, offers traditional pub food, say, home-made garlic mushrooms or leek and potato soup, and then roasted lamb shank, fillet steak and Stilton and walnut pie. Draught Flowers IPA, Wadworth 6X and a guest ale, plus eight wines by the glass. Accommodation is also available.
Open *winter Mon to Fri 11 to 2.30, 6 to 11, Sat 11 to 11, Sun 11.45 to 2.30, 6 to 10.30; summer 11 to 11 (10.30 Sun)*

CHACOMBE

Northamptonshire   map 5
George & Dragon
Silver Street, Chacombe OX17 2JR
TEL: (01295) 711500
off A361, just N of M40 junction 11
This is a friendly sixteenth-century sandstone inn with interior to match: low beams, flagged floors and open fires in season. Theakston Best and Courage Directors are on handpump, plus a guest from the likes of Black Sheep or Timothy Taylor; in addition, eight fruit wines are offered alongside the trio of conventional wines served by the glass. The blackboard menu changes every three weeks, but always includes four fish and three vegetarian dishes, and there are sandwiches and stuffed baguettes at lunchtime. Two rooms available.
Open *12 to 11, Sun 12 to 10.30*

CHALE

Isle of Wight   map 2
Wight Mouse Inn
Chale PO38 2HA
TEL: (01983) 730431
on B3399, 5m W of Ventnor
Badger has taken over the Wight Mouse, and some refurbishment was in progress as the Guide went to press, so things were somewhat in a state of flux. But six handpumps dispense Badger's range of ales plus guests, the lists of whiskies and wines have both been pared down, and food continues to be served all day, every day. Reports please.
Open *11 to 11.45, Sun 12 to 10.30*

CHARLTON

Wiltshire   map 2
Horse and Groom
The Street, Charlton SN16 9DL
TEL: (01666) 823904
on B4040 Malmesbury to Cricklade road, 2½m E of Malmesbury
This sixteenth-century hostelry in the comfortable honey-sandstone and pantile vernacular has parasol-shaded tables in front. There's also a garden with picnic tables on the lawn and a wooded area with a giant climbing

frame. Three regular real ales are offered – Wadworth 6X, Archer's Village, Smiles Best – plus a guest (maybe Smiles seasonal Mayfly), and eight wines come by the glass. Food ranges from spinach and mushroom roulade to beef, Stilton and Guinness pie, plus frozen orange soufflé, or blueberry spotted dick to finish. Two bedrooms available.

Open *12 to 3, 7 to 11, Sat 12 to 11, Sun 12 to 10.30*

CHARTHAM HATCH

Kent   map 3

Chapter Arms
New Town Street, Chartham Hatch CT4 7LT
TEL: (01227) 738340
turn off A28 2m S of Canterbury

A new extension has made more room for drinkers at this modern pub in a street of modern houses – and now that it is a freehouse that might mean a pint of Master Brew, London Pride or Adnams, or a glass of wine from the range of around ten. Diners can enjoy substantial bar snacks or adjourn to the softly lit restaurant offering both table d'hôte and à la carte menus. Reports please.

Open *11 to 3, 6.30 to 11, Sun 12 to 3*

CHEDINGTON

Dorset   map 2

Winyard's Gap
Chedington DT8 3HY
TEL: (01935) 891244
off A356, between Crewkerne and Dorchester, at Winyard's Gap

This inn, tucked under an ancient earthwork on a ridge above the source of the Axe, has a stunning view towards the Quantock Hills that inspired Thomas Hardy's poem 'At Winyard's Gap'. You too can see this from the pleasantly modernised bar or the terrace over Wadworth 6X or one of two changing guest ales: maybe the own-label Winyard's Gypsy's Alibi (the pub figured in a steamy eighteenth-century case involving gypsies, prostitution and the Lord Mayor of London). A standard pub menu is

served, with families welcome in a designated dining area.

Open *11 to 2.30, 6.30 to 11, Sun 12 to 2.30, 7 to 10.30; closed eve 25 Dec and 1 Jan*

CHEDWORTH

Gloucestershire   map 5

Seven Tuns
Chedworth GL54 4AE
TEL: (01285) 720242
off A429, 8m N of Cirencester

Roman villas can be thirsty work, but just a step away from Chedworth's is this attractive stone-built inn of 'circa 1690', with a restored water wheel in its walled garden. Smiles IPA and Best, and Young's Bitter and Special are complemented by a guest – maybe Young's Waggle Dance. A dozen wines come by the glass, and food ranges from baguettes and pizzas to reasonably priced, daily-changing dishes like pigeon breast on red cabbage with black pudding and smoked bacon. Children are welcome. Accommodation is planned.

Open *summer 11 to 11, winter 11 to 3, 6 to 11, Sun all year 12 to 3, 7 to 10.30*

CHERITON BISHOP

Devon   map 1

Old Thatch Inn
Cheriton Bishop EX6 6JH
TEL: (01647) 24204
off A30, between Exeter and Okehampton, 7m SW of Crediton

Dark thatch and black window surrounds contrast with white walls to give this substantial sixteenth-century building a piebald look. There's a garden outside and, inside, a beamed bar with a log fire. Regular brews are local – Branscombe Vale (Branoc) and Otter – and the guest may be Palmers from Dorset, or Adnams Broadside from distant Suffolk; six wines come by the glass. A daily-changing menu offers the likes of pan-fried duck breast, and children are welcome in eating areas. Three rooms available.

Open *11.30 to 3, 6 to 11, Sun 12 to 3, 7 to 10.30; closed 25 Dec*

CHESTER

Cheshire   map 7

Union Vaults

Egerton Street, Chester CH1 3ND
Tel: (01244) 400556

Unpretentious local boozer ten
minutes from the city centre, made up
of three knocked-through cottages,
with a 'mellow, lived-in' feel and a
warm welcome for regulars and
visitors alike. The traditional vault is
the heart of the pub, with an energetic
cast of regulars who enjoy their horse
and pigeon racing, and other sports
and games – as well as a large-screen
TV, there are facilities for more-
traditional pub pastimes, including a
rare bagatelle table. Greenalls Bitter
and Plassey Bitter are the regular real
ales, joined by a regularly changing
guest. Food is limited to pub snacks.
Open *11 to 11, Sun 12 to 10.30*

CHIDDINGSTONE

Kent   map 3

Castle Inn

Chiddingstone TN8 7AH
Tel: (01892) 870247

off B2027, 4½m E of Edenbridge
In the centre of a heavily (and
genuinely) half-timbered village, this
imposing edifice of old red bricks
became an inn in 1730. Beers are
Chiddingstone-brewed Larkin's
Traditional (and Porter in winter),
Harveys Best and Young's Bitter, and a
vast wine list offers three by the glass –
not including the Ch. Latour. In
summer you can drink in a pretty
courtyard at the back, or the garden
beyond; in winter use the beamy saloon
bar. There's a restaurant too, but bar
menus list long-standing pub favourites
plus more contemporary dishes.
Open *11 to 11, Sun 12 to 10.30*

CHILMARK

Wiltshire   map 2

Black Dog

Chilmark SP3 5AH
Tel: (01722) 716344

just S of B3089, 10m W of Salisbury
Worth tracking down for its unspoilt
atmosphere, appealing décor, good real
ales and promising food: the Black
Dog is a classic fifteenth-century
stone-built pub. Drink draught Bass,
Hopback GFB or Wadworth 6X in the
main bar, with its black and terracotta
tiled floor, sturdy wooden tables and
large fireplace, or head for the huge
rear garden on warmer days. Children
are welcome in the dining areas and
garden. Menus list dishes such as
warm chicken and bacon salad,
mushroom and chestnut tagliatelle and
fish and chips. Reports please.
Open *12 to 2.30, 6 to 11, Sun 12 to 2.30,
7 to 10.30*

CHURCHILL

N.W. Somerset   map 2

Crown Inn

The Batch, Churchill BS25 5PP
Tel: (01934) 852995

off A368, 3m S of Congresbury
Set beside a track at the base of the
Mendip Hills, this 400-year-old pub
was originally a coaching inn and once
housed the village grocer's and
butcher's shops. Both unspoilt bars
have flagstoned floors, stone walls,
heavy beams and open fires. Five
handpumps dispense regular brews
(Palmers IPA, Hop Back GFB, RCH
Brewery's PG Steam, Bath SPA, plus
Bass), and three more deliver guests –
from Church End, for example.
Traditional pub fare at lunchtime only,
and a delightful walled front terrace for
al fresco drinking.
Open *12 to 11, Sun 12 to 10.30*

CHURCH KNOWLE

Dorset   map 2

New Inn

Church Knowle BH20 5NQ
Tel: (01929) 480357

off A351, 4m S of Wareham
The ambience is pleasantly relaxed at
this sixteenth-century inn, near to
Corfe Castle, with views of the
Purbeck Hills from the garden. Three
interconnecting rooms have open fires
and Turkish carpets, and the long
menu features fresh fish, perhaps sea
bass or black bream, and local produce
like Blue Vinny cheese in a soup. Real
ales kept are Flowers Original,
Wadworth 6X and Old Speckled Hen,

while the wine cellar offers a choice of around 1,000 bottles; ten wines are served by the glass.

Open *11 to 3, 6.30 to 11, Sun 12 to 3, 6.30 to 10.30*

CLIFTON HAMPDEN

Oxfordshire   map 2

Plough Inn

Abingdon Road, Clifton Hampden OX14 3EG
TEL: (01865) 407811
on A415 in Clifton Hampden between Abingdon and Dorchester

Farming implements – among them (of course) a plough – are at the front of this pretty thatched seventeenth-century pub, and inside, low-beamed ceilings, black wooden doors and deep-red tiled floors set the tone. Traditional pub food turns up dishes such as ham, egg and chips, or fillet steak with peppercorn and brandy sauce, or might extend to Thai green chicken curry. To drink are wines from a mainly French list (six by the glass), and for beer drinkers John Smith's and Directors. No smoking throughout pub. Accommodation available. The current licensee has plans to sell, so updates please.

Open *11am to midnight, Sun noon to 10.30*

CONDER GREEN

Lancashire   map 8

Stork Hotel

Conder Green LA2 0AN
TEL: (01524) 751234

This large white-painted sixteenth-century coaching inn is bedecked with window boxes in summer. Situated on the banks of the Conder and Lune estuary, the pub looks out on mudflats with a large bird population – and at very high tides is on the water's edge. Ales include Boddingtons, Timothy Taylor Landlord and various guest beers, and the printed menu is supplemented by blackboard specials: mushroom stroganoff, deep-fried goujons of sole, and liver and onions, for example. Children welcome.

Open *11 to 11, Sun 12 to 10.30*

CONISTON

Cumbria   map 8

Black Bull

1 Yewdale Road, Coniston LA21 8DU
TEL: (015394) 41335 or 41668
off A593, 6m SW of Ambleside

This old coaching inn, built around the time of the Spanish Armada, is now a pub, restaurant and 15-bedroom hotel with its own brewery. Home brews include Old Man ale (the 'big toe' of the Old Man mountain, which overlooks the inn, is a large piece of stone set into the wall of the residents' lounge) and Bluebird Bitter (Donald Campbell used Coniston for his water speed record attempts); plus Opium, Blacksmith's and Premium Bluebird. Guest ales and scrumpy are also available. An extensive range of food is offered, sometimes featuring local fish.

Open *11 to 11, Sun 12 to 10.30*

COOKHAM

Berkshire   map 3

Bel and the Dragon

High Street, Cookham SL6 9SQ
TEL: (01628) 521263
on A4094, off A404 just N of Marlow

Devotees of Cookham artist Stanley Spencer and walkers on the Thames Path will find this fascinating fifteenth-century inn right on their route, opposite the Stanley Spencer Gallery. The door opens on to a warren of well-refurbished, low-ceilinged rooms, ultimately leading to a galleried barn. The apocryphal story that is the source of the intriguing name is the subject of a series of illustrations adorning the bar area and the menu. Food is contemporary British, beers are from Courage, Marston's and Brakspear, and a decent list of wines has ten available by the glass. Children welcome.

Open *11.30 to 11, Sun 12 to 10.30; closed eve 25 and 26 Dec, 1 Jan*

CORFE CASTLE

Dorset   map 2

Fox Inn

West Street, Corfe Castle BH20 5HD
TEL: (01929) 480449

on A351, SE of Wareham

Visitors to this unspoilt village inn will
find the mature, sun-trap rear garden
particularly appealing in summer,
especially as it enjoys fine views of the
dramatic ruined castle. Inside is a very
snug little front bar and a slightly
larger lounge with a thirteenth-century
fireplace and a bustling, often smoky
atmosphere. Enjoy Young's Special,
Greene King Abbot Ale, Wadworth
6X, Fuller's London Pride, Old
Speckled Hen and Burton Ale, all
tapped straight from the cask.
Straightforward pub food. No children
inside.
Open *11 to 2.30 (3 summer), 6.30 to 11,
Sun 12 to 2.30 (3 summer), 7 to 11*

Greyhound Inn

The Square, Corfe Castle BH20 5EZ
TEL: (01929) 480205

on A351 in village centre

The characterful interior of this
sixteenth-century coaching inn, with
low beams, oak panelling, sturdy
furnishings and cosy alcoves, is the
setting for ales such as Timothy Taylor
Landlord, Fuller's London Pride and
Marston's Pedigree. Pub food includes
lamb shank, and fillet of cod with
avocado and prawns. Fine views of the
castle ruins and the Purbeck Hills can
be enjoyed from the rear garden.
Children are welcome and B&B
accommodation is offered.
Open *winter Mon to Fri 11 to 3, 6 to 11,
Sat 11 to 11, Sun 12 to 10.30; summer 11 to 11,
Sun 12 to 10.30*

CORFTON

Shropshire   map 5

Sun Inn

Corfton SY7 9DF
TEL: (01584) 861239

on B4368, 4½m NE of Craven Arms

At the back of this seventeenth-century
pub under Wenlock Edge landlord
Norman Pearce brews his award-
winning Corvedale ales, Norman's

Pride and Secret Hop among them.
These he serves in the two bars and
restaurant along with guest beers and
14 wines by the glass. His wife
Theresa's food includes a large
vegetarian selection. Much extended
over the years, the pub offers good
facilities for the disabled and, for
children, an obstacle course in the
large garden.
Open *12 to 2.30, 6 to 11, Sun 12 to 3, 7
(6 summer) to 10.30; open all day bank hols*

COTTERED

Hertfordshire   map 3

Bull

Cottered SG9 9QP
TEL: (01763) 281243

on A507, between Buntingford and Baldock

This is a Greene King pub, with IPA
and Abbot Ale on draught: part of the
appeal that draws people to this village
hostelry from the surrounding area,
including nearby Stevenage. Two fires
in winter contribute to the warm
atmosphere, and the food is another
attraction: perhaps duck with sweet
chilli sauce, 'piggley' pie (sausage,
bacon and leeks in gravy under a puff
pastry lid), and fish on Tuesdays.
Three wines are available by the glass.
Open *12 to 2.30, 6.30 to 11, Sun 12 to 3,
7 to 10.30*

COTTON

Suffolk   map 6

Trowel & Hammer

Mill Road, Cotton IP14 4QL
TEL: (01449) 781234

6m N of Stowmarket, just off B1113

The village is a maze of lanes heading
in all directions, which makes this not
the easiest pub to find. Once you do
track it down, you will be rewarded
with a fine selection of real ales from
regional breweries like Adnams,
Greene King, Mauldons and
Nethergate. There is also a wide-
ranging menu: expect salad of warm
garlic sausage and Gruyère, deep-fried
Brie with onion marmalade, sautéed
scallops in garlic butter, and pork fillet
en croûte with apple and onion
stuffing, as well as a few more exotic
dishes like onion bhajis and samosas

with mango chutney, or kangaroo fillet with a Madeira and redcurrant reduction.

Open *Mon to Fri 12 to 3, 6 to 11, Sat 12 to 11, Sun 12 to 10.30*

CRANBORNE

Dorset   map 2

Fleur de Lys

5 Wimbourne Street, Cranborne
BH21 5PP
TEL: (01725) 517282
on B3078 in centre of Cranborne

This creeper-covered village inn dates from the sixteenth century. It's a popular place, the cooking contributing to the appeal: perhaps steak and ale pie, rack of lamb, and veal escalope with a white wine and mushroom sauce, with, say, grilled trout, or crumbed prawn Mornay among fish options. Four wines by the glass, as well as well-kept Badger Best Bitter and Tanglefoot, add to the attraction.

Open *11 to 3, 6.30 to 11, Sun 12 to 3, 7 to 10.30*

CRASTER

Northumberland   map 10

Jolly Fisherman

Craster NE66 3TR
TEL: (01665) 576461
off B1339, 6m NE of Alnwick

A white-painted harbourside pub serving food all day during the summer. Seafood features strongly, and the speciality is crab soup with cream and whisky. Also on the menu are various sandwiches and rolls, simple snacks like home-made Craster kipper pâté with toast, and light meals such as potato skins, or a Geordie stottie cake pizza. Beers include Tetley and Marston's.

Open *winter 11 to 3, 6 to 11, Sun 12 to 4, 7 to 10.30; summer 11 to 11, Sun 12 to 10.30*

CRAY

North Yorkshire   map 8

White Lion

Cray BD23 5JB
TEL: (01756) 760262
off B6160, 2m N of Buckden

At 1,000 feet above sea level, this stone-built former drovers' inn is the highest pub in Wharfedale. Nestling beneath Buckden Pike opposite a stream, and surrounded by open moorland and stunning scenery, it is popular with walkers and people out for the day. Moorhouses Premier Bitter and Pendle Witches Brew and Timothy Taylor Landlord are on draught, together with a guest such as No-Eyed Deer from Goose Eye or Blonde from Daleside. Around a dozen wines by the glass complement such culinary experiences as duck breast in red wine and raspberry sauce, loin of lamb with garlic and rosemary, and chicken with cashew nuts and ginger. Eight en suite bedrooms are available.

Open *11 to 11, Sun 12 to 10.30; closed 25 Dec*

CROSCOMBE

Somerset   map 2

Bull Terrier

Croscombe BA5 3QJ
TEL: (01749) 343658
on A371, between Wells and Shepton Mallet

First licensed in 1612, nowadays the Bull Terrier dispenses Winchester's Buckland Best Bitter and three guests – perhaps Adnams Bitter, Ruddles County and Palmers IPA – and four wines by the glass. There are three welcoming bars: the Snug, the Common bar, and the Inglenook. To the rear of the attractive stone-built pub, originally a priory, the elevated garden backs on to the church, which has Jacobean beams, and overlooks the surrounding countryside. An interesting walk leads across fields to the Bishop's Palace at Wells. Accommodation is available.

Open *12 to 2.30, 7 to 11 (10.30 Sun); closed Mon Oct to Mar*

CUMNOR

Oxfordshire   map 2

Vine Inn

11 Abingdon Road, Cumnor OX2 9QN
TEL: (01865) 862567

off A420, 4m W of Oxford

This eighteenth-century vine-covered
inn has a pleasantly relaxed atmosphere
even when it's busy, with comfortable
settees and a fireplace. Wadworth 6X,
Old Speckled Hen, Hook Norton Best
Bitter and Adnams Bitter may be
among the real ales on draught, and six
wines are sold by the glass. The menu
leans towards classic dishes of fillet
steak with brandy sauce, Dover sole,
and sea bass with butter sauce. There is
a climbing frame in the garden for
younger visitors, plus picnic tables.
Open *Mon to Fri 11 to 3, 6 to 11,*
Sat (and Fri in summer) 11 to 11,
Sun 12 to 10.30

DALWOOD

Devon   map 2

Tuckers Arms

Dalwood EX13 7EG
TEL: (01404) 881342

1m N of A35, between Honiton and
Axminster

Uneven stone floors, low beamed
ceilings and open log fires set the scene
at this flower-decked and part-
thatched thirteenth-century inn,
situated in the centre of a delightful
Axe Valley village. Formerly a
farmhouse, hunting lodge and a
residency for stonemasons working on
the nearby church, it serves Otter
Bitter, O'Hanlon's Fire Fly and
Courage Directors; 12 wines are
available by the glass. Fresh fish and
game dishes might feature, and
overnight accommodation is offered in
four en suite bedrooms.
Open *12 to 3, 6.30 to 11, Sun 12 to 3, 6.30 to*
10.30; closed 26 Dec

DARTINGTON

Devon   map 1

White Hart

Dartington Hall, Dartington TQ9 6EL
TEL: (01803) 847111

from A384 follow signs for Dartington and
then for Dartington Hall

Dartington Hall, with its art college,
gallery, theatre and 1,000-acre estate,
also houses this fine bar and restaurant.
Open all the way up to the ancient
dark rafters in the roof with high
arched windows, it has a church-like
feel. Tables are laid for eating, but the
mood is easy-going. Beers include
White Hart Ale, Bass and
Worthington; the wine list favours
organic producers. Bar food is available
at lunchtimes only, with a restaurant
menu in the evenings. The kitchen
uses top-quality materials, mostly
local, free-range and organic. A new
chef has taken over since we last
inspected, so reports would be
especially welcome.
Open *11 to 11, Sun 12 to 12.30*
(3 winter); closed Christmas to New Year and
Mon winter

DENT

Cumbria   map 8

Sun

Main Street, Dent LA10 5QL
TEL: (015396) 25208

in Dentdale, 4m SE of Sedburgh

Standing in a Dales village street lined
with fifteenth- and sixteenth-century
cottages, this charming old white-
painted inn serves all the beers from
the Dent brewery, which was opened
in 1990 by the Sun's licensee in a
converted stone barn at nearby
Cowgill: Bitter, Aviator and lager-style
Rambrau in cask, and three strong ales
in both cask and bottle. The pub
welcomes children and serves daily
specials in addition to a range of snacks
and bar meals. Four rooms are
available for B&B. The pub's opening
hours are unpredictable in winter, so
please phone to check.
Open *winter Mon to Fri 11 to 2.30, 7 to 11,*
Sat 11 to 11, Sun 12 to 10.30; summer 11 to 11,
Sun 12 to 10.30

DOBCROSS

Greater Manchester   map 7

Swan Inn

The Square, Dobcross OL3 5AA
TEL: (01457) 873451
off M62 junction 22, down A6052, turn left
just after Delph on to A62 and take first
right, follow for 1m

The 'glorious' setting of this fine old
village local, dating from 1765, is one of
the most scenic old weaving villages of
the southern Pennines. An ultra-
traditional feel pervades the main bar,
with its wood panelling, flagstone
floors and ornate moulded plaster
ceilings. Bar menus major in curries –
at least six different versions are usually
available – but there are also traditional
pub staples such as fish and chips,
gammon and egg and chilli. Beers are
the full range from fine Lakeland
brewery Jennings, plus a guest ale.
There is also a short wine list.
Open *Mon to Wed 12 to 3, 5.30 to 11, Thur to*
Sat 12 to 3, 5 to 11, Sun 12 to 4, 7 to 10.30
(no food Sun eve)

DORSTONE

Herefordshire   map 5

Pandy Inn

Dorstone HR3 6AN
TEL: (01981) 550273
off B4348 Hay-on-Wye to Hereford road,
5m E of Hay-on-Wye

This snug, white-painted inn sits near
the head of the Golden (Dore) Valley,
between the gardens of Abbey Dore
and the bookshops of Hay. The low-
ceilinged interior features exposed
walls and stone floor. Butty Bach and
Dorothy Goodbody ales from the Wye
Valley Brewery are served, along with
Stowford Press cider. Building and
setting may be English traditional, but
the landlady's native South Africa
influences the menu, with bobotie
offered as well as Herefordshire rump
steak; specialities are fish and
vegan/vegetarian dishes. The wine list
has four by the glass and includes
several South Africans.
Open *Mon 6 to 11, Tue to Fri 12 to 2.30, 6 to*
11, Sat 12 to 11, Sun 12 to 3, 6 to 10.30; closed
Mon nights from end Jan to Mar

DUNCTON

West Sussex   map 3

Cricketers

Duncton GU28 0LB
Tel: (01798) 342473
on A285, 3m S of Petworth

This white sixteenth-century pub was
once known as the Swan, until
renamed in the nineteenth century
when Sussex all-rounder Jem Dean
turned from cricket to innkeeping.
Outside it has a green and pretty
garden, inside there's one big, beamy
room with a log fire where drinkers
can enjoy Fuller's London Pride,
Harveys Sussex Best Bitter and
Young's Bitter. For those who've come
to eat, there's black pudding, or
chicken liver Cognac pâté, then
bangers and mash, cheeseburgers, or
maybe prune-stuffed pork tenderloin,
with Bakewell tart to finish. Five wines
are served by the glass. New owners
arrived in early 2003; reports please.
Open *Mon to Sat 11 to 2.30, 6 to 11,*
Sun 12 to 3

DUNTISBOURNE ABBOTS

Gloucestershire   map 2

Five Mile House

Duntisbourne Abbots GL7 7JR
TEL: (01285) 821432

The kind of place for which the words
'characterful' and 'individual' were
invented, this former coaching inn on
the original Roman Ermine Street
(parallel to the noisy A417) seems
virtually unchanged since the
seventeenth century. Tiny higgledy-
piggledy bars, furnished with high-
backed settles and dark wood, are thick
with locals' pipe and cigar smoke. A
more formal dining room in the
Georgian extension is painted deep
maroon and the steeply sloping garden
has wonderful views. Beers are
typically Donnington's BB, Young's
Bitter and Timothy Taylor Landlord,
plus occasional guests. Home-made
food combines traditional dishes with
unusual innovations.
Open *12 to 3, 6 to 11, Sun 12 to 3, 7 to 10.30*

DURLEY

Hampshire   map 2

Robin Hood

Durley SO32 2AA
TEL: (01489) 860229

1m W of Bishop's Waltham off B2177

The Robin Hood is not so much a pub
as a modern bar/bistro, though it does
stock good real ales, including Old
Speckled Hen and Greene King IPA.
The unconventional menu offers
eclectic tapas-style bar snacks: spicy
chicken wings, deep-fried squid with
garlic mayonnaise, faggots with prune
and onion gravy, and chorizo and lentil
stew, for example. As nibbles to
accompany drinks, the format works
well, but for a full meal pick a selection
of these and add a portion of chips. In
the evening the menu works on more
familiar starter/main-course lines, with
perhaps leek and potato soup with a
poached egg and truffle oil, followed
by grilled calf's liver with black
pudding and parsnip risotto.

Open *12 to 11, Sun 12 to 10.30*

DUXFORD

Cambridgeshire   map 6

John Barleycorn

Moorfield Road, Duxford CB2 4PP
TEL: (01223) 832699

on B1379, close to M11 junction 10

Built in 1660 as a coaching inn, the
John Barleycorn is on the main road
through the village, not far from
Duxford Air Museum. A good line-up
of real ales runs from regulars from
Greene King and Ruddles, plus Old
Speckled Hen, to specials like Bateman
XXXB and Caledonian 80/-. On the
menu might be beef Wellington, Irish
stew, or fillet of lemon sole, with
puddings of spotted dick, or apple pie.
Four en suite rooms available.

Open *11 to 11, Sun 12 to 10.30*

EARL SOHAM

Suffolk   map 6

Victoria Inn

The Street, Earl Soham IP13 7RL
TEL: (01728) 685758

on A1120, 3m W of Framlingham

The Street in Earl Soham is unusual: a
Roman road with a kink (to

circumvent boggy ground). This neat
white pub on the village green offers
beers from the Earl Soham brewery
(which until 2001 was out the back –
now it's in larger premises down the
road), including Victoria Bitter, Albert
Ale, Gannet Mild and Sir Roger's
Porter. There is also local apple juice,
and five wines by the glass. Food is
traditional pub fare, from ploughman's
to casseroles, via salads and fish
specials. Children are welcome
throughout the pub.

Open *11.30 to 3, 6 to 11, Sun 12 to 3,
7 to 10.30*

EAST BERGHOLT

Essex   map 3

Kings Head

Burnt Oak, East Bergholt CO7 6TL
TEL: (01206) 298190

off B1070, follow signs to Flatford Mill

Its setting – a splendid part of
Constable country – is a plus at the
Kings Head, as are the real ales:
Adnams Bitter and Broadside, and
Greene King IPA. Food is served all
week except Sunday and Monday
evenings and might include pan-fried
duck breast with red wine sauce served
on creamy mash, or beer-battered
deep-fried haddock with chips. Three
red and three white wines come by the
glass.

Open *12 to 3, 6.30 to 11, Sun 12 to 3, 7.30 to
10.30*

EASTBRIDGE

Suffolk   map 6

Eel's Foot Inn

Eastbridge IP16 4SN
TEL: (01728) 830154

off B1122, 2m N of Leiston

The Eel's Foot is an Adnams pub,
stocking the brewery's full range;
wines, with three by the glass, are
supplied by the same company. The
pub is popular with walkers, visitors to
the nearby RSPB reserve at Minsmere
and holidaymakers, and caravanning
and camping facilities are provided in
the grounds; there's also one double en
suite letting room inside. The menu is
a fairly standard list of pub favourites.

Children and dogs are welcome throughout.

Open *winter Mon to Fri 12 to 3, 6 to 11, Sat 12 to 11, Sun 12 to 10.30; summer 12 to 11*

EAST ILSLEY

Berkshire   map 2

Crown & Horns

East Ilsley RG16 0LH
TEL: (01635) 281545

just off A34, 9m N of Newbury

Those walking the Ridgeway path, five minutes away, will find food and refreshment aplenty at this pub in a horse-racing village. As well as decent choice on the menu, there is also a good selection of seasonally changing ales: perhaps including Wadworth 6X, Fuller's London Pride and Theakston Old Peculier. In addition, 17 wines are sold by the glass. The skittle alley has been converted into B&B accommodation.

Open *11 to 11, Sun 11 to 10.30*

EAST LYNG

Somerset   map 2

Rose & Crown

East Lyng TA3 5AU
TEL: (01823) 698235

on A361, 5m NE of Taunton

A large inglenook takes up one wall of this comfortable, well-kept village pub, which also has low beams, stone floors and a grandfather clock. The menu offers few surprises except among desserts, where speciality ice creams include maple pecan fudge and Beaulieu blackberry. On draught are Butcombe Bitter and Gold and Palmers 200, and four wines are served by the glass. At the back is an attractive garden.

Open *11 to 2.30, 6.30 to 11, Sun 12 to 3, 7 to 10.30*

EAST RUSTON

Norfolk   map 6

Butcher's Arms

East Ruston NR12 9JG
TEL: (01692) 650237

Stick together three cottages and an old butcher's shop and you get the Butcher's Arms, a complex of bar and child-friendly restaurant areas (non-smoking, too) with plenty of outdoor space. Bass is the mainstay beer but weekly-changing guests might be Nelson's Revenge, Woodforde's Wherry or a fine pint of Adnams. The specials board offers good-value home-cooked food, and there are £2 lunches during the week.

Open *12 to 2.30, 7 to 11 (10.30 Sun)*

EXTON

Rutland   map 6

Fox and Hounds

19 The Green, Exton LE15 8AP
TEL: (01572) 812403

2m off A606, between Stamford and Oakham

New licensees in summer 2002 are making a few changes to this handsome seventeenth-century coaching inn on the village green: three rooms are to have en suite facilities. The wine list is to be extended in terms of both numbers and quality too, although Greene King IPA and Samuel Smith Old Brewery Bitter are still on handpump and there's a broad range of food. Rutland Water is just two miles away.

Open *9 to 3, 6 to 11, Sun 12 to 4, 7 to 10.30; may stay open all day summer*

FADDILEY

Cheshire   map 7

Thatch Inn

Wrexham Road, Faddiley CW5 8JE
TEL: (01270) 524223

on A534, 3m W of Nantwich

Built in 1457, the Thatch Inn has rustic appeal in the shape of beams and exposed brickwork and a cornucopia of flowers at the front. The menu has been broadened from typical pub food to include fish specials: scallop thermidor, for instance, or butter-fried breadcrumbed lemon sole with mussels and prawns. On draught are Weetwood Best Bitter and Ambush Ale, Courage Directors and Wells Banana Bread Beer, and more than 20 wines are served by the glass. As the Guide went to press, plans were in hand to build two large accommodation blocks, and the pub may stay open all day once the work is complete.

Open *12 to 3, 6.30 to 11, Sun 12 to 10.30*

FALSTONE

Northumberland   map 10

Blackcock Inn

Falstone NE48 1AA
TEL: (01434) 240200

off B3620 8m W of Bellingham

The Blackcock stocks an impressive line-up of real ales: John Smith's Magnet, Theakston Cool Cask, perhaps Cains Dr Duncan's IPA and other guests from Jennings, Wylam and Brakspear. Traditional pub dishes are what to expect on the food front, and two wines are sold by the glass. Walkers, and other less energetic visitors to Kielder reservoir and forest, enjoy the warmth of this snug old-time local with its traditional atmosphere.

Open *winter Mon to Fri 7 to 11, Sat 12 to 3, 7 to 11, Sun 12 to 3, 7 to 10.30; summer 12 to 3, 7 to 11 (10.30 Sun)*

FEERING

Essex   map 3

Sun Inn

Feering CO5 9NH
TEL: (01376) 570442

off A12, 5m NE of Witham

Six real ales are on tap at any one time at this sixteenth-century inn: the selection might be Crouch Vale Brewers Gold, Young's Bitter, Mighty Oak IPA and Icebreaker, Ridleys Old Bob and Archers Black Jack Porter. Six wines are sold by the glass, and there are more than 40 single-malt whiskies. Among the dishes on the imaginative, ever-changing menus might be rabbit in red wine and caper sauce, haggis, mushroom and whisky pie, and wild boar in apple and Calvados sauce. No cards.

Open *12 to 3, 6 to 11 (10.30 Sun)*

FELSHAM

Suffolk   map 6

Six Bells

Church Road, Felsham IP30 0PJ
TEL: (01449) 736268

off A14, 7m SE of Bury St Edmunds

This Greene King pub serves IPA and Abbot Ale, and whenever possible fresh local produce appears on the menu: expect game pie, baked cod, and steak and kidney pie. When you find the old inn, reached along country lanes, you will be rewarded with a friendly atmosphere. It has a garden and welcomes children throughout.

Open *12 to 3, 6.30 to 11, Sun 12 to 2.30, 7 to 10.30*

FIR TREE

Co Durham   map 10

Duke of York

Fir Tree DL15 8DG
TEL: (01388) 762848

on A68, 4m S of Tow Law

Dating from the 1740s, this coaching inn by the village green was traditionally a stopping-off point on the main route to Scotland. A comfortable, homely feel pervades the main bar and the sumptuously decorated lounge, and if you look closely at the bar counter you will spot the trademark carved mouse of 'Mouseman' Thompson. Menus, listed on blackboards, deal mainly in old-fashioned pub cooking – things like gammon and pineapple with chips, pork Normandie, and cod and chips. One visitor enjoyed a roll filled with a substantial portion of tender roast beef. Beers are from Black Sheep.

Open *11 to 2.30 (3 summer), 6.30 to 10.30 (11 summer); closed 25 Dec*

FITZHEAD

Somerset   map 2

Fitzhead Inn

Fitzhead TA4 3JP
TEL: (01823) 400667

off B3227, 7½m NW of Taunton

Lost in the lanes between Wiveliscombe and Taunton, this quirky pub is closed for weekday lunchtimes, but otherwise offers such dishes as fillet of turbot, rack of lamb, or fillet steak stuffed with Stilton, and maybe lime and ginger crème brûlée to follow. On the bar's three pumps may be Exmoor Fox, Exmoor Gold, or beers from Butcombe Brewery, and there are half a dozen wines available by the glass.

Open *Mon to Fri 7 to 11, Sat and Sun 12 to 3, 7 to 11 (10.30 Sun)*

FLAUNDEN

Hertfordshire   map 3

Bricklayers Arms

Long Lane, Hogspit Bottom, Flaunden HP3 0PH

TEL: (01442) 833322

3m SW of Hemel Hempstead; village signposted off A41

Fuller's London Pride, Marston's Pedigree and Morrells Oxford Blue are the regular ales at this charming, Virginia creeper-covered little pub, with guests from breweries like Cottage and Archers. Cottage pie and scampi and chips are on the menu, together with other traditional offerings, while lamb's liver or seafood platter might be among the specials. Around a dozen wines are served by the glass.

Open *11.30 to 3, 6 to 11, Sun 12 to 2.30, 6.30 to 10.30*

FORD

Gloucestershire   map 5

Plough Inn

Ford GL54 5RU

TEL: (01386) 584215

on B4077, 5m E of Winchcombe

This sixteenth-century, slate-roofed Cotswold-stone inn contains the remains of some indoor stocks (as in wooden frames with holes) – from the time when it did duty as a courthouse, and sheep-stealers were incarcerated in the cellars rather than beer. Today's customers, including local jockeys and stable hands, come in for Donnington SPA and BB, Addlestone cider and four wines by the glass. Simple, homely food includes fresh fish, steaks, pies and highly popular

asparagus suppers in season. Three guest rooms available.

Open *11 to 11, Sun 12 to 10.30*

FORDCOMBE

Kent   map 3

Chafford Arms

Spring Hill, Fordcombe TN3 0SA

TEL: (01892) 740267

on B2188, off A264, 4m W of Tunbridge Wells

This 1850s tile-hung pub with steeply sloped roofs is partly wreathed in creeper and lies in a colourful garden brimming with flowers. Ales are Larkins, Bass and Shepherd Neame Spitfire, and of the 40-odd wines eight come by the glass. It offers bar and restaurant menus, the latter focusing on fish. Children are welcome. No food Sun and Mon evenings.

Open *11.45 to 11, Sat 11 to 11, Sun 12 to 10.30*

FORTY GREEN

Buckinghamshire   map 3

Royal Standard of England

Forty Green HP9 1XT

TEL: (01494) 673382

off B474 out of Beaconsfield at Knotty Green

This place is literally showing its age, with eleventh-century timbers, thirteenth-century plaster and a name bestowed by Charles II, who sheltered here en route for France after defeat at Worcester. More recently, stained-glass from blitz-damaged London churches was added. Even the ale is historic: Owd Roger, brewed here for three centuries, is now made by Marston's, but bottles are sold here alongside the cask ales: Marston's Pedigree, Greene King Old Speckled Hen, Brakspear Bitter and Fuller's London Pride and Chiswick Bitter.

Open *11 to 3, 5.30 to 11, Sun 12 to 3, 7 to 10.30*

FOWNHOPE

Herefordshire   map 5

Green Man Inn

Fownhope HR1 4PE
TEL: (01432) 860243
on B4424, 6m SE of Hereford

Half a mile from the meandering
middle Wye, this inn dates from 1485
and has black and white half-timbering
inside and out. With 20 bedrooms and
a leisure complex it is really more hotel
than pub, but it has a friendly feel and
is well placed for salmon-fishers. In
the two bars a wide choice of simple
pub food complements ales from
Tetley and Hereford's Spinning Dog
Brewery, plus Green Man from
Bartrams in Suffolk and Courage
Directors. Children are welcomed.
Open *11 to 11, Sun 12 to 10.30*

FRESHWATER

Isle of Wight   map 2

Red Lion

Church Place, Freshwater PO40 9BP
TEL: (01983) 754925

Look for the church – next to it is this
pub, which reputedly has its origins in
the eleventh century. Most of the
current building is more recent,
although inside are suitably ancient-
looking stone floors, brick pillars and
beams, with lanterns hanging from the
ceiling. Black Sheep Best Bitter,
Fuller's London Pride, Flowers
Original and locally brewed Goddards
Special constitute a pretty good line-up
of real ales, and fortunately the
cooking is better than the menu's puns
might lead you to expect – 'mules'
marinière, for example. Rabbit stew
with dumplings is a typical main
course, and you might finish with
chocolate 'taught'.
Open *Mon to Fri 11.30 to 3, 5.30 to 11,
Sat 11 to 3, 6 to 11, Sun 12 to 3, 7 to 10.30*

FRILSHAM

Berkshire   map 2

Pot Kiln

Frilsham RG18 0XX
TEL: (01635) 201366
*off B4009; from Yattendon go over motorway
bridge and straight on – do not turn right to
Frilsham*

Behind this seventeenth-century red-
brick pub on a narrow country lane
used to be the West Berkshire
Brewery. It has now moved to
Yattendon, but still produces Brick
Kiln Bitter exclusively for the Pot Kiln,
which serves it alongside Arkell's BBB
and Morland Original Bitter. There
are also three wines by the glass.
Hungry walkers are often in evidence,
eating the simple home-cooked meals
available from both a printed menu
and regularly changing specials
blackboard.
Open *Wed to Sat and Mon 12 to 3, Mon to Sat
6.30 to 11, Sun 12 to 3, 7 to 10.30; no food Tue
eve*

FROXFIELD

Hampshire   map 2

Trooper Inn

Alton Road, Froxfield GU32 1BD
TEL: (01730) 827293
*from Petersfield, follow signs to Steep and
continue climbing to Froxfield; pub on right*

This substantial white-painted
building is deep in the country at
Hampshire's highest point. Inside, in
the light, wood-floored bar, Ringwood
Best or Fortyniner might be among
the frequently changing guest beers on
offer (over 400 different ones have
appeared in the last half-dozen or so
years). In the two pine-furnished
dining areas and restaurant the
speciality is half-shoulder of lamb,
along with fresh fish and game dishes.
Eight bedrooms available.
Open *Tue to Sat 12 to 3.30, 6 to 12, Sun 12 to
2.30*

FULLER STREET

Essex   map 3

Square & Compasses
Fuller Street CM3 2BB
TEL: (01245) 361477
off A131 or A12, 5m W of Witham

This unassuming whitewashed pub in a pleasant part of agricultural Essex is worth seeking out. The back and front gardens are pleasant places to sit and sup Ridley's IPA and Nethergate Suffolk County in summer. Inside, walls covered with stuffed birds and old farming tools are almost a museum of rural bygones. Food, in bar or upstairs eating area (used mainly for large groups) is 'hearty country' style, with game well represented (home-prepared gravad lax, or whole roast mallard, for example), and four wines are available by the glass.

Open *11.30 to 3, 6.30 to 11 (7 to 11 winter), Sun 12 to 3, 7 to 10.30*

GARRIGILL

Cumbria   map 10

George & Dragon
Garrigill CA9 3DS
TEL: (01434) 381293
off B6277, 3m S of Alston

This seventeenth-century inn catered for workers at long-gone lead mines in these majestic hills; now it refreshes walkers crossing the Tyne/Tees watershed on the Pennine Way or cyclists on the C2C route. In the flag-floored bar there's Adnams Broadside, Deuchars IPA from Caledonian, and Black Sheep brews to drink, and bar snacks and packed lunches to be had. There are also evening meals and four bedrooms for weary travellers.

Open *Mon to Fri 12 to 2, 7 to 11, Sat 12 to 11, Sun 12 to 4.30, 7 to 10.30*

GAWSWORTH

Cheshire   map 8

Harrington Arms
Gawsworth SK11 9RR
TEL: (01260) 223325
down A536 from Macclesfield towards Congleton, take second left after Warren and pub is 200yds down road

The Harrington Arms is actually part of a working family-run farm. It is also a real gem and oozing with atmosphere. The creeper-covered three-storey red-brick building dates from the late seventeenth century, and the no-frills taproom has simple seating and a quarry-tiled floor. There is no menu as such, but food is available at lunchtimes – just ask the landlady what is available and she will provide soup, sandwiches, and pies. Celery soup has been praised, and properly home-made pork pies are a far cry from the run-of-the-mill mass-produced items. Robinson's supplies the beer.

Open *12 to 3, 6 to 11, Sun 12 to 3, 7 to 10.30*

GESTINGTHORPE

Essex   map 3

Pheasant
Gestingthorpe CO9 3AX
TEL: (01787) 461196
off B1058, from A131, 5m SW of Sudbury

In a pleasantly rural part of north Essex, this pale pink pub with a protuberant bow window offers three regular ales – Adnams Bitter and Greene King IPA and Abbot Ale – plus a guest such as Fuller's London Pride, and four wines by the glass. A log fire and bar billiards provide the background for bar and à la carte menus that offer the likes of boeuf bourguignonne and lamb shank, plus weekend fish specials like whole grilled sea bass with butter and capers.

Open *Tue to Sat 12 to 3, Mon to Sat 6.30 (5.30 Fri) to 11, Sun 12 to 3, 7 to 10.30; no food Sun and Mon eve*

GLOOSTON

Leicestershire   map 5

Old Barn Inn
Andrews Lane, Glooston LE16 7ST
TEL: (01858) 545215
off A6, 6m N of Market Harborough

Glooston may be off the beaten track now, but the Roman road from Colchester to Leicester ran past it, and the Old Barn began as a sixteenth-century coaching inn (you cannot tell that from outside, but the inside is appropriately cosy and beamy).

Alongside Shepherd Neame Spitfire
and Bateman XB Bitter there are a
couple of guests, like Ridleys IPA and
Timothy Taylor Landlord, and a full-
dress menu focuses on fish but also
includes steaks and vegetarian choices.
Open *12 to 3, 7 to 11 (10.30 Sun); closed
Mon L*

GREAT BARRINGTON

Gloucestershire   map 2

Fox Inn

Great Barrington OX18 4TB
TEL: (01451) 844385
off A40, 3m W of Burford
Set between Great and Little
Barrington and beside the River
Windrush is this seventeenth-century
inn with lovely gardens that make it a
splendid summer pub (the gardens
hold more people than the pub).
Donnington's Bitter and Special Ale
are on tap, along with seven wines by
the glass. Blackboard menus offer the
likes of beef and ale pie, and chicken
piri-piri, with crème brûlée, or a fruit
crumble to follow.
Open *11 to 11, Sun 12 to 10.30*

GREAT EVERSDEN

Cambridgeshire   map 6

The Hoops

2 High Street, Great Eversden CB3 7HN
TEL: (01223) 264008
Standing at a crossroads in a peaceful
rural setting is this cream-painted pub
with beer garden, reached from the car
park over a tiny footbridge and equally
small stream. Inside, an airy open-plan
bar serves Greene King Abbot Ale and
IPA and Old Speckled Hen. Choose
from filled baguettes, chef's steak and
ale pie, or spicy macaroni cheese at
lunchtime, and in the evening perhaps
plump for beef Wellington with black
cherries, or mushroom risotto. A
dessert of rum and raisin chocolate
torte was met with 'appreciative noises'
and mulled wine pudding was 'a
successful variation'.
Open *12 to 2 (3 Sun), 6 to 11 (10.30 Sun);
closed Mon L*

GREAT LANGDALE

Cumbria   map 8

Old Dungeon Ghyll Hotel

Great Langdale LA22 9JY
TEL: (015394) 37272
on B5343, 6m from Skelwith Bridge on A593
What's special here is the magnificent
setting, which has long made this a
magnet for serious walkers and
climbers. Thirsts can be quenched
with Theakston XB and Old Peculier,
Jennings Cumberland, Black Sheep
Special and Yates Bitter, plus guests
like Brains SA or Moorhouses Pendle
Witches Brew; for cider drinkers there
is Weston's Old Rosie, and the wine
list has three by the glass. Filling pub
food is available (curry, chilli con
carne, Cumberland sausage), and once
a month there are folk music evenings.
The hotel has 13 rooms.
Open *Mon to Fri 11 to 11, Sat and Sun 9am
to 11pm (10.30pm Sun)*

GREAT OUSEBURN

North Yorkshire   map 9

Crown

Main Street, Great Ouseburn YO26 9RF
TEL: (01423) 330430
off B6265 5m S of Boroughbridge
Ouseburn lies between the Ouse and
the Nidd, beside the Roman road from
York to the Brigantian capital at
Aldborough (and quite close to the A1
too). It's a nice-looking eighteenth-
century building, white with red
pantiles, and the interior is pleasantly
traditional. As well as John Smith's,
Black Sheep, Tetley and Timothy
Taylor Landlord, there are ten wines
by the glass, and the blackboard
specials always include seafood – king
scallops, perhaps – along with the likes
of chicken and smoked bacon Caesar
salad.
Open *Mon to Fri 5 to 11, Sat 11.30 to 11,
Sun 12 to 10.30*

GRITTLETON

Wiltshire   map 2

Neeld Arms Inn

The Street, Grittleton SN14 6AP
TEL: (01249) 782470

*from M4 junction 17 take A429 N and
follow signs to Grittleton*

Dating from the seventeenth century,
the Neeld Arms is an unpretentious
pub built of Cotswold stone standing
opposite Grittleton House, its interior
decorated in rustic style. Wadworth 6X
and Buckley's Best Bitter, from Brains,
are the regulars on handpump, with a
couple of guests that might include
Young's Bitter. Venison casserole,
braised lamb shank, or pork fillets in
mustard sauce are what to expect on
the interesting blackboard menu. Four
wines are sold by the glass.
Accommodation available.

Open *Mon to Fri 12 to 3, 5.30 (5 Fri) to 11,
Sat 12 to 3.30, 5 to 11, Sun 12 to 3.30, 7
(6 summer) to 10.30*

HAPPISBURGH

Norfolk   map 6

Hill House

Happisburgh NR12 0PW
TEL: (01692) 650004

on B1159, 7m E of North Walsham

Dating from the sixteenth century, this
is a family-run freehouse and B&B
where Conan Doyle stayed in 1903
and wrote *The Dancing Men*.
Elementary Ale is brewed locally to the
pub's own recipe; they also offer
Shepherd Neame Spitfire, plus four
regularly changing guest ales, and
wines include a dozen moderately
priced bins. Food on the printed menu
leans towards the plain and simple, to
which you can add your own speciality
'house sauce', while a board above the
bar lists the specials.

Open *winter Mon to Wed 12 to 3, 7 to 11,
Thur to Sat 11 to 11, Sun 12 to 10.30; summer
12 to 11, Sun 12 to 10.30*

HARBERTON

Devon   map 1

Church House Inn

Harberton TQ9 7SF
TEL: (01803) 863707

*off A381 Totnes to Kingsbridge road, 2½m S
of Totnes*

Built around 1100 to house the
builders of the church next door, this
was later a monks' chantry, and finally
passed into secular hands only in 1950.
Centuries of clerical association are
reflected in the magnificently evocative
interior. Pews from redundant
churches support imbibers of Palmers
IPA and Charles Wells Bombardier,
regularly changing guest beers like
Palmers 200 or Tetleys Imperial, and
locally made farm cider. Ten wines are
on offer by the glass from a reasonable
list. Food like steak and ale pie, rabbit
pie, or spinach, leek and blue cheese
gâteau focuses on local raw materials.
There are three en suite bedrooms.

Open *12 to 3 (3.30 Sat), 6 to 11,
Sun 12 to 4, 6 to 10.30*

HARRINGWORTH

Northamptonshire   map 6

White Swan

Seaton Road, Harringworth NN17 3AF
TEL: (01572) 747543

off B672, 4m N of Corby

Greene King IPA and, usually,
Timothy Taylor Landlord and Old
Speckled Hen are served at this stone-
built fifteenth-century coaching inn
tucked away in a pretty and unspoilt
village in the Welland Valley. It is close
to the impressive 82-arch viaduct that
traverses the valley and is a handy
refreshment stop for tourists exploring
Uppingham and Oakham or visiting
nearby Rockingham Castle. The pub
has a traditional interior with stone
walls, open fires and two eating areas
where whole roast partridge or pan-
fried sea bass might be on the menu.

Open *11.45 to 2.30, 6.30 to 11, Sun 12 to 3,
7 to 10.30; closed eve 25 Dec and lunchtime
26 Dec*

HARROGATE

North Yorkshire   map 8

Old Bell Tavern

6 Royal Parade, Harrogate HG1 2SZ
TEL: (01423) 507930

An extensive choice of speciality beers is one of the attractions listed on boards outside this town-centre pub. The standard repertoire of Black Sheep Best Bitter, Deuchars IPA and Timothy Taylor Landlord is supplemented by various guests, usually including some from local microbreweries, plus a couple of draught foreign beers and a good choice of Belgian bottled beers. There are two bare-floorboarded bar areas, one of which was once home to Farrah's famous Harrogate toffee. Food is served both in the downstairs bar and the upstairs restaurant; braised lamb shank, Cumberland sausage and leek mash, Whitby fish pie and a range of sandwiches.
Open *12 to 11 (10.30 Sun)*

HARTFIELD

East Sussex   map 3

Anchor Inn

Church Street, Hartfield TN7 4AG
TEL: (01892) 770424
village is on junction of B2026 and B2110, 6m SE of East Grinstead

For walkers in the Ashdown Forest and Pooh-sticks players (that bridge is close by) the small village of Hartfield makes a good starting – and refuelling – point. The Anchor offers five real ales, including brews from Harveys, Fuller's London Pride and Adnams Bitter, and the food on the specials board majors on fish dishes like prawn and crab curry. Children are welcome. Two rooms are available for B&B.
Open *11 to 11, Sun 12 to 10.30*

HASCOMBE

Surrey   map 3

White Horse

Hascombe GU8 4JA
TEL: (01483) 208258
on B2130, 3m SE of Godalming

A mecca for families – children love climbing the venerable old trees in the garden, and there is a family room indoors – this attractive-looking pub caters to the well-heeled local clientele. Adnams Best, Flowers Original and Harveys are on draught, with five wines available by the glass. The bar menu might include beef and ale pie, or Thai-style salmon and prawn fishcakes.
Open *Mon to Fri 11 to 3, 5.30 to 11, Sat 11 to 11, Sun 12 to 10.30; closed 25 Dec*

HEATH

West Yorkshire   map 9

Kings Arms

Heath Common, Heath WF1 5SL
TEL: (01924) 377527
from A638 between Wakefield and Crofton take A655, then turn left to Heath and Kirkthorpe

This early-eighteenth-century inn in a particularly picturesque village overlooks Heath Common, a 100-acre area of grassland, ideal for walkers. The partly panelled bar retains an old black range. The beers are Tetley, John Smith's, Clark's Traditional and Timothy Taylor Landlord, plus a guest, and there is a short wine list. Bar food ranges from snacks to main courses and the specials board always offers meat, fish and vegetarian dishes; there is also a separate restaurant with a more upmarket menu.
Open *Mon to Fri 11.30 to 3, 5.30 to 11, Sat 11.30 to 11, Sun 12 to 10.30*

HECKINGTON

Lincolnshire   map 6

Nags Head

34 High Street, Heckington NG34 9QZ
TEL: (01529) 460218
off A17, 5m E of Sleaford

Standing by the village green, this seventeenth-century pub supposedly includes Dick Turpin among its former customers. A regular crowd of locals give the place a friendly, informal atmosphere and staff are 'affable'. Traditional pub food is along the lines of whitebait, steak and kidney pie, lamb chops, sausage with egg and chips, and jacket potatoes, and there is a good range of desserts – trifle, or lemon meringue ice cream, for example. Beers are a decent bunch, including Adnams Broadside and Black Sheep Bitter, and several wines are served by the glass.

Open *11 to 11 (12.30 Sun)*

HELFORD

Cornwall   map 1

Shipwrights Arms

Helford TR12 6JX

TEL: (01326) 231235

on S side of Helford River, 7m E of Helston

This thatched pub's terraced gardens, dropping down to the water's edge, offer a peaceful view of the Helford River and the wooded creek on which the village lies. Sit among palm trees and flowers on a summer's day or relax in the bar – oak settles, open fire, nautical memorabilia – with Castle Eden Ale, Flowers IPA, or Sharp's Doom Bar Bitter, or one of the five wines sold by the glass. Children are welcome, and there are memorable summer evening barbecues. The bar menu changes daily, and there's a restaurant too.

Open *11 to 2.30, 6 to 10.30 (11 summer); closed Sun eve*

HELSTON

Cornwall   map 1

Blue Anchor

50 Coinagehall Street, Helston TR13 8EL

TEL: (01326) 565765

Dating back to the early fifteenth century when it was a rest home for monks – it became a tavern after Henry VIII's Dissolution of the Monasteries – the Blue Anchor is one of the oldest pubs in the country to brew its own beer. The potent ales are Spingo Best, Spingo Middle and Special, and Spingo also turns up in a beef dish on a menu where hearty pies, pan-fried duck, lamb and fishcakes also feature. Accommodation available.

Open *11 to 11, Sun 12 to 10.30; closed eve 25 Dec*

HERMITAGE

West Sussex   map 3

Sussex Brewery

36 Main Road, Hermitage, Emsworth PO10 8AU

TEL: (01243) 371533

on A259, just out of Emsworth towards Chichester

Once a brew pub, this rustic seventeenth-century hostelry is now a Young's house and offers their range of beers, plus Smiles Heritage and Bristol IPA. Over 40 kinds of additive-free sausages form the backbone of the menu, among them chicken, orange and walnut, and pork, port and Stilton. Expect few frills – simple furnishings and a thick coat of sawdust on the floor. Walled garden.

Open *11 to 11 (10.30 Sun)*

HILDERSHAM

Cambridgeshire   map 6

Pear Tree

Hildersham CB1 6BU

TEL: (01223) 891680

off A1307, 8m SE of Cambridge

Quiet, unpretentious one-room local, brown of décor and featuring a brick-built bar, a small wood-burning stove and an old coin-operated gaming machine. Nowadays, tables have legs but they used to be suspended on chains, some of which remain dangling from the ceiling. Among the drinks available are Greene King IPA, Abbot Ale and a changing guest beer, plus a modest selection of wines (six by the glass). Food is simple, along the lines of steak and kidney pudding.

Open *11.45 to 2, 6.30 (6 Fri and Sat) to 11, Sun 12 to 2, 7 to 10.30*

HOLBETON

Devon   map 1

Mildmay Colours

Holbeton PL8 1NA

TEL: (01752) 830248

off A379 Plymouth to Modbury road, 1m after National Shire Horse Centre, signposted Mothecombe and Holbeton

At this white, sixteenth-century pub, the horse-racing motif carries through from the pub sign to the menu

('starter's orders', 'nosebag nibbles').
Food is largely locally sourced, and
Wednesday night is curry night.
Regular beers, Colours Best Bitter and
SP from Skinner's in Truro, are
supplemented by guests like Sharp's
Eden Ale, or Old Speckled Hen. At the
August bank holiday beer festival there
are eight on tap.

Open *11 to 2.30 (3 summer), 6 to 11, Sun 12
to 3, 7 to 11*

HOLYPORT

Berkshire   map 3

Belgian Arms
Holyport SL6 2JR
TEL: (01628) 634468

off A330, 2m S of Maidenhead

This is close enough to the M4 to
make it a useful alternative to
motorway service stations for
personal refuelling. It is white and
creeper-fronted, with a garden set
next to the village pond. Inside there
are some low beams along with
Brakspear Best Bitter and Special
(also five wines by the glass).
Blackboards may offer dishes like
chicken suprême or a half-shoulder
of lamb, and there is always bread-
and-butter pudding plus a crumble of
some sort to finish with.

Open *Mon to Fri 11 to 3, 5.30 to 11, Sat 11 to
3, 6 to 11, Sun 12 to 3, 7 to 10.30*

HOLYWELL

Cambridgeshire   map 6

Old Ferry Boat Inn
Holywell PE27 4TG
TEL: (01480) 463227

off A1123, 3m SE of St Ives

Those driven to distraction by the
traffic on the A14 might seek out one
of England's oldest inns: a low,
whitewashed and thatched pub beside
the Ouse that was originally a ferry
house. Said to have sold liquor since
AD 560, it boasts both Domesday
Book entry and a ghost – Juliet,
suicidal victim of unrequited love for a
wood-cutter, who walks at midnight
on the anniversary of her death on
17 March 1078. On sunny terrace or in
beamy interior there are Greene King
IPA and Abbot Ale, plus Old Speckled

Hen and dishes like bacon and
Speckled Hen pie, or banoffi pie.
Seven rooms for B&B.

Open *11.30 to 11, Sun 12 to 10.30*

HOOK NORTON

Oxfordshire   map 5

Pear Tree Inn
Scotland End, Hook Norton OX15 5NU
TEL: (01608) 737482

off A361, 5m NE of Chipping Norton

The Pear Tree operates a child-
friendly policy, with a children's
licence until 9pm, and an outdoor
chess set and a Wendy house in the
large garden. The pub is tied to the
Hook Norton Brewery, just along the
lane, and stocks the brewer's full
range. The welcoming wooden-
floored bar sports a rustic mix of
furnishings, an open log fire and a
loyal following. Straightforward food
along the lines of pub snacks, steaks
and scampi are what to expect,
although at weekends the specials
might be more enterprising: smoked
salmon fishcakes, perhaps, or pork in
Madeira sauce. Five wines come by the
glass, with a further dozen country
fruit wines. B&B available.

Open *Mon to Fri 11.30 to 2.30, 6 to 11,
Sat 11.30 to 4, 6 to 11 (11 to 11 summer),
Sun 12 to 4, 7 to 10.30*

HORSEBRIDGE

Devon   map 1

Royal Inn
Horsebridge PL19 8PJ
TEL: (01822) 870214

off A388, 5m W of Tavistock

This white-painted former nunnery
had become an inn by the time
Charles I reputedly patronised it; then
it had a Gothic makeover in the
nineteenth century, to judge from the
windows. It sits close to a superb
fifteenth-century bridge over the
Tamar in the back roads between
Launceston, Callington and Tavistock.
The beers – from Bass, Sharp's in
Wadebridge (Doom Bar Bitter) and
perhaps from Launceston's Ring
O'Bells Brewery – might be
accompanied by a ploughman's, filled

baguettes, steaks, or chilli tortillas.
Children welcome lunchtimes only.
Open *12 to 3, 7 to 11, Sun 12 to 3,
7 to 10.30*

HORSEY

Norfolk   map 6
Nelson Head
Beach Road, Horsey NR29 4AD
TEL: (01493) 393378
off B1159, 9m NE of Acle

Tucked away down a cul-de-sac close
to the beach and Horsey Mere, the
Nelson Head is an unpretentious
brick-built pub with open log fires and
nautical and farming implements.
Children are allowed to use the family
room, and the restaurant has a no-
smoking area. The menu in here, also
served in the bar, makes good use of
local produce, and fish is something of
a speciality. Woodforde's Wherry Best
Bitter and Nelson's Revenge are
regularly stocked, with occasionally a
third ale from the same brewery.
Three wines are served by the glass, 15
by the bottle.
Open *Mon to Wed 11 to 2.30, 6 to 11, Thur to
Sat 11 to 2.30, 7 (6 summer) to 11, Sun 12 to 3,
6 to 10.30; closed eve 25 and 26 Dec*

HUNDON

Suffolk   map 6
Plough Inn
Hundon CO10 8DT
TEL: (01440) 786789
*off A143, 2m N of Haverhill, take right turn
to Kedington, then 1m towards Hundon*

A pink-painted country pub set on one
of the relatively high points of the area,
with views of the Stour valley, the
Plough has an unspoilt bar, a more
formal restaurant, eight guest
bedrooms and a conference centre. On
draught are Woodforde's Wherry and
Greene King IPA plus a guest ale,
perhaps Shepherd Neame Spitfire;
about 30 malt whiskies are stocked,
and ten wines are served by the glass.
As well as the bar menu of
straightforward pub fare, the restaurant
menu majors on fish, steaks and
traditional desserts. Children welcome.
Open *11 to 2.30, 6 to 11, Sun 12 to 3,
7 to 10.30*

HURLEY

Berkshire   map 2
Dew Drop
Batts Green, Hurley SL6 6RB
TEL: (01628) 824327
*take Honey Lane off A423, just outside
Hurley between Maidenhead and Henley-on-
Thames, continue past council houses and
through farm until wood; at T-junction take
right turn on to smaller lane; inn is a few
hundred yards on right*

In a rustic setting in woods just outside
the village, with a large garden for
summer eating and drinking, this is a
Brakspear tied house, selling the
brewery's range of ales, including
seasonal ones. Dating from the
seventeenth century, the pub has two
bars (children allowed in one). Both a
printed menu and a board announce
what food is on offer: from sandwiches
to home-made pies and fish specials,
with occasional game dishes in season.
Three wines are sold by the glass.
Open *12 to 3, 6 to 11, Sun 12 to 3, 7 to 10.30*

HYDE

Gloucestershire   map 2
Ragged Cot Inn
Cirencester Road, Hyde GL6 8PE
TEL: (01453) 884643
*take B4077 from Stow-on-the-Wold towards
Toddington, turn left towards Temple Guiting
and Hyde is around 1m down road, pub is on
left*

The 'very Cotswolds' Ragged Cot
occupies an isolated position at the
junction of two very minor roads –
roads which, judging by the packed car
park, are seeing a sight more traffic
since this pub/hotel's recent makeover.
A seventeenth-century coaching inn of
honey-coloured stone, all interlinked
snugs with exposed stone walls, it now
has a fine conservatory/dining room
built of excellent old materials, and
extensive outdoor seating with a very
modern fountain. Traditional pub food
comes with cheery but courteous
service, and real ales include Cotswold
Way, Smiles Best and Very Old Spot.
Open *11 to 11, Sun 12 to 10.30*

INGLEBY

Derbyshire   map 5

John Thompson

Ingleby DE73 1HW
TEL: (01332) 862469
off A514, 3m NW of Melbourne

JTS Bitter and JTS Summer Ale are
produced on the premises of this
homely, traditionally furnished pub,
which dates from the fifteenth century,
and an ale from the Burton Bridge
Brewery is normally on tap too, with
four wines by the glass. Visitors can
enjoy carvery-style meals at lunchtime,
when children are welcome
throughout (there's a family room for
use in the evening).
Open *Tue to Sat 10.30 to 2.30, Mon to Sat
7 to 11, Sun 12 to 2.30, 7 to 10.30; closed eve
25 Dec*

INGS

Cumbria   map 9

Watermill

Ings LA8 9PY
TEL: (01539) 821309
just off A591, 2m E of Windermere

Food is served throughout this 250-
year-old converted wood mill, with a
menu and a large specials board offering
such dishes as bobotie, venison
sausages, and braised Barbary duck with
a red berry and whisky sauce. Eight
full-time and eight guest ales are on the
go at the same time; among the former
are Theakston Best Bitter and Jennings
Cumberland Ale, with Moorhouses
Pendle Witches Brew and Yates Winter
Fever among the latter. Seven wines are
served by the glass. The pub has seven
en suite bedrooms. Children – and dogs
– are welcome, and there are tables
outside by the River Gowan.
Open *12 to 11, Sun 12 to 10.30*

INKBERROW

Worcestershire   map 5

Old Bull

Inkberrow WR7 4DZ
TEL: (01386) 792428
*off A422, Worcester to Stratford-upon-Avon
road, 5m W of Alcester*

In a quiet village, close to the church,
the Old Bull is known to listeners of

The Archers as the model pub for the
Bull at Ambridge. It is a fine half-
timbered Tudor building and well
worth visiting for its splendid beamed
interior, notably the impressive collar-
beam-framed roof, and for the wealth
of memorabilia relating to the
programme. Flowers IPA, Courage
Directors and Marston's Pedigree are
on handpump, and eight wines are
served by the glass. Traditional pub
food is found on the menu and specials
board, and fish and chips is still a
feature on Fridays.
Open *12 to 11 (10.30 Sun)*

KELD

North Yorkshire   map 9

Tan Hill Inn

Keld DL11 6ED
TEL: (01833) 628246
off B6270 at Keld, then 4m N

At around 1,700 feet above sea level, this
is Britain's highest pub – and one of its
remotest. It's on the Pennine Way,
offering a welcome haven for walkers,
who can thaw out in front of an open
fire and seek revival from traditional pub
food (with Yorkshire puddings to the
fore), and from Theakston Old Peculier
and XB, and one of the guest ales. A
generator provides power for the pub, as
it does not have mains electricity.
Open *11 to 11, Sun 12 to 10.30*

KINGSBRIDGE

Devon   map 1

Crabshell Inn

Embankment Road, Kingsbridge TQ7 1JZ
TEL: (01548) 852345
off A381, 8m SW of Totnes

This waterside pub has a quay 125 feet
long, some of it for seating, some a car
park, but all for mooring boats. If the
weather is inclement, the popular bar
areas offer a genuinely friendly
atmosphere, and children – and dogs –
are welcome, especially in the well-
equipped games room. Bass, Crabshell
Bitter and Flowers IPA are on
handpump, along with guest ales,
especially in summer, like Wadworth
6X or Fuller's London Pride. The long
menu offers plenty of choice, and four
wines are sold by the glass.
Open *11 to 11, Sun 12 to 10.30*

KINGSTEIGNTON

Devon   map 1

Old Rydon Inn

Rydon Road, Kingsteignton TQ12 3QG
Tel: (01626) 354626
*from A380 take Kingsteignton turn-off, then
first turning left into Brook Way, which
becomes Rydon Road*

This Grade II listed former farmhouse
dates back to the sixteenth century and
the bar, with log fire and whitewashed
walls, features an original cider loft. As
we go to press the new owner is
planning to maintain the separation
between the informal atmosphere of
the bar – where beers are Bass and
London Pride (plus a guest) and spicy
dishes feature on the menu – and the
separate, smarter restaurant with its
more traditional à la carte menu. The
popular garden is due for a makeover
and a summer barbecue is on the
cards. Reports please.
Open *11 to 2.30, 6 to 11, Sun 12 to 3,
7 to 10.30*

KINGSTON NEAR LEWES

East Sussex   map 3

Juggs

The Street, Kingston near Lewes
BN7 3NT
Tel: (01273) 472523
off A27, 2m SW of Lewes

A terrace and a children's play area
make the Juggs a popular summer
destination, but you will be greeted all
year round with the full range of ales
from Shepherd Neame as well as
around 15 wines by the glass.
Traditional pub fare is the principal
business of the kitchen, but see also
the blackboard specials, which might
take in tempura-battered hake fillet on
a bed of sautéed potatoes, peppers,
leeks and chillies, or slow-braised lamb
shank with red wine gravy, shallots and
cinnamon mash.
Open *11 to 11, Sun 12 to 10.30*

KNEBWORTH

Hertfordshire   map 3

Lytton Arms

Park Lane, Old Knebworth SG3 6QB
Tel: (01438) 812312
*from Knebworth on B197, take side road
signposted Old Knebworth*

New licensees have refurbished the
Lytton Arms and invigorated the
kitchen, so as well as traditional pub
dishes you can now expect main
courses along the lines of fillet of
plaice stuffed with leeks and
mushrooms with a cheese and red
onion sauce; braised lamb shank; or
poached salmon with hollandaise. Real
ales take in regulars Woodforde's
Wherry Best Bitter, Fuller's London
Pride and Adnams Bitter, joined by
guests from breweries like Burton
Bridge, Milton, Mighty Oak and
Church End. Draught ciders, eight
wines by the glass, up to 20 bottled
beers and the same number of malt
whiskies complete the drinks picture.
Open *Mon to Sat 11 to 11, Sun 12 to 10.30;
closed eve 25 Dec*

KNIPTON

Leicestershire   map 5

Red House

Croxton Road, Knipton NG32 1RH
Tel: (01476) 870352
off A607, 6m SW of Grantham

This Regency building, handy for
Belvoir Castle, sits on a hill looking
down towards the village church. It is a
pub with a split personality:
extravagantly decorated restaurant on
the one hand; busy, informal bar on
the other. In the latter Adnams Bitter
and Everards Beacon Bitter, plus a
changing guest like Wadworth 6X or
Marston's Pedigree, accompany a long
menu of snacks and grills, while the
restaurant might offer roast pheasant
in redcurrant sauce, or pork tenderloin
with a cream, mushroom and Marsala
sauce.
Open *Wed to Sat 12 to 2, Mon to Sat 6 to 11,
Sun 12 to 2, 6 to 10.30*

LACOCK

Wiltshire   map 2

Red Lion

1 High Street, Lacock SN15 2LQ
TEL: (01249) 730456

on A350, 3m S of Chippenham

Dating from the 1700s, the Red Lion is
a large, red-brick building set on the
main road running through the village.
Window seats overlook 200-year-old
grey-stone houses and half-timbered
cottages. There is the Abbey too, and a
museum of the work of pioneering
photographer Fox Talbot. Décor in the
bar of this spacious pub includes
agricultural implements, bellows and a
vast fireplace, while menus offer
traditional cooking in the form of beef
and ale pie, and lamb and port
casserole. Badger Tanglefoot,
Wadworth 6X or IPA and a seasonal
guest ale are kept, and around ten
wines are available by the glass.
Accommodation available.

Open *winter 11.30 to 3, 6 to 11, Sun 12 to 3,*
7 to 10.30; summer 11 to 11, Sun 12 to 10.30

LANGTON HERRING

Dorset   map 2

Elm Tree

Shop Lane, Langton Herring DT3 4HU
TEL: (01305) 871257

off B3157, 5m NW of Weymouth

Set in the heart of Dorset farmland,
this cream-painted pub with a slate
roof grabs the attention of passers-by
with its colourful floral displays.
Inside, high-backed settles and an open
fire give a warm, traditional feel. Beers
are Marston's Pedigree and Bass, and
everything on the wine list is available
by the glass. Hearty pub dishes chalked
up on a blackboard include steak and
ale pie, crab Mornay, spinach and
ricotta cannelloni and the Elm Tree's
own mustardy chicken.

Open *12 to 3, 6 to 11, Sun 12 to 3, 8 (6.30*
summer) to 10.30

LANLIVERY

Cornwall   map 1

Crown

Lanlivery PL30 5BT
TEL: (01208) 872707

off A390, 2m W of Lostwithiel

Reputedly Cornwall's oldest pub, this
rough-stone former longhouse dates
from the twelfth century and is worth
tracking down for the tiptop ales –
Doom Bar Bitter and Eden – from
Sharp's Brewery. Tucked away down a
narrow lane close to the parish church
it boasts an impressive black slate-
floored bar with ancient beams, old
settles and a priest hole in the
chimney. Overnight accommodation
in two bedrooms and a peaceful
secluded garden.

Open *11 to 3, 6 to 11, Sun 12 to 3,*
6.30 to 10.30

LAPWORTH

Warwickshire   map 5

Navigation Inn

Old Warwick Road, Lapworth
BN4 6NA
TEL: (01564) 783337

on B4439, 1m SE of Hockley Heath

The garden of this friendly, family-
orientated pub (children welcome
throughout, with their own menu) runs
down to the Grand Union Canal.
Inside, stuffed fish are a feature in the
bar, where two regular ales, including
Bass, are joined by four or five guests
that change every couple of days, among
them Badger Tanglefoot, Greene King
Abbot Ale and Hanby Nutcracker. Two
wines are served by the glass, and on the
daily-changing menus might be
pheasant, or fish and chips.

Open *Mon to Fri 11 to 3, 5.30 to 11,*
Sat 11 to 11, Sun 12 to 10.30

LEEDS

West Yorkshire   map 9

Whitelocks

Turks Head Yard, Briggate LS1 6HB
TEL: (0113) 245 3950

Slip off the main drag of Briggate,
down an alleyway beside Marks and
Spencer for a marvellous escape from
the world of the high street. This long,

narrow pub glories in its unmodernised charms – black-painted woodwork, painted mirrors and brass rails, with an original Victorian luncheon bar soon to be back in service. Real ales are the draw for locals and students alike, with regulars from Theakston, Ruddles and John Smith's plus four guests. Nine wines come by the glass and you can fill up on sandwiches, steak pie, fish and chips, or the ever-popular Yorkshire pudding with onion gravy.

Open *11 to 11, Sun 12 to 10.30*

LITTLE BARRINGTON

Oxfordshire   map 2

Inn For All Seasons

The Barringtons, Little Barrington
OX18 4TN
TEL: (01451) 844324

The traffic screams past on the A40, but this prosperous-looking, creeper-clad freehouse offers instant respite with snug and traditional Cotswold-stone walls, varnished wooden tables and flagstones in the bar. Wadworth 6X is joined by a guest such as Doom Bar, Bass Cask or Wychwood on the handpumps, while wines run to 14 by the glass and over 100 on the list. The trump card is the fish – maybe grilled sardines with port and garlic butter followed by whole sea bass on a bed of roasted fennel with a light Pernod butter sauce.

Open *11 to 2.30, 6 to 11, Sun 12 to 2.30, 7 to 10.30*

LITTLE CHEVERELL

Wiltshire   map 2

Owl

Low Road, Little Cheverell SN10 4JS
TEL: (01380) 812263
on B3098 ¼ m W of A360

The Owl is in a tiny hamlet surrounded by farmland with views of Salisbury Plain. French windows open on to decking that extends right along the pub, and a peaceful garden runs down to the Cheverell Brook. A number of menus give plenty of choice on the food front – expect anything from Thai green chicken curry to game pie or sea bass – and among the handpumped ales might be Fuller's

London Pride, Greene King IPA, or Cotleigh Tawny Bitter. Twenty-one wines are sold by both glass and bottle. Children are welcome, and B&B is available.

Open *Mon to Fri 11 to 3, 6 to 11, Sat 11 to 11, Sun 12 to 4, 7 to 10.30 (12 to 10.30 summer); closed eve 25 Dec*

LITTLE HADHAM

Hertfordshire   map 6

Nags Head

The Ford, Little Hadham SG11 2AX
TEL: (01279) 771555
between B1004 and A120, 3m W of Bishop's Stortford

This white-painted pub, dating from 1595, is in a picturesque village opposite a footbridge over the River Ash (little more than a stream at this point). Inside are beams, part-brick walls and horsy pictures, with a no-smoking restaurant area down some steps. The lengthy menu ranges from traditional English fare to classic Anglo-French dishes, with a concentration on fish: coquilles St-Jacques, or smoked salmon pâté, followed by skate wing deep-fried in beer batter, or seafood platter. Finish with something like hazelnut meringue. Greene King ales are on handpump, and seven wines are served by the glass.

Open *11 to 3, 6 to 11, Sun 12 to 3, 6 to 10.30*

LITTLEHEMPSTON

Devon   map 1

Tally Ho!

Littlehempston TQ9 6NF
TEL: (01803) 862316
off A381, 2m NE of Totnes

The Tally Ho! is a fourteenth-century, creeper-covered pub by the village church. The single bar has open fires in winter, and in summer you can enjoy the sun and the flowers on the patio. Bass is joined by regularly changing guest ales: perhaps Dartmoor IPA from Princetown, or Marston's Pedigree. Apart from snacks, the menu and weekly-changing boards offer such things as steaks and fillets of lemon sole. B&B available.

Open *winter 12 to 2.30, 6.30 to 11 (10.30 Sun); summer 12 to 3, 6 to 11 (10.30 Sun)*

LITTLE LONGSTONE

Derbyshire   map 8

Packhorse Inn

Little Longstone DE45 1NN
TEL: (01629) 640471

off B6465, 2m NW of Bakewell

Built as two cottages in the sixteenth
century and converted to an inn in
1787, the Packhorse is in prime Peak
District walking country, on the
Monsal trail between Bakewell and
Miller's Dale. It offers simple old-
fashioned character, with log fires and
local prints and photos on the walls.
Two handpumps dispense Marston's
Bitter and a guest: perhaps Greene
King Abbot Ale. The daily menu deals
in traditional home-made food, and a
couple of wines are sold by the glass.
Children are welcome in the lounge
and restaurant.
Open *Mon to Fri 12 to 2.30, 5 to 11, Sat 11 to
11, Sun 12 to 10.30*

LITTLE SHELFORD

Cambridgeshire   map 6

Navigator

63 High Street, Little Shelford CB2 5ES
TEL: (01223) 843901

*off M1 at junction 11, take A10 towards
Royston; pub is 2m S of Hauxton*

This pink-painted cottage on the main
road through the village is a friendly,
unassuming local, 'the sort of place
you'd be happy to have within easy
reach'. Its main attraction is its
extensive Thai menu, offering
authentic favourites like chicken satay,
crispy prawns with sweet chilli sauce
and green chicken curry. There is a
lighter lunch menu at weekends.
Drink Thai Singha beer, one of the
cask-conditioned English ales, or one
of the ten wines by the glass listed on a
blackboard.
Open *Mon 6 to 11, Tue to Fri 12 to 2, 6 to 11,
Sat 6 to 11, Sun 12 to 2, 7 to 10.30*

LITTLE STRETTON

Shropshire   map 5

Ragleth Inn

Little Stretton SY6 6RB
TEL: (01694) 722711

*on B4370, off A49, just SW of Church
Stretton*

Built in 1663, this handsome brick pub
is in a pleasant wooded valley at the
foot of Long Mynd. It's popular with
walkers, among others, seeking out
traditional pub food – perhaps a
hotpot, or beef in ale – and draught
Hobsons Best Bitter or something
from the Wye Valley or Eccleshall
Breweries, served in the oak-beamed
lounge or restaurant. Four wines are
sold by the glass from a list of around a
dozen bottles. Pleasant summer garden
with an unusual tulip tree.
Open *Mon to Fri 12 to 2.30, 6 to 11, Sat 12 to
11, Sun 12 to 10.30; closed eve 25 Dec*

LIVERPOOL

Merseyside   map 7

Brewery Tap

35 Stanhope Street, Liverpool L8 5XJ
TEL: (0151) 709 2129

Cains is the brewery in question here:
it's right next door and a tour can be
combined with a visit to the pub. From
the outside, red brick and high etched
windows make traditional promises,
and these are now fulfilled by the
refurbished interior. Unsurprisingly
Cains beers dominate. Food is served
at lunchtimes only.
Open *11 (12 Sat and Sun) to 11 (10.30 Sun)*

The Dispensary

87 Renshaw Street, Liverpool L1 2SP
TEL: (0151) 709 2160

It may look like an old chemist's shop,
but fear not: look up at the blackboard
and you'll see that you're in the right
place for a full range of Cains beers
and guests such as Ceres Red Erik and
Hopf Weisse. The refurbishment was a
Cains brainwave, but this is still a
friendly Victorian corner pub at heart.
Open *11.30 to 11, Sun 12 to 10.30*

Doctor Duncan's

St John's Lane, Liverpool L1 1HF
TEL: (0151) 709 5100

Just 100 yards from the hubbub of
Queen Square, in the shadow of the
mighty Marriot hotel, this outpost of
the expanding Cains empire enjoys
calming views of St George's Hall
gardens – and the Mersey Tunnel.
The eponymous doctor, a Victorian
health campaigner, would feel right at
home with the traditional décor of
high ceilings, tiled walls and pillars,
but what he would make of the
tightly packed eclectic crowd is
another matter. Beers are a strong
point – with Faxe, Red Erik, lots of
Cains offerings, Gordon's stout and
more – and food is pub standards
with a twist.
Open *11.30 to 11, Sun 12 to 10.30*

Everyman Bistro

9–11 Hope Street, Liverpool L1 9BH
TEL: (0151) 708 9545

The Everyman Theatre, in whose
basement this bar-bistro is located, is
on one of the city's most famous
streets, with the Catholic cathedral at
one end and the Anglican cathedral at
the other. The canteen style is aimed
to get people in and out before
performances begin. Expect eclectic
dishes such as Angus beef stroganoff,
chicken tikka biryani, and tuna pizza.
Though not really a pub in the
traditional sense, it has an informal
pub-like buzz as well as a host of good
beers, including quality foreign
examples (such as Liefman's
Frambozenbier) and some good
British real ales – perhaps Timothy
Taylor Landlord, or Drawwell Bitter
from Hanby Ales.
Open *Mon to Wed 12 to 12, Thur 12 to 1am,
Fri and Sat 12 to 2am*

Old Post Office

Old Post Office Place, Liverpool L1 3DH
TEL: (0151) 707 8880

A cosy city-centre pub behind the
main branch of Littlewoods, close to
the Neptune Theatre and Bluecoat
Chambers, this is a useful little bolt-
hole to avoid the crowds. It's also an
ideal place for 'those who like a decent
steak at a ridiculously reasonable price'.
Apart from huge steaks, the menus run
to roast chicken, ribs and combinations
of those three items, bolstered with
chips or a jacket potato and side orders
of mushrooms, garlic bread and onion
rings. Wash the protein down with
local Cains real ales.
Open *Mon to Thur 11 to 11, Fri and Sat 11 to
2am, Sun 12 to 12.30*

Ship and Mitre

133 Dale Street, Liverpool L2 2JH
TEL: (0151) 236 0859

The Ship has stayed on course despite
a change of owners in early 2003. The
main draw in the galley-like bar is the
constantly changing line-up of a dozen
real ales that might include Jigsaw,
Yardstick and Hyde Mild, but there's
also food at lunchtime and teatime
snacks.
Open *12 to 11 (10.30 Sun)*

Vernon Arms

69 Dale Street, Liverpool L2 2HJ
TEL: (0151) 236 4525

The strong points of this city-centre
boozer opposite the Municipal
Building are the fine range of real ales
such as Wonky Donkey, Gunpowder
and the Cottage Whippet series, and
the 'tasty chips' served alongside
simple lunchtime toasties or more
substantial peppered steak. A mix of
professionals, regulars and students
settle into the dark wood and red
leather seats – with booths for diners –
and the Vernon is consequently busy
and smoky at lunchtimes as well as in
the evening.
Open *11.45 to 11 (10.30 Sun)*

LLANYBLODWEL

Shropshire   map 5

Horse Shoe Inn

Llanyblodwel SY10 8NQ
TEL: (01691) 828969
just off B4396, 5m SW of Oswestry

Dating from the sixteenth century, the
Horse Shoe Inn is a half-timbered
building next to the ancient bridge
over the River Tanat in a quiet hamlet
a mile from the Welsh border. The
open-plan interior has open fires, low,

blackened beams, and bare wooden floors. Bass and Worthington are on handpump, and the menu, with daily specials, features plenty of game in season; otherwise there might be sea bass or duckling, for instance. Children are welcome, and picnic tables on the river bank are ideal for peaceful summer drinking.
Open *11.30 to 3, 6.30 to 11, Sun 12 to 3, 7 to 10.30; closed Mon lunchtime, eve 25 Dec*

LONG PRESTON

North Yorkshire   map 8

Maypole Inn
Long Preston BD23 4PH
Tel: (01729) 840219
on A65 Skipton to Settle road
This comfortably refurbished 300-year-old inn is set in a pretty dales village overlooking the green and maypole and is noted for its choice of North Country ales. Sup a pint of Moorhouses Premier or Timothy Taylor Landlord; alternatively if your tipple is real cider try Saxon Ruby Tuesday. Relax by the log fire in the neat carpeted bar where the food menu runs to a selection of light snacks (sandwiches, salads, baked potatoes) and main courses of chicken with prawns and ginger, local game and fish. Children are welcome, and the pub has six en suite rooms.
Open *11 to 2.30 (3 summer), 6 to 11, Sat 11 to 11, Sun 12 to 10.30*

LOW CATTON

East Riding of Yorkshire   map 9

Gold Cup Inn
Low Catton YO41 1EA
Tel: (01759) 371354
off A166, just S of Stamford Bridge
The spacious beer garden has access to the river Derwent at this modernised whitewashed pub in a small village at the foot of the Yorkshire Wolds. Real ales include John Smith's and Tetley Bitter, and food consists of traditional pub fare and an à la carte menu in the restaurant area. Well patronised by walkers trekking the Wolds Way near Thixendale, the unpretentious interior comprises a rambling three-roomed lounge, each with welcoming log fires

and a wealth of bric-à-brac, and a games room to the rear.
Open *Mon to Fri (exc Mon lunchtime) 12 to 2.30, 6 to 11, Sat 12 to 11, Sun 12 to 10.30; closed eve 25 and 26 Dec*

LOWICK

Northamptonshire   map 6

Snooty Fox
Main Street, Lowick NN14 3BS
Tel: (01832) 733434
just off A6116, 2m NW of Thrapston
This solid-looking stone pub with a tiled roof dates from 1530, although it became an inn as *recently* as 1671. It presents a warm and welcoming impression, with a wood-burning stove, and cooking that encompasses mainly traditional pub fare such as steaks and familiar dishes of lamb, chicken and perhaps swordfish. Banks's Bitter and Original and Marston's Pedigree are joined on handpump by a guest ale such as Fuller's London Pride or Greene King Abbot Ale, and three wines are normally available by the glass.
Open *12 to 3, 6.30 to 11, Sun 12 to 3, 7 to 10.30; closed 25 Dec*

LUDGVAN

Cornwall   map 1

White Hart
Churchtown, Ludgvan TR20 8EY
Tel: (01736) 740574
from A30 N of Penzance at Crowlas, take turning signposted Ludgvan, continue 1m
From this fourteenth-century pub next to the sixteenth-century church in an inland village you can see St Michael's Mount two and a half miles away. Within are beamed ceilings and panelled walls, a wood-burning stove and an inglenook fireplace. Menus, displayed on an upright piano, offer egg and chips or T-bone steaks, while the specials board might include rabbit casserole, quiche or steak and kidney pie. Whiskies are something of a bar speciality, while cask ales offer a choice of Bass, Flowers IPA or Marston's Pedigree.
Open *11 to 2.30, 6 to 11, Sun 12 to 3, 7 to 10.30*

LUDLOW
Shropshire   map 5
Unicorn Inn
Lower Corve Street, Ludlow SY8 1DU
Tel: (01584) 873555

The Unicorn is a traditional-looking pub with plenty of clues to its venerable status: half-timbering and, inside, huge ancient beams and an enormous hearth, for example. Extensive blackboard menus typically list starters of seafood and crab pot, or chicken liver pâté, followed by venison sausages with ale and onion gravy and mustard mash, rack of lamb with redcurrants, orange and port, or rainbow trout with a caper, pink peppercorn and pine-nut butter. Hancock's HB, Bass and Old Speckled Hen are dispensed, and there are eight wines by the glass.

Open *12 to 3, 6 to 11, Sun 12 to 3.30, 7 to 10.30*

LUGWARDINE
Herefordshire   map 5
Crown & Anchor
Cotts Lane, Lugwardine HR1 4AB
Tel: (01432) 851303
off A438, 3m E of Hereford

This unpretentiously old-fashioned pub is decorated with interesting vintage photographs of Weston's Cider Company staff, farming implements, a bunch of fishing rods, and hop garlands on beamed walls and ceiling. Especially attractive is the paved patio in a flowery garden, which clearly shows the power of some very green fingers. On draught are Worthington Best Bitter, Marston's Pedigree, Timothy Taylor Landlord and Butcombe Ale, and there are eight wines by the glass.

Open *12 to 11 (10.30 Sun)*

LYDFORD
Devon   map 1
Castle Inn
Lydford EX20 4BH
Tel: (01822) 820241
off A386, 7m N of Tavistock

Head for the castle at the end of the village and look for the pink walls of this ancient building. Traditional pub décor includes collections of china and farm implements, and a warm welcome is helped along in wintertime by a roaring log fire. London Pride and Old Speckled Hen ales and seven wines by the glass can accompany hearty fare such as chicken and vegetable broth followed by bubble and squeak with bacon and fried eggs.

Open *11.30 to 3.30, 6 to 11, Sun 12 to 3, 7 to 10.30; no food served 25 Dec*

LYNMOUTH
Devon   map 1
Rising Sun Hotel
Harbourside, Lynmouth EX35 6EQ
Tel: (01598) 753223
on A39, 12m W of Porlock

This thatched inn overlooking a picture-book harbour in the Exmoor National Park has a situation to appeal to Romantic littérateurs: Blackmore wrote part of *Lorna Doone* while staying here, and Shelley is believed to have spent his honeymoon in what is now one of the guest rooms. You could seek to fuel inspiration with handpumped regulars Exmoor Gold or Cotleigh Tawny Bitter in the bar, or guest beers like Young's Bitter or Timothy Taylor Landlord. Four wines by the glass are offered from an enterprising list. The menu has a gamey streak, with Exmoor venison burgers, or rabbit, leek and bacon pie, or maybe wild boar, apple and cider sausages and mash.

Open *11 to 3, 5.30 to 11, Sun 12 to 2, 7 to 10.30*

MANCHESTER
Greater Manchester   map 8
Dukes 92
Castle Street, Manchester M3 4LZ
Tel: (0161) 839 8642
turn right off A57 in to Chester Road; 500 metres on left is Castle Street

Canalside warehouse conversion in the Castlefield district of Manchester, next to a lock keeper's house. Outside, it has plenty of space for fine weather drinking, while the inside is spacious and livened up with lots of greenery in pots. Food-wise, there's a counter offering cheeses and pâtés, while the printed menu lists a range of options from toasties and sandwiches, through various pasta and salad dishes to themed buffet selections – Mexican, Indian or oriental, for example. Blackboard specials might include minted lamb casserole or vegetable stroganoff. Not much of interest on the beer front but a reasonable choice of wines.

Open *11.30 to 11 (12 Fri and Sat), Sun 12 to 10.30*

Rain Bar

80 Great Bridgewater Street, Manchester M1 5JY
TEL: **(0161) 235 6500**

This tall Victorian red-brick building with a terrace overlooking the Rochdale Canal is a fixture on Manchester's bar scene in the evenings. Lunchtimes see a quieter pace and some real bargains on the comfort-food menu of soup, steak and chips, hot sandwiches and the like. Dark wood, leather and exposed brickwork suit both moods and service in the bar (with food servery) and upstairs restaurant is friendly and efficient. Beers stretch beyond lagers to decent real ales and 20 wines come by the glass.

Open *Mon to Thur 11 to 11, Fri and Sat 11 to 12, Sun 12 to 10.30*

Royal Oak

729 Wilmslow Road, Didsbury, Manchester M20 6WF
TEL: **(0161) 434 4788**

Surrounded by Didsbury's chain café-bars and brasseries, the Royal Oak upholds the virtues of the traditional English pub. The walls in the main bar are decorated with framed theatre programmes from the early twentieth century, but this is not a place given to drama. Instead, it takes a down-to-earth approach: at lunchtimes (weekdays only), the bar is stacked with an array of cheeses, pâtés, a leg of roast ham, pickled onions and breads. Marston's Pedigree and Banks's Original are perfect for washing down such simple, hearty fare.

Open *11 to 11, Sun 12 to 10.30*

MARSHWOOD

Dorset   map 2

Bottle

Marshwood DT6 5QJ
TEL: **(01297) 678254**
on B3165 between Crewkerne and Lyme Regis, 4m SW of Broadwindsor

Home to the famous annual nettle-eating competition ('The Nettlerash Bash'), the Bottle is a pub where the food philosophy leans towards an organic and vegetarian way of thinking. But there are also plenty of meat and fish dishes, so alongside goats' cheese en croûte with honey and hazelnuts you will also find grilled Barnsley chops with redcurrant sauce, Thai filo prawns with sweet chilli sauce, and baked whole plaice with lemon and herb butter. A fine selection of beers is offered, such as Old Speckled Hen and London Pride, and Weymouth organic sometimes makes an appearance – this organic approach even extends to some wines and soft drinks.

Open *all week 12 to 3.30, Tue to Sun 6.30 to 11 (10.30 Sun)*

MARSWORTH

Buckinghamshire   map 3

Red Lion

90 Vicarage Road, Marsworth HP23 4LU
TEL: **(01296) 668366**
off B489, 2m N of Tring

On the Grand Union Canal, the Red Lion is not only popular with narrowboat users but with walkers and twitchers from the nearby Tring Reservoir too. Thirst-quenching Fuller's London Pride and the Vale Brewery's Notley Ale might be among the three ales normally on offer, and four wines are sold by the glass. The cooking is built around classic pub fare such as ploughman's, ham, egg and chips, and cod and chips, with spotted dick, apple pie, or cherry pie to finish.

Open *11 to 3, 5 (6 Sat) to 11, Sun 12 to 3, 7 to 11*

MELLOR

Lancashire   map 8

Millstone Hotel

Church Lane, Mellor BB2 7JR
TEL: (01254) 813333
off A677, 3m NW of Blackburn

In a village overlooking the Ribble
Valley, the Millstone is an old coaching
inn that now has more of the feel of a
country-house hotel than an inn, and
is also under new ownership. Thwaites
Lancaster Bomber and cask ale are the
draught beers offered, and there is a
menu of modern pub food taking in
starters of deep-fried Brie with chilli
jam, smoked chicken Waldorf salad,
and warm black pudding salad with
bacon and mortadella, while main
courses might be poached salmon on
Caesar salad with new potatoes, penne
with pesto and oyster mushrooms, and
chargrilled minted lamb shank with
salad and chips. To finish there may be
crème brûlée with berry compote.
Reports please.
Open *11 to 11 (10.30 Sun)*

MEYSEY HAMPTON

Gloucestershire   map 2

Masons Arms

Meysey Hampton GL7 5JT
TEL: (01285) 850164
off A417, 1½m W of Fairford

In a village on the southern edge of the
Cotswolds, the Masons Arms dates
from the seventeenth century. Bass
and Hook Norton Best Bitter are
joined by two guest ales – perhaps
Kamikaze from the Dent Brewery in
Cumbria – and around half a dozen
wines are sold by the glass. Those with
an appetite may dine on a starter of
bacon, avocado and prawn salad, or
chicken Caesar salad, and then chicken
casseroled in creamy Stilton and bacon
sauce, and finish with fruit pancakes or
treacle tart. Accommodation is
available.
Open *11.30 to 2.30, 6 to 11, Sun 12 to 4, 7 to
10.30; closed Sun eve Nov to Mar; no food Sun
eve all year*

MICHAELCHURCH ESCLEY

Herefordshire   map 5

Bridge Inn

Michaelchurch Escley HR2 0JW
TEL: (01981) 510646
*Michaelchurch Escley signposted off B4348
about 6m SE of Hay-on-Wye*

From the church, take the lane down
the hill and over the brook and you
will soon arrive at this un-signed pub –
its remote location means that it is
mostly used by locals and residents of
the neighbouring campsite. It is
divided into a popular, lively bar and a
no-smoking dining area, but you can
eat in either. The bar menu deals
mainly in snacks, from baguettes or a
burger to Chinese-style spare ribs,
while the main menu, which makes
good use of local produce,
encompasses prawn cocktail, or dried
ham with figs, followed by smoked
haddock rarebit or cannelloni with
ricotta and spinach. On the drinks
front there is a good wine list and a
decent selection of beers.
Open *11 to 11, Sun 12 to 10.30*

MONKSILVER

Somerset   map 2

Notley Arms

Monksilver TA4 4JB
TEL: (01984) 656217
on B3188, 5m S of Watchet

Fair prices and a homely, child-
friendly atmosphere are the chief
attractions of this comfortable, popular
pub, a white-pebbledash building at
the centre of this village on the edge of
the Brendon Hills. The family room is
packed with games, toys and books,
and high chairs are provided. Dogs are
welcome too. Straightforward bar food
includes prawns with mayonnaise,
traditional ploughman's, and moules
marinière, as well as a few more
ambitious dishes like Italian-style roast
pork with rosemary and juniper,
roasted vegetables and tomatoes. There
are seven or so house wines by the
glass, plus a couple of country wines,
and beers include Wadworth 6X and
Smiles Best.
Open *11.30 to 2.30, 6.30 to 11, Sun 12 to
2.30, 7 to 10.30 (11 summer)*

MONTACUTE

Somerset   map 2

Kings Arms

Montacute TA15 6UU
TEL: (01935) 822513

just off A3088, 4m NW of Yeovil

In an unspoilt village close to the gates
of Montacute House (NT) is a
sixteenth-century coaching inn built of
golden-coloured local hamstone. It
was once a staging post on the
Plymouth–London route, and horses
were changed here before the gruelling
climb up Ham Hill. The civilised
interior has a good pubby bar – serving
Greene King IPA – with pleasing
village views, a candlelit restaurant and
comfortable accommodation in 15 en
suite bedrooms. Children welcome.
Open *11 to 11, Sun 12 to 10.30*

MORWENSTOW

Cornwall   map 1

Bush Inn

Crosstown, Morwenstow EX23 9SR
TEL: (01288) 331242

3m W of A39, 9m N of Bude

Hunched against westerly gales, this
haunted inn sits under a mile from
Higher Sharpnose Point and close to
the fine church of St Morwenna and St
John the Baptist. Initially a hermit's
cell in AD 950 (there's a Celtic piscina
in one wall), it was extended by
thirteenth-century Cistercians. The
interior is unspoilt and traditional,
with flagstones, built-in settles, stone
fireplace, and St Austell HSD and
Duchy tapped from the cask. Food is
served at lunchtime only.
Open *12 to 2.30 (3 summer), 6 (7 summer) to
11, Sun 12 to 3, 7 to 10.30; closed Mon winter,
closed eve 25 Dec*

MUCH WENLOCK

Shropshire   map 5

George & Dragon

2 High Street, Much Wenlock TF13 6AA
TEL: (01952) 727312

*on A458, between Shrewsbury and
Bridgnorth, 8m NW of Bridgnorth*

'Very traditional, very ancient, very
English,' thought one visitor to this
black and white half-timbered

property on the high street. A new
licensee has taken over since the last
edition but beers remain a draw, with
Hobsons Town Crier, Ringwood
Fortyniner and Timothy Taylor
Landlord among the range on offer.
The chef has not changed though, and
the menu still offers ploughman's,
jacket potatoes, baguettes and
sandwiches at lunchtime, as well as a
couple of variations on Welsh rarebit.
In the evening, start with garlic
mushrooms, before chicken breast in
apricot, mead and cream sauce, and
finish with sticky toffee pudding.
Two rooms are available on a B&B
basis.
Open *winter Mon to Thur 12 to 3, 6 to 11,
Fri and Sat 12 to 11, Sun 12 to 10.30; summer
12 to 11 (10.30 Sun)*

NAUNTON

Gloucestershire   map 5

Black Horse

Naunton GL54 3AD
TEL: (01451) 850565

off B4068, 5½m W of Stow-on-the-Wold

Tucked away up the Windrush from
Bourton-on-the-Water, Naunton is
delightfully rural, and well placed for
walkers on the Warden's Way and
Windrush Way. The Black Horse, on
the main street of this honey-coloured
village, dates from the 1870s and
retains its original flagged floors and
open fireplaces. The wine list has four
by the glass, and real ales are
Donnington SPA and BB from Stow-
on-the-Wold, plus cider from
Weston's and Stowford Press. Daily-
changing specials may include coq au
vin, local trout, and local game in
season. Children welcome.
Open *11.30 to 3, 6 to 11, Sun 12 to 3,
7 to 10.30*

NEAR SAWREY

Cumbria   map 8

Tower Bank Arms

Near Sawrey LA22 0LF
TEL: (015394) 36334

on B5285, 2m SE of Hawkshead

On the edge of Grizedale Forest and
close to Esthwaite Water is a small,
unassertive building familiar to

Jemima Puddleduck fans. Now one of the National Trust's few pubs (it is close to Beatrix Potter's home, Hill Top), it has beams, flagged floors and five real ales: regulars Theakston Best Bitter and Old Peculier and Charles Wells Bombardier, plus guests that include local brews from Barngate and Hawkshead. Seven wines by the glass can also accompany food that includes steaks, and wild boar and pheasant pie.

Open *11 to 3, 6 (5.30 summer) to 11, Sun 12 to 3, 6 to 10.30 (12 to 10.30 summer); closed eve 25 Dec*

NESSCLIFFE

Shropshire   map 7

Old Three Pigeons
Nesscliffe SY4 1DB
TEL: (01743) 741279
on A5, 8m NW of Shrewsbury

A short distance from the Welsh border lies this ancient pub, built in 1405. Blackboard menus list plenty of seafood, perhaps plainly served oysters and lobster to soused mackerel, and also home-made sausages and Welsh lamb. The real ale selection changes regularly – typical ales include Old Stockport Bitter from Robinson's, Everards Beacon Bitter and Moles Bitter – as does the wine list. Children are welcome.

Open *Tue to Sun 12 to 3, 6 to 11 (10.30 Sun)*

NEWCASTLE UPON TYNE

Tyne & Wear   map 10

Crown Posada
31 The Side, Newcastle upon Tyne
NE1 3JE
TEL: (0191) 232 1269

One of the oldest and best pubs in Newcastle, the music-free Crown Posada is a bastion of tradition in the midst of the manic Quayside scene, easily identified by the gold crown above the entrance. Oak panelling, stained glass and an ornate ceiling make for a fine interior. The pub is long and narrow and easily filled by a combination of locals, office workers and weekend revellers in search of an excellent-value and well-kept pint,

such as Workie Ticket, Tanglefoot or Magus from the Durham Brewery.

Open *Mon to Fri 11 to 11, Sat 12 to 11, Sun 7 to 10.30*

Free Trade Inn
St Lawrence Road, Newcastle upon Tyne
NE6 1AP
TEL: (0191) 265 5764

This time-honoured hide-out for Geordies and students united in the belief that pubs are for beer and smoking, rather than posing and shouting, occupies one of the last remaining stretches of undeveloped Newcastle quayside. Nothing to look at in itself, it enjoys fine views down river to the Baltic arts centre, the Millennium Bridge and the older Tyne bridges. Excellently kept local real ales from Mordue (Workie Ticket, Geordie Pride) and a range of microbreweries, plus a renowned jukebox and notorious toilet graffiti, draw visitors from across the city and beyond. Tuesday pub quizzes are particularly popular.

Open *11 to 11, Sun 12 to 10.30*

NEW MILLS

Derbyshire   map 8

Pack Horse Inn
Mellor Road, New Mills SK22 4QQ
TEL: (01663) 742365
follow Market Street then Spring Bank Road N out of New Mills, turn left at White Hart pub and continue for about ½m

With extensive views of some of the Peak District's highest points, this seventeenth-century former farmhouse is a popular spot with walkers. Curries are featured on blackboards, while the main menu goes in for mostly traditional items: steak and kidney pie, lasagne, baked salmon, and seafood casserole. Tetley Bitter is the regular real ale, supplemented by three guests from regional microbreweries, such as Ossett and Frankton Bagby.

Open *Mon to Fri 12 to 3, 5 to 11, Sat 12 to 11, Sun 12 to 10.30*

NEWNHAM

Kent   map 3

George Inn

44 The Street, Newnham ME9 0LL
TEL: (01795) 890237

off A2, 5m SW of Faversham

This pub started life as a farmhouse in
1540 and became a coaching inn in the
eighteenth century; in summer its
brick ground floor and tile-hung first
floor are festooned with flowers in
window boxes and hanging baskets. As
a Shepherd Neame house, it serves
Master Brew, Spitfire and Bishop's
Finger, plus a good selection of Old
and New World wines (12 by the
glass). Tempting dishes, such as
shoulder of lamb, or Baileys crème
brûlée focus on local produce.
Children are welcome in the eating
areas and garden.
Open *11 to 3, 6.30 to 11, Sun 12 to 4, 6.30 to
10.30*

NEWTON

Cambridgeshire   map 6

Queens Head

Fowlmere Road, Newton CB2 5PG
TEL: (01223) 870436

on B1368, 6m S of Cambridge

Overlooking the five-way junction in
the village centre since the eighteenth
century, this is just about the
archetypal country village pub. The
Short family have run it, to continuous
acclaim, for some 40 years, with
Cambridge dons and farm workers
filling the settle and benches in the
bow-windowed bar, or playing shove-
ha'penny and other games at the back.
They come for the unpretentiously
relaxed atmosphere, the gravity-fed
Adnams ales (including their seasonal
brews), and satisfying, no-nonsense
bar food: notably mugs of hearty soup
and good-value, cut-to-order
sandwiches.
Open *11.30 to 2.30, 6 to 11, Sun 12 to 2.30,
7 to 10.30; closed 25 Dec*

NEWTON UNDER ROSEBERRY

Redcar   map 10

King's Head

Newton under Roseberry TS9 6QR
TEL: (01642) 722318

on A173, 3m SW of Guisborough

The main focus at this red-brick and
stone inn is on food; choose from the
printed menu, daily blackboard
specials, or a good-value mid-week
lunch option. Dishes include wood
pigeon casseroled in red wine, fillet of
mackerel on a leek mash, and baked
Alaska. Theakston Best Bitter is the
only real ale, but there is a wide
selection of Old and New World
wines, including 17 by the glass. It gets
busy at weekends, and is popular with
walkers following the Cleveland Way.
Open *11.30 to 3, 5.30 to 11, Sun 11.45 to 4,
7 to 10.30*

NORTHLEACH

Gloucestershire   map 5

Wheatsheaf Inn

Northleach GL54 3EZ
TEL: (01451) 860244

just S of junction of A40 and A429

This sixteenth-century former
coaching inn is set in a pretty
Cotswolds village with a 'very lovely'
parish church. The décor is stylish and
classy, with an interesting pale toffee
colour scheme and wood panelling.
The pub acts as the headquarters for a
fine wine shippers, so there is a very
respectable list of 42 bottles, and on
draught are Wadworth 6X, Marston's
Pedigree and Hook Norton Best
Bitter. Food aims to make a trendy
impression with the likes of crab
risotto, braised lamb shank with Puy
lentils, and pan-fried duck breast with
a thyme and onion marmalade filo
parcel and orange jus. More reports
please.
Open *12 to 11 (10.30 Sun)*

NORTH SHIELDS

Tyne & Wear   map 10

Tap and Spile

184 Tynemouth Road, North Shields
NE30 IEG
TEL: (0191) 257 2523

opposite magistrates' court

This corner pub with a traditional
décor is an excellent venue for ale fans,
with an impressive line-up of
handpumps dispensing Caledonian
Deuchars IPA, Ruddles County, John
Smith's Magnet and up to seven
guests. There is also a reasonable
choice of wines by the glass, some in
single-serving bottles. Food is served at
lunchtimes only during the week, and
until early evening at weekends. The
style sticks largely to a well-trodden
route that leads to smoked haddock
and onion fishcakes with chips and
salad, Thai red vegetable curry with
rice, and stalwarts such as lasagne or
jacket potatoes.
Open *12 to 11, Sun 12 to 10.30*

Tynemouth Lodge Hotel

Tynemouth Road, North Shields
NE30 4AA
TEL: (0191) 257 7565

Despite the name, this traditional
eighteenth-century hostelry is not a
hotel, but it is a haven for real ale fans.
Typically, the selection of beers might
include draught Bass, Belhaven 80/-
and Deuchars IPA, plus a guest ale
such as Old Cornelius from a local
microbrewery in Jarrow. The décor is
fairly unprepossessing, but there is a
pleasant beer garden. Food is not
served, and just two wines are available
by the glass.
Open *11 to 11, Sun 12 to 10.30*

NORTH WOOTTON

Dorset   map 2

Three Elms

North Wootton DT9 5JW
TEL: (01935) 812881

on A3030, 2½m SE of Sherborne

On the fringes of Blackmoor Vale,
with great views towards Bulbarrow
Hill (Dorset's highest point), this pub
conspicuously reflects its landlord's
passions. It contains over 1,300 model

cars and other vehicles from bygone
days, among other memorabilia.
Originally a cider house, the building
has been extended by the present
owner, and there is a pleasant garden.
As well as several handpumped real
ales – including Otter Bitter,
Butcombe Bitter, Fuller's London
Pride – Burrow Hill cider is available,
along with 15 wines by the glass. The
menu includes 12 club sandwiches,
liver and bacon or beef Wellington for
carnivores, and an extensive choice for
vegetarians.
Open *11 to 2.30, 6.30 (6 Fri and Sat) to 11,
Sun 11 to 2.30, 7 to 10.30*

NORWICH

Norfolk   map 6

Fat Cat

West End Street, Norwich NR2 4NA
TEL: (01603) 624364

*from centre of Norwich follow A1074 out of
city, turn right on to Nelson Street, pub on
first corner*

The Fat Cat is a top-class beer pub,
tucked away down a side street west of
the city centre but easy to spot due to
the large black cat painted on the
outside wall. As many as 30 real ales
are on draught at any time, along with
a good selection of bottled beers from
Belgium, Scotland and Ireland. It
won't be a surprise to find the place
packed to overflowing with
enthusiastic beer aficionados,
especially at weekends. There are a few
wines too. Food is not available.
Open *12 (11 Sat) to 11, Sun 12 to 10.30*

NOTTINGHAM

Nottinghamshire   map 5

Olde Trip To Jerusalem

I Brewhouse Yard, Castle Road,
Nottingham NGI 6AD
TEL: (0115) 947 3171

Famously, this atmospheric inn at the
foot of Castle Rock claims to be the
oldest in England, with a licence dating
back to 1189. The ground floor has
flagstone floors and beams that are
covered in foreign coins and banknotes
left by visitors, while the first-floor
Rock Lounge is partly set into the
original castle caves. An extensive

menu offers mostly straightforward cooking along the lines of Mexican chilli, garlic and herb chicken, cheesy leek and potato bake, and chicken tikka masala. Beers are Hardys & Hansons Old Kim, Kimberley Classic and Best Mild, and there is a short list of wines.
Open *11 to 11, Sun 12 to 10.30*

NUNNEY

Somerset   map 2
George
11 Church Street, Nunney BA11 4LW
TEL: (01373) 836458
off A361, 2m SW of Frome
If you happen by the George spare a thought for victims of the Bloody Assizes. Some of the condemned were tried in one of its rooms and then hanged by the neck in the garden. Back in the twenty-first century help yourself from the lunchtime carte, or head for the restaurant to eat sticky pork ribs, deep-fried Camembert with raspberry coulis, a fish speciality such as silver bream, red snapper or swordfish – with maybe tiramisù to finish. Alternatively choose from one of the many real ales on tap, including perhaps something from Exmoor Ales or Wadworth, or Highgate Saddlers Celebrated Best Bitter or Black Sheep Best Bitter.
Open *12 to 3 (4 summer), 6.30 to 11.30, Sun 12 to 3, 6 to 11*

ONECOTE

Staffordshire   map 5
Jervis Arms
Onecote ST13 7RU
TEL: (01538) 304206
on B5053, 1m off A523 Leek to Ashbourne road, 4m E of Leek
On the bank of the River Hamps on the edge of the Peak District National Park is this seventeenth-century stone inn, popular with holidaymakers. A small footbridge over the stream connects the car park with the pub and riverside garden, where picnic tables and a play area draw families in summer – the welcome to children extends to three family rooms. Devotees of well-kept real ale will

rejoice at the sight of five handpumps on the bar, including Whim Arbor Light and several guest brews. A selection of pub food is available along the lines of home-made pies.
Open *11 to 3, 7 (6 Sat) to 11, Sun 12 to 10.30; 25 Dec lunchtime drinks only*

ORFORD

Suffolk   map 6
Jolly Sailor
Quay Street, Orford IP12 2NU
TEL: (01394) 450243
at end of B1084, 11m E of Woodbridge
The Suffolk coast has seen centuries of seafaring, and this was a quayside pub in a busy port until the harbour silted up in the sixteenth century. Nowadays it's mostly landsmen who appreciate the warmth generated by wood-burning stoves and low ceilings, aided and abetted by the Adnams Bitter and Broadside. Old-fashioned hatches and counters serve the series of cosy little rooms that feature genuine old timbers from wrecked seventeenth-century ships. Those after food will find the blackboards feature at least four local dishes, and, in season, local game as well. No children inside. Accommodation available.
Open *11.30 to 2.30, 7 to 11, Sun 12 to 2.45, 7 to 10.30*

OSWALDKIRK

North Yorkshire   map 9
Malt Shovel
Oswaldkirk YO62 5XT
TEL: (01439) 788461
on B1363, 4m S of Helmsley
Just within the North York Moors National Park, not far from Rievaulx Abbey, the Malt Shovel was built as a manor house in 1610 and became a coaching inn during the eighteenth century. It is now a Grade II listed building, worth visiting not just for its location but for its characterful interior: the taproom boasts a huge inglenook and a lofty beamed ceiling, and roaring log fires warm the two little bars. Samuel Smith Old Brewery Bitter is on handpump, and three wines are available by the glass. Note

that no food is served on Wednesdays or Sunday evenings.

Open *Mon to Fri 11 to 3, 6 to 11, Sat 11 to 11, Sun 12 to 3, 7 to 10.30*

OVING

West Sussex   map 3

Gribble Inn

Gribble Lane, Oving PO20 6BP
TEL: (01243) 786893
off A259, 3m E of Chichester

This old thatched building has been a pub only since 1980 but is making up for lost time by being the home of the Gribble Brewery (owned by Hall & Woodhouse). Its six handpumps offer the brewery's four regular brews, from Fursty Ferret to Reg's Tipple, plus seasonals like Plucking Pheasant and Porterhouse. There's also a list of 12 wines that includes eight by the glass. The pub has a non-smoking family room as well as a pleasant garden where children are welcome (they do a children's menu too). Daily blackboard specials supplement the printed menu, and there are always vegetarian options.

Open *11 to 3 (4 summer), 5.30 to 11, Sun 12 to 3 (4.30 summer), 7 to 10.30*

PAGLESHAM

Essex   map 3

Plough & Sail

East End, Paglesham SS4 2EQ
TEL: (01702) 258242
off B1013, 4m E of Rochford

Home-made pies are something of a speciality at this 400-year-old weatherboarded pub, and pudding and pie evenings are held occasionally on Thursday evenings in winter. Fish and shellfish are also strong points of the blackboard menus. A brew from Mighty Oak and perhaps something from Ridleys or Greene King IPA are on draught, and 10 wines are served by the glass. The pub, in a peaceful spot just a short walk from the River Roach, has a spacious garden.

Open *11.30 to 3 (3.30 Sat), 7 to 11, Sun 12 to 3.30, 7 to 10.30*

PEACEMARSH

Dorset   map 2

Dolphin Inn

Peacemarsh SP8 4HB
TEL: (01747) 822758
on B3095, just N of Gillingham and 6m NW of Shaftesbury

Formerly a farmhouse, this creeper-clad building is near enough to the A303 to make a pleasant pit stop. It has a garden (with play area) for summer al fresco sipping. Inside, four pumps dispense Badger Best Bitter, Tanglefoot, Sussex Bitter, and a guest from the Hall & Woodhouse portfolio, or there are seven wines by the glass. The menu is supplemented by specials, many of which are fish from Cornwall or the South Coast: mussels, monkfish, skate or sea bass.

Open *11 to 3, 6 to 11, Sun 12 to 10.30*

PELDON

Essex   map 5

Peldon Rose

Mersea Road, Peldon CO5 7QJ
TEL: (01206) 735248
off B1025, 5m S of Colchester

This attractive old pub is in a picturesque location less than a mile from the causeway to Mersea Island and lays on all the fifteenth-century timber beams and wonky angles you could wish for – until you pass through to the airy modern conservatory dining room at the back. Food is reliable if not adventurous, but the combination of Adnams beers and Lay & Wheeler wines (25 offered by the glass) hits the bull's-eye.

Open *11 to 11, Sun 12 to 10.30*

PELYNT

Cornwall   map 1

Jubilee Inn

Pelynt PL13 2JZ
TEL: (01503) 220312
on B3359, 4m NW of Looe

This long, low, white-painted medieval farmhouse-turned-pub dropped The Axe for Jubilee Inn in 1887, and the décor celebrates Queen Victoria. Bass is one of four well-kept regular real ales, alongside local brews from Sharp's (Doom Bar Bitter), Skinner's (Betty Stogs Bitter) and perhaps St Austell (there are three wines by the glass too). Menu and blackboards feature fresh local fish and game when available. There are 11 en suite rooms and a large garden.

Open *Mon to Fri 12 to 3, 6 to 11, Sat 12 to 11, Sun 12 to 10.30*

PENELEWEY

Cornwall   map 1

Punch Bowl & Ladle

Penelewey TR3 6QY
TEL: (01872) 862237

from A39 3m S of Truro, take B3289 towards King Harry Ferry

Formerly a courthouse and a meeting place for Customs and Excise men, this rambling fifteenth-century thatched and rose-covered cottage is handy for Trelissick Gardens (NT) and the King Harry Ferry. Inside is a charming series of interconnecting, low-beamed rooms with open fires, sofas and easy chairs, and a collection of rural bygones. This St Austell house has Tinners Ale and Tribute (plus Bass) as regular ales, with HSD on occasion and guests like Goddards Winter Warmer on the other three pumps. Wine bibbers can choose from 30 bottles, and locally sourced food favours fish (scallops, sea bass, smoked haddock) and game in season.

Open *11.30 to 3, 5.30 to 11, Sat 11.30 to 11, Sun 12 to 10.30; open all day June to mid-Sept*

PENRITH

Cumbria   map 10

Agricultural

Castlegate, Penrith CA11 7JE
TEL: (01768) 862622

Local affection for the 'Aggie' is much in evidence at busy Sunday lunchtimes, when hearty, good-value traditional pub grub seems to hit the spot. For visitors it is easily found by following signs for the ruins of Penrith castle, which stand opposite this town-centre hotel. It's an imposing building but in the bar red upholstery, wheel-back chairs and etched-glass panels make for comfortably pubby surroundings. New licensees have taken over since our last inspection,

but continue to serve the full range of local Jennings ales. Reports please.

Open *11 to 11, Sun 12 to 10.30*

PERRY GREEN

Hertfordshire   map 5

Hoops Inn

Bourne Lane, Perry Green SG10 6EF
TEL: (01279) 843568

off B180, just before Much Hadham, 5m N of Ware

This seventeenth-century inn is conveniently placed for visitors to the Henry Moore Foundation sculpture park. The large garden includes a paddock for horse-riders to rest their mounts in while they tuck into the house speciality sizzlers – maybe flame-grilled steak or a prawn stir-fry. Regular guest beers are Greene King IPA, Woodforde's Wherry, Fuller's London Pride and Young's Bitter.

Open *11.30 to 3, 6 to 11, Sun 12 to 3, 7 to 10.30*

PIERCEBRIDGE

Co Durham   map 10

George Hotel

Piercebridge DL2 3SW
TEL: (01325) 374576

on B6275, 5m W of Darlington

A white-painted, red-tiled sixteenth-century inn by the bridge where Adnams Broadside and Timothy Taylor Landlord are on handpump, and there's a choice of around 30 wines (six by the glass). Food emphasises local produce: fresh game in season, plus seafood dishes like Whitby crab or lemon sole, and chocolate and Grand Marnier mousse to finish. Children are welcome, and there are 35 en-suite rooms.

Open *11 to 11, Sun 12 to 10.30*

PILLATON

Cornwall   map 1

Weary Friar

Pillaton PL12 6QS
TEL: (01579) 350238

2m W of A38, between Saltash and Callington

This white twelfth-century inn nuzzles the church of St Odolphus (it began as a hostel for the church's builders) in the valley of the Lynher above Saltash. Three pumps offer the local Weary Ale and either Wadworth 6X or Sharp's Doom Bar, plus a guest (maybe Blackawton 44 Special); four wines come by the glass too. Children are welcome if dining, and the food emphasises local fish and game. The pub has a garden and a no-smoking area, plus 12 rooms for B&B.

Open *11.30 to 3.30, 6.30 to 11, Sun 12 to 3, 7 to 10.30*

PITTON

Wiltshire   map 2

Silver Plough

White Hill, Pitton SP5 1DU
TEL: (01722) 712266
off A30, 5m E of Salisbury

Say you're belting along the A30 and suddenly fancy a games of skittles …. Well, anyway, if you *were*, they've got a skittle alley here, as well as a nice garden. Badger IPA, Best Bitter and Tanglefoot are the regular ales, and eight of the 30-odd wines listed are offered by the glass, as are another 15 fruit wines. Food, served in both bar and restaurant, takes in chicken curry and salmon fillet, not to mention the produce of the village smokehouse.

Open *11 to 3, 6 to 11, Sun 12 to 3, 6 to 10.30*

PLUMLEY

Cheshire   map 7

Smoker

Plumley WA16 0TY
TEL: (01565) 722338
off A556, 4m SW of Knutsford

Smoker was the Prince Regent's favourite racehorse, so the name of this thatched, white-walled pub, which dates from Elizabethan times, is younger than the building. Its comfortable sofas and open fires create a welcoming atmosphere. Robinson's Best and Old Stockport Bitters are joined by monthly-changing guest beers like Cwmbran's Double Hop, and supplemented by over 30 malt whiskies and 21 wines (ten of them available by the glass). As well as snacks, there are traditional dishes prepared from local ingredients

(including beef, game and salmon) and a children's menu as well.

Open *11.30 to 3, 6 to 11, Sun 12 to 10.30*

PLUSH

Dorset   map 2

Brace of Pheasants

Plush DT2 7RQ
Tel: (01300) 348357
off B3143, 2m N of Piddletrenthide

The country-cottage appearance – neat thatch, brilliant white-painted walls and wreaths of greenery – may be timeless, but big changes have come to this sixteenth-century inn with the arrival of new owners Toby and Suzie Albu and chef Noel Ashbourne, formerly of London restaurant Ransome's Dock. Food is the focus, but there's a serious line-up of cask beers from Butcombe, Ringwood, Bass, Fuller's and Adnams, and seven wines from the 24-strong list are available by the glass. The pub also claims to have the fastest skittle alley in Dorset. Children welcome. Reports please.

Open *12 to 2.30, 7 to 11, Sun 12 to 3, 7 to 10.30*

POLKERRIS

Cornwall   map 1

Rashleigh Inn

Polkerris PL24 2TL
TEL: (01726) 813991
off A3082, 2½m W of Fowey

This former coastguard station in deepest Du Maurier country (aka the Inn on the Beach) overlooks a tiny cove beside an isolated beach and restored jetty. Sit on the terrace watching the sunset over St Austell Bay, quaffing the (Sharp's-brewed) own-label Rashleigh Bitter, Sharp's Doom Bar Bitter or Timothy Taylor Landlord, or one of three ever-changing guests (some 300 annually). Eight wines come by the glass. Bar food and the Monday-to-Saturday evening carte make the most of local fish and game, but include barracuda and swordfish also.

Open *11 to 11, Sun 12 to 10.30, 25 Dec 12 to 2*

POLPERRO

Cornwall   map 1

Blue Peter

Quay Road, Polperro PL13 2QZ
TEL: (01503) 272743

on A387, 3m SW of Looe

With a fine view of the delightful
fishing village of Polperro from its
eyrie in the cliff face overlooking the
harbour, this charmingly old-
fashioned pub nevertheless focuses on
what really matters – well-kept real
ales. Regulars are Sharp's Doom Bar
Bitter and St Austell HSD while guests
such as Cotleigh Golden Eagle or
Sharp's Special extend the range to
around five in summer, when Colin
Vincent's scrumpy is also available.
Seafood is the mainstay of the
lunchtime-only menu, in adventurous
combinations such as pilchard
bruschetta with roasted peppers,
spinach and olives.
Open *11 to 11, Sun 12 to 10.30*

POSTBRIDGE

Devon   map 1

Warren House Inn

Postbridge PL20 6TA
TEL: (01822) 880208

*on B3212 1½m E of Postbridge towards
Moretonhampstead*

One of England's highest inns, this is
in the middle of nowhere with
magnificent views to match; reputedly,
one of the bar's two fires has burned
continuously since the place was built
in 1845! Regular brews are Moor
Beer's Old Freddy Walker, Sharp's
Doom Bar Bitter and Butcombe Gold,
plus changing guests like Shepherd
Neame Spitfire or Badger Tanglefoot.
Rabbit pie and game pie may be on the
different lunchtime and evening
menus or on the specials boards.
Open *Mon to Thur 11 to 3, 6 to 11,
Fri and Sat 11 to 11, Sun 12 to 10.30; all week
11 to 11 in summer*

POWERSTOCK

Dorset   map 2

Three Horseshoes

Powerstock DT6 3TF
TEL: (01308) 485328

off A3066 at Gore Cross, 4m NE of Bridport

Reached down winding country lanes
overhung with trees, village locations
don't come any more idyllic than this.
But just along the road from the
church change is afoot at this stone-
built pub, where new licensees have
plans to reinvigorate the bar and dining
room. Palmers beers (IPA and
Coppers) are complemented by six
wines. Reports please.
Open *11 to 3, 6 to 11, Sun 12 to 3,
7 to 10.30*

POYNINGS

West Sussex   map 3

Royal Oak Inn

The Street, Poynings BN45 7AQ
TEL: (01273) 857389

off A281, 4m NW of Hove

This white old inn below the Devil's
Dyke has an atmospheric beamed bar,
and is especially appealing to families,
as children are welcome (except at the
bar) and have a special play area. Ales
on draught are Old Speckled Hen and
Courage Directors, plus one from
Harveys, and eight wines come by the
glass. The specials boards change twice
a week, and they have barbecues at
summer weekends.
Open *11.30 to 11, Sun 12 to 10.30*

PRIORS DEAN

Hampshire   map 2

White Horse Inn

Priors Dean GU32 1DA
TEL: (01420) 588387

*off A3 or A32, 3m N of Petersfield and ½m
N of Steep*

A hard one to find (OS ref.
SU726265). The empty iron inn-sign
frame outside prompts the local
nickname, the Pub With No Name.
Inside, there's a warm atmosphere
with stuffed sofas, leather armchairs,
candles in bottles and farm gadgets.
Real ales are the draw, with six regulars
(Ringwood Fortyniner, Fuller's
London Pride, Gale's Butser Bitter and

HSB, and a couple of own-labels: No
Name Best and Strong) and three or
four guests; there are also 21 country
fruit wines by the glass. Food (not
available on Sunday evenings or
Mondays) stresses local produce.
Open *11 to 2.30, 6 to 11, Sun 12 to 3,
7 to 10.30*

RATTERY

Devon   map 1

Church House Inn
Rattery TQ10 9LD
TEL: (01364) 642220
off A385, 4½m W of Totnes

This is one of Britain's oldest pubs;
some parts of the building date to 1028
when it housed craftsmen building the
parish church next door. Inside are
reminders of its past – a massive oak
screen, beams and standing timbers.
Real ales are Greene King Abbot, St
Austell's Dartmoor Best Bitter, Wells
Bombardier and Adnams Broadside,
plus occasional guests. Children are
welcomed, and there are a patio and
garden. Locally sourced food includes
game in season and lots of fish.
Open *Mon to Fri 11 to 3, 6 to 11, Sat 11 to 3,
6 to 11 (11 to 11 summer), Sun 12 to 3,
6 to 10.30 (12 to 10.30 summer)*

RATTLESDEN

Suffolk   map 6

Brewers Arms
Lower Road, Rattlesden IP30 0RJ
TEL: (01449) 736377
off A14, 5m W of Stowmarket

This attractive old pub, both inside and
out, is at the centre of the small village
and has a smartly attired bar and a
separate restaurant, though the same
menus are available throughout. The
cooking blends old and new ideas:
moules marinière, onion and Stilton
tartlet, and main courses of gammon
steak with honey and mustard sauce,
lamb and coriander burger on ciabatta,
and poacher's pot (boar, rabbit,
pheasant and venison cooked in ale
and red wine gravy). The pub is tied to
local brewery Greene King, so expect
Abbot Ale and IPA on draught.
Open *11.30 to 2.30, 6 to 11, Sun 12 to 3,
7 to 10.30*

REEDHAM

Norfolk   map 6

Reedham Ferry Inn
Ferry Road, Reedham NR13 3HA
TEL: (01493) 700429
off A47, 6m S of Acle

For almost 50 years the Archers have
run this seventeenth-century inn next
to the chain ferry across the Yare (the
only crossing for cars between
Yarmouth and Norwich). To
customers from road or river (or the
caravan site behind) they serve
Woodforde's Wherry, Adnams Best
and Broadside and a weekly-changing
guest (St Peter's Mild, perhaps, or
Ferryman from Reedham's own
Humpty Dumpty Brewery). Stowford
Press cider is also available, plus three
wines by the glass, not to mention
mulled wine and sangria. Food
includes local game (duck, partridge),
fish and veggie alternatives, and there
is a children's menu too.
Open *11 to 2.30 (3 summer), 7 (6.30 summer)
to 11, Sun 12 to 10.30*

RIDGEWELL

Essex   map 6

White Horse
Mill Road, Ridgewell CO9 4SG
TEL: (01440) 785532
on A1017, 6m SE of Haverhill

Despite its plain exterior, this child-
friendly pub on the main street has a
welcoming atmosphere, an unusual
bar counter covered in old pennies and
a spacious dining room. A menu of
familiar pub dishes also includes
chicken Dijon and home-made pies,
alongside ploughman's and organic
baguettes. Two pumps dispense a
twice-weekly-changing array of guest
ales, from locals such as Ridleys and
Nethergate or incomers like Archers
or Caledonian. Then there's twelve
wines by the glass, and Pimm's or
sangria for heliotropes.
Open *Wed to Sat 11 to 3, Mon to Sat 6 to 11,
Sun 12 to 10.30*

RINGLESTONE

Kent   map 3

Ringlestone Inn

Ringlestone, nr Harrietsham ME17 1EX
TEL: (01622) 859900

off A20, 3m N of Harrietsham

Built in 1533 as a monks' hospice, this
became an alehouse after the
Reformation. There's a pleasant eight-
acre garden outside, and the brick and
flint interior and stout wooden
furniture make an atmospheric setting
for food and drink. Theakston Old
Peculier, Greene King IPA, and
Shepherd Neame Bishops Finger are
available, plus a wide range of
Ringlestone fruit wines. The latter
reappear in dishes like chicken and
asparagus in cowslip wine, beef in
black beer and raisin wine, and salmon
and prawns in elderflower wine.
Open *Mon to Fri 11 to 3, 6 to 11, Sat 11 to
11, Sun 12 to 10.30; closed 25 Dec*

RINGMER

East Sussex   map 3

Cock

Uckfield Road, Ringmer BN8 5RX
TEL: (01273) 812040

just off A26, 2m NE of Lewes

With views of the South Downs, this
sixteenth-century inn makes for a
pleasant real ale pub. The beer range
takes in Harveys Sussex Best Bitter,
Fuller's London Pride, Flowers
Original and Harveys seasonal brews.
Half a dozen wines from a list of about
20 are served by the large or small
glass. Blackboards list a fair selection of
traditional pub food including
vegetarian options. Children are
welcome.
Open *11 to 3, 6 to 11, Sun 12 to 3, 7 to 10.30*

RINGSTEAD

Norfolk   map 6

Gin Trap Inn

High Street, Ringstead PE36 5JU
TEL: (01485) 525264

off A149, 2m E of Hunstanton

In January 2003 new owners stepped
in at this beautifully maintained
seventeenth-century coaching inn

situated on the Peddar's Way close to
the north Norfolk coast. It is a popular
stop-off for walkers and tourists alike
and offers a range of traditional pub
food. The bar has low-beamed
ceilings, and a cosy, welcoming
atmosphere; here East Anglian ales
take pride of place and include those
from Woodforde's, and the specially
brewed, by Woodforde's, Gin Trap
Bitter. Three en suite rooms are
available.
Open *11.30 to 2.30, 6 to 11, Sun 11.45 to
2.30. 6.45 to 10.30; summer 10.30 to 11, Sun
12 to 10.30*

ROBIN HOOD'S BAY

North Yorkshire   map 9

Laurel Inn

New Road, Robin Hood's Bay
YO22 4SE
TEL: (01947) 880400

*at end of B1447 (off A171), 5m SE of
Whitby*

The tall and narrow Laurel Inn is one
of the tiniest pubs in Yorkshire.
Standing among fishermen's cottages
in this much-loved cliffside village,
famed for its narrow streets and
dramatic seascapes, it is worth
searching out after a stroll along the
beach. Theakston ales are served in the
beamed bar which is carved from solid
rock, and during opening hours soup
and sandwiches are available. Self-
catering flat for two people is available.
Open *Mon to Sat 12 to 11, 25 Dec
12 to 2*

ROKE

Oxfordshire   map 2

Home Sweet Home

Roke OX10 6JD
TEL: (01491) 838249

*turn at the signpost 'Home Sweet Home' on
B4009, between Benson and Watlington*

Tranquilly set next to a field where you
might spot sheep, this thatched pub has
a fine beer garden enclosed by low stone
walls. Inside, the atmosphere is relaxed
and friendly. Blackboards give bar
specials, and there's a separate à la carte
restaurant. Henry's Original IPA from
Wadworth is on tap, and five wines

from a 20-bottle list are available by the glass. Children are welcome throughout.
Open *11 to 3, 6 to 11, Sun 12 to 3; closed 25 and 26 Dec*

ROMALDKIRK

Co Durham   map 10
Kirk Inn
Romaldkirk DL12 9GD
TEL: (01833) 650260
on B6277, 6m NW of Barnard Castle
New licensees took over the rustic Kirk Inn, a real community local set on the village green, in early 2003. This tiny one-room pub doubles as the village post office each morning and is a favoured walkers' retreat; the Pennine Way and splendid walking country are close by. Home-made soup, sandwiches and jam roly-poly feature alongside heartier far, and real ales from independent North Country breweries, in particular Black Sheep, White Boar and Timothy Taylor Landlord. Reports please.
Open *12 to 3, 7 to 10.30 (11 summer exc Sun)*

ROTHERFIELD PEPPARD

Oxfordshire   map 2
Greyhound
Gallowtree Road, Rotherfield Peppard RG9 5HT
TEL: (0118) 972 2227
off B481 N of Sonning Common
The Greyhound is an ancient brick and timber building, its tiled roof as wonky as ever, and, despite a change of ownership, bar snacks still look interesting enough: lamb stewed in Guinness with dumplings, smoked bacon and black pudding salad with a poached egg, and salmon fillet on a mussel and tiger prawn stir-fry, for example. There is also a separate restaurant with a more ambitious menu. Real ales are from Brakspear, Fuller's and Hook Norton. Reports please.
Open *11 to 3.30, 6 to 11, Sun 12 to 6.30*

RYE

East Sussex   map 3
Mermaid Inn
Mermaid Street, Rye TN31 7EY
TEL: (01797) 223065
This lovely old inn, dating from Elizabethan times, is set among other fine buildings on one of the cobbled streets of Rye. Enter through imposing old doors and continue down a corridor hung with portraits of Elizabethan and Tudor greats – Sir Walter Raleigh, the Earl of Leicester and some of Henry's wives for good measure. In the bar a huge inglenook fireplace virtually takes up one wall, and there are pikes and swords and good-quality furnishings and fabrics. The bar menu offers up seafood platter, spaghetti and baguettes; there's a children's menu too. Drink Old Speckled Hen or Courage Best. Accommodation available.
Open *11 to 11, Sun 12 to 10.30*

ST AGNES

Isles of Scilly   map 1
Turk's Head
St Agnes TR22 0PL
TEL: (01720) 422434
Set on a tiny island popular with wildlife watchers, who flock here in search of seals and seabirds, is a nineteenth-century slate-roofed cottage overlooking the harbour and quay: the Turk's Head is a 20-minute boat journey from the main island. Bedecked with nautical memorabilia, the pub serves traditional beers – Dartmoor Best and Turks Ale – and a favoured tipple here is hot chocolate laced with St Agnes brandy. Menus include local fish and home-made pies. Children are welcome. One bedroom for overnight guests.
Open *11 to 11, Sun 12 to 10.30; closed some days winter*

ST BREWARD

Cornwall   map 1

Old Inn

St Breward PL30 4PP
TEL: (01208) 850711
off B3266, 4m S of Camelford

The Old Inn, at one time a staging post for smugglers hauling contraband along the north Cornish coast, now plies a more respectable trade. Among the handpumped beers are Sharp's Doom Bar Bitter and Special and traditional scrumpy is drawn from a barrel; eight wines served by the glass. A specials menu includes Barbary duck in plum sauce, a selection of seasonal fish and to conclude perhaps ginger pudding or summer fruit brûlée.
Open *Mon to Thur 11 to 3, 6 to 11, Fri and Sat 11 to 11, Sun 12 to 10.30; open 11 to 11 Mon to Thur June to Sept*

ST EWE

Cornwall   map 1

Crown Inn

St Ewe PL26 6EY
TEL: (01726) 843322
between B3287 and B3273, 5m SW of St Austell

This attractive, flower-bedecked sixteenth-century local, not far from the Lost Gardens of Heligan, is set in a village named after the local saint. Inside, a slate floor and open fire set the tone for drinkers who – given this is a St Austell house – will find Tinners, HSD, Duchy and Tribute the regulars on tap. For overspill there's a sheltered garden with heated marquee. No bar food is on offer, but a separate dining room serves ocean pie, Barnsley lamb chop, and game. Children are welcome, and there's accommodation in one double room.
Open *12 (11 summer) to 3, 5 to 11, Sun 12 to 3, 5 to 10.30*

ST JUST

Cornwall   map 1

Star Inn

Fore Street, St Just TR19 7LL
TEL: (01736) 788767
on A3071/B3306, 4m N of Land's End

This is a friendly place, jam-packed with atmosphere and local characters.

Granite-built and beamed within, the eighteenth-century Star stands in a terrace on the narrow road through the village, and is the scene of live accordion music some nights, perhaps singing or joke-telling others. There's a family room, and hearty simple pub fare is available throughout lunchtimes. Beer enthusiasts will find St Austell's brews: Tinners Ale straight from the barrel, plus HSD, Dartmoor and Black Prince. Accommodation in three rooms.
Open *11 to 11, Sun 12 to 10.30; closed lunchtime 25 Dec*

SALFORD

Greater Manchester   map 8

Mark Addy

7 Stanley Street, Salford M3 5EJ
TEL: (0161) 832 4080

A busy, attractive, modern warehouse conversion overlooking the River Irwell in the city centre, with terraces outside for fine-weather drinking. Best bet are the good-value, generously portioned cold platters of cheeses and pâtés with granary bread or focaccia, which are served all day. Options run to a fairly standard range of cooked dishes – pasta, pies and steaks – as well as salads and hot sandwiches. Drink Boddingtons, Moorhouses Pride of Pendle, or something off the blackboard of 'wines of the week'.
Open *11.30 to 11, Sun 12 to 10.30*

SCALES

Cumbria   map 10

White Horse Inn

Scales CA12 4SY
TEL: (01768) 779241
just off A66 Keswick to Penrith road, 5m NE of Keswick

The White Horse's elevated position provides a haven from the traffic – the inn and the house next door are on a bend of the old meandering A66 before it was straightened out into a dual carriageway. It is seemingly a must-do for fell walkers fresh from a conquest of Saddleback. Long, low, beamed and homely, it offers comfort food along the lines of grilled black pudding in pepper sauce, venison haunch steak, pork fillet, vegetarian butter-bean casserole, and perhaps

home-made apple pie to round things off. Jennings ales and Black Sheep Best Bitter are served, and the wine list numbers around 30 bottles.
Open *12 to 3, 6.30 to 11 (10.30 Sun)*

SCAWTON

North Yorkshire   map 9

Hare Inn
Scawton YO7 2HG
TEL: (01845) 597289
off A170, 7m E of Thirsk
Situated within the North York Moors National Park and convenient for the Cleveland Way and Rievaulx Abbey, this low, cream-painted pub stands in a charming village of stone cottages. Eccentric collections of radios, puppets and crockery vie with a cottagey-style dining area. The menu is mainly traditional with some European ideas – perhaps a starter of crab with celeriac rémoulade, followed by salmon steak with tomato and basil sauce. Sandwiches and snacks are lighter lunchtime options. Black Sheep Best Bitter and Timothy Taylor Landlord are on draught, plus guests. Wines are good value with nine by the glass. A new licensee was expected as the Guide went to press, so reports please.
Open *12 to 3, 6.30 to 11 winter, 12 to 11 summer; closed 25 Dec, Mon winter*

SEVERN STOKE

Worcestershire   map 5

Rose and Crown
Church Lane, Severn Stoke WR8 9JQ
TEL: (01905) 371249
on A38 between Worcester and Tewkesbury
An ancient black and white half-timbered pub at the centre of the village, opposite the village green – the pub has an extensive children's play area which is tacked on to this area. Décor is conventional (horse brasses, hop wreaths, and so on) but bottles of flavoured oils on tables hint at an ambitious kitchen. On the menu might be warm salad of seared scallops in a light ginger dressing, then rosemary-roasted rack of lamb in a garlic, mint and Pinot Noir reduction. Lunches are simpler. Drink from a short, good-value wine list, or one of

the varying guest ales – London Pride, Bateman XB and Wells Bombardier.
Open *Mon to Fri 12 to 3, 6 to 11, Sat and Sun 12 to 11 (10.30 Sun)*

SHAMLEY GREEN

Surrey   map 3

Red Lion Inn
Shamley Green GU5 0UB
TEL: (01483) 892202
on B2128, 4m SE of Guildford
Neat white-painted pub opposite the green itself with upmarket bar food: for example, half a roast duck in black cherry sauce or ribeye steak, followed by strawberry and passion-fruit cheesecake. There is a separate restaurant. Marston's Pedigree, Adnams Broadside and Young's ales are regular beers, and six of the 30 wines listed are available by the glass. Open for breakfast, guest accommodation.
Open *Mon to Fri 7.30am to 11.30pm, Sat 8.30am to 11.30pm, Sun 8.30am to 10.30pm*

SHARDLOW

Derbyshire   map 5

Malt Shovel
The Wharf, Shardlow DE72 2HG
TEL: (01332) 799763
off A6, 6m SE of Derby
As its name suggests the Malt Shovel is part of a converted and greatly extended eighteenth-century maltings, situated on the banks of the Trent & Mersey Canal. Expect tables outside for warmer days and Marston's Pedigree, Adnams Bitter and Banks's Bitter on handpump; straightforward pub food is served lunchtimes only. Children are welcome.
Open *11 to 11, Sun 12 to 10.30; closed 25 Dec*

SHEEPSCOMBE

Gloucestershire   map 2

Butchers Arms
Sheepscombe GL6 7RH
TEL: (01452) 812113
Marvel at the glorious views over the rolling Stroud valley from this seventeenth-century mellow-stone pub, at the heart of *Cider with Rosie* country. In summer sit on the steeply

sloping lawn, and in winter gather around log fires in the characterful bars. Order a pint of Hook Norton Best, Wye Valley Dorothy Goodbody or Uley Old Spot and select from the interesting range of food, which includes home-cooked daily specials.
Open *11.30 to 3, 6.30 (6 summer) to 11, Sun 12 to 4, 7 to 10.30*

SHEEPWASH

Devon   map 1
Half Moon Inn
Sheepwash EX21 5NE
TEL: (01409) 231376
off A3072, 4m W of Hatherleigh
This long, white-painted village inn near the River Torridge, with its ten miles of fishing rights, attracts fishermen eager to cast a line for salmon and sea and brown trout. Facilities include a rod room, tackle shop and personal tuition. The classic, slate-floored main bar has a huge inglenook, Ruddles, Courage and Sharp's ales on draught, a 200-strong wine list, and an impressive selection of malt whiskies. Simple lunchtime snacks in the bar; à la carte restaurant dinners evening only. Twelve en suite bedrooms.
Open *11.30 to 2.30, 6 to 11, Sun 12 to 2.30, 7 to 10.30*

SHENINGTON

Oxfordshire   map 5
Bell
Shenington OX15 6NQ
TEL: (01295) 670274
off A422, 6m W of Banbury
Very much at the heart of village life is the Bell, a cottagey, stone-built pub dating from the seventeenth century and fronting a three-acre green in a sleepy Oxfordshire village. A tip-top pint of Hook Norton Best is served in the lively locals' bar, and a snug and welcoming lounge/restaurant area is the setting for a good choice of freshly prepared food, using local produce where possible. Accommodation is available in three letting bedrooms.
Open *12 to 2.30, 6.30 to 11, Sun 12 to 3, 7 to 10.30; closed Mon lunchtime, eve 25 Dec*

SHIPTON-UNDER-WYCHWOOD

Oxfordshire   map 5
Shaven Crown Hotel
High Street, Shipton-under-Wychwood OX7 6BA
TEL: (01993) 830330
on A361, 4m NE of Burford
Addlestone's cider is served alongside Hook Norton and a guest ale of perhaps Old Speckled Hen or London Pride at this honey-coloured stone hotel built in the fourteenth century. It was formerly a monks' hospice, and retains several original features including the medieval hall now used as a residents' lounge. Stables have been converted into a small bar. The bar menu might list stir-fried beef with cashew nuts or venison sausages with celeriac mash. Children are welcome, nine en suite rooms are available.
Open *11 to 2.30, 5 to 11 (10.30 Sun)*

SHRALEYBROOK

Staffordshire   map 5
Rising Sun
Knowle Bank Road, Shraleybrook ST7 8DS
TEL: (01782) 720600
Three beers with recipes devised by a group of local ale enthusiasts and named on a civil war theme are produced here at the Shraley Brook Brewery. They are joined by regularly changing real ales, such as Abbot Ale and Old Speckled Hen, and 10 wines by the glass. Bar food is straightforward stuff; as well as omelettes, burgers, salads and various pizzas are main courses along the lines of venison in red wine, chicken Kiev, or salmon in asparagus sauce. Vegetarians have their own better-than-average menu.
Open *Mon to Thur 6 to 11, Fri and Sat 11.45 to 11, Sun 12 to 10.30*

SHREWSBURY

Shropshire   map 5
The Armoury
Victoria Quay, Welsh Bridge, Shrewsbury SY1 1HH
TEL: (01743) 340525
This 'fabulous' warehouse-like pub overlooking the River Severn was

indeed once an armoury. It has also been a bakery, and with all the books that line the walls, it could even pass for a library. In between the books are framed collections of pipes and explosives, but perhaps of more interest is the remarkable collection of real ales: Wadworth 6X, Wood Shropshire Lad and Thwaites Lancaster Bomber are just some of the names you might find. This is very much a socialising and drinking environment, but food is worth a mention: try salmon and tarragon fishcakes, pan-fried duck breast stuffed with coriander and ginger and conclude with warm treacle tart.

Open *12 to 11 (10.30 Sun)*

Three Fishes

4 Fish Street, Shrewsbury SY1 1UR
TEL: (01743) 344793

At the heart of Shrewsbury, Fish Street is a steep, seriously cobbled thoroughfare lined with ancient half-timbered buildings, including this Grade II listed fifteenth-century pub. It has a 'brilliant' atmosphere and an excellent range of beers on tap, including Adnams Bitter and Fuller's London Pride, plus ever-changing locally brewed guest ales such as Proud Salopian, and Wye Valley HPA. The long, colourful printed menu has sections titled 'light bites' (things like spicy chicken wings, or duck and port pâté), 'salad bowls' (hot bacon and Stilton), and 'hearty meals' – everything from lamb cutlets with mint gravy to chicken curry.

Open *Mon to Thur 11.30 to 3, 5 to 11, Fri and Sat 11.30 to 11, Sun 12 to 10.30*

SHUSTOKE

Warwickshire   map 5

Griffin

Shustoke B46 2LB
TEL: (01675) 481205

on B4114, 2½m E of Coleshill

A former oak-framed coaching inn harking back to the early seventeenth century with ten ales on tap including Marston's Pedigree, Theakston Old Peculier, Wells Bombardier and Banks's Original, with scrumpy (in summer). The short menu concentrates on snacks

and traditional pub dishes. Food is only served at lunchtime and not on Sundays. Children are welcome in the conservatory.

Open *12 to 2.30, 7 to 11, Sun 12 to 2.30, 7 to 10.30*

SLEDMERE

East Riding of Yorkshire   map 9

Triton Inn

Sledmere YO25 3XQ
TEL: (01377) 236644

village on B1253 16m W of Bridlington

In 2,000 acres laid out by Capability Brown is Sledmere House, which contains remarkable antique furniture and a room which is a copy of a sultan's apartments in Istanbul. The Triton was built in the mid-eighteenth century as the coach house just within the grounds. Food on the bar menu offers standard pub fare, two or three daily specials and a set menu. On draught are Tetley and John Smith's Bitter and Stowford Press cider.

Open *Mon to Sat (exc Mon lunchtime) 11.30 to 2.30, 7 to 11.30, Sun 12 to 3, 7.30 to 10.30*

SMARDEN

Kent   map 3

Bell Inn

Bell Lane, Smarden TN27 8PW
TEL: (01233) 770283

off A274, 7m SW of Charing; pub is ½m outside village (signposted from village)

The age of this half-tiled pub is apparent in the ancient-looking red-brick walls, gnarled beams and tiled floors in the warren of small linked rooms. Menus are listed on blackboards, and the choice of dishes is wide but doesn't seem to change that often. Typically, expect things like duck breast with game chips and black cherry sauce, grilled plaice with creamy prawn and white wine sauce, tuna steak on stir-fried vegetables with soy sauce, and lamb shank on sweet potato with redcurrant and rosemary sauce. There is also a good range of draught real ales: Flowers IPA, London Pride, Shepherd Neame Spitfire, Marston's and a seasonally changing guest ale.

Open *11.30 to 3, 6 to 11, Sun 12 to 10.30; closed 25 Dec*

SMART'S HILL

Kent   map 3

Spotted Dog Inn

Smart's Hill TN11 8EE

TEL: (01892) 870253

off B2188, 1m S of Penshurst

Dating from 1520, this
weatherboarded inn, under new
management, is popular with walkers
and locals alike. Inside are low ceilings
and quarry-tiled or oak-boarded floors;
outside is an attractive garden, and
from the rear of the pub are wonderful
views across the valley. Larkins
Traditional Ale and Harveys Sussex
Best Bitter are the regular real ales,
with a guest such as Greene King
Abbot Ale or Old Speckled Hen; half a
dozen wines are available by the glass.
Bar snacks are served at lunchtimes,
and the full menu is complemented by
blackboards of specials. Penshurst
Place is worth visiting for its great hall
alone.

Open *Mon to Wed 11 to 3, 6 to 11
(11 to 11 summer), Thur to Sat 11 to 11,
Sun 12 to 10.30*

SNAPE

Suffolk   map 6

Golden Key

Priory Road, Snape IP17 1SG

TEL: (01728) 688510

just off B1069, 3m S of Saxmundham

Beer at the Golden Key is Adnams
Best Bitter and Broadside, and guests
are Fisherman and Tally Ho. Adnams
supply the wines too, 12 are offered by
the glass, or choose from 12 single
malts. The menu might include Stilton
and mushroom royale, grilled sardines,
steak and Guinness pie and seasonal
fish and game. Home-made puddings
might run to chocolate brandy cake.
Music is played all year round at
nearby Snape Maltings.

Open *11 to 3, 6 to 11, Sun 12 to 3,
7 (6 summer) to 10.30*

SOUTHWOLD

Suffolk   map 6

Harbour Inn

Blackshore Quay, Southwold IP18 6TA

TEL: (01502) 722381

Facing on to the harbour and
extending into neighbouring
buildings, this large pub does a roaring
trade for a mixed bag of Southwold
locals and visitors. Beers and wines
come from the commendable Adnams
stable. The kitchen pumps out a huge
amount of food from a long menu and
service can be rather impersonal.
However, basics like bangers and
mash work well and fresh veg is of a
high standard.

Open *11 to 3, 6 to 11, Sun 12 to 3, 7 to 10.30*

SOUTH WOODCHESTER

Gloucestershire   map 2

Ram Inn

Station Road, South Woodchester
GL5 5EL

TEL: (01453) 873329

off A46, 2m S of Stroud

The Ram Inn is over four hundred
years old and boasts four hundred
different guest ales over a year. Regular
tipples include Archers Golden Bitter,
Uley Old Spot Prize Ale and Wickwar,
and house wines are Australian. Hearty
pub cooking of the likes of kangaroo or
fillet steak, gammon or grilled fish is
rounded off by banoffi pie, or syrup
roly-poly. An Irish beer festival is held
annually.

Open *11 to 11, Sun 12 to 10.30*

SOUTH ZEAL

Devon   map 1

Oxenham Arms

South Zeal EX20 2JT

TEL: (01837) 840244

off A30, 4m E of Okehampton

When the Oxenham Arms (named
after a family that subsequently owned
the property) was built in the twelfth
century, a prehistoric standing stone
was incorporated into the fabric of the
building, and it can still be seen set in a
wall. Other features are a granite
fireplace in the lounge and a granite
pillar supporting a beam in the dining

room. Contemplate these and more while drinking one of three ales drawn straight from the cask: something from Dartmoor's Princetown Brewery, or from the St Austell or Sharp's Breweries in Cornwall.

Open *11 to 2.30, 5 to 11, Sun 12 to 2.30, 7 to 10.30*

SPELDHURST

Kent   map 3

George & Dragon

Speldhurst TN3 0NN
TEL: (01892) 863125
between A26 and A264, 2m NW of Tunbridge Wells

Dating from 1213, this magnificent black and white timbered inn set back from the village lane is reckoned to be one of the oldest in southern England. The claim is probably true, judging by the massive flagstones, heavy carved ceiling beams, ancient wall panelling and huge inglenook in the main bar. A range of real ales includes local Harveys Sussex Best and Larkins Traditional, and 11 wines are available by the glass. Bar food dishes include moules marinière and sausage and mash, and a separate restaurant is open Friday and Saturday evenings and Sunday lunch.

Open *11 to 11, Sun 12 to 10.30*

SPROTBROUGH

South Yorkshire   map 9

Boat Inn

Nursery Lane, Sprotbrough DN5 7NB
TEL: (01302) 857188
just off A1(M), 3m W of Doncaster

Pleasant walks upstream to a nature reserve can be taken from this Don valley pub which enjoys a riverside location and garden. Once a farmhouse, it now offers pub food – steak and ale pie, seasonal game, and chicken wrapped in pancetta, and a separate restaurant menu (à la carte and set meals). John Smith's, Courage Directors and Theakston are the ales on tap, and a wine list represents both Old and New Worlds.

Open *winter 11 to 3, 6 to 11, summer 11 to 11, Sun all year 12 to 10.30*

STANBRIDGE

Bedfordshire   map 6

Five Bells

Station Road, Stanbridge LU7 9JF
TEL: (01525) 210224

Steel-grey paintwork on the windows and doors suggests a modern outlook at this otherwise traditional white-painted building set back from the road through the village. The style is pursued inside, where a smart restaurant in cool greys contrasts with wooden bar furniture, while candles, cacti and oriental rugs add some offbeat charm. Beers are Bass Cask, Marston's Pedigree and Hook Norton, sometimes with the addition of Black Sheep, while sandwiches and sausages typify the straight-ahead pub food. All-day opening makes this a useful afternoon stopover.

Open *11 to 11, Sun 12 to 10.30*

STOCKPORT

Greater Manchester   map 8

Arden Arms

23 Millgate, Stockport SK1 2LX
TEL: (0161) 480 2185

This traditional old pub, 'a good solid Georgian block of matured Cheshire brick' decorated colourfully with hanging baskets and shrubs in tubs, is tucked away behind a large modern supermarket. Inside are several rooms, each full of individual character and charm. Beers are from Robinson's brewery, which is just a few hundred yards away so quality and freshness are guaranteed. Food is limited but represents good value. The menu offers various sandwiches (such as Brie and grape, or turkey with stuffing) and hot filled ciabattas (hot beef, tomatoes and fried onions), plus daily specials: perhaps grilled tuna on mash with spicy tomato sauce, or broccoli and Brie crêpes.

Open *12 to 11 (10.30 Sun)*

STOKE ABBOTT

Dorset   map 3

New Inn

Stoke Abbott DT8 3JW
TEL: (01308) 868333

signposted off B3163 SW of Beaminster

This large seventeenth-century grey-stone inn is advertised accurately as a 'traditional village pub'. Family-run, with a friendly and unpretentious atmosphere, it looks the part, having red-brick hearths with iron stoves, flagstone floors and walls lined with horse brasses, copper pans and decorative plates. The menu offers 'a mix of the ordinary and the extraordinary', ranging from prawn cocktail and breaded plaice to grilled Stilton-topped apricots, wild mushroom and fennel pie, and salami and mushroom muffin. Vegetarians are notably well catered for. This is a Palmers pub offering that brewery's ales.

Open *Mon to Thur 11.30 to 3, 6.30 to 11 (7 to 11 winter), Fri and Sat 11.30 to 3, 6.30 to 11, Sun 12 to 3, 6.30 to 10.30 (7 to 10.30 winter)*

STOKE BRUERNE

Northamptonshire   map 5

Boat Inn

Stoke Bruerne NN12 7SB
TEL: (01604) 862428

just W of A508, 4m E of Towcester

Owned and run by the Woodward family since around 1868, this much-extended seventeenth-century thatched inn is a popular destination for families and narrowboat enthusiasts. It boasts a prime location beside the Grand Union Canal, opposite the fascinating Canal Museum. Boat trips can be arranged by the licensees, and traditional pub food is served all day. Six real ales are on handpump, there is a characterful flagstoned bar, and a no-smoking room. Children are welcome.

Open *winter Mon to Thur 9.30am to 3, 5 to 11; summer 9am to 11pm (10.30pm Sun)*

STOKE FLEMING

Devon   map 1

Green Dragon

Church Road, Stoke Fleming TQ6 0PX
TEL: (01803) 770238

take A379 S from Dartmouth

The nautical theme of this large, custard-coloured village-centre pub is evidence of the landlord's past as a round-the-world yachtsman. It is a busy place with a relaxed but raucous atmosphere, and there always seems to be one event or another going on – live music, for example. The 'Mess Deck' offers a varied and reasonably priced bistro-style menu: among starters are Normandy livers (cooked in cider) and 'Quiddle' (battered squid rings with chilli jam), while main courses run to fish pie, chicken bonne femme, and Thai duck satay with noodles. A good number of real ales are on tap, along with eight wines by the glass.

Open *11 to 3, 5.30 to 11, Sun 12 to 3, 6.30 to 10.30*

STOUGHTON

West Sussex   map 3

Hare and Hounds

Stoughton PO18 9JQ
TEL: (023) 92631433

off B2147 at Walderton, 5m NW of Chichester

Built about 300 years ago as two cottages, the Hare and Hounds is hidden away in downland, with excellent walking, lovely views and Kingley Vale Nature Reserve nearby. Inside, the three knocked-through rooms feature flagstone floors, log fires and pine furniture. Supplementing the standard printed menu is a blackboard of specials: perhaps a fish of the day, vegetarian choices, and game in season running to pheasant casserole, partridge and venison. Six handpumps dispense, among other real ales, Timothy Taylor Landlord, Fuller's London Pride and Gale's HSB, and the wine list includes four by the glass.

Open *11 to 3, 6 to 11, Sun 12 to 3, 7 to 10.30; open all day Sun summer*

STRATTON

Dorset   map 2

Saxon Arms

The Square, Stratton DT2 9WG
Tel: (01305) 260020

off A37 3m NW of Dorchester

In contrast to the many 'New' Inns
that tend to be ancient, this pub with
an ancient-sounding name is just a
couple of years old. It's a huge flint
building with a thatched roof and a
spacious, open-plan interior. Light
snacks of deep-fried mushrooms in
beer batter, and grilled black pudding
with pear and ginger chutney, are
offered alongside main meals such as
chicken curry and vegetable lasagne.
Locally produced ice creams are the
dessert speciality. Four real ales and
eight wines by the glass are listed on
blackboards.

Open *Mon to Fri 11 to 2.30, 5.30 to 11, Sat
11 to 2.30, 6 to 11, Sun 12 to 3, 6.30 to 10.30*

STRINESDALE

Greater Manchester   map 8

Roebuck Inn

Brighton Road, Strinesdale OL4 3RB
Tel: (0161) 624 7819

*from Oldham take A62 Huddersfield road,
then left on to A672 Ripponden road, then
right after 1m on to Turf Pit Lane; follow for
1m*

Set in open country just outside
Oldham, climbing towards the moors,
the Roebuck is a cosy village pub with
walls of exposed stone, and
comfortable banquette seating in a
separate dining room, although food
may also be eaten in the bar. Plenty of
seafood is in evidence among starters,
while mains bring on the likes of
steaks, chilli con carne, pies, and
specialities such as duck or veal.
Marston's Pedigree and Boddingtons
Bitter are on handpump, and there are
seven wines by the glass.

Open *12 to 3, 5 to 11, Sun 12 to 10.30*

STURMINSTER MARSHALL

Dorset   map 2

Red Lion Inn

Sturminster Marshall BH21 4BU
Tel: (01258) 857319

The window boxes are brimming over
outside this neatly presented pub
opposite the churchyard. Beers and
food are bountiful too, with Badger
Best, Tanglefoot and guests such as
Fursty Ferret on the handpumps and a
menu that ranges from kangaroo with
port wine sauce to whole lemon sole.
Service is attentive, and many will
welcome the no-smoking bar areas and
a full no-smoking restaurant. The
wine list runs to 30 bins.

Open *12 to 2.30, 7 to 11, Sun 12 to 3,
7 to 10.30*

SUSWORTH

Lincolnshire   map 9

Jenny Wren

East Ferry Road, Susworth DN17 3AS
Tel: (01724) 784000

off A519, 3m W of Scotter

Picturesque early-eighteenth-century
inn with open log fires and a large beer
garden by the river. In addition to John
Smith's there are two or three guest
ales, and a selection of New World and
European wines. Blackboard specials
and a printed menu offer seafood or
game in season. Children welcome in
lounge and garden.

Open *12 to 3, 5.30 to 11 (10.30 Sun)*

TEMPLE GRAFTON

Warwickshire   map 5

Blue Boar

Temple Grafton B49 6NR
Tel: (01789) 750010

off A46, 3m W of Stratford-upon-Avon

Children are welcome at this creeper-
covered seventeenth-century inn,
where you can enjoy a drink on the
flower-decked patio in summer.
Theakston Best, XB and Old Speckled
Hen are supplemented by a weekly-
changing guest beer, and nine wines
from the extensive list are available by
the glass. The Blue Boar is close to
where William Shakespeare was
married, and its window seats, open

fires and exposed stone seem a reminder of the era. Food is standard bar fare. B&B provided in 16 en suite rooms.

Open *11 to 11, Sun 11 to 11.15*

TESTCOMBE

Hampshire   map 2
Mayfly
Testcombe SO20 6AX
TEL: (01264) 860283
on A3057, between Stockbridge and Andover, by River Test

A lovely honey-coloured brick-built riverside pub, especially inviting in summer when you can sit in the garden and watch the ducks and swans swim past. Inside, various eating and drinking areas are set with wooden tables and chairs, plus open fires in winter. Ales are Wadworth 6X, Marston's Pedigree and one guest ale, perhaps Ringwood Best. Alternatively a generous selection of wines by the glass is offered.

Open *10 to 11, Sun 12 to 10.30*

THOMPSON

Norfolk   map 6
Chequers Inn
Griston Road, Thompson IP24 1PX
TEL: (01953) 483360
1m off A1075, 3m S of Watton

Festooned with colourful hanging baskets, this pretty sixteenth-century thatched pub has a lengthy menu offering mostly standard pub fare, from jacket potatoes and sandwiches to beef stroganoff and sirloin steak. More interesting is the blackboard of daily specials, which feature plenty of local game in season, perhaps wild boar, pheasant and partridge, or maybe ostrich with Madeira sauce. Beers are from Adnams, Fuller's and Greene King, with occasional guests.

Open *11.30 to 2.30, 6.30 to 11, Sun 12 to 3, 7 to 10.30*

THORNBOROUGH

Buckinghamshire   map 5
Lone Tree
Bletchley Road, Thornborough
MK18 2DZ
TEL: (01280) 812334
just off A421; approx 3m E of Buckingham, pub signposted on left; do not go into village

The name seems appropriate: the pub, parts of which date from the seventeenth century, stands apart from the village surrounded by fields. Old beams and brick fireplaces characterise the main bar and give away the age of the place. Menus don't veer too far from the standard pub repertoire – expect steak, ale and mushroom pie, and sausages with bubble and squeak and onion gravy – although some items are given an unusual twist, such as fish and chips, which is in fact monkfish tempura with a lattice of potato batons. There is also a good choice of sandwiches at lunchtimes, and a selection of real ales to wash it all down, together with around ten wines by the glass.

Open *12 to 3, 6 to 11, Sun 12 to 10.30*

THREE LEGGED CROSS

East Sussex   map 3
Bull
Dunster Mill Lane, Three Legged Cross
TN5 7HH
TEL: (01580) 200586
take Three Legged Cross road signposted in centre of Ticehurst, off B2099

In a peaceful and attractive location at the junction of two lanes is a typical Sussex pub, built of brick and hung with tiles. The Bull has a large lawn in front and excellent views to the rear; colourful love birds can be seen in the wooden aviary and there is a children's play area. Real ales include examples from local breweries Harveys and Rother Valley; eight wines by the glass. Bar snacks and blackboards list chicken, fish, game and vegetarian options. A separate restaurant menu is available in the evening only. The inn offers B&B.

Open *11 to 11, Sun 12 to 10.30*

THURGARTON

Nottinghamshire   map 5

Red Lion

Southwell Road, Thurgarton NG14 7GP
TEL: (01636) 830351

on A612, 3m S of Southwell

A sixteenth-century village inn, which
began life as an alehouse for the monks
of Thurgarton Priory and was the
scene of a gruesome murder in 1936;
inside, framed newspaper accounts are
testament to this. Today's customers
are less ecclesiastical, and will find
well-kept real ales to sup, including
Banks's Mansfield Cask, Black Sheep
and Jennings Cumberland Ale, and
traditional pub food (served all day at
weekends). Children are welcome
throughout.

Open *Mon to Fri 11.30 to 2.30, 6 to 11,
Sat 11.30 to 11, Sun 12 to 10.30*

TICHBORNE

Hampshire   map 2

Tichborne Arms

Tichborne SO24 0NA
TEL: (01962) 733760

off A31 or B3046, 2m SW of Alresford

This heavily thatched red-brick pub,
set in a tranquil hamlet in the Itchen
valley, was rebuilt in 1939 after fire
destroyed the original thatched
building. Village photographs and
documents relating to the famous
Tichborne Claimant court case adorn
one of the bars. Ringwood Best and
several guest ales are served from the
cask, food takes in ploughman's and
jacket potatoes, and there is a specials
board, perhaps steak, ale and Stilton
pie. Seek it out in summer for the
splendid, flower-filled rear garden.
Excellent local walks.

Open *11.30 to 2.30, 6 to 11, Sun 12 to 3, 7 to
10.30; closed 25, 26 Dec and eve 31 Dec*

TIVETSHALL ST MARY

Norfolk   map 6

Old Ram Coaching Inn

Ipswich Road, Tivetshall St Mary
NR15 2DE
TEL: (01379) 676794

on A140, S of Norwich

Comfortable en suite accommodation
is provided at this sympathetically
restored seventeenth-century coaching
inn where food is served all day,
including breakfast from 7.30am, to
travellers using the A140 between
Norwich and Ipswich. A spacious and
well-maintained interior features
standing timbers, brick floors, pine
furnishings, wood-burning stoves and
old farming implements. Ales on
handpump include Adnams Bitter,
Bass and Hancocks HB. A good range
of wines lists 22 by the glass. Separate
bar and restaurant menu and daily
specials.

Open *11 to 11, Sun 12 to 10.30 (breakfast
from 7.30); closed 25 and 26 Dec*

TOLLARD ROYAL

Wiltshire   map 2

King John Inn

Tollard Royal SP5 5PS
TEL: (01725) 516207

on B3081 (off A354), 14m SW of Salisbury

Children get their own menu and a
non-smoking family room at this
unpretentious inn in picturesque
Tollard Royal. All food is served in
both the restaurant and bar, from
sandwiches and rolls to fish – perhaps
Mediterranean-style hake – and meat
dishes like a trio of lamb chops in
minted yoghurt, mixed grill, or
vegetarian stuffed peppers. Five wines
are available by the glass, and among
the line-up of real ales on handpump
might be Wadworth 6X, Wells
Bombardier Premium Bitter, Fuller's
London Pride or Marston's Pedigree.
The inn, built in 1859 to house the
workforce of the village's iron foundry,
is well placed for walkers exploring the
ancient forests nearby. Reports please.

Open *11 to 3, 6 to 11, Sun 12 to 4, 7 to 10.30
(12 to 10.30 summer)*

TOOT HILL

Essex   map 3
Green Man
Toot Hill CM5 9SD
TEL: (01992) 522255
*off A414, between North Weald and
Chipping Ongar*
Between Epping and Ongar is a
refurbished Victorian coaching inn set
down narrow lanes in rolling Essex
countryside. Four real ales on
handpump, including Adnams,
Fuller's London Pride and Young's
Bitter, sit alongside a monthly-
changing guest ale, and a
comprehensive 120-bin wine list. Food
is available from an extensive menu,
served in two restaurant areas. Starters
of scallops or mussels along with main
dishes of calf's liver and bacon, black
bream, halibut and pheasant. An
award-winning floral courtyard is a
great place for summer imbibing.
Open *11 to 3, 6 to 11, Sun 12 to 4, 7 to 10.30*

TOPSHAM

Devon   map 1
Bridge
Topsham EX3 0QQ
TEL: (01392) 873862
Up to ten real ales, including
Branscombe Vale Bitter, Exmoor Valley
and Black Autumn, are drawn straight
from barrels at this mainly sixteenth-
century pub. The original building goes
back another half a millennium, and the
village museum is devoted to the
ecology of the Exe estuary and the
history of shipbuilding. Traditional pub
food includes ploughman's,
sandwiches, pasties, and soup in winter.
Open *12 to 2, 6 to 10.30 (11 Fri and Sat),
Sun 12 to 2, 7 to 10.30*

TREBURLEY

Cornwall   map 1
Springer Spaniel
Treburley PL15 9NS
TEL: (01579) 370424
*on A388 halfway between Launceston and
Callington*
This is a friendly roadside pub with a
relaxing atmosphere and an interesting
menu that might offer up

bouillabaisse, or sautéed scallops with
bacon and shallots, then Cornish crab
pasty, pan-fried duck breast with a
blackberry and Cassis sauce, or loin of
lamb forestière. Seasonal game is a
speciality. Beers, provided by Cornish
brewery Sharp's, include Cornish
Coaster, Doom Bar Bitter and the
house brew, Springer Ale, and eight
wines are available by the glass.
Reports please.
Open *11 to 3, 6 to 11; closed eve 25 Dec
(drinks only lunchtime)*

TRESCO

Isles of Scilly   map 1
New Inn
Tresco TR24 0QQ
TEL: (01720) 422844
The New Inn makes a good base for
exploring this lovely car-free island
very much geared to holidaymakers,
and reached by ferry or helicopter
from Penzance via St Mary's. Set
meals and specials boards in the bar,
and a separate restaurant menu, feature
lots of local fish – 'succulent scallops'
among them. Real ales are from
mainland Cornish brewers St Austell
and Skinner's, alongside Fuller's
Chiswick Bitter; Hoegaarden wheat
beer is also available, together with
draught cider, 20 malt whiskies and 36
wines (eight by the glass). The hotel
has 15 guest rooms, many with a view
to the sea. Children welcome.
Open *winter 11 to 3, 6 to 11, Sun 12 to 3, 6 to
10.30; summer 11 to 11, Sun 12 to 10.30*

TRURO

Cornwall   map 1
Old Ale House
7 Quay Street, Truro TR1 2HD
TEL: (01872) 271122
'Certainly a pub for the traditionalists,'
thought one visitor. It is also one for
real ale fans, providing up to eight at
any time, served under gravity, often
including several from local breweries –
Skinner's Kiddleywink and Sharp's
Doom Bar, for example. They keep the
food fairly simple, with a regular menu
featuring 'sizzling' dishes, such as
Cantonese prawns or Cajun chicken,
served in cast-iron pans with bread.

Daily blackboard specials might be
Italian-style chicken or bacon and
mushroom pasta, while desserts offer
up steamed puddings and ice cream
sundaes.
Open *11 to 11, Sun 12 to 10.30*

TUNBRIDGE WELLS

Kent   map 3
The Beacon
Tea Garden Lane, Tunbridge Wells
TN3 9JH
TEL: (01892) 524252
Making the best of an excellent location
outside Tunbridge Wells, this rambling,
turreted oddity of a building revels in
views of the dramatic High Rocks,
whether through its large windows or
from the many outside terraces.
Drinkers young and old are very much
welcome in the large, smoky bars, with
beers from the likes of Harveys,
Timothy Taylor and Larkins and a
dozen wines by the glass. Rather pricey
restaurant food includes complex
combinations such as crisp duck on
mango and water chestnut salad with
champagne vinaigrette and a blackboard
of fish specials.
Open *11 to 11, Sun 12 to 10.30*

TURVEY

Bedfordshire   map 6
Three Cranes
High Street, Turvey MK43 8EP
TEL: (01234) 881305
on A428, 7m W of Bedford
Children are welcome throughout this
300-year-old stone pub next to the
parish church in a pretty village. Food is
served in all areas too, with lunchtime
bar snacks of sandwiches, pies and
ploughman's joined by daily-changing
specials like lamb jalfrezi and pork
medallions with apricots. As many as
ten wines are available by the glass, and
the regular real ales on handpump,
Greene King IPA and Abbot Ale, are
joined by three guests that change twice
a week: perhaps Old Speckled Hen,
Wychwood Hobgoblin and Elgood's
Golden Newt. Reports please.
Open *winter Mon to Thur 11 to 3, 6 to 11, Fri
and Sat 11 to 11, Sun 12 to 10.30; summer 11 to
11, Sun 12 to 10.30*

UPPERMILL

Greater Manchester   map 8
Cross Keys Inn
Off Running Hill Gate, Uppermill
OL3 6LW
TEL: (01457) 874626
A 'very traditional' 300-year-old pub
set between Saddleworth Moor and
the Tame Valley – views are
spectacular. Focal point of the main
bar is a grand fireplace, while the
flagstone-floored taproom has a vast
blackened range stove. Home-cooked
food is good value, including some
'unforgettable' suet puddings and pies:
steak, mushroom and ale, perhaps, or
chicken and leek. The rest of the menu
deals in old favourites like chilli,
battered cod or haddock and
sandwiches. This is a JW Lees pub
with that brewery's range of beers on
draught.
Open *11 to 11, Sun 12 to 10.30*

VENTNOR

Isle of Wight   map 2
Spyglass Inn
The Esplanade, Ventor PO38 1JX
TEL: (01983) 855338
This ramshackle old pub enjoys a
plum location, right on the sea wall at
the western end of the esplanade.
Extensions have been designed to
make the most of the views and there
is an outdoor terrace for use in
summer. The regular printed menu of
standard pub food (baguettes, scampi,
chicken Kiev) is supplemented by
more interesting blackboard specials
such as crab, cheese and tomato tart.
Real ales are Badger Dorset Best and
Tanglefoot, and Golden from the very
local Ventnor brewery.
Open *10.30 to 11 (10.30 Sun)*

WAMBROOK

Somerset   map 2

Cotley Inn

Wambrook TA20 3EN
TEL: (01460) 62348
off A30, just W of Chard

Friendly, unpretentious pub with
reasonably priced food served in hefty
portions. It has a somewhat domestic
feel with bright décor featuring an
assortment of oil paintings, vintage
photos and china animals. The lengthy
and rather old-fashioned menu offers
starters such as crispy whitebait or
melon and grape cocktail, which may
be followed by steak with port and
Stilton sauce or perhaps chicken
cordon bleu, and concluded with
bread-and-butter pudding. Otter Ale is
the one real ale served. Service is
'courteous and sincere'. Events
advertised on posters have included
quiz nights and more rural pursuits
such as hedge-laying contests. Guest
accommodation available.
Open *11 to 3, 7 to 11; closed Sun eve*

WARBLETON

East Sussex   map 3

War-Bill-in-Tun

Warbleton TN21 9BD
TEL: (01435) 830636
off B2096, S of Punnett's Town

Harveys Sussex Best and Shepherd
Neame – Bishops Finger, Master Brew
– are on draught at this inn whose
name may be a play on the village's
name, or may refer to civil war events.
Food is served throughout; vegetarians
are well provided for, with stuffed
mushrooms, nut roast and vegetable
bake, and omnivores also have a wide
choice, from stuffed duck breast, lamb
chops or steaks to poached salmon.
Children welcome and small portions
served.
Open *11 to 3, 6.30 to 11, Sun 12 to 3,
7 to 10.30; closed eve 25, 26 Dec and 1 Jan*

WARDLOW MIRES

Derbyshire   map 8

Three Stags Heads

Wardlow Mires SK17 8RW
TEL: (01298) 872268
*at junction of B6465 and A623, 2m E of
Tideswell*

On a main road through the Dales but
otherwise fairly remote, this is an
unassuming, unpretentious and fairly
simple type of pub. It is on several
walking routes and feels like the sort of
place where passing hikers would be
very much at home – but don't expect
much in the way of frills. Menus focus
on seasonal game and hearty, rustic-
sounding dishes like oxtail in chestnut
soup, as well as more standard fare
such as chicken curry and cottage pie.
Beers are from good regional brewers
such as Abbeydale and Broadstone.
Open *Fri 7 to 11, Sat and Sun 12 to 11; also
open bank hols*

WARESIDE

Hertfordshire   map 3

Chequers Inn

Wareside SG12 7QY
TEL: (01920) 467010
2m W from Ware on B1004

The Chequers is a good-looking
country pub in the middle of nowhere,
complete with requisite low beams,
real wood fires and a relaxing
atmosphere, plus a couple of friendly
resident dogs. Daily specials chalked
up on a blackboard might be pea and
ham soup, rabbit stew, and fruit
crumble, while the printed menu goes
in for prawn cocktail, garlic
mushrooms, chicken pie, steak, and
roasted vegetable lasagne. Beers are
from Adnams and Greene King.
Open *Mon to Fri 12 to 3, 6 to 11,
Sat 12 to 11, Sun 12 to 10.30*

WASDALE HEAD

Cumbria   map 8

Wasdale Head Inn

Wasdale Head CA20 1EX
TEL: (019467) 26229

*off A595, between Gosforth and Holmbrook;
follow signs for 8m*

Great Gables Brewing Company are
now located on the premises,
extending the list of ales served here
from Scawfell, Burnmore Pale Ale,
Wrynose and Yewbarrow to include
Great Gable and Wasdale. For
Europhiles they keep Hoegaarden,
German wheat beers and Scottish
heather ales. The area is a remote,
unspoilt part of Lakeland, and a haven
for ramblers, walkers and climbers.
The bar was named after the first
landlord, the 'world's biggest liar', and
there is a garden with beck-side tables.
Food is traditional: steak and ale pie,
local lamb, rabbit and pheasant.
Alternatively the restaurant offers a
four-course set menu. Children
welcome. Accommodation available.
Open *11 to 10 (11 summer), Sun 12 to 10*

WATLINGTON

Oxfordshire   map 2

Chequers

Love Lane, Watlington OX49 5RA
TEL: (01491) 612874

*take B4009 from M40 junction 6 and turn
right down Love Lane just before Watlington,
signposted Icknield School*

This Brakspear house keeps the
brewery's Bitter and Special, plus
seasonal ales. Watlington, in the
Chilterns, makes a useful stop-off
from the M40 – especially the garden
and vine-decked conservatory of this
old pub. The latter is one of the eating
areas for bar food that runs from
sandwiches and jacket potatoes to lamb
shank and balti chicken.
Open *12 to 2.30, 6 to 11, Sun 12 to 3,
7 to 10.30; closed eve 25 and 26 Dec*

WEST HUNTSPILL

Somerset   map 2

Crossways Inn

Withy Road, West Huntspill
TA9 3RA
TEL: (01278) 783756

on A38, 3m S of Burnham-on-Sea

In this haven of real ale amid the
watery Somerset Levels there's a
breezy ambience. The three regular
ales are Bass, London Pride and
Flowers IPA, while three guests might
include Cotleigh Barn Owl Bitter,
Exmoor Stag and Church End Vicar's
Ruin. Six wines from the short list are
offered by the glass, and bar food on
blackboards runs to ploughman's,
home-made pies and fresh fish.
Open *11 to 3, 5.30 to 11, Sun 12 to 3,
7 to 10.30*

WEST TANFIELD

North Yorkshire   map 9

Bull Inn

Church Street, West Tanfield HG4 5JQ
TEL: (01677) 470678

on A6108 Ripon to Masham road

The terraced garden of this pleasant
seventeenth-century village pub runs
down to the River Ure – a popular spot
in summer. Children are also welcome
in the restaurant, where there's a full
menu. Hand-pulled local Black Sheep
Best Bitter and Tetley Bitter, joined in
summer by another ale, are served in
the open-plan bar, where snacks like
baguettes are possibilities at weekends.
Three wines are available by the glass,
with the full list of around 15 bottles
focusing on the New World. Five en
suite letting bedrooms, recently
refurbished. Reports please.
Open *Mon 11 to 3, Tue to Fri 11 to 3, 5 to 11,
Sat 11 to 11, Sun 12 to 10.30*

WHALTON

Northumberland   map 10

Beresford Arms

Whalton NE61 3UZ
TEL: (01670) 775225

on B6524 from Morpeth

In a country village of mainly Georgian
houses is this very attractive

nineteenth-century stone building.
Family-run, it attracts a mature
lunchtime clientele in the bar and
comfortably furnished restaurant. A
wide variety of fish and game in season
feature on the long menu, perhaps
pheasant and rabbit pie or cod and
prawn Mornay. There are no real ales.
Open *11 to 3, 6 to 11, Sun 12 to 3, 7 to 10.30;
closed Sun eve winter*

WHITSTABLE

Kent   map 3
Prince Albert
Sea Street, Whitstable CT5 1AN
TEL: (01227) 273400
The Prince Albert is a tiny backstreet
pub, literally a stone's throw from the
beach at the centre of this seaside town
famous for its oysters. First-class real
ales served in tip-top condition are the
main draw: Greene King IPA and
Fuller's London Pride, plus a changing
guest ale. There is also a short bar
menu of decent home cooking. One
visitor was well pleased with steak and
oyster pie containing plenty of large
chunks of tender meat and a huge
whole oyster. Other menu stalwarts
include fish and chips, and the special
of the day might be gnocchi with
Gorgonzola. Food is served all day at
weekends.
Open *11 to 11, Sun 12 to 10.30*

WILDBOARCLOUGH

Cheshire   map 8
Crag Inn
Wildboarclough SK11 0BD
TEL: (01260) 227239
off A54, 5m SE of Macclesfield
Walkers are asked to remove muddy
boots before coming in for
Worthington Bitter or guest ales like
London Pride and Shepherd Neame
Spitfire at this seventeenth-century
stone-built pub. Traditional food is
served in the bar and separate
restaurant; on Friday evenings and
over the weekend there is a carvery.
The dictionary says that clough is a
valley or ravine, but locals say it's no
good fishing for wild boar in the

stream as it's actually a wild boar that
runs up it.
Open *12 to 3, 7 to 11, Sun 12 to 6 (closed Sun
eve); closed Mon all year*

WISBOROUGH GREEN

West Sussex   map 3
Cricketers Arms
Wisborough Green RH14 0DG
TEL: (01403) 700369
village on A272 W of Billingshurst
Watch the cricket on the green outside
this pub, and drink Fuller's London
Pride, Greene King IPA and Young's at
the tables provided. Alternatively go
inside for the relaxed and atmospheric
nooks and crannies of an old-style pub
decorated with sporting prints and
with a stove in a double-sided
fireplace. Bar snacks and daily-
changing blackboards include smoked
haddock kedgeree, pies and local fish.
Live music sessions are held regularly.
Open *Mon to Fri 11 to 2.30, 5.30 to 11,
Sat 11 to 11, Sun 12 to 10.30; closed eve 25 Dec*

WISTANSTOW

Shropshire   map 5
Plough
Wistanstow SY7 8DG
TEL: (01588) 673251
*off A49 Church Stretton to Ludlow road,
2m N of Craven Arms*
Seats outside this village local overlook
the Shropshire hills and Wenlock
Edge. Real ale buffs travelling on the
A49 would be advised to find time for
a visit as the Plough stands right next
to the Wood Brewery, one of the best
small independent country breweries
in Britain. You can arrange to tour the
brewery and sample the full range of
ales – Shropshire Lad, Special and
Parish – in the simply furnished bar.
Traditional English cooking includes
venison steak with celeriac purée, steak
and kidney pie and coffee and walnut
sponge.
Open *Tue to Sat 11.30 to 2 (2.30 summer),
7 (6.30 summer) to 11, Sun 12 to 2.30,
7 to 10.30; closed 25 Dec*

WOODBASTWICK

Norfolk   map 6

Fur & Feather Inn

Slad Lane, Woodbastwick NR13 6HQ
TEL: (01603) 720003

1½m N of B1140, 8m NE of Norwich

The brewery is next door to this
thatched Norfolk Broads pub,
subsequently beers from Woodforde's
are well represented. The full range
of eight brews is offered –
occasionally used in the cooking, e.g.
bangers and mustard mash with
Wherry gravy – and there are nine
wines by the glass. The printed menu
and blackboard offers a range of
traditional pub food; start with pea
and ham soup and move on to steak
and kidney pie.

Open *winter 11.30 to 3, 6 to 11, Sun 12 to
10.30, summer 11.30 to 11, Sun 12 to 10.30*

WOOLLEY MOOR

Derbyshire   map 5

White Horse Inn

Badger Lane, Woolley Moor DE55 6FG
TEL: (01246) 590319

*on W side of Ogston Reservoir, off B6014,
between Matlock and Stretton*

A 'real Dales pub', high up in 'the
middle of nowhere', this squat, stone-
built inn is worth knowing about for
its real ales: the regularly changing
selection of four might include
Adnams Best and Broadside, and
Bateman XXXB. Those with children
will also appreciate the outdoor play
area. The lounge bar and the modern
conservatory are used mainly for
dining, and the vast menu (printed and
blackboard) includes a few home-
made items.

Open *winter 12 to 3, 6 to 11, Sun 12 to 10.30;
summer 11.30 to 3, 6 to 11, Sun 12 to 10.30*

WOOLSTHORPE

Lincolnshire   map 5

Chequers

Woolsthorpe, by Belvoir NG32 1LU
TEL: (01476) 870701

off A52 or A607, 6m W of Grantham

Confusingly there are two
Woolsthorpes in the area. This one sits
a mile and a half from Belvoir Castle
in prosperous farming country close to
the Grantham Canal. Follow signs off
the main street to a sandy-coloured
stone building with tables outside.
Heavy beams, country prints and a
roaring fire in the bar contribute to a
thoroughly English, faintly manorial
feel sustained in the snug, dining areas
and more formal restaurant. The
drinks choice is wide-ranging: well-
kept Banks's Original, Marston's
Pedigree and local guest beers, 50-odd
whiskies and a dozen wines by the
glass from a list of 40. A smart menu
includes starters like grilled scallops
with Parma ham, followed perhaps by
confit of duck. A new licensee took
over in spring 2003, so reports please.

Open *12 to 2, 7 to 11, Sun 12 to 2*

WRENINGHAM

Norfolk   map 6

Bird in Hand

Church Road, Wreningham NR16 1BH
TEL: (01508) 489438

off B1113, 5m S of Norwich

Despite being close to Wymondham
and the Lotus car factory, this extended
and tastefully refurbished red-brick
pub with a sheltered rear terrace enjoys
an isolated rural position. It's a popular
country destination for its friendly
atmosphere, good range of real ales,
including Woodforde's Wherry Best
Bitter, Adnams Best Bitter and Fuller's
London Pride, and a choice of wines:
seven are available by the glass. There
are separate bar and restaurant menus
which change regularly, plus
interesting daily specials.

Open *11.30 to 3, 6 to 11, Sun 12 to 3, 7
(6 summer) to 10.30*

YARDE DOWN

Devon   map 1

Poltimore Arms

Yarde Down EX36 3HA
TEL: (01598) 710381

take Blackmoor Gate road A361 for 1m,
then follow signs for Simonsbath for 4m

An isolated pub built over 300 years
ago as a coaching inn, set high up on
the edge of remote Exmoor. Poltimore
Arms has great views across Devon
countryside, and in keeping with the
rustic location the interior is simply
furnished and the atmosphere relaxed.
Local farmers, huntsmen and visitors
enjoy the range of pub food – venison
casserole, beef stroganoff or perhaps
sea bass with ginger and spring onions.
Cotleigh Tawny and guest ales in
summer are drawn straight from the
barrel.

Open *12 to 2.30, 6.30 to 11, Sun 12 to 2.30,*
7 to 10.30; closed all day Mon and lunchtimes
Tue to Fri from Jan to Mar

YEALAND CONYERS

Lancashire   map 8

New Inn

40 Yealand Road, Yealand Conyers
LA5 9SJ
TEL: (01524) 732938

off A6, 2m N of Carnforth

A collection of antique watering cans
adorns one side of this ivy-clad pub,
which can be found at the bottom of a
hill at one end of the village. And
inside the cosy bar the decorative
theme is wooden spoons. Good value
and generous portions are chief
characteristics of the food. Among
starters might be mussels with white
wine, cream and garlic, and Cajun
potato skins with melted Cheddar,
while main courses include beef in
beer with mushrooms and smoked
bacon, and salmon fillet in a herby
cream and Chardonnay sauce.
Robinson's Hartleys XB is the regular
beer, supplemented by a seasonal ale –
Old Tom in winter.

Open *11.30 to 11, Sun 12 to 10.30*

SCOTLAND

ARDFERN

Argyll & Bute   map 11

Galley of Lorne
Ardfern PA31 8QN
TEL: (01852) 500284
*on B8002, reached from A816 N of
Lochgilphead*
Beautiful scenery taking in views over
Loch Craignish can be enjoyed from
the terrace of this traditional
eighteenth-century inn. Inside, the
atmosphere is friendly and welcoming,
with warming log fires. By Scottish
standards, the selection of draught real
ales is impressive, taking in Deuchars
IPA, Teuchter from Houston and
Highlander from Fyne Ales. There is
also a wide range of malt whiskies. Bar
food is along the lines of chicken liver
pâté with whisky marmalade, or grilled
goats' cheese salad with tomato salsa,
with main courses of deep-fried
scampi, beef, ale and mushroom pie,
or haddock and chips, and to finish
there's sticky ginger pudding.
Open *winter 12 to 3, 5 to 12; summer 12 to 12;
closed 25 Dec*

BADACHRO

Highland   map 11

Badachro Inn
Badachro IV21 2AA
TEL: (01445) 741255
With a plum location on the jetty,
looking out past the boats to two small
islands, the Badachro brings together
locals, walkers, yachts-people and just
about anyone who doesn't mind
squeezing in close to their neighbours
to enjoy the seafood and a good
selection of beers, wines and whiskies.
Food prices can be a bit high, but the
atmosphere and view are something
special.
Open *12 to 12; closed 25 Dec*

BROUGHTY FERRY

Dundee   map 11

Fisherman's Tavern
10–14 Fort Street, Broughty Ferry
DD5 2AD
TEL: (01382) 775941
off A930 (shore road)
An established destination for real ale
fans, the Fisherman's Tavern also does
well by wine drinkers, with 25 by the
glass. McEwan 80/- is the regular ale,
while guests might include Belhaven
St Andrew's Ale and IPA, Inveralmond
Ossian's Ale and Fraoch Heather Ale,
or others from south of the border.
This listed seventeenth-century house
was once a fisherman's cottage and fish
remains the kitchen's speciality,
supported by straightforward bar
snacks.
Open *11am to midnight (1am Thur to Sat)*

CLOVENFORDS

Borders   map 11

Clovenfords Hotel
1 Vine Street, Clovenfords TD1 3LU
TEL: (01896) 850203
on A72, 3m W of Galashiels
A statue outside this eighteenth-
century coaching inn commemorates
Sir Walter Scott's frequent use of one
of its rooms. Clovenfords, set in a
small village in the tweed and woollen
country around Galashiels, takes real
ale seriously, with Caledonian 80/- as
the regular draught, joined by eight
guests – perhaps something from the
Isle of Skye or Orkney. The printed
menu and blackboard display hearty
food including haggis, steak, scampi
and fish and chips.
Open *Mon to Thur 11 to 11,
Fri and Sat 11 to 12, Sun 12 to 11*

EDINBURGH

Edinburgh   map 11

Abbotsford
3 Rose Street, Edinburgh EH2 2PR
TEL: (0131) 225 5276
The Abbotsford is a traditional
Victorian pub with wood panelling,
and bench seating around all four sides
of the island bar. There is a separate

restaurant upstairs, although the same menu is available throughout: the daily-changing soup, roast, pie and curry might be, respectively, tomato, beef, steak and lamb; otherwise expect things like avocado and prawns with lemon and dill mayonnaise, mixed grill, and chicken breast stuffed with haggis with whisky cream sauce. This is a good real ale pub, with five cask beers, perhaps including Belhaven 80/.
Open *Mon to Sat 11 to 11*

Starbank Inn
64 Laverockbank Road, Edinburgh
EH5 3BZ
TEL: (0131) 552 4141

The Starbank enjoys a great location with a view across the Firth of Forth to Fife. A wide choice of wines by the glass and a selection of changing guest beers make it a good pub for drinkers, and children are welcome. Value is fair for the traditional food: starters like prawns marie-rose, chicken liver pâté, and cured herring salad, and main courses of mince and tatties, steak and ale pie, and halibut with orange sauce.
Open *11 to 11 (12 Thur to Sat),*
Sun 12.30 to 11

GATEHEAD

East Ayrshire   map 11

Cochrane Inn
45 Main Road, Gatehead KA2 0AP
TEL: (01563) 570122
on A759 just SW of Kilmarnock

On a T-junction on the Kilmarnock to Troon road is this white-painted, unshowy pub with neat flower borders. Inside, flagstoned floors, dark beams and dark wooden tables with wrought-iron legs create the right impression. Cooking revolves around an extensive choice of traditional Scottish fare, such as Cullen skink, Scotch broth, and haggis with neeps and tatties, as well as dishes such as sea bass or mussels. Children welcome in restaurant.
Open *11 to 3, 5 to 11 (12 Sat and Sun)*

GLASGOW

Glasgow   map 11

Lismore
206 Dumbarton Road, Glasgow G11 6UN
TEL: (0141) 576 0103

Fans of good beers – from Caledonian and perhaps Kelburn Red Smiddy – and whiskies (wine too, these days) flock from the university to the nearby Lismore. The décor is traditional stained glass and dark wood, the atmosphere convivial and there's live music two or three times a week, but you won't find any food served here.
Open *11 to 11 (12 Fri and Sat),*
Sun 12.30 to 11

GLENCOE

Highland   map 11

Clachaig Inn
Glencoe PH49 4HX
TEL: (01855) 811252
just off A82, Crianlarich to Fort William road

Some of the most spectacular views in Britain are to be enjoyed from this inn, including some of Scotland's highest peaks. The Clachaig describes itself as 'the outdoor inn', and certainly serves the outdoor fraternity of walkers and climbers. A printed menu features traditional pub food including salmon and steak. Unusually for this isolated area there is a good selection of Scottish cask-conditioned beers, including Fraoch Heather Ale and Isle of Skye beers. Children are welcome in lounge bar, and B&B is offered.
Open *11 to 11, Fri 10.30 to 12,*
Sat 10.30 to 11.30, Sun 12.30 to 12

ISLE OF WHITHORN

Dumfries & Galloway   map 11

Steam Packet
Harbour Row, Isle of Whithorn
DG8 8HZ
TEL: (01988) 500334
off A750, 12m S of Wigtown

Its harbour-side setting is an attraction here, and seafood is something of a speciality of the menu too, taking in anything from langoustines and scallops to sole and sea bass. Theakston XB is the regular real ale, joined by a

guest like Caledonian Deuchars IPA,
and a respectable selection of around
forty wines includes seven by the glass.
Children are welcome, and there's a
beer garden.
Open *winter Mon to Thur 11 to 2.30,
6 to 11, Fri and Sat 11 to 11, Sun 12 to 11;
summer 11 to 11, Sun 12 to 11; 25 Dec drinks
only 11 to 3, 7 to 11*

KIRKTON OF GLENISLA

Angus   map 11
Glenisla Hotel
Kirkton of Glenisla PH11 8PH
TEL: (01575) 582223
*from Alyth head N on B954, turn left on to
B951 and follow signs*
Built as a coaching inn in the
seventeenth century, the Glenisla
nowadays refreshes travellers with its
real ales, all Scottish: perhaps Ossian's
Ale or Lia Fail from the Inveralmond
Brewery, or Peter's Well from the
Houston Brewing Company. Fifty
malt whiskies and forty wines, with
two by the glass, are also worth
thinking about. The restaurant menus
use plenty of home-grown produce,
including Glamis duck, hill lamb, local
beef and seasonal game, while in the
bar (where you can also order from the
restaurant menu) you can expect
fishcakes with lime and coriander, or
venison burgers. Children have their
own menu. Reports please.
Open *Mon to Thur 11 to 11, Fri 11 to 12,
Sat 11 to 1am, Sun 12 to 11; closed Mon to Fri
afternoons Jan to Easter*

LINLITHGOW

West Lothian   map 11
Four Marys
65 High Street, Linlithgow EH49 7ED
TEL: (01506) 842171
The name refers to four ladies-in-
waiting of Mary Queen of Scots,
whose life and death are
commemorated in the fascinating
décor. The complicated history of this
tall town house starts about 1500, but
it remained unlicensed until 1975.
Now it's a monument to Scottish
brewing with Caledonian Deuchars
IPA, and Belhaven 70/-, 80/- and
St Andrews as regulars; guests might

be from other well-respected Scottish
breweries like Harviestoun,
Broughton, or Orkney. Food offers
specials such as chicken in pepper
sauce and lamb shank, along with
traditional pub meals, Scottish style.
Open *Mon to Wed 12 to 11, Thur to Sat 12 to
11.45, Sun 12.30 to 11*

MINNIGAFF

Dumfries & Galloway   map 11
Creebridge House Hotel
Minnigaff DG8 6NP
TEL: (01671) 402121
off A75, just N of Newton Stewart
'Tranquillity in the heart of bonnie
Galloway' is promised at this splendid
country-house hotel, built in 1760 and
originally home to the Earl of
Galloway. The informal beamed bar is
where you can enjoy beers from the
local Sulwath brewery, including
Criffel and Knockendoch. The wine
list is also respectable, with eight by
the glass. The eclectic menus offer
everything from lamb fillet on herb
taboulleh with a caramelised shallot,
date and tomato sauce to deep-fried
haddock in ale batter with chips and
mushy peas, or pasta with wild
mushrooms and feta. The Garden
Restaurant is a more upmarket affair.
Open *12 to 2.30, 6 to 11.30*

RATHO

Edinburgh   map 11
Bridge Inn
27 Baird Road, Ratho EH28 8RA
TEL: (0131) 333 1320
*off M8 and A8, 8m W of Edinburgh; follow
signs for Edinburgh Canal Centre from
Newbridge roundabout; pub is alongside
canal*
The Bridge boasts a warren of small
rooms and is the setting for Belhaven
80/- Ale (which is always available),
and a couple of guest beers, together
with three wines by the glass. It is
located about 20 minutes out of
Edinburgh and close to the canal. The
'Pop Inn' bar menu offers burgers,
battered fish, sausages and the like for
mains, with a more unusual dish of the
day, which might be fillet steak with
haggis in Drambuie and mushroom

sauce. Cranachan is one way of finishing.

Open *Mon to Thur 12 to 11, Fri 12 to 12, Sat 11 to 12, Sun 12.30 to 11*

ROSLIN

Midlothian   map 11

Roslin Glen Hotel
2 Penicuick Road, Roslin EH25 9LH
TEL: (0131) 440 2029

At this stone-built inn set at the foot of the Pentland Hills, drinkers will find Deuchars IPA and Belhaven Best on draught, plus four wines by the glass and a selection of malts. A short menu nonetheless offers both traditional and more unusual dishes: haggis dish of the week, or toasted nachos, then move on to Thai vegetable and coconut curry, haddock in a light beer batter with home-made chips, or 'house pie' – venison in port and Stilton gravy. Accommodation available.

Open *11 to 11 (12.30 Fri and Sat)*

ST MARY'S LOCH

Borders   map 11

Tibbie Shiel's Inn
St Mary's Loch TD7 5LH
TEL: (01750) 42231

100yds off A708, 13m W of Selkirk

Looking over St Mary's Loch and gorgeous scenery, an area not that well known to tourists, is this idyllically situated cottage. The Inn takes its name from Isabella (Tibbie) Shiel who moved to the property in 1823, and it was a favourite haunt of poets in the nineteenth century looking for food and a bed. Today the clientele is more likely to comprise walkers and windsurfers. Scottish real ales on tap

here are from Greenmantle and Belhaven, alongside Stowford Press cider, and a great many single-malt whiskies. Three dozen wines are on offer, but only two by the glass. Homely Scottish fare includes traditional high teas as well as hearty main dishes and snacks. Children are welcome. B&B is available too.

Open *summer Mon to Thur 11 to 11, Fri and Sat 11am to midnight, Sun 12.30 to 11; winter Thur 11 to 11, Fri and Sat 11am to midnight, Sun 12.30 to 6*

STROMNESS

Orkney   map 11

Ferry Inn
John Street, Stromness, Orkney
KW16 3AA
TEL: (01856) 850280

take the ferry from Aberdeen or Scrabster

As its name suggests, this tall, steep-roofed pub overlooks the bustling harbour where the ferries dock. In the bar, fitted out in mahogany to resemble the interior of a schooner, you can enjoy the Orkney Brewery's Dark Island and Red MacGregor, plus another real ale perhaps from further afield. Three wines are sold by the glass from a list of around twenty bottles. The same food is served in both the bar and the restaurant, and the daily-changing choices, mainly traditional in style, are based on local produce. Children are welcome, and 20 bedrooms are available for B&B. Stromness is an attractive town of narrow winding streets; views over the harbour extend to Scapa Flow, a naval base in both World Wars.

Open *Mon to Wed 9am to midnight, Thur to Sat 9am to 1am, Sun 9.30am to midnight*

WALES

ABERGORLECH

Carmarthenshire   map 4
Black Lion Inn
Abergorlech SA32 7SN
TEL: (01558) 685271
on B4310, S of Llansawel

An unassuming village pub which has
successfully maintained its sixteenth-
century period charm. The
characterful bar is furnished with a
large oak table and pair of high-backed
settles, while outside the river Cothi
flows past the garden. Brains Rev
James is the real ale kept, and every
few months guests are brought in. Eat
traditional food in the bar or
restaurant.

Open *Tue to Fri 12 to 3.30, 7 to 11.30, Sat 12
to 11.30, Sun 12 to 5; closed Mon exc bank hols*

BODFARI

Denbighshire   map 7
Dinorben Arms
Bodfari LL16 4DA
TEL: (01745) 710309
off A55, 4m NE of Denbigh

Up a steep hill followed by a sharp
right turn is this heavily timbered
seventeenth-century inn in the heart of
the Vale of Clwyd, with views to
match. Noted for its amazing flower-
filled terraced gardens, the mind-
boggling collection of over 200
whiskies behind the bar, and the
popular lunchtime self-served
smorgasbord. Ale aficionados will find
Banks's Mansfield Cask Ale and
Marston's Pedigree on handpump
along with a guest such as Caledonian
Deuchars IPA, while the cellar choice
will delight wine drinkers. Children
are welcome throughout; dogs in the
gardens only.

Open *Mon to Fri 12 to 3.30, 6 to 11,
Sat 12 to 11, Sun 12 to 10.30*

BWLCH-Y-CIBAU

Powys   map 7
Stumble Inn
Bwlch-y-Cibau SY22 5LL
TEL: (01691) 648860
on A490, 3m SE of Llanfyllin

A small village in the Welsh Marches
near the Vyrnwy river might seem an
unlikely setting, but the Stumble Inn's
specials board features Eastern dishes
of Peking duck with noodles,
Szechuan-style prawns, and mild to
hot curries, although whole Dover
sole, and salmon in prawn and saffron
sauce may make an appearance on the
menu. Four wines are available by the
glass, fourteen by the bottle, and
among the ales might be something
brewed by Marston's, Greene King,
Hook Norton or Adnams. Children
are welcome if eating.

Open *winter Wed to Sat 6 to 11, Sun 12 to 2;
summer Wed to Fri 6 to 11, Sat 12 to 2, 6 to 11,
Sun 12 to 2, 6 to 10.30*

CILGERRAN

Pembrokeshire   map 4
Pendre Inn
Cilgerran SA43 2SL
TEL: (01239) 614223
off A478, 3m S of Cardigan

Ancient whitewashed inn not far from
Cardigan Bay and Cilgerran Castle
offering outstanding value for money.
The food delivers some unusual ideas,
perhaps délices of trout with apple and
vermouth cream, or liver and bacon
with lime pickle, tomato and onion.
Fixed-price 'gourmet night' dinners
are a steal at £19 for three courses, plus
a cheeseboard, Buck's Fizz and petits
fours. Tomos Watkin Whoosh is a beer
with a name to conjure with, and three
house wines are served by the glass.
Children welcome.

Open *Mon to Sat 11 to 3, 6 to 11*

EAST ABERTHAW

Vale of Glamorgan   map 4

Blue Anchor Inn

East Aberthaw CF62 3DD
TEL: (01446) 750329

off B4265, between St Athan and Barry

A warren of charming rooms bristle
with nooks and alcoves, and in the
main bar the ancient walls have been
darkened by smoke from the massive
open fire. Parts of this brown-
thatched, creeper-covered inn date
from 1380 and it is said to have been
the haunt of smugglers.Custom is
attracted from miles around,
particularly at weekends and in the
evenings. Ales include Buckley's Best,
Wadworth 6X and one regularly
changing guest beer; three wines are
offered by the glass. Food runs to lamb
and leek casserole and Cumberland
sausages.

Open *11 to 11, Sun 12 to 10.30*

LLANDDAROG

Carmarthenshire   map 4

Butchers Arms

Llanddarog SA32 8NS
TEL: (01267) 275330

off A48, 5m E of Carmarthen

This Victorian pub is very near the
National Botanic Garden of Wales.
Halibut fillet with prawn and lobster
sauce might be on the fresh fish menu,
alongside sea bass, lemon sole and
salmon; otherwise, go for something
like crispy stuffed duck with orange
and Grand Marnier sauce, or pork
steaks in garlic and mushroom sauce.
Children are welcome in the no-
smoking restaurant, although the same
menus are available throughout.
Felinfoel Best Bitter and Double
Dragon Ale, brewed in Llanelli, are on
draught, and four wines are sold by the
glass. Note that the pub is closed on
Sundays.

Open *Mon to Fri 12 to 3, 6 to 11, Sat 11.30 to
3, 5 to 11; closed 25 and 26 Dec*

White Hart Inn

Llanddarog SA32 8NT
TEL: (01267) 275395

The White Hart, 600 years old, is an
attractive stone building with a
thatched roof, with flower-filled
hanging baskets and tubs outside. The
home-brew beers are a real draw, with
Cwrwblafuf Ale regularly on
handpump and up to three others,
such as Roasted Barley Stout or, in
summer, a fruit beer like plum or
nettle. Five wines come by the glass,
five times that number by the bottle.
Lots of local produce shows up on the
long menus, including Welsh black
beef and fish, although it's equally
possible just to have a snack. Sit on
picnic tables outside and admire the
fine views over the countryside.

Open *11.30 to 3, 6.30 to 11, Sun 12 to 3,
7 to 10.30; closed 25 and 26 Dec*

LLANDINAM

Powys   map 4

Lion Hotel

Llandinam SY17 5BY
TEL: (01686) 688233

*on A470 in village centre, 8m SW of
Newtown, 6m N of Llanidloes*

The Lion's kitchen uses a notable
amount of local produce in its cooking:
Welsh beef (perhaps in a casserole) and
lamb, and wild trout and salmon, with
something like a vegetable roast with
mango and lime for vegetarians and
moules marinière among starters. In
summer you can eat in the garden,
separated only by a meadow from the
Upper Severn. Old Speckled Hen is a
fixed feature on the ales front, joined
by a guest such as Wells Bombardier
Premium Bitter.

Open *12 to 3, 6.30 to 11, Sun 12 to 3,
7 to 10.30; closed eve 25 Dec, Mon winter*

LLANGYBI

Monmouthshire   map 4

White Hart

Llangybi NP15 1NP
TEL: (01633) 450258

just off A449, between Newport and Usk

In a tiny village in the lovely Vale of
Usk, the White Hart dates from the
twelfth century, and the unspoilt
interior features heavy beams,
flagstones and open fires. The same
menu is served in the bar areas as well
as in the no-smoking restaurant:
perhaps local pheasant, beef stroganoff,
Jamaican-style chicken, salmon with
prawn and ginger sauce, or one of the
vegetarian choices. Butty Bach, Tomos
Watkin Old Style Bitter and Bass are
on draught, and three wines come by
the glass.

Open *Mon to Fri 11.30 to 3, 6.30 to 11,
Sat 11 to 11, Sun 12 to 4, 7 to 10.30*

LLANGYNWYD

Bridgend   map 4

Old House

Llangynwyd CF34 9SB
TEL: (01656) 733310

off A4063, 2m S of Maesteg

Flowers IPA, Worthington, Bass and
an ale from Cardiff's Brains brewery
are the usual ales on offer at this
thatched pub dating from the twelfth
century, and they are joined in
summer by a guest like Shepherd
Neame Spitfire Premium Ale. Around
a dozen wines are served by the glass
from a list approaching 30 bottles, so
finding something appropriate to
match the food should be little
problem. The printed menu is
complemented by a list of daily
specials, among them fish dishes,
mostly grilled or pan-fried Dover or
lemon sole, halibut, hake or trout. The
beer garden, which has a children's
play area, overlooks the Llynfi.

Open *11 to 11, Sun 12 to 10.30*

LLANHENNOCK

Monmouthshire   map 2

Wheatsheaf

Llanhennock NP18 1LT
TEL: (01633) 420468

off B4236, 2m N of Caerleon

At one time a farmhouse, this old,
L-shaped stone pub is at the top of the
hill running through the tiny village.
Tables and chairs in the front garden,
where there's also a Wendy house and
a slide, make a good spot for summer
eating (lunchtimes only): perhaps fish
chowder, a pie, faggots and peas,
boiled ham with parsley sauce, or one
of the fish specials. Bass and
Worthington are the regular draught
beers, and one of the frequently
changing guests could be the Full
Malty from the Cwmbran Brewery.

Open *winter Mon and Wed 11 to 3, 5.30 to
11, Tue, Thur, Fri and Sat 11 to 11, Sun 12 to
3, 7 to 10.30; summer; 11 to 11, Sun 12 to 3,
7 to 10.30*

LLANTHONY

Monmouthshire   map 4

Llanthony Priory

Llanthony NP7 7NN
TEL: (01873) 890487

off A465, 9m N of Abergavenny

Once part of a twelfth-century
Augustinian abbey, this remote pub is
in a stunning setting surrounded by
beautiful trees and soaring mountains.
Approach through a wall straight into
the open cloisters, and there you find
this old prior's house, built into the
ruins – worth a visit in their own right
– its old stone now lichen-covered and
highly atmospheric. The tiny bar in the
vaulted crypt offers Bass, Flowers
Original and Felinfoel ales, plus a
blackboard menu of simple, hearty
fare; vegetarian options, local lamb and
pheasant in season. Accommodation
available.

Open *summer Mon 10 to 3, Tue to Fri 11 to 3,
6 to 11, Sat 11 to 11, Sun 12 to 10.30 (open 11
to 11 every day in July and Aug); winter Fri 6 to
11, Sat 11 to 11, Sun 12 to 4*

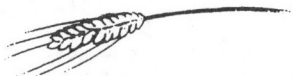

MOLD

Flintshire   map 7

Glasfryn

Raikes Lane, Sychdyn, Mold CH7 6LR
TEL: (01352) 750500

Opposite the civic centre and theatre, this red-brick building recalls its farmhouse origins with views over rolling countryside to the rear. A cheerful buzz fills the honeycomb of rooms, each with its own decorative theme, centred on a big, oak-panelled bar. Real ales are taken seriously, with Flowers, Timothy Taylor Landlord and Plassey joined by two guests, and there's an upbeat wine list with at least ten by the glass. Food is a modern take on pub grub – perhaps grilled red bream with ricotta and spinach tortellini, or a lighter chicken and cranberry salad tortilla wrap.
Open *11.30 to 11, Sun 12 to 10.30*

MONTGOMERY

Powys   map 4

Dragon Hotel

Montgomery SY15 6PA
TEL: (01686) 668359

on B4385, 3m E of A483 Newtown to Welshpool road

This former coaching inn with 20 en suite rooms, and dating from the seventeenth century, is notable for its black and white façade and prime location on the market square. The restaurant has both a printed menu and a blackboard list of daily specials, and the kitchen uses as much local produce as possible. Shropshire's Wood Brewery supplies some of the real ales dispensed in the bar, and five wines are sold by the glass. Children welcome. Offa's Dyke Path is nearby.
Open *11 to 11, Sun 12 to 10.30*

NEVERN

Pembrokeshire   map 4

Trewern Arms

Nevern SA42 0NB
TEL: (01239) 820395

on B4582, 2m E of Newport

Dating from the seventeenth century, this picturesque, creeper-covered inn, with a patio and garden, is on the bank of the River Nevern in a village notable for its medieval church and ancient bridge. Snacks are served in the atmospheric bar, with a full menu in the restaurant (Thursday to Saturday, dinner only) offering such main courses as beef stroganoff, braised lamb shank and salmon in dill sauce. Wadworth 6X, Flowers Original and Castle Eden Ale are among the rotating real ales on handpump, and three wines are sold by the glass. Ten en suite guests' rooms are available.
Open *11 to 3, 6 to 11, Sun 12 to 3, 7 to 10.30; no food 25 Dec*

OLD RADNOR

Powys   map 4

Harp Inn

Old Radnor LD8 2RH
TEL: (01544) 350655

off A44, between New Radnor and Kington

With a 500-year history, the Harp is of a similar age to the church it looks over. In a peaceful spot on a hillside in the Marches, not far from Offa's Dyke Path, it offers a warm and welcoming haven. The one handpump dispenses a constantly changing real ale, including something from local brewers like Six Bells in Bishop's Castle, and three wines are served by the glass. The two dining rooms, one no-smoking, have blackboard menus that include steaks, cod in beer batter, home-made faggots, and pork and leek sausages. Children are welcome, with their own menu, and five rooms, one a four-poster, are available for B&B.
Open *Tue to Fri 7 (6 summer) to 11, Sat and Sun 12 to 3, 7 to 11; also open bank hol Mon*

REYNOLDSTON

Swansea   map 4

King Arthur

Higher Green, Reynoldston SA3 1AD
TEL: (01792) 390775

Located at the base of Cefn Bryn on the Gower Peninsula, this black and white building dotted with hanging baskets looks out on grassland to the front and woodland to the rear. When the moon is full the ghost of King Arthur is said to emerge from the Cromlech and traverse this scenic

landscape. The pub's interior is traditional and the views splendid. Sporting memorabilia is much in evidence. Real ales are Bass, Worthington and Felinfoel Double Dragon. Children are welcome and a self-catering cottage is available.
Open *11 to 11*

RHYD-DDU

Gwynedd   map 7

Cwellyn Arms
Rhyd-Ddu LL54 6TL
TEL: (01766) 890321
on A4085, between Caernarfon and Beddgelert

Up to nine beers are dispensed at this stone-built pub within the Snowdonia National Park, among them perhaps Brains Arms Park, Dark and Bitter, Bass and Worthington cask. Three wines are available by the glass, with the full list approaching 20 bottles. Snacks as well as a full restaurant menu are on offer. Outside is a beer garden and children's playground. The pub has three en suite bedrooms, a self-catering cottage, a campsite and a bunkhouse.
Open *11 to 11, Sun 12 to 10.30*

RUTHIN

Denbighshire   map 7

Ye Olde Anchor Inn
2 Rhos Street, Ruthin LL15 1DX
TEL: (01824) 702813
at junction of A525 and A494

This large, white, slate-roofed hotel stands in the centre of the medieval town on the Clwyd. Inside, it has all the olde worlde trimmings: prints and plates on the wall, low oak beams and inglenooks. It also has an excellent reputation for food – on offer in the past were starters like chicken liver parfait with date and apple chutney, and main courses such as sweet-and-sour vegetable stir-fry with Thai egg noodles, or Cumberland sausage with whole-grain mustard mash – though menus were being amended under a new licensee as the Guide went to press. Bass and Timothy Taylor Landlord, the real ales on draught, may change too. Wines are supplied by

Tanners of Shrewsbury. Reports please.
Open *12 to 3, 5.30 to 11*

SOLVA

Pembrokeshire   map 4

Cambrian Inn
Main Street, Solva SA62 6UU
TEL: (01437) 721210
off A487, 3m W of St David's

Felinfoel Double Dragon Ale is on draught, along with a guest such as Bass or Brains Bitter, at this unpretentious pub set in a small fishing village at the bottom of a steep valley within the Pembrokeshire Coast National Park. Traditional pub grub – fishcakes and cottage pie, for example – is supplemented by two daily specials, one normally a fish dish. In the evening the restaurant menu comes into play (also served in the bar). Four wines are available by the glass.
Open *12 to 3, 6.30 to 11, Sun 12 to 2, 6.30 to 10.30; closed 25 Dec*

TAFF'S WELL

Rhondda Cynon Taff   map 4

Fagins
8 Cardiff Road, Taff's Well CF4 7RE
TEL: (029) 2081 1350

Fagins is one of a chain of idiosyncratic pubs and restaurants across the South Wales valleys, each with its own character. The one thing they all have in common is an excellent range of beers. Expect to find as many as fourteen real ales at any time: six are dispensed by handpump, while a further eight are served direct from the cask behind the bar. Food, listed on blackboards, is inexpensive and straightforward, along the lines of minted lamb pie, sausage, egg and chips, and spicy sausage sizzler, plus various baguettes and tortilla wraps; there is also a separate steak menu.
Open *11 to 11, Sun 12 to 10.30*

TALYBONT

Powys   map 4

Star Inn

Talybont LD3 7YX
TEL: (01874) 676635
½m off A40, 6m SE of Brecon

Llangorse Lake, Talybont Reservoir,
the Usk and the Monmouthshire and
Brecon Canal are all attractions near
this eighteenth-century stone pub in
the Brecon Beacons. The impressive
line-up of real ales is a draw too,
among them something from Cardiff
breweries Brains and Bullmastiff, plus
perhaps Theakston Old Peculier,
Felinfoel Double Dragon or Everards
Original. Food is generally familiar
renditions of pub favourites using
mostly local produce: perhaps roast
lamb or beef. Live music is performed
on Wednesday evening. Two en suite
guest rooms; children welcome.

Open *Mon to Fri 11 to 3, 6.30 to 11,
Sat 11 to 11, Sun 12 to 3, 6.30 to 10.30
(12 to 10.30 summer)*

Index

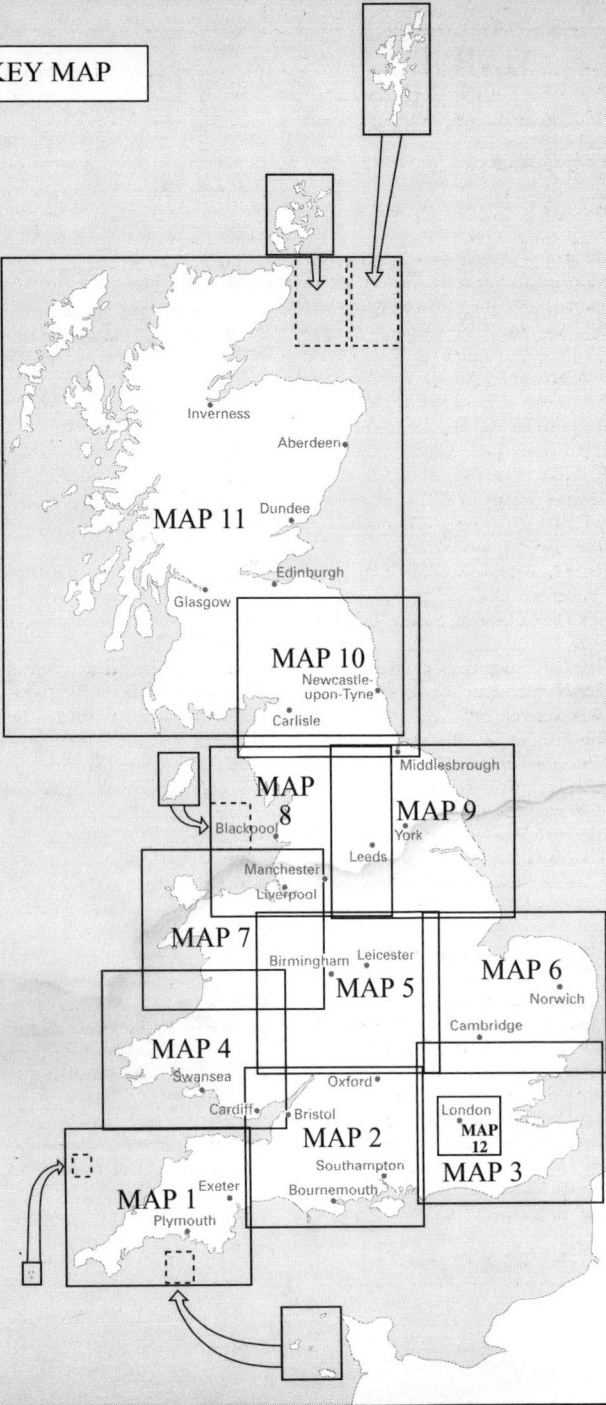

KEY MAP

MAP 11

Inverness
Aberdeen
Dundee
Edinburgh
Glasgow

MAP 10
Newcastle-upon-Tyne
Carlisle

Middlesbrough

MAP 8
Blackpool

MAP 9
York
Leeds

Manchester
Liverpool

MAP 7
Birmingham
Leicester

MAP 5

MAP 6
Norwich

Cambridge

MAP 4
Swansea
Oxford
Cardiff
Bristol

MAP 2
Southampton
Bournemouth

London
MAP 12

MAP 3

MAP 1
Exeter
Plymouth

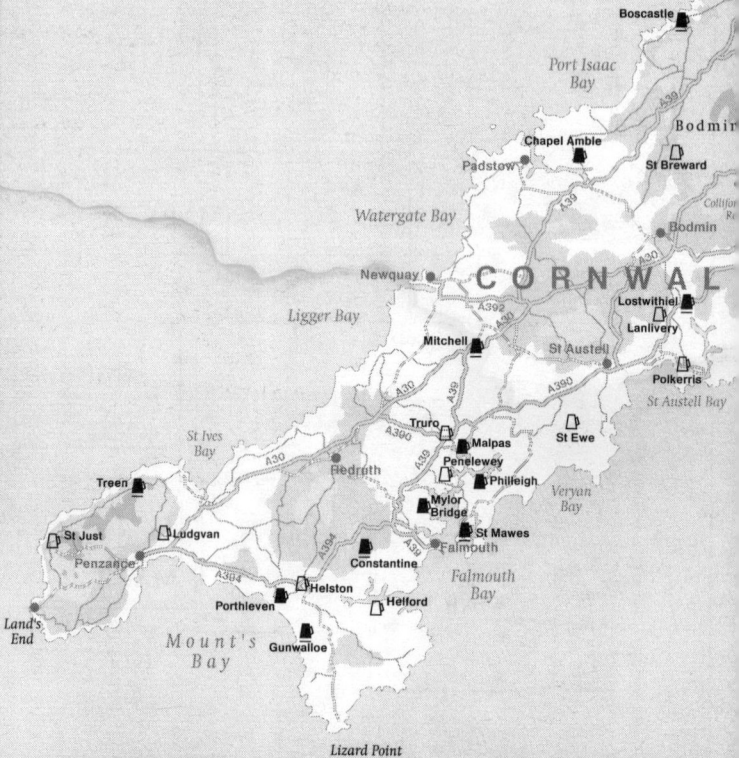

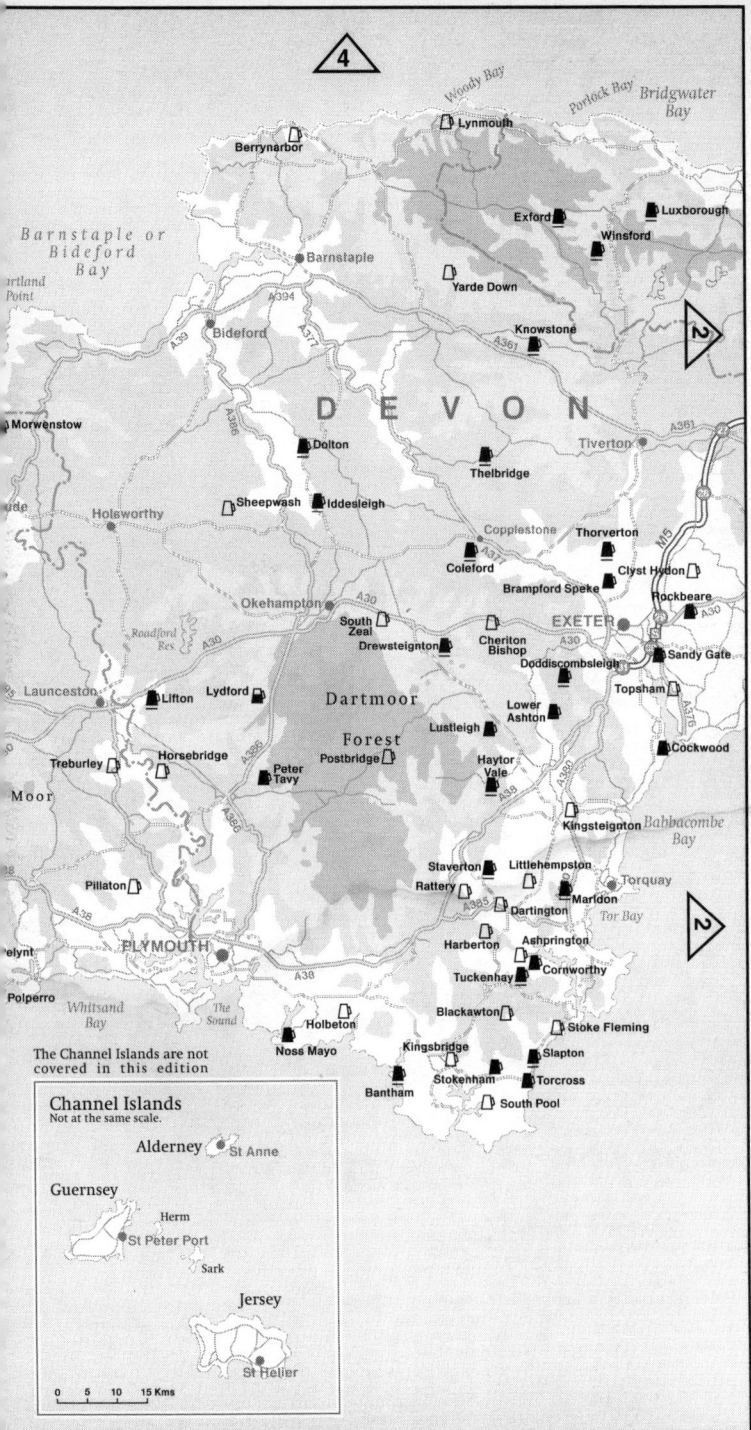

4

Woody Bay · Porlock Bay · Bridgwater Bay

Lynmouth

Berrynarbor

Barnstaple or Bideford Bay

artland Point

Barnstaple

Exford · Luxborough

Winsford

Yarde Down

Bideford

Knowstone

D E V O N

Morwenstow

Tiverton

Dolton

Thelbridge

Holsworthy

Sheepwash · Iddesleigh

Copplestone

Thorverton

Coleford

Brampford Speke

Clyst Hydon

Okehampton

Rockbeare

Roadford Res

South Zeal

Cheriton Bishop

EXETER

Drewsteignton

Doddiscombsleigh

Sandy Gate

Launceston

Lower Ashton

Topsham

Lifton · Lydford

Dartmoor

Lustleigh

Cockwood

Treburley

Horsebridge

Forest

Postbridge

Haytor Vale

Peter Tavy

Moor

Kingsteignton · *Babbacombe Bay*

Pillaton

Staverton · Littlehempston

Rattery

Torquay

PLYMOUTH

Dartington

Marldon

Tor Bay

Harberton

Ashprington

elynt

Tuckenhay · Cornworthy

Polperro

Whitsand Bay

The Sound

Holbeton

Blackawton

Stoke Fleming

Noss Mayo

Kingsbridge

Slapton

Stokenham · Torcross

Bantham

South Pool

The Channel Islands are not covered in this edition

Channel Islands
Not at the same scale.

Alderney · St Anne

Guernsey

Herm

St Peter Port

Sark

Jersey

St Helier

0 5 10 15 Kms

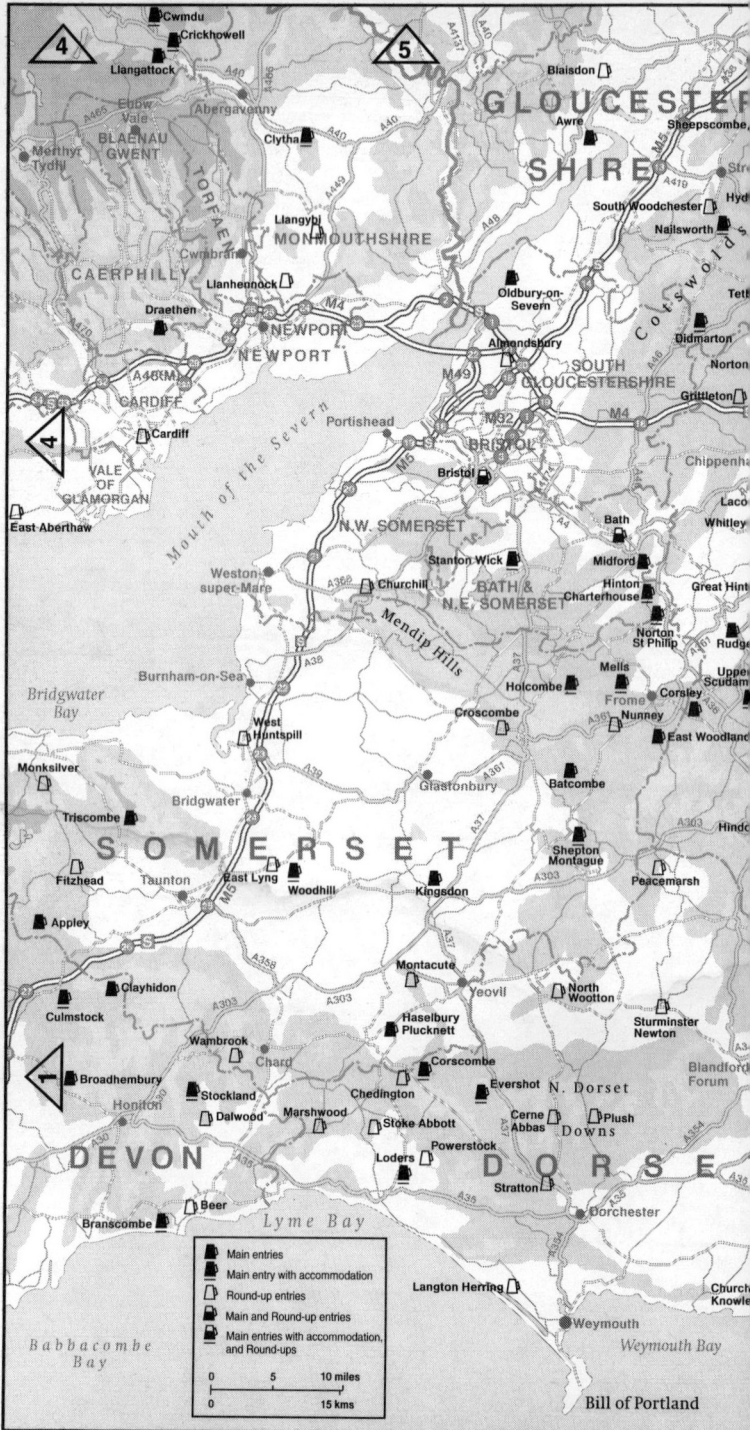

4

Cwmdu
Crickhowell
Llangattock
Ebbw Vale
BLAENAU
GWENT
Merthyr Tydfil
Abergavenny
Clytha

5

Blaisdon
GLOUCESTER
SHIRE
Awre
Sheepscombe
Stroud
South Woodchester
Hyd
Nailsworth
Tetb
Didmarton
Norton
Grittleton

Langybi
MONMOUTHSHIRE
Cwmbran
TORFAEN
CAERPHILLY
Llanhennock
Draethen
NEWPORT
NEWPORT
Oldbury-on-Severn
Almondsbury
SOUTH
GLOUCESTERSHIRE
Cardiff
CARDIFF
4
Cardiff
VALE
OF
GLAMORGAN
East Aberthaw
Portishead
Mouth of the Severn
BRISTOL
Bristol
N.W. SOMERSET
Chippenha
Laco
Whitley
Bath
Midford
Hinton
Charterhouse
Great Hint
Norton
St Philip
Rudge
Upper
Scudam
Corsley
East Woodland
Mells
Frome
Nunney
Weston-super-Mare
Churchill
BATH &
N.E. SOMERSET
Stanton Wick
Mendip Hills
Burnham-on-Sea
Holcombe
Croscombe
Batcombe
Bridgwater Bay
West
Huntspill
Glastonbury
Shepton
Montague
Hind
Peacemarsh
Monksilver
Triscombe
S O M E R S E T
Fitzhead
Taunton
East Lyng
Woodhill
Kingsdon
A303
Appley
Montacute
Yeovil
North
Wootton
Sturminster
Newton
Clayhidon
Culmstock
Haselbury
Plucknett
Wambrook
Chard
Corscombe
Evershot
N. Dorset
Blandford
Forum
Broadhembury
Stockland
Dalwood
Honiton
Marshwood
Chedington
Stoke Abbott
Cerne
Abbas
Plush
Downs
DEVON
Loders
Powerstock
D O R S E
Beer
Stratton
Branscombe
Lyme Bay
Dorchester
Babbacombe
Bay
Langton Herring
Church
Knowle
Weymouth
Weymouth Bay
Bill of Portland

Main entries
Main entry with accommodation
Round-up entries
Main and Round-up entries
Main entries with accommodation,
and Round-ups

0   5   10 miles
0   15 kms

MAP 2

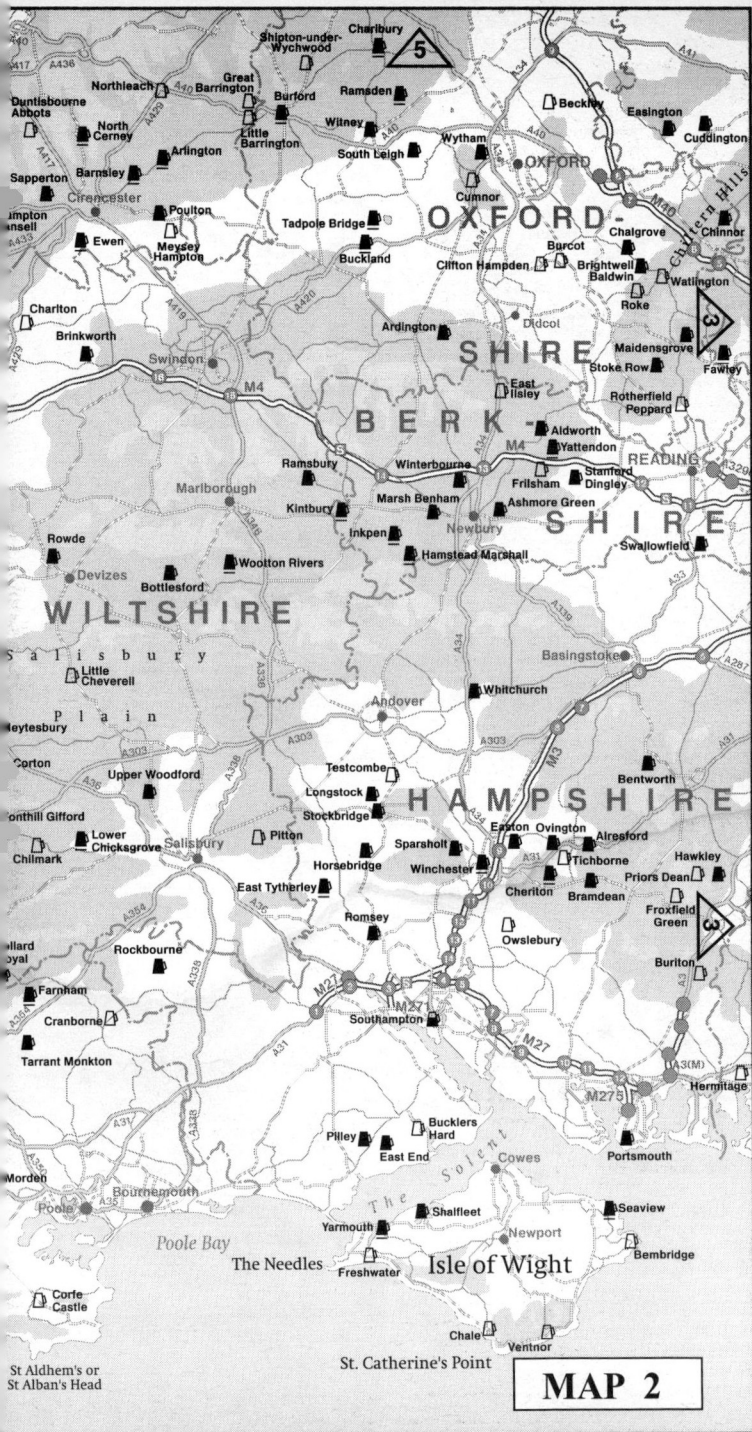

Charlbury
Shipton-under-Wychwood
5
Northleach
Great Barrington
Burford
Ramsden
Beckley
Easington
Duntisbourne Abbots
North Cerney
Little Barrington
Witney
Wytham
Cuddington
Sapperton
Arlington
Barnsley
South Leigh
OXFORD
Cirencester
Poulton
Tadpole Bridge
Cumnor
OXFORD-
Chalgrove
Chinnor
...mpton ...nsell
Ewen
Meysey Hampton
Buckland
Burcot
Brightwell Baldwin
Watlington
Clifton Hampden
Roke
Charlton
Brinkworth
Ardington
Didcot
SHIRE
Maidensgrove
Stoke Row
Fawley
Swindon
East Ilsley
Rotherfield Peppard
3
M4
BERK-
Aldworth
Yattendon
READING
Ramsbury
Winterbourne
M4
Stanford Dingley
Marlborough
Marsh Benham
Frilsham
Ashmore Green
SHIRE
Kintbury
Newbury
Rowde
Inkpen
Hamstead Marshall
Swallowfield
Devizes
Wootton Rivers
Bottlesford
WILTSHIRE
S a l i s b u r y
Basingstoke
Little Cheverell
P l a i n
Heytesbury
Whitchurch
Corton
Upper Woodford
Andover
...onthill Gifford
Testcombe
Bentworth
HAMPSHIRE
Lower Chicksgrove
Salisbury
Longstock
Stockbridge
Easton Ovington
Alresford
Hawkley
Chilmark
Pitton
Sparsholt
Tichborne
Priors Dean
East Tytherley
Horsebridge
Winchester
Cheriton
Bramdean
Froxfield Green
...llard ...oyal
Rockbourne
Romsey
Owslebury
3
Buriton
Farnham
Cranborne
M27
M27
Tarrant Monkton
Southampton
Hermitage
Morden
M275
M27
Poole
Bournemouth
Pilley
Bucklers Hard
Cowes
Portsmouth
East End
Poole Bay
Shalfleet
Seaview
The Needles
Yarmouth
Newport
Freshwater
Isle of Wight
Bembridge
Corfe Castle
St Aldhem's or St Alban's Head
Chale
Ventnor
St. Catherine's Point
The Solent

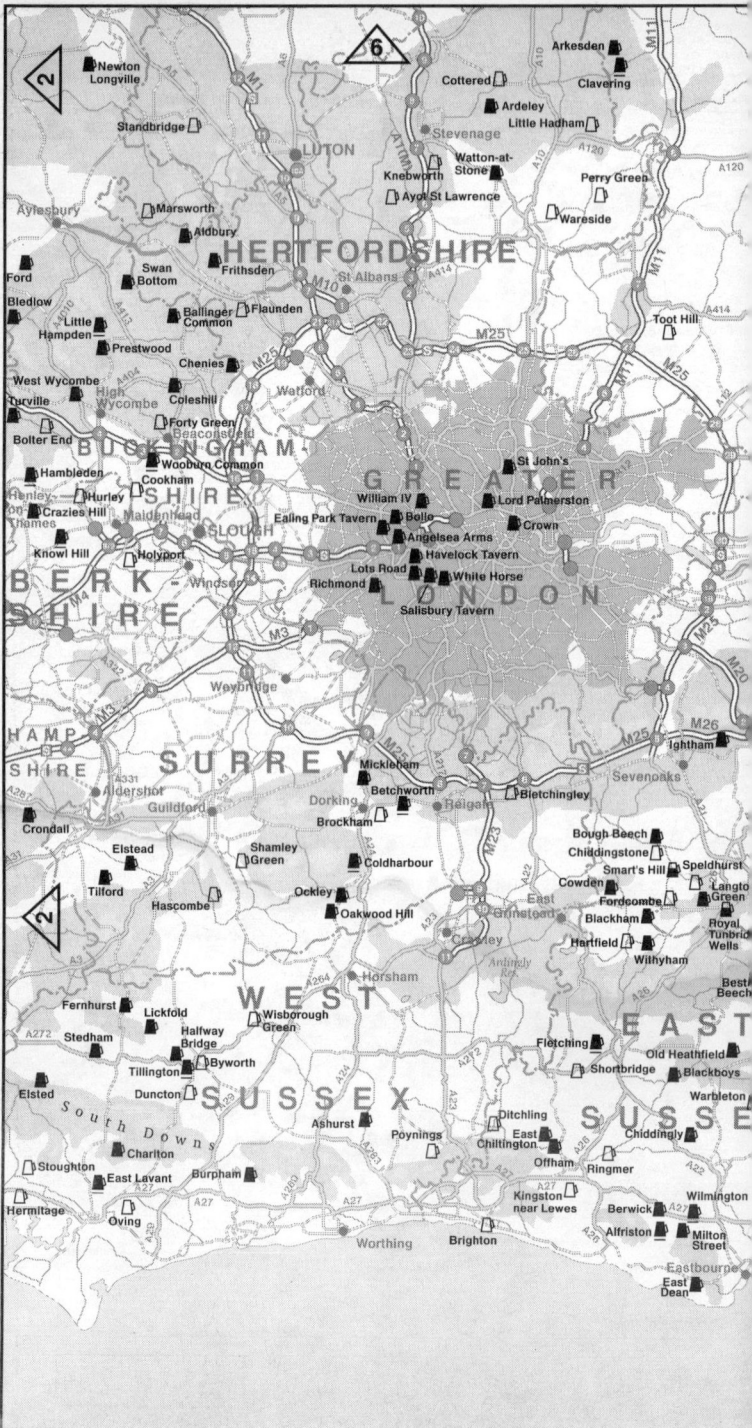

6

HERTFORDSHIRE

GREATER LONDON

BUCKINGHAM-SHIRE

BERK-SHIRE

HAMP-SHIRE

SURREY

WEST SUSSEX

EAST SUSSEX

Newton Longville
Standbridge
Arkesden
Clavering
Cottered
Ardeley
Little Hadham
Stevenage
Knebworth
Watton-at-Stone
Perry Green
Aydi St Lawrence
Wareside
Marsworth
Aldbury
Aylesbury
LUTON
Swan Bottom
Frithsden
Ford
Bledlow
St Albans
Little Hampden
Ballinger Common
Flaunden
Toot Hill
Prestwood
Chenies
West Wycombe
Coleshill
Watford
Turville
High Wycombe
Forty Green
Beaconsfield
Bolter End
Woobum Common
Cookham
Hambleden
Henley-on-Thames
Hurley
Crazies Hill
Maidenhead
St John's
Lord Palmerston
William IV
Belle
Crown
Ealing Park Tavern
Angelsea Arms
Havelock Tavern
Knowl Hill
Holyport
SLOUGH
Lots Road
White Horse
Richmond
Windsor
Salisbury Tavern
Weybridge
Aldershot
SHIRE
Guildford
Mickleham
Betchworth
Bletchingley
Dorking
Reigate
Brockham
Sevenoaks
Ightham
Crondall
Elstead
Shamley Green
Coldharbour
Bough Beech
Chiddingstone
Speldhurst
Tilford
Hascombe
Ockley
Smart's Hill
Cowden
Fordcombe
Langto Green
Oakwood Hill
East Grinstead
Blackham
Royal Tunbridge Wells
Crawley
Hartfield
Withyham
Horsham
Best Beech
Fernhurst
Lickfold
Wisborough Green
Fletching
Old Heathfield
Stedham
Halfway Bridge
Shortbridge
Blackboys
Tillington
Byworth
Warbleton
Elsted
Duncton
SUSSEX
Ashurst
Ditchling
Chiddingly
Poynings
East Chiltington
Charlton
Burpham
Offham
Ringmer
Stoughton
East Lavant
Oving
Kingston near Lewes
Berwick
Wilmington
Hermitage
Alfriston
Milton Street
Worthing
Brighton
Eastbourne
East Dean
South Downs

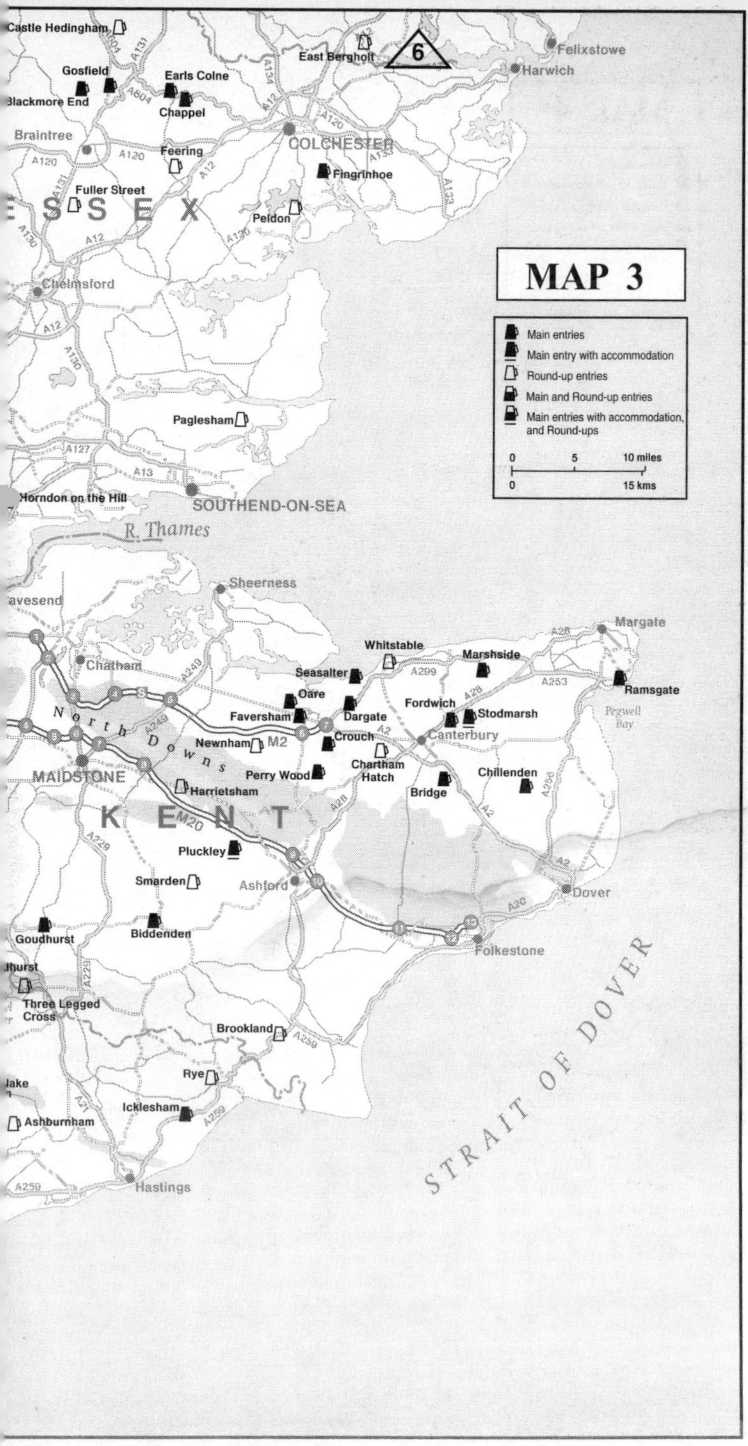

MAP 3

Legend:
- Main entries
- Main entry with accommodation
- Round-up entries
- Main and Round-up entries
- Main entries with accommodation, and Round-ups

0   5   10 miles
0   15 kms

Locations shown:

Castle Hedingham
Gosfield
Earls Colne
Blackmore End
Chappel
Braintree
Feering
Fuller Street
Fingrinhoe
Peldon
ESSEX
Chelmsford
East Bergholt
6
Felixstowe
Harwich
COLCHESTER
Paglesham
Horndon on the Hill
SOUTHEND-ON-SEA
R. Thames
Sheerness
Gravesend
Chatham
Whitstable
Seasalter
Oare
Faversham
Newnham
Perry Wood
Harrietsham
MAIDSTONE
KENT
Pluckley
Smarden
Goudhurst
Biddenden
Ashford
Marshside
Dargate
Fordwich
Stodmarsh
Crouch
Canterbury
Chartham
Hatch
Bridge
Chillenden
North Downs
Margate
Ramsgate
Pegwell Bay
Dover
Folkestone
Three Legged Cross
Brookland
Rye
Icklesham
Ashburnham
Hastings
STRAIT OF DOVER

MAP 4

Main entries
Main entry with accommodation
Round-up entries
Main and Round-up entries
Main entries with accommodation, and Round-ups

| 0 | 5 | 10 miles |
| 0 | | 15 kms |

7

CARDIGAN

BAY

Aberaeron

A487

Newport Bay

Fishguard Bay

Cilgerran

Nevern

Abercych

A487

Newcastle
Emlyn

Porthgain

PEMBROKESHIRE

CARMA

Solva

Carmarthen

A40

St. Brides
Bay

A40

A40

A477

Broad Sound

Pembroke Ferry

Carew

A477

Lamphey

Carmarthen
Bay

Stackpole

BRISTOL

1

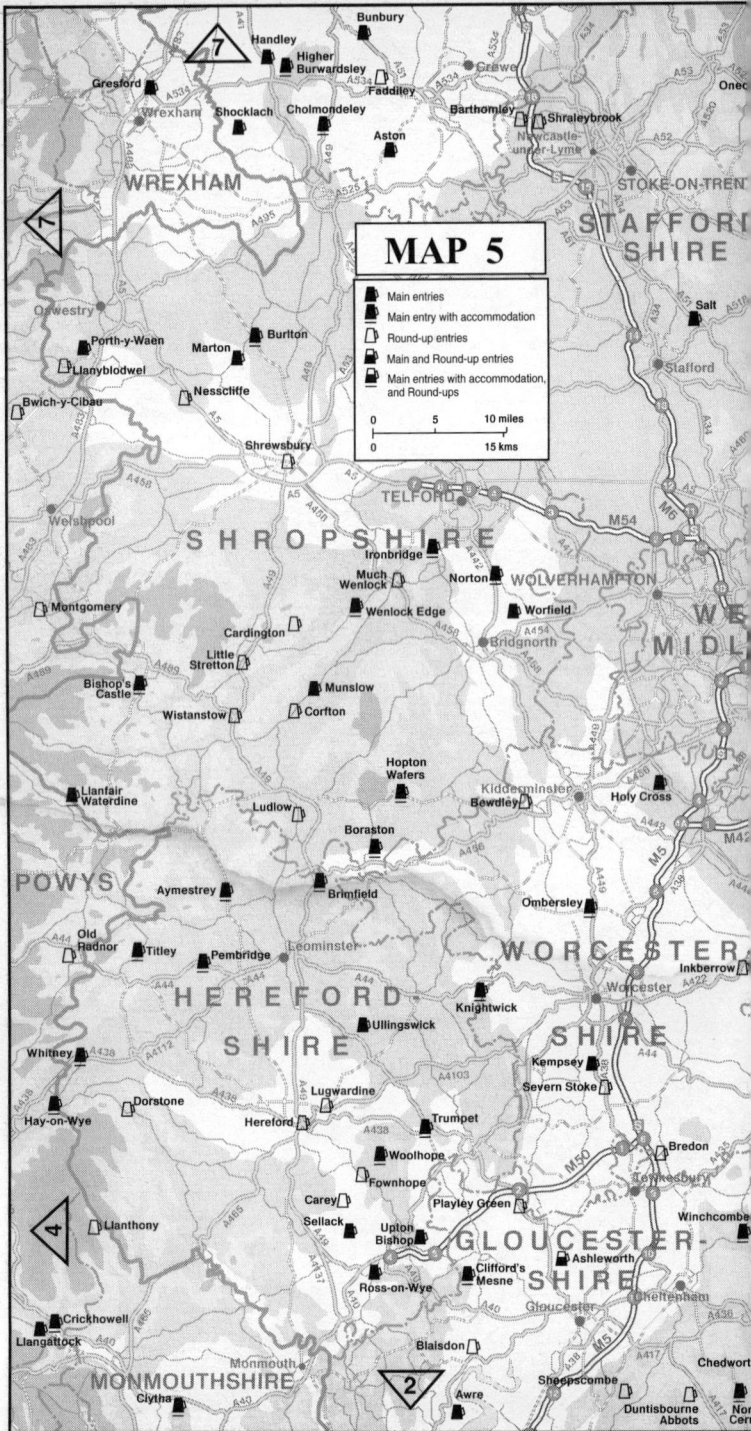

MAP 5

- ■ Main entries
- ■ Main entry with accommodation
- □ Round-up entries
- ◨ Main and Round-up entries
- ◪ Main entries with accommodation, and Round-ups

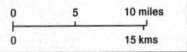

0   5   10 miles
0   15 kms

WREXHAM

STAFFORDSHIRE

STOKE-ON-TRENT

SHROPSHIRE

WOLVERHAMPTON

WEST MIDLANDS

POWYS

WORCESTERSHIRE

HEREFORDSHIRE

GLOUCESTERSHIRE

MONMOUTHSHIRE

Bunbury, Handley, Higher Burwardsley, Faddiley, Crewe, Gresford, Wrexham, Shocklach, Cholmondeley, Barthomley, Shraleybrook, Newcastle-under-Lyme, Aston, Onec...

Oswestry, Salt, Stafford, Porth-y-Waen, Marton, Burlton, Llanyblodwel, Nesscliffe, Bwlch-y-Cibau, Shrewsbury, Telford, M54, M6

Welshpool, Ironbridge, Much Wenlock, Norton, Worfield, Montgomery, Cardington, Wenlock Edge, Bridgnorth, Little Stretton, Munslow, Bishop's Castle, Wistanstow, Corfton, Llanfair Waterdine, Hopton Wafers, Kidderminster, Bewdley, Holy Cross, Ludlow, Boraston, Aymestrey, Brimfield, Ombersley, Old Radnor, Titley, Pembridge, Leominster, Worcester, Inkberrow, Ashleworth, Whitney, Ullingswick, Knightwick, Kempsey, Severn Stoke, Dorstone, Lugwardine, Hereford, Trumpet, Bredon, Hay-on-Wye, Woolhope, Fownhope, Carey, Playley Green, Tewkesbury, Winchcombe, Llanthony, Sellack, Upton Bishop, Clifford's Mesne, Cheltenham, Crickhowell, Ross-on-Wye, Gloucester, Llangattock, Blaisdon, Chedwort..., Monmouth, Clytha, Awre, Sheepscombe, Duntisbourne Abbots, Nor Cern...

Birchover
Woolley Moor
Caunton
Collingham
MANSFIELD
9
Butterton
Brassington
Upton
Cauldon
Hognaston
NOTTINGHAM-
SHIRE
DERBY-
SHIRE
Thurgarton
Hollington
Nottingham
DERBY
Colston Bassett
Redmile
Grantham
Shardlow
Cavendish Bridge
Woolsthorpe
Knipton
Tutbury
Ingleby
Castle Donnington
Stathern
Abbots Bromley
Burton upon Trent
Loughborough
6
Wymondham
Market Overton
Cottesmore
Exton
Rutland Water
LEICESTERSHIRE
Upper Hambleton
RUT-
LAND
Wing
LEICESTER
Lyddington
Glooston
Shustoke
Nuneaton
East Langton
Thorpe Langton
DS
Berkswell
Market Harborough
Barston
COVENTRY
Chadwick End
Rugby
Kettering
Lapworth
Birmingham
East Haddon
Wellingborough
Preston Bagot
Warwick
Ashby St Ledgers
Daventry
NORTHAMPTON
Aston Cantlow
Stratford-upon-Avon
Badby
Farthingstone
Temple Grafton
Alveston
NORTHAMPTON-
SHIRE
Stoke Bruerne
WARWICKSHIRE
Oxford
Alderminster
Chacombe
Chicheley
Bretforton
Ilmington
Shenington
MILTON KEYNES
Broadway
Shipston on Stour
Banbury
Bodicote
3
Broad Campden
Paxford
Great Wolford
Hook Norton
Ford
Swerford
Thornborough
Great Tew
Preston Bissett
Stow-on-the-Wold
Upper Oddington
Lower Oddington
OXFORDSHIRE
Naunton
Bledington
Chadlington
Bicester
Marsh Gibbon
BUCKINGHAMSHIRE
Great Barrington
Charlbury
Ramsden
Beckley
Marsworth
Fletcherleigh
Little Barrington
Burford
Witney
2
Aylesbury
Weston Turville
Coln St Aldwyns
South Leigh
Wytham
Easington
Cuddington
Ford
Swan Bottom
OXFORD

LINCOLNSHIRE

Lincoln
Coleby
Fulbeck
A158
A16
A52
Skegness

Heckington
Aswarby
Boston
The Wash
Thornha
Ringstead
Snettisham

Grantham
Gedney Dyke
King's Lyn

Grimsthorpe
The Fens
Stow Bardolph
Barto
Bendi

Market Overton
Stretton
Clipsham
Cottesmore
Exton
RUTLAND
Empingham
Upper Hambleton
Stamford
Wisbech

Wing
Barrowden
Harringworth
Lyddington
PETERBOROUGH

Elton
Fotheringhay
Stilton
CAMBRIDGE-

Lowick
Kettering
SHIRE
Ely
Fordham

Keyston
Sutton Gault
Huntingdon
Hemingford Grey
Holywell
Fenstanton
Fen Drayton
Godmanchester
Wellingborough
Grafton Water

Keysoe
St Neots
Madingley
Cambridge
Kirtling
Lidg

Odell
Great Eversden
Little Shelford
Hildersham
Ridgewel

Turvey
Newton
Fowlmere
Whittlesford
Duxford

BEDFORDSHIRE
Bedford
Biggleswade
Chicheley
Houghton Conquest
Broom
Heydon

MILTON KEYNES
Cottered
Arkesden
Clavering
Little Hadham
Ardeley
Standbridge
LUTON
Knebworth
Stevenage
Watton-at-Stone

ESSEX

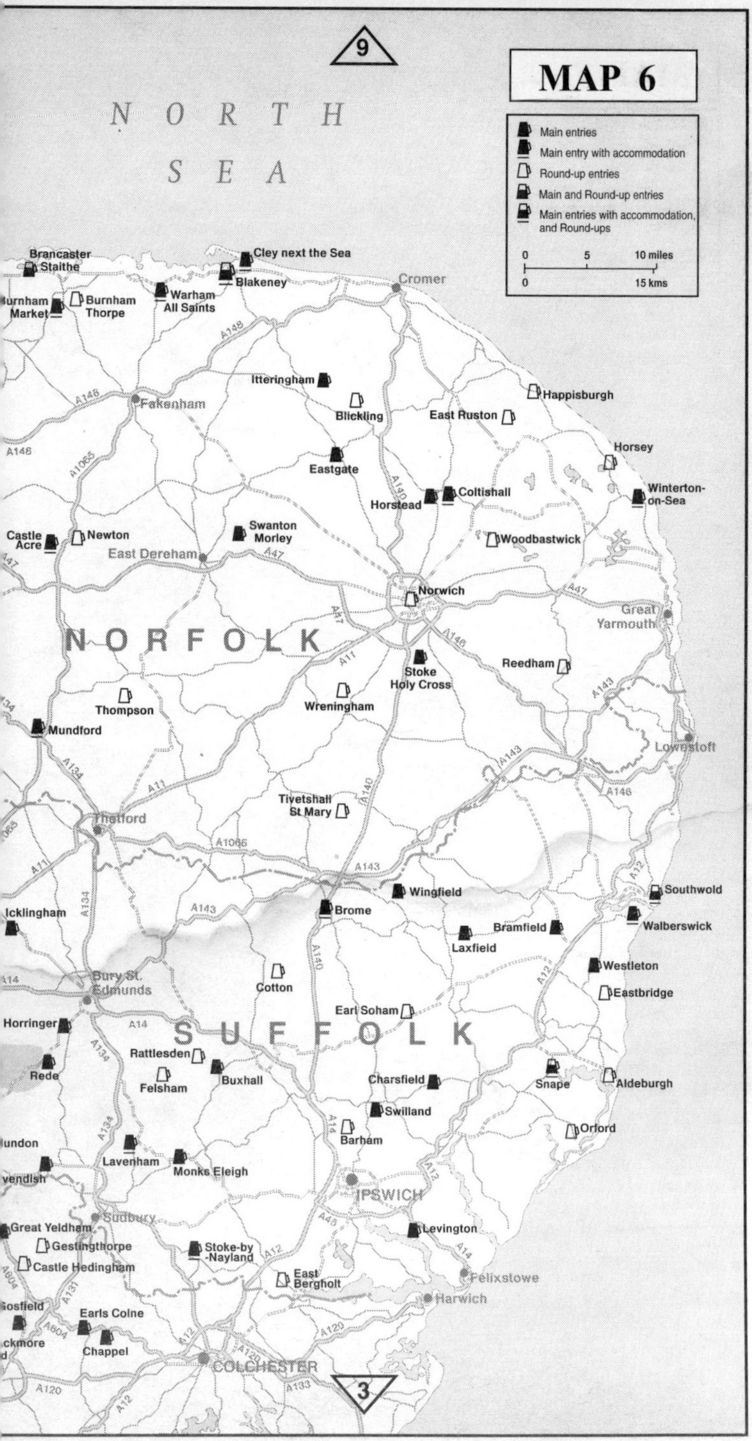

MAP 6

Main entries
Main entry with accommodation
Round-up entries
Main and Round-up entries
Main entries with accommodation, and Round-ups

| 0 | 5 | 10 miles |
| 0 | | 15 kms |

NORTH
SEA

NORFOLK

SUFFOLK

Brancaster Staithe
Burnham Market
Burnham Thorpe
Warham All Saints
Cley next the Sea
Blakeney
Cromer
Itteringham
Fakenham
Blickling
East Ruston
Happisburgh
Eastgate
Horsey
Horstead
Coltishall
Winterton-on-Sea
Castle Acre
Newton
Swanton Morley
East Dereham
Woodbastwick
Norwich
Great Yarmouth
Thompson
Stoke Holy Cross
Reedham
Mundford
Wreningham
Lowestoft
Thetford
Tivetshall St Mary
Wingfield
Southwold
Icklingham
Brome
Bramfield
Walberswick
Bury St. Edmunds
Cotton
Laxfield
Westleton
Eastbridge
Horringer
Rattlesden
Earl Soham
Rede
Felsham
Buxhall
Charsfield
Snape
Aldeburgh
Swilland
Orford
Lundon
Lavenham
Barham
Cavendish
Monks Eleigh
IPSWICH
Great Yeldham
Gestingthorpe
Sudbury
Levington
Castle Hedingham
Stoke-by-Nayland
East Bergholt
Felixstowe
Gosfield
Earls Colne
Harwich
ckmore
Chappel
COLCHESTER

MAP 7

Main entries
Main entry with accommodation
Round-up entries
Main and Round-up entries
Main entries with accommodation, and Round-ups

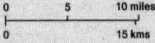

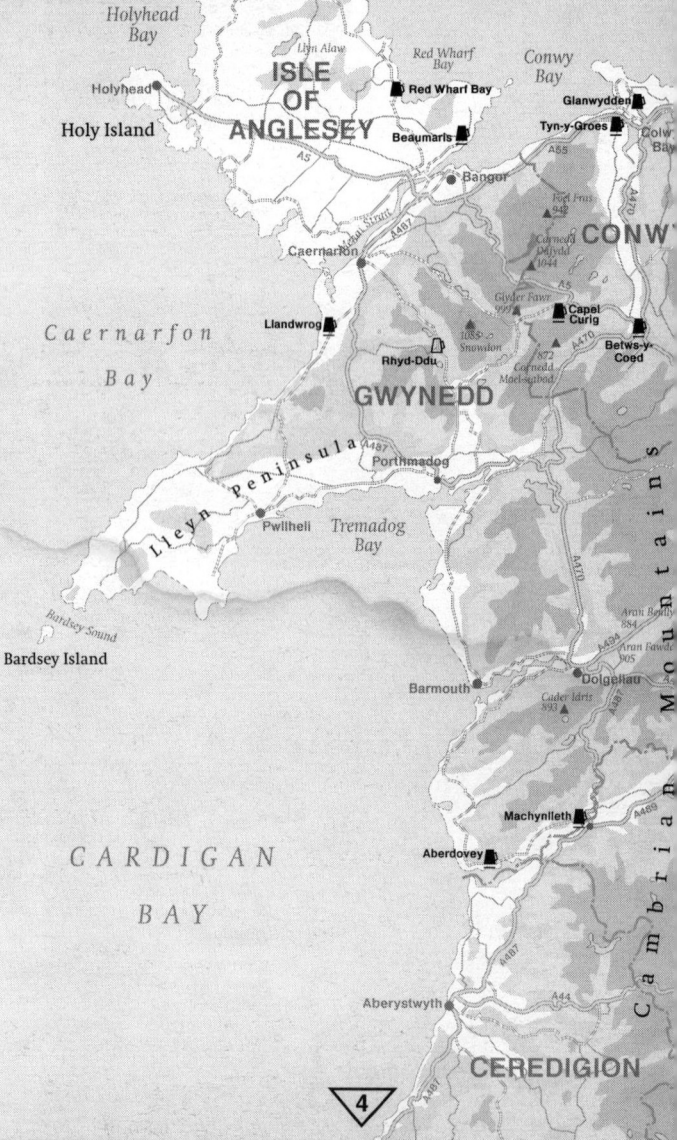

0   5   10 miles
0   15 kms

IRISH

SEA

Holyhead Bay

Llyn Alaw

Red Wharf Bay

ISLE OF ANGLESEY

Red Wharf Bay

Conwy Bay

Glanwydden

Tyn-y-Groes

Colw
Bay

Holyhead

Holy Island

Beaumaris

A5

Bangor

A55

Foel Fras

CONW

Menai Strait

Caernarfon

A4087

Carnedd Dafydd
1044

A5

Glyder Fawr
999

Capel
Curig

Caernarfon

Bay

Llandwrog

1085
Snowdon

872
Carnedd
Moel-siabod

Betws-y-
Coed

Rhyd-Ddu

GWYNEDD

A4710

A487

Lleyn peninsula

Porthmadog

A470

Tremadog

Pwllheli

Bay

Aran Benllyn
884

A494

A493

Aran Fawddwy
905

Bardsey Sound

Bardsey Island

Barmouth

Cader Idris
893

Dolgellau

Cambrian Mountains

CARDIGAN

BAY

Machynlleth

A489

Aberdovey

A487

Aberystwyth

A44

CEREDIGION

A4

4

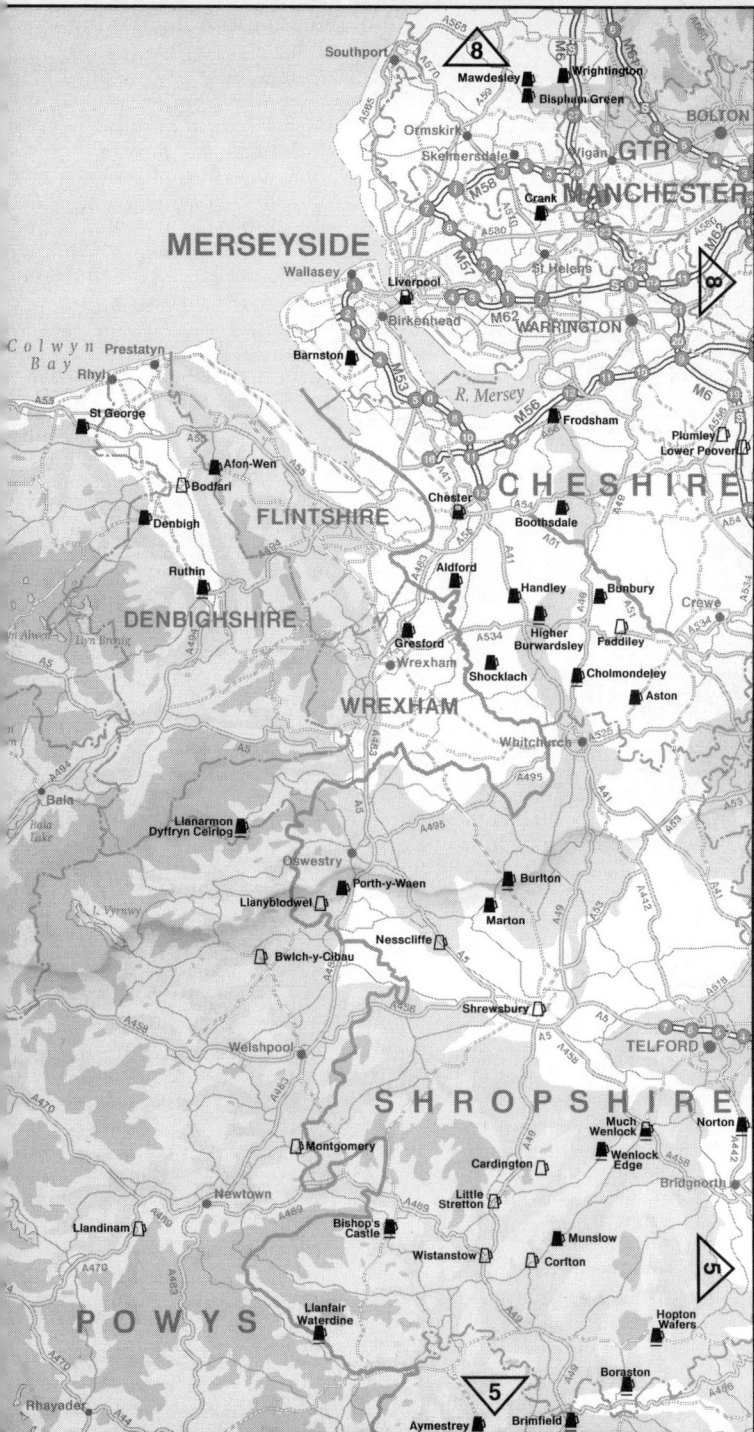

Southport

Mawdesley Wrightington

Bispham Green

BOLTON

Ormskirk

Skelmersdale Wigan GTR

MANCHESTER

Crank

MERSEYSIDE

Wallasey St Helens

Liverpool WARRINGTON

Birkenhead M62

Colwyn Bay Prestatyn

Rhyl Barnston R. Mersey

St George Frodsham Plumley
Lower Peover

Afon-Wen

Bodfari CHESHIRE

Denbigh Chester

FLINTSHIRE Boothsdale

Ruthin Aldford

Handley Bunbury

DENBIGHSHIRE Crewe

Gresford Higher Faddiley
Wrexham Burwardsley

Shocklach Cholmondeley

WREXHAM Aston

Whitchurch

Llanarmon
Dyffryn Ceiriog

Bala Oswestry

Bala Porth-y-Waen Burlton
lake

Llanyblodwel Marton

Bwlch-y-Cibau Nesscliffe

L. Vyrnwy Shrewsbury TELFORD

Welshpool

SHROPSHIRE Norton

Much
Wenlock

Montgomery Cardington Wenlock
Edge Bridgnorth

Newtown Little
Stretton

Llandinam Bishop's
Castle Munslow

Wistanstow Corfton

POWYS Llanfair
Waterdine Hopton
Wafers

Boraston

Rhayader Aymestrey Brimfield

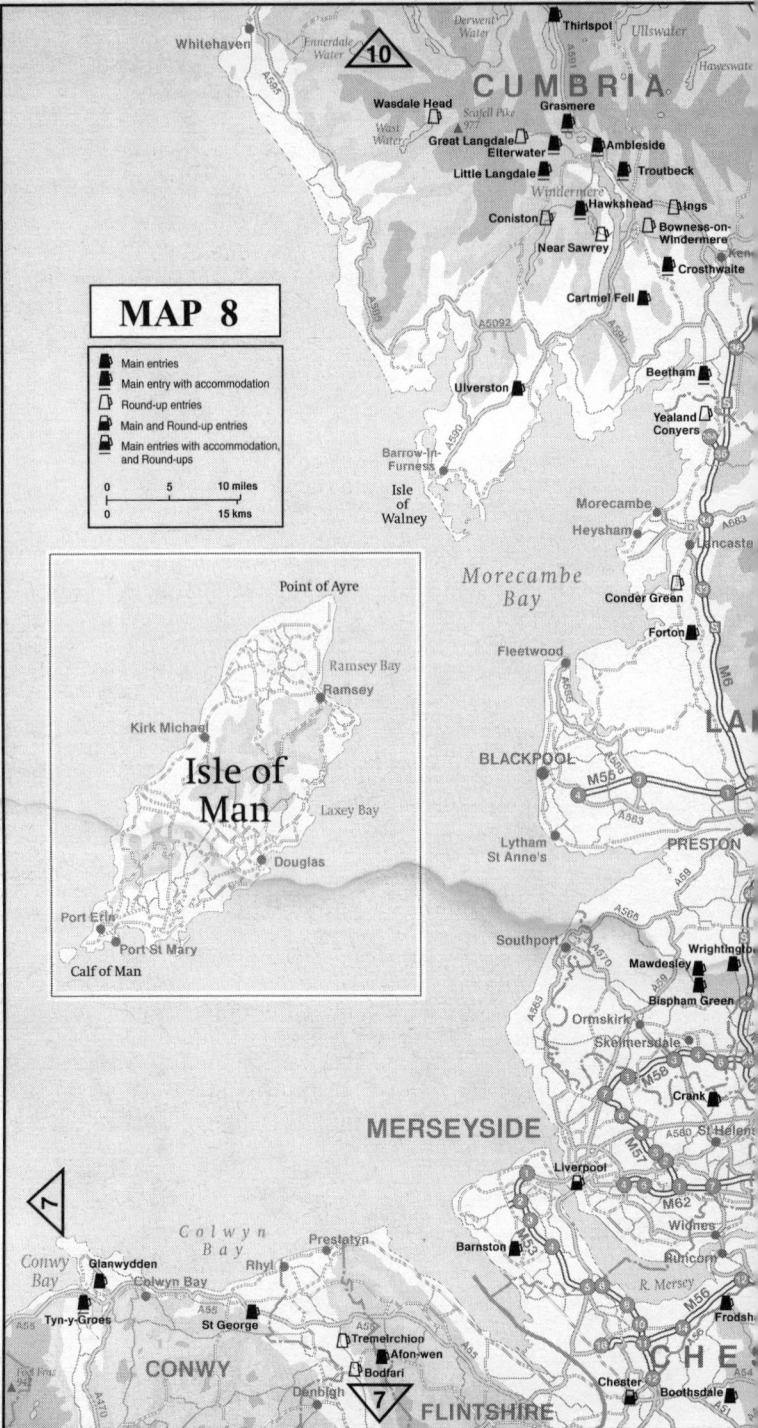
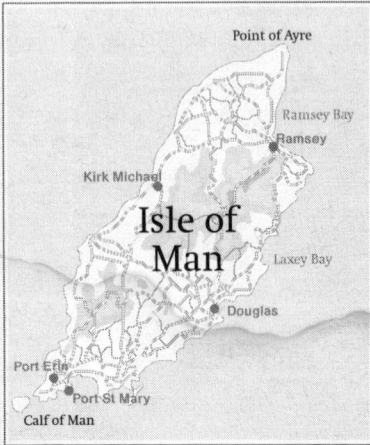
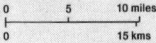

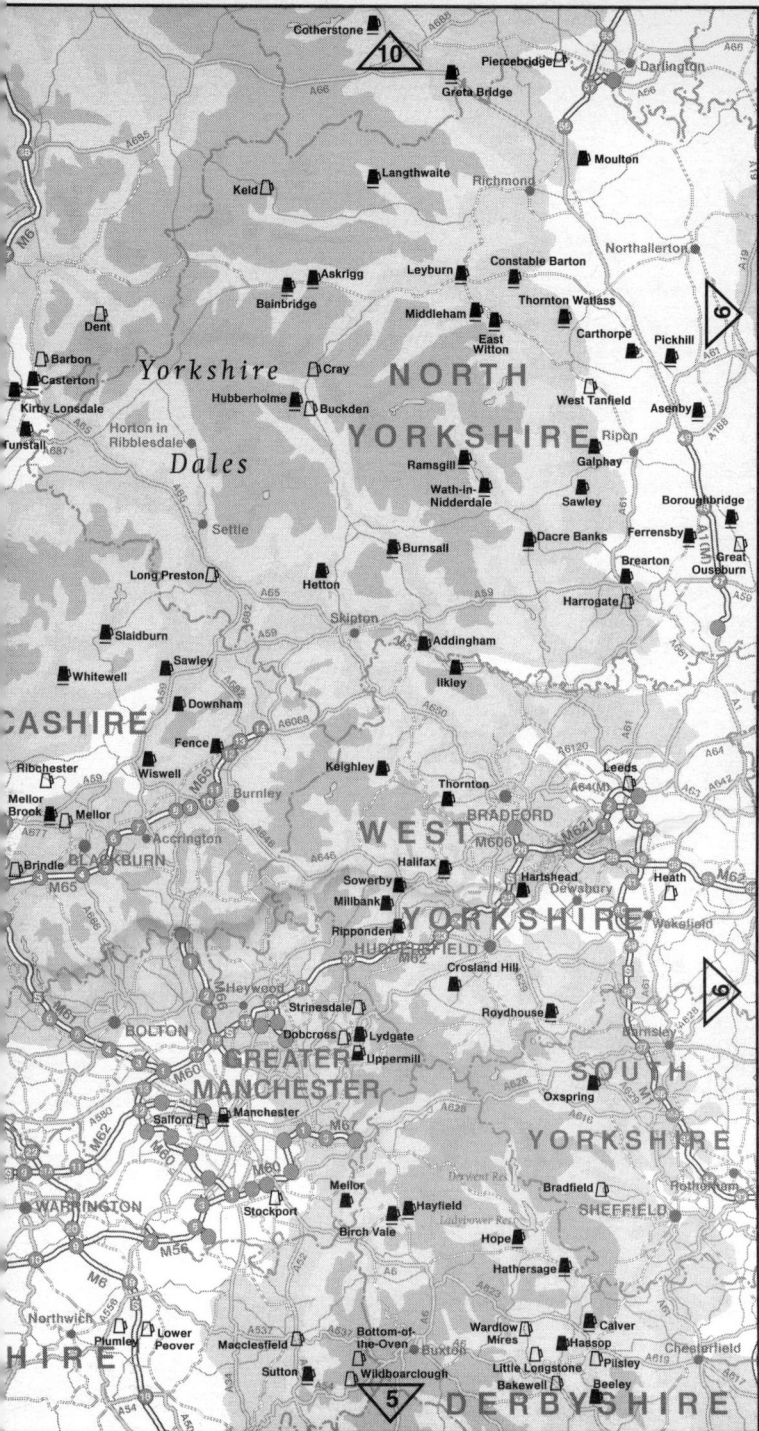

Cotherstone
10
Piercebridge
Greta Bridge
Darlington
Moulton
A66
Richmond
Langthwaite
Keld
Northallerton
Askrigg
Leyburn
Constable Barton
6
Bainbridge
Thornton Watlass
Middleham
Carthorpe
Pickhill
East Witton
Dent
Barbon
Cray
NORTH
Casterton
Hubberholme
Buckden
West Tanfield
Asenby
Kirby Lonsdale
Tunstall
Horton in Ribblesdale
YORKSHIRE
Ripon
Yorkshire
Galphay
Ramsgill
Dales
Settle
Wath-in-Nidderdale
Sawley
Boroughbridge
Dacre Banks
Ferrensby
Great Ousseburn
Burnsall
Brearton
Long Preston
Hetton
Harrogate
Slaidburn
Skipton
Sawley
Addingham
Whitewell
Downham
Ilkley
LASHIRE
Fence
Ribchester
Wiswell
Keighley
Leeds
Mellor Brook
Mellor
Burnley
Thornton
BRADFORD
Brindle
BLACKBURN
Accrington
WEST
Halifax
Hartshead
Heath
Sowerby
Dewsbury
Millbank
YORKSHIRE
Wakefield
Ripponden
HUDDERSFIELD
Crosland Hill
Heywood
Roydhouse
6
Strinesdale
Dobcross
Lydgate
BOLTON
Uppermill
Oxspring
GREATER
SOUTH
MANCHESTER
Salford
Manchester
YORKSHIRE
WARRINGTON
Barnsley
Stockport
Mellor
Bradfield
Rotherham
Hayfield
SHEFFIELD
Birch Vale
Hope
Northwich
Hathersage
Plumley
Lower Peover
Wardlow Mires
Calver
HIRE
Macclesfield
Bottom-of-the-Oven
Buxton
Hassop
Chesterfield
Little Longstone
Pilsley
Sutton
Wildboarclough
Bakewell
Beeley
5
DERBYSHIRE

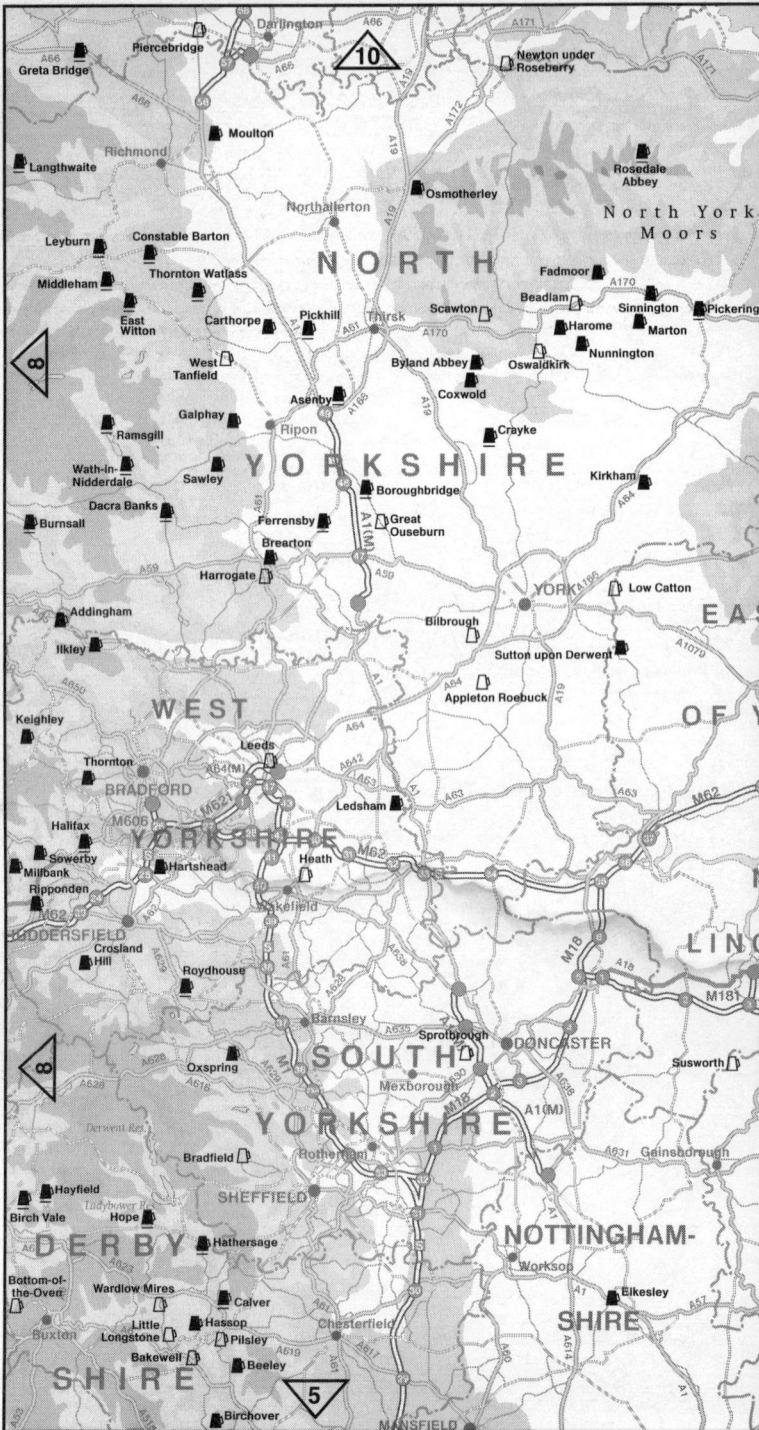

Darlington
Piercebridge
Greta Bridge
Newton under Roseberry
10
Moulton
Richmond
Langthwaite
Osmotherley
Rosedale Abbey
North York Moors
Leyburn
Constable Barton
Thornton Watlass
Middleham
Fadmoor
Beadlam
Sinnington
Pickering
East Witton
Carthorpe
Pickhill
Thirsk
Scawton
Harome
Marton
Nunnington
West Tanfield
Byland Abbey
Oswaldkirk
8
Galphay
Asenby
Coxwold
Ramsgill
Ripon
Crayke
YORKSHIRE
Kirkham
Wath-in-Nidderdale
Sawley
Dacra Banks
Boroughbridge
Burnsall
Ferrensby
Great Ouseburn
Brearton
Harrogate
YORK
Low Catton
Addingham
Bilbrough
EA
Ilkley
Sutton upon Derwent
OF Y
Appleton Roebuck
Keighley
WEST
Thornton
Leeds
BRADFORD
YORKSHIRE
Ledsham
Halifax
Sowerby
Millbank
Ripponden
HUDDERSFIELD
Heath
Wakefield
LINC
M181
Crosland Hill
Roydhouse
Barnsley
Sprotbrough
DONCASTER
8
Oxspring
SOUTH
Mexborough
Susworth
Bradfield
YORKSHIRE
Rotherham
A1(M)
Geinsborough
Hayfield
Birch Vale
Hope
SHEFFIELD
DERBY
Hathersage
NOTTINGHAM-
Worksop
Bottom-of-the-Oven
Wardlow Mires
Calver
Elkesley
Buxton
Little Longstone
Hassop
Pilsley
Chesterfield
SHIRE
Bakewell
Beeley
SHIRE
Birchover
5
MANSFIELD

MAP 9

10

- Main entries
- Main entry with accommodation
- Round-up entries
- Main and Round-up entries
- Main entries with accommodation, and Round-ups

0   5   10 miles
0   15 kms

Whitby
Robin Hood's Bay
Scarborough
Flamborough Head
Sledmere
Bridlington
Bridlington Bay
Driffield
Yorkshire Wolds
RIDING
Lund
RKSHIRE
KINGSTON UPON HULL
KINGSTON UPON HULL
Humber
Barton-upon-Humber
RTH
Winterton
LNSHIRE
cunthorpe
M180
Grimsby
Cleethorpes
Spurn Head
N.E. LINCOLNSHIRE
Market Rasen
Louth
Mablethorpe
The Wolds
Lincoln LINCOLNSHIRE
6
Skegness

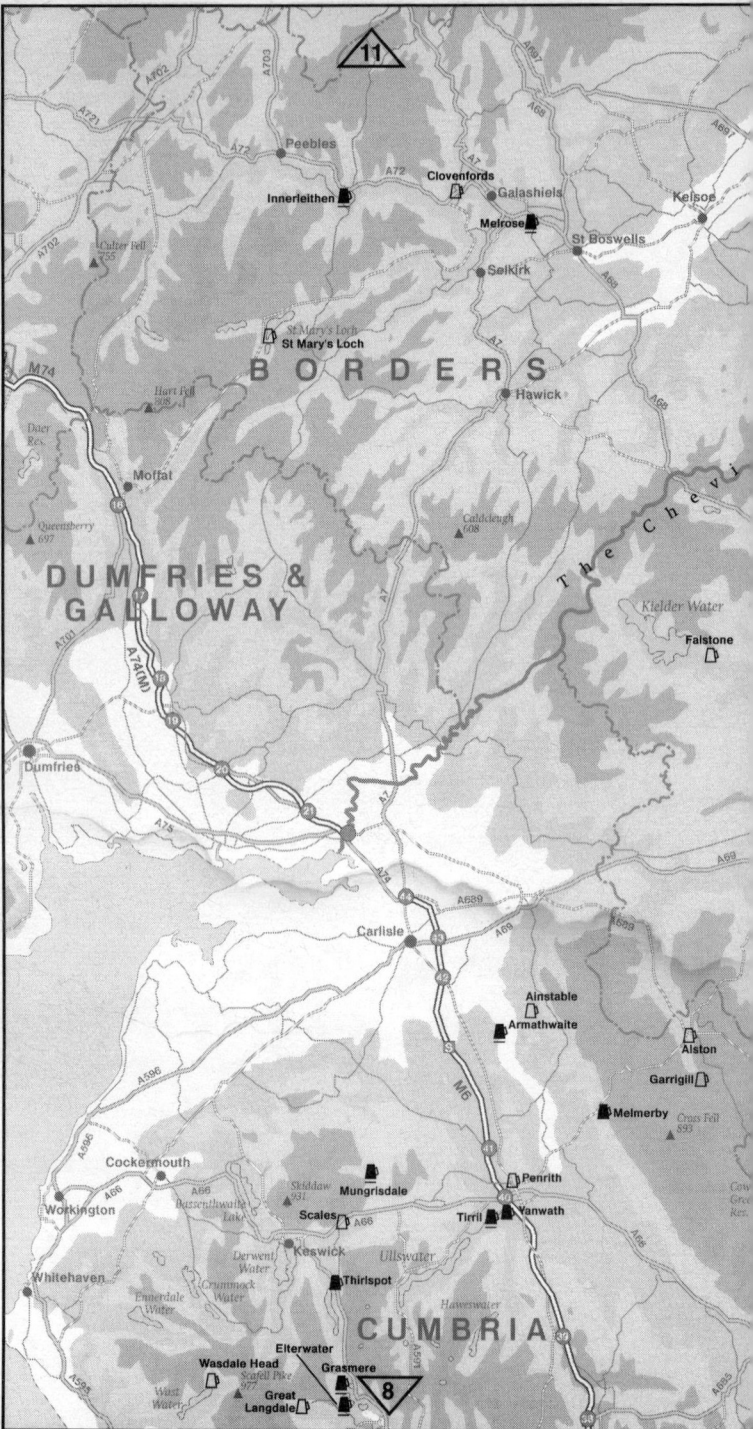

MAP 10

Main entries
Main entry with accommodation
Round-up entries
Main and Round-up entries
Main entries with accommodation, and Round-ups

| 0 | 5 | 10 miles |
| 0 | | 15 kms |

Berwick-upon-Tweed

Coldstream
Yark

Holy Island
Holy Island

Farne Is.

Seahouses

The Cheviot
815

Eglingham

Low Newton
-by-the-Sea

Craster
Dunstan

Alnwick

Ainmouth

Newton-on-the-Moor

NORTHUMBERLAND

Morpeth

Whalton

Haydon
Bridge

Anick

Great Whittington

Hexham

Hedley
on the Hill

Carterway
Heads

Derwent Res.

Newcastle
upon Tyne

North Shields Tynemouth

**TYNE
&
WEAR**

SUNDERLAND

A194(M)

Stanley

Consett

Chester-le-
Street

DURHAM

Durham

Shincliffe

Bishop
Auckland

Fir Tree

Romaldkirk

Cotherstone

Aycliffe

Piercebridge

Greta Bridge

Darlington

Hartlepool

HARTLEPOOL

Tees Bay

Redcar

**STOCKTON-
ON-TEES**

MIDDLESBROUGH

**MIDDLES
BROUGH**

REDCAR

Newton under
Roseberry

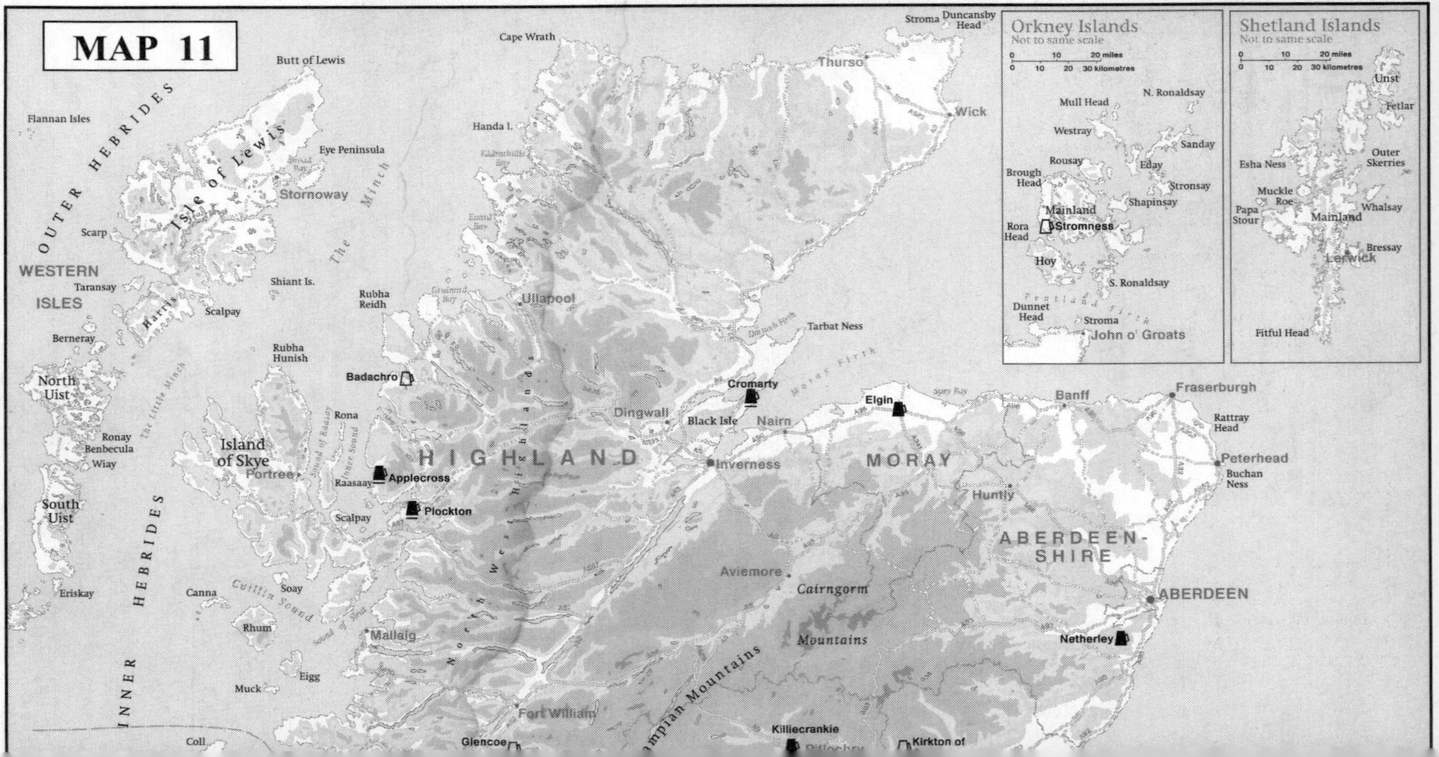

MAP 11

Shetland Islands
Not to same scale

0   10   20   30 kilometres
0   10   20 miles

Unst
Fetlar
Outer Skerries
Whalsay
Muckle Roe
Papa Stour
Esha Ness
Mainland
Bressay
Lerwick

Fitful Head

Orkney Islands
Not to same scale

0   10   20   30 kilometres
0   10   20   30 miles

N. Ronaldsay
Westray
Sanday
Eday
Stronsay
Rousay
Shapinsay
Brough Head
Mainland
Stromness
S. Ronaldsay
Hoy
Stroma
John o' Groats
Dunnet Head

Cape Wrath
Handa I.
Stroma   Duncansby Head
Thurso
Wick

Butt of Lewis
Flannan Isles
Eye Peninsula
Stornoway
Scarp
Taransay
Harris
Scalpay
Shiant Is.

WESTERN ISLES
ISLE OF LEWIS

OUTER HEBRIDES

Berneray
North Uist
Ronay
Benbecula
Wiay
South Uist
Eriskay

Flannan Isles

The Minch

Rubha Reidh
Rubha Hunish
Badachro
Applecross
Plockton
Raasay
Inner Sound
Scalpay
Island of Skye
Portree
Crowlin Is.
Sound of Raasay
Iona

INNER HEBRIDES

Canna
Rhum
Eigg
Muck
Coll
Soay
Mallaig

HIGHLAND

Ullapool

Dingwall
Inverness
Black Isle
Cromarty
Nairn
Tarbat Ness

MORAY
Elgin

Banff
Fraserburgh
Rattray Head
Peterhead
Buchan Ness

ABERDEEN-SHIRE
ABERDEEN
Netherley

Huntly

Aviemore
Cairngorm Mountains
Grampian Mountains
Killiecrankie
Kirkton of

Fort William
Glencoe

Netherley

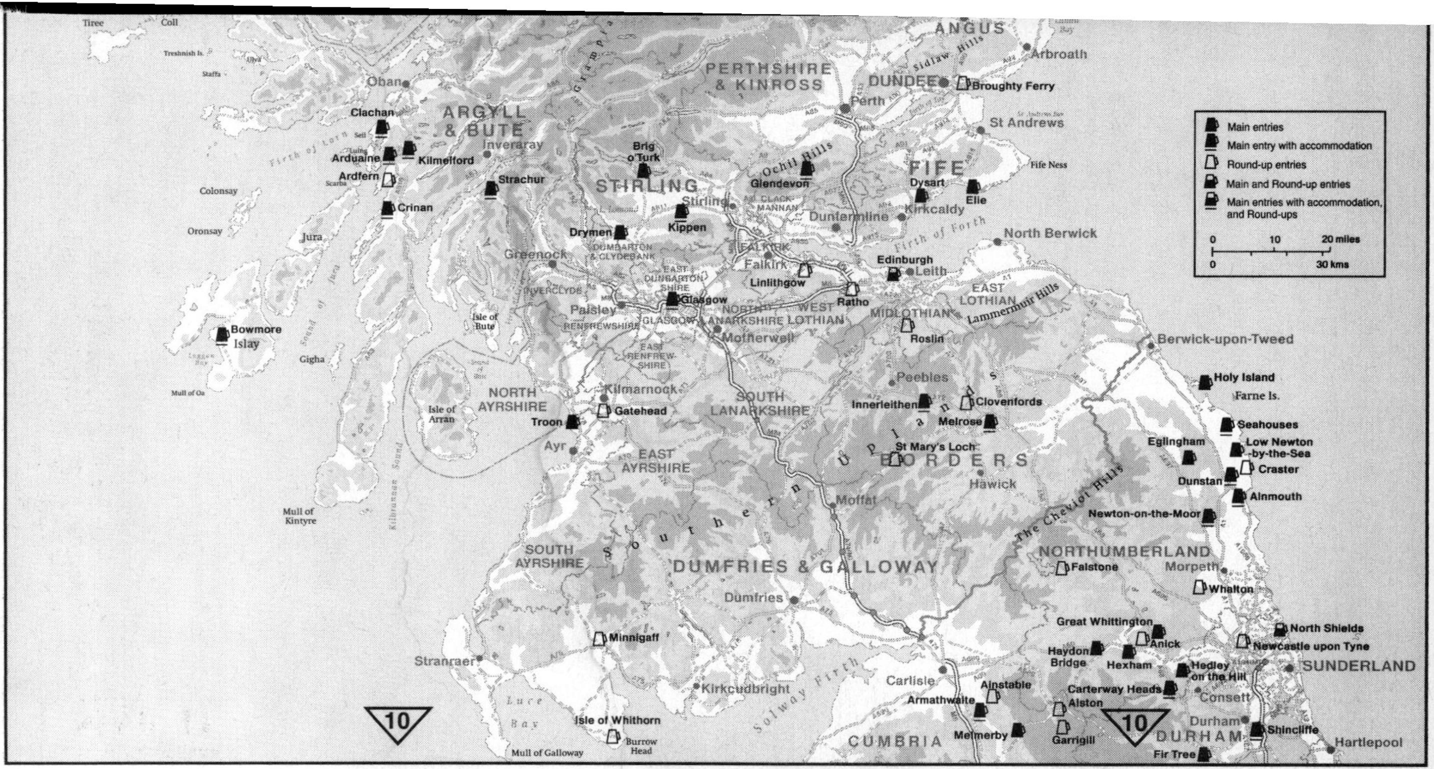
Main entries
Main entry with accommodation
Round-up entries
Main and Round-up entries
Main entries with accommodation, and Round-ups
0 10 20 miles
0 30 kms
ANGUS
PERTHSHIRE & KINROSS
DUNDEE
Broughty Ferry
Arbroath
Perth
St Andrews
Fife Ness
FIFE
Dysart
Elie
Kirkcaldy
Dunfermline
Firth of Forth
North Berwick
Ochil Hills
Glendevon
Sidlaw Hills
Oban
Clachan
ARGYLL & BUTE
Inveraray
Arduaine
Kilmelford
Ardfern
Strachur
Crinan
Firth of Lorn
Brig o'Turk
STIRLING
Stirling
Kippen
Drymen
DUMBARTON & CLYDEBANK
Greenock
FALKIRK
Falkirk
Linlithgow
Edinburgh
Leith
Ratho
EAST LOTHIAN
Lammermuir Hills
MIDLOTHIAN
Roslin
INVERCLYDE
EAST DUNBARTON SHIRE
Glasgow
Paisley
RENFREWSHIRE
GLASGOW
NORTH LANARKSHIRE
WEST LOTHIAN
Motherwell
EAST RENFREWSHIRE
Tiree
Coll
Treshnish Is.
Ulva
Staffa
Colonsay
Oronsay
Jura
Sound of Jura
Bowmore
Islay
Gigha
Mull of Oa
Isle of Bute
Isle of Arran
NORTH AYRSHIRE
Kilmarnock
Gatehead
Troon
Ayr
EAST AYRSHIRE
SOUTH LANARKSHIRE
Kilbrannan Sound
Mull of Kintyre
Berwick-upon-Tweed
Holy Island
Farne Is.
Peebles
Innerleithen
Clovenfords
Melrose
St Mary's Loch
BORDERS
Hawick
Southern Uplands
Moffat
Seahouses
Eglingham
Low Newton -by-the-Sea
Craster
Dunstan
Alnmouth
Newton-on-the-Moor
The Cheviot Hills
NORTHUMBERLAND
Falstone
Morpeth
Whalton
SOUTH AYRSHIRE
DUMFRIES & GALLOWAY
Dumfries
Minnigaff
Stranraer
Kirkcudbright
Solway Firth
Luce Bay
Isle of Whithorn
Burrow Head
Mull of Galloway
10
Carlisle
Ainstable
Armathwaite
Melmerby
CUMBRIA
Great Whittington
Anick
Haydon Bridge
Hexham
Hedley on the Hill
Carterway Heads
Alston
Garrigill
Consett
Durham
DURHAM
Fir Tree
Shincliffe
Hartlepool
North Shields
Newcastle upon Tyne
SUNDERLAND
10

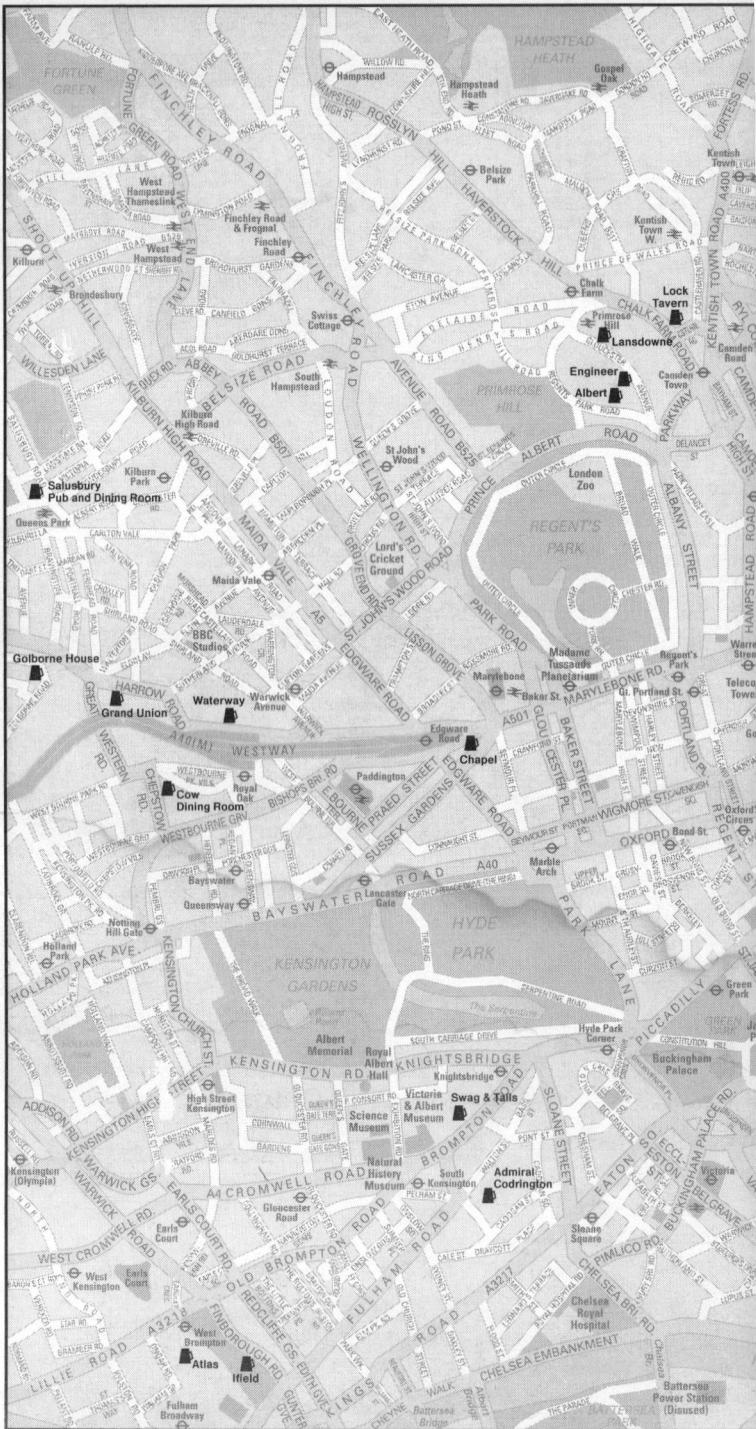

A map of central and north-west London showing locations including:

- FORTUNE GREEN
- HAMPSTEAD HEATH
- Hampstead
- Hampstead Heath
- Gospel Oak
- Belsize Park
- Kentish Town
- Kentish Town W
- Chalk Farm
- Lock Tavern
- Primrose Hill
- Lansdowne
- Engineer
- Albert
- Camden Town
- West Hampstead Thameslink
- Finchley Road & Frognal
- Finchley Road
- Swiss Cottage
- South Hampstead
- West Hampstead
- Kilburn
- Brondesbury
- PRIMROSE HILL
- St John's Wood
- London Zoo
- REGENT'S PARK
- Regent's Park
- Salusbury Pub and Dining Room
- Queens Park
- Kilburn Park
- Kilburn High Road
- BELSIZE ROAD
- Maida Vale
- Lord's Cricket Ground
- Madame Tussauds
- Marylebone
- Baker St.
- Gt. Portland St.
- Warren Street
- Telecom Tower
- BBC Studios
- Golborne House
- Waterway
- Warwick Avenue
- Grand Union
- WESTWAY
- Edgware Road
- Chapel
- Paddington
- Royal Oak
- Cow Dining Room
- Bishop's Bridge
- Bayswater
- Queensway
- Lancaster Gate
- Marble Arch
- Oxford Circus
- Bond St.
- Notting Hill Gate
- Holland Park
- HYDE PARK
- The Serpentine
- Green Park
- KENSINGTON GARDENS
- Albert Memorial
- Royal Albert Hall
- KNIGHTSBRIDGE
- Knightsbridge
- Hyde Park Corner
- Buckingham Palace
- High Street Kensington
- Science Museum
- Victoria & Albert Museum
- Swag & Tails
- Kensington (Olympia)
- Natural History Museum
- South Kensington
- Gloucester Road
- Admiral Codrington
- Sloane Square
- Victoria
- Earls Court
- West Kensington
- West Brompton
- Atlas
- Ifield
- Fulham Broadway
- Chelsea Royal Hospital
- CHELSEA EMBANKMENT
- Battersea Power Station (Disused)
- Battersea Bridge

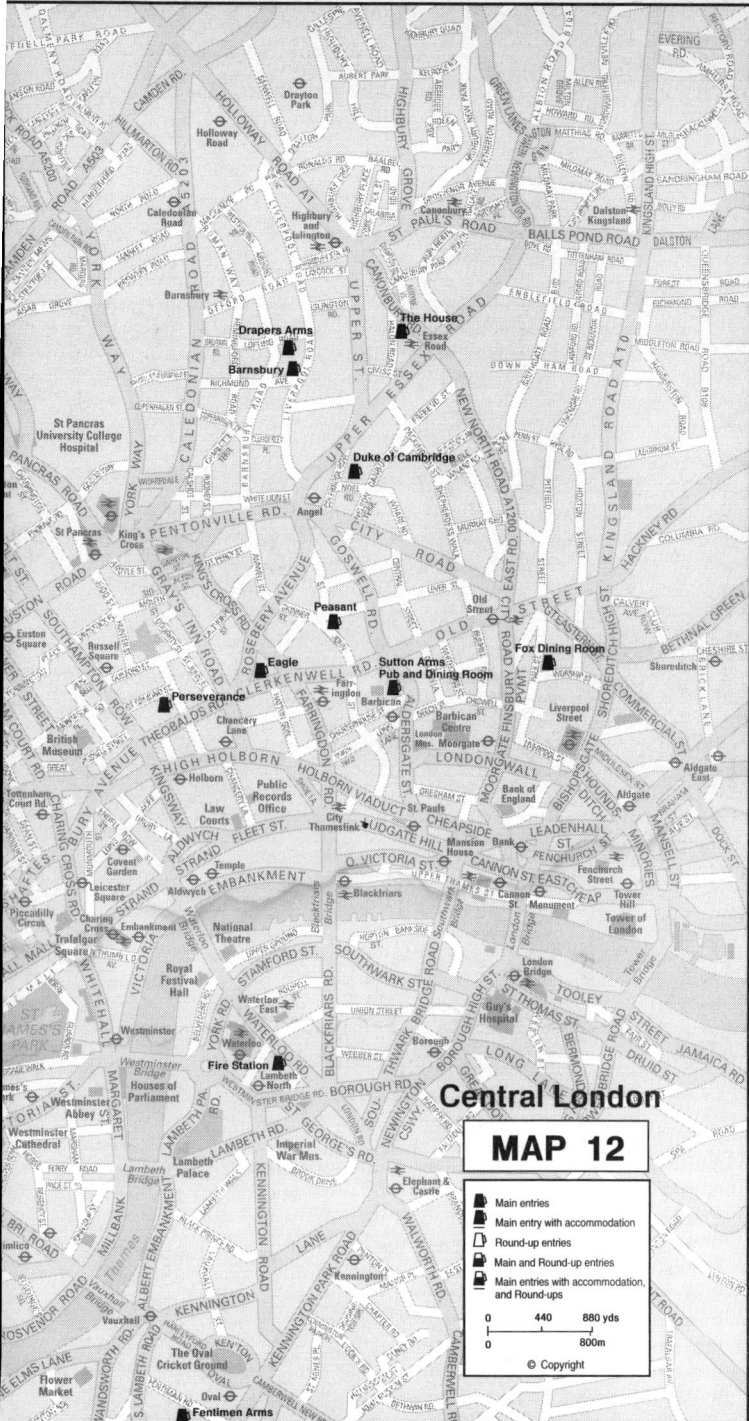

Central London

MAP 12

Main entries (map labels):

- Drayton Park
- Holloway Road
- Caledonian Road
- Highbury and Islington
- Canonbury
- Dalston Kingsland
- Barnsbury
- Drapers Arms
- Barnsbury
- The House
- St Pancras University College Hospital
- Duke of Cambridge
- King's Cross
- St Pancras
- Angel
- Peasant
- Old Street
- Fox Dining Room
- Euston Square
- Russell Square
- Eagle
- Sutton Arms Pub and Dining Room
- Farringdon
- Barbican
- Liverpool Street
- Perseverance
- Barbican Centre
- London Mus. Moorgate
- Shoreditch
- British Museum
- Chancery Lane
- Aldgate East
- Holborn
- Public Records Office
- Holborn Viaduct
- St Pauls
- Cheapside
- Bank of England
- Aldgate
- Tottenham Court Rd.
- Law Courts
- Fleet St.
- City Thameslink
- Ludgate Hill
- Mansion House
- Bank
- Leadenhall St.
- Fenchurch Street
- Covent Garden
- Leicester Square
- Strand
- Temple
- Aldwych
- Embankment
- Q. Victoria St.
- Cannon St.
- Cannon St.
- Monument
- Tower Hill
- Piccadilly Circus
- Charing Cross
- Blackfriars
- Tower of London
- Trafalgar Square
- Embankment
- National Theatre
- London Bridge
- Royal Festival Hall
- Stamford St.
- Southwark St.
- Tooley St.
- Westminster
- Waterloo East
- Union Street
- Guy's Hospital
- Houses of Parliament
- Waterloo
- Borough
- Long La.
- Westminster Abbey
- Fire Station
- Lambeth North
- Westminster Cathedral
- Lambeth Palace
- George's Rd.
- Imperial War Mus.
- Elephant & Castle
- Vauxhall
- Kennington
- Kennington
- The Oval Cricket Ground
- Oval
- Flower Market
- Fentimen Arms

Legend

- ■ Main entries
- ▮ Main entry with accommodation
- ◨ Round-up entries
- ◨ Main and Round-up entries
- ▦ Main entries with accommodation, and Round-ups

0	440	880 yds
0		800m

© Copyright

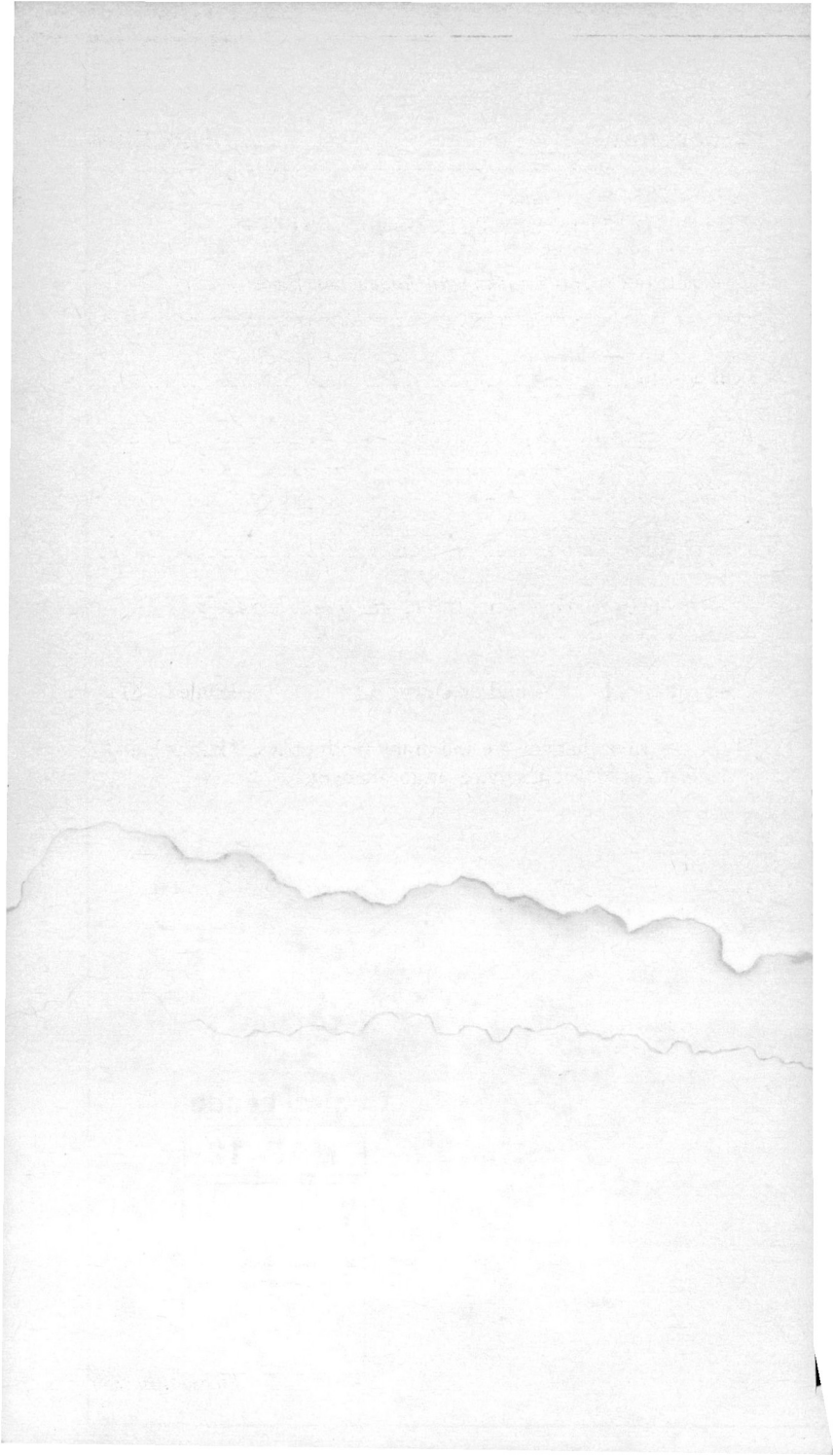

Report form

To *The Which? Pub Guide,*
FREEPOST, 2 Marylebone Road, London NW1 4DF

Or email your report to: *whichpubguide@which.net*

PUB NAME _____

Address _____

_____ Telephone _____

Date of visit _____

From my personal experience this establishment should be
(please tick)

main entry ❑   Round-up entry ❑   excluded ❑

Please describe what you ate and drank (with prices, if known), and
give details of location, service, atmosphere etc.

Please turn over

My meal for ___ people cost £___ Value for money? yes ❏ no ❏

I am not connected in any way with the management or proprietors.

Name and address (BLOCK CAPITALS) _____

_____

_____

Signed